The CME Group Risk Management Handbook

Founded in 1807, John Wiley & Sons is the oldest independent publishing company in the United States. With offices in North America, Europe, Australia, and Asia, Wiley is globally committed to developing and marketing print and electronic products and services for our customers' professional and personal knowledge and understanding.

The Wiley Finance series contains books written specifically for finance and investment professionals as well as sophisticated individual investors and their financial advisors. Book topics range from portfolio management to e-commerce, risk management, financial engineering, valuation, and financial instrument analysis, as well as much more.

For a list of available titles, please visit our Web site at www.WileyFinance .com.

The CME Group Risk Management Handbook

Products and Applications

JOHN W. LABUSZEWSKI
JOHN E. NYHOFF
RICHARD CO
PAUL E. PETERSON

WILEY

John Wiley & Sons, Inc.

Published by John Wiley & Sons, Inc., Hoboken, New Jersey.
Published simultaneously in Canada.

Library of Congress Cataloging-in-Publication Data:
  The CME group risk management handbook: products and applications/John W.
Labuszewski . . . [et al.].
    p. cm. – (Wiley finance series)
  Includes bibliographical references and index.
  ISBN 978-0-470-13771-0 (cloth)
  1. Futures. 2. Risk management.   I. Labuszewski, John.
  HG6024.A3C587 2010
  332.64'52–dc22

                                                            2009054060

Printed in the United States of America

10 9 8 7 6 5 4 3 2

Contents

Foreword

However we view it, the twentieth century must be assessed as remarkable. Although it recorded a new low in the history of violence—with two world wars and the Holocaust—it was also a century that bespoke of unprecedented advances in human endeavor: At its outset, Joseph J. Thompson's detection of the electron proved that atoms were at the foundation of matter just as the Greeks believed; Emmeline Pankhurst lit the torch on behalf of women's right to vote; Gregor Mendel discovered how inherited traits are passed on; Wilbur and Orville Wright transformed human transportation at Kitty Hawk; Sigmund Freud unlocked the mysteries of our subconscious; and Albert Einstein, the foremost scientist of the century, recorded his earth-shaking three papers. The combination of these breakthroughs fulfilled their promise and directed the destiny of humankind. Metaphorically speaking, the twentieth century propelled civilization from the horse and buggy to the moon and beyond.

To put it another way, the technology of the last century moved humankind from the vast to the infinitesimal. In physics, Einstein's theory of general relativity dealt with the universe—the big. As the century progressed we journeyed to quantum physics—the little. Similarly, we moved from macro to the micro in biology—from individual cells to gene engineering. And just as technology brought us to subatomic particles in physical science, just as technology brought us to molecules in biological science, so in financial markets when computer technology was applied to established investment strategies, the evolution from the big to the little was strikingly similar. With computer science, the most complicated risk-management structure could be broken down into its separate components. Financial engineers disaggregated, repackaged, and redistributed risks and their corresponding rewards, exchanging one set of risks and rewards for another that responded better to investors' preferences. We moved from macro to micro applications. In other words, the over-the-counter (OTC) derivatives market with its attendant risks was born. Indeed, derivatives were the financial equivalents to particle physics and molecular biology. Charles Sanford, the former chairman of Bankers Trust, dubbed it "particle finance."

Derivatives in OTC venues and those on regulated futures exchanges are used by the largest and most sophisticated financial institutions in the world—domestic and international banks, public and private pension funds, investment companies, mutual funds, hedge funds, energy providers, asset and liability managers, mortgage companies, swap dealers, and insurance companies. Financial entities that face foreign exchange, energy, agricultural, or environmental exposure use our markets to hedge or manage their price risk. Financial intermediaries that have exposure in equities use our markets to hedge or to benchmark their investment performance. Financial institutions that have interest rate exposure from lending and borrowing activities, or their dealing in OTC interest rate instruments, swaps, and structured derivatives products, or their proprietary trading activities use our markets to hedge or arbitrage their exposure in money market swaps or to convert their interest rate exposure from a fixed rate to a floating rate or vice versa.

Few would argue that the modern era of futures markets was born with the launch of financial futures at the International Monetary Market (IMM) of the Chicago Mercantile Exchange (CME). This first-mover advantage provided the momentum that ultimately brought the CME Group to today's pinnacle of futures markets. The metamorphosis ensued directly after August 15, 1971, the date when President Nixon dropped the U.S. dollar convertibility to gold. By closing the gold window, Nixon's action led to an irreversible breakdown of the system of fixed exchange rates, initiated the modern era of globalization, and provided the rationale for the CME and other futures exchanges to prove that the traditional idea about use of futures markets in physical commodities was applicable to instruments of finance and beyond.

Our birthright in futures markets was to mediate risk during a narrow window for a few big agricultural products. Upon adulthood we extended this heritage into finance. With the advent of the digital age we launched CME Globex, becoming electronic and international. Now we provide risk-management capabilities on a nearly round-the-clock basis on a vast array of products that cover the gamut from finance to energy, from securities to the environment, from banking to agriculture. We provide alternative investments coverage, maintain strategic alliances with other exchanges, serve as a global benchmark for valuing and pricing risk, provide most transparent markets, offer an array of mini products for individual investors, and maintain educational facilities along with a complement of banking services. Most importantly, we manage an efficient, financially sophisticated central-party clearinghouse that guarantees, clears, and settles every trade within a no-debt structure.

Although OTC derivatives experienced problems during the 2007–2008 financial breakdown, the financial safeguards in regulated futures markets proved solid and demonstrated our market's undeniable value in the management of complex business risks.

Our introduction of Globex near the end of the twentieth century transported the trading pit to every corner of the globe. Whereas as little as six years ago American futures exchanges were still limited to floor-based execution, now the trading screen enables customers around the globe to execute trades without the need for physical representation on the floor of an exchange. The impact on growth is evidenced in the quantum leap in our annual transaction volume since the launch of CME Globex. Not so long ago if a financial official, say, in China, made a statement that affected the value of the dollar, it could take hours if not days before that knowledge was translated into market action. Today, nobody of consequence can say anything anywhere without the potential of it being instantly reduced into a buy or sell on a screen. You can execute a complex spread or do an entire panoply of connected transactions that includes markets across multiasset classes as fast as your fingers press the keys. The digital age reduced the Globex execution speed from 2,500 milliseconds a decade ago to less than 10 milliseconds today.

Indeed, advanced technology has dramatically altered the nature and definition of the trader, morphing the computer into an instrument that uses artificial intelligence and algorithms that direct the execution of the trade itself. These apply advanced proprietary mathematical models to execute countless sophisticated trading strategies to capture even minute profits based on price correlations, price distortions, and value associations between markets. Housed within proprietary trading enterprises throughout the globe—sometimes referred to as high-frequency trading operations—they are an extension of the digital revolution and supply enormous liquidity and breadth to market structures both in equities and futures and options markets.

The preceding brief historical sketch of financial markets provides a clear understanding that OTC derivatives and exchange-traded futures are a product of the dramatic changes in the science and technology of the twentieth century. The same can be said for the modern Chicago Mercantile Exchange—now CME Group. Clearly, during the last century the "House That Pork Bellies Built" in the 1960s evolved into today's "House That Innovation Built." Far less known, however, is the fact that during the same time span it was also the "House That Education Built." Among its achievements was the CME's commitment to advance market education. Beginning in the early 1970s, and continuing throughout its ensuing four-decade march to the top of the futures world, the CME was and remains a leading force in advancing academic education, courses, textbooks, studies, learning centers, workshops, and symposia in the field of futures and options.

It was the first exchange to promote a center for futures education in partnership with the Commodity Exchange, Inc. at Columbia University in the early 1970s, to establish in 1978 a prize in financial writing at the University of Chicago, and to endow chairs for the study of futures at both the University of Chicago and Northwestern University in the 1990s. In 2003, it founded the CME Center of Innovation. Among its accomplishments is the establishment of the Fred Arditti Innovation Award to individuals who have made significant conceptual or practical contributions to commerce or markets. The Innovation Center also teamed up with the Mathematical Sciences Research Institute (MSRI) to create a prize for the innovation of mathematical, statistical, or computational methods in the study and behavior of markets. In 2007, the original Chicago Mercantile Exchange Trust Trust (created in 1969) was converted into the CME Charitable Trust with a primary goal of promoting, teaching, and learning about financial markets, futures, and derivatives. Indeed, it would be impossible to attempt to enumerate the number of books, textbooks, magazines, journals, and periodicals about financial markets that have been published as a result of these initiatives.

As the expansion of futures markets continues into the twenty-first century, so will the need for education. The present publication, *The CME Group Risk Management Handbook* by principal authors John W. Labuszewski, John E. Nyhoff, Richard Co, and Paul E. Peterson, is a continuation of CME's grand educational tradition. Labuszewski, Nyhoff, Co, and Peterson are extremely well qualified for this undertaking, having spent their professional lives in our industry at this exchange and with brokers and asset managers that utilize exchange products. The handbook, with contributions by Dale Michaels, Jim Moran, Brett Vietmeier, Fredrick Stum, and Charles Piszczor, contains information, data, details, facts, and background of a vital nature concerning the use and application of the most notable products traded at CME and beyond. The material includes consummate intelligence with respect to both the underlying fundamentals that affect the instruments described as well as technical analysis and interpretations of price movements. This handbook, a long sought-after work, will in my opinion become an indispensable reference textbook for futures and option markets.

Leo Melamed
Chairman Emeritus
CME Group

Prologue

The financial marketplace continuously grows more complex and exciting as new technologies and products emerge. Since the recent economic crisis, transparency, liquidity and security have become increasingly important.

CME Group has always evolved to match the technological needs of our markets and to offer reliable risk management tools to our customers. For example, the launch of CME Globex, our high-speed electronic trading platform, created a 24-hour marketplace. This launched CME Group into the global markets, where we continue to flourish with extensive product listings and strategic partnerships.

The reliability of our markets was also further demonstrated with the 2002 introduction of CME ClearPort, a central counterparty clearinghouse that settles and guarantees every trade. Risk is distributed among clearing members, allowing the clearinghouse to guarantee the performance of every transaction – and the security of every clearing member's customer.

This evolution has spanned 160 years. *The CME Group Risk Management Handbook:* Products and Applications collects our product history and illustrates the development of our innovative risk management applications. The CME Group Research and Product Development team worked with Clearing, Market Regulation and Products and Services senior staff members to create a comprehensive reflection of our history, products and business model.

CME Group has always been a proponent of market education and active in developing academic courses, textbooks, learning centers and workshops to advance the futures and options field. This book is another excellent resource for market participants, which will be especially useful during these rapidly changing times.

Terry Duffy
Executive Chairman
CME Group Inc.

Acknowledgments

In 1979, I was fortunate enough to be hired on to the staff of the Chicago Board of Trade (CBOT) as a junior economist. I consider myself fortunate because, at the time, I don't believe I could accurately have articulated the differences between the CBOT and the Chamber of Commerce. At the time, the futures industry largely was regarded as a provincial Chicago-based curiosity dominated by agricultural contracts and locally based brokerage firms specializing exclusively in commodities. Financial futures had only recently been introduced, options were banned in the industry, and electronic trading was inconceivable.

A great deal has changed in the 30 intervening years. To begin, I'd like to think that I've learned to distinguish the functions of a derivatives exchange and the Chamber of Commerce during that period! But more importantly, these markets have grown far beyond a provincial curiosity. Today, the most significant institutions in the world routinely use futures and options on futures as a component of their risk-management and trading programs. Countless innovative products and structures have been introduced by the industry. Electronic trading technologies have promoted internationalization of the marketplace, facilitating active participation by traders from every corner of the globe. Trading activity has grown tremendously as a result of these developments.

The story is not only one of growth but of consolidation. It wasn't too long ago that the Chicago Mercantile Exchange (CME) was regarded as second fiddle to the venerable CBOT. But exchanges began to demutualize in the early 2000s, setting the stage for consolidation as the CME, CBOT, and New York Mercantile Exchange (NYMEX) were reorganized under the CME Group holding company umbrella. Thus, a single derivatives exchange began to offer the most diverse array of products running the gamut from interest rates, equities, currencies, agricultural commodities, and energy to metals, all offered on the same trading platform and processed through the same clearing mechanism.

This book was developed as the Research & Product Development Department of CME Group began to document the many functions and products provided by the newly consolidated exchange. It is intended to serve as a primer and reference regarding the most significant of CME Group products and the applications to which they may be deployed. (Please note that the specific terms and conditions of particular futures or option contracts are subject to amendment. Please consult the current version of the CME, CBOT, or NYMEX Rulebooks for the most up-to-date specifications.)

This book was very much a group effort. Principal authors include John E. Nyhoff, Richard Co, Paul E. Peterson, and myself. Contributing authors include Dale Michaels, James Moran, Charles Piszczor, Fred Sturm, and Brett Vietmeier. (Principal authors are those who have developed material appearing in more than one chapter, whereas contributing authors have provided material appearing in a single chapter.)

We would further like to express our gratitude to a variety of supporters who have provided encouragement or insights that have found their way into the text. These include (alphabetically) Lori Aldinger, Peter Barker, David Boberski, Jim Boudreault, Jack Bourodijian, Scott Brusso, Jack Cook, Kate Darcy, Phupinder Gill, Larry Grannan, Dan Grombacher, Matt Kelly, Matt Kluchenek, Dave Lehman, Tina Lemieux, Craig LeVeille, Bob Levin, Gene Mueller, Bill Parke, Rick Redding, Jerry Roberts, Derek Samman, Jack Sandner, Fred Seamon, Sayee Srinivasan, Sabrina Su, Kim Taylor, Bob Turner, Lucy Wang, Scot Warren, Julie Winkler, David Wong, and Steve Youngren. (We extend apologies to those whose names may inadvertently have been omitted.)

Finally, a special acknowledgment goes to CME Group Chairman Emeritus Leo Melamed, who shaped and molded the industry as we know it today, and to CME Group's Executive Chairman Terry Duffy and Chief Executive Officer Craig Donohue, who are guiding CME Group into the future.

John W. Labuszewski
November 2009

Introduction

As Chief Executive Officer of CME Group, I am proud to present *The CME Group Risk Management Handbook: Products and Applications*. This book is a reflection of our collective wisdom on CME Group products and their risk management applications gleaned over the past 160 years.

Since the mid-nineteenth century, CME Group's exchanges have been where the world comes to manage risk. During this time, the risks that businesses and investors face have evolved. Financial, agricultural commodity, energy and metals markets, as well as alternative markets such as real estate and weather, have become increasingly complex and global. CME Group has kept pace with this evolution, providing an ever-growing range of sophisticated products and services for both the listed and over-the-counter markets. Our futures and options products enjoy global distribution across more than 85 countries and territories and trade electronically virtually 24 hours a day.

Equally important is our business model. The liquidity and transparency that are hallmarks of the CME Group marketplace stem from our central counterparty clearing model. CME Clearing stands at the center of this model, serving as the buyer to every seller and the seller to every buyer, thereby guaranteeing the performance of every transaction. No customer has ever lost any money as the result of a clearing member default at CME Group, including during the Great Depression and up through the most recent global economic crisis. Even under the most turbulent conditions, our markets have proven to be safe, sound, secure, and reliable.

This book draws on the considerable knowledge and talent of the CME Group Research and Product Development department, supplemented by the expertise of senior staff members from our Clearing, Market Regulation, and Products and Services departments. On behalf of our senior management team, I applaud their efforts.

The world is increasingly realizing the importance of risk management. For both new and experienced market participants, this book can serve as a road map for developing a sound understanding of risk and a successful strategy for managing it across any asset class.

Craig S. Donohue
Chief Executive Officer
CME Group Inc.

CHAPTER 1

Futures Market Fundamentals

John W. Labuszewski

The precise origins of the futures markets are obscure but arguably might be traced back to ancient Greece or medieval Europe or perhaps Japan. Modern futures markets as we know them today emerged from the North American grain trade as it evolved during the nineteenth century, driven in large part by the development of grain transportation patterns in the central and eastern United States. In more recent times since the early to mid-1970s, a variety of financial futures have been introduced in addition to the more traditional agricultural or physical commodity futures markets. These instruments now cover products as diverse as interest rate, equity, and foreign exchange markets but have been extended to include somewhat more esoteric items including real estate values, economic indicators, and even weather conditions.

Whereas futures were once regarded as arcane trading vehicles largely used by speculators in search of outsized profits, they are now widely regarded and accepted by institutional and retail traders alike as a legitimate and even essential component of many investment and risk-management programs. The popularity of these instruments has in fact grown to achieve immense scale. The notional value of futures transacted frequently exceeds the values traded in the underlying markets to which these futures are tied. In the process, these instruments have focused attention and interest on Chicago as the epicenter of futures market developments and innovation.

CME Group stands out as the leader in this regard, representing the amalgam of futures exchanges including Chicago Mercantile Exchange (CME), Chicago Board of Trade (CBOT), New York Mercantile Exchange (NYMEX), and Commodity Exchange (COMEX).

It is beyond the scope of this chapter to discuss the many direct and less subtle uses of these versatile risk management and investment tools. Rather,

1

it is our intent to introduce and discuss the fundamental terminology and concepts associated with the futures markets in general and the specific instruments traded on CME Group as the leading derivatives trading organization whose products are distributed worldwide and attract active participation from all parts of the globe.

WHAT IS A FUTURES CONTRACT?

Perhaps the first and most fundamental question to consider is simply, "What is a futures contract?" A simple answer is that a futures contract represents a standardized commitment to make or take delivery of a specific quantity and quality commodity or security during a specified future delivery month. For example, one may transact CME Group futures contracts based on $1 million face value of Eurodollars; or $100,000 face value of 10-year Treasury notes; or based on a value equal to $50 times the venerable Standard & Poor's 500 (S&P 500) stock price index; or, 12.5 million Japanese yen; or 40,000 pounds of live cattle; or 1,000 barrels of crude oil. Actually, the question becomes a bit more complicated to the extent that not all futures contracts actually call for the physical delivery of the underlying product or security. As discussed later, many futures contracts are settled in cash and never actually entail a physical delivery.

Because futures contracts trading on a particular exchange are standardized or generic, they are *fungible* and readily offset. A fungible item is one that is precisely alike another. Futures are fungible in the sense that one (for example) March 2008 CME Eurodollar futures contract is exactly like every other March 2008 CME Eurodollar futures contract and can be used to offset a previous transaction. That is, a market participant may buy, or "go long," a March 2008 CME Eurodollar futures contract and subsequently sell a March 2008 CME Eurodollar contract at the prevailing market price before entering the delivery or cash settlement process. As a result, the original commitment to buy is canceled. Or a market participant may sell, or "go short," futures and subsequently buy at the prevailing market price before entering the settlement or delivery process. This series of transactions means that the original commitment to sell is canceled.

Although we often speak of the futures markets in the generic, it is noteworthy that futures exchanges also typically offer options on futures contracts. Options generally come in the form of call options and put options. A *call option* conveys the right to buy, or go long (for example), one Eurodollar futures contract at a specific strike or exercise price on or before a specific expiration date. A *put option* conveys the right to sell, or go short (for example), one Japanese yen futures contract at a specific strike or exercise price on or before a specific expiration date. One may either buy or sell (or *write*) puts or calls and, as such, there are four fundamental transactions one may engage in with respect to options. The buyer of an option pays a negotiated premium or price to the seller or writer of an option in consideration for rights received by the buyer and obligations assumed by the seller.

Futures and options on futures contracts (or, simply put, futures markets) are generally considered exchange-traded derivatives. That is, they are developed by organized exchanges authorized by the appropriate government agencies to offer futures trading to an institutional and retail public audience. Exchanges exist fundamentally to allocate access to the trading process. Not too many years ago, futures were largely traded via "open outcry" in physical trading pits that were crowded by many local traders and floor brokers. Accordingly, exchanges sold memberships in an auction-like process to allocate access to the physically confined space in a trading pit. Today, however, roughly 85% of volume in CME Group products is conducted completely electronically through the CME Globex electronic trading platform. Many other futures exchanges around the world operate on a completely electronic basis. As such, distribution and access to the trading process is much enhanced relative to conditions just a few short years ago. Thus, futures market activity in the form of volume or number of contracts traded and open interest or the number of contracts entered into but not yet closed through an offsetting or opposite transaction has been growing very rapidly in the early part of the twenty-first century.

Once a futures trade is executed or matched, records of such transaction are reported to the exchange clearinghouse. The classic explanation is that, once executed and cleared, regardless of the actual counterparty to the specific transaction, the clearinghouse steps in to act as buyer to every seller and seller to every buyer. This is the fundamental nature of a multilateral clearing mechanism that allows transactions to be offset and stricken from the books regardless of who the actual counterparty may be in the opening and closing transactions. Subsequently, a clearinghouse takes on a bookkeeping and surety role by maintaining records of each executed and outstanding futures trade in coordination with the network of brokerage houses and other proprietary trading organizations that act as clearing members of the clearinghouse. These clearing members act on behalf of their ultimate customers by taking financial responsibility for each and every transaction. Market participants holding open futures positions are required to post performance bonds or, in slang, "margins." These margins are generally determined to cover the maximum one day's price movement from close to close with perhaps a 95 to 99% statistical level of confidence.

Futures exchanges are generally closely regulated by the appropriate government agency. In the United States, the Commodity Futures Trading Commission (CFTC) acts as the primary regulator of the futures industry, and the Securities and Exchange Commission (SEC) acts as the primary regulator of the securities industry. This dichotomy is rather unique because a single regulator serves both purposes in most other jurisdictions around the world. In addition, the National Futures Association (NFA) serves as an industry self-regulatory organization to supplement the activities of the CFTC as well as the self-regulatory functions of the exchanges themselves. Note that the CFTC monitors and scrutinizes the rules and operating procedures of U.S. exchanges.

Historical Development of Futures

Although the origins of futures trading may arguably be traced to ancient Greek or Phoenician times, we recount the development of these markets with a Chicago-centric viewpoint beginning in the early 1800s. Chicago is located at the base of the Great Lakes, close to the farmlands and cattle country of the U.S. Midwest, making it a natural center for transportation, distribution, and trading of agricultural produce. Gluts and shortages of these products caused chaotic fluctuations in price. This led to the development of a market enabling grain merchants, processors, and agriculture companies to trade in "to arrive" or "cash forward" contracts to insulate them from the risk of adverse price change and enable them to hedge.

Forward contracts were quite commonplace at the time. However, forward contracts were quite frequently defaulted on by either the buyer or the seller. For example, consider the execution of a forward contract that calls for the delivery of corn at a fixed price at a fixed date in the future. But if the price of corn dramatically increases by the time the delivery date rolls around, there is a possibility that the seller might default on such delivery, selling his or her corn into the open market at the current higher market price. Or if the price of corn declines dramatically, there is the possibility that the buyer may refuse delivery, opting to purchase his or her corn requirements in the open market at a reduced price. Exacerbating the problem was the fact that these early forward contracts were negotiated bilaterally between two counterparties and were often quite illiquid. An exchange was needed that would bring together potential buyers and sellers of a commodity instead of shifting the burden of finding counterparties to the individual market participants.

The epicenter for much of the early trade in grain forward contracts (nearly futures contracts) was in the city of Buffalo, New York. Buffalo was strategically located as an important bulk grain transshipment hub upon the completion of the Erie Canal in 1825 that linked the Great Lakes to the Hudson River and on to New York City and European export centers. In fact, forward trading in grain sprung up at several cities on the Great Lakes system, including Chicago, Duluth, Toledo, and Milwaukee. Forward trading of various types of grain and other agricultural produce grew up at many other important hubs along other U.S. waterways along the Mississippi and its tributaries, such as Minneapolis, Kansas City, Memphis, and New Orleans; along the Atlantic in New York and Baltimore; and eventually by the early twentieth century on the West Coast in Seattle, Portland, San Francisco, and Los Angeles.

But Chicago emerged as a particularly strategic transshipment point by 1848 with the completion of the Illinois and Michigan Canal along with the completion of the Chicago and Galena Union Railroad. These transportation routes effectively linked the Great Lakes with the Mississippi River system. Eventually, railroad transport proved more economical and became preferred over waterway transport, enhancing Chicago's importance to the extent that a large number of railway systems used Chicago as a key hub in connecting the fertile Midwest farm fields to the bulk of the consuming population on the East Coast and beyond to European export markets.

Thus, the Chicago Board of Trade (CBOT) was formed in 1848 and emerged over time as the preeminent grain exchange. Trading was originally in forward contracts; the first contract on corn was written on March 13, 1851. Standardized futures contracts were introduced on the CBOT in 1865.

In a parallel development, the Chicago Produce Exchange (CPE) was established in 1874, specializing in the cash trade of butter and eggs. The year 1882 witnessed the first use of "time contracts," essentially a futures contract, on the CPE. Several reorganizations saw the introduction of the Produce Exchange Butter & Egg Board (1895) and then the Chicago Butter and Egg Board as a splinter group in 1898. Eventually, in 1919, the Chicago Butter and Egg Board became formally known as Chicago Mercantile Exchange (CME), adopting renewed resolve to promote the use of time or futures contracts and with the foresight that other commodities could be added to the product line in coming years.

The Great Depression of the 1930s, followed by strict price controls of agricultural products during World War II, put a damper on commodity trading. In particular, the postwar support price of $0.25 effectively did away with butter as a viable futures contract. Trading in other agricultural commodities, including potatoes and onions, was introduced but eventually discontinued, sometimes amid turbulent circumstances. Throughout this period, CME's fortunes were flagging. But the 1960s saw renewed vigor at the exchange, led by a group of so-called young Turks including Leo

Melamed, along with a commitment to develop new product lines. As a result, CME launched products in pork bellies (1961), live cattle (1965), and live hogs (1966), breathing new life into the institution.

Deflated grain prices in the postwar period led to some degree of stagnation at the CBOT as well. By the early 1970s, the CBOT was looking far from its origins for new sources of growth. It financed the development of organized stock option trading by creating the Chicago Board Options Exchange (CBOE). As such, "financial" in additional to agricultural or physical commodities started to become fair game for the nation's futures exchanges.

Financial futures trace their origins from the early 1970s and established a revolutionary new direction for the industry. Leo Melamed created the International Monetary Market (IMM) in 1971 for the purpose of developing financial futures. The concept took form in 1972 with the introduction of foreign currency futures including the British pound, Canadian dollar, German mark, Japanese yen, Mexican peso, and Swiss franc. This roughly coincided with the breakdown of the postwar Bretton Woods system, which generally had provided for fixed international exchange rates, in favor of floating market-driven exchange rates. These products quickly emerged as the first successful financial futures products, opening up new vistas for the futures industry. (The IMM was merged with CME by 1976.)

Subsequent years saw the development of financial futures contracts focused on trading in interest rates. These contracts included the GNMA CDR contract introduced on the CBOT in 1975 as the very first interest rate futures contract. This initiative was quickly followed in the late 1970s and throughout the 1980s by products including CME Treasury bills, CBOT Treasury bonds, 10-year, 5-year, and 2-year Treasury notes, and the 90-day Eurodollar contract introduced on CME in 1981. These interest rate contracts had an enormous impact on the financial landscape in general and served to invigorate the development of other derivatives on an over-the-counter (OTC) basis including the interest rate swap (IRS) market. Stock index futures followed soon thereafter with the development of the Value Line Composite Average (VLCA) futures contract on the Kansas City Board of Trade, followed quickly by CME's Standard & Poor's 500 (S&P 500) contract as well as the Nasdaq 100 and Russell 2000 contracts and the Dow Jones Industrial Average (DJIA) offered on CBOT.

Despite the development of financial futures in the early 1970s, the decade proved to be one during which physical commodity trading reigned supreme. In particular, the 1970s witnessed a tremendous surge of inflation that pervaded the U.S. economy to the point that we saw double-digit inflation in the United States in 1979 for the first and only time on record to date. The roots of this massive inflation date back to the 1960s and President Johnson's Great Society social programs, the cost of financing the Vietnam War, and resulting federal spending deficits, generally financed through growth in money supplies. Upward pressure on grain values was further heightened with the Russian grain deal of 1973, which permitted large-scale grain exports from the United States to the then Soviet Union.

As a result, trading of physical commodity futures thrived in the 1970s, led by commodities including grains (soybeans and its derivatives, corn, and wheat on the CBOT) and precious metals (traded on the COMEX in New York as well as on the Chicago exchanges). Brokerage of these markets was led in large part by parochial and often family-owned firms, many headquartered in Chicago and concentrating on retail brokerage activities. This retail clientele viewed futures trading, rightly or wrongly, as a means of hedging against the ravages of inflation.

By the early 1980s, the federal government had begun to take steps to combat this inflation. In one of his last and most enduring acts, President Carter appointed Paul Volcker to step in as chairman of the Federal Reserve. Volcker took bold steps to control inflation by crimping the growth of money supplies, which in the process provided a huge impetus for the acceptance and growth of financial futures.

A fundamental macroeconomic concept balances money supplies with gross domestic product (GDP) or the cost multiplied by the supply of goods and services available in an economy. Further, federal spending must be financed through the aggregation of taxes collected plus funds raised through debt issuance plus money supply growth. If federal spending is financed by large growth in money supplies and productivity in an economy, that is, the availability of goods and services cannot expand to match money supply growth, then the cost of such goods and services must increase. In other words, inflation will be observed.

By establishing limited targets for money supply growth, Volcker essentially forced the federal government to finance deficits through new taxes or by issuing debt. Politicians frequently find it difficult to raise taxes, so, at least in the short term, it was obvious that federal debt issuance would increase sharply and interest rates would soar. This was tough but courageous medicine for an economy accustomed to liberal federal spending programs.

Interest rates did indeed soar in the early 1980s with the prime bank lending rate increasing to over 20%. As a result, commodity price increases were curbed. Those retail speculators who had embraced physical commodities as a hedge against inflation soon found that they could open a money market account and earn upward to 20% in annual interest with little or no risk. Thus, a simple money market investment drew significant interest away from those physical commodity markets.

But in the process, it created tremendous risks for financial institutions holding Treasury, corporate, mortgage, or other debt instruments. As interest rates soared, the price of those debt instruments plummeted. Compounding the problem was a general inversion in the shape of the interest rate yield curve. While interest rates generally increased, short-term rates increased far more sharply than long-term rates. Many banks and savings and loan (S&L) institutions accustomed to borrowing short and lending long found themselves in a massive squeeze. The government reacted by liberalizing the approved activities of federally insured S&Ls. But this prompted some to engage in ever riskier investment activities, sometimes to excess. The fallout of this situation was the eventual collapse of many S&Ls and a resulting large-scale federal bailout with the formation of the Resolution Trust Corporation (RTC), established to liquidate the assets of those failed institutions.

In the short term, Volcker's policies caused much financial turmoil. But in the long term, this courageous policy of tough love, in a monetary policy sense, was effective. Inflation fell from dangerous double-digit territory in 1979 to –3% by 1985. In the process, institutions came to embrace financial futures as an everyday part of their risk-management activities. This policy further breathed life into the domestic stock market, which had stagnated in a long-term holding pattern since the late 1960s. By 1982, equities commenced on a long-term bull trend that continued into the twenty-first century. Finally, the Plaza Hotel Accord of 1985, in which the major economic powers agreed to a long-term devaluation of the U.S. dollar versus other major currencies, led to a long-term bull market in currency futures. The Basel Accord of 1988, which established reserve requirements for international banks, provided breaks for investment in low-risk government securities. This began a long-lived bull trend in government-issued securities across the globe.

The upshot of these developments and market trends is that those retail speculators of the 1970s were largely replaced in the 1980s by institutional risk managers in the futures markets. Retail commodity investors generally began to find a commodity outlet in managed accounts or commodity funds operated by trading professionals. Those family-owned commodity boutique brokerage firms were superseded by New York–based broker-dealers, who viewed futures as one part of the mix of financial products they must offer to their customers to remain competitive. International investors soon found use for financial futures as well. In particular, Japanese corporations were earning huge dollar-denominated revenues and investing those dollars in Treasury securities to the point where Japanese investors were routinely taking upward of 50% of new Treasury auctions. Thus, Japanese and European broker-dealers were joining the Chicago exchanges as clearing members by the late 1980s.

Options on futures contracts were added to the product offerings of futures exchanges by 1982. These contracts offer an added level of sophistication to the risk-management activity of institutional investors. Adding even greater depth has been the development of OTC derivatives in the form of interest rate swaps, currency forwards, credit derivatives, and other instruments that have developed on a generally parallel and largely complementary basis to exchange-traded futures and options on futures.

Futures exchanges outside of the United States have been developed with a nod to EUREX, a subsidiary of the Deutsche Bourse; the London International Financial Futures Exchange (LIFFE) affiliated with Euronext, the European exchange conglomerate; the Singapore Exchange Ltd. (SGX); and numerous others. Interestingly, these exchanges have largely adopted the framework and contract designs established by the Chicago exchanges as the model for their development.

The early to mid-1990s saw another interesting trend in the form of the widespread adaptation of electronic trading systems. These systems, including the CME Globex electronic trading platform, provide exchanges with a way to enhance distribution of, and access to, their product lines. Exchanges are no longer constrained to offering products on a time-zone specific basis in a physical trading environment, intensifying competition among the global exchange community. As of this writing, approximately 85% of the volume on CME Group is directed through the Globex system, and many other exchanges are completely electronic.

Coming hand in hand with the widespread acceptance of electronic trading mechanisms has been a trend toward demutualization among the exchange community. In the past, exchanges were typically organized for the purpose of developing trading opportunities for the express benefit of the exchange membership. But CME, for example, demutualized by adopting a for-profit corporate structure in 2000 and engaged in an initial public offering (IPO) in 2002. Because exchange goals are focused on the profit motive, this is further intensifying competition among derivatives exchanges.

Inevitably, mergers, acquisitions, and other partnership combinations have become relatively common within the exchange community. The IntercontinentalExchange (ICE) had its origins in the late 1990s in the OTC energy derivatives markets but eventually entered the futures markets by acquiring the International Petroleum Exchange (IPE), now ICE Futures, a prominent energy futures exchange. ICE further acquired the New York Board of Trade (NYBOT), specializing in the trade of international "soft" commodities including coffee, cocoa, and sugar as well as cotton. In 2006, the venerable New York Stock Exchange (NYSE) took steps to acquire the LIFFE's "Euronext" electronic exchange to form the first transcontinental securities and derivatives exchange.

CME implemented an historic common clearing link with the CBOT in 2003. As such, CME began providing clearing and settlement services for all CBOT products. In 2006, CME began hosting trading of New York Mercantile Exchange (NYMEX) energy and COMEX metals products on the CME Globex electronic trading platform. These alliances eventually evolved into full-fledged acquisitions. CME was reorganized under the auspices of CME Group and the CME and CBOT holding companies were merged in 2007. This brought together CME's short-term interest rates, stock indexes, currency, and livestock businesses with CBOT's Treasury and grain businesses. Soon thereafter in 2007, CME Group acquired NYMEX and COMEX, bringing together a vast array of energy and metals products under the same roof. The CME, CBOT, NYMEX, and COMEX continue to operate as Self-Regulatory Organizations (SROs) under the auspices of CME Group as the holding company.

As such, the futures markets have transcended their modest midwestern agricultural origins. They have risen in stature to become essential risk-management and trading tools of international financial institutions in all corners of the globe. They are distributed widely, and there is intense competition to find new and innovative futures products that will appeal to the growing audience of market participants.

Chicago as Futures Innovation Epicenter

Although Chicago is by no means the only venue for successful futures trading, noting that the concept has spread far and wide across the globe, Chicago is nonetheless generally viewed as the epicenter of the futures world. And for good reason: The product designs that have been pioneered in Chicago have been widely mimicked across the globe.

This extends to several basic financial futures contract designs including (1) the so-called IMM Index methodology for quoting short-term interest rate futures first deployed by CME in the context of its T-bill futures introduced in 1977; (2) the CBOT's bond/note contract design featuring a conversion factor invoicing system; (3) the cash settlement mechanism first successfully deployed by CME in the context of its Eurodollar futures in 1981; and (4) the now universal design for stock index futures, which introduced the concept of cash settlement to a fixed monetary multiplier times the index value.

These concepts have been applied to a wide variety of contracts. In particular, CME Group boasts of perhaps the most widely diversified product line of any derivatives exchange worldwide. Principal CME Group product lines and specific product offerings include (1) interest rates including Eurodollars and Treasury contracts; (2) stock index futures including the

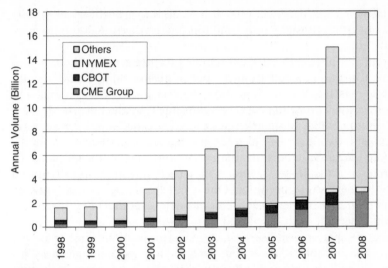

EXHIBIT 1.1 Worldwide Futures Annual Contract Volume
Note: CBOT folded into CME Group by 2008.

S&P 500, Nasdaq 100, DJIA, Nikkei 225, and MSCI EAFE; (3) currencies including the euro, Japanese yen, British pound, Swiss franc, Canadian dollar, Chinese renminbi, and South Korean won; (4) agricultural commodities including grains such as corn, wheat, soybeans, soybean meal, and soybean oil, along with livestock such as live cattle and lean hogs; (5) energy products including crude oil, natural gas, gasoline, and heating oil; (6) metals such as gold, silver, and copper; and (7) so-called alternative products including weather, economic indicators, and real estate.

Other important futures contracts based domestically and abroad include German Bunds and Bobls; Euribor rates; stock indexes, including the euro STOXX, FTSE 100, CAC 40, and DAX; energy products, including crude oil, natural gas, heating oil, and gasoline; soft commodities such as coffee, sugar, and cocoa; and metals including gold, silver, and copper. Worldwide growth of the futures industry (excluding single-stock futures) is depicted in Exhibit 1.1.

Physical Delivery versus Cash Settlement

A particularly important innovation that enabled the futures markets to grow sharply over the years was the development of cash settlement. Prior to the first successful application of a cash settlement mechanism with the introduction of Eurodollar futures on the CME in 1981, futures contracts generally culminated or were satisfied with an actual physical delivery of a commodity or book entry delivery of a security (e.g., delivery of 40,000 pounds of cattle, transfer of 12.5 million Japanese yen, 5,000 bushels of soybeans, etc.).

Actually, a physical settlement remains the preferred method of constructing a futures contract from the perspective of many financial engineers. The reason is simple: A physical delivery guarantees that cash and futures prices will come together, or "converge," by the time the delivery period comes around. This convergence is a key requirement for a futures contract lest the contract fails to track or price or correlate closely with the commodity, security, or other instrument on which the contract is based.

Before an actual delivery, futures may trade at either a premium or a discount to the cash or spot value. Often, the difference, or *basis*, between cash and futures prices represents "cost of carry" considerations; that is, the basis will reflect the costs associated with buying, carrying, and eventually delivering the spot or cash instrument in satisfaction of an expiring futures contract. For example, one may buy gold bullion and simultaneously sell gold futures with the intent of delivering that gold in the future in satisfaction of the futures contract. In the process, one may finance the carry of the gold bullion by borrowing at prevailing short-term interest rates. The cost of carrying that gold may be reflected in a futures price that is higher than, or in excess of, the spot value of gold bullion. Gold futures calling for delivery in subsequent or deferred months may be priced at higher and higher levels, reflecting greater accruals of interest charges over extended periods of time.

Sometimes, and this is frequently the case in the context of financial futures, the underlying instrument generates a return or a payout of income. For example, a Treasury note generates semiannual coupon payments, stocks generate dividend income, and a foreign currency may be invested at the prevailing foreign interest rate. Receipt of such income reduces the cost of buying and holding the underlying instrument. Thus, futures prices may reflect the spot value of the underlying instrument plus finance charges minus any payout.

$$\text{Futures Price} \cong \text{Spot Value} + \text{Finance Charges} - \text{Payouts}$$

Sometimes those payouts may exceed finance charges, and sometimes the reverse is true. For example, in a normal upwardly sloped yield curve environment where long-term rates exceed short-term financing rates, the price of Treasury bond or note futures should be less than and run to successively lower and lower levels in successively deferred months out into the future. This condition is known as *positive carry* because the payout associated with buying and carrying the bond or note may exceed short-term financing rates.

Consider the normal situation in stock index futures in which dividend yields are less than short-term interest rates. Under these circumstances, stock index futures will be expected to trade at higher and higher levels out into the future. This condition is known as *negative carry* because the payout associated with buying and carrying stocks is less than the cost of financing. Currency futures may price at either positive or negative carry depending on the relationship between interest rates in the two countries whose currencies are represented. For example, a Japanese yen futures contract essentially represents the value of Japanese yen priced in U.S. dollars, and the relationship between Japanese short-term rates (the payout) and U.S. short-term rates (finance charges) dictates whether positive or negative carry prevails.

The terms *positive carry* and *negative carry* are typically applied in the context of financial futures. Positive and negative carry is enforced by arbitrageurs who monitor the value of the basis and take action where profits are possible. For example, if futures were to price at a value that was much greater than the "carry price," then arbitrageurs might be expected to buy cash and sell futures, eventually delivering the underlying instrument in satisfaction of the futures contract. In the process, the arbitrageur would bid up cash prices and/or push down futures, eventually reestablishing "equilibrium" pricing conditions. Or if futures were to price at values much less than the carry price, arbitrageurs might sell cash and buy futures, eventually taking repossession of the subject instrument through the futures delivery process and, once again, reestablishing equilibrium pricing conditions.

Physical commodities, including grains, metals, or energy futures, do not produce a payout of any sort. Theoretically, their values should price at higher and higher levels in successively deferred contract months to reflect the cost of financing. This would be known as a *contango*. But other times, these physical commodities may price at levels that are equal to or even lower than the spot commodity value. A *backwardation* is said to occur when these commodities price at levels less than the spot or cash price.

Why might a backwardation occur? Cost of carry pricing conditions are enforced by arbitrage. But where an arbitrage is difficult or costly or possibly impossible altogether, cost of carry pricing may break down. Instead, market pricing may simply be dictated by the influx of buy and sell orders into the market. The volume and timing of those buy and sell orders may be dictated by investor expectations regarding the future course of prices (i.e., traders anticipate future market trends and act accordingly). We may refer to this condition as an "anticipatory pricing model."

Some physical commodities price very closely in accordance with cost of carry. For example, the arbitrage is quite efficient in the context of gold and silver futures. Thus, gold and silver futures prices and the spreads between those prices closely reflect prevailing short-term interest rates. But how easy is it to conduct an arbitrage in the context of West Texas Intermediate (WTI) crude oil futures? The NYMEX WTI contract calls for the delivery of 1,000 barrels of oil in Cushing, Oklahoma. But without the requisite infrastructure to facilitate such delivery, one is generally best advised to refrain from participation in a delivery. As such, crude oil futures may resort to an anticipatory pricing model to a larger extent than futures where the arbitrage is facile and inexpensive to conduct.

Still, cash and futures prices must come closer and closer together, and the basis must converge as delivery approaches. But the lynchpin to such convergence and to a cost of carry pricing model is the delivery mechanism. The threat, if not the actual realization of a delivery, is key to the arbitrage that enforces the cost of carry pricing model in a futures market. As such, futures contract designers go to some lengths to develop facile delivery mechanisms.

But sometimes it becomes exceedingly cumbersome to facilitate a delivery. Consider, for example, the S&P 500 stock index, which references 500 different equities. Or the MSCI EAFE, which references in the neighborhood of 1,000 stocks from 21 countries. To the extent that the bookkeeping associated with the delivery of 500 or 1,000 stocks in the appropriate ratios as reflected in the index weightings would be exceedingly difficult, the futures industry developed the cash settlement mechanism.

A cash settlement implies that the futures market is marked-to-market (MTM) on a daily basis just like all futures contracts. In other words, both buyers and sellers pay any losses or collect any profits daily based on the closing or settlement value of the futures contract relative to the prior day's settlement value. But on the final day, the futures settlement price is established at the final settlement value (e.g., the spot value of the S&P 500 or MSCI EAFE). Buyers and sellers are subject to a final mark-to-market at such value, and their positions are liquidated or stricken from the books. That is, their positions simply expire and are settled at the spot value of the underlying index or instrument.

For many years, the futures industry had refrained from adopting this simple but effective mechanism. This hesitancy was due to a number of factors, not the least of which was concern that a cash-settlement mechanism might fall under the jurisdiction of state gambling statutes. These legal and regulatory concerns were laid to rest in the early 1980s, however, and the Eurodollar futures contract was established. This contract is settled to the spot value of Three-Month Eurodollar Interbank Time, a key rate to which many bank loans and OTC interest rate swaps are settled.

This development paved the way for the introduction of myriad stock index futures contracts and many other contracts cutting across all futures market sectors, including commodities, interest rates, equities, currencies, and alternative investment markets such as weather and real estate. History has proven that a cash settlement can be equally effective in ensuring cash/futures convergence as a traditional physical delivery provided that the value to which the contract is finally settled is essentially insusceptible to manipulation.

Regulatory Landscape of Derivatives Markets

Derivatives may generally be thought of as products that are, quite simply, derived or based off another existing cash or spot or other type of product or financial instrument of a securitized or nonsecuritized nature. Although we focus on exchange-traded futures contracts, they are certainly not the sole form of derivative instrument.

A vast number of derivatives are traded on an OTC basis as well. These OTC derivatives may take the form of forward contracts, swaps, options, and possibly other formats that may not be so readily classified. Further, a variety of derivatives may be registered as securities including stock options and exchange-traded funds (ETFs) based on popular stock indexes, frequently the very same stock indexes that form the basis for popular futures contracts. In some cases, these instruments serve similar purposes or functions. Still, there are some important fundamental distinctions not only in terms of the regulatory environment in which these products reside but also in terms of operation and function (see Exhibit 1.2).

A futures contract may be considered quite similar to an OTC forward contract. Both call for the deferred delivery of, or cash settlement against, some specified financial instrument, value, or commodity. But they are quite different in some significant respects. A forward contract is generally negotiated privately between two counterparties on a bilateral basis as opposed to a multilateral auction-like market that typifies the exchange trading model. However, the OTC market is making growing use of electronic trading platforms to negotiate transactions, blurring the distinction between OTC derivatives and exchange-traded futures.

The financial integrity of OTC derivatives is generally not guaranteed by a clearinghouse although there is movement in that direction in many market sectors. Rather the counterparties generally rely on each other's creditworthiness to secure the transaction. It has become increasingly commonplace, however, for OTC derivative dealers to require collateral resembling a performance bond or margin in a futures context from their customers. Frequently, large institutions establish bilateral netting agreements whereby the cash flows associated with all the various bilateral derivatives deals between the two counterparties are netted for purposes of simplifying money transfers (see Exhibit 1.3).

EXHIBIT 1.2 Financial Market Regulatory Ecosystem

	OTC Derivatives	Futures	Securities
Primary products	Interest rate products, primarily swaps (IRSs), account for 70% of market; 8% currencies; 7% in credit derivatives with the rest in equity, and commodity derivatives	Dominated by interest rate and stock index markets; currencies, energy products, grains, livestock, precious and industrial metals also traded	Primarily equities, fixed-income securities, mutual funds, stock options, ETFs
Product structure	Very flexible; negotiated bilaterally between counterparties	Generally highly defined structures with limited flexibility	Generally highly defined structures with limited flexibility
Regulation	Largely exempt from direct regulation but participation generally restricted to institutions	Closely regulated by government agencies; the CFTC is the relevant U.S. regulator	Closely regulated by government agencies; the SEC is the relevant U.S. regulator
Market structure	Sold through loose networks of dealers mostly on a "voice" basis with growing use of electronic trading platforms	Traded on regulated exchanges and sold through "Futures Commission Merchants" (FCMs) per U.S. regulation	Traded on regulated security exchanges and through OTC activities of broker/dealers
Participants	Banks, broker/ dealers, funds	Institutional and qualified retail traders	Institutional and qualified retail traders
Clearing	Contracts held bilaterally; counterparty credit risk becomes a prime concern	Cleared on multilateral basis, guaranteed by a clearinghouse (e.g., CME Clearing House)	Generally cleared on multilateral basis; guaranteed by a clearinghouse (e.g., DTCC or OCC)

EXHIBIT 1.3 Notional Value of Over-the-Counter Derivatives Market (Billions USD)

	Dec-03	Dec-04	Dec-05	Dec-06	Dec-07	Dec-08
TOTAL OTC CONTRACTS	197,167	257,894	297,666	414,845	595,341	591,963
Foreign exchange contracts	24,475	29,289	31,360	40,271	56,238	49,753
Forwards and FX swaps	12,387	14,951	15,873	19,882	29,144	24,562
Currency swaps	6,371	8,223	8,504	10,792	14,347	14,725
Options	5,717	6,115	6,984	9,597	12,748	10,466
Interest rate contracts	141,991	190,502	211,970	291,582	393,138	418,678
Forward rate agreements	10,769	12,789	14,269	18,668	26,599	39,262
Interest rate swaps	111,209	150,631	169,106	229,693	309,588	328,114
Options	20,012	27,082	28,596	43,221	56,951	51,301
Equity-linked contracts	3,787	4,385	5,793	7,488	8,469	6,494
Forwards and swaps	601	756	1,177	1,767	2,233	1,632
Options	3,186	3,629	4,617	5,720	6,236	4,862
Commodity contracts	1,406	1,443	5,434	7,115	8,455	4,427
Gold	344	369	334	640	595	395
Other commodities	1,062	1,074	5,100	6,475	7,861	4,032
Forwards and swaps	420	558	1,909	2,813	5,085	2,471
Options	642	516	3,191	3,663	2,776	1,561
Credit default swaps		6,396	13,908	28,650	57,894	41,868
Single-name instruments		5,117	10,432	17,879	32,246	25,730
Multi-name instruments		1,279	3,476	10,771	25,648	16,138
Unallocated	25,508	25,879	29,199	39,740	71,146	70,742
Exchange-traded derivatives	36,788	46,594	57,789	70,444	79,099	59,797
Interest rate contracts	33,917	42,769	52,297	62,593	71,051	54,432

(*continued*)

EXHIBIT 1.3   (*Continued*)

	Dec-03	Dec-04	Dec-05	Dec-06	Dec-07	Dec-08
Foreign exchange contracts	118	164	174	240	291	227
Equity index contracts	2,753	3,660	5,318	7,611	7,757	5,138
CME Group contracts	14,289	19,135	25,713	29,432	39,083	27,651

Source: Bank for International Settlements (BIS).

OTC derivative transactions are generally not fungible. That is, once the transaction is entered, it may generally only be offset by mutual agreement of both parties. Frequently, even offsetting transactions reside on the books of both counterparties until the transaction comes to full term. This is different than a futures transaction in which offsetting transactions are stricken from the books through the multilateral clearing process. Still, there are some "tear-up" services that identify offsetting transactions in the records of one or more institutions as a means of cleaning up the books. Further, there is a growing trend to extend full-blown multilateral clearing or processing services to the OTC derivatives industry.

Whatever the differences, the usefulness of OTC and exchange-traded derivative products is reflected in terms of their sheer size, rapid growth, and acceptance. As of the end of 2008, the Bank for International Settlements (BIS) estimated there was $592 trillion in outstanding notional value of OTC derivatives worldwide, with another $60 trillion in outstanding notional value in exchange-traded derivatives. If we add those numbers together, we might estimate the notional value of outstanding derivatives of the OTC and exchange-traded variety at $652 trillion as of the conclusion of 2008 or approximately double the $355 trillion counted just three years earlier in December 2005.

That $652 trillion in outstanding notional value of the worldwide derivatives market dwarfs the size of the global spot or cash capital markets by a margin of perhaps 2 to 1 or better, which may give some cause for concern. Note, however, that these are notional values. The notional amount associated with a derivative represents "the amount on which interest and other payments are based. Notional principal typically does not change hands; it is simply a quantity used to calculate payments. Although notional principal is the most commonly used measure in derivatives markets, it is not an accurate measure of credit exposure . . . which is typically far less than reported notional amounts outstanding."[1]

Why the apparent disparity between the notional value of OTC and exchange-traded markets? Actually, these numbers can be a bit misleading because of differences in accounting practices associated with OTC derivatives and exchange-traded derivatives. OTC derivatives are typically transacted as bilateral agreements between the two counterparties. Thus, it is commonplace for a trader, for example, to purchase an interest rate swap from one counterparty and subsequently sell a swap with the same terms to another counterparty, thus offsetting one's risk exposure completely. Still, both transactions are typically carried on one's books until the full term of the agreement, possibly many years later. This creates more reported notional value outstanding.

In the words of Alan Greenspan, "notional values are not meaningful measures of the risks associated with derivatives. Indeed it makes no sense to talk about the market risk of derivatives; such risk can be measured meaningfully only on an overall portfolio basis, taking into account both derivatives and cash positions, and the offsets between them."[2]

Exchange-traded derivatives such as futures, however, use multilateral clearing facilities where transactions among all parties are assigned to a central clearinghouse and offset, thereby reducing open interest or reported notional values outstanding. Thus, it is not strictly accurate to compare reported outstanding notional values of OTC and exchange-traded derivatives. Greenspan explains that a risk comparison "depends critically on the extent to which netting and margining procedures are employed to mitigate the risks. In the case of exchange-traded contracts, of course, daily variation settlements by clearing houses strictly limit, if not totally eliminate, such counterparty risks."[3]

A more reasonable comparison may be found in reported turnover or volume statistics. Although derivatives volume on exchanges is reported on a daily and even on a real-time basis, volume in the (fragmented) OTC markets is not frequently reported to any central facilities. But the BIS conducts a triennial survey of activity as shown in Exhibit 1.4. Note that activity in exchange-traded derivatives at $6,173 billion on a daily basis in April 2007 exceeded the $4,198 billion recorded in OTC derivatives markets by almost a 2-to-1 margin.

Many derivatives are registered and transacted in the United States and in other jurisdictions as securities. Certainly, the stock option markets have grown up in the United States since the early 1970s as a vibrant industry replete with a half-dozen exchanges competitively trading options on the very same equity instruments, including the American Stock Exchange (AMEX), Boston Options Exchange (BOX), Chicago Board Options Exchange (CBOE), International Securities Exchange (ISE), Pacific Stock Exchange (PCX), and the Philadelphia Stock Exchange (PHLX). As you can see in Exhibit 1.5, volumes in 2008 exceeded 3.5 billion contracts.

EXHIBIT 1.4 Turnover in Over-the-Counter Derivatives Market (Average Daily Turnover in April, Notional Value in Billions)

	1995	1998	2001	2004	2007
Foreign exchange turnover	$688	$959	$853	$1,303	$2,319
Outright forwards and FX swaps	$643	$862	$786	$1,163	$2,076
Currency swaps	$4	$10	$7	$21	$32
Options	$41	$87	$60	$117	$212
Other	$1	$0	$0	$2	$0
Interest rate turnover	$151	$265	$489	$1,025	$1,686
Forwards (FRAs)	$66	$74	$129	$233	$258
Swaps	$63	$155	$331	$621	$1,210
Options	$21	$36	$29	$171	$215
Other	$2	$0	$0	$0	$1
Estimated gap in reporting		$39	$43	$92	$193
Total derivatives turnover	$880	$1,265	$1,385	$2,420	$4,198
Turnover at 4/07 FX rates		$1,410	$1,700	$2,550	$4,198
Exchange-traded derivatives	$1,221	$1,382	$2,198	$4,547	$6,173
Currency contracts	$17	$11	$10	$22	$72
Interest rate contracts	$1,204	$1,371	$2,188	$4,524	$6,101

Source: Bank for International Settlements (BIS).

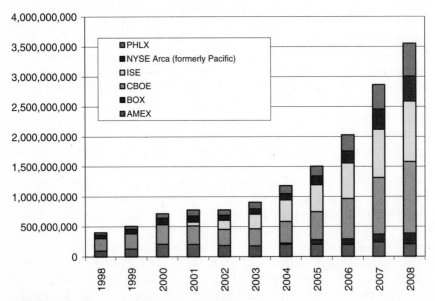

EXHIBIT 1.5 Domestic Stock Option Volume

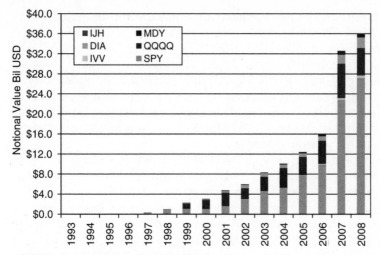

EXHIBIT 1.6 Volume in Popular ETFs

In the early 1990s, the concept of an exchange-traded fund (ETF) was introduced, and it has grown to become a very popular means of gaining exposure to a portfolio of stocks that comprise popular stock indexes including the Standard & Poor's 500 (Ticker: SPY and IVV), the Nasdaq 100 (Ticker: QQQQ), Dow Jones Industrial Average (Ticker: DIA), S&P Mid-Cap 400 (Tickers: MDY and IJH), and hundreds of other indexes. These securities are akin to futures in the sense that they are highly regulated (by the SEC), traded on organized exchanges, and subject to a multilateral clearing system. Growth in the ETF market has been nothing short of spectacular in recent years (see Exhibit 1.6).

OVERVIEW OF POPULAR FINANCIAL FUTURES CONTRACTS

Whereas the futures trade has its roots in agriculture, the most popular and fastest growing contracts tend to be financial in character. Thus, let us review the characteristics of some of the most popular currency, interest rate, and stock index futures contracts.

Currency Futures

Currency futures were the very first financial futures contracts, successfully introduced on CME in 1972. They are available on a variety of foreign currencies, the most popular of which are futures based on the British pound, Canadian dollar, euro, Japanese yen, and Swiss franc. These particular contracts call for the actual delivery of these currencies on deposit at designated foreign financial institutions through the Continuous Linked Settlement (CLS) system, which may be thought of as essentially an escrow service ensuring that payment of one currency is made versus the other currency. Currency or FX futures generally call for delivery during the months of March, June, September, and December (the "March quarterly cycle").

Japanese yen futures may be quoted as shown in Exhibit 1.7. Note that the contract is quoted in "American" terms (i.e., in terms of dollars per foreign unit). This is at variance from the typical interbank practice of quoting foreign exchange transactions in terms of foreign unit per U.S. dollar. Of course, you can convert these quotes from dollars per foreign unit to foreign units per dollar by simply taking the reciprocal. For example, if September Japanese yen futures close at 0.008832 dollars per yen, this may readily be converted into 113.22 Japanese yen per 1 U.S. dollar (1/0.008832).

Take a look at Exhibit 1.8. Traders who "go long," or buy, Japanese yen futures are committed to take or accept delivery of 12,500,000 Japanese yen, whereas traders who "go short," or sell, Japanese yen futures are committed to make delivery of 12,500,000 Japanese yen. The short making delivery is compensated by the buyer accepting delivery by an amount equal to the futures settlement price quoted in U.S. dollars on the last day of trading.

Noting that the Japanese yen futures contract is based on 12,500,000 marks, this means that the September contract was valued at $110,400.00 (= 12,500,000 yen × 0.008832 dollars/yen). The minimum allowable price fluctuation, or "tick," in yen futures is $0.000001 yen per dollar or $12.50 (= $0.000001 × 12,500,000 yen). Exhibit 1.8 illustrates the contract specifications associated with Japanese yen futures along with some of other most actively traded CME currency futures.

Many currency futures traded at CME Group call for the actual or physical delivery of the currency in question. But oftentimes it becomes impractical to provide for such delivery when, for example, exchange restrictions are in force with respect to a particular currency. Under such cases, the currency may trade as a non-deliverable forward (NDF) in the OTC or interbank currency markets. There are, in fact, some currency futures contracts based on non-deliverable currencies that are settled in cash upon futures contract expiration. These contracts include the Chinese renminbi, the Russian ruble, and others.

EXHIBIT 1.7 Quoting Japanese Yen Futures (June 30, 2006)

Month	Open	High	Low	Settlement	Change	Volume	Open Interest
Sep 2006	0.008817–0.008816	0.008855	0.008809A	0.008832	+40	73,027	147,195
Dec 2006	0.008962	0.008963B	0.008962	0.008946	+40	164	20,509
Mar 2007				0.009056	+42		2
June 2007				0.009162	+41		15
Sep 2007				0.009266	+45		10
TOTAL						67,873	167,731

EXHIBIT 1.8 Specifications of Popular Foreign Exchange Futures

	EuroFX Futures	Japanese Yen Futures	British Pound Futures	Swiss Franc Futures
Trade unit	125,000 euros	12,500,000 yen	62,500 pounds	125,000 francs
Minimum price fluctuation (tick)	$0.0001 per euro ($12.50)	$0.000001 per yen ($12.50)	$0.0001 per pound ($6.25)	$0.0001 per franc ($12.50)
Price limits	No limits			
Contract months	First six months in March quarterly cycle (March, June, Sep, and Dec)			
CME Globex trading hours	Sunday through Monday: 5:00 PM to 4:00 PM the following day (Chicago time)			
Trading ends at	Second business day before third Wednesday of contract month			
Delivery	Through Continuous Linked Settlement (CLS) facilities			
Position limits	No limits			
Ticker	EC	JY	BP	SF

Short-Term Interest Rate Futures

T-bill futures were introduced at CME in 1977 and represent the very first short-term interest rate (STIR) futures contract. This contract is notable because it established the model on which many other STIRs traded domestically and abroad were developed. Still, it is the CME Group Eurodollar contract that emerged after an inauspicious beginning in 1981 to become the predominant STIR contract worldwide.

Eurodollar futures are based on a $1 million face-value short-term debt instrument. The contract is settled in cash based on the British Bankers Association (BBA) surveyed rate for three-month Eurodollar interbank time deposits. Of course, a Eurodollar is simply a U.S. dollar on deposit with a bank outside of the United States. A Eurodollar rate may be subtly distinguished from the London Interbank Offered Rate (LIBOR) by reference to the fact that a Eurodollar might technically be held anywhere outside the United States and not simply in a London-domiciled institution.

Exhibit 1.9 illustrates how Eurodollar futures prices are quoted. Eurodollar futures use the IMM index quotation model, originally established in the context of the T-bill contract. Specifically, the IMM index is equal to 100 less the yield on the security. For example, if the yield equals 0.41%, the index equals 99.59. The minimum price fluctuation is generally equal to

EXHIBIT 1.9 Quoting Eurodollar Futures (November 27, 2009)

Month	Open	High	Low	Settlement	Change	Volume	Open Interest
Dec 2009	99.6925	99.7100	99.6900	99.6975	−4.5	266,412	1,022,850
Jan 2010				99.6700	−4.5	7,395	23,075
Feb 2010				99.6300	−5.0	278	7,534
Mar 2010	99.5800	99.6050	99.5800	99.5900	−4.0	298,050	1,013,560
Apr 2010				99.5450	−4.0		265
May 2010				99.5000	−3.5		69
Jun 2010	99.4550	99.4700	99.4500	99.4550	−4.5	281,544	1,013,560
Sep 2010	99.2150	99.2150	99.2000	98.2050	+1.0	253,810	759,757
Dec 2010	98.8900	98.8900	98.8550	98.8750	+4.5	245,380	842,695
Mar 2011	98.5600	98.5600	98.5200	98.5500	+7.0	200,026	546,715
Jun 2011	98.2200	98.2200	98.1800	98.2150	+8.0	146,344	525,174
Sep 2011	97.9100	97.9100	97.8700	97.9150	+9.0	146,169	485,362
Dec 2011	97.6150	97.6150	97.5850	97.6250	+9.0	64,643	264,883

. . .

one-half basis point, or 0.005%. Based on a $1 million face-value 90-day instrument, this equates to $12.50, or $25.00 for one full basis point (0.01%). On this day, March 2010 futures fell by 4.0 basis points. This is equal to $100.00 (= 4.0 × $25).

Eurodollar futures (Exhibit 1.10) generally mature during the months of March, June, September, or December (the "March quarterly cycle") plus some intervening "serial months." These contracts are actually listed out upward to 10 years into the future. These long-term listings distinguish Eurodollars, and to a certain extent other STIR contracts, such as the Euribor contract listed on the Euronext LIFFE exchange, from other futures contracts. Most futures contracts are most actively traded in the nearby or front month or months with little activity in the back or deferred months. But STIR futures such as Eurodollars are tied closely to the OTC interest

EXHIBIT 1.10 Eurodollar Futures Specifications

Unit	$1 million face-value, 90-day Eurodollar Time Deposits.
Cash settlement	Cash settlement based on a British Bankers Association rate for three-month Eurodollar Interbank Time Deposits
Quote	In terms of the IMM index or 100 less the yield (e.g., a yield of 3.39% is quoted as 96.61)
Minimum price fluctuation or "tick"	One-half basis point (0.005) equals $12.50, except in nearby month where tick is one-quarter basis point (0.0025), or $6.25
Months	March quarterly cycle of March, June, September, and December; plus, the first four "serial" months not in the March quarterly cycle
Hours of trade	Trading on the floor is conducted from 7:20 AM to 2:00 PM. Trading on the CME Globex electronic trading platform is conducted on Mondays to Thursdays from 5:00 PM to 4:00 PM and 2:00 PM to 4:00 PM; Shutdown period from 4:00 PM to 5:00 PM; Sundays and holidays from 5:00 PM to 4:00 PM
Final trading day	The second London bank business day immediately preceding the third Wednesday of the contract month. If it is a bank holiday in New York City or Chicago, trading terminates on the first London bank business day preceding the third Wednesday of the contract month. If an exchange holiday, trading terminates on the next preceding business day.
Ticker	ED or GE on electronic system

rate swap markets, noting that an IRS may be listed out for many years into the future. Thus, there is frequent use of "back-month" Eurodollar futures contracts, enough so to warrant deferred listings out upward to 10 years.

Long-Term Interest Rate Futures

Bond and note futures call for delivery of debt securities during the months of March, June, September, or December, extending outward more than two years into the future. In fact, most *financial* futures trade for delivery in the March quarterly cycle. Traders who "go short," or sell futures, are committed to make delivery of $100,000 face-value securities; traders who "go long," or buy futures, are committed to take delivery of the $100,000 face-value securities. The terms and conditions associated with the most popular Treasury contracts are depicted in Exhibits 1.11A and 1.11B.

The very first interest rate futures contract was introduced on the CBOT in 1975 with the introduction of the GNMA CDR contract based on mortgage-backed securities. Although this contract did not ultimately survive, it did establish a model for long-term interest rate futures contracts worldwide. It was only a few years later in 1977 that the CBOT rolled out its long-term 30-year Treasury bond futures and, subsequently, its 10-, 5-, 3-, 2-year and Treasury note and ultra Treasury bond contracts that were similarly constructed. The insight associated with these contracts is to provide for the delivery of any of a number of eligible-for-delivery securities at the discretion of the short, with an adjustment to the invoice price paid from long to short upon delivery of any particular security.

Treasury futures contracts are quoted, unlike money market instruments such as T-bills and Eurodollars that are quoted on a yield basis, in percent of par to the nearest 1/32nd of 1% of par (see Exhibit 1.12). For example, one may quote a note at 108-12, or 112% of par plus 12/32nds (112.375 on a decimal basis). Thus, a $100,000 face-value security might be priced at $112,375. If the price moves by 1/32nd from 108-12 to 108-13, this equates to a movement of $31.25. Sometimes these instruments, particularly those of shorter maturities, are quoted in finer increments than 1/32nd. For example, one may quote the security to the nearest half of 1/32nd (or 1/64th) or to the nearest quarter of 1/32nd (or 1/128th). A quote in the Treasury futures markets of 108-122 means 112% of par plus 12/32nds plus 1/128th. A quote of 108-125 means 108% of par plus 12/32nds plus 1/64th. Finally, a quote of 108-127 means 108% of par plus 12/32nds plus 3/128ths.

EXHIBIT 1.11A Specifications of T-Note Futures

	2-Year Note Futures	3-Year Note Futures	5-Year Note Futures	10-Year Note Futures
Contract size	$200,000 face-value U.S. Treasury notes		$100,000 face-value U.S. Treasury notes	
Delivery grade	T-notes with original maturity of not more than 5 years and 3 months and remaining maturity of not less than 1 year and 9 months from first of delivery month but not more than 2 years from last day of delivery month	T-notes with original maturity of not more than 5-1/4 years and a remaining maturity of not more than 3 years but not less than 2 years, 9 months, from last day of delivery month	T-notes with original maturity of not more than 5 years and 3 months and remaining maturity of not less than 4 years and 2 months as of first day of delivery month.	T-notes maturing at least 6-½ years but not more than 10 years, from first day of delivery month.
Invoice price	Invoice price = settlement price × conversion factor (CF) plus accrued interest; CF = price to yield 6%			
Delivery method	Via Federal Reserve book-entry wire transfer			
Contract months	March quarterly cycle: March, June, September, December			
Trading hours	Open auction: 7:20 AM to 2:00 PM, Monday to Friday; electronic: 6:00 PM to 4:00 PM, Sunday to Friday (Central Standard Times)			
Last trading and delivery day	Business day preceding last 7 business days of month; last delivery day is last business day of delivery month			
Price quote	In percent of par to one quarter of 1/32nd of 1% of par ($15.625 rounded up to nearest cent)		Quoted in percent of par to one half of 1/32nd of 1% of par ($15.625 rounded up to nearest cent)	

EXHIBIT 1.11B Specifications of T-Bond Futures

	Ultra T-Bond Futures	30-Year Bond Futures
Contract size	$100,000 face-value U.S. Treasury bonds	
Delivery grade	T-bonds with minimum of 25 years from the first day of delivery month.	T-bonds not callable for 15 years from first day of delivery month; if callable, a minimum maturity of 15 years from first day of delivery month.
Invoice price	Invoice price = settlement price × conversion factor (CF) plus accrued interest; CF = price to yield 6%	
Delivery method	Via Federal Reserve book-entry wire transfer	
Contract months	March quarterly cycle: March, June, September, December	
Trading hours	Open auction: 7:20 AM to 2:00 PM, Monday to Friday; electronic: 6:00 PM to 4:00 PM, Sunday to Friday (Central Standard Times)	
Last trading and delivery day	Business day preceding last 7 business days of month; last delivery day is last business day of delivery month	
Price quote	Quoted in percent of par to 1/32nd of 1% of par ($31.25)	

EXHIBIT 1.12   Quoting 10-Year T-Note Futures (March 27, 2007)

Month	Open	High	Low	Settlement	Change	Volume	Open Interest
Jun 2007	108-140	108-175	108-105	108-125	−0-045	921,370	2,359,230
Sep 2007	108-160	108-160	108-155	108-145	−0-045	7,297	24,020

Bond and Note Delivery Grade

Delivery months, price quotations, contract size and margins are uniform for Treasury bond and note futures contracts. What differs are the securities that may be delivered against the contracts (see Exhibits 1.11A and 1.11B). Bond and note futures call for the delivery of *nominally* 6% securities with a particular maturity or range of maturities. T-bond futures, for example, call for the delivery of U.S. Treasury bonds that mature or are noncallable for at least 15 years from the date of delivery. Ultra T-bond futures call for the delivery of U.S. Treasury bonds with at least 25 years from the date of delivery. Ten-year note futures call for the delivery of nominally 6% Treasury securities that mature within 6-1/2 to 10 years from delivery. The 5-year note futures contract calls for the delivery of nominally 6% Treasury securities, originally issued as five-year notes, with at least 4 years, 2 months, to maturity. The 3-year note futures contract calls for the delivery of a nominally 6% coupon Treasury security with between 2-3/4 to 3 years until maturity. The two-year note futures contract calls for the delivery of a nominally 6% Treasury security with between 1-3/4 and 2 years until maturity.

These contracts are based on "nominally" 6% instruments. But this does not imply that shorts are required to deliver 6% coupon securities. Ten-year T-note futures, for example, permit the delivery of *any* note with between 6-1/2 and 10 years until maturity regardless of the coupon. At any given time, there may be a wide variety of securities varying widely in coupon and maturity that meet that qualification. Of course, high-coupon securities are worth more than comparable low-coupon securities. Thus, the "invoice price" paid by buyer to seller upon delivery is calculated to reflect the varying values of different coupon and term securities. Accordingly, bond and note futures employ a "conversion factor" invoicing system to reconcile these differences to the standard 6% coupon. Upon delivery of a note or bond, the "principal invoice price" is calculated as the futures settlement price times $1,000 times the conversion factor.

$$\text{Principal Invoice Price} = \text{Futures Settlement} \times \$1,000 \times \text{Conversion Factor}$$

Conversion factors equal the price of the bond or note to be delivered to yield 6%. Thus, securities with coupons in excess of 6% will have conversion factors greater than 1.0. Securities with coupons under 6% will have conversion factors less than 1.0. (See Exhibit 1.13.)

The conversion factor for the delivery of the 4 5/8% Treasury note of February 2017 against the June 2007 T-note futures contract equals 0.9015. This implies that this 4-5/8% note is worth roughly 90% as much as a 6% note. If June futures settle at 108-125, the principal invoice price may be calculated as follows. Interest accrued since the last semiannual interest payment date is added to the principal invoice price to arrive at a final price that the short invoices the long upon delivery.

$$\text{Principal Invoice Price} = 108\text{-}125(108.390625) \times \$1{,}000 \times 0.9015$$
$$= \$97{,}714.15$$

The conversion factor for the delivery of the 4-3/4% Treasury note of May 2014 against the June 2007 T-note futures contract equals 0.9314. This implies that this 4-3/4% note is worth roughly 93% as much as a 6% note. If June futures settle at 108-125, the principal invoice price may be calculated as follows.

$$\text{Principal Invoice Price} = 108\text{-}125(108.390625) \times \$1{,}000 \times 0.9314$$
$$= \$100{,}955.03$$

The conversion factor invoicing system is intended to render equally economic the delivery of any of the deliverable securities. In other words, one should theoretically be indifferent between the delivery of any eligible for delivery security. In practice, however, a single security generally stands out as "cheapest" or most economic to deliver in light of the relationship between cash and futures prices.

The 4 5/8%-17 note may be purchased in the cash market for 100-03 or $100,093.75 for $100,000 face value; the 4-3/4%-14 note may be purchased for 101-04 or $101,125.00 for $100,000 face value (not including accrued interest). Let's compare these values to the previous principal invoice prices.

	4-5/8%-17	4-3/4%-14
Futures	108-125	108-125
× CF	0.9015	0.9314
= Invoice	$97,714.15	$100,955.03
− Cash	($100,093.75)	($101,125.00)
= Return	($2,379.60)	($169.97)

EXHIBIT 1.13 Eligible for Delivery 10-Year T-Notes and Conversion Factors

Coupon	Maturity Date	Mar-07	Jun-07	Sep-07	Dec-07	Mar-08	Jun-08
4-1/4%	11/15/13	0.9069					
4%	2/15/14	0.8902	0.8937				
4-3/4%	5/15/14	0.9294	0.9314	0.9335			
4-1/4%	8/15/14	0.8983	0.9012	0.9040	0.9069		
4-1/4%	11/15/14	0.8955	0.8983	0.9012	0.9040	0.9069	
4%	2/15/15	0.8774	0.8806	0.8837	0.8870	0.8902	0.8937
4-1/8%	5/15/15	0.8822	0.8851	0.8881	0.8910	0.8941	0.8971
4-1/4%	8/15/15	0.8873	0.8901	0.8927	0.8955	0.8983	0.9012
4-1/2%	11/15/15	0.9013	0.9034	0.9058	0.9080	0.9105	0.9128
4-1/2%	2/15/16	0.8990	0.9013	0.9034	0.9058	0.9080	0.9105
5-1/8%	5/15/16	0.9398	0.9410	0.9424	0.9436	0.9450	0.9463
4-7/8%	8/15/16	0.9209	0.9226	0.9242	0.9259	0.9275	0.9293
4-5/8%	11/15/16	0.9015	0.9034	0.9054	0.9074	0.9095	0.9115
4-5/8%	2/15/17	0.8995	0.9015	0.9034	0.9054	0.9074	0.9095

This implies that if you deliver the 4-5/8s, a loss of $2,379.60 will result. Delivery of the 4-3/4s results in a loss of only $169.97. Thus, the 4-5/8s are more economic or cheaper to deliver than the 4-3/4s. By performing this analysis for all eligible for delivery securities, one may find the single security that stands out as cheapest or most economic to deliver. Futures prices tend to track or price or correlate most closely with the price of the cheapest to deliver cash security.

What makes one security cheaper to deliver than another? Although the conversion factor system goes a long way toward reconciling the price of a particular security with the 6% standard, certain biases may render a single security as cheapest. When yields are in excess of 6%, the conversion factor system tends to slightly favor the delivery of relatively low-coupon, long-maturity securities. When yields are less than 6%, high-coupon, short-maturity securities may become cheaper. Cash market biases play a strong role as well. For example, some investors prefer discount as opposed to premium securities for tax reasons. The shape of the yield curve can be quite influential as well.

Stock Index Futures

The most significant stock index based futures contract traded domestically is the S&P 500 or, more specifically, E-mini S&P 500 futures. Other popular stock index futures include the E-mini Nasdaq 100 contract, the MSCI EAFE contract, and the $5 DJIA contract. All of these contracts share similar design characteristics because all are settled in cash based on the product of the spot index value and a fixed contract multiplier.

In the case of the E-mini S&P 500 contract (Exhibit 1.14), that multiplier equals $50 times the index value. Thus, if the futures contract were trading at 1,428.40 index points, that implies a contract value of $71,420 (= 1,428.40 × $50). Note that these contracts are simply quoted in terms of index points.

This particular contract is considered a "mini" contract to the extent that the original S&P 500 futures contract listed on CME in 1982 was

EXHIBIT 1.14 Quoting E-mini S&P 500 Futures (December 29, 2006)

Month	Open	High	Low	Settlement	Change	Volume	Open Interest
Mar 2007	1,434.25	1,437.50	1,425.50	1,428.40	−5.40	527,676	1,481,743
Jun 2007	1,446.25	1,450.00	1,439.00	1,441.10	−5.40	424	12,788
						528,100	1,494,531

based on the value of $500 times the index, later amended in 1997 to $250 times the index. Around the same time in 1997, CME also listed a mini-sized version valued at $50 times the index and offered exclusively on the CME Globex electronic trading platform as opposed to a floor or pit trading environment. Thus, the contract was dubbed an "E-mini," and the concept was subsequently deployed with respect to other successful futures including the E-mini Nasdaq 100, E-mini S&P MidCap 400, CBOT's $5 DJIA contract and others (see Exhibit 1.15).

Although these contracts share similar design characteristics, they differ of course with respect to the underlying subject. For example, the S&P 500 is a capitalization-weighted index of 500 stocks listed domestically on the NYSE, Nasdaq system, and the American Stock Exchange (Amex). The S&P 500 may be considered a very broadly representative grouping of large capitalization, or large cap, stocks. The DJIA is a price-weighted index of 30 industrial stocks that represents a relatively narrow grouping of so-called blue-chip stocks. The Nasdaq 100 represents the top 100 nonfinancial stocks listed on Nasdaq and weighted per a

EXHIBIT 1.15 Specifications for Popular Stock Index Futures

	E-mini S&P 500	E-mini NASDAQ 100	E-mini MidCap 400	E-mini ($5) DJIA
Contact multiplier	$50 × S&P 500 Index	$20 × NASDAQ 100 Index	$100 × S&P MidCap 400	$5 × Dow Jones Industrial Average
Minimum price fluctuation (tick)	0.25 index points ($12.50)	0.50 index points ($10.00)	0.10 index points ($10.00)	1.00 index points ($5.00)
Price limits	Limits at 10%, 20%, 30% moves			
Contract months	First 5 months in March quarterly cycle			
Trading hours	Monday to Thursday: 5:00 PM to 3:15 PM the following day and 3:30 to 4:30; Sunday: 5:00 PM to 3:15			
Trading ends at	8:30 AM on third Friday of month			
Cash settlement	Versus Special Open Quote (SOQ)			
Position limits or accountability	20,000 standard S&P contracts	10,000 standard NASDAQ contracts	5,000 standard MidCap contracts	50,000 contracts
Symbol	ES	NQ	EMD	YM

modified capitalization weighting scheme. The Nasdaq 100 is often considered a high-tech index because the index is dominated by technology issues such as Microsoft. The S&P/MidCap 400 includes 400 leading mid-cap stocks listed domestically.

Although cash settlement was deployed with respect to the Eurodollar contract prior to the development of stock index futures in 1982, it is perhaps the cash settlement mechanism that enables and defines these contracts. Of course, the cash settlement system is a necessary development in the context of stock index futures. Consider the alternative of delivering a basket of all the stocks represented in the index. This, of course, is quite impossible where you may have upward to 2,000 stocks represented in the index.

ANATOMY OF A FUTURES TRANSACTION

The processes by which a futures transaction is executed has been changing rapidly over the past decade as the industry transitions from a floor-based, open outcry trading environment to an electronic trading environment. Once visitors to a futures exchange would witness frantic activity, noise, and commotion on the floor of the exchange as the orders of buyers and sellers interacted in a physical trading environment. As of this writing, that activity is diminishing and being replaced by electronic trading platforms and trading rooms that appear to be less frantic, at least superficially.

But this is deceptive because the pace of activity has actually much increased. Of course, the purpose of an exchange is to allocate access to, and otherwise manage, the trading process. In a physical pit trading environment, access is limited to the number of traders who can squeeze into a confined space on a trading floor. Electronic trading systems vastly increase access and distribution so that the ultimate customer can enter orders from virtually anywhere in the world and receive fills in seconds or even fractions of a second.

Although the dominant trend is toward the adaptation of completely automated, electronic trading methods, open outcry still endures. In particular, there are still some situations in which the application of human intervention continues to add value, notably in the context of option markets where one may pursue some very complex strategies involving multiple options. As such, open outcry still thrives in certain markets. But as electronic trading systems inevitably develop to become more flexible with enhanced functionality, it is likely that open outcry will disappear altogether. And not without some regret because this change will spell the end of many long-standing traditions that have defined the futures markets for many years.

Open Outcry

Traditionally, and before the advent of electronic trading systems, futures were traded exclusively in a manner known as "open outcry" (i.e., a physical open auction environment where a number of traders may simultaneously be voicing a bid and an offer). Only members of the exchange are permitted to participate directly in the auction-like proceedings that take place on the exchange floor. Exchange members generally are independent businesspeople who make a living by trading commodities.

There are essentially two types of participants or "locals" on the trading floor: the floor trader, or scalper, and the floor broker. Brokers tend to be the less numerous of the two categories of participants. Brokers stand in a pit and execute trades on behalf of outside customers. In return for this service, they accept a fee for each contract traded.

Traders, or scalpers, provide a critical function by essentially acting as market makers. Sometimes these traders take a position in the market either long or short in anticipation of a bullish or bearish price movement. Most of the time, however, they are content to capture the bid/ask spread out of the market. That is, they stand ready to buy at the bid or sell at the offer in order to capture the bid/ask spread. For example, a scalper may buy at the bid against market orders to sell. Then, they will look for buy market orders against which to sell. If they succeed in trading against a market buy order by selling at the offer, they will have bought at the bid and sold at the offer, thereby capturing the bid/ask spread. Because a large number of scalpers are operating competitively, this bid/ask spread is typically very tight. Scalpers, however, assume some measure of risk during the time between the point at which they bought at the bid and are able to sell at the offer. If, for example, the market falls between those two transactions, the scalper's long position is declining in value. If market conditions become unstable, the bid/ask spread may increase.

Thus, these floor traders perform a valuable service. By taking the opposite side of customers' orders, they assure that these outside orders will be filled quickly and at a narrow spread. Although the activity of these locals is often the center of attention for visitors to an exchange floor, it is important to realize that this activity is intended primarily to serve the needs of outside customers.

How do these customer orders reach the trading floor? A customer with an account open with a futures broker typically calls the broker and verbally conveys an order. That order is recorded and stamped with the time at which it was received by the broker. The order is then conveyed directly to the order desk of the brokerage firm for execution on the floor. Many brokerage firms wire the instructions associated with smaller orders or retail orders to the floor. Large orders are typically conveyed verbally through a telephone line to a clerk at the firm's order desk. The clerk records and time-stamps the order. It is handed to a floor messenger, or runner, or is signaled by hand to the floor broker in the pit who will execute the order. Once executed, the information surrounding the order is conveyed backward through the original chain to the customer.

Throughout the course of the day, locals on the floor who have executed business on the floor take their transaction cards to the brokerage firm that is clearing their trades. This information is entered into computer terminals and transmitted to the exchange clearinghouse, at which point the clearinghouse attempts to match buyers and sellers. For every buyer there must be a seller; for every seller, a buyer. If these trading records fail to match, in other words, if the details recorded in connection with each transaction do not coincide, then the trade does not clear. If, subsequent to a number of opportunities to reconcile the trade, it does not clear, it becomes an "out-trade" and is not valid. Once a trade clears, the clearinghouse formally stands as buyer to every seller and seller to every buyer.

Electronic Trading

Although the legacy of the open outcry system is still available in some markets, electronic trading has become increasingly commonplace. As of this writing, approximately 85% of all transactions in CME Group products are completed through the CME Globex electronic trading platform. Electronic trading platforms offer the advantage of much broader distribution and access to the trading mechanism. Although its primary location is in Chicago, the Globex system maintains numerous connections and offers access through hubs located in London, Dublin, Amsterdam, Paris, Milan, Singapore, Sao Paulo, and Seoul.

As such, direct access to the trading process, which was once limited by physical space constraints on the floor, is much expanded. Further, there are often numerous ways to connect to an exchange electronic trading platform. Most customers connect through a commercial ISV, or independent software vendor, or through a brokerage firm's proprietary system. ISVs are companies that offer front-end trading platforms, frequently Internet enabled, through which customers may trade on a variety of exchanges. In other words, ISVs may in turn connect with any number of futures or securities exchanges. These front-end systems often have unique features and are functionality designed to make trading easy and provide ancillary analytical, accounting, or risk-management services.

Of course, customers must have permission to trade on any particular exchange. CME Group, for example, offers an "open access" policy whereby any customer may trade directly on the exchange's electronic trading platform provided the customer maintains an account with, and their activities are financially backed by, a clearing member.

Actually, the reference to the Globex system refers to the matching engine maintained by CME Group that matches buyers and sellers. This matching process is generally accomplished through a variety of matching or allocation algorithms. The most obvious matching algorithm is "first in, first out," or FIFO. This simply means that the first buy or sell order received in the system at a more aggressive price will be filled first. But sometimes other algorithms are employed for a variety of purposes. For example, a pro rata algorithm may fill orders at the same price proportionate to the size of the order.

Sometimes exchanges use a market maker priority, or "preferencing system," that allocates a certain proportion of each order to designated electronic market makers regardless of whether they were the first market participant to show a more aggressive price (i.e., a higher bid or reduced offer price). Of course, anyone with access to the system can enter both bids and offers and attempt to capture the bid-offer spread in much the same way as locals do on the floor of an exchange trading per an open outcry system. However, there are many proprietary trading firms that specialize in acting as electronic, or cyber, market makers. These traders provide liquidity, an essential element in any successful market, by continuously showing a bid and an offer. As a result, exchanges may offer preferencing as an incentive for these "cyber locals."

Once a customer's order has been filled and reported back to the customer through the electronic trading system, it is reported to the exchange's clearinghouse. Unlike trade records that come from the floor and must be matched, these trade records are already matched, and therefore there are no out-trades in an electronic context. Exhibit 1.16 provides a flowchart for an electronically executed futures transaction.

Acceptable Orders

A variety of different types of orders may be accepted on the floor of the exchange or through electronic trading systems. These orders may vary in terms of the price at which they are to be executed and the time at which they may be executed. Typical orders are described next.

A *market order* is simply an open order to buy or sell. Once placed, the broker has discretion to buy or sell at the best available price prevailing in the pit. A customer might expect a market order to buy to be filled at the

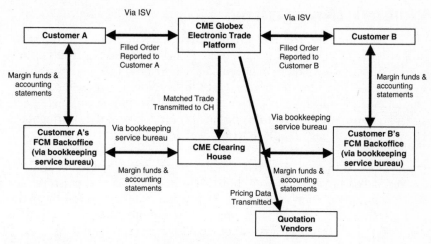

EXHIBIT 1.16 Anatomy of an Electronic Futures Transaction

prevailing offer, a market sell order to be filled at the bid. But electronic trading systems may not recognize a market order per se and may require one to place orders with a price attached.

A *limit order* is specific with respect to the price at which it may be executed. For example, one may place a limit buy in the Eurodollar futures market at 99.59. This means that the transaction may only be executed if the broker is able to buy at 99.59 or less. A limit sell at 99.595 may only be executed if the broker is able to sell at 99.595 or more.

A *stop*, or *stop-loss*, order is generally placed in conjunction with an order to establish a new position. Assume, for example, that you establish a long position at 99.59. You might place a stop-sell order at 99.54 *below* the market. Or if you sold at 99.595, you may place a stop-buy order at 99.645 *above* the market. A *market if touched* order is an instruction to the broker to execute the buy or sell order at the best available price if the market trades at a particular price at least once.

Orders may also be placed instructing the broker to buy or sell at a particular time of day. For example, a *market on open* (MOO) order instructs the broker to buy or sell on the opening. A *market on close* (MOC) order instructs the broker to buy or sell at the close. An OCO, or *one cancels the other*, order may be thought of as two limit orders or a limit and a stop order. If one of the two orders is executed, then the other becomes invalid. Assume, for example, that the Eurodollar market is at 99.59. You may put in a limit order to buy at 99.54 and a stop buy at 99.64. If the limit order is executed, the stop is canceled or vice versa.

Multilateral Clearing System

Once orders are executed, they are sent to the exchange's clearinghouse for processing and bookkeeping purposes. Generally speaking, transactions executed in an open outcry environment may require manual intervention to enter the trades into the system. Once in the system, buys and sells must be matched per all the particulars of the trade, including product, price, size, and so on. An electronically executed trade comes to the clearinghouse already matched, negating the possibility of an out-trade.

Whether trades are matched by the clearinghouse or are submitted on a prematched basis, once accepted, the clearinghouse steps in to act as buyer to every seller and seller to every buyer. This is the process of *novation*. Because each futures contract is fungible, they may readily be offset by an opposite transaction regardless of whether the counterparty to the trade is identical or not. This is the essence of a multilateral clearing system.

Futures Margin Requirements

Eurodollar futures were trading in our previous example at 99.59 and are based on a three-month $1 million face-value instrument. But that $1 million face value is not the amount needed to establish a futures position. When you establish a futures position, long or short, you are required to make an *initial* performance bond or margin deposit. Initial margins may be deposited in cash, T-bills, or other qualifying securities. The customer is entitled to continue to earn the float or interest associated with collateral posted to secure a position. This margin is generally paid into the customer's account with a futures broker firm or futures commission merchant (FCM). The FCM may act as a clearing member of the exchange or might act through another correspondent firm that is a clearing member. The clearing member in turn posts such collateral with the exchange.

Once an initial margin is deposited, futures traders "mark to market"; that is, they are required to pay any losses and entitled to collect any gains daily in cash. "Variation" margins must be met in cash. But these variation margin payments are only required if the account balance falls below the "maintenance" margin level.

For example, assume that a long futures position is established at 99.59. Assume that an initial margin of $750 is required. Note that margin requirements change from time to time based on market volatility and other conditions. On the next day, futures decline 5 basis points to 99.54 for a loss of $125. Now, there is only $625 in equity in the account. Still, no additional funds are required because (we assume) the maintenance margin is $550. On the next day, assume that futures decline another 5 basis points to 99.49 for a loss of an additional $125. The account is now depleted by $250 to $500 and below the initial margin requirement of $750. As such, the trader must replenish the depleted account to the initial level with a $250 cash deposit. Assume that on the next day, futures rally 12 basis points to 99.61 for a gain of $300. This releases $300 to the trader's account in cash.

Futures margins are unlike stock margins. When you purchase stock, you may margin up to 50% of that purchase. That is, you make a down payment equal to at least half the value of the stock and borrow the balance at interest from your broker. Futures margins, however, are unlike stock margins because the character of the transaction is quite different. When you buy or sell futures you do not assume an equity interest in any particular instrument. Rather, you have simply entered into a commitment to make or take delivery of a particular commodity or security. As such, futures margins may reflect a much lower proportion of the value of the underlying instrument. Futures margins may be thought of as good faith deposits or performance bonds, not as a down payment on the purchase of equity. Because futures are *marked to market* daily, they are intended to cover one day's maximum price movement.

Financial Safeguards

This collateral or margin is required to secure the financial integrity of each transaction on the exchange. Ultimately, the exchange clearinghouse guarantees the financial integrity of transactions on the part of its clearing member firms. It is important to note that the CME Clearing House, which operates as a wholly owned and integrated division of CME, has never experienced a default on the part of its clearing members during its entire history dating from 1898.

If, in the rather unlikely event of a default, the CME Clearing House may draw on its considerable financial safeguards package to cure any possible defaults. As of the conclusion of September 30, 2009, the CME Clearing House held some $85.8 billion in performance bond deposits or collateral on the part of its clearing members. Further, the clearinghouse may draw on the market value of CME Group stock shares and trading rights pledged by member firms, CME surplus funds, the security deposits of clearing members, and, finally, may wield limited assessment powers to cure any possible default.

CONCLUSION

This chapter provides an introduction to the world of commodity and financial futures. The development of our markets has accelerated in the past few decades. Where once futures were considered a rather provincial market-place centered in Chicago and concentrating on agricultural commodities, today the market is global and features the trade of financial futures including currency and both short-term and long-term interest rate futures as well as stock index products. But futures are not the only type of derivative product available. In addition to futures, there are also OTC derivatives (e.g., IRSs) available along with securitized derivatives (e.g., ETFs).

Not only has the range of products available in the form of derivatives expanded considerably over the years, but the way in which these markets are traded and accounted for has also evolved. Nowhere is this evolution seen more dramatically than in the development of electronic trading technologies. To the extent that electronics allow an exchange to distribute its product quite efficiently across the globe, volume activity has increased tremendously within the last decade. Finally, we have seen credit issues emerge from time to time including the so-called subprime mortgage crisis. This episode highlights the necessity to maintain a high degree of financial surety as provided by a multilateral clearing system.

Subsequent chapters will flesh out these issues and many more associated with modern futures markets.

NOTES

1. Thomas F. Seims, "10 Myths about Financial Derivatives," September 11, 1997.
2. Speech by Alan Greenspan, Futures Industry Association, Boca Raton, Florida, March 19, 1999.
3. Ibid.

CHAPTER 2

Order Entry and Execution Methodologies

Richard Co
John W. Labuszewski

The process of entering and executing orders on exchanges has been subject to dramatic change over the past decade or so as trading activity has largely migrated from a physical pit or open outcry environment to the realm of electronic trading.

Exchanges such as Chicago Mercantile Exchange (CME), Chicago Board of Trade (CBOT), and New York Mercantile Exchange (NYMEX), all currently part of the CME Group holding company umbrella, were originally organized for the purpose of allocating and maintaining efficient access to the trading process. Before the development of computerized trading processes, trading literally required face-to-face interaction at a centralized location.

However, there may be a physical limitation on the size of any indoor trading venue or a practical limitation on the number of human beings who may efficiently interact before the crowd fragments and competitive trading ceases to exist. Accordingly, exchanges would allocate direct access to the trading process and limit the size of the crowd via membership requirements. These memberships are themselves assets subject to public valuation and may be allocated to those who value direct access through a bidding process. That is, the highest bidder is awarded a membership and direct access to the trading venue.

Exchanges continue to allocate direct access to the trading process even in the era of electronic trading. Of course, direct access may be much more widely distributed through electronics. As such, traders and their entered orders may interact even if they originate from the farthest reaches of the globe. This does not imply that access is unlimited. Rather, the demands placed on electronic trading systems may be such that exchanges are compelled to allocate "bandwidth" to traders using a variety of criteria. Still, it is clear that modern exchanges including CME Group have been successful in widening access and growing their businesses over the past decade with the use of electronic trading systems.

Our discussion is organized as follows. We delve briefly into the venerable open outcry trading process, despite its declining importance. It serves as the context for the development of the CME Globex electronic trading platform. Next, we consider the process of electronic trade matching on CME Globex, noting that different trade matching algorithms are used in different markets. We concentrate on the most significant of these matching algorithms including enhancements necessitated by options trading, which is inherently more demanding in terms of system functionality.

OPEN OUTCRY/PIT TRADING

Although the importance of open outcry trading has diminished with the advent of electronic trading, it may nonetheless be instructive to provide an abbreviated discussion of the process. We highlight the aspects of trading that endure even after the transition to electronic trading methodologies. This further provides a context to our discussion regarding the origins and development of the CME Globex electronic trading platform. Note that many electronic trade matching procedures are more than vaguely reminiscent of pit trading practices as they originally evolved in the context of open outcry, or "pit," trading.

The Pit

The center of gravity for open outcry trading is the trading pit. The size and shapes of trading pits may vary to accommodate specific trading needs. But in Chicago, the pit has traditionally been configured as an octagonal area with risers that are successively elevated as one moves from the flat base or center to the periphery of the pit.

"Local traders," or simply locals, are typically independent businesspeople who traditionally purchase membership on the exchange that grants them rights to enter the pit and trade. Floor traders may trade on their own behalf using their own capital or the capital of a sponsor. Floor brokers execute orders on behalf of outside customers, earning a negotiated pit broker or execution fee in the process.

Floor traders congregate in the center of the pit. They are surrounded by floor brokers around the pit on the elevated steps. Brokerage firms station representatives in booths surrounding these pits. These individuals are in communication with the brokers of the firm, who are stationed away from the exchange (upstairs brokers) via telephone or through some alternative means of communication. Sometimes brokerage firms permit larger customers to call direct to these stations on the floor to facilitate a speedy execution.

Executing an Order

Classically, a customer may place an order via telephone. The brokerage firm's representative fields and records the call. The order is relayed to an executing floor broker in the trading pit with which the brokerage firm has concluded an agreement to execute trades. The relay may be via the physical delivery of the order by a "runner" or the order may more commonly be communicated via hand signals between the booth and a clerk employed by the executing floor broker and stationed near the upper rim of the pit. This clerk relays order instructions to the floor broker. The clerk, by virtue of a vantage point such that he or she may see downward into the pit, may further communicate market information to brokerage firm employees stationed at booths, and the information may further be conveyed to upstairs brokers or to customers.

The executing broker may request quotes from floor traders within the pit. These locals, either individually or collectively, serve the critical function of providing liquidity in the form of a two-sided market (i.e., both bids and offers) for the instrument in question. This process is continuous and fluid. Locals quote markets based on all information available to them including their own inventory of positions. An "inside market" is formed by identifying the best bids and offers from the locals, who collectively may be referred to as "the crowd."

Provided that a mutually agreeable price is reached, the executing broker may consummate the trade with the local(s) who is quoting an acceptable price. Occasionally, a trade is consummated between executing brokers at a price that splits the difference between the prevailing bid/offer spread, affording both customers some measure of price improvement. The executing broker might also split up a larger order among two or more locals. This is more prevalent in markets where price volatility is generally lower and ticket size is bigger.

Immediately following such agreement, both the executing broker and the floor trader record the details of the trade on a trading card. Information includes an identification of the instrument(s) that is being traded, the quantity and price of the trade, as well as information identifying the opposing trader and the clearing firm associated with the trader, and finally the time (15-minute) bracket in which the trade is consummated. This "fill" is relayed back by the executing broker's clerk and then back to the booth to confirm the trade with the ultimate customer. The action may be initiated and concluded within a matter of mere seconds.

Although traders abide by the motto "my word is my bond," further processing is nonetheless necessary to complete the documentation of the trade. Information documented on the trading cards is submitted by clearing firms to the CME Clearing House for purposes of trade matching. The clearinghouse then pieces together the trades based on information by matching counterparties in the trades. Unmatched trades due to mismatched information, or "out-trades," are resolved in reconciliation sessions.

Pit trading is subject to well-defined rules intended to protect customers from potential trading abuses. Compliance with such rules is closely monitored and enforced by the Market Regulation Department. In fact, activity in the trading pits at CME Group are monitored in real time and recorded through an elaborate video system. Violators are subject to disciplinary action initiated by the exchange with possible sanctions that vary from fines to expulsion from the exchange.

Market reporters employed by the exchange are stationed at strategic points at the periphery of the pit. Their function is to record transacted values into a computer system for subsequent automated entry into the market data stream. This data flows into the systems of literally hundreds of quotation vendors for dissemination across the globe. This data is completely independent of the information entered into clearing systems, which may lag the market data stream considerably and therefore be of little use in the context of real-time trading applications.

INTRODUCTION OF THE CME GLOBEX PLATFORM

Having provided a brief overview of how trades may be consummated in a classic trading pit environment, we now turn our attention to the development of modern electronic trading systems. CME operates a world-class system referred to as the CME Globex electronic trading system. As of this writing, upward of 85% of all trades at CME Group are consummated electronically on CME Globex, far exceeding the trading volume in the pits.

Arguably, the gestation period for the electronic trading system as we know it today was very long. One could argue that the development of electronic trading system mirrored the development of the computing environment in general. Although we do not intend to recount the entire history of the CME Globex electronic trading system, certain important milestones that shaped the current landscape of electronic trading are worthy of mention.

After-Hours Convenience

In the early days, electronic trading systems were intended to represent a supplementary outlet for open outcry trading, to be activated during non-U.S. trading hours. Indeed, the CBOT introduced evening trading on its trading floor in the late 1980s to accommodate the growing demand for Treasury futures from overseas customers during non-U.S. hours. Keeping the trading floor open to service the evening trading session was not necessarily optimal, given the physical demands imposed on locals as a result.

The CME Globex concept was introduced by Exchange leadership in 1987 as a "low-impact" means of providing after-hours market coverage. In particular, interbank currency markets had been, and remain, effectively a 24-hour market. Trading continues regardless of whether traders in Chicago are awake or asleep. Thus, deploying an electronic trading system could capture some of the volume that would otherwise elude the Exchange.

The first iteration of CME Globex was operational in 1992, with currency futures the primary focus at the outset. This initiative was modestly successful in providing electronic access to a futures market while open outcry trading was not available. But playing second fiddle is not a viable way to succeed in anything. Just like any other technological development, it would require a compelling application to propel the technology onto the main stage.

Breakthrough Product

That compelling application arrived on the scene in 1997, in the form of the E-mini Standard & Poor's (S&P) 500 Index futures. Ironically, the advent of the E-mini S&P 500 Index futures had less to do with electronic trading than other factors. The "mini" part was just as significant, if not more, as the "E" in the moniker. By 1997, the S&P 500 Index futures had grown in notional contract size with the meteoric advance of stock prices to the point of excluding all but the largest traders with substantial economic backing. In other words, the E-mini S&P 500 Index futures was introduced as a smaller version of the standard S&P 500 futures in an effort to encourage broader participation in the market.

Equally important was the decision to allow the E-mini S&P 500 Index futures to trade concurrently with the standard S&P 500 Index futures

EXHIBIT 2.1   Milestones in CME Globex History

1987	CME Globex concept approved for after-hours trading
1992	Currency and interest rate products launched on CME Globex
1995	Stock index products launched on CME Globex
1997	E-mini S&P 500 futures launched
	Monthly CME Globex volume exceeds 100,000 for first time
1999	Side-by-side Eurodollar trading introduced
2000	CME Globex open access policy implemented
2002	Average daily volume exceeds 1 million for first time
2003	Implied spread functionality introduced in Eurodollar futures
	International access hubs activated
2004	CME Globex volume exceeds pit volume for first time
	Spread-friendly Eurodollar options matching engine developed
2006	NYMEX products listed on CME Globex
2007	CBOT products listed on CME Globex after merger
	CME Globex volume exceeds 1 billion

during the daylight hours, albeit exclusively on CME Globex. As such, much of the original flow of business for the E-mini S&P 500 came from the computer terminals surrounding the S&P 500 Index futures pit.

The two alternatively sized contracts were rendered fungible with each other, and the goal of broadening participation was achieved. Participants in the standard-sized contract could "lean on" the E-mini S&P 500 market for supplemental liquidity, and E-mini traders would look to the standard S&P 500 market for directional guidance. Exhibit 2.1 shows the milestones through CME Globex since 1987.

Open Access Policy

In the early days of CME Globex, access to the electronic market was confined to dedicated terminals. As such, ultimate customers were unlikely to possess one such terminal and would still require brokers physically to relay trading instructions. With the advent of the Internet, it became progressively apparent that this requirement was the gating factor. In other words, the intervention of the human hand was becoming unnecessary and actually getting in the way of electronic communication. In 2000, CME leadership introduced an open access policy that allows ultimate customers to enjoy direct access to CME Globex rather than requiring that their orders be handled by brokers.[1]

The concept of open access is rather simple. Customers are permitted to route their orders directly to the CME Globex trading system, provided that a clearing member of the exchange grants them financial guarantees for their trading activities.

To provide this credit intermediation service effectively, clearing members naturally require the ways and means to monitor and supervise these trading activities. But this does not pose a significant challenge in the era of electronic trading. "Front end" trading software may be procured from various independent software vendors (ISVs). Instructions can be transmitted through these vendors' or the brokers' portals to the exchange. For more sophisticated trading operations, custom-written software is employed to fulfill the tasks.

The open access policy also ushered in the era of *algorithmic trading*. Stripping away the daunting moniker, algorithmic, or "algo," trading is nothing more than the deployment of computer programs designed to submit order instructions to CME Globex (or any other electronic markets) based on data and information of all related financial markets gathered electronically.

As of this writing, algorithmic trading is particularly prevalent in equity markets (i.e., index futures, stocks, options on stocks, and indexes). All of these closely associated markets are heavily automated in the sense that data and orders may be relayed and processed electronically, making algorithmic trading a very viable practice. Thus, it is no coincidence that algorithmic trading has supplanted more traditional point-and-click trading as the largest source of trading volume. See Exhibits 2.2 and 2.3.

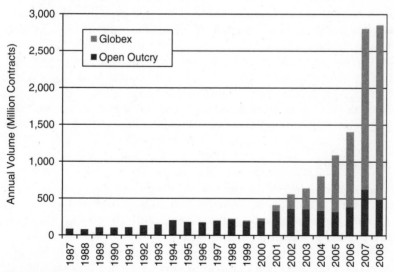

EXHIBIT 2.2 CME Group Annual Volume (1987–2008)

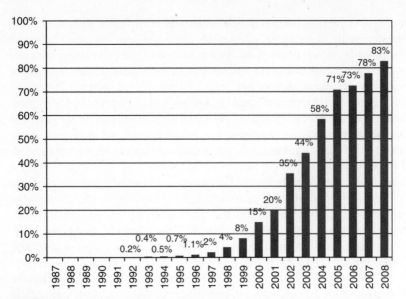

EXHIBIT 2.3 Percentage of CME Group Volume on Globex (1987–2008)

TRADE MATCHING ALGORITHMS

The manner in which buy and sell orders are brought together in the context of an electronic trading environment is often much different than the parallel process in an open outcry environment. The trade matching process may be concluded using many different methodologies or algorithms. In fact, CME Group deploys several different algorithms all within the auspices of its CME Globex electronic trading platform and tailored to the specific demands of particular markets. Noting that trade matching algorithms are subject to ongoing development, it is advisable to consult the rules and regulations of the exchange for a full understanding of the mechanism currently deployed.

Limit Order Book

A working understanding of the electronic trade matching process necessarily begins with a discussion of limit orders. Sometimes referred to as price orders, *limit orders* are simply orders entered with the contingency that they must be filled at a specific price or better.

For example, a limit buy order at the price of 100 is an order to buy at a price no higher than 100. This is also known as a *limit bid order*. Likewise, a *limit sell order* (alternatively known as a limit ask or a limit offer) at the price of 101 is an order to sell at a price no lower than 101. Of course, these orders are further associated with a specified order quantity. The current outstanding collection of all open limit bids and offers constitutes the limit order book, sometimes known as the central limit order book (CLOB) or simply as the "order book" for brevity.

It is noteworthy that one cannot explicitly enter a market order in an electronic trading system as one might in an open outcry system. A market order is simply an order to buy or sell at the best available price (i.e., at the prevailing offer or bid, respectively). But orders placed in an electronic trading system such as CME Globex must necessarily be accompanied by a specified price. One could enter a limit buy order at the prevailing offer or a limit sell order at the prevailing bid and come close to entering a market order. But there are no explicit market orders when trading electronically. Of course, there are many other order types (e.g., stop orders). These order types are discussed later in the context of how these orders are handled in the CME Globex electronic trading system.

The order book is displayed to the trading public via electronic means of communication. A snapshot of the limit order book is provided for September 2009 E-mini S&P 500 futures on August 20, 2009, for purposes of illustration, as seen in Exhibit 2.4.

Order books may be displayed using many different formats. But the most significant elements of the order book tend to be included in most formats. These significant elements include the current bid and offer (or asking) price, the volume bid or offer at each value, and the volume traded at any particular level.

The central column in the exhibit displays the "Price" for E-mini S&P 500 futures. Note that E-mini S&P 500 futures are traded with a minimum price fluctuation, or "tick," of 0.25 index points. In this situation, the market last traded at a value of 1,004.00 index points, which is highlighted on the display to indicate as such.

Immediately to the left of the price column is a column labeled "Bid Size." This column depicts the total quantity of bids at each admissible price level. In our illustration, the total amount of currently outstanding bids at the price of 1,004.00 is 707 contracts. Immediately to the right of the price column is a column labeled "Ask Size," depicting the total quantity of offers at each admissible price. Some 1,615 contracts are currently being offered at a price of 1,004.25.

A quick glance at the display indicates that the current bid-offer spread is 1,004.00 bid and 1,004.25 offer. Of course, the highest or most competitive bid necessarily must be below the lowest or most competitive offer or ask price. If a bid should rise to equal or exceed the lowest offer or if an offer should equal or fall below the highest bid, then a matched trade

EXHIBIT 2.4 Limit Order Book for Sep-09 E-mini S&P 500 Futures (9:45 AM on August 20, 2009)

Cumulative Bid	Bid Size	Price	Ask Size	Cumulative Ask	Volume	Trades
		1,006.50	1,495	17,774		
		1,006.25	1,712	16,279		
		1,006.00	1,825	14,567		
		1,005.75	1,386	12,742		
		1,005.50	1,824	11,356		
		1,005.25	1,592	9,532		
		1,005.00	3,367	7,940		
		1,004.75	2,147	4,573	2,682	248
		1,004.50	1,838	2,426	11,979	675
		1,004.25	588	588	12,708	1,141
707	707	1,004.00			5,153	506
2,321	1,614	1,003.75			2,879	421
4,005	1,684	1,003.50			6,540	733
5,904	1,899	1,003.25			6,759	797
7,193	1,289	1,003.00			18,230	1,468
8,222	1,029	1,002.75			30,432	2,538
9,267	1,045	1,002.50			30,472	3,231
11,247	1,980	1,002.25			30,446	3,549
12,290	1,043	1,002.00			39,507	3,891
13,649	1,359	1,001.75			32,897	3,099

Source: CME E-quote System.

results. Thus, the bid and offer that matches are immediately stricken from the order book. The bid-offer spread represents a very quick indication regarding liquidity in the market. In our example, the bid and offer diverges by one minimum price fluctuation and as such represents the "tightest" market possible.

To the left and right of the bid and offer size columns is information regarding the cumulative bid and offer sizes, respectively. For example, the quantities bid at the two most competitive bid prices of 1,004.00 and 1,003.75 total 1,614 contracts. The quantities offered at the two most competitive asking prices of 1,004.25 and 1,004.50 total some 2,426 contracts. These cumulative totals tell us about the "depth" of the book and the extent to which one may move the market if entering a large size order.

The columns to the far right are labeled "Volume" and "Trades." These fields represent the total number of contracts traded at each price level, as well as the number of transactions at said level. For example, some 248 transactions with a total quantity of 2,682 contracts traded at the price of 1,004.75 during the current trading session. Because no trades or volume are indicated at prices above 1,004.75, one may surmise that value represents the high of the day. This information may be considered supplementary to the extent that it has no impact on the trade-matching process moving forward. It is included in the display to the extent that it may be useful for traders attempting to formulate their trading decisions, perhaps by reference to technical trading methods.

Matching an Order

When a bid or an offer is routed to CME Globex at an executable limit value versus standing limit orders in the order book, a trade is concluded. For example, assume that an offer with a price of 1,004.25 arrives at the CME Globex system. Because there are standing offers at the same price, a match is made and a transaction is concluded at 1,004.25.

If the incoming bid at 1,004.25 is for a quantity less than the current total outstanding offers at that price, then the total outstanding offered quantity subsequent to the matched transaction is simply reduced by the quantity bid.

Example Assume a bid at 1,004.25 is received with a quantity of 100 contracts, noting that 588 contracts are offered at 1,004.25. The resulting matched transaction reduces the offered quantity by 100 contracts so that 488 contracts remain offered at 1,004.25.

Assume the quantity of the incoming bid at 1,004.25 exceeds the quantity of currently outstanding offers at the same price. In that case, the bid will exhaust the entirety of the standing bids at 1,004.25. The remaining unfilled bid is retained in the limit order book at the price.

Example Assume a bid at 1,004.25 is received with a quantity of 1,000 contracts when 588 are offered at 1,004.25. Thus, 588 contracts are matched at 1,004.25. The remaining unfilled 412 contracts bid at 1,004.25 are then displayed as the highest or most competitive bid in the book.

Should the incoming bid be specified at a price greater than the lowest offer price, it will be matched first against the lowest offered price. The remaining unfilled quantity will then be matched at the next higher price, and so on, until either the entire order has been filled or until the remaining offer prices in the system exceed the bid.

Example Assume one enters a bid for 2,000 contracts at 1,004.50. Some 588 contracts are filled at 1,004.25 while the remaining 1,412 contracts are filled at 1,004.50. This leaves 426 contracts offered at 1,004.50, noting there were originally 2,426 offered at or below that level.

Example   Assume one enters a bid for 4,000 contracts at 1,004.50. Some 588 contracts are filled at 1,004.25 while another 1,838 contracts are filled at 1,004.50 for a total of 2,426 filled contracts. The remaining 1,574 contracts bid at 1,004.50 will remain in the order book as an open limit bid.

As of this writing, the CME Globex electronic trading platform permits market participants to enter a so-called iceberg order, which refers to a limit order that is placed with a total quantity in excess of the size that will be displayed in the order book. For example, a bid of 1,000 contracts at 1,004.00 may be submitted with instructions publicly to display no more than 100 contracts at a time. If the publicly displayed portion of the order is transacted, the next 100 contracts will be displayed, and so on. The immediate implication is that the "displayed liquidity" of a market represents a conservative estimate of true market depth.

Market with Protection

E-mini S&P 500 futures are one of the most liquid futures markets available today with significant quantities of standing bids and offers throughout the day and night. There are, however, markets in which the standing bids and offers are less abundant. In those thinner markets, it is possible for a large incoming buy (sell) order with a price far away from the current market to exhaust all of the best offers (bids) at multiple price levels.

This situation is known as "sweeping the book" in the vernacular of trading. Given the immediate consummation of transactions using electronic trading platforms, it may be impossible for market participants to enter orders and thereby replenish the limit order book before trade matching for a currently working order ceases. Thus, one might possibly observe whipsaws in the market caused by such orders. However, there are certain safeguards built into the CME Globex electronic trading platform to mitigate this volatility.

As mentioned earlier, a true "market order" represents an instruction to execute a trade at the best available price in the order book without limitation on the order price. This order type is not supported by the CME Globex electronic trading platform. However, such orders may be approximated by entering a limit order with certain adjustments to the order price.

When a trader issues a market order to buy ("buy at market") the intent is to buy the prescribed quantity even if a portion of the trade may only be executable above the current best offer. This intention may be simulated on an electronic order entry system through entry of a limit bid that is a few ticks above the best offer price. Likewise, a market order to sell ("sell at market") may be simulated with the entry of a limit sell that is a few ticks below the best bid price. Still, there remains the possibility that some portion of the order may not be executable immediately and may continue to reside in the order book.

The CME Globex system supports an order type referred to as "market with protection." This order is entered with a price buffer, known as protection points, which may vary from product to product. Note that this price buffer is identified in relationship to the current market price and therefore changes dynamically in accordance with prevailing market conditions. Traders should consult exchange documents for the currently enforced protection points in any particular market. Alternatively, traders can make their own adjustments to their orders to accomplish the same objective, or modify their own trade entry system to make the adjustment.

Further, the CME Globex uses another form of protection called *price banding*. Banding is generally enforced regardless of the type of order that is entered. This protection is seen in Exhibit 2.5.

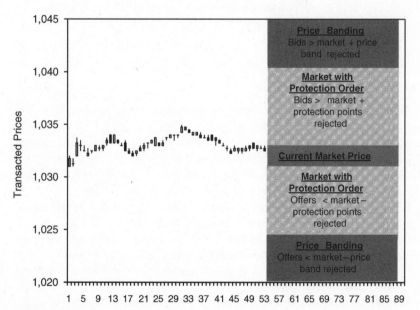

EXHIBIT 2.5 Price Bands and Market Protection Limits

Allocation among Resting Orders

Thus far we have focused on the disposition of the incoming order that precipitates a match or the "aggressive" order. The other side of the equation is how these aggressive orders are matched up against the "passive" standing orders previously residing in the order book. How are matches allocated among those orders that may be received at various times from multiple market participants?

The answer to this question is very "market specific." A variety of matching algorithms are used per the discretion of the exchange and in light of the specific needs and circumstances of the market in which the algorithm may be deployed.

Most markets use a simple and intuitive matching or trade allocation algorithm commonly known as first in, first out (FIFO). For example, E-mini S&P 500 futures are traded per the FIFO convention. But this is far from universal. The Eurodollar futures market uses an algorithm referred to as a "modified pro rata" convention. Other markets, particularly nascent markets, may use a "market maker" algorithm in an attempt to foster the development of liquidity.

Let's consider the machinations, rationale, and consequences of each of these three algorithms. However, you must realize that, in addition to these three matching conventions, it is entirely possible to create other more or less elaborate formulas. You may keep abreast of any such developments by consulting the exchange rulebooks that provide details, rules, and procedures in this regard.

First In, First Out Algorithm

The FIFO, or strict price/time priority convention, is the most straightforward and intuitive of trade allocation mechanisms in use. This algorithm operates per the simple logic that the oldest limit order residing in the order book at any particular price should be accorded priority over all others in the matching process versus incoming orders. This is CME Group's default matching algorithm unless otherwise specified by the exchange.

Although we do not intend to consider game theories as applied to order placement strategies, it is noteworthy that, for each trade-matching algorithm, there are corresponding nuances in order placement that may inspire interesting patterns in the dynamics of the limit order book.

For example, consider that traders placing limit orders are attempting to execute trades at *their* prices. That is, they hope the market will gravitate to their preferred execution price. Thus, such traders may be motivated to place their orders early to assure priority in the trade-matching process and thereby increase the probability of receiving a fill. If an order should be canceled and subsequently reentered at the same price, the new order will rejoin the queue with subordinated time priority. The probability of receiving a fill is diminished. As such, time priority becomes a valuable asset to be managed.

Traders are generally free to enter orders at multiple price levels. They may attempt to secure time priority by entering orders early at various price levels, canceling such orders only when they are certain they no longer wish to be filled at such levels. However, this type of strategy may be subject to some restrictions imposed by the customers' clearing members. As discussed earlier, clearing members perform a credit intermediation function by guaranteeing the performance of customer accounts. They may impose limitations on account activity as part and parcel of the credit management process, including the total quantity that can remain open at any point in time.

Although a trader may be uncertain where an order resides in the queue dictated by temporal priority, it may not be terribly difficult to hazard a guess. When an order is initially placed, temporal priority is clear because the order resides at the back of the queue. But as time marches on, consummated transactions at the order price level will diminish the queue in front of any resting orders. Other customers may cancel their resting orders at a particular price level, thereby further diminishing the queue. Still, it may be impossible to know precisely whether canceled orders are in front or behind one's own order. But a probabilistic assessment may provide a reasonable indication.

Completely computerized trading systems, referred to as automated trading systems (ATSs) or algorithmic (algo) trading systems, are frequently employed. These systems may be programmed to account for these considerations and may operate on a completely automated basis using whatever logic is preferred by the programmers and without the operational intervention of the human hand.

Pro Rata Allocation

As indicated earlier, CME Eurodollar futures are matched according to a modified pro rata allocation convention. First, let's describe how a "straight" pro rata allocation operates and then add in the modifications as applied by CME Group.

A straight pro rata convention provides that an incoming order is matched against standing limit orders at the same price in proportion to the size of those standing limit orders. This practice of rationing participation harkens back to the pit practice of splitting fills between locals on very large futures orders.

The exchange has applied some modifications to this process including integer restrictions, minimum allocations, and "market turner" priority.

Integer restrictions are necessary to the extent that futures contracts must be traded in integral multiples of one contract unit. Thus, a precisely pro rata share of an allocation is rounded down to the nearest integral multiple unit of one futures contract. The exchange does not round up the share to the extent that the quantity to be filled cannot exceed the total order quantity.

Markets that use a pro rata allocation methodology often attract large numbers of orders that may result in a very large quantity being bid or offered at each allowable price level. Thus, there may be a number of allocations of one contract each. As such, limit orders may reside in the system for extended periods of time or traders may have a long wait before their resting orders are filled in any meaningful quantities. As such, the exchange applied a minimum quantity restriction to such allocated fills. As of this writing, the minimum allocated quantity is two contracts.

The term *market turner* is a reference to the aggressive order that "turns" the market or represents the first order to establish a higher bid or lower offer. These aggressive orders are critical to ensure a tight and competitive marketplace. Thus, the pro rata matching algorithm provides an incentive to be the market turner. Specifically, the algorithm provides a feature such that the market turning order must be filled in its entire quantity before others "joining the bid" or "joining the offer," as the case may be, may be filled. There can only be a single market turner.

Essentially, this is a form of FIFO in the sense that the first order recorded at a particular price point is filled first. Subsequent to the fulfillment of the market turning order, however, no other orders receive such priority. In other words, they are all subject to standard pro rata matching.

For example, the first order to be bid at a price of 100 is designated the market turner. Other orders may join the bid at 100. But no subsequent orders at 100 will be considered to have turned the market.

Assume that a subsequent order is entered to buy at 101. Thus, that order becomes the market turner at 101. The market turning order entered at 100 is no longer accorded priority even if all bids at 101 are exhausted and the highest outstanding bid stands back at 100. That is, once market turning status is stripped, it cannot be reestablished by the same order. If, however, all bids at 100 are exhausted and the best bid falls to 99, a new bid entered at 100 may be considered the market turning order for purposes of the modified pro rata matching convention. The procedures associated with market turning designation in the context of offers to sell orders are analogous.

To summarize, the following sequence of events occurs when an incoming order is entered into the limit order book.

1. If there is a market turner at a particular price level, the market turning order will be matched first in its entire quantity.
2. Nonmarket turning orders that remain after the market turner is filled are allocated using the pro rata mechanism, subject to a minimum allocation of two contracts for Eurodollar futures.
3. Any remaining unfilled quantities subsequent to the pro rata allocation are matched to the oldest standing order.
4. If there are any remaining unfulfilled quantities in the incoming order, it continues to reside in the limit order book and is considered a market turning order subject to priority matching against subsequent incoming orders.

As already mentioned, traders frequently deploy order entry strategies in response to the allocation algorithm applied to any particular market. Traders operating in a FIFO environment, for example, may take pains to establish their time priority in the order queue. But the value of time priority is diminished per a pro rata allocation convention to the extent that only a small quantity of the allocation may be allotted to older orders that are not the market turning order. In fact, latecomers may essentially establish a priority over earlier orders by entering very large orders in the pro rata matching algorithm, noting that the fill is proportional to the order size. Thus, traders may attempt to win bigger shares by entering larger orders, noting that the balance of any unfilled order may subsequently be canceled.

Of course, every trader may share a similar incentive to inflate the order size. Thus, when more orders join the queue, traders who submitted earlier orders may have an incentive to increase their order sizes to preserve their claim on the order flow. Similarly, if quantities residing in the book should diminish because of a flurry of fills or order cancellations, everyone may share a motivation to cancel portions of their outstanding orders.

Traders who strategize in this way, however, may run the risk of an "overfill." For example, a trader who submits a 1,000 lot order in the hopes of being filled for 100 contracts must consider the possibility that the entirety of the order may be filled before he or she has an opportunity to react. This represents an offsetting risk that may prevent some traders from overreaching with their entered order quantities.

Market Maker Allocation

Thus far we have discussed trade matching algorithms deployed in the context of flagship CME Group contracts including E-mini S&P 500 futures and Eurodollar futures. Of course, not all markets are as actively traded or as liquid as these products.

Thus, the exchange may solicit commitments from market makers to show tight two-sided markets (a bid and an offer) in reasonable quantities. In some cases, the exchange will attempt to provide tangible incentives for market makers to provide this service. One of the most popular means of incentivizing market makers is to provide preferential treatment in the order queue.

The Market Maker Allocation, also known as the Lead Market Maker (LMM) program, provides that a portion of any incoming order is allocated to the designated market maker or market makers provided that their bid or offer matches the best bids and offers, respectively, in the system. This preference is established regardless of the time at which the market maker order was entered into the system. The exchange establishes a specified proportion of the incoming order that will be allocated in this way. Generally, this proportion is established at less than 50%. Or it may be allocated among market makers. For example, if there are two designated market makers, each may be entitled to 20% of any incoming order; if there are three designated market makers, each may be entitled to 15% of any incoming order, and so on.

Subsequent to this allocation to market makers, incoming orders are allocated according to FIFO or pro rata allocation, depending on the parameters selected for the particular market in question. Market turner designation may or may not apply, again depending on the parameters selected for any particular market.

It is possible that the market makers will be allocated a higher proportion of the trade than the specified market maker allocation. In particular, if the only orders at the best price levels are entered by the market makers, they will of course be allocated the entire trade.

Fat Finger Protections

Despite the best of intentions and the efficiency of electronic trading systems, sometimes mistakes are made in the order entry process. As a result, the exchange has adopted a number of protections to address various so-called fat finger issues whereby an order may be entered erroneously in terms of the price or order quantity.

One of the most widely reported instances of an erroneous order entry in recent years occurred when a Japanese brokerage firm attempted to sell one share of a particular stock at 610,000 yen in December 2005. The order was erroneously entered as a sale of 610,000 shares at 1 yen each. The widely publicized error cost the brokerage firm 27 billion yen, and it sent waves of shock and dismay through the global stock and derivatives marketplace.

Trivial errors may always occur during the order entry process and likely cannot be prevented entirely. However, systems can be programmed to scan entered orders to detect aberrations beyond certain fixed or even dynamic parameters. The CME Globex electronic trading system has developed two major safeguards to address potentially catastrophic human errors in the form of quantity restrictions and "price banding." We consider the two protocols together to the extent that they are highly related.

It is quite simple to include a system restriction on the maximum order entry quantity. This protocol is obviously intended to prevent the entry of abnormally sized orders. For example, the current quantity restriction on the entry of an E-mini S&P 500 futures order is 2,000 contracts. This does not imply that traders are prevented from buying or selling more than 2,000 contracts. A 4,000-contract order may easily be entered as two 2,000 lot orders. By requiring entry of two orders, the system implicitly increases the probability that the entry of the two orders will be a conscious and willful act and reduces the probability of a typo. Quantity limits vary from product to product and are subject to change in response to conditions prevailing in any particular market.

Whereas quantity restrictions obviously address the possibility of a fat-fingered quantity entry, price banding is intended to address the possibility that limit orders may be entered at price levels that are quite far from prevailing prices. As such, the system is programmed to reject bids that are above the current price plus a specified band or offers that are below the current price less a specified band.

Bids below and offers above the market are not rejected to the extent that they do not imply any price destabilizing effects but rather add depth to the marketplace. Further, such orders do not represent a risk or danger to the errant order.

Cascading Stops

A stop order, sometimes referred to as a stop-loss order, is entered at a particular price below the market, in the case of a sell stop, or above the market, in the case of a buy stop. They are typically used to offset existing positions where the market is moving adversely. For example, a stop sell may be entered below the market to prevent excessive losses on an existing long position. A stop buy may be entered above the market to prevent excessive losses on an existing short position. In an open outcry environment, these orders are triggered if even a single trade is recorded at the stop level. Once activated, these orders become market orders.

It has been argued that stop orders may tend to contribute to marketplace volatility. This argument may hold some validity to the extent that such orders, once activated, tend to chase the market. If there is a large series of stops at graduated levels in a market, this may cause the market to continue the chase in a particular direction for some time. Note further that stop orders may not be visible in the book to the extent that they are not activated until and unless a transaction is recorded at the stop price.

As noted earlier, there are no true market orders in the context of an electronic trading system such as CME Globex. This logic extends into stop orders insofar as, once a stop is triggered, the order cannot be entered or activated in the form of a true market order. As an alternative, the system offers two ways of handling stop orders in an electronic context.

1. *Stop limit orders:* Per a stop limit order, traders must specify two values, a stop price and a limit price. For example, a buy stop order may be entered with a stop price of 1,020.00 and a limit price of 1,025.00. This means that the stop is triggered if the market reaches 1,020.00 and activates a limit buy order at a price no higher than 1,025.00.
2. *Stop with protection order:* A stop with protection order is the functional equivalent to a stop limit order with the proviso that the gap between the stop price and the limit price automatically is set to the default protection point in force for the particular market in question.

In either case, stop orders are effectively converted into limit orders. The limiting aspect of the stop order is intended to prevent the activation of a series of cascading stops that may drive the market sharply in one direction or the other as a chain reaction, as seen in Exhibit 2.6.

EXHIBIT 2.6   Cascading Series of Stops

Price	Order Quantity	Cumulative Quantity	Stop Qty	
1,006.50	1,495	17,774		
1,006.25	1,712	16,279		
1,006.00	1,825	14,567	8,000	8,000-lot stop pushes prices up
1,005.75	1,386	12,742		even further
1,005.50	1,824	11,356		
1,005.25	1,592	9,532		
1,005.00	3,367	7,940		
1,004.75	2,147	4,573	10,000	10,000-lot stop pushes price
1,004.50	1,838	426		up thru 1,005.00
1,004.25	588	588	5,000	5,000-lot stop pushes price up
1,004.00				thru 1,005.00

For example, consider the possibility that the market is trading near 1,004.00 but ticks up to 1,004.25 where a 5,000-lot stop order resides. The order is triggered and pushes the market upward to a level of 1,004.75 where another 10,000-lot stop order resides. That order is triggered in turn, and the market continues its upward advance. As the market encounters more stops in sequential fashion, it continues to rally in a chain reaction fashion.

The possibility that a cascading series of stops may result in a rapid price movement in one direction or the other is hardly unique to electronic order books. It is quite possible that a cluster of stop orders is activated in an open outcry environment. But unlike an electronic order book, a trading pit does not necessarily operate in a strictly regimented sequential fashion. Thus, it is possible that one or more local traders may recognize what is triggering the price action and step in to take the other side of these cascading positions.

In contrast, the rapid and automated executions that are made possible by electronic order systems make the possibility of cascading stops a source of concern. Because of the sequential nature of electronic trading, buy stops could sweep through several price levels triggering additional stops that must be processed in sequential fashion. This possibility may be particularly acute in thin markets where the probability of sweeping through the book may be greater than in more liquid markets.

The CME Globex electronic facility combats this possibility with a stop cascade moderating logic. When stops are triggered, causing the price to move too far beyond current market levels, the system goes into a temporary reserve state, or "time-out," during which time trade matching is suspended but the system continues to process order entries. The market then reopens and trade matching resumes following the momentary suspension.

Trading Spreads

Futures are most frequently traded outright. However, spreads between contract months (intramarket or calendar spreads) and spreads between different commodities (intermarket spreads) are also frequently practiced. Spreads are generally executed in two different ways: (1) one may "leg in" to the spread by executing trades in both spread components separately, or (2) one may trade a listed spread quoted as a spread value.

If one legs into a spread, that implies the execution of two separate transactions. These two separate transactions will be documented with two separate trade instructions. Of course, traders who attempt to leg into spreads risk the possibility that one or both legs of the spread will not be filled or possibly filled at unsynchronized points in time.

As an alternative, the exchange often lists popular spreads to be traded as a unified whole. Locals in a pit may make markets quoting spreads between two (or more) separate items. Once filled as a spread, prices are assigned in the outright legs of the spread per exchange conventions. Spreads may also be listed in an electronic environment in a spread book or a central limit order book composed of orders to execute spread trades between the two contract months. The trade is explicitly negotiated on a spread basis (i. e., priced in terms of the spread). If a spread order is filled, then execution of both legs of the spread is guaranteed, and prices in the outright legs of the spread are assigned per exchange conventions.

But these practices may have the effect of fragmenting spread markets from outright markets. Clearly, spread and outright markets are highly related and trade in one market should contribute to liquidity in the other market. This fragmentation may become severe where there are many spread combinations available.

Consider, for example, the Eurodollar futures market in which contracts are listed a full 10 years out into the future. Thus, there are 40 quarterly Eurodollar futures listed at any given time and far more potential combinations of those futures in the form of calendar spreads between two different contract months.

The underlying subject of a Eurodollar futures contract is the London Interbank Offer Rate (LIBOR) for three-month Eurodollar deposits. This represents an important benchmark for U.S. denominated interest rates. The term structure or forward curve of these rates extending out 10 years into the future provides an important market view of the trajectory of future interest rates. Thus, the relative performance of different contract months quoted as a spread is of much interest to market participants. The forward curve observed in other markets such as crude oil and agricultural products is of similar interest.

Calendar spreads in various markets may be quoted with different conventions. But if you were to "buy a calendar spread" in Eurodollar futures, that implies that you are simultaneously buying a near-term contract month and selling a deferred contract month in Eurodollar futures. For example, buying the December 2009/March 2010 spread means you are buying December 2009 and selling March 2010 Eurodollar futures. "Selling a calendar spread" in Eurodollar futures means you are selling a near-term contract month and buying a deferred contract month (e.g., selling December 2009 and buying March 2010 futures).

The price of a Eurodollar calendar spread is quoted as the price of the near-term or nearby contract less the price on the deferred contract. This number could be either positive or negative depending on conditions in the interest rate markets. In a typical upwardly sloped yield curve environment, however, rates increase out into the future, and Eurodollar futures, quoted as 100 less yield, tend to decline in successively deferred months out into the future. Thus, the Eurodollar calendar spread quoted as nearby less deferred futures tends (conveniently) to be quoted as a positive number.

Consider the possibility that you "leg into" the December 2009/March 2010 spread by either buying or selling the spread. If you buy the spread, you may buy the nearby contract (presumably) at the current offer price and sell the deferred contract at the current bid price. If you sell the spread, you may sell the nearby contract at the bid and buy the deferred contract at the offer.

Example You may buy the December 2009/March 2010 Eurodollar calendar spread on September 1, 2009, by buying December 2009 futures at the offer of 99.505 and selling March 2010 at the bid of 99.285. This results in a quote of 0.220, or 22 basis points.

Example You may sell the December 2009/March 2010 Eurodollar calendar spread on September 1, 2009, by selling December 2009 futures at the bid of 99.500 and selling March 2010 at the bid of 99.290. This results in a quote of 0.210, or 21 basis points. See Exhibit 2.7.

EXHIBIT 2.7 Eurodollar Dec-09, Mar-10 and Spread Order Books (September 1, 2009, 12:50 PM Central Time)

Dec-09 Eurodollar Futures				Mar-10 Eurodollar Futures			
Bid Size	Bid	Ask	Ask Size	Bid Size	Bid	Ask	Ask Size
557	99.500	99.505	1,876	1,873	99.285	99.290	1,487
4,188	99.495	99.510	1,926	4,134	99.280	99.295	5,068
1,134	99.490	99.515	1,038	678	99.275	99.300	606
1,037	99.485	99.520	906	1,169	99.270	99.305	404
732	99.480	99.525	762	230	99.265	99.310	661

Dec-09/Mar-10 Eurodollar Spread			
Bid Size	Bid	Ask	Ask Size
3,271	0.210	0.215	921
3,250	0.200	0.220	2,526
1,549	0.200	0.225	1,466
200	0.190	0.230	1,851
210	0.190	0.235	598

In other words, you may currently leg into a long calendar spread at 22 basis points or leg into a short calendar spread at 21 basis points. This may be referred to as the "implied spread" in the sense that it is implied from the bids and offers prevailing in the outright markets.

However, we see that the quoted values in the calendar spread traded as a spread were actually tighter than the implied spread on this particular day. In fact, the calendar spread was bid at 21.0 basis points and offered at 21.5 basis points.

Implied Spread Functionality

The implied spread trade matching functionality of the CME Globex system effectively links the liquidity of these three separate order books together in a unified whole. This functionality populates the spread book with bids and offers that are effectively created by reference to the individual spread legs as well as orders entered directly into the spread book (the "implied in" process). Similarly, the functionality recognizes that the combination of an outright plus a spread may effectively create a bid or offer in the other outright leg of the spread (the "implied out" process).

This functionality has the effect of brokering trades involving three parties. To illustrate, assume that trader A wants to buy the calendar spread (i. e., buy December and sell March), trader B wants to sell December futures outright, and trader C wants to buy March futures outright. If one combines the offer in March entered by trader B with the bid in December entered by trader C, the system can effectively create or imply the value of a calendar spread. Assuming that the spread price implied by the combination of B's offer and C's bid matches the actual spread value bid by A, a match may occur and a transaction is consummated. See Exhibit 2.8.

The CME Globex system will construct implied bids and offers in spreads from the limit order books of the individual contract months. These implied quotes are commingling with actual bids and offers entered into the spread order book. Quantities that may be executable are shown on the system as the aggregate of the implied and actual spreads that are executable as a result.

Just as one may "imply in" bids and offers in spreads from the outright prices in the two legs of the spread, one may "imply out" outright bids and offers from spread prices. For example, one might sell a December 2009 Eurodollar futures contract and buy a December 2009/March 2009 spread to effectively create a short position in March 2009 futures. Alternatively, one may buy a December 2009 contract and sell the December 2009/March 2009 spread effectively to create a long position in March 2010.

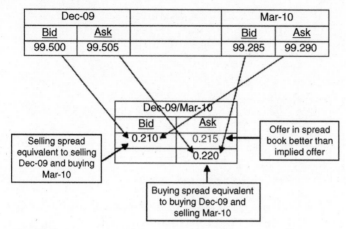

EXHIBIT 2.8 "Implying in" Spread Bid/Ask

Example On September 1, 2009, you may have sold December 2009 futures at the prevailing bid of 99.500 and bought the December 2009/March 2010 Eurodollar calendar spread at 0.215, or 21.5 basis points. This effectively creates a short position in March 2010 futures at a price of 99.285.

Sell Dec-09 Eurodollar futures @	99.500
Buy Dec-09/Mar-10 spread (buy Dec-09 and sell Mar-10) @	0.215
EQUALS Short Mar-10 Eurodollar futures @	99.285

Example On September 1, 2009, you may have bought December 2009 futures at the prevailing offer of 99.505 and sold the December 2009/March 2010 Eurodollar calendar spread at 0.210 or 21.0 basis points. This effectively creates a long position in March 2010 futures at a price of 99.295.

Buy Dec-09 Eurodollar futures @	99.505
Sell Dec-09/Mar-10 spread (sell Dec-09 and buy Mar-10) @	0.210
EQUALS Buy Mar-10 Eurodollar futures @	99.295

Thus, the CME Globex system creates implied outright positions in futures contracts by combining outrights and spreads. The system commingles these implied bids and offers with "real" bids and offers entered for any individual futures contract. Quantities bid and offered in an outright futures contract will reflect the aggregate of the implied and real executable orders entered into the system.

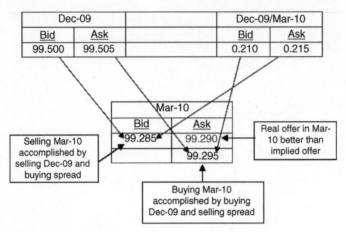

EXHIBIT 2.9 "Implying Out" an Outright Bid/Ask

As discussed, matching in Eurodollar futures is subject to the modified pro rata algorithm. Implied orders are included in the book just as a real order and receive their allocations accordingly. See Exhibit 2.9.

It is theoretically possible to imply even more complicated structures than calendar spreads. Indeed, spreads involving three contract months (or more) may be "implied." A butterfly spread may be created through the combination of positions in three contract months.[2] Or a butterfly may be implied from the three individual legs. Or a butterfly spread may be implied using a combination of outright positions and calendar spreads.

In the interest of operational trackability, however, CME Globex may not attempt to imply transactions based on all possible combinations. Thus, butterfly spread books in Eurodollar futures include implied orders based on the three individual component contract months. But the order books for the component contract months may not contain orders implied out from the butterfly spreads.

Not all spread markets are conducive to the application of implied spread functionality. For example, the pricing convention of the market may render implied functionality difficult or impossible. Consider that E-mini S&P 500 futures are quoted in minimum increments of 0.25 index points, whereas associated calendar spreads are quoted in minimum increments of 0.05 index points. Creation of implied outs into the outright markets could result in quotes that fell between the permissible increments in the outright market. Thus, implied spread functionality is only applied where outright and spread pricing conventions are compatible.

It is further possible to apply implied spread functionality in the context of intermarket spreads, subject to compatibility considerations. Again, it is important that the two markets are quoted on a compatible basis. It is further important to preserve the economics of the spread. For example, one may spread 5-year and 10-year U.S. Treasury note futures on a one-for-one basis to the extent that both contracts are based on a $100,000 face value unit and quoted compatibly in percent of par. But institutions often trade this spread in a ratio that reflects the relative volatility of the more volatile 10-year contract versus the less volatile 5-year contract.[3] That ratio will drift over time and will require monitoring and adjustment. Thus, implied spread functionality may be lost on an intermarket spread between 5- and 10-year Treasury futures.

ABOUT OPTIONS MARKETS

Our discussion thus far has focused on futures markets. But options on futures represent a much different instrument that necessitates certain adjustments in electronic trading methodologies.

In particular, options are inherently a spread market in the sense that they are priced by reference to the underlying futures contract for which they may be exercised. Further, they are often priced by reference to, or spread against, other options. In fact, there are a very wide variation of option spreads and combinations that trade frequently (e.g., vertical spreads, horizontal spreads, straddles, strangles, butterflies, condors, etc.). The sheer numbers of such spreads and combinations is daunting, so much so that a simple limit order book may not be up to the task of effectively supporting option trade.

Thus, several special features and functionalities have been developed to support options within the CME Globex electronic trading platform.

Mass Quotes

Traders, and particularly market makers, participating in option markets often find themselves faced with daunting operational challenges.

Consider that option traders must monitor and react to dynamic market conditions in myriad option series spread out over put options, call options, many different contract months, and many different strike prices. The number of series in any particular market may total into the dozens or hundreds. Still, all of the options in any particular market generally will respond to the same dynamic market conditions, notably including fluctuations in the value of the underlying futures contract, simultaneously. As such, market makers and other traders would prefer to update their orders in all these options simultaneously.

This means that option traders may wish to enter orders in a wide variety of option series with the ability to cancel and replace those orders quickly in response to dynamic conditions. In fact, this may become a risk management imperative if one suddenly begins to accumulate a large position as resting orders are suddenly filled in a variety of option series.

Accordingly, CME Globex has been programmed to include a functionality referred to as mass quoting. A *mass quote* represents a single or unified order message that incorporates bids and offers on a large number of options to be entered simultaneously.

Because these mass quotes may be transmitted in a single package, this conserves system "bandwidth," or capacity. Note that although telecommunications systems can be very fast and operate with very high capacities, systems may nonetheless be taxed with high message traffic in active markets. Electronic exchanges typically go to great lengths to upgrade speed and capacity. But there are still limits, and sometimes exchanges must "throttle back" or allocate message traffic as a result.

But perhaps the most important benefit of mass quoting is found in its contribution to enhanced risk management. The mass quoting functionality includes a feature to cancel all remaining orders when the aggregate order fulfillment across the entire mass quote exceeds a certain threshold. Traders establish this parameter when the mass quote is placed. This addresses concerns that traders who participate in many different option series simultaneously may get in over their heads from a risk perspective.

Options Spreads and Combos

Spread or combination trading in options can become exceedingly complex. Because of the large number of option series available, the number of spread and combination trades that may be created using those series may be extremely large. As a result, it may become impractical to create a limit order book for each and every spread or combination in which traders may be interested.

As a result, the CME Globex system has been adapted to accept instruction from users to create on-the-fly combinations of options not prelisted or created by another user. Once a combination of options is created, it can be traded on CME Globex as a free-standing instrument with its own limit order book.

Of course, traders may debate the merit of entering a spread trade in its entirety versus the prospect of legging into all the individual components of the trade separately. But often, and certainly for more common option trading strategies, the bid/offer in the spread market may be tighter than the bid/offer implied by the sum total of bid/offers in each of the individual legs.

Call Markets

The ability to create spreads on the fly sometimes leads to another problem. Specifically, once the previously unlisted combination is created, how would other traders know about it? Certainly if market makers are unaware of the availability of a particular spread or combination, they cannot be expected to populate the book with quotes. Three features have been developed to address this problem.

1. *Request for Quotes (RFQs):* An RFQ is a message transmitted by market participants throughout the CME Globex system to call attention to a particular instrument or market. Subsequent to the creation of a user-defined spread on the system, a trader may issue an RFQ to solicit bids and offers from other market participants including market makers.[4]
2. *Market Maker Allocations:* As an incentive to respond to RFQs in any particular market, the exchange may offer certain inducements to market markers. This may include financial incentives in strategic markets or, as discussed earlier, deployment of the market maker matching algorithm that provides market makers priority in the order queue.
3. *Formal Trade Crossing Requirements:* The exchange generally requires market participants to trade competitively through CME Globex or via open outcry. These trading environments generally do not permit traders to "cross" or fill transactions until and unless one or both orders is exposed to the competitive open market. This may be particularly important in less liquid markets including arcane user-defined spreads. Further, exchange rules generally prohibit "preexecution discussions" between prospective counterparties except under some very well-defined conditions.[5]

In certain markets, including Eurodollar options, the exchange offers a request for cross (RFC) facility. Per an RFC, an otherwise matching bid and offer may be set aside temporarily. The rest of the marketplace is alerted to the fact that a cross is being attempted and is invited to submit more bids or offers, ideally resulting in market improvement. Following the elapse of a specified amount of time, the RFC may be crossed in its entirety if it resides strictly inside the published bid/offer spread. If the incoming quotes offer price improvement on either side of the RFC order, the cross cannot take place. Instead, the RFC order will be matched to the improved quotation.

Delta Hedging

Option traders often use futures contracts as a means of hedging the price sensitivity inherent in an option premium. Because this hedging transaction typically is concluded in a ratio of futures to options dictated by the option delta, the trade is often known as a delta-neutral trade.

For example, if one buys 100 call options with a delta of 0.50, the position will perform somewhat like a position of 50 long futures. Thus, traders may sell 50 futures against the option position to create a "delta-neutral" position. Some traders, certainly including option market makers, would enjoy the convenience of placing an offsetting hedge in combination with a fill in the option market.

Electronic trading systems may be programmed to facilitate that convenience, although there are some complications. Specifically, the requisite number of futures needed to offset the price risk of an option position infrequently works out to a nice round number. Matters are complicated when pro rata trade matching algorithms are deployed to the extent that a pro rata allocation tends to fragment large trades, rendering it difficult to be assured of a fill in the correct ratio. Finally, of course, futures prices are dynamic and may run away from the levels at which they were trading at the moment when the option transaction is filled.

CME Group has developed functionality to address this issue called the covered user-defined spread (covered UDS). This system feature is currently deployed in the Eurodollar option market.

The covered UDS system represents an extension of the user-defined spread environment for option-only spreads. But the system is refined to define the limiting element of the order by reference to an option premium and the futures price.

Upon definition of a covered UDS, an RFQ is issued and broadcast to all market participants to solicit the entry of bids and offers. The system subsequently observes most standard UDS and RFQ procedures. Once a match is made, the system determines the appropriate number of futures to allocate to the covered UDS. For example, a transaction for 100 long calls with a delta of 0.50 suggests that one needs to sell 50 futures. Those 50 futures may be filled at a price level specified in the original covered UDS definition. The 50 contracts are then allocated to the contra side of the transaction in proportion to the size of each order. Thus, if the position is matched with two orders to buy 60 contracts each, both of those orders are allocated 25 contracts.

Fluctuations in the value of the futures contract may be handled by market participants by adjusting the specification of the limit futures price. Note that otherwise identical covered UDSs at two different limit prices on the futures side of the transaction are entered as, and considered to be, two separate instruments. Thus, the two separate instruments populate two separate limit order books. This may have the effect of fragmenting liquidity, so it is advisable to determine if there is a similarly constructed covered UDS before defining a new specification.

Volatility Quotes

Options on futures are normally quoted by reference to the option premium using the same currency and quote conventions associated with the underlying futures contract. For example, an option on a EuroFX futures contract is quoted in terms of dollars and cents per one euro just like EuroFX futures.

But sometimes option traders prefer to quote in terms of volatility. Volatility is one of several major inputs into mathematical option on futures pricing models including the underlying market price, strike price, term until expiration, and short-term interest rates. CME Globex accommodates this by offering a distinct limit order book in which options are quoted on the basis of volatility defined in terms of an annualized standard deviation of day-to-day percentage price movements (vol quotes) rather than premium.

Once a trade is matched in terms of volatility, the trade must be booked and accounted for in terms of an option premium quoted using standard pricing conventions. Accordingly, the system determines the option premium based on a standard mathematical option pricing formula referencing the traded volatility as the input. That price is booked into the system.

The vol quote system also includes the functionality to include an offsetting futures position in the transaction. The ratio of futures to options as indicated by delta is likewise determined by reference to a standard mathematical option pricing formula. Any covering futures position is booked at the same futures price used for determining the option premium.

The volatility-based quoting system is conceptually straightforward, whereas the covered UDS is more flexible but entails more effort on the part of the trader.

EX-PIT TRADING

The preceding discussion focused on the competitive trading venues hosted by the exchange. Indeed, the bulk of the volume in listed futures and options is consummated in either an open outcry or electronic trading environment. In recent years, activity has shifted strongly in favor of the latter trading venue. As such, the plurality of trading is conducted in an open, transparent, and competitive manner that permits CME Group contracts to be used for purposes of price discovery.

But there are some circumstances in which a privately negotiated or "ex-pit" trade may be warranted. The term *ex-pit trade* refers to any transaction that is executed on a noncompetitive basis and outside of a traditional open outcry or electronic trading environment. The several varieties of ex-pit transactions serve slightly different purposes and may be subject to somewhat different rules. These transactions are known by a variety of names including exchange for physicals (EFPs), exchange for risk (EFRs), block trades, and cleared-only, or ClearPort, contracts. Whatever the nomenclature, they may collectively be referred to as "ex-pit" transactions.

Exchange for Physicals

Exchange for physicals (EFP) transactions originated over a century ago in grain and other physical commodity markets. An EFP is a transaction that is privately negotiated between two counterparties and involves the simultaneous exchange of a futures position for an economically offsetting position.

Although traditionalists in the futures industry are accustomed to referring to EFPs, sometimes terms become fine-tuned so that more descriptive terminology is used to distinguish these types of trades on the basis of the nature of the offsetting position. Technically, an EFP refers to a transaction in which a futures position is assumed in juxtaposition to an offsetting cash or spot transaction. The term *exchange for risk* (EFR) may be used to identify similar transactions in which a futures position is offset by an over-the-counter (OTC) derivatives position. Over the years, these practices have been adopted in the context of futures markets and generalized as *exchange of futures for related positions* (EFRPs).

Still, apart from a rather fine distinction regarding the nature of the offsetting position, EFPs and EFRs are almost identical, representing two forms of EFRP transactions. Other terms that have been used over the years to refer to similar types of transactions include *exchange for swap* (EFS) and exchange basis facility (EBF). But veterans of the industry sometimes apply the term *EFP* in a generalized sense, and we conform to that tradition here.

EFPs may be thought of as privately negotiated "basis trades." The futures trade is bilaterally negotiated, apart from a competitive trading environment such as the CME Globex electronic trading platform or the exchange floor, and subsequently novated to the CME Group Clearing House, where it is accounted for just like any other futures position. Note that the exchange plays no role in facilitating the execution of, or subsequent bookkeeping for, the cash, spot, or OTC position. Rather, that is contingent on the two counterparties to the EFP.

The cash, spot, or OTC position that is traded opposite to the futures contract must be a product that represents a legitimate economic offset. The exchange identifies acceptable offsets for any particular listed market. For example, in the context of stock index futures, recognized offsetting positions include baskets of stock, exchange-traded funds (ETFs), or OTC equity swaps.

Stock baskets must be "highly correlated" to the underlying index with a correlation of 0.90 or greater to be part of an EFP. Further, these stock baskets must represent at least 50% of the underlying index by weight or include at least 50% of the names of the underlying index. The notional value of the basket must be functionally equivalent to the value of the futures component of the trade.

Exchange-traded funds (ETFs) are also acceptable as part of an EFP provided that they mirror the stock index on which the futures contract is based. For example, SPDRs represent an acceptable mirror for S&P 500 futures insofar as the SPDR Trust holds the stocks that constitute the index in a (near) exact match. Likewise, QQQQs represent an acceptable mirror for Nasdaq 100 futures. Equity swaps that mirror stock index futures are likewise acceptable as a component of an EFP transaction.

An EFP may be transacted at any time and at any price agreed on by the two counterparties. Two customers may transact an EFRP among themselves provided that the resulting futures position is subsequently submitted to the CME Clearing House (CH) through the facilities of a clearing member. More commonly, however, a customer establishes a relationship with a dealer who is inclined to make a market, that is, show a bid and an offer, in the particular market(s) in question. These dealers normally require the customer to carry a futures account as well as a securities account in which the resulting futures and cash positions may reside. A variety of firms may make markets in EFPs, although the exchange assumes a neutral posture and does not offer recommendations in this regard.

After the two counterparties consummate the transaction, the futures position is reported to the CH through a clearing member via electronic systems. The cash position continues to be held in appropriate accounts established by the EFP counterparties and is not reported to the exchange upon execution. If called on during the course of a periodic audit, however, clearing members may be required to produce statements that show the offsetting position was transacted and meets exchange standards as a valid offsetting position.

Although dealers often show bids and offers on EFPs to customers directly, the exchange does not post such quotes or otherwise facilitate the execution of these transactions. CME Group cannot facilitate the transaction of stock index EFPs where the cash side of the transaction represents a basket of securities or ETFs. In particular, one must be registered as a securities exchange to facilitate the public trade of securities under U.S. law, noting that CME Group operates as a registered futures exchange and not as a securities exchange.

EFPs are generally used by institutional traders who find themselves with existing cash positions that they may wish to offset using futures transactions. For example, market makers in ETFs may find themselves either long or short large inventories that they may wish to hedge. By using an EFRP transaction, these market makers may readily transform a preexisting ETF position into a futures position, thereby enjoying the liquidity and financial sureties associated with trading at CME Group. So-called program traders who seek to arbitrage possible temporary pricing discrepancies between cash and futures markets may find EFPs to be a convenient way to liquidate or reduce possible long or short stock basket holdings.

Ex-pit transactions including EFRPs are allowed by CME Group as an accommodation to traders who find this a convenient and expeditious way of conducting business. They are not intended to represent the mainstream way of trading futures. Rather, the exchange expects that the plurality of trading will be conducted in an open, competitive trading venue such as open outcry or on Globex.

Price discovery represents a primary function of the futures market. Thus, it is important to promote a transparent trading venue as the primary trading venue where values may readily be referenced. Liquidity is a necessary prerequisite for the efficient discovery of equilibrium prices. In fact, only a small proportion of volume in CME Group markets is transacted as EFPs. Still, EFPs represent a useful and convenient outlet for some traders and therefore remain consistent with the exchange's mission of providing customers with an efficient source of price discovery as well as hedging utility.

Block Trade Facility

A block trade represents an outright trade or spread in a futures or option contract that is privately negotiated between two eligible counterparties. Unlike an EFP or EFR, a block trade does not involve an offsetting cash or OTC transaction. Once executed on this basis, the transaction is submitted or novated to the CH for trade processing, bookkeeping, and the application of financial safeguards.

Block trades serve a useful purpose, particularly in the context of very large transactions that may not be executable quickly at a single price in an open outcry or electronic trading environment. The concept of "best execution" has traditionally been used to refer to a situation where one may obtain the absolute best available price. But best execution may mean somewhat different things to different traders. Some customers value other factors in addition to the best available price (e.g., speed of execution or a fill at a single price as opposed to a "split" fill among many prices). Block trades are further useful in the context of very complicated transactions such as multi-legged spreads.

Block trades are subject to unique rules that govern their trade including eligibility, minimum quantities, and pricing requirements. The exchange identifies which markets are eligible for block trading. For example, S&P 500 futures are currently ineligible for block trading. Block trades are limited to so-called eligible contract participants (ECPs) as defined by CFTC regulation. This essentially limits block trading to institutions or very well-heeled individuals.

Block trading is limited to "large" quantities relative to normal trading patterns in the particular market as identified by the exchange. As of this writing, for example, Eurodollar futures have a minimum threshold of 4,000 contracts during U.S. trading hours, assuming that all futures expirations in the trade are within the 20 nearest quarterly expirations. These thresholds are subject to review and revision by the Exchange. Finally, block transactions must be concluded at prices that are "fair and reasonable" in light of prevailing market conditions.

Cleared-Only Contracts

Some CME Group contracts are offered on a "cleared-only" basis. This facility is intended to allow transactions executed in an OTC regulatory environment to be submitted or novated to the CH for purposes of trade processing and the application of financial safeguards. The exchange generally uses the CME ClearPort facility for purposes of these transactions.

Although this concept may be applied to any number of commodity and financial markets, the service has been most widely accepted to date within the context of the NYMEX energy markets. ClearPort was originated in the early 2000s at NYMEX but was relabeled CME ClearPort subsequent to the CME Group's acquisition of NYMEX Holdings, Inc. in 2008.

CME ClearPort should not be thought of as a trading platform or as a clearing service. Rather it is best understood as an Internet or web-based gateway. The CME ClearPort system currently provides traders a wide degree of latitude to conduct transactions in literally hundreds of energy, metals, and other contracts. These transactions are executed off exchange in a bilateral transaction directly between buyer and seller. This is much like the execution of any other OTC derivatives contract. Subsequently, the transaction is submitted or "novated" to the CH for purposes of processing and clearance. This is accomplished through the EFP, EFS, or substitution (SUB) process. The SUB process represents the transaction of an OTC derivative that is subsequently novated to the CH and transformed into a futures position and may be thought of as akin to an EFP or EFS.

Whatever nomenclature is used, the net result is that the original OTC derivative is extinguished in favor of a corresponding futures position with economically equivalent terms and conditions. Once the transaction is accepted and processed in the exchange's multilateral clearing system, it is subject to initial and periodic variation margin requirements like any other futures contract. Like any other futures contract and unlike an OTC derivatives contract, it may be offset with an opposite transaction with any other counterparty and not just with the original counterparty.

By submitting OTC transactions to the CME ClearPort process, one enjoys the financial sureties afforded by the CH. Thus, one may effectively address counterparty credit risks, which of course have become heightened in the wake of the so-called subprime mortgage crisis.

CME ClearPort currently facilitates the processing of a very wide variety of contracts linked to natural gas; crude oil; petroleum by-products; ethanol; freight rates; "green" products; electricity; coal; metals; currencies; so-called softs including coffee, cocoa, and sugar; commodity indexes including the S&P/GSCI Index; uranium; petrochemicals; and grains.

These contracts may be based on the outright values for these products or may use alternative structures. A "basis swap" is a very common structure that essentially represents a spread between the values of a commodity at two different locations. For example, one might trade a basis swap between the values of natural gas at the benchmark Henry Hub location versus the Houston ship channel. Index swaps, swing swaps, and options may also be available.

Although the ClearPort concept has been deployed with the most success to date in the context of energy products, the exchange intends to extend the process to other markets including interest rates, credit derivatives, currencies, equities, agricultural, and other markets.

CONCLUSION

This chapter provides an overview of order entry and execution methodologies as they have evolved over the years. In particular, the transition from a pit-based, open outcry environment to electronic trading platforms has dramatically altered the nature of futures and option trading. Electronics facilitate direct access on a globalized basis. As a result of this widespread distribution, volumes in the industry have skyrocketed over the past decade.

Electronic trading systems provide much more flexibility than a physical trading environment. They allow traders to automate their strategic trading and order entry approaches using so-called algorithmic trading methodologies. CME Group has responded by developing market-specific matching algorithms to meet the specific circumstances in various markets.

In addition to offering access through its legacy open outcry and electronic trading platforms, the exchange also offers so-called ex-pit trading with the use of EFP and blocks trades. Finally, CME Group is active in accepting transactions originally executed as an OTC derivative for purposes of processing and clearing through its CME ClearPort facility.

NOTES

1. Granting ultimate customers the ability to access CME Globex directly does not necessarily imply that customers will opt for self-execution. Some institutional customers may elect to retain brokers to submit their orders on their behalf. Self-execution necessitates some level of staffing and supporting equipment. One must further consider the possibility of erroneous trade executions when trading directly. Finally, some brokers may provide valuable advice regarding trading or execution strategies that might not be accessible when directing one's own trading activities.
2. Eurodollar futures butterfly spreads reflect the curvature of the yield curve, which is, in itself, a subject of trading interest. Buying a butterfly spread means one buys equal quantities in the first and third contract months and sells twice those quantities in the second or middle contract month. Selling a butterfly spread, of course, is just the opposite transaction.
3. The spread between the 5-year and 10-year U.S. Treasury note futures reflects the yield spread between the T-notes that underlie each contract. Those underlying Treasury securities are mismatched in terms of duration and therefore will exhibit very different price movements in response to a given change in yield. Thus, the spread needs to be weighted properly so it will be sensitive only to changes in the yield spread as opposed to parallel shifts in the yield curve. This suggests that one needs more 5-year Treasury futures and fewer 10-year Treasury futures given that longer term fixed-income instruments are generally more sensitive to changing yields than are shorter term fixed-income instruments.
4. Note that RFQs are not confined to options spreads. They may be issued in the context of any listed contract for purposes of soliciting actionable quotations.
5. See, for example, Rule 539.C in the CME Rulebook for the complete description of the rules governing preexecution discussion.

CHAPTER 3

Role of the Clearinghouse

Dale Michaels
Jim Moran
John W. Labuszewski

The Chicago Butter and Egg Board was founded in 1898 and evolved into the Chicago Mercantile Exchange (CME), a not-for-profit Illinois corporation, in 1919, at which time a clearinghouse was introduced. In 2000, CME transformed into a for-profit Delaware corporation called the Chicago Mercantile Exchange Inc. In 2001, CME completed a reorganization to create Chicago Mercantile Exchange Holdings Inc. ("CME Holdings"), which became the parent company of CME. In 2002, CME Holdings underwent an initial public offering, and its stock is now listed on the Nasdaq Global Select Market under the ticker symbol CME. CME Holdings was the surviving company in the 2007 merger of CME Holdings and CBOT Holdings, Inc. (CBOT) and was renamed CME Group Inc. (CME Group). CME Group serves the risk-management requirements of customers around the globe. Subsequently, in 2008, CME Group acquired the New York Mercantile Exchange (NYMEX) and the Commodity Exchange (COMEX). CME Group offers a broad array of significant interest rate, equity, currency, commodity, and alternative investments products such as weather and real estate on the floor of the exchange and through the CME Globex electronic trading platform.

The Clearing House Division (CME Clearing) of CME (or the Exchange) operates as an integrated operating division of the exchange. It has been registered as a Derivatives Clearing Organization (DCO) as defined by Section 1a(9) of the Commodity Exchange Act since December 21, 2000. This corresponds to the date on which DCO registrations were recognized per the Commodity Futures Modernization Act [CFMA] of December 2000.

FINANCIAL SAFEGUARDS

The accounts of individual members, clearing firms, and nonmember customers must be carried and guaranteed to CME Clearing by a clearing member. For every transaction received by or matched through its facilities, CME Clearing is substituted as the counterparty, guaranteeing performance on the opposite side. Clearing members assume full financial and performance responsibility for all transactions executed through them and all positions they carry. CME Clearing, dealing exclusively with clearing members, holds each clearing member accountable for every position it carries regardless of whether the position is being carried for the account of an individual member, for the account of a nonmember customer, or for the clearing member's own customer account. Conversely, as the contra-side to every position, CME Clearing is held accountable to the clearing members for the net settlement from all transactions on which it has been substituted as provided in CME Rules.

Ensuring Financial Integrity

CME Clearing does not look to individual customers for performance or attempt to evaluate their creditworthiness or market qualifications. CME Clearing monitors clearing member firms for the adequacy of credit monitoring and risk management of their customers. CME Clearing looks solely to the clearing member firm carrying and guaranteeing the account to secure all payments and performance bond obligations. Clearing members provide a clearing guarantee to an individual and act as the guarantor of last resort for all resulting trades.

The financial safeguards package encompasses all activity cleared by CME Group to maximize capital efficiencies. As CME Clearing has begun to offer clearing services to over-the-counter (OTC) markets, financial safeguard standards have been aligned to best serve the unique attributes of each market. In spite of market differences, CME Clearing employs mark-to-market, performance bond requirements, and account identification as standard risk management practices for all markets served.

The risk management and financial surveillance techniques employed by CME Clearing are comprehensive and specifically designed to:

- Anticipate potential market exposures;
- Ensure that sufficient resources are available to cover future obligations;
- Result in the prompt detection of financial and operational weaknesses;

■ Allow swift and appropriate action to be taken to rectify any financial problems and protect the clearing system; and
■ Prevent the accumulation of losses.

These techniques are consistent with risk-management recommendations and industry best practice standards such as those promulgated by the CPSS/IOSCO Task Force on Securities Settlement Systems and the Group of Thirty.

Mark-to-Market

CME Clearing derives its financial stability in large part by removing debt obligations among market participants as they occur. This is accomplished by determining a marking price at the close of each settlement cycle twice daily, for each contract, and marking all open positions to that price. Debt obligations from option contracts are also immediately removed because the purchaser of an option must pay the premium (cost of the option) in full at the time of purchase.

Each business day, CME Clearing performs two full settlement cycles, marking to the market once in the late morning and once again in the late afternoon. Actual settlement of the late morning mark-to-market occurs at midday, and actual settlement of the late afternoon mark-to-market occurs in the very early morning hours of the next day.

Two distinct processes occur during a settlement cycle. Initially, at each settlement cycle, all new trades are captured, cleared, and marked-to-market. All open positions are marked-to-market at this time. Cash settlement flow occurs for the mark-to-market on open futures positions and the option premium associated with new option positions. The mark-to-market on open option positions can be satisfied with collateral as part of performance bond requirements. The resulting cash flows between clearing member firms and CME Clearing are known as settlement variation.

Simultaneously, forward looking collateral requirements are reevaluated for all open positions. The combination of these two processes, including the cash payments that move between CME Clearing and its clearing members and the resetting of performance bond coverage, ensure that all accumulated debt obligations are removed from the system, and that CME Clearing holds sufficient collateral to protect against any losses clearing members may accumulate prior to the subsequent settlement cycle.

In times of extreme price volatility, CME Clearing has the authority to perform additional mark-to-market calculations on open positions and call for immediate payment of settlement variation. Settlement variation payments through CME Clearing averaged $2.1 billion per day in 2007 and peaked at $10.3 billion in August 2007. CME Clearing's mark-to-market settlement system stands in direct contrast to the traditional settlement systems implemented by many other financial markets that are not centrally cleared, including interbank currency, Treasury security markets, various OTC markets based on interest rate, currency, credit, equity and commodity instruments, where participants regularly assume credit exposure to each other. In those markets, the failure of one participant can have a ripple effect on the solvency of the other participants. Conversely, CME Clearing's mark-to-market system does not allow losses to accumulate over time or allow a market participant the opportunity to defer losses associated with market positions.

Performance Bonds

Performance bond requirements represent good faith deposits to guarantee performance on open positions and are often referred to as *margin*. CME Clearing establishes minimum initial and maintenance performance bond levels for all products cleared through its facilities. CME Clearing bases these requirements on historical and implied price volatilities, market composition, current and anticipated market conditions, and other relevant information. Performance bond levels vary by product and are adjusted periodically to reflect changes in price volatility and other factors. Maintenance performance bond levels represent the minimum amount of protection against potential losses at which the exchange will allow a clearing member to carry a position or portfolio. Initial performance bond reflects the minimum deposit a clearing member must obtain from a customer opening a new position. Should performance bonds on deposit at the customer level fall below the maintenance level, Exchange rules require that the account be re-margined at the required higher initial performance bond level. Initial performance bond enables a customer to absorb some losses before issuance of another performance bond call. Clearing members may impose more stringent performance bond requirements than the minimums set by the exchanges. At the CME Clearing level, clearing members must post at least the maintenance performance bonds for all positions carried. This requirement applies to positions of individual members, nonmember customers, and the clearing member itself.

In setting performance bond levels, CME Clearing monitors both current and historical price and volatility movements covering short-, intermediate- and longer-term data. CME Clearing uses several different methods of statistical parametric and nonparametric analyses that typically establish futures maintenance performance bond levels covering expected one-day price moves of at least 95 to 99% of the days during these time periods. Actual performance bond requirements may exceed this level for some products. Performance bond requirements for options reflect movements in the underlying futures price, volatility, time to expiration, and other risk factors and adjust automatically each day to reflect the unique and changing risk characteristics of each option series. In addition, long options must be paid for in full. CME Clearing also mandates stringent minimum performance bonds for short option positions. Option sellers are assessed risk requirements as determined by CMEG's Standard Portfolio Analysis of Risk (SPAN) system, in addition to the value of the option.

CME Clearing calculates performance bonds using the SPAN system that was developed and implemented by CME in 1988. SPAN bases performance bond requirements on the overall risk of the portfolios using parameters as determined by CME Clearing, and it represents a significant improvement over other performance bond systems, most notably those that are "strategy based" or "delta based." SPAN simulates the effects of changing market conditions and uses standard options pricing models to determine a portfolio's overall risk. It treats all products uniformly while recognizing the unique features of options. In standard options pricing models, three factors most strongly affect options values: the underlying price, volatility (variability of the underlying price), and time to expiration. As these factors change, positions may gain or lose value. SPAN constructs scenarios of price and volatility changes to simulate what the entire portfolio might reasonably lose over a one-day time horizon. The resulting SPAN performance bond requirement covers this potential loss. CME has licensed SPAN to other exchanges and clearing organizations around the world and has successfully established SPAN as the industry's standard performance bond system.

CME Clearing requires "gross" performance bonds for customer segregated positions in products traded on CME Group's exchanges. The clearing member must deposit performance bonds for each open position (long or short) held at each clearing cycle, with appropriate allowances for spreads. CME Clearing allows for optimal margining for customer segregated positions in CBOT products as a continuation of the market practices for those products, giving clearing member firms the choice of modified "net" performance bonds that exclude long option value or "gross" performance bonds that include long option value. CME Clearing allows for "net" performance bonds for nonsegregated or proprietary positions. If a clearing member does not have sufficient performance bond collateral on deposit with CME Clearing, then the clearing member must meet a call for cash performance bond deposits by the designated time after each settlement cycle, which results in a direct debit to the clearing member's account at one of CME Clearing's settlement banks. Active clearing members may meet performance bond requirements using a wide variety of collateral, including:

- Cash (denominated in U.S. dollars and selected foreign currency);
- U.S. Treasury securities;
- Letters of credit;
- Stocks selected from the Standard & Poor's 500 (S&P 500) Stock Price Index;
- Selected sovereign debt;
- Selected agencies and mortgage-backed securities;
- Selected money market mutual funds; and
- Bank-sponsored cash management program, through selected banks.

Securities are revalued every day and are subject to prudent haircuts. Additionally, foreign cash is subject to haircuts in selected circumstances. Various forms of collateral are also subject to limits. CME Clearing also offers a choice of several different collateral management programs, providing efficient and cost-effective solutions for clearing member firms collateral management needs.

Concentration Performance Bond

CME Clearing maintains a concentration performance bond program, which allows CME Clearing to charge additional performance bond requirements when clearing firms' potential market exposures become large relative to the financial resources available to support those exposures.

Cross-Margining

In recognition of the growing linkages among the markets for exchange-traded equity derivative products, as well as the need to promote efficient clearing procedures and to focus on the true intermarket risk exposure of clearing members, CME Clearing, in conjunction with the Options Clearing Corporation (OCC) offers a cross-margining program with respect to market professionals and proprietary accounts. Combination of the positions of joint or affiliated clearing members in certain broad-based equity index futures and options into a single portfolio and the application of sophisticated risk-based margining systems of each clearing organization results in a single performance bond requirement across both markets. The clearing organizations jointly hold a first lien on, and security interest in, the positions in cross-margined accounts. All performance bond deposits associated with these accounts are jointly held. The cross-margining program significantly enhances both the efficiency and financial integrity of the clearing system by allowing gains accruing to futures or options positions to be immediately available to meet the requirements for funds from losing positions.

In the event that a clearing organization suspends a cross-margining member, the positions in the cross-margin accounts would be liquidated and all performance bond collateral would be converted to cash and applied toward each clearing organization's costs of liquidating the cross-margin accounts. CME Clearing and the OCC are each entitled to half of any surplus to apply toward other obligations of the clearing member; if one clearing organization did not need its entire share of the surplus, the excess would be made available to the other clearing organization.

Clearing also maintains a cross-margin agreement, the Fixed Income Clearing Corporation. This program involves the cross-margining of selected short-term interest rate and fixed-income products. The design of this cross-margin program differs from the OCC program mentioned earlier in that performance bond collateral is held separately at each respective clearing organization. In the event that a clearing organization suspends a cross-margining participant, the cross-margined positions would be liquidated and performance bond collateral would be converted to cash at each respective clearing organization. If as a result of the liquidation of cross-margined positions and performance bond there is a resulting cross-margin loss, there will be a cross-margin guarantee payment from one clearing organization to the other to share the loss.

Segregation of Customer Funds

Regulations governing the U.S. futures and options on futures markets require that customer positions and monies be separately accounted for and segregated from the positions and monies of the clearing member. The regulations are designed to protect customers in the event of the insolvency or financial instability of the clearing member through which they conduct business. The requirements of separate accounting and segregation of customer positions and monies extend to CME Clearing. Based on specific written instructions from a clearing member, CME Clearing maintains separate accounting of the aggregate positions and monies of the clearing member's customers.

CME's Audit Department routinely inspects the books and records of clearing members to ensure, among other things, their compliance with segregation requirements. The integrity of segregation relies on the accuracy and timeliness of the information provided to CME Clearing by member firms. Violations by a clearing member of its segregation requirements are considered serious infractions and can result in major penalties imposed by the Exchange.

Cleared OTC markets generally are unregulated and therefore not subject to the segregation of customer funds. However, OTC products clearing through CME Clearing are subject to CME Clearing's standard risk-management practices and may under certain circumstances qualify for segregation.

Capital Requirements for Clearing Members

CME Group clearing members subject to Commodity Futures Trading Commission (CFTC) regulation are required to maintain adjusted net capital (ANC) at prescribed levels.

Clearing members generally must maintain ANC in excess of the greatest of the following.

- $2,500,000;
- CFTC minimum regulatory capital requirements (see later); or
- Securities and Exchange Commission (SEC) minimum regulatory capital requirements.

Note that certain clearing members with restricted clearing privileges, including inactive clearing members, may be subject to reduced capital requirements.

CME Group and the CFTC have adopted a risk-based capital requirement as the regulatory minimum capital requirement. This requirement is computed as 8% of domestic and foreign domiciled customer and 4% of noncustomer (excluding proprietary) risk maintenance performance bond requirements for all domestic and foreign futures and options on futures contracts excluding the risk margin associated with naked long option positions. ANC is computed based on the following formula:

$$\text{Adjusted Net Capital (ANC)} = \text{Current Assets} - \text{Adjusted Liabilities} - \text{Capital Charges}$$

Where "current assets" refers to cash and other assets that are reasonably expected to be realized as cash, or sold, during the next 12 months.

However, certain assets such as prepaid expenses, deferred charges, and unsecured receivables from customers, noncustomers, subsidiaries, and affiliates, which would be classified as current under generally accepted accounting principles, are deemed noncurrent. Exchange memberships and assigned shares are also reflected as noncurrent assets.

Adjusted liabilities is a reference to the clearing member's total liabilities less the liabilities that have been subordinated to the claims of general creditors. Finally, *capital charges* refer to regulatory capital charges that primarily encompass percentage deductions ("haircuts") on the following:

- Speculative proprietary futures and options positions;
- Proprietary inventories, fixed-price commitments, and forward contracts;
- Undermargined customer, noncustomer, and omnibus accounts; and
- Marketable securities.

CMEG Group's risk-based capital requirements are identical to those imposed by the CFTC, except inactive clearing members are not subject to risk-based capital requirements. Capital requirements are monitored by CMEG Group's Audit Department. ANC requirements vary to reflect the risk of each clearing member's positions as well as CME Group's assessment of each clearing member's internal controls, risk-management policies, and back office operations.

In order to clear products at one or more CME Group exchanges, you are required to own a certain number of memberships at the exchange along with a certain number of Class A equity shares. This requirement may vary depending upon the nature of one's business. These requirements may be subject to change and it is recommended that the reader consult current CME Group requirements for specific information.

An OTC clearing member must be in compliance with all applicable regulatory capital requirements; however, an OTC clearing member must maintain a minimum of $50 million in capital if it clears only commodity OTC derivatives and $300 million in capital if it clears financial or credit (i.e., equity, interest rate, etc.) derivatives. A CME, CBOT, NYMEX, and COMEX clearing member must maintain $300 million in capital if it clears interest rate swaps or credit default swaps.

Finally, CME Group rules generally require owners of 5% or more of the equity securities of a clearing member to guarantee obligations arising out of house (noncustomer and proprietary) accounts of clearing members to the extent of their ownership interest. Owners of 50% or more must guarantee 100% of the house obligations. This parent guarantee provides a high level of assurance that obligations arising out of trades made and positions held by owners of clearing members are promptly discharged.

FINANCIAL SURVEILLANCE

Recognizing the need to monitor the financial condition of clearing members, the CME Audit Department, in conjunction with other self-regulatory organizations, operates a sophisticated financial surveillance program. The program has several important aspects including (1) reporting; (2) notification; (3) inspection; (4) information sharing; and (5) intraday monitoring activities, as outlined next.

Reporting

Clearing members must calculate segregation requirements and ensure compliance with capital requirements daily. In addition, firms must submit to the Audit Department full financial statements monthly, provide certified financial statements once a year, and make more frequent reports (daily) as directed.

Notification

Clearing members are required to report any failure to meet segregation or minimum capital requirements. Clearing member firms must notify CME Clearing prior to any significant business transaction or significant change in operations.

Inspection

Generally each clearing member is subject to a financial/operational review every year. The reviews are tailored to focus on the specific risks of the clearing member. All such inspections are performed without prior notification.

Information Sharing

CME Clearing participates in formal agreements with other clearing and self-regulatory organizations, domestic and foreign, regularly exchanging financial and operational information about joint common clearing members with other participating markets. Recognizing that the financial marketplace spans the globe, CMEG was instrumental in developing the International Information Sharing Memorandum of Understanding, which established a framework for 65 exchanges and clearing organizations worldwide to share information relevant to managing global market emergencies. CME Clearing also seeks broader cooperation between clearing organizations through such industry forums as the Unified Clearing Group, the Joint Audit Committee, CCP 12, the Intermarket Financial Surveillance Group, and the DCO Risk Committee.

Intraday Monitoring

CME Clearing monitors intraday price movements throughout the trading session. To assess the impact of these price changes on clearing members, intraday mark-to-market calculations are performed on clearing member positions and reviewed by CME Clearing throughout the day and overnight. Large or concentrated positions on the losing side of the market receive special attention. CME Clearing monitors its clearing member firms' settlement variation and performance bond activities at non-CMEG cleared exchanges and clearing organizations daily. The risk-management team may contact the exchanges or clearing organizations to follow up on this activity. The Audit Department may either contact or visit a clearing firm to determine whether proper performance bonds have been collected for positions and to determine their impact on the clearing member's capital position and liquidity.

CME Clearing conducts stress testing of clearing member positions daily. Numerous stress scenarios have been modeled to reflect a diverse set of possible market events. Stress results are evaluated against performance bond on deposit and also with clearing member adjusted net capital. Results of stress tests may lead CME Clearing to request that the clearing member provide additional information about its customer accounts such as whether there are non-CME Group offsetting positions in other markets. In some cases stress test results may cause CME Clearing to increase a clearing member's performance bond requirement or reduce or transfer positions.

Market Regulation

Through CME Group's Division of Market Regulation, the risk-management team has daily access to specific account position information regarding individual members, nonmember customers, and clearing members, all of which is kept highly confidential. Such critical information allows the identification of concentrated positions as they arise and the aggregation of positions that may be owned by common principals through several different clearing members. Knowledge of concentrated or high-risk positions, coupled with information routinely gathered on the cash and/or related derivative markets, enables CME Clearing to respond rapidly to market situations that might adversely affect the clearing system and/or the financial stability of a clearing member. Account-level information is monitored for both regulated and non-regulated activity.

Clearing Member Risk Reviews

CME Clearing periodically visits clearing member firms to review financial, operational, credit, and market risk-management procedures and capabilities. Senior CME Clearing professionals evaluate how well each firm's procedures and capabilities correspond to its line of business. Senior professionals from Audit, Clearing, Risk Management, and Market Regulation follow up with the clearing member's senior management if deficiencies are found in their risk management procedures and capabilities.

DEFAULT BY A CLEARING MEMBER

CME Group continues to maintain the financial safeguards system and general default procedures for both regulated and OTC markets. Additionally, bankruptcy provisions have been reviewed to remain consistent with the application to each class of clearing member. Although the risk management and financial surveillance techniques of CME Clearing are specifically designed to prevent a clearing member firm from defaulting on its obligations, CME Clearing, by rule and by operational practice, has prepared contingencies to deal expeditiously with such an event. The following summarizes the steps that may be taken in the event a clearing member failed to meet its financial obligations to CME Clearing.

Proprietary Account Default

If a clearing member was unable to meet its financial obligations to CME Clearing and a default occurred in its house (proprietary, noncustomer, or nonregulated OTC) account, CME Clearing may act immediately to:

- Attempt to transfer all segregated customer positions and monies to another clearing member;
- Take control of or liquidate the positions in the house account;
- Apply the clearing member's security deposit and house performance bond deposits to the failed obligation;
- Attach all other assets of the clearing member that are available to the exchange (e.g., shares and memberships); and
- Invoke any applicable parent guarantee.

Customer segregated assets (positions and/or monies) on deposit with or in the control of CME Clearing may not be used or impaired by CME Clearing in the case of a clearing member default resulting from house account activity.

Customer Account Default

If a clearing member was unable to meet its financial obligations to CME Clearing and a default occurred in its customer account, CME Clearing may act immediately to:

- Attempt to transfer noninvolved customer positions and monies to another clearing member;
- Take control of or liquidate involved customer positions and house positions;
- Apply the clearing member's security deposit and house performance bond deposits to the failed obligation; and
- Attach all other assets of the clearing member that are available to the exchange (e.g., shares and memberships).

Although CME Clearing segregates customer performance bond deposits from the clearing member's proprietary performance bond deposits, the customer performance bond deposits for each clearing member are held in the aggregate, without identifying specific ownership of the deposits. If a default occurred in the clearing member's customer account, CME Clearing has the right to apply toward the default all customer performance bond deposits and positions in the defaulting clearing member's customer account at CME Clearing. Accordingly, positions and performance bonds deposited by customers not causing the default are potentially at risk if there is a default in the customer account of their clearing member. Additionally, customer account positions are held in aggregate without identifying which positions are held by specific customers. CME Clearing has the right to liquidate all customer positions and collateral. Accordingly, positions and collateral of customers not causing the default may be liquidated.

Temporary Liquidity Facility

CME Clearing has a 364-day, $1 billion, fully secured, confirmed line of credit agreement with a consortium of domestic and international banks that is expandable to $1.5 billion under an accordion feature. Under the terms of the credit agreement, CMEG may borrow up to the full amount, by giving notice no later than 3:45 PM Chicago time. The credit facility may be used if there is a temporary problem with the domestic payments system that would delay payments of settlement variation between CME Clearing and clearing members or in the unlikely event of a clearing member default. The line of credit thus provides a high level of assurance that CME Clearing has the capacity to pay settlement variation to all clearing members even if a clearing member may have failed to meet its financial obligations to CME Clearing.

Unsatisfied Obligation

Should the defaulting clearing member's obligation not be fully satisfied by CME Clearing activity as previously discussed, CME would next apply its surplus funds and the security deposits of the clearing members. CME Clearing stands out among clearing organizations with regard to this use of both internal and external financial resources.

Each month, CME Group's chief financial officer determines the maximum amount of surplus funds that CME could contribute to satisfy any remaining default obligation while retaining a prudential amount of working capital for continuing exchange operations. The amount is targeted at a minimum of $100 million.

CME Rules are designed to maximize the liquidity and safety of the pool of security deposits. In general, each clearing member is required to maintain a security deposit equal to the greater of $500,000 or the results of a formula under which 84.25% of the total requirement is based on the clearing member's proportionate contribution to aggregate risk performance bond requirements over the preceding three months, 15% is based on the clearing member's contribution to risk-weighted volume over the preceding three months, and 0.75% is based on foreign currency settlement requirements. CME Clearing revaluates clearing member security deposit requirements at the beginning of each quarter for these purposes. If the default continued to remain unsatisfied after the surplus funds and aggregate security deposits were applied, CME Clearing would then invoke its right to assess clearing members for any unsatisfied obligations. The balance of the unsatisfied default would then be allocated among the clearing membership up to an amount equal to 275% of the aggregate security deposit requirement across all clearing members. The allocation would be based on each clearing member's share of the security deposit pool.

Insolvency Law Protections

In the case of a bankruptcy of a full clearing member (typically an FCM or broker-dealer), the U.S. Bankruptcy Code and CFTC regulations contain a number of provisions that provide preferential treatment to a clearing member's public customers and to CME Clearing. Recent history has highlighted the advantage that customers of a centrally cleared and regulated entity hold. In a bankruptcy situation, CME Clearing member firms' customers are afforded the protections of a CFTC-regulated central clearing counterparty, whereas customers of any noncentrally cleared and regulated entity are not provided such protections. These provisions include special priority rules for distribution of property to customers and certain exceptions to the automatic stay and voidability provisions of the U.S. Bankruptcy Code. A general overview of these provisions follows.

The Bankruptcy Code offers a number of protections to CME Clearing when a clearing member is bankrupt regardless of whether the bankrupt clearing member holds public customer accounts or only clears proprietary trades. For example, a trustee may not void pre-bankruptcy payments of original performance bond or settlement variation made to CME Clearing (except in the event of a fraudulent transfer). In addition, the filing of a bankruptcy petition will not stay a setoff by CME Clearing of claims for original performance bond or settlement variation payments owed by a clearing member against cash, securities, or other property of a clearing member that CME Clearing holds. These provisions establish a priority for CME Clearing with respect to performance bond deposits, which protect all clearing members. Further, the Bankruptcy Code provides that neither a clearing member's bankruptcy nor any order of a bankruptcy court can prevent CME Clearing from exercising any contractual right it has to liquidate a commodity contract.

With respect to distribution of customer property, the CFTC's bankruptcy rules classify a clearing member's customers as either "public" or "nonpublic." Nonpublic customers include certain account holders that are affiliated with or related to the clearing member such as the clearing member officers, directors, general partners, or 10% or greater owners. All other customers are considered "public," and their property on deposit with the clearing member is subject to the Commodity Exchange Act (CEA) and CFTC segregation requirements. Customer classes are further divided by account class as futures accounts, foreign futures accounts, leverage accounts, or delivery accounts.

The Bankruptcy Code affords claims of public customers the highest priority, subject only to the payment of claims relating to the administration of customer property. First, the customer segregated property of the bankrupt clearing member is to be distributed pro rata among the clearing member's public customers. In determining the pro rata distribution, all property segregated on behalf of, or otherwise traceable to, a particular account class is allocated to that class. Property is distributed pro rata notwithstanding that it can be specifically identifiable to particular customers.

Second, if the segregated assets are insufficient to satisfy all public customer claims in full, the clearing member's remaining assets are to be used to satisfy such claims before they are available for distribution to the clearing member's general creditors. After the claims of public customers are paid in full, the same allocation formula is applied to distribute any remaining property to nonpublic customers.

The applicability of these and other bankruptcy-related provisions depend on the circumstances of each situation. For example, CME Group's outside counsel has indicated that in no instance of an insolvency of a foreign bank clearing member would CME be subject to an obstacle preventing immediate termination of all contracts with the defaulting bank, liquidation of all obligations on a broad netting basis, and satisfaction of any net obligations to CME from the bank's security deposits. As discussed earlier, the applicability of these various laws will be fact specific and depend on the entities involved.

RESOURCES BACKING CME GROUP CLEARING SYSTEM

Under no circumstances will customer segregated performance bond deposits held by CME Clearing for one clearing member be used to cover either a house or customer default of another clearing member. Customers doing business through a clearing member not involved in a default are insulated from losses incurred by the failure of another clearing member. In the event of a default, as of September 30, 2009, CME Group may draw on all or a portion of the following resources to satisfy the outstanding obligation. See Exhibit 3.1.

CUSTOMER PROTECTION

Customers face credit risk in doing business through any particular clearing member. Consequently, the selection process for a suitable clearing member is important. Although the policies applicable to segregation of customer monies for products traded in regulated markets are specifically designed to

EXHIBIT 3.1 Customer Protection

Aggregate performance bond deposits*	$85,788,000,000
Market value of CME pledged shares/Trading rights	$647,000,000
Surplus funds	$100,000,000
Guarantee fund	$1,973,000,000
Assessment power	$5,426,000,000
Total	$93,934,000,000

*Only the performance bond deposits of the defaulting firm would be available to CME. Because performance bond deposits reflect position risk, a larger outstanding obligation typically would be met by a larger share of these aggregate deposits.

protect customers from the consequences of a clearing member's failure, they do not always provide complete protection should the default be caused by another customer at that firm.

Protection against a customer-caused default rests primarily with the management of the clearing member and the importance placed on its internal risk-management controls. Generally, a clearing organization's role in the customer protection process is to require all customers to post adequate performance bonds, to administer financial surveillance programs designed to monitor the financial viability of clearing members, and, when necessary, to impose specific remedies in an effort to avert the consequences of financial deterioration.

DISASTER RECOVERY AND BUSINESS CONTINUITY

CME Clearing maintains and routinely tests a comprehensive Disaster Recovery & Business Continuity Plan designed to provide protection against a broad spectrum of physical disaster types and to guarantee the survivability of core trading and clearing functions. Key components of the plan include the following:

- Multiple-redundant systems components, maintained at separate geographically dispersed facilities;
- Multiple-redundant network connectivity between clearing firms and CME Clearing, into those separate geographically dispersed facilities;
- Real-time mirroring of data storage between separate facilities;
- Physical dispersion of operations-oriented staff;
- Multiple electricity feeds as well as back-up generator capability; and
- Redundant voice telecommunications lines with automatic switching to backup facilities.

The plan provides survivability even in the event of complete destruction of CME Group's primary facilities in downtown Chicago. Routinely tested scenarios include both the completion of the daily clearing cycle on the day of such a physical disaster and the resumption of normal clearing processing on the following business day.

RULE ENFORCEMENT

The exchange relies on its Market Regulation Department to actively monitor market participants and their trading practices and to enforce compliance with Exchange rules. Market Regulation is composed of a number of highly trained and experienced units. One unit conducts trade practice surveillance that monitors individual transactions executed on the Exchange, whether done electronically, via open outcry, or by an allowed privately negotiated transaction. Another unit reviews large positions held at the Exchange, focusing on overall market directions and trends to detect and prevent manipulations and other disruptive events. Another unit focuses on the integrity of the data submitted to the Exchange.

Any violations of the rules can be prosecuted through an enforcement group within Market Regulation or by referral to the appropriate government or law enforcement agency.

Systems Development is also a large part of Market Regulation because the analyses conducted by the department are highly dependent on having powerful computer tools and databases. Market Regulation also works closely with the Audit Department and the Clearing House Risk Management Group in monitoring potential risks and with the Legal Department on rule amendments and guidance.

Further, the department is responsible for handling customer complaints and administering an arbitration program for the resolution of disputes. The department employs investigators, attorneys, trading floor investigators, data analysts, and an in-house computer programming and regulatory systems design staff.

Surveillance Tools

The Regulatory Division has created some of the most sophisticated tools in the world to assist with the detection of possible rule violations and monitoring of the market. In addition to access to "live" activity in the CME Globex system or in the clearing system, the department also has various "exception" processes to monitor for potential rule violations. Further, the department uses extensive databases containing the detail of trading activity going back years that allows for research into trading patterns over time.

To prevent manipulation, the Market Surveillance unit constantly monitors positions based on percentage of open interest and historic user participation in each contract, and it aggregates positions across clearing members, with the use of its position reporting systems, to account for all large positions held by any single participant. This daily review permits the surveillance analyst to identify unusual market activity promptly.

For trading floor activity, the exchange has employed video surveillance since 1992. This system is controlled by and allows Market Regulation to monitor activity on the trading floor to detect possible abuses in the open outcry markets and use the video evidence at disciplinary proceedings.

Enforcement Powers

The Exchange has disciplinary committees made up of both member and nonmember representatives. The Probable Cause Committee considers investigation reports from Market Regulation and acts as the "grand jury" to determine if charges of a rule violation are warranted. When charges are issued, they are referred to the applicable exchange's Business Conduct Committee, which will follow procedures to conduct a hearing. The Business Conduct Committee can issue a fine up to a million dollars per violation, plus it can order restitution for the amount of benefit received as a result of the violation. Further, the committee may restrict, suspend, or expel a person or firm from membership, and it can order full restitution when it finds that a customer has been financially harmed from the conduct. CME was the first exchange to implement nonmember panelists to sit on and chair disciplinary panels.

Arbitration

CME offers a forum for the resolution of disputes per the strictures of Chapter 6 of the Exchange Rulebook. This forum calls for a binding arbitration administered through the Market Regulation Division of claims against members of a division of the Exchange and/or their employees, CME clearing member firms and/or their employees, or introducing brokers and/or their employees in instances where the introducing broker is guaranteed by a CME clearing member firm.

Exchange Rule 606 empowers an arbitration panel to convene a hearing to investigate the matter and to award actual damages and interest. The panel can award punitive damages of up to twice the actual damage. The panel may also award some or all of the administrative costs of the proceeding and the reasonable and necessary expenses, including, but not limited to, attorneys' fees incurred by a party by reason of another party's frivolous or bad faith claim, defense, or conduct during the arbitration, or provided that a statutory or contractual basis exists for awarding such fees. Requests for attorneys' fees and costs incurred in the arbitration proceeding must be raised in the proceeding or they are waived.

In setting another industry precedent, CME was the first exchange to implement a Market Regulation Oversight Committee (MROC), which is composed of public directors from the CME Group board of directors. The MROC regularly reviews budgets, work processes and systems, and case work of both the Market Regulation and the Audit Departments.

FINANCIAL AND REGULATORY INFORMATION SHARING

CME Group participates in formal agreements with other futures and securities clearing organizations and with other self-regulatory organizations, domestic and foreign, regularly exchanging financial information about joint clearing members with other participants.

Note that CME Group is a leading participant in the Joint Audit Committee (JAC), and in the Intermarket Financial Surveillance Group (IFSG). Both of these agreements facilitate information sharing with respect to the financial condition of exchange participants.

The JAC includes representatives from all domestic futures exchanges and the National Futures Association (NFA). The committee assigns primary regulatory oversight responsibility for particular clearing firms to a single self- regulatory organization (SRO), which, in turn, audits that firm and shares its conclusions with all exchanges on which that firm clears. These audits include an assessment of the financial condition of the firm, including capital, segregation, and secured status; results of all other audits and examinations; results of any special reviews; the margin condition of accounts held by the firm; and the general operating condition and internal controls applied by the firm.

The IFSG is composed of the JAC members and all securities exchanges. This group shares information on common member firms with respect to their financial condition including capital, segregation, secured, and customer reserve status; status of margin accounts; status of omnibus or carrying broker accounts; pay/collect information; general operating condition; and other high-level information on the results of any other audits or examinations of the firm.

CME Group was the first futures exchange to participate in the Intermarket Surveillance Group (ISG) and today is an active member of this increasingly international group. The ISG consists of 35 domestic and foreign SROs that have formally agreed to share information. As such, CME Group participates in a bilateral exchange of information between exchanges to detect possible abuses.

CME Group also participates in the Joint Compliance Committee (JCC), which is a group of domestic exchange SROs that meets to discuss common rules and share best regulatory practices.

CME Group was instrumental in developing the International Information Sharing Memorandum of Understanding, which established a framework for 65 exchanges and clearing organizations worldwide to share information relevant to managing global market emergencies. CME Group also seeks broader cooperation between clearing organizations through such industry forums as the Unified Clearing Group.

CONCLUSION

The CME Clearing House, Audit Division, and Market Regulation Division act in concert to ensure the financial integrity of transactions processed through CME Group's exchanges.

The Clearing House establishes minimum performance bond levels for all futures, options, and OTC positions cleared at the Exchange, marks all open positions to market twice daily, and continually monitors the financial viability of its clearing members to ensure a well-functioning marketplace.

Customer protection is of paramount importance at CME Group. CME's Audit Department routinely inspects the books and records of clearing members to ensure, among other things, their compliance with segregation requirements.

The Exchange relies on its Market Regulation Department to actively monitor market participants and their trading practices and to enforce compliance with exchange rules.

CME also participates in formal agreements with other futures and securities clearing organizations and with other self-regulatory organizations, domestic and foreign, regularly exchanging financial information about joint clearing members with other participants.

CHAPTER 4

Currency Futures: The First Financial Futures

John W. Labuszewski

Currencies represent the most basic of commodities and have been traded in many different formats and venues from time immemorial. The modern era of currency trading may be thought of as beginning in the early 1970s following the collapse of the Bretton Woods agreement. Traditional trading formats include spot, outright forward, and foreign exchange (FX) swaps on an over-the-counter (OTC) basis. Many other inventive exchange-traded currency products, including CME Group currency futures and options, likewise emerged as a means of coping with the risks attendant to a floating exchange rate regime.

Now, some 30 years later, the currency markets are in the midst of another sea change. Buy-side traders have emerged as important sources of liquidity, electronic and algorithmic trading technologies are enhancing the speed and efficiency of the markets, and centralized clearing increasingly is viewed as an attractive means of managing credit risks.

This chapter provides an overview of the growth and development of this most basic and fundamental of commodities and reviews available trading formats, venues, and possible future market trends.

EVOLUTION OF FOREIGN EXCHANGE MARKETPLACE

The history of currency trading extends far into the distant past. Certainly the minting of silver coins was common prior to 2500 BCE, and gold coinage emerged not more than 2,000 years later. The Romans minted vast quantities of coins in two basic units; the aureus and the solidus coins contained in the vicinity of 7 and 4 grams of gold, respectively. But by the collapse of the western Roman Empire, the gold content of coinage was compromised severely by the inclusion of base metals.

As a result, the gold dinar and the silver dirham from Muslim regions became accepted as the currency of choice. As European civilization emerged from the Dark Ages, its gold coins, including the ducat, florin, zloty, and guinea, became accepted as benchmarks of value followed later by the Spanish gold escudo.

In the period from the Middle Ages up to World War I, and arguably until World II, the world's currency markets were dominated by the British pound, which reigned as the recognized benchmark against which other currencies were valued.

The appellation *pound* originally had literal meaning because it was a reference to 1 troy pound of sterling silver. The pound sterling was adopted as a standard by Elizabeth I in 1560 as a reaction to the so-called Great Debasement when the silver content of pennies was compromised by blending silver with base metals, causing runaway inflation in the process. Elizabeth recalled the debased coinage at the discounted value and reissued coins per the true standard. As such, the pound sterling became trusted as the European currency of choice even through the many and perhaps inevitable periods of financial crisis faced by the empire.

Gold Standard

The adoption of a gold standard in England may be considered a gradual event. But historians generally agree that Sir Isaac Newton's assay of 1717, establishing a fixed ratio between the value of gold coins and English silver pennies, was a key enabling event. By the late 1700s, the cost of colonial and Napoleonic wars and the cost of the China trade depleted the nation's silver reserves, prompting the minting of token silver coins. But between 1816 and 1821, England began to mint gold sovereigns and silver crowns. In 1833, notes of Bank of England were declared legal tender. The Bank Charter Act of 1844 decreed that those notes were fully backed by gold, thus, the empire completely adopted a gold standard.

Other countries followed suit, so by 1900 the world had essentially adopted a universal gold standard. The gold standard had the effect of stimulating trade between conforming nations and encouraging industrialization. However, the human costs of that industrialization were not necessarily cheap. Although the dynamics are still not well understood by economists, the populations of developed nations grew sharply, creating large demand for cheap agricultural products, in turn pressuring nations to reduce tariffs. As tariff revenues decreased, income and sales taxes rose while wages were pressured downward. Panics and depressions seemed to occur frequently during the early industrialization age.

The outbreak of World War I in 1914 saw Britain terminate convertibility of English bank notes. War costs led to inflation, and the victorious allies imposed punitive reparations on Germany in an attempt to rebuild. By 1925, England reinstituted the gold standard at prewar convertibility rates. Deflation finally caused Britain to abandon the standard by 1931, followed by other industrialized countries. The United States reacted strongly by banning private ownership of gold.

Depression

The Great Depression led to severe deflation, widespread economic hardship, and the abandonment of the gold standard with the London Conference of 1933. In particular, the United Kingdom and United States had been accused of attempting to maintain an artificially low convertibility rate to gold, exacerbated by a proliferation of exchange controls and high trade tariffs. Global trade stagnated as attempts to devalue one's currency relative to the currency of one's trading partners led to further deflationary spirals. Public management of the economy emerged as an ordinary and natural role for central governments.

World War II saw massive depletion of UK gold reserves to fund the war effort, providing a clear indication that Britain could not lead a postwar revival of the gold standard. Rather, the United States emerged from the war as the world's leading economy, having built a massive manufacturing infrastructure, marketing weaponry and other supplies during the era. U.S. output more than doubled during the war and led the world in production and exports with 80% of the world's gold reserves. The United States was uniquely positioned to prosper from liberal international trade, unfettered from untoward exchange rate controls and trade tariffs. Further, the Allied powers, largely devastated by the war effort, were disposed to accept U.S. economic leadership.

Bretton Woods

Forty-four nations met in the small town of Bretton Woods, New Hampshire, in July 1944 for the United Nations Monetary and Financial Conference. The delegation emerged from that historic meeting having hammered out a new monetary order that became operational by 1946 after general ratification of the treaty.

The goals of the accord were generally spelled out by the earlier Atlantic Charter of 1941, which called for openness in world trade practices.

Despite their inclination to revert to 1930s-style protectionism, both the United Kingdom and France grudgingly made trade concessions in return for U.S. economic aid immediately after the war.

The central premise of the new monetary order was an obligation on the part of central banks to peg their currencies at an established fixed value ±1% versus the benchmark U.S. dollar. If an exchange rate were to fall outside of that ±1% band, the central bank was obligated to intervene to restore parity. The lynchpin of the system was the U.S. dollar's convertibility to gold at a fixed rate of $35 per ounce. Central banks were permitted to exchange dollars for gold with the U.S. Treasury. Thus, as seen in Exhibit 4.1, the U.S. dollar became the world's benchmark and reserve currency of choice.

The pegged or par value of a currency could be altered but only with the approval of the newly established International Monetary Fund (IMF). Such approval required a determination of a fundamental disequilibrium in the balance of payments by the IMF. The IMF further operated to attempt to control inflation and introduce austerity programs in nations that could not maintain equilibrium.

The system was reasonably effective in controlling trade disputes and promoting global economic growth, at least until the late 1960s when a number of factors coalesced to undermine the dollar. U.S. federal spending grew rapidly in this era as a result of the Vietnam War and President Johnson's Great Society social programs. Tax revenues did not keep pace, resulting in inflation and a reversal of U.S. balance of payments and eventually a burgeoning trade deficit. The dollar was overvalued while the currencies of European and Japanese trade partners, having recovered nicely from the war, became undervalued with no haste to revalue lest their exports suffer. Thus, the dollar had rivals threatening its singular benchmark status.

The 1960s further saw growing globalization of the banking system, which facilitated the ability of banks and banking consortium to move vast amounts of capital in and out of any particular currency. Speculation ensued based on perceived disequilibrium and the prospect of a subsequent devaluation (downward) or revaluation (upward) of a currency. Thus, the foundations for today's interbank or over-the-counter (OTC) currency markets were formed.

These factors applied increasing pressure on U.S. gold reserves as dollars were eagerly traded for gold. Tensions grew and provisional measures failed. By 1970, gold coverage declined to 22%, signaling the inevitable collapse of Bretton Woods. The ax fell on August 15, 1971, when President Nixon unilaterally closed the gold window.

The so-called Nixon shock was followed in December 1971 with the Smithsonian Agreement, devaluing the U.S. dollar to $38 per ounce with

EXHIBIT 4.1 Currency Marketplace Timeline

1560	Elizabeth I establishes the pound sterling, which tied the British currency to silver.
1844	Adoption of gold standard by Great Britain with passage of Charter Bank Act, which tied the value of notes issued by the Bank of England to gold.
1933	Great Depression leads to the London Conference and collapse of international gold standard.
1944	Bretton Woods Accord ratified with the aim of stabilizing global exchange rates and stimulating economic recovery in the post–World War II era. The system featured rates pegged to the value of gold with a U.S. dollar within a ±1% band and convertibility of U.S. dollars into gold at a fixed rate.
1971	Bretton Woods Accord is replaced by Smithsonian Agreement that permits wider currency fluctuations within a fixed band as President Nixon abandons the gold standard.
1972	Chicago Mercantile Exchange (CME) introduces futures trading in seven major currencies.
1973	Smithsonian Agreement breaks down, issuing in a new modern age of currency trading generally featuring floating rate currency values.
1979	Europe adopts the European Monetary System (EMS) in an attempt to develop greater independence from the U.S. dollar as the world's key reserve currency.
1984	CME introduces options on currency futures products.
1993	The EMS liberalizes pricing bands, giving further impetus to a global free-float currency exchange rate system.
1999	Trading in so-called European legacy currencies (including the Deutsche mark, French franc, Italian lira, etc.) are halted in favor of the EuroFX as the standard currency throughout most of Western Europe.
Current	Electronic and algorithmic trading technologies are being embraced as efficient trading mechanisms; buy-side firms are stepping in as liquidity providers; centralized clearing is increasingly viewed as a viable means to manage credit risks.

±2.25% bands. But this had little effect on U.S. government policies, and the price of gold continued to advance.

Free-Floating Currencies

By March 1973, the Bretton Woods Agreement could be considered effectively dead. It was replaced by the system of free-floating currencies that endures today. Although central banks have frequently attempted to intervene to control fluctuations in the value of their currencies, a so-called dirty float, such intervention has typically been ineffectual and costly.

The free float system fostered the development of more elaborate means by which to trade currencies. Chicago Mercantile Exchange (CME), led by its then chairman Leo Melamed, successfully introduced futures trading in seven major currencies in 1972 while OTC or interbank spot and forward currency trading began to flourish.

But the inclination to link currency valuations was not put to bed for long. By 1979, the European Monetary System (EMS) was established, linking the value of currencies within the European Economic Community (EEC) to each other through the mechanism of the European Currency Unit (ECU). The ECU was a basket of currencies to which European currencies were intended effectively to remain pegged within a $\pm 2.25\%$ band (or $\pm 6\%$ for the Italian lira). The key mechanism to maintain parity was interest rate adjustment. Some nations could not maintain the discipline required to ensure smooth functioning of the system. Bands were widened to $\pm 15\%$ per the Brussels Compromise of 1993. By 1999, the ECU was eliminated in favor of a unified currency in the form of the euro.

OVER-THE-COUNTER CURRENCY TRADING VEHICLES

A free-floating currency pricing regime that allows for unconstrained price fluctuations creates risks. And traders have been very inventive in developing new and increasingly specialized mechanisms to address those risks. Currencies now trade in the OTC markets as well as on exchanges. Electronic trade is increasingly becoming the norm in both these venues. Further, a variety of trading structures have emerged as described next.

Spot

A spot, or outright currency transaction, is simply the exchange of one currency for another currency, transacted at the spot rate. Although the transaction may be concluded immediately in a variety of OTC markets, usually over the telephone or increasingly via electronic trading systems, payment or settlement typically is concluded two business days hence. It is possible, if mutually agreed, to settle or value a transaction on a one business day basis. In fact, this is the convention with transactions between Canadian and U.S. dollars, which are normally settled one business day hence.

Quotes may be in either "American terms" or "European terms." For example, one may quote the value of the Swiss franc in dollars ($0.7628 per one Swiss franc as of November 22, 2005) or the value of the U.S. dollar in francs (1.3110 Swiss francs per $1.00). Clearly one quote is the reciprocal of the other. Since 1978, convention has been to quote most currencies in European terms in the interest of standardization with some exceptions such as the euro, the British pound, and other British Commonwealth currencies such as the Australian dollar and New Zealand dollar, which are generally quoted in American terms. The table in Exhibit 4.2 provides indicative quotes for a variety of major currencies by way of illustration.

EXHIBIT 4.2   Select Spot and Forward Exchange Rates (Tuesday, November 22, 2005)

ISO 4217	Country	USD Equivalent	Currency per USD
AED	United Arab Emirates, Dirhams	0.2723	3.6724
ARS	Argentina, Pesos	0.3397	2.9438
AUD	Australia, Dollars	0.7375	1.3559
BHD	Bahrain, Dinars	2.6525	0.3770
BRL	Brazil, Brazil Real	0.4448	2.2482
CAD	Canada, Dollars	0.8513	1.1747
1-month forward		0.8520	1.1737
3-months forward		0.8536	1.1715
6-months forward		0.8555	1.1689
CHF	Switzerland, Francs	0.7628	1.3110
1-month forward		0.7628	1.3070
3-months forward		0.7696	1.2994
6-months forward		0.7759	1.2888
CLP	Chile, Pesos	0.001896	527.43
CNY	China, Yuan Renminbi	0.1237	8.0839
COP	Colombia, Pesos	0.0004389	2278.42
CZK	Czech Republic, Koruny	0.04031	24.808
DKK	Denmark, Kroner	0.1583	6.3171
EGP	Egypt, Pounds	0.1737	5.7564
EUR	EuroFX	1.1812	0.8466
GBP	United Kingdom, Pounds	1.7220	0.5807
1-month forward		1.7215	0.5809
3-months forward		1.7213	0.5810
6-months forward		1.7221	0.5807
HKD	Hong Kong, Dollars	0.1290	7.7538
HUF	Hungary, Forint	0.004656	214.78
IDR	Indonesia, Rupiahs	0.0000996	10040
INR	India, Rupees	0.02184	45.788

(*continued*)

EXHIBIT 4.2 *(Continued)*

ISO 4217	Country	USD Equivalent	Currency per USD
JOD	Jordan, Dinars	1.4094	0.7095
JPY	Japan, Yen	0.008416	118.82
1-month forward		0.008447	118.39
3-months forward		0.008512	117.48
6-months forward		0.008606	116.20
KRW	Korea (South), Won	0.0009583	1043.51
KWD	Kuwait, Dinars	3.4240	0.2921
LBP	Lebanon, Pounds	0.0006651	1503.53
MTL	Malta, Liri	2.7514	0.3635
MXN	Mexico, Pesos	0.0941	10.6304
MYR	Malaysia, Ringgits	0.2646	3.7793
NOK	Norway, Krone	0.1500	6.6667
NZD	New Zealand, Dollars	0.6913	1.4465
PEN	Peru, Nuevos Soles	0.2949	3.3910
PHP	Philippines, Pesos	0.01839	54.377
PKR	Pakistan, Rupees	0.01675	59.702
PLN	Poland, Zlotych	0.2972	3.3647
RUB	Russia, Rubles	0.03467	28.843
SEK	Sweden, Kronor	0.1236	8.0906
SGD	Singapore, Dollars	0.5889	1.6981
SKK	Slovakia, Koruny	0.03051	32.776
THB	Thailand, Baht	0.02426	41.220
TRY	Turkey, New Lira	0.7331	1.3640
TWD	Taiwan, New Dollars	0.02974	33.625
USD	U.S.A., Dollars	1.0000	1.0000
UYU	Uruguay, Pesos	0.04230	23.641
VEB	Venezuela, Bolivares	0.000466	2145.92
XDR	International Monetary Fund (IMF) Special Drawing Rights	1.4198	0.7043
ZAR	South Africa, Rand	0.1515	6.6007

Source: Wall Street Journal, November 23, 2005.

As illustrated, most currencies are quoted to the fourth place past the decimal, or 0.0001, also known as a "pip" or a "tick." However, practices may vary with respect to currencies whose values are very small or very large in relative terms.

It is also, of course, possible to trade *cross rates,* or transactions that do not involve U.S. dollars and are not quoted as such, as seen in Exhibit 4.3. For example, one may trade the British pound/euro rate. Either currency

EXHIBIT 4.3 Select Cross Rates (November 22, 2005)

	U.S. dollar	Euro	British pound	Swiss franc	Mexican peso	Japanese yen	Canadian dollar
U.S. Dollar	—	1.1812	1.7220	0.76280	0.09407	0.00842	0.85130
Euro	0.84660	—	1.4578	0.64578	0.07964	0.00712	0.72071
British Pound	0.58072	0.6859	—	0.4430	0.05463	0.00489	0.49437
Swiss Franc	1.311	1.5485	2.2575	—	0.12332	0.01103	1.1160
Mexican Peso	10.6304	12.5566	18.306	8.1089	—	0.08947	9.0496
Japanese Yen	118.82	140.35	204.61	90.637	11.178	—	101.153
Canadian Dollar	1.1747	1.3875	2.0228	0.8960	0.11050	0.00989	—

Source: Wall Street Journal, November 23, 2005.

might be used as the base rate, but there are some conventions that tend to prevail such as euro/yen or sterling/franc. The quote may readily be interpreted by noting that the base currency is mentioned first.

Outright Forwards

An outright forward contract is almost identical in operational terms to a spot transaction with the significant difference that the value or settlement date is deferred. Rather than settle two days hence, outright forwards are typically traded for settlement in 1 week, 2 weeks, 1 month, 2 months, 3 months, 6 months, 12 months forward, also referred to as "straight dates." Although the outright forward contract may be settled some days, weeks, or months later, no consideration is necessarily passed between buyer and seller when the transaction is consummated. However, many dealers demand that customers post some acceptable collateral to cover market risks in the interim, particularly if a trade goes "underwater."

OTC instruments may be configured to the demands of the moment. Thus, one may closely match the quantity traded and the value date to one's specific needs. Of course, dealers may make their customers pay a price for such customization in the form of a wider bid/ask spread.

The value of an outright forward relative to the spot value of the currency may be modeled by taking into consideration the costs and benefits associated with purchasing and carrying the currency over the life of the forward transaction. Consider, for example, the prospect of buying British pounds with U.S. dollars on a forward basis. The forward value may be calculated as follows, where R_{term} represents the short-term rate that may be earned by investing the "term" currency, R_{base} represents the short-term rate associated with the "base" currency, and d represents the number days until full term.

$$\text{Forward Rate} = \text{Spot Rate} \times \left(\frac{1 + [R_{term} \times (d/360)]}{1 + [R_{base} \times (d/360)]} \right)$$

Assume that the U.S. short-term rate is 4.40% and the applicable U.K. short-term rate is 4.60%; the spot rate is \$1.7220/£1. A 90-day forward rate may be calculated as 1.7214 as follows. The convention in most markets is to calculate short-term rates based on a 360-day count assumption, but some short-term rate markets, including the United Kingdom, employ a 365-day count.

$$\begin{aligned} \text{Forward Rate} &= 1.7220 \times \left(\frac{1 + [0.0440 \times (90/360)]}{1 + [0.0460 \times (90/365)]} \right) \\ &= 1.7214 \end{aligned}$$

Some central banks do not facilitate the actual exchange of their currencies by imposing restrictions on foreign ownership or similar measures. Some of the most significant currencies that are not deliverable include the Chinese renminbi, Indian rupee, and Russian ruble. Still, these currencies are frequently traded as nondeliverable forwards (NDFs). Rather than culminating in a delivery of currency, NDFs are settled with a cash payment for the net profit or loss denominated in the readily negotiable currency.

Foreign Exchange Swaps

An FX swap may be thought of as a combination of two offsetting currency transactions separated by time and constitute the largest segment of the FX marketplace in terms of daily turnover. An FX swap is executed when one currency is swapped for another on a nearby value date ("near date") only to reverse the transaction on a subsequent value date ("far date").

A large proportion of FX swaps entail a spot trade as the near date transaction, a "short-dated FX swap." Frequently, the far date transaction occurs within a week. But dealers often quote FX swaps with the full range of straight dates (e.g., 1 week, 2 weeks, 1 month, 2 months, etc.) as the far date. Dealers often offer a high degree of flexibility and may be willing to quote prices for odd dates and forward swaps where the near-term leg is executed as a forward rather than a spot transaction.

A *spot-next FX swap* is executed by delivering a currency one day and reversing the trade on the subsequent business day. Note that the spot transaction is typically settled two business days subsequent to the deal date. A *tom-next swap* is transacted by executing the spot transaction on a "pre-spot" basis or one day earlier than normal convention (i.e., tomorrow as opposed to two business days hence), reversing the trade on the subsequent business day. Or one may execute a "spot-week" or "spot-2 week" FX swap. A *forward FX swap* is generally considered one where the near date transaction is settled not on a spot basis two days hence but on some forward date.

A *buy-sell swap* implies the purchase of a fixed quantity of the base currency on the near date only to be offset with the sale of a fixed quantity of the base currency on the far date. Conversely, a *sell-buy swap* implies the opposite: the sale of a fixed quantity of the base currency subsequently offset with its repurchase.

FX swaps may be thought of as akin to repurchase or repo agreements in fixed-income markets where one borrows or lends cash temporarily collateralized with an equivalent value of a fixed-income item, most often a U.S. Treasury security. Like a repo or an FX forward transaction, the value of an FX swap reflects an interest rate or, more accurately, the interest rate differential between the two currencies. FX swaps are typically quoted in terms of pips as follows, where R_{term} represents the short-term rate that may be earned by investing the "term" currency; R_{base} represents the short-term rate associated with the "base" currency; and d represents the number of days between the far and near dates.

$$\text{Swap Points} = \text{Spot Rate} \times \left(\frac{1 + [R_{term} \times (d/360)]}{1 + [R_{base} \times (d/360)]} \right) - 1$$

Returning to our previous example, assume that the U.S. short-term rate is 4.40% and the applicable U.K. short-term rate is 4.60%; the spot rate is $1.7220/£1. A one-month or 31-day swap rate may be calculated as −2 pips as follows. In other words, one might be expected to pay 2 pips for the privilege of holding British pounds and, therefore, the opportunity to earn a slightly superior rate of interest over the 31-day term of the FX swap.

$$\begin{aligned} \text{Swap Points} &= 1.7220 \times \left(\frac{1 + [0.0440 \times (31/360)]}{1 + [0.0460 \times (31/365)]} \right) - 1 \\ &= -0.0002 \end{aligned}$$

FX swap transactions are often used to manage one's currency positions on a short-term basis or to speculate on fluctuations in the interest rate differentials between two countries.

An FX swap must be distinguished from a so-called currency swap transaction. A currency swap entails an element of an FX swap as well as an element of an interest rate swap. Parties to a currency swap initially exchange two currencies on a spot basis, swap a series of periodic floating interest rate payments denominated in the respective currencies involved in the transaction, and ultimately conclude the transaction by re-exchanging the two currencies.

Currency swaps differ from interest rate swaps (IRSs) to the extent that an IRS typically implies the periodic exchange of a stream of fixed versus floating rate payments in a single currency rather than in two different currencies. But like an IRS, there are many variations on the theme including fixed versus fixed rate, fixed versus floating rate, or floating versus floating rate currency swaps.

Over-the-Counter Currency Options

The FX markets became quite aggressive and inventive with respect to the use of options beginning in the early 1980s. Options provide a very flexible structure that may be tailor made to meet the risk management or speculative needs of the moment.

Options may generally be categorized as two types: calls and puts. Call options convey the right, but not the obligation, to buy a specified quantity currency at a particular strike or exercise price on or before an expiration date. One may either buy a call option, paying a negotiated price or premium to the seller, writer, or grantor of the call, or sell, write, or grant a call, thereby receiving that premium.

Put options convey the right, but not the obligation, to sell a specified quantity currency at a particular strike or exercise price on or before an expiration date. Again, one may buy or sell a put option, either paying or receiving a negotiated premium or price.

Options may be configured as European- or American-style options. A European-style option may be exercised only on its expiration date, whereas an American-style option may be exercised at any time up to and including the expiration date.

The purchase of a call option is an essentially bullish transaction with limited downside risk. If the market should advance above the strike price, the call is considered "in-the-money" and one may exercise the call by purchasing currency at the exercise price even when the exchange rate exceeds the exercise price. This implies a profit that is diminished only by the premium paid up front to secure the option. If the market should decline below the strike price, the option is considered "out-of-the-money" and may expire, leaving the buyer with a loss limited to the premium.

The risks and potential rewards that accrue to the call seller or writer are opposite that of the call buyer. If the option should expire out-of-the-money, the writer retains the premium and counts it as profit. If the market should advance, the call writer is faced with the prospect of being forced to sell currency when the exchange rate is much higher; such losses are cushioned to the extent of the premium received upon option sale. See Exhibit 4.4.

The purchase of a put option is essentially a bearish transaction with limited downside risk. If the market should decline below the strike price, the put is in-the-money and one may exercise the put by selling currency at the exercise price even when the exchange rate is less than the exercise price. If the market should advance above the strike price, the option is out-of-the-money, implying a loss equal to the premium. See Exhibit 4.5.

The risks and potential rewards that accrue to the put writer are opposite that of the put buyer. If the option should expire out-of-the-money, the writer retains the premium and counts it as profit. If the market should advance, the put writer is faced with the prospect of being forced to buy currency when the exchange rate is much lower; such losses cushioned to the extent of the premium received upon option sale.

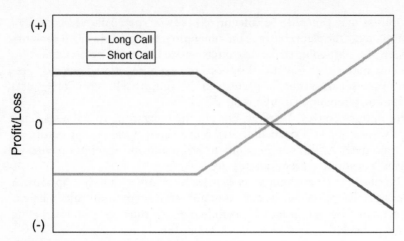

EXHIBIT 4.4 Profit/Loss for Call Option

Although one may dispose of an option through an exercise or abandonment (expiration sans exercise), there is also the possibility that one may liquidate a long/short option through a subsequent sale/purchase. As such, option traders use a variety of mathematical pricing models to identify appropriate premium values, not the least of which is the Black-Scholes option pricing model. Several factors, including the relationship between market and exercise price, term until expiration, market volatility, and interest rates, impact the formula. Frequently, options are quoted in terms of volatility and converted into monetary terms with use of these formulas.

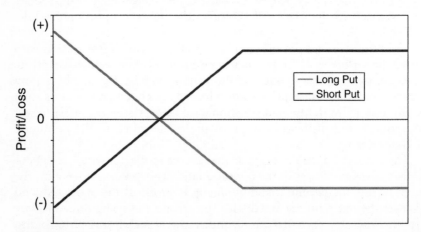

EXHIBIT 4.5 Profit/Loss for Put Option

By combining options of varying types (puts or calls), exercise prices, and expiration dates, one may create an almost infinite variety of strategies that may be tailored to suit one's unique needs.

EXCHANGE-TRADED CURRENCY FUTURES AND OPTIONS

Currency futures were developed in 1972 by CME chairman Leo Melamed working in concert with the Nobel Prize–winning economist Milton Friedman. This development may be considered a direct response to the breakdown of the Bretton Woods Accord and represented the first financial futures contract ever successfully introduced.

Over the years, many currency contracts have been added, and the listings now include contracts on EuroFX, Japanese yen, British pound, Swiss franc, Canadian dollar, Australian dollar, Mexican peso, New Zealand dollar, Russian ruble, South African rand, Brazilian real, Polish zloty, Norwegian krone, Swedish krona, Hungarian forint, Czech koruna, and Israeli shekel. Most recent additions to the lineup include the Chinese renminbi and Korean won. Further, CME Group lists smaller size, or "E-micro," versions of major currency contracts including the EuroFX and Japanese yen. The contracts just mentioned are generally quoted versus, and denominated in, the U.S. dollar. Major cross-rate contracts included Euro/BP, Euro/JY, Euro/SF, BP/SF, BP/JY, and many others. CME Group further offers options on many of these currency futures contracts.

Mechanics of Currency Futures

Futures may be considered akin to a forward contract, and typically they are priced as such, except they are traded on a regulated futures exchange subject to standardized terms and conditions. Exchange-traded currency futures have historically been distinguished from OTC FX transactions by their standardization versus flexibility or customization inherent in working with a dealer. But exchanges are introducing greater degrees of flexibility in their trading practices.

FX futures are traded on the CME Globex electronic trading platform and on the floor of the exchange in an open outcry environment, although the predominant mode of trade is electronic. These contracts generally call for delivery of a specified quantity of a specified currency, or a cash settlement, during the months of March, June, September, and December (the "March quarterly cycle"). Thus, one may buy or sell 12,500,000 Japanese yen for delivery on the third Wednesday of December 2006 or 125,000

EXHIBIT 4.6   Specifications of Popular Foreign Exchange Futures

	EuroFX Futures	Japanese Yen Futures	British Pound Futures	Swiss Franc Futures
Trade unit	125,000 euros	12,500,000 yen	62,500 pounds	125,000 francs
Minimum price fluctuation (tick)	$0.0001 per Euro ($12.50)	$0.000001 per yen ($12.50)	$0.0001 per pound ($6.25)	$0.0001 per franc ($12.50)
Price limits	No limits			
Contract months	First six months in March quarterly cycle (March, June, Sep, & Dec)			
CME Globex trading hours	Sundays through Mondays: 5:00 PM to 4:00 PM the following day (Chicago time)			
Trading ends at	Second business day before third Wednesday of contract month			
Delivery	Through Continuous Linked Settlement (CLS) facilities			
Position limits	No limits			
Symbol	EC	JY	BP	SF

euros for delivery on the third Wednesday of March 2007. For example, traders who "go long" or buy Japanese yen futures are committed to take or accept delivery of 12,500,000 Japanese yen, whereas traders who "go short" or sell EuroFX futures are committed to make delivery of 125,000 euros. The short making delivery is compensated by the buyer accepting delivery by an amount equal to the futures settlement price quoted in U.S. dollars on the last day of trading. See Exhibit 4.6.

Noting that the Japanese yen futures contract is based on 12,500,000 yen, this means that the September contract was valued at $110,400.00 (= 12,500,000 yen × 0.008832 dollars/yen). The minimum allowable price fluctuation, or "tick," in yen futures is $0.000001 per yen or $12.50 (= $0.000001 × 12,500,000 yen). Exhibit 4.7 illustrates quotation practices in four of the most significant of these currency futures markets.

Digging in a bit more deeply, Exhibit 4.8 illustrates how Japanese yen futures may be quoted. Note that the contract is quoted in "American" terms (i.e., in terms of dollars per foreign unit). This is at variance from the typical interbank practice of quoting foreign exchange transactions in terms of foreign unit per U.S. dollar.

Of course, you can convert these quotes from dollars per foreign unit to foreign units per dollar by simply taking the reciprocal. For example, if September Japanese yen futures close at 0.008832 dollars per yen, this may

EXHIBIT 4.7 Select Foreign Exchange Futures (June 30, 2006)

	Open Range	High	Low	Settlement	Volume	Open Interest
British pounds (62,500 pounds sterling)						
Sep-06	1.8406–1.8403	1.8532	1.8403	1.8508	66,982	78,992
Dec-06		1.8550B		1.8549	224	242
Mar-07						1
EuroFX (125,000 euros)						
Dec-05	1.27830–1.27840	1.28550B	1.27800	1.28500	167,015	154,334
Mar-06	1.29260	1.29260	1.29200A	1.29220	546	1,104
Jun-06				1.29880	2	80
Japanese yen (12,500,000 yen)						
Dec-05	0.008817–0.008816	0.008855	0.008809A	0.008832	73,027	147,195
Mar-06	0.008962	0.008963B	0.008962	0.008946	164	20,509
Jun-06				0.009056		2
Swiss franc (125,000 francs)						
Dec-05	0.8183–0.8182	0.8246	0.8182	0.8241	54,497	60,560
Mar-06		0.8319B		0.8318	100	208
Jun-06				0.8392		7

Note: B = bid; A = ask.

EXHIBIT 4.8 Quoting Japanese Yen Futures (June 30, 2006)

Month	Open	High	Low	Settlement	Chg	Volume	Open Interest
Sep-06	0.008817–0.008816	0.008855	0.008809A	0.008832	+40	73,027	147,195
Dec-06	0.008962	0.008963B	0.008962	0.008946	+40	164	20,509
Mar-07				0.009056	+42		2
Jun-07				0.009162	+41		15
Sep-07				0.009266	+45		10
TOTAL						67,873	167,731

EXHIBIT 4.9 Translating from American to European Term (June 30, 2006)

CME Group Quotes	American Terms	European Terms
USD per EUR	1.28500 USD/EUR	0.7782 EUR/USD
USD per JPY	0.008832 USD/JY	113.22 JY/USD
USD per GBP	1.8508 USD/GBP	0.5403 GBP/USD
USD per CHF	0.8241 USD/CHF	1.2134 CHF/USD

readily be converted into 113.22 Japanese yen per one U.S. dollar (1/0.008832) as illustrated in Exhibit 4.9.

These popular currency futures tend to be smaller than most typical institutional interbank currency transactions in the range of perhaps $100,000 to $160,000 in notional value. This is intended to render the contracts accessible to retail in addition to institutional traders and thereby add another element of liquidity to the marketplace, noting that one might readily trade in multiples of a single standard contract size. See Exhibit 4.10.

Like any futures contract, FX futures are secured by performance bonds posted by both buyers and sellers. The performance bond or margin requirement reflects one day's maximum anticipated price movement. Subsequently, these positions are marked-to-market (MTM) daily by the exchange clearinghouse. That is, any profits or losses are posted to the trader's account daily. Thus, there are no paper profits or losses in futures.

Deliverables versus Non-Deliverable Futures

The four major currency futures just highlighted call for the actual delivery of these currencies on deposit at designated foreign financial institutions through the CLS system. CLS may be thought of as essentially an

EXHIBIT 4.10 Sizing Major Futures Contracts (June 30, 2006)

	Contract Size	Sep 2006 Contract	Contract Value	Tick Size	$ Value of Tick
EuroFX	125,000	1.28500	$160,625.00	$0.0001	$12.50
Japanese yen	12,500,000	0.008832	$110,400.00	$0.000001	$12.50
British pounds	62,500	1.8508	$115,675.00	$0.0001	$6.25
Swiss francs	125,000	0.8241	$103,012.50	$0.0001	$12.50

escrow service ensuring that payment of one currency is made versus the other currency.

But oftentimes it becomes impractical to provide for such delivery when, for example, exchange restrictions are in force with respect to a particular currency. Under such cases, the currency may trade as an NDF in the OTC or interbank currency markets as described earlier. There are in fact some currency futures contracts based on nondeliverable currencies that are settled in cash upon futures contract expiration. This provision allows CME Group to extend the futures product line to currencies including the Chinese renminbi, the Russian ruble, and others. These contracts are cash settled versus a representative price surveyed from the interbank spot markets.

Fair Value Concept and Arbitrage

Futures are most closely compared to outright FX forward transactions and are priced in accordance with the same cost of carry considerations discussed earlier. However, some unique terminology is often applied to the futures markets. In particular, futures market participants often speak of "the basis" or the relationship between futures and spot prices in a very specific way. The basis may be thought of as the futures price less the spot or cash price of the currency in question.

$$\text{Basis} = \text{Futures Price} - \text{Spot Price}$$

The basis may be either positive or negative contingent on the relationship between short-term interest rates prevailing with respect to the base and terms currencies. Because CME Group FX futures are generally quoted in terms of U.S. dollars (USD) per the named currency, USD becomes the "terms" currency, and the named currency is base currency in this context. The appropriate level for the futures contract, or the "fair market value," may be calculated per the following formula:

$$\text{Futures} = \text{Spot Price} \times \left(\frac{1 + [R_{term} \times (d/360)]}{1 + [R_{base} \times (d/360)]} \right)$$

Where the terms rate exceeds the base rate, futures should trade at premium to the spot price of the currency. This is a condition known as "negative carry" in futures markets because costs are incurred to buy and carry base currency. But when the terms rate is less than the base rate, futures should trade at discount to spot. This is a circumstance known as "positive carry" because earnings accrue from buying and carrying base currency. Note that the futures basis is analogous to "forward points" as quoted in interbank markets and described earlier.

As an example, consider the fair market value for a March 2007 EuroFX futures contract as of January 22, 2007. At the time, note that the spot value of the Euro (EUR) was 1.2953 EUR per USD. There were 58 days until the March 21, 2007, futures delivery date. The term rate (or USD rate) stood at 5.31% per a 360 rate convention and the base rate (EUR rate) was at 3.66%, likewise with 360 rate convention. As such, the March 2007 EuroFX futures price could have been calculated as 1.2987.

$$\text{Futures} = \text{Spot Rate} \times \left(\frac{1 + [R_{term} \times (d/360)]}{1 + [R_{base} \times (d/360)]} \right)$$

$$\text{Futures} = 1.2953 \times \left(\frac{1 + [5.31\% \times (58/360)]}{1 + [3.66\% \times (58/360)]} \right)$$

$$= 1.2987$$

The basis may be quoted at 34 points (= 1.2987 – 1.2953). Note that the futures price exceeds the spot price and that the basis will tend to increase in further deferred futures contract months; that is, futures in successively deferred months run to higher and higher levels. This is a condition of negative carry because costs are incurred when borrowing USD to buy EUR because U.S. rates ("terms rate") exceed euro rates ("base rate").

$$\text{Basis} = \text{Futures Price} - \text{Spot Price}$$
$$= 1.2987 - 1.2953$$
$$= 0.0034, \text{ or } 34 \text{ points}$$

Exhibit 4.11 depicts this condition in deferred months. Note that although the March 2007 contract traded at a basis of 34 points, the June 2007 basis is higher at 80 points and the December 2007 basis is even higher at 119 points. Note further that we apply different short-term rates to different terms in recognition of the shape of the U.S.- and euro-denominated short-term yield curve.

EXHIBIT 4.11   Forward Pricing of EuroFX Futures (January 22, 2007)

	Price	Basis	"Fair Value"	Maturity	Days	Term Rate	Base Rate
Spot	1.2953			1/22/07			
ECH7	1.2987	0.0034	1.2987	3/21/07	58	5.31%	3.66%
ECM7	1.3033	0.0080	1.3033	6/20/07	149	5.36%	3.84%
ECZ7	1.3072	0.0119	1.3072	9/19/07	240	5.40%	3.98%

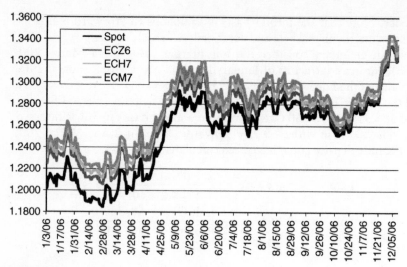

EXHIBIT 4.12   Spot EuroFX versus Futures

Over time as we approach expiration of a futures contract, that basis will tend to converge toward zero. This is attributed to the fact that the impact of the differential short-term rates becomes less relevant as expiration approaches. Finally, by the time the futures contract becomes deliverable, the futures contract becomes a direct proxy for the spot delivery of the currency in question, and the basis is said to converge to zero.

Exhibits 4.12 and 4.13 depict this convergence on an outright basis and by following the basis directly. Despite some minor flutter, these basis relationships are really quite predictable. That is because arbitrageurs monitor and promptly act on situations where futures and spot prices are misaligned.

Assume that futures prices were to be trading above their fair value. Under those circumstances, an arbitrageur may sell futures and buy an equivalent amount of the spot currency, eventually making delivery of the currency in satisfaction of the futures contract.

For example, if March 2007 EuroFX futures were priced above their fair value of 1.2987, one might buy 125,000 euros in the spot markets (or the equivalent of one futures contract) at the spot value of 1.2953 euros per U.S. dollar as of January 22, 2007, and eventually make delivery against the futures contract. If one leverages the transaction by borrowing at prevailing short-term U.S. rates to purchase the euros, holding the position over the next 58 days until the March 21, 2007, futures contract expiration, one would incur $1,385 in associated USD finance costs

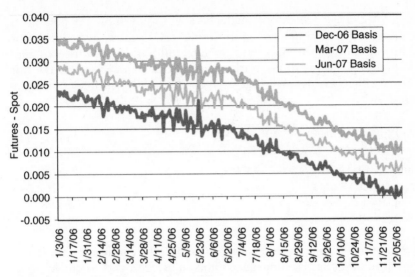

EXHIBIT 4.13 Convergence of EuroFX Basis

at a rate of 5.31%. Presumably, one invests those euros over the next 58 days at 3.66%, earning $955. The net cost associated with buying and carrying those euros over the 58-day period equals $162,343 or 1.2987. Any excess over that 1.2987 at which one might be able to sell EuroFX futures represents a potential profit. By buying and carrying spot euros and selling EuroFX futures, arbitrageurs' trading activities may be expected to bid up the spot currency and/or push down futures to re-establish equilibrium pricing levels.

Buy 125,000 euros @ 1.2953 EUR/USD	–$161,913
USD finance charges @ 5.31% over 58 days	–$1,385
Invest euros @ 3.66% over 58 days	$955
Net cost over 58 days	–$162,343
Divided by 125,000 euros	1.2987
Expected futures price	1.2987

If, in contrast, futures prices were to trade below their fair value, one might buy futures and sell an equivalent amount of the currency in the spot markets, eventually taking repossession of the currency by accepting delivery of the currency in satisfaction of the futures contract. Of course, by selling euros for U.S. dollars, one enjoys the opportunity to invest those dollars at the prevailing U.S.-denominated rate of 5.31%, forgoing the opportunity to invest in euros at 3.66%. Any amount under fair value of 1.2987 at which one might be able to buy futures represents a potential profit on the part of an arbitrageur. Of course, by selling euros and buying futures, this may have the effect of pushing down euros and/or bidding up futures to establish an equilibrium price level at the fair value. In other words, arbitrage activity essentially enforces fair value pricing.

Sell 125,000 euros @ 1.2953 EUR/USD	$161,913
Invest USD @ 5.31% over 58 days	$1,385
Finance Euros @ 3.66% over 58 days	–$955
Net cost over 58 days	+$162,343
Divided by 125,000 euros	1.2987
Expected futures price	1.2987

As a practical matter, of course, one must also consider costs attendant to arbitrage, that is, slippage, commissions, fees, and so on. As such, futures tend to trade within a "band" above or below its theoretical fair value, and the width of that band is a reflection of the amount of those costs. Thus, when futures fall below that band, arbitrageurs may be recommended to buy futures and sell spot. When futures rise above that band, arbitrageurs may be recommended to sell futures and buy spot. In the context of currency futures, that band tends to be rather tight because the arbitrage is rather straightforward and the attendant costs are low.

Fair Value – Arbitrage Costs < Futures Price < Fair Value + Arbitrage Costs

Spreading Currency Futures

Currency futures contracts are frequently used as part of a spread transaction. See Exhibit 4.14. Perhaps the most actively spread currency futures include the British pound, euro, Japanese yen, and Swiss franc contracts. For example, one might wish to spread the British pound versus the Japanese yen or the euro currency versus the Swiss franc.

Because these major currency futures contracts trade at quite different levels, it is generally necessary to structure, or "weight," these intermarket spreads by adjusting the number of futures contracts held in each market. In particular, the goal is to balance the monetary value of each contract that forms the intermarket spread. To do so, one must reference the value of each contract as a function of the contract multiplier and the price of each leg of spread.

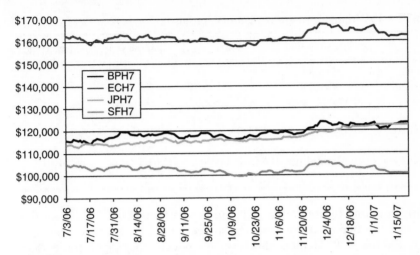

EXHIBIT 4.14 CME Currency Futures Performance (USD)

$$\text{Multiplier}_1 \times \text{Price}_1 \sim \text{Multiplier}_2 \times \text{Price}_2$$
$$\text{Spread Ratio} = (\text{Multiplier}_1 \times \text{Price}_1) \div (\text{Multiplier}_2 \times \text{Price}_2)$$

For example, assume that we wanted to place an intermarket spread with British pounds and Japanese yen futures on January 22, 2007. At the time, March 2007 British pounds futures (BPH7) were trading at 197.58 for a contract value of $123,488 (= 62,500 pounds × 197.58). March 2007 Japanese yen futures (JYH7) were trading at 0.009793 for a contract value of $122,413 (= 12,500,000 yen × 0.009793). The appropriate spread ratio is calculated as 1:1 or one British pound futures contract for every one Japanese yen futures contract.

$$
\begin{aligned}
\text{Spread Ratio} &= (\text{Multiplier}_{BPH7} \times \text{Price}_{BPH7}) \div (\text{Multiplier}_{JYH7} \times \text{Price}_{JYH7}) \\
&= (\$625 \times 197.58) \div (\$1,250 \times 0.9793) \\
&= \$123,488 \div \$122,413 \\
&= 1.0088 \text{ or } \sim 1:1 \text{ spread ratio}
\end{aligned}
$$

Because these types of intermarket spreads are so commonplace, the CME Group Clearing House offers reduced performance bond (or "margin") requirements in recognition of the fact that the risks associated with a spread are often reduced relative to the risks associated with an outright position. Exhibit 4.15 depicts outright speculative and hedge/member/maintenance performance bond requirements as of January 2007 and further shows the spread credit (i.e., credit on spread between

EXHIBIT 4.15 Margining Currency Futures Spreads

	British pound	Euro	Japanese yen	Swiss franc
British pound	$1,688 ($1,250)			
Euro	75% 3:2 ratio	$2,565 ($1,900)		
Japanese yen	65% 1:1 ratio	70% 3:4 ratio	$2,430 ($1,800)	
Swiss franc	65% 1:1 ratio	85% 2:3 ratio	70% 1:1 ratio	$1,620 ($1,200)

1 British pound futures versus 1 Japanese yen futures is 65%). Note that performance bond requirements are subject to frequent amendment. Further, Exhibit 4.15 depicts the ratio on which one might trade these spreads as the basis for the margin break. Thus, the hedge/member/maintenance margin on our British pound/Japanese yen spread is equal to $1,067.50 (= 35% of $1,250 + $1,800).

Let's look at another intermarket spread example. In this case, one might have placed an intermarket spread by buying three British pound futures for every two EuroFX futures sold. By placing the spread on January 9, 2007, and liquidating it a few weeks later on January 22, 2007, one might actually have made money on both sides of the spread for a tidy profit.

1/9/07   Buy 3 BPH7 @ 194.02   Sell 2 ECH7 @ 1.3042
1/22/07 Sell 3 BPH7 @ 197.58   Buy 2 ECH7 @ 1.2987
         +$6,675 (= 3 × $625 × 3.56)   +$1,375 (= 2 × $125,000 × 0.0055)
         +$8,050

In addition to facilitating intermarket spread opportunities through a weighted approach, CME Group also directly lists a variety of cross-rate futures contracts including the Euro/BP, Euro/JY, Euro/SF, BP/SF, BP/JY, and many others. These contracts are quoted in terms of a major non-USD currency and are accounted for in those terms. As such, they facilitate a direct and precise cross-rate transaction without resorting to the weighting structures as described earlier. You can also see this in Exhibit 4.16.

Hedging with Currency Futures

A firm faced with the risk of volatile exchange rates has many alternative means to address those risks. One of the most efficient and effective

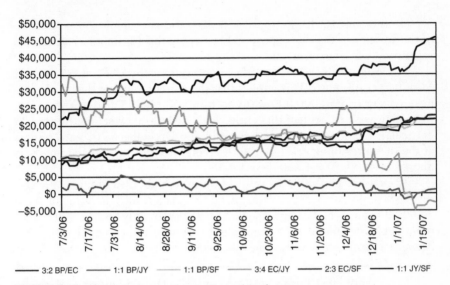

EXHIBIT 4.16 CME Currency Futures Spread Performance

risk-management tools in this regard is found in the form of CME Group currency futures contracts. Let's explore the possibilities.

The first thing that must be considered when constructing a hedging strategy is the amount of risk exposure. That is intuitive to the extent that the purpose of a hedge is to offset possibly adverse price fluctuations in one market with an (ideally) equal and opposite exposure in the hedging vehicle such as futures.

Actually, the identification of a "hedge ratio" (HR) in the context of currencies is rather straightforward and generally a simple function of the relationship between the exposure to be hedged and the futures contract size.

Assume, for example, that a company domiciled in the United States and whose financial statements are denominated in U.S. dollars, agrees to sell goods to be delivered a few months later for a future payment of €50,000,000. As a result, said company is exposed to the risk of a declining euro versus the U.S. dollar. The appropriate strategy might be to sell EuroFX futures to address the risk exposure. The hedge ratio is found by comparing that €50,000,000 risk exposure with the €125,000 futures contract size.

$$\text{Hedge Ratio} = \text{Value of Risk Exposure} \div \text{Futures Contract Size}$$
$$= €50,000,000 \div €125,000$$
$$= 400 \text{ Euro FX futures contracts}$$

In other words, the appropriate hedge ratio is a simple linear function of the amount of the risk exposure. Let's apply this formula to an example using some actual market data.

It is August 18, 2008, and the spot value of the USD/euro rate is at $1.4704 per one euro. This implies that the current value of that forthcoming payment of €50,000,000 was worth $73,520,000. Of course, the company may wish to protect this anticipated cash flow by selling futures. In particular, the company might have sold 400 December 2008 euro futures at the then prevailing price of 1.4605. Note that the basis at the time was quoted at –0.0099 (= 1.4605 less 1.4704).

By October 17, 2008, the value of the euro had fallen dramatically versus the U.S. dollar to a spot value of 1.3425. As a result, the value of those 50,000,000 euros had declined some $6,395,000 to only $67,125,000. That represents a decline of 8.7% and might very well represent the difference between a profit and a loss on the sale.

	Spot USD/Euro	€50MM in USD	Dec-08 Futures	Basis
8/18/08	1.4704	$73,520,000	Sell 400 @ 1.4605	–0.0099
10/17/08	1.3425	$67,125,000	Buy 400 @ 1.3420	–0.0005
		($6,395,000)	+$5,925,000	+0.0094
		Net Loss of $470,000		

But by selling those 400 futures contracts, the company might have generated a sizable profit to offset its spot market losses. Note that futures likewise declined from 1.4605 to 1.3420. This translated into a futures market profit of $5,925,000 for the company. This profit did not quite offset the $6,395,000 loss in the spot market. Still, a net loss of $470,000 is far superior to an unhedged loss of $6,395,000.

Why did the transaction result in a net loss? Note that the futures/spot basis fluctuated from its original level of –0.0099 to –0.0005 (= 1.3425 less 1.3420). Our company was effectively short the basis because it was short euros in the futures market and long euros in the spot market.

The advance in the basis was largely a function of declining European short-term rates in the period from late August to late October 2008. Note that European economic conditions were slumping to match similar conditions in the United States during this period. As a result, European central bankers were easing to reflect this economic weakness and European rates were pushed down to levels more closely resembling those prevailing in the United States. Of course, it could very well have gone the other way and the basis might have become more negative, a circumstance that would have worked to the benefit of the hedger in our example.

Our prior example focused on a situation involving the sale of futures to offset the possibility that the euro might decline relative to the U.S. dollar, or a "short hedge." But we might likewise examine the opposite situation involving the purchase of futures, or a "long hedge."

To illustrate, consider the plight of a U.S.-based importer who has contracted to purchase goods from a Japanese company and who has agreed to pay ¥10 billion in return. In this case, the importer must be wary about the possibility that the value of the Japanese yen will advance versus the U.S. dollar in the interim between the time the contract is executed and the payment is due.

Our first order of business is to identify the appropriate hedge ratio. Note that the CME Group Japanese yen futures calls for the delivery of 12.5 million Japanese yen and is quoted in USD per JPY. Thus, the appropriate hedge ratio is calculated at 800 futures contracts as follows:

$$\text{Hedge Ratio} = \text{Hedged Value Futures} \div \text{Futures Contract Size}$$
$$= ¥\,10,000,000,000 \div ¥\,12,500,000$$
$$= 800 \text{ euro FX futures contracts}$$

On August 18, 2008, the Japanese yen (JPY) versus the U.S. dollar was quoted at 109.97 yen per dollar. Note, however, that CME Group currency futures are generally quoted in "American" terms. Thus, we take the reciprocal of that number and quote the spot rate at 0.009093 USD per JPY. As such, ¥10 billion equates to $90,930,000, and it is that value that our company wishes to lock up by buying Japanese yen futures contracts.

By October 17, 2008, the exchange rate declines to 101.54 yen per dollar. Taking the reciprocal of this figure consistent with the specifications of the CME Group Japanese yen futures contract, this equates to a value of 0.009848 USD per JPY. Thus, that ¥10 billion is now worth the U.S. dollar equivalent of $98,848,000. This implies an unhedged loss of $7,918,000.

	Spot USD/JPY	¥10 bil in USD	Dec-08 Futures	Basis
8/18/08	0.009093	$90,930,000	Buy 800 @ 0.009141	0.000048
10/17/08	0.009848	$98,848,000	Sell 800 @ 0.009880	0.000032
		($7,918,000)	+$7,390,000	– 0.000016
		Net Loss of $528,000		

Of course, our company had executed a long hedge by buying 800 December 2008 Japanese yen futures at the prevailing price of 0.009141. A few months later, the value of the December contract rose to 0.009880. This translates into a profit in the futures market of $7,390,000 and a net loss of $528,000.

Although our company still experienced a net loss on the hedged transaction, it is far preferable to absorb a $528,000 loss as opposed to the unhedged loss of $7,918,000. Why did our company experience a hedge loss on a hedged basis? Note that the basis defined as futures less cash declined from its original value of 0.000048 (= 0.009141 less 0.009093) to a value of 0.000032 (= 0.009880 less 0.009848) over the two-month duration of the hedge.

But our hedger was effectively short the basis by virtue of being long cash and essentially short futures. The basis declined because Japanese short-term interest rates were soft during this period as the economic conditions weakened in Japan, reflecting general weakness in the United States and elsewhere in the world. Whereas U.S. short-term rates were relatively low, Japanese rates were even lower and sinking. As such, basis movement worked against the hedger. But it could easily have gone the other way.

Options on Currency Futures

In addition to operating the primary venue for the trade of currency futures, CME Group also offers options exercisable for futures. Note that upon exercise, rather than delivering actual currency, these contracts contemplate the establishment of a currency futures position. These contracts are accessible through the CME Globex electronic trading platform and are offered on an American-style and European-style basis.

Exchange-traded options are similar to exchange traded futures with respect to their relatively high degree of standardization. And like currency futures, trading volumes in options on currency futures have been growing very quickly in recent years.

FOREIGN EXCHANGE MARKET GROWTH AND TRENDS

As a result of these product innovations, volatility, globalization, and use of electronic trading platforms, worldwide currency trade has grown rapidly. It is interesting to note that currency derivative trade (i.e., forward, swaps, futures, and options) had overtaken spot trade of currencies by the early 1990s. In fact, OTC FX swaps now comprise approximately half of all currency trading on an OTC or exchange-traded basis. See Exhibit 4.17.

EXHIBIT 4.17 Turnover in Foreign Exchange Derivatives Market (average daily turnover in April; notional value in billions)

	1995	1998	2001	2004	2007
Outright forwards and FX swaps	$643	$862	$786	$1,163	$2,076
Currency swaps	$4	$10	$7	$21	$32
Options	$41	$87	$60	$117	$212
Other	$1	$0	$0	$2	$0
OTC foreign exchange turnover	688	959	853	1,303	2,319
Exchange-traded FX contracts	17	11	10	22	72
Exchange-traded share (%)	2.4%	1.1%	1.2%	1.7%	3.0%

Source: Bank for International Settlements (BIS).

Exchange-traded currency derivatives (i.e., futures and options on futures) currently account for a relatively small slice of the pie. But volumes have generally been growing. This growth may be attributed in large part to the deployment of futures and options on globally distributed electronic trading platforms. See Exhibit 4.18.

The FX markets operate 24 hours a day. Some currency dealers specialize in certain aspects of the business, and many are happy to accommodate demand for flexible or customized instruments on the part of their customers. Financial institutions including banks, hedge funds, other asset managers, and corporations are active participants. Banks and other major security broker/dealers, acting as either traders or market makers, are the most active participants. Many carry large positions in FX, shifting the attendant risk management responsibilities from their London to New York

EXHIBIT 4.18 Outstanding Notional Value of Over-the-Counter FX Derivatives (Billions USD)

	Dec-03	Dec-04	Dec-05	Dec-06	Dec-07	Dec-08
OTC FX derivatives	24,475	29,289	31,360	40,271	56,238	49,753
Outright forwards, FX swaps	12,387	14,951	15,873	19,882	29,144	24,562
Currency swaps	6,371	8,223	8,504	10,792	14,347	14,725
Options	5,717	6,115	6,984	9,597	12,748	10,466
Exchange-traded FX contracts	118	164	174	240	291	227
Exchange-traded share (%)	0.48%	0.56%	0.55%	0.59%	0.51%	0.46%

Source: Bank for International Settlements (BIS).

EXHIBIT 4.19 Outstanding Notional Value of Over-the-Counter Foreign Exchange Derivatives by Currency(Billions USD)

	Dec-04	Dec-05	Dec-06	Dec-07	Dec-08
All Currencies	29,289	31,360	40,271	56,238	44,200
Australian dollar	1,092	1,315	1,502	2,227	1,360
Canadian dollar	1,172	1,379	1,768	2,404	1,568
Danish krone	119	136	148	241	195
Euro	11,900	12,857	16,037	21,806	18,583
Hong Kong dollar	605	493	631	988	608
Japanese yen	7,076	7,575	9,490	12,857	11,292
New Zealand dollar	14	22	48	60	28
Norwegian krone	140	134	281	420	369
Pound sterling	4,331	4,424	6,135	7,979	4,732
Swedish krona	957	1,067	1,220	1,525	1,178
Swiss franc	1,452	1,689	2,311	3,662	3,034
U.S. dollar	25,726	26,295	33,755	46,947	37,516

Source: Bank for International Settlements (BIS).

to Asian offices throughout the day. Although trading is actively pursued in multiple money centers throughout the world, London stands out as the epicenter of currency trade. See Exhibit 4.19.

Although London may be the most important OTC FX trading center due to the fact that it straddles both European and U.S. trading hours, it remains a very U.S. dollar–centric world. Note that the proportion of OTC FX derivatives featuring the U.S. dollar as one side of the transaction has been fading just a bit over the years and checked in at 42% in December 2008. The euro, Japanese yen, and British pound check in at approximately 21, 13, and 5%, respectively.

Electronic Trading

Most OTC FX trading is probably still conducted the old-fashioned way, via telephone between a variety of dealers and their customers. But traditional trading practices are giving way to electronic trading, fueled by the buy-side demand on the part of hedge funds, commodity trading advisors (CTAs), and proprietary trading companies.

These customers are drawn to electronic trade for the following reasons: ease of access, multiple liquidity channels, central clearing (in the case of futures), transaction speed, reduced cost, and straight through processing (STP).

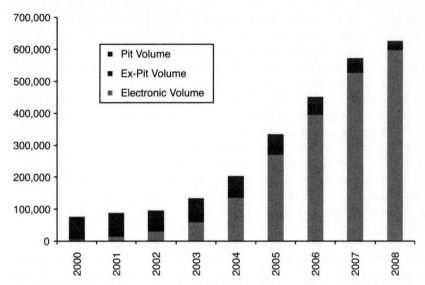

EXHIBIT 4.20 Average Daily Volume of CME Foreign Exchange Futures and Options

Three of the largest electronic platforms are EBS with an estimated $227 billion in average daily volume (ADV), Reuters at an estimated $140 billion, and CME Globex, the CME Group's electronic platform, at an estimated $90 billion in 2007. See Exhibit 4.20.

In addition, there are a number of electronic communication networks (ECNs) specializing in FX, including FXConnect, Fxall, Currenex, Hot Spot, and eSpeed. These systems facilitate direct market access and customer-to-customer in addition to dealer-to-customer trade. There are also a number of single bank electronic portals offered by primary FX banks including UBS, Deutsche Bank, Dresdner, Barclays, and Citigroup, where the bank acts as a singular market maker.

In particular, exchange-traded futures and options have now almost completely migrated to CME Group's Globex electronic trading platform. See Exhibit 4.20. In years past, the bulk of the trade was done in an open outcry or pit environment, requiring "high-touch" order handling on the part of brokers on the floor of the exchange. Note that trading may also be conducted on an "ex-pit" basis as a so-called exchange for physical (EFP) transaction. EFP transactions entail a privately negotiated currency transaction in the OTC markets that are subsequently novated to the CME Group for purposes of clearing.

As a result of this electronic activity, a fundamental paradigm shift is occurring in the FX market. Major banks, acting as spot dealers, are seeing their stature as a single source of liquidity diminish. Many new buy-side customers no longer depend on the advice, liquidity, or credit traditionally supplied by these dealer-banks. Hedge funds are attracting vast amounts of capital without the assistance of the banks, which had traditionally bound the hedge funds to prime broker operations.

But many high net worth individuals, pension funds, and money managers are seeking enhanced Alpha directly from top-performing hedge funds, bypassing investment banks. Once hedge funds are free to execute their FX business where they please, they tend to focus on optimizing their fills and minimizing costs.

CME Group's Globex system may potentially offer the greatest value proposition to the FX market. Large traders are discovering that CME Group offers liquidity on par or exceeding the platforms just mentioned with additional benefits not available elsewhere. These benefits include price transparency, transaction fees equal to or less than prime brokerage, millisecond transaction times, complete anonymity, and a clearinghouse guarantee as discussed later. FX futures are closely regulated by the Commodity Futures Trading Commission (CFTC), providing a complete paper trail and clearly posted MTM settlement each day that facilitates risk-management and position valuation capabilities.

The evolution of the FX marketplace from direct phone dealing to electronic trading has also caused intense discussion about whether or not the entire market will eventually transform into an exchange model. Traditional sell-side participants naturally resist these developments. But if buy-side customers are no longer willing to pay away a spread to execute their business or need trade advice, what becomes of the traditional spot dealer's value proposition? Some banks are addressing these issues by aggregating the feeds of electronic platforms into a single feed to their customers while continuing to offer traditional service to those who demand it. Further, buy-side firms are themselves becoming market makers, providing the same tight spreads to the marketplace as traditional sell-side dealers.

The deployment of sophisticated algorithmic trading models is further changing the landscape. Originally conceived by equity arbitrage traders, "algo" strategies have been applied successfully to FX markets. From black box "quants" at investment banks and hedge funds, to turnkey software solutions from companies like Trading Technologies X Trader application, algo trading is booming.

This has exerted some strain on electronic platforms that are incapable of handing the ensuing massive message traffic generated, noting that many more unfilled order messages may be generated than volume executed. The more robust systems such as CME Globex handle this traffic with relative ease. The challenge going forward to all electronic platforms will be how to manage the massive message traffic without detracting from system response time or losing essential trading logic.

Finally, we may consider whether these developments call into question the utility of the spot market versus futures or other derivatives. Many hedge funds cite the liquidity in spot markets as a prime attraction. Still, they frequently transition into forward trade after spot trades, incurring additional processing and risk-management costs and consuming credit lines. As traders realize that futures and other derivatives offer comparable liquidity, the need to look to spot may further diminish.

Clearinghouse

Exchange-traded FX products offer an important advantage over OTC products to the extent that they are cleared and guaranteed by the CME Group Clearing House (CH). The CH acts as the central counterparty for all transactions. Thus, credit risk concerns associated with holding FX positions with a variety of counterparties are minimized.

When establishing a futures position, you are required to post a margin and MTM daily any profits or losses on a net basis with the CH acting as a single point of contact. Because futures are margined and MTMed daily, credit risks are mitigated and no capital requirements need be set aside per the Basle Accord.

Specifically, the Basle Accord includes futures contracts among the various off-balance sheet items that require "special attention because banks are not exposed to credit risk for the full value of their contracts, but only to the potential cost of replacing the cash flow (on contracts showing positive value) if the counterparty defaults."[1] Further, note that "[i]nstruments traded on exchanges may be excluded where they are subject to daily receipt and payment of cash variation margin."[2]

CONCLUSION

Currencies may be the most fundamental of all commodities because they represent the basic units in which transactions of all types are denominated. Currencies have been exchanged or traded in one way or another since the concept of a currency was created.

CME and its chairman emeritus Leo Melamed, responding to the breakdown of the Bretton Woods agreement and free-floating currency values, was a pioneer by creating the first successful financial futures based on major currencies. Since then, currency derivatives in the form of futures, options on futures, and a variety of interbank-traded instruments have flourished.

These markets will likely continue to evolve and adapt to dynamic market conditions and advancing technologies. In particular, the widespread acceptance of electronic trading technologies has opened up new vistas for the currency markets by offering widespread distribution of products as well as the opportunity to apply automated or algorithmic trading methodologies.

NOTES

1. "International Convergence of Capital Measurement and Capital Standards," Basle Committee on Banking Supervision, July 1988.
2. "Basle Capital Accord: Treatment of Potential Exposure for Off-Balance-Sheet Items," Basle Committee on Banking Supervision, April 1995.

CHAPTER 5

Stock Index Futures Fundamentals

John W. Labuszewski
Brett Vietmeier

Stock index futures were introduced in 1982 on domestic futures exchanges and have since grown to become perhaps the second most significant sector, after interest rates, within the futures trading community. Actually, the concept of a stock index futures contract had been discussed and analyzed for many years prior to 1982, but a variety of regulatory and intellectual property rights issues held the concept back. In particular, there had been much discussion regarding the application of a cash settlement mechanism, jurisdictional issues between the Commodity Futures Trading Commission (CFTC) and the Securities and Exchange Commission (SEC); as well as the rights accruing to independent index publishers.

However, these issues were addressed by 1982, leading to the introduction of futures based on the Value Line Composite Average (VLCA) on the Kansas City Board of Trade (KCBT) in 1982, followed in short order by futures based on the Standard & Poor's 500 Index (S&P 500) on the Chicago Mercantile Exchange (CME). The basic model established by these exchanges for the trade of stock index futures was ultimately adapted on a domestic and global basis by many other exchanges. As a result, we now enjoy a vibrant array of stock index futures for access by institutional and retail traders alike.

MECHANICS OF STOCK INDEX FUTURES

For purposes of exposition, we focus on several extraordinarily successful stock index futures contracts that share some common mainstream design characteristics. We are referring to the "E-mini" line of stock index futures products as introduced on the CME in 1997. These contracts are traded exclusively on electronic trading platforms such as the CME Globex system and constructed with relatively modest contract sizes relative to the original or "standard"-sized stock index futures based on the particular index.

Note that the original CME S&P 500 futures contract introduced in 1982 was based on a value of $500 times the index value. Over the years, of course, the stock market has generally risen, exceeding inflation rates by a wide margin. Thus, by 1997, CME found it was offering a contract with a very high and unwieldy contract value. As a result, CME "split" the original S&P 500 contract such that the contract multiplier was halved from $500 to $250 times the Index. Still, the contract value was relatively high, and CME offered an alternative "E-mini" S&P 500 contract valued at $50 times the index. The E-mini design was widely accepted and rapidly grew to become the most popular line of stock index futures available, as illustrated in Exhibit 5.1.

Although reasonably simple, the E-mini design was widely imitated by many exchanges. Like all stock index futures contracts, they are valued at a specified contract multiplier times the spot or cash index value. They call for a cash settlement at said value generally during the contract months of March, June, September, and December (the "March quarterly cycle"). For example, the CME Group E-mini S&P 500 futures contract features a contract multiplier of $50 times the index. The resulting final

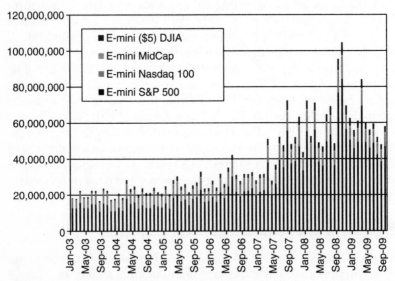

EXHIBIT 5.1   Growth of Major Mini Stock Index Figures

EXHIBIT 5.2 Specifications of Popular Stock Index Futures Contracts

	E-mini S&P 500	E-mini Nasdaq 100	E-mini MidCap 400	E-mini ($5) DJIA
Contact multiplier	$50 × S&P 500 Index	$20 × Nasdaq 100 Index	$100 × S&P MidCap 400	$5 × Dow Jones Industrial Avg
Minimum price fluctuation (tick)	0.25 index points ($12.50)	0.50 index points ($10.00)	0.10 index points ($10.00)	1.00 index points ($5.00)
Price limits	Limits at 10%, 20%, 30% moves			
Contract months	First five months in March quarterly cycle			
Trading hours	Mon–Thu: 5:00 PM to 3:15 PM the following day and 3:30 to 4:30; Sun: 5:00 PM to 3:15			
Trading ends at	8:30 AM on third Friday of month			
Cash settlement	Versus. special open quote (SOQ)			
Position limits or accountability	20,000 standard S&P contracts	10,000 standard NASDAQ contracts	5,000 standard MidCap contracts	50,000 contracts
Symbol	ES	NQ	EMD	YM

settlement value is generally relatively modest compared to "standard-sized" stock index contracts, and they are all traded on electronic trading platforms for most of the 24-hour weekday period beginning on Sunday evenings. See Exhibit 5.2.

Quotation Practices

Stock index futures are quoted in terms of the underlying or spot or cash index value in index points. For example, the March 2007 E-mini S&P 500 futures contract settled at 1,428.40 index points on December 29, 2006. By taking the product of the $50 contract multiplier and the settlement value of 1,428.40, we can calculate the notional value represented in the contract as $71,420.

$$
\begin{aligned}
\text{Futures Contract Value} &= \text{Contract Multiplier} \times \text{Quoted Value} \\
&= \$50 \times 1{,}428.40 \\
&= \underline{\$71{,}420}
\end{aligned}
$$

EXHIBIT 5.3 Quoting E-mini S&P 500 Futures (12/29/06)

Month	Open	High	Low	Settlement	Change	Volume	Open Interest
Mar-07	1,434.25	1,437.50	1,425.50	1,428.40	−5.40	527,676	1,481,743
Jun-07	1,446.25	1,450.00	1,439.00	1,441.10	−5.40	424	12,788
TOTAL						528,100	1,494,531

Further, these contracts are quoted in a specified minimum increment, or "tick" value, as seen in Exhibit 5.2. The minimum allowable price fluctuation in the context of the E-mini S&P 500 futures contract is equal to 0.25 index points, or $12.50 per tick (= contract multiplier of $50 × 0.25 index points).

We may value these four popular stock index futures as seen in Exhibit 5.4. Note that the associated contract values range, as of December 29, 2006, from $35,500 upward to $79,490. These contracts are branded as "E-mini" contracts on the CME because they represent a one-fifth-sized version of the so-called standard contracts. For example, the standard S&P 500 contract is valued at a contract multiplier of $250 times the index value. Thus, although the E-mini contract was valued at $71,420, the standard-sized contract was valued at five times that amount, or $357,100 (= $250 × 1,428.40). See Exhibit 5.4.

Of course, these contract values are subject to change minute by minute as futures prices fluctuate up and down. Values for the underlying spot or cash stock index are actually updated every 15 seconds during the course of a normal trading day in domestic stock markets and made available by the

EXHIBIT 5.4 Pricing Popular Stock Index Futures (12/29/06)

	Contract Multiplier	Mar-06 Contract	Contract Value	Tick (Index Points)	$ Value of Tick
Standard S&P 500	250x	1,428.40	$357,100	0.10	$25.00
E-mini S&P 500	$50x	1,428.40	$ 71,420	0.25	$12.50
E-mini Nasdaq 100	$20x	1,775.00	$ 35,500	0.50	$10.00
E-mini S&P MidCap 400	$100x	811.30	$ 81,130	0.10	$10.00
$5 DJIA	$5x	12,539	$ 62,695	1.00	$ 5.00

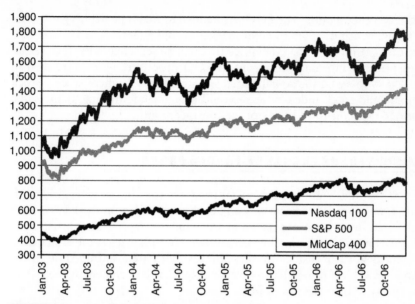

EXHIBIT 5.5 Nasdaq 100, S&P 500, MidCap 400

index publishers through a variety of commercially available electronic quotation or ticker systems. See Exhibit 5.5.

Cash Settlement Mechanism

Stock index futures do not call for the delivery of the actual stocks associated with the stock index. Such delivery would be cumbersome to say the least, considering the fact that a stock index may be composed of hundreds or even thousands of constituents. Potential delivery problems are compounded to the extent that one would have to weight the delivery of the various stocks by reference to their exacting weights as represented in the stock index. As a result, the industry addressed this problem by introducing the concept of a cash settlement mechanism.

The cash settlement mechanism is actually quite simple. After establishing a long or short position, market participants are subject to a normal "mark-to-market" (MTM) like any other day; that is, they pay any losses or collect any profits daily and in cash. Subsequent to the final settlement day, positions simply expire and are settled at the spot value of the underlying index or instrument.

Domestic stock index futures typically employ a final settlement price that is marked to a "special opening quotation" (SOQ) on the third Friday of the contract month. The SOQ is intended to facilitate arbitrage activity by allowing arbitrageurs to enter market on open (MOO) orders to liquidate cash positions at the same price that will be reflected in the final settlement price. A morning settlement or SOQ procedure was established in late 1980s to avoid the so-called triple witching hour where stocks, stock options, and stock index futures would all conclude trading at the same time of day on the third Friday of the contract month.

E-MINIS VERSUS EXCHANGE-TRADED FUNDS

Two of the most significant financial products to debut in recent years include E-mini stock index futures and exchange-traded funds (ETFs). Both of these products are based on major stock indexes representing broad market movements, and both allow an investor to capitalize on the anticipated movement in various stock market indexes. Both are also traded on major exchanges subject to regulatory oversight by U.S. government agencies and a full array of financial safeguards.

Still, there are some important differences between the two investment approaches. Let's compare and contrast the advantages and disadvantages of these investment vehicles, focusing in particular on the futures and ETFs associated with two of the most significant and widely referenced domestic stock indexes: the S&P 500 Index and the high-tech Nasdaq 100 Index.

How Does an Exchange-Traded Fund Work?

An ETF represents ownership in a unit investment trust patterned after an underlying index, and it is a mutual fund that is traded much like any other fund. Unlike most mutual funds, however, but akin to futures contracts, ETFs can be bought or sold throughout the trading day, not just at the closing price of the day. ETFs generate dividends but are also subject to annual management fees, in addition to the commissions and other transaction costs associated with their purchase or sale. ETFs on both the S&P 500 and the Nasdaq 100 are offered on various stock exchanges including the American Stock Exchange (AMEX), New York Stock Exchange (NYSE), and Nasdaq.

Standard & Poor's 500 Depositary Receipts, or "SPDRs," are traded at approximately a tenth the value of the index. Thus, a single SPDR was quoted at $141.62, or approximately a tenth the value of the S&P 500 at 1,418.30, on December 29, 2006. On the same day, the PowerShares QQQ, based on the Nasdaq 100 and often referred to by its ticker symbol QQQQ, traded at approximately a fortieth of the value of the index. Thus, a single QQQQ was quoted at $43.16, approximately a fortieth of the value of the Nasdaq 100 at 1,756.90.

Of course, futures are settled in cash versus the value of the underlying index on the final settlement day, whereas ETFs represent ownership in unit trusts designed to parallel the underlying index. As such, both futures and ETFs closely parallel movement in the underlying stock index.

Rapid Growth

Both stock index futures and ETFs have experienced remarkable growth in the relatively short periods that they have been available. The first ETFs were introduced in the early 1990s, but it took until the mid- to late 1990s to achieve a good deal of market penetration. In 2006, SPDRs traded $9.23 billion on an average daily basis; QQQQs posted some $4.36 billion. E-mini stock index futures debuted in 1997 and have become one of the fastest growing futures products in history. The dollar value of average daily trading volume during 2006 was $67.98 billion for E-mini S&P futures; E-mini Nasdaq 100 futures posted $10.59 billion. Thus, one might safely conclude that both product lines are quite attractive. Still, there are distinctions that can be considered significant for the investing public, as discussed later.

ETFs may be attractive to the small investor in that they are sized at small values. For example, a SPDR was recently quoted at $141.62, whereas a E-mini S&P 500 futures contract had a much higher nominal (cash equivalent) value of $71,420. To illustrate this point, consider that it would require 500 SPDRs to equate with the value of one E-mini S&P 500 contract, and 800 QQQQs to equate with the value of one E-mini Nasdaq 100 contract. Clearly, ETFs permit one to trade in smaller unit sizes with greater flexibility than do E-mini futures.

Leverage

The capital requirements or margin rules are applied very differently with ETFs and E-mini futures. Like other equity securities, ETFs are subject to the Federal Reserve's Regulation T (Reg T) margin requirements. This means that one must margin a security holding with an initial minimum deposit of 50% of the purchase price, the balance of which may be borrowed at interest. When customers short an ETF, they must put up 50% of the sale price and retain the short sale proceeds in their account.

By contrast, futures traders put up an initial margin deposit or performance bond to secure the transaction, not the amount implied by the nominal value. The performance bond or margin requirements associated with E-mini futures are designed to reflect the maximum anticipated risk associated with the position from day to day. Although the exchange minimum margin requirements are subject to adjustment, the initial speculative performance bond requirement to the E-mini S&P 500 contract was at $3,500 or ~4.9% of the contract value (= $3,500/$71,420) as of December 29, 2006.

Consider the implications of such margin on the purchase of an E-mini S&P futures contract relative to the purchase of 500 SPDRs. Assume that an investor buys one futures contract at a price of 1,420, which equates to a value of $71,000, on margin of $3,500. The market rallies by 40 index points to 1,460 and the investor sells the contract for a profit of $2,000, a profit of 57.1% on the initial margin of $3,500 (not counting fees and commissions).

Buy one E-mini S&P 500 futures @ 1,420	$71,000 (= $50 × 1,420)
Sell @ 1,460	$73,000 (= $50 × 1,460)
Profit (Loss)	$2,000 (= $71,000 − $73,000)
Initial Margin	$3,500
Percentage Profit	57.1% (= $2,000/$3,500)

Now, assume that the investor buys the rough equivalent of that E-mini contract by purchasing 500 SPDRs at a price of $140, subsequently selling at $144, for a profit of $2,000. Per Reg T, the initial margin requirement is 50% of the $70,000 purchase price, or $35,000, which translates into a profit of 6.8% on initial margin. And, of course, the investor still owes interest to his or her broker.

Buy 500 SPDRs @ $140.00	$70,000 (= 500 × $140.00)
Sell @ $144.00	$72,000 (= 500 × $144.00)
Profit (Loss)	$2,000 (= $72,000 − $70,000)
Initial Margin	$35,000 (= 50% of $70,000)
Percentage Profit	5.7% (= $2,000/$35,000)

E-mini futures provide the opportunity to leverage one's capital to a greater extent than ETFs. Of course, care must be taken when applying such leverage to control one's risk exposure and avoid overextending one's financial resources. Leverage cuts both ways. It can be used to enhance one's percentage returns when a trade becomes profitable, but likewise it increases one's percentage losses in unfavorable market circumstances.

Open Competition versus Specialist System

CME Group E-mini futures are traded on the CME Globex electronic trading platform. The system provides for fast, efficient order entry and reporting of resulting fills to the customer without favoritism or regard to the identity of the customer. ETFs were pioneered on the floor of the AMEX. But the popularity of the concept was such that other exchanges, including the NYSE and Nasdaq, took steps to offer a trading forum for ETFs. Further, electronic communication networks (ECNs) may offer trading in ETFs through their electronic trading platforms. On a traditional stock exchange such as the AMEX, trade flows through the specialist's station. In other words, there is a human hand involved, which is not the case with E-mini products.

Trading Costs

The costs associated with trading either E-mini stock index futures or ETFs represent a rather small proportion of the value of the instruments, or the potential profit, or possible loss, associated with such trading activities. Still, active traders should be sensitive to these costs because they have a way of adding up over time and over a sizable volume of trades.

The most obvious costs associated with trading either E-mini futures or ETFs are brokerage commissions that accrue to the broker. Commissions vary widely in futures and security markets, and they range from deep discount to full-service brokerage firms. Deep discounters often require investors to operate completely online with little or no support, whereas full-service brokers may take on the role of personal financial consultants. However, commissions generally represent a very small proportion of the actual cost of trading. The major cost of doing business is implied in the bid/offer spread, to the extent that a market order to buy may be filled at the prevailing offer, whereas a market order to sell may be filled at the prevailing bid.

ETFs are distinguished from futures in that they entitle the holder to the receipt of dividends. (Of course, dividends tend to be quite small in the context of high-tech stocks as represented in the Nasdaq 100.) But futures prices will trade to levels that reflect the value of the underlying stock index, plus finance charges, less anticipated dividends. This is referred to as "cost of carry." Because futures prices tend to be discounted to reflect the lack of dividend receipts, there is no reason to believe that ETFs are superior in this respect. ETFs are charged ordinary expenses, or a management fee, by the firm that administers the underlying unit investment trust. SPDRs entailed a management fee of 10 basis points (0.10%), and QQQQs a fee of 20 basis points (0.20%) at year's end 2006, noting that these fees have been trending down over the years.

Although futures are not subject to annual fees as such, there is an implicit cost in maintaining a futures position for an extended period of

EXHIBIT 5.6 Estimated Costs of Futures versus ETFs versus Stocks (in BPs per $100 mil notional)

	E-mini S&P 500	SPDRs	E-mini Nasdaq 100	QQQQs
Commission	0.8	2.8	1.6	8.8
One-way market impact/ Trans cost	6.0	6.0	15.0	12.0
Total entry cost	6.8	8.8	16.6	20.8
ETF Mgt fee/Futures roll costs	2.5	10.0	−16.8	18.0
Additional commission from roll	5.0	0.0	9.8	0.0
Total holding cost	7.5	10.0	−7.0	18.0
Commission	0.8	2.8	1.6	8.8
One-way market impact/ Trans cost	6.0	6.0	15.0	12.0
Total exit cost	6.8	8.8	16.6	20.8
Total cost for 1 year	21.1	27.5	26.2	59.5

Source: Goldman Sachs Global Derivatives and Trading Research (July 26, 2004).

time. Typically, futures are most actively traded in the lead or most current contract month (e.g., in November 2006, most trading volume and open interest would have been in the December 2006 contract). But traders typically "roll" forward their positions by liquidating December futures in favor of establishing a position in March futures as the December expiration approaches. The costs associated with the roll are reflected in the spread between the nearby and deferred futures contract and in any additional commissions associated with the transaction, as illustrated in Exhibit 5.6.

Goldman Sachs recently tallied up the costs associated with E-mini futures and ETFs, concluding that the cost of holding a $100 million position for one year in E-mini S&P 500 futures totaled 21.1 basis points annually versus 27.5 basis points for SPDRs. The advantage associated with E-mini futures was even greater in Nasdaq 100 markets, where a $100 million position in E-mini Nasdaq 100 cost 26.2 basis points to maintain versus 59.5 basis points in QQQQs.[1]

Carr Futures conducted a similar study and tallied up the relative cost savings associated with trading various quantities of E-mini Nasdaq 100 futures over the course of a year versus the cost of trading QQQQs. The savings were considerable, as detailed in Exhibit 5.7.[2]

EXHIBIT 5.7 Potential Monthly Savings Using E-mini Nasdaq 100 Futures Instead of QQQQ Exchange-Traded Funds

	Round-Turn Trading Cost per QQQQ Share			
QQQQ shares traded/month	$0.04	$0.06	$0.08	$0.10
100,000	$ 1,750	$ 3,750	$ 5,750	$ 7,750
500,000	$ 8,750	$ 18,750	$ 28,750	$ 38,750
1,000,000	$17,500	$ 37,500	$ 57,500	$ 77,500
5,000,000	$87,500	$187,500	$287,500	$387,500

Source: "EMini Futures Can Reduce the Cost of Trading Equities," Carr Futures Research Note, January 20, 2004.

Holding Period Considerations

A trader considering a long-term "buy-and-hold" strategy must consider the perpetual nature of an ETF versus the somewhat more transitory nature of a futures contract. Futures contracts are traded for cash settlement on a quarterly basis. And although one might trade futures for a deferred delivery month, the nearby futures contracts are typically the most liquid and, therefore, the trading vehicle of choice.

But because futures expire, they must be "rolled over" to maintain a "buy-and-hold" strategy. In other words, the expiring contract must be liquidated and the position reestablished in a deferred futures month, at least on a quarterly basis. This implies certain trading costs, such as commissions and bid/offer spreads, as discussed earlier. A position in ETFs, by contrast, can be held indefinitely with the management fees representing the only costs. We note, however, that the average holding period in SPDRs is currently only 24 days. The average holding period in QQQQs is only five days. Thus, the advantage that ETFs offer in this respect may be more theoretical than practical.

Finally, when adding up the respective advantages and disadvantages, the value implied by average daily trading volume in E-mini futures tends to be some multiple of the value associated with ETFs, specifically $67.98 billion in E-mini S&P 500 futures versus $9.23 billion in SPDRs. Although both investment vehicles have unique merits, we suggest that this figure is most telling.

PRICING STOCK INDEX FUTURES

Stock index futures cannot be expected to trade at a level that is precisely aligned with the spot or cash value of the associated stock index. The difference between the futures and spot values is often referred to as the *basis*. We generally quote a stock index futures basis as the futures price less the spot index value.

$$\text{Basis} = \text{Futures Price} - \text{Spot Index Value}$$

For example, the March 2007 E-mini S&P 500 futures price was 1,428.40 with the spot index value at 1,418.30 as of December 29, 2006. Thus, the basis may be quoted as 10.10 index points (= 1,428.40 − 1,418.30). The basis will generally reflect "cost of carry" considerations, or the costs associated with buying and carrying the index stocks until futures contract expiration. These costs include financing costs per the assumption that one is a leveraged buyer of the equities and a payout represented by the dividends that are expected to accrue until the futures expiration date. Thus, the futures price may be estimated as follows:

$$\text{Futures Price} = \text{Spot Index Value} + \text{Finance Charges} - \text{Dividends}$$

Fair Value

This difference reflects the premium or discount at which futures are theoretically expected to trade relative to the spot index value, often referred to as *fair value*. In other words, the level at which futures prices should be expected to trade, albeit not necessarily where they will trade relative to the spot index value. In the context of stock index futures, fair value is normally expected to be greater than zero (Futures − Spot > 0). That is due to the fact that we normally expect finance charges as reflected in short-term interest rates such as the London Interbank Offered Rate (LIBOR) to exceed dividend yields.

Negative carry is said to prevail where short-term interest rates exceed dividend yields. This may be understood by considering that this implies it costs more to finance the purchase and carry of a basket of stocks as represented in an index than the direct payout associated with the stock basket. As such, stock index futures tend to price at higher and higher levels in successively deferred months extending out into the future.

Positive carry is said to prevail under circumstances where short-term interest rates are less than dividend yields. Under these conditions, the payouts or dividends associated with the basket of stocks represented in the index provide a superior return to short-term interest rates; hence one may earn a positive return by buying and carrying the basket. Although not altogether unheard of, this condition is reasonably rare, noting that if a stock were to provide a dividend yield that was in excess of short-term rates, that implies the corporation cannot apply those funds in such as way as to earn a return in excess of short-term rates, not a favorable signal. Under these conditions, stock index futures tend to price at lower and lower levels in successively deferred months extending out into the future.

Basis Convergence

Regardless of whether positive or negative carry prevails, the design of a stock index futures contract assures that the basis or difference between futures prices and spot index values will fall to zero by the time futures contract maturity rolls around. This is assured because, of course, the futures contract is settled in cash at the spot index value on its final settlement date. The process by which futures and spot value come together over time is known as *convergence*. Note that, regardless of whether equity prices in general are trending upward or downward, the basis is steadily converging toward zero. See Exhibits 5.8 and 5.9.

That is not to say that basis convergence is always completely smooth or predictable. In fact, there may be considerable "flutter" in the process on a day-to-day basis. Some of that flutter may be attributed to the fact that stock index futures are often traded some minutes beyond the time of day that the cash stock exchanges close and settle equity values. In particular, CME Group routinely offers stock index futures some 15 minutes after the close of the NYSE on a daily basis. Although 15 minutes is not a terribly long period of time, there is always some probability that breaking news

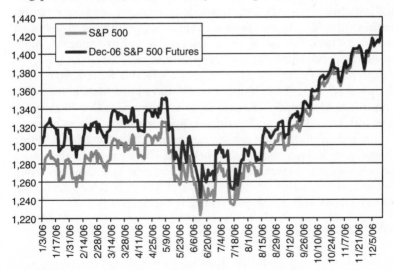

EXHIBIT 5.8 Convergence of S&P 500 and Dec-06 Futures

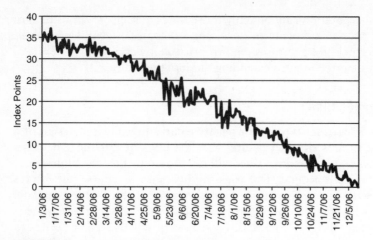

EXHIBIT 5.9 December 2006 S&P 500 Futures Basis

may push futures prices upward or downward to diverge from movements in the underlying stock markets.

As a result, CME Group has implemented a "fair value settlement procedure" on the last day of each calendar month with respect to its domestic stock index futures contracts. On a normal day, the daily settlement value is established by reference to an indicative market price that may have been executable during the final minutes of trade on that particular day. But the fair value settlement procedure provides that, regardless of where futures prices are in relationship to the spot index value, they will be settled at their fair value (FV). That FV is calculated based on a survey of applicable interest rates and dividends to accrue until expiration date.

For example, on December 29, 2006, the applicable short-term interest rate was surveyed at 5.332%; there were 76 days until March 16, 2007, expiration of the March 2007 futures contract; the spot value of the S&P 500 index was at 1,418.30; and dividends accruing until futures contract expiration were estimated at 5.901 index points. The FV of the March 2007 futures contract was calculated as below at 10.064 over the spot index value. In other words, March 2007 futures should be at 10.064 premium over the spot index value of 1,418.30, and were therefore settled at 1,428.40 index points (or 1,428.36 rounded to the nearest tick).

$$
\begin{aligned}
\text{Fair Value} &= \text{Finance Charges} - \text{Dividends} \\
&= \text{Rate} \times (\text{days}/360) \times \text{Index Value} - \text{Dividends} \\
&= 5.332\% \times (76/360) \times 1{,}418.30 - 5.901 \\
&= \underline{10.064}
\end{aligned}
$$

Enforcing Cost of Carry Pricing

Despite some level of flutter, liquid stock index futures markets do in fact tend to price efficiently and in reasonable close conformance with their fair values. That is due to the fact that many market participants are prepared to "arbitrage" any apparent mispricing or pricing anomalies between spot and futures markets.

For example, if futures prices were to rally much above their fair market value, an astute arbitrageur may act to buy the stock portfolio and sell stock index futures in an attempt to capitalize on that mispricing. Frequently enough, these arbitrageurs may attempt to trade in a basket or subset of the stocks included in a stock index. Or, the state of electronic trading systems may provide them the means to trade in all or virtually all of the constituents of a particular stock index as part of the arbitrage transaction. In the process of buying stocks and selling futures, the arbitrageur may bid up the stocks or push futures prices down to reestablish an equilibrium pricing situation where arbitrage is ostensibly not profitable. For example, on December 29, 2006, one might have bought the stocks in the S&P 500 at levels reflecting the spot index value of 1,418.30, incurring finance charges of 5.332% or 15.965 index points, carrying the stocks and earning dividends equivalent to 5.901 index points. The net cost is 1,428.36 and, therefore, futures should price at this level.

Buy stocks @ levels reflecting spot index value	(1,418.30)
Incur finance charges @ 5.332%	(15.965)
Receive dividends of 5.901 index points	5.901
Net cost over 76 days	(1,428.36)
Expected futures price	1,428.36

Or, if futures were to be trading significantly below their fair value, one might sell stocks and buy futures. This arbitrage should have the effect of bidding futures prices upward and pushing stock prices downward to reestablish equilibrium pricing.

Sell stocks @ levels reflecting spot index value	1,418.30
Invest proceeds @ 5.332%	15.965
Forgo dividends of 5.901 index points	(5.901)
Net cost over 76 days	1,428.36
Expected futures price	(1,428.36)

In practice, one must also consider costs attendant to arbitrage (i.e., slippage, commissions, fees, bid-offer spreads, etc.). As such, futures tend to trade within a "band" above and below its theoretical fair value. Again, when futures fall below that band, one might be recommended to buy futures and sell a parallel or replicating stock portfolio. Or, when futures rise above that band, one might be recommended to sell futures and buy a parallel or replicating stock portfolio.

Fair Value − Arbitrage Costs < Futures Price < Fair Value + Arbitrage Costs

This band may vary from stock index to stock index, but it would not be unreasonable to assume that the costs attendant to "arbing" S&P 500 futures fall into the vicinity of perhaps 1.25 index points. Thus, futures may very well trend upward and downward within that band, fundamentally reflecting the influx of buy-and-sell orders, without engendering an arbitrage transaction.

SPREADING STOCK INDEX FUTURES

A wide variety of broad-based stock index futures are available in today's marketplace. The most popular of these contracts tend to track a broad spectrum of the equity marketplace rather than a specific industrial sector (e.g., energy, high-tech, consumer goods, etc.). Still, these indexes represent somewhat different slices of the market and serve somewhat different purposes.

The S&P 500 Index represents 500 leading blue-chip U.S. equities weighted by market capitalization. Think of the S&P 500 as a high-cap, blue-chip stock index.

The Nasdaq 100 represents the top 100 nonfinancial stocks traded on the Nasdaq system, which uses a modified capitalization weighting system. Although the index reflects any industry excluding financials, the most actively traded stocks on the Nasdaq system tend to be high-tech stocks and, therefore, the Nasdaq 100 is often referenced as a proxy for the technology sector of the equity marketplace.

The S&P/MidCap 400 represents the 400 most significant stocks in the domestic equity markets after the top 500 as represented in the S&P 500. As such, they reflect the value of so-called midcap, or middling capitalized, corporations.

Finally, the venerable Dow Jones Industrial Average (DJIA) represents 30 leading blue-chip equities weighted by price.

There are, in fact, reasonably high correlations among these four leading stock indexes. Note that the highest level of correlation from 2001 through 2006 was observed between the S&P 500 and DJIA or the two

EXHIBIT 5.10 Correlation between Popular Stock Index Futures (2001–2006)

	S&P 500	Nasdaq 100	MidCap 400	DJIA
S&P 500	—			
NASDAQ-100	0.8499	—		
MidCap 400	0.9205	0.8143	—	
DJIA	0.9632	0.7567	0.8698	—

blue-chip indexes at 0.9632. The lowest degree of correlation was observed between the Nasdaq 100 and the DJIA at 0.7567. See Exhibit 5.10.

Cyclical Spread Patterns

Speculators often attempt to take advantage of the relative movements between these indexes by spreading stock index futures (i.e., taking a long position in one market versus a short position in another market).

This is often referred to as an intermarket spread. These speculative positions are frequently motivated by fundamental market conditions that may impact different portions of the equity market in somewhat different ways. Often these conditions are cyclical, and we have observed some long-term market trends over the years.

Exhibit 5.11 illustrates how various spreads including the S&P 500 over the Nasdaq 100; the MidCap 400 over the S&P 500, and the MidCap 400 over the Nasdaq 100 intermarket spreads have performed in the years 2001 to 2006.

Note that for the first couple of years, the MidCap over Nasdaq spread performed quite well. This is attributed to the fact that the stock market was falling quickly in the wake of the burst of the so-called tech bubble of the late 1990s and the Nasdaq 100 was very weak. Smaller cap stocks as represented in the S&P/MidCap 400 were comparatively stronger as the Federal Reserve aggressively pushed interest rates downward with the Fed Funds rate falling to 1% by 2002. Small-cap stocks are often more sensitive to borrowing costs than large-cap stocks and tend to do well in an easing monetary environment.

After a relatively brief recessionary period, the stock market began to bounce back sharply by 2003. Despite the fact that the Federal Open Market Committee (FOMC), the policy-making body of the Federal Reserve, instituted a series of measured rate hikes, small cap stocks continued to outperform large caps and high-tech issues. In particular, credit was relatively easy to secure, favoring small or middling capitalized companies. Thus, the MidCap over Nasdaq and MidCap over S&P 500

EXHIBIT 5.11 High-Cap, Small-Cap, and Tech Stock Market Cycles

2003–	Recession ends, corporate profits and stock values begin to bounce back. Small caps outperform in low-rate environment. Federal Open Market Committee (FOMC) begins series of measured tightening in late 2004.
2000–2002	Stock market declines sharply as tech "bubble" collapses. FOMC aggressively eases Fed funds rate down to 1%. This favors small caps where borrowing costs are typically more problematic over high caps. Still, credit concerns mount by 2002 and small caps tumble.
1995–2000	High caps outperform as investment managers are compelled to park huge amounts of new investment in high caps. Russian and Asian financial crises stimulate flight to quality. Tech stocks lead the way, given emergence of telecomm technologies such as the Internet.
1990–1993	Post–Gulf War era exerts very positive effect on small caps. Interest rates decline to lowest levels in decades as U.S. T-bill rates dip below 3% by November 1993 and 30-year U.S. T-bond yields fall below 6%.
1983–1990	Most significant bull market since the 1950s begins as high-cap stocks race ahead. Weakness in U.S. dollar favors large-cap stocks with international market presence (e.g., Merck, Coca-Cola, Philip Morris)
1973–1982	Small-cap stocks outperform high-cap stocks by wide margin lead. Small energy stocks lead the way as OPEC crimps oil supplies.

intermarket spreads turned very good performances over the next few years. See Exhibit 5.12.

Some rather mixed performances were realized during calendar year 2005. Let's focus specifically upon the relationship between middling-cap versus high-cap stocks as represented in the MidCap 400 over S&P 500 intermarket spread. The spread rallied considerably early in 2005. But by March 2005, the spread was fading to bottom in early May close to where it began the year. Exhibit 5.13 shows how the spread subsequently strengthened considerably through July and ended the year considerably higher than where it began the year.

These trends nicely illustrate the relative sensitivity of mid- or small-cap versus high-cap stocks to credit concerns. In particular, smaller cap stocks tend to be much more responsive to such concerns than the more resilient high-cap sector of the market. This may be illustrated by correlating the performance of the spread between corporate bond and Treasury yields, as illustrated in Exhibit 5.14. This spread may be illustrated by comparing the Moody's A Corporate Bond Index versus a 10-year Constant Maturity

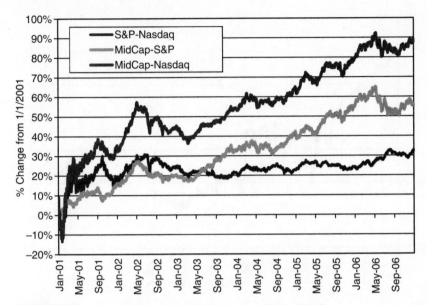

EXHIBIT 5.12 Equity Index Spread Performance (2001–2006)

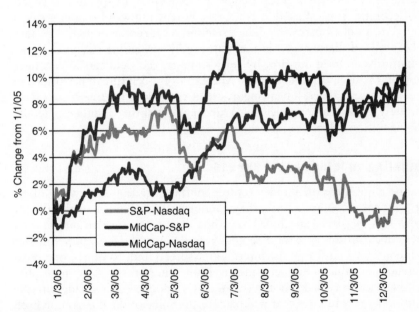

EXHIBIT 5.13 Equity Index Spread Performance (2005)

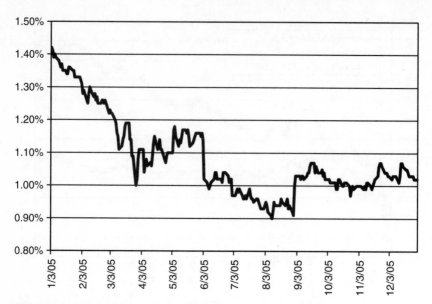

EXHIBIT 5.14   Moody's A Corp Bond Index less 10-Year Treasury Yield

Treasury (CMT) yield as illustrated below. Note that the spread was generally declining, suggesting that corporate borrowing was becoming easier relative to public borrowing. The premium of corporate versus Treasury yields declined sharply early in the year. But by springtime this yield spread temporarily reversed upward. By early summer, the yield spread was once again on the decline. Note that the MidCap over S&P spread performed in a near inverse manner, advancing as credit conditions became more favorable early in the year, experiencing a hiccup in the spring and then generally rallying for the balance of the year.

Weighting an Intermarket Spread

Because all of these stock index futures contracts trade at somewhat different notional monetary values, they cannot necessarily be traded on a 1:1 basis. This begs the question: How should one structure an intermarket stock index futures spread? The goal is to balance the monetary value of each contract that forms the intermarket spread and, to do so, one must reference the value of each contract as a function of the contract multiplier and the price of each leg of the spread. By so doing, one may identify the appropriate spread ratio that will balance the value of the position on both sides of the intermarket spread.

$$\text{Multiplier}_1 \times \text{Price}_1 \sim \text{Multiplier}_2 \times \text{Price}_2$$
$$\text{Spread Ratio} = (\text{Multiplier}_1 \times \text{Price}_1) \div (\text{Multiplier}_2 \times \text{Price}_2)$$

For example, consider the application of a S&P 500/Nasdaq 100 spread on May 20, 2005. The June 2005 E-mini S&P 500 contract (ES) has a contract multiplier of $50 and was trading at a price of 1,190.25 index points. The June 2005 E-mini Nasdaq-100 contract (NQ) has a contract multiplier of $20 and was trading at a price of 1,530.50 index points. The appropriate spread ratio may be calculated at 2:1 as illustrated below.

$$
\begin{aligned}
\text{Spread Ratio} &= (\text{Multiplier}_{ES} \times \text{Price}_{ES}) \div (\text{Multiplier}_{NQ} \times \text{Price}_{NQ}) \\
&= (\$50 \times 1,190.25) \div (\$20 \times 1,530.50) \\
&= \$59,512 \div \$30,610 \\
&= 1.9446 \text{ or } \sim 2:1 \text{ spread ratio}
\end{aligned}
$$

In other words, this calculation recommends that a trader use two single E-mini Nasdaq 100 contracts (NQ) against a single E-mini S&P 500 (ES) contract. Note that the CME Clearing House offers margin breaks for spreads placed in this ratio in recognition of the fact that the spread is generally less volatile than an outright position in either leg of this spread.

Another example may be constructed in the context of a MidCap 400/ S&P 500 spread also on May 20, 2005. The June 2005 E-mini S&P/Mid-Cap 400 contract (EMD) has a contract multiplier of $100 and was trading at a price of 662.50 index points. The appropriate spread ratio may be calculated at 1:1 as illustrated below.

$$
\begin{aligned}
\text{Spread Ratio} &= (\text{Multiplier}_{EMD} \times \text{Price}_{EMD}) \div (\text{Multiplier}_{ES} \times \text{Price}_{ES}) \\
&= (\$100 \times 662.50) \div (\$50 \times 1,190.25) \\
&= \$66,250 \div \$59,512 \\
&= 1.1132 \text{ or } \sim 1:1 \text{ spread ratio}
\end{aligned}
$$

Assume you had placed the spread on May 20 by buying one E-mini S&P/MidCap 400 contract and selling one E-mini S&P 500 contract, subsequently unwinding the spread on June 20. Under these circumstances, a trader may have realized a profit on both legs of the spread as the E-mini S&P/MidCap 400 index was appreciating while the large-cap S&P 500 index was rallying but at a slower rate.

5/20/05	Buy 1 EMD @ 662.50 or $66,250	Sell 1 ES @ 1,190.25 or $59,512
6/10/05	Sell 1 EMD @ 679.80 or $67,980	Buy 1 ES @ 1,199.00 or $59,950
	+$1,730	($438)

Net Profit of + $1,292

HEDGING WITH STOCK INDEX FUTURES

The primary raison d'être of any futures contract is for use in the context of risk-management activities, and stock index futures, of course, are no exception. In fact, the academic literature has provided a robust framework for understanding how stock index futures may be used in the context of risk abatement programs. We are alluding, of course, to the capital asset pricing model (CAPM).

Capital Asset Pricing Model

The CAPM represents a way of understanding how asset values fluctuate or react to various economic forces driving the market. In particular, the model suggests that the total risk associated with a particular equity may be broken down into two elements: systematic and idiosyncratic or unsystematic risks.

$$\text{Total Risk} = \text{Systematic Risks} + \text{Unsystematic Risks}$$

Systematic risk refers to "market risks" reflected in general economic conditions and that affect all equities to one degree or another. For example, all stocks may be affected to a degree by Federal Reserve monetary policies, by the robustness of the economy, by foreign trade policies, and so on. Unsystematic risk, or "firm-specific risks," represent factors that uniquely impact a specific stock. For example, a particular company may have created a unique new product or its management may have introduced new policies or direction that will affect the company to the exclusion of others.

The degree to which systematic and unsystematic risks impact on the price behavior of a particular company may be analyzed through a beta analysis, or a statistical regression to define the relationship between individual stock and market returns. In particular, one may regress the daily returns of the subject stock (R_{stock}) against the daily returns of the relevant market index (R_{market}).

$$R_{stock} = \alpha + \beta \, (R_{Market}) + \text{error}$$

Note that "market returns" are frequently often defined by reference to an index such as the S&P 500. By-products of the regression analysis include beta (β) and R-squared (R^2). Beta (β) identifies the expected relative movement between an individual stock and the market. For example, if beta equals 1.1, that suggests the stock may be expected to rally by 11%

provided that the market rallies by 10%, or that the stock will decline in value by 11% if the market declines by 10%. In other words, stocks whose betas exceed 1.0 are more sensitive than the market in general and are considered "aggressive" stocks. If beta equals 0.9, that suggests the stock may be expected to rally by 9% in response to a 10% rally in the market, or decline by 9% in response to a 10% decline in the market. Stocks whose betas are less than 1.0 are considered "conservative" stocks because they are less sensitive than the market in general.

$$\text{If } \beta > 1.0 \Rightarrow \text{It's considered an } aggressive \text{ stock}$$
$$\text{If } \beta < 1.0 \Rightarrow \text{It's considered a } conservative \text{ stock}$$

R^2 is another by-product of the regression and identifies the reliability with which stock returns are explained by market returns. Note that R^2 will vary between 0 and 1.0. If R^2 equals 1.0, this implies that 100% of the stock returns are explained by market returns. In other words, there is perfect correlation, and one might execute a perfect hedge using a derivative instrument that tracks the market perfectly. If R^2 was zero, this implies a complete lack of correlation and an inability to hedge using a derivative that fails to track the market.

$$\text{If } R^2 = 1.0 \Rightarrow \text{This implies a perfect hedge}$$
$$\text{If } R^2 = 0 \Rightarrow \text{This implies no correlation or no "hedgeability"}$$

An "average" stock might have an R^2 of perhaps 0.30, which implies that perhaps 30% of its movements are explained by systematic factors and are "hedgeable." Thus, the remaining 70% of unsystematic risks are not hedgeable with broad-based stock index futures.

Stock Index Hedge Ratio

To the extent that stock index futures are based on broad-based market indexes that proxy for "the market," they can be used to hedge systematic market risks. However, to the extent that only a fraction of the risk associated with any particular stock is traced to systematic risks while generally a larger proportion of the attendant risks are unsystematic, these stock index futures may represent poor hedging vehicles for individual stocks.

However, the capital asset pricing model underscores the power of diversification. By creating a portfolio of stocks, instead of limiting one's investment to a single stock, one may effectively diversify away most unsystematic risks from the portfolio. In particular, academic literature suggests that one may create an "efficiently diversified" portfolio by randomly combining as few as perhaps eight individual equities. The resulting portfolio taken as a whole may reflect market movements with little observable impact from those firm-specific risks. That may be understood by considering that those unsystematic factors that uniquely impact on specific corporations are expected to be independent one from the other. Thus, we might conclude that stock index futures can be used effectively to hedge the systematic risks associated with diversified stock portfolios.

Still, some analysis is required to place a hedge position effectively. In particular, practitioners identify the appropriate "hedge ratio" (HR), or the number of stock index futures required effectively to hedge equity portfolios from systematic risks.

Hedge Ratio (HR) = [Stock Value (V_{stock}) ÷ Index Value (V_{Index})] × Beta (β)

Where . . .

V_{stock} = Monetary value of stock portfolio
V_{Index} = Index value (e.g., for E-mini S&P 500 futures)
V_{Index} = $50 × Index
Beta (β) = Weighted beta of portfolio

Consider the hypothetical stock portfolio depicted in Exhibit 5.15. The portfolio is valued at $17,602,550 and has a weighted beta equal to 1.05. Assume that the investor in this portfolio believed the market is overvalued and likely to decline in the near term. Thus, the investor may take steps to protect the portfolio from risk of loss by selling E-mini S&P 500 futures. On January 18, 2007, the March 2007 E-mini S&P 500 futures was trading at 1,433.00. The S&P 500 Index was valued at 1,426.37. Thus, the Index Value associated with one futures contract would have been valued at $71,318.50 (= $50 × 1,426.37). The appropriate hedge ratio may be calculated as 258 contract as shown below.

$$HR = (V_{stock} \div V_{futures}) \times \beta$$
$$= (\$17,602,550 \div \$71,318.50) \times 1.05$$
$$= 259 \text{ E-mini S\&P 500 futures}$$

Let's simulate the possible performance of the hedged position assuming that the market (as measured by the S&P 500 Index) declines 4.65% over the next few months. This implies an anticipated 4.89% decline in the value of the stock portfolio as predicted by the beta of 1.05 (−4.89% = −4.65% × 1.05). The loss in the stock market is offset by a profit in the futures market. Note that the investor still benefits from dividends accruing from the portfolio. Further, the hedger benefits

EXHIBIT 5.15 Hypothetical Stock Portfolio with β = 1.05 (January 18, 2007)

	Stock	Ticker Symbol	Price	Shares	Value	Beta
1	Anheuser Busch	BUD	$ 50.76	15,000	$ 761,400	0.66
2	Best Buy	BBY	$ 49.18	50,000	$ 2,459,000	1.61
3	Chevron Corp	CVX	$ 70.92	9,000	$ 638,280	1.06
4	Chicago Mercantile Exchange	CME	$577.50	2,000	$ 1,155,000	1.14
5	Coca-Cola	KO	$ 48.35	8,000	$ 386,800	0.80
6	Dow Chemical	DOW	$ 40.94	40,000	$ 1,637,600	1.25
7	Halliburton	HAL	$ 28.63	25,000	$ 715,750	1.26
8	International Business Machines	IBM	$ 99.45	10,000	$ 994,500	1.06
9	McClatchy Co	MNI	$ 39.86	12,000	$ 478,320	0.44
10	Merck	MRK	$ 45.74	65,000	$ 2,973,100	0.88
11	Microsoft	MSFT	$ 31.00	50,000	$ 1,550,000	0.95
12	Novell Networks	NOVL	$ 6.72	65,000	$ 436,800	0.62
13	Procter & Gamble	PG	$ 65.54	15,000	$ 983,100	0.57
14	Unisys CP	UIS	$ 8.27	105,000	$ 868,350	1.34
15	Walt Disney	DIS	$ 35.85	20,000	$ 717,000	0.89
16	Waste Management	WMI	$ 36.85	23,000	$ 847,550	0.99
					$17,602,550	1.05

from the convergence in the value of the spot stock index values and the stock index futures price.

On January 18, 2007 . . .

Long stock portfolio with β = 1.05	($17,602,550)	
Sell 259 Mar-07 E-mini S&P 500 futures		1,433.00
S&P 500 @ 1,426.37; Basis @ 6.63		
(= 1,433.00−1,426.37)		

Hypothetically on March 16, 2007 . . .

S&P 500 @ 1,360.00 (−4.65%); portfolio down −4.89% (=1.05 × −4.65%)	$16,742,538
Accrued dividends @ (assumed) 2% dividend yield	$55,741
Loss in stock portfolio	($804,271)

EXHIBIT 5.16 Hypothetical Hedged and Unhedged Returns

	S&P 500 at		
	1,360	**1,426**	**1,490**
Unhedged	−28.86%	1.83%	31.58%
Short futures hedge	5.06%	5.08%	5.10%

Futures converge to spot value of 1,360.00	(1,360.00)
Profit in futures = 259 cnts × $50 ×	$945,359
(1,433.00 − 1,360.00)	
Hedged Profit/Loss	$141,079
Hedged Return (on $17,602,550 over	5.06%
57 days)	

The net result is that the investor is anticipating the ability to "lock-in" a return of 5.06% or approximating the short-term rate of return, often represented by LIBOR. That is, a futures hedge provides one with the ability effectively to transform a stock market investment into an investment that will return a rate approximating prevailing short-term interest rates. Or we might simulate the hedged and unhedged returns on an annualized basis, as illustrated in Exhibits 5.16 and 5.17.

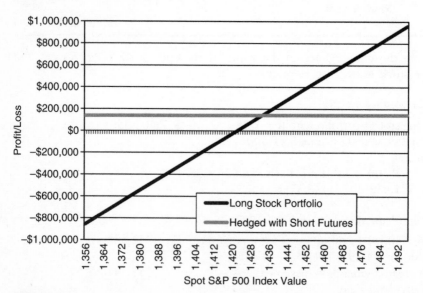

EXHIBIT 5.17 Stock Portfolio Hedged with Futures

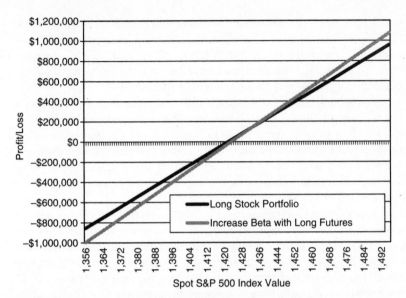

EXHIBIT 5.18 Adjusting Stock Portfolio Beta with Futures

Although it is certainly possible to price protect the value of the equity portfolio almost completely using stock index futures, it may be much more common for portfolio managers to use stock index futures to adjust their risk exposures on a less radical basis.

Assume, for example, that an investor anticipates a near-term market advance and wishes strategically to increase the portfolio beta from 1.05 to 1.20 while maintaining current holdings. The appropriate hedge ratio may be calculated as follows. This calculation suggests that one should buy 37 futures in order to increase, at least temporarily, the risk exposure to take advantage of the anticipated market advance. Of course, one may use this type of partial hedge to either increase or decrease one's risk exposure as measured by the effective portfolio beta. See Exhibit 5.18.

$$\begin{aligned}
HR &= (V_{stock} \div V_{Index}) \times (\text{Target } \beta - \text{Current } \beta) \\
&= (\$17,602,550 \div \$71,318.50) \times (1.20 - 1.05) \\
&= 37 \text{ E-mini S\&P 500 futures}
\end{aligned}$$

PORTABLE ALPHA STRATEGIES

Terms such as alpha and beta are used as explained earlier in reference to the source of returns associated with an individual stock or a portfolio of stocks. But they have also come to have some slightly different meanings. "Portable alpha" investment strategies first emerged soon after the introduction of stock index futures in 1982. But in recent years, these strategies have come to carry that moniker and have become very popular and the topic of much discussion within the "indexing community."

Portable alpha strategies distinguish the total returns of a portfolio by reference to an alpha and a beta component. The beta component of those returns is tied to a general market benchmark such as a popular stock index (e.g., the S&P 500 or S&P MidCap 400). Additional returns are generated by devoting a portion of one's assets to another more ambitious trading strategy that is intended to generate a superior return over the base or benchmark "beta" returns.

Stock index futures have proven to be ideal vehicles for achieving those benchmark or beta returns represented by a popular stock index. They are ideal to the extent that (1) futures may be traded on leverage, freeing a portion of one's assets for application to an associated alpha strategy; and (2) trading costs associated with futures are typically very low and frequently superior to alternative strategies for capturing benchmark beta returns.

Traditional Investment Strategy

A traditional and typical fund management strategy requires an investor to allocate funds among different asset classes such as stocks, bonds, real estate, and alternative investments, as seen in Exhibit 5.19. That mix among

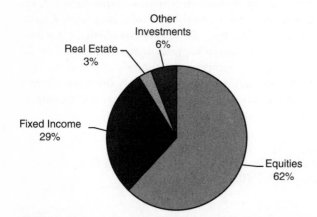

EXHIBIT 5.19 Typical Market Exposure of S&P 500 Defined Benefit Pension Plans ($1.3 bil in assets, December 2004)
Source: Credit Suisse Asset Management, "Alpha Management Revolution or Evolution, a Portable Alpha Primer," November 2005.

various asset classes may be determined based on the investor's return objectives, risk tolerance, investment horizon, and other factors. Generally speaking, conservative investors may apply a larger proportion of available funds to fixed-income investments and a smaller proportion to riskier equities. A more aggressive investor may apply more funds to equities and possibly to other alternative investment applications.

Beyond establishing those allocations, investors often retain the services of active fund managers to manage portions of a portfolio, noting there are many fund managers who specialize in stocks, bonds, real estate investments, and the various subsectors within those asset classes. In particular, investors often hope to retain managers who are capable of generating some excess return beyond the "benchmark" return in specific asset classes, as measured by indexes such as the S&P 500 in the equity market or the Barclays Capital U.S. Aggregate Index in the bond market.

However, this approach frequently fails to generate returns in excess of benchmark returns, often because of high management fees. Accordingly, the past few decades have seen widespread acceptance of index funds whose only objective is to keep pace with the benchmark return with no hope of actually achieving superior returns.

Capturing Alpha

Portable alpha strategies are designed specifically in the hopes of achieving (alpha) returns in excess of the applicable benchmark (or beta) returns. Thus, there are two components of a portable alpha strategy: alpha and beta.

Alpha returns, in excess of prevailing short-term rates as often represented by LIBOR, are generated by applying some portion of one's capital to an active trading strategy. A variety of proprietary trading methodologies, including the retention of a hedge fund, are typically used to generate beta. Some commonly used alpha-generating investment strategies include (1) tactical asset allocation programs that attempt to shift capital from less to more attractive investments; (2) programs that attempt to generate attractive absolute returns such as hedge funds, commodity funds, and real estate investment vehicles; and (3) traditional active management strategies within a particular asset class or sector of an asset class.

Of course, more active alpha-generating strategies tend to require more trading skill. Although they may generate more attractive returns, they may also entail higher management fees. And still, it is difficult to find an investment strategy that consistently delivers attractive alpha and is truly distinct from the benchmark class that forms the core beta returns. As such, the major and most obvious risk associated with portable alpha strategies is the possibility that the alpha strategy fails to outperform LIBOR.

Capturing Beta

A portable alpha strategy suggests that the bulk of one's capital be applied to generate beta returns that reflect some applicable benchmark (e.g., the S&P 500, Barclays Capital U.S. Aggregate Bond Index, MSCI EAFE, etc.). Such beta is typically created in a passive manner with the use of derivatives such as futures or over-the-counter swaps at a cost that is reflective of LIBOR.

Because derivatives can be leveraged, funds are freed to apply to the alpha strategy. Note, for example, that the performance bond requirement associated with an E-mini S&P 500 futures contract was $3,500 as of December 29, 2006. This represented 4.9% of the contract value at the time. Further, that 4.9% may be posted in form of T-bills or other collateral on which a portfolio manager continues to earn interest. Exhibit 5.20 shows that this leaves the residual 95.1% of contract value or some fraction thereof to be applied to an alpha-generating strategy. See also Exhibit 5.21.

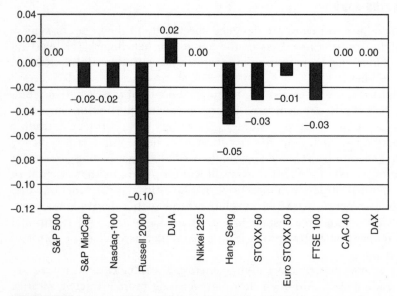

EXHIBIT 5.20 Percent Deviation from Fair Value (2006)
Source: Goldman Sachs "Equity Products Strategy, Futures Focus," January 17, 2007.

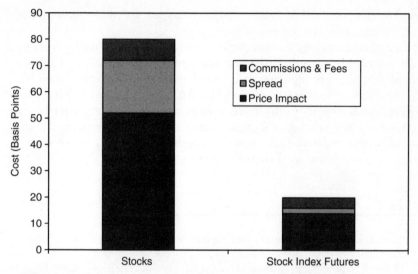

EXHIBIT 5.21 Estimated Trading Friction (for $30 mil portfolio)
Source: Credit Suisse Asset Management, "Alpha Management Revolution or Evolution, a Portable Alpha Primer," November 2005.

Still, there is the potential risk that the costs associated with the capture of beta may be too high or that tracking error of the derivative instrument is too great. Note, however, that one analyst has estimated the average deviation from "fair value" of S&P 500 futures during 2006 as essentially zero. It is also noteworthy that the CME Group essentially eliminates month-to-month tracking error by implementing "fair value" settlements on the last day of each month. This ensures that funds holding CME Group stock index futures deliver a "true" beta from month to month.

As discussed earlier, futures generally represent a very economic way of capturing beta. "Trading friction" including commissions, fees, the bid/offer spread and the price impact of executing an order are much reduced in the context of stock index futures relative to a similar beta-replicating strategy using actual equities.

CONCLUSION

Stock index futures represent an efficient tool to gain exposure to or manage the risks associated with volatile equity market movements. CME Group offers stock index futures based on the most significant of U.S. stock indexes including the Standard & Poor's 500, the Nasdaq 100, Dow Jones Industrial Average, and many others.

In addition to outright speculation on the direction of equity markets, stock index futures are also used as a means of taking a position on the relative value of different segments of the stock market in the form of intermarket spreads. Asset managers use stock index futures to hedge against the risk of adverse movements in the stock market and to adjust the beta or risk exposure of their portfolios in anticipation of market movement. Finally, portable alpha strategies have become increasingly popular in response to extremely competitive conditions in the investment arena.

NOTES

1. "Equity Derivatives Strategy, Futures and Swaps," Goldman Sachs, July 26, 2004.
2. "E-Mini Futures Can Reduce the Cost of Trading Equities," Carr Futures Research Note, January 20, 2004.

CHAPTER 6

Eurodollar Futures

Interest Rate Market Building Blocks

John W. Labuszewski
Richard Co

Eurodollar futures have achieved remarkable success since their introduction at Chicago Mercantile Exchange (CME) in December 1981. Much of this growth may directly be attributed to the fact that Eurodollar futures represent fundamental building blocks of the interest rate marketplace. Indeed, they have often been characterized as the "Swiss Army knife" of the futures industry to the extent that they may be used in any number of ways to achieve diverse objectives.

This chapter provides an appreciation as to how and why Eurodollar futures may be used to achieve these diverse ends. We begin with some background on the fundamental nature of Eurodollar futures including a discussion of pricing and arbitrage relationships. We move on to an explanation of how Eurodollar futures may be used to take advantage of expectations regarding the changing shape of the yield curve or dynamic credit considerations. Finally, we discuss the symbiotic relationship between Eurodollar futures and over-the-counter (OTC) interest rate swaps. In particular, Eurodollar futures are often used to price and to hedge interest rate swaps with good effect.

EURODOLLAR FUTURES MARKET

Eurodollar futures were introduced on the CME in December 1981. Although they have since become CME Group's flagship product offering, they were virtually pronounced dead soon after launch by *Institutional Investor*: "Eurodollar contracts do not appear to have much of a future. . . . Five months after their noisy launch on the Chicago Mercantile Exchange, Eurodollar contracts still haven't caught on."

Of course, Eurodollar futures have since silenced the critics by becoming the most active short-term interest rate (STIR) futures contract traded worldwide with an average daily volume of 2.3 million contracts in calendar year 2007.

Pricing and Quotation

Eurodollar futures are based on a $1 million face-value, three-month maturity Eurodollar Time Deposit. It is settled in cash on the second London bank business day just prior to the third Wednesday of the contract month based on the British Banker's Association Fixing for three-month Eurodollar Interbank Time Deposits.

These contracts mature during the months of March, June, September, or December, extending outward 10 years into the future. However, the exchange also offers "serial" contract months in the four nearby months that do not fall into the March quarterly cycle. See Exhibit 6.1 for contract specifications.

Trading is conducted on the floor of the exchange using traditional open outcry methods during regular daylight hours and simultaneously on the CME Globex electronic trading platform virtually around the clock. Increasingly, the market is shifting to trading on an electronic basis such that, as of 2008, the majority of all Eurodollar volume traded is concluded on the CME Globex platform.

These contracts are quoted in terms of the "IMM Index."[1] The IMM Index is equal to 100 less the yield on the security (e.g., if the yield equals 3.39%, the index equals 96.61). The minimum price fluctuation generally equals one-half basis point, or 0.005%. Based on a $1 million face-value 90-day instrument, this equates to $12.50. However, in the nearby expiring contract month, the minimum price fluctuation is set at one-quarter basis point, or 0.0025%, equating to $6.25 per contract.

As seen in Exhibit 6.2, September 2005 futures rose by 4 full basis points to settle the day at a price of 96.61. Noting that each basis point is worth $25 per contract based on a $1 million 90-day instrument, this implies an increase in value of $100 for the day. Note that the value of a basis point may be computed as $25 = $1,000,000 × (90 days/360 days) × 0.01%.

Shape of the Yield Curve

Pricing patterns in the Eurodollar futures market are very much a reflection or mirror of conditions prevailing in the money markets and moving outward on

EXHIBIT 6.1 Eurodollar Contract Specifications

Unit	$1 million face-value, 90-day Eurodollar Time Deposits.
Cash settlement	Cash settlement based on a British Bankers Association Rate for 3-month Eurodollar Interbank Time Deposits.
Quote	In terms of the "IMM Index" or 100 less the yield (e.g., a yield of 3.39% is quoted as 96.61).
Minimum price fluctuation, or "tick"	One-half basis point (0.005) equals $12.50; except in nearby month, where tick is one-quarter basis point (0.0025) or $6.25.
Months	March quarterly cycle of March, June, September, and December, plus the first four "serial" months not in the March quarterly cycle.
Hours of trade	Trading on the floor is conducted from 7:20 AM to 2:00 PM. Trading on the CME Globex electronic trading platform is conducted on Mondays to Thursdays from 5:00 PM to 4:00 PM; shutdown period is from 4:00 PM to 5:00 PM, Sundays and holidays from 5:00 PM to 4:00 PM.
Final trading day	The second London bank business day immediately preceding the third Wednesday of the contract month. If it is a bank holiday in New York City or Chicago, trading terminates on the first London bank business day preceding the third Wednesday of the contract month. If an exchange holiday, trading terminates on the next preceding business day.

the yield curve. But before we explain how Eurodollar futures pricing patterns are kept in lockstep with the yield curve, let us consider that the shape of the yield curve may be interpreted as an indicator of the direction in which the market as a whole believes interest rates may fluctuate. Three basic theories are referenced to explain the shape of the yield curve: the expectations hypothesis, the liquidity hypothesis, and the segmentation hypothesis.

Let's start with the assumption that the yield curve is flat; that is, short-term rates and longer-term interest rates are equivalent and investors are expressing no particular preference for securities on the basis of maturity. The expectations hypothesis modifies this assumption with the supposition that rational investors may be expected to alter the composition of their fixed-income portfolios to reflect their beliefs with respect to the future direction of interest rates.

Thus, investors move from long-term into short-term securities in anticipation of rising rates and falling fixed-income security prices, noting

EXHIBIT 6.2 Eurodollar Futures Activity (November 30, 2004)

Month	Open	High	Low	Settlement	Change	Volume	Open Interest
December 2004	97.5200	97.5250	97.5175	97.5225	—	35,218	957,652
January 2005	—	—	—	97.3800	—	—	5,735
February 2005	—	—	97.2400	97.2350	−1	—	638
March 2005	97.1100	97.1250	97.0950	97.1100	+1	61,000	1,019,810
April 2005	—	—	—	97.0400	—	—	50
June 2005	96.8250	96.8550	96.8000	96.8400	+3.5	54,539	983,437
September 2005	96.5850	96.6300	96.5650	96.6100	+4	47,282	837,948
December 2005	96.3800	96.4300	96.3550	96.4150	+5.5	52,726	646,746
March 2006	96.2250	96.2800	96.2000	96.2600	+5.5	36,699	477,888
June 2006	96.1050	96.1550	96.0700	96.1350	+5	26,392	351,868
September 2006	96.0000	96.0400	95.9700	96.0250	+4.5	26,087	274,414
December 2006	95.8900	95.9200	95.8600	95.9050	+3	21,686	219,979
March 2007	95.8100	95.8250	95.7700	95.8100	+1.5	17,866	167,460
June 2007	95.7100	95.7200	95.6800	95.7050	+0.5	18,349	157,484
September 2007	95.6100	95.6150	95.5750	95.5900	−1	19,151	127,935
December 2007	95.5050	95.5150	95.4600	95.4850	−2	13,082	94,485
March 2008	95.4300	95.4300	95.3700	95.3850	−3.5	13,792	87,279
June 2008	95.3400	95.3400	95.2750	95.2850	−4.5	12,776	84,760
September 2008	95.2250	95.2550	95.1750	95.1900	−5.5	12,270	87,394
December 2008	95.1350	95.1450	95.0650	95.0750	−6	8,890	66,532
March 2009	95.0500	95.0600	94.9700	94.9850	−6.5	7,813	53,156
June 2009	94.9350	94.9700	94.8750	94.8900	−7	6,623	40,034
September 2009	94.8350	94.8850	94.7900	94.8050	−7	6,843	32,754
December 2009	94.7350	94.7450	94.6950	94.7200	−7.5	2,068	15,655
March 2010	94.6400	94.6450	94.6350	94.6450	−7.5	426	13,735

June 2010	94.5750	94.5750	94.5650	94.5700	−8	385	5,852
September 2010	94.4750	94.4750	94.4750	94.4950	−8	1,080	7,181
December 2010	—	—	94.4150	94.4200	−8.5	245	6,115
March 2011	—	—	94.3550	94.3600	−8.5	395	6,350
June 2011	—	—	94.2950	94.3000	−8.5	245	5,647
September 2011	—	—	94.2400	94.2450	−8.5	395	4,519
December 2011	—	—	94.1650	94.1850	−9	5	1,635
March 2012	—	—	94.1150	94.1300	−9.5	5	1,330
June 2012	—	—	94.0650	94.0800	−9.5	5	1,504
September 2012	—	—	94.0350	94.0500	−9.5	354	1,491
December 2012	—	—	94.0000	94.0150	−9.5	5	612
March 2013	—	—	93.9550	93.9700	−9.5	5	410
June 2013	—	—	93.9100	93.9250	−9.5	5	393
September 2013	—	—	93.8800	93.8950	−9.5	5	269
December 2013	—	—	93.8400	93.8550	−9.5	55	347
March 2014	—	—	93.8100	93.8250	−9.5	55	224
June 2014	—	—	93.7800	93.7950	−9.5	55	144
September 2014	—	—	93.7500	93.7650	−9.5	55	124
TOTAL						504,932	6,848,975

that the value of long-term instruments reacts more sharply to shifting rates than short-term instruments or by moving from short-term into long-term securities in anticipation of falling rates and rising fixed-income prices.

In the process of shortening the maturity of one's portfolio, investors bid up the price of short-term securities and drive down the price of long-term securities. As a result, short-term yields decline and long-term yields rise: The yield curve steepens. In the process of extending maturities, the opposite occurs and the yield curve flattens or inverts.[2]

Yields expected to rise → Yield curve is steep

Yields expected to fall → Yield curve is flat or inverted

The liquidity hypothesis modifies our initial assumption that investors may generally be indifferent between short- and long-term investments in a stable rate environment. Rather, we must assume that investors generally prefer short- over long-term securities to the extent that short-term securities roll over frequently, offering a measure of liquidity by virtue of the fact that one's principal is redeemed at a relatively short-term maturity date. As such, long-term securities must pay a liquidity premium to attract investment, and long-term yields typically exceed short-term yields, a natural upward bias to the shape of the curve. See Exhibit 6.3.

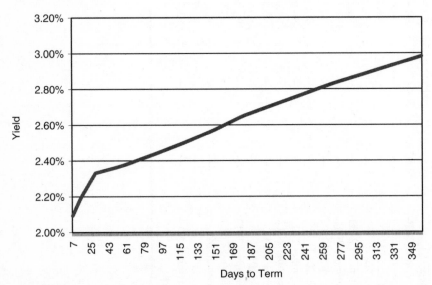

EXHIBIT 6.3   U.S. LIBOR Yield Curve (11/2004)

Finally, the segmentation hypothesis suggests that investors may be less than fully capable of modifying the composition of their portfolios quickly and efficiently in order to take advantage of anticipated yield fluctuations. In particular, investors sometimes face internally or externally imposed constraints: the investment policies of a pension fund or regulatory requirements. Thus, "kinks" sometimes are observed in the yield curve.

Implied Forward Rates

A lot of useful information regarding market expectations of future rates is embedded in the shape of the yield curve. But how might one unlock that information? The answer is found in the *implied forward rate,* or IFR. An IFR might be used to identify what the market believes that short-term rates will be in the future (e.g., what will 180-day investments yield 90 days from now?).

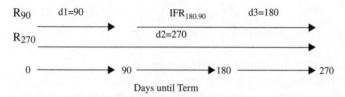

Days until Term

The anticipated 180-day rate 90 days from now, or $IFR_{180,90}$, may be found as a function of the 90-day term rate R_{90} and the 270-day term rate R_{270}. Let's denote the length of each period as d1 = 90 days; d2 = 270 days, and d3 = 180 days. A baseline assumption is that investors may be indifferent between investing for a 9-month term or investing at a 3-month term and rolling the proceeds over into a 6-month investment 90 days from now. As such, the IFR may be calculated as follows:

$$IFR_{d3,d1} = \frac{[1 + R_{d2}\,(d2/360)]}{(d3/360)\,[1 + R_{d1}\,(d1/360)]} - \frac{1}{(d3/360)}$$

Example Assume that the 90-day rate equals $R_{90} = 2.75\%$ and the 270-day rate equals $R_{270} = 3.00\%$. What is the IFR for a 180-day investment 90 days from now?

$$\begin{aligned}
IFR_{d3,d1} &= \frac{[1 + R_{d2}\,(d2/360)]}{(d3/360)\,[1 + R_{d1}\,(d1/360)]} - \frac{1}{(d3/360)} \\
&= \frac{[1 + 0.03\,(270/360)]}{(180/360)\,[1 + 0.0275\,(90/360)]} - \frac{1}{(180/360)} \\
&= 0.031037 \text{ or } 3.10\%
\end{aligned}$$

Example Assume that $R_{90} = 3.25\%$ and the 270-day rate equals $R_{270} = 3.00\%$. What is the implied forward rate for a 180-day investment 90 days from now?

$$
\begin{aligned}
IFR_{d3,d1} &= \frac{[1 + R_{d2} (d2/360)]}{(d3/360) [1 + R_{d1} (d1/360)]} - \frac{1}{(d3/360)} \\
&= \frac{[1 + 0.03 (270/360)]}{(180/360) [1 + 0.0325 (90/360)]} - \frac{1}{(180/360)} \\
&= 0.028518 \text{ or } 2.85\%
\end{aligned}
$$

Example Assume that $R_{90} = 3.00\%$ and the 270-day rate equals $R_{270} = 3.00\%$. What is the implied forward rate for a 180-day investment 90 days from now?

$$
\begin{aligned}
IFR_{d3,d1} &= \frac{[1 + R_{d2} (d2/360)]}{(d3/360) [1 + R_{d1} (d1/360)]} - \frac{1}{(d3/360)} \\
&= \frac{[1 + 0.03 (270/360)]}{(180/360) [1 + 0.03 (90/360)]} - \frac{1}{(180/360)} \\
&= 0.029777 \text{ or } 2.98\%
\end{aligned}
$$

Exhibit 6.4 summarizes the results of our examples. As such, a steep yield curve suggests a general market expectation of rising rates. An inverted yield curve suggests a general market expectation of falling rates.

Finally, a flat yield curve suggests that the market expects slight declines in rates. This is consistent with our liquidity hypothesis that suggests the market will generally favor short- over long-term rates in the absence of expectations of rising or falling rates. It is the slightly inclined yield curve that reflects an expectation of stable rates in the future.

This result may further be understood by citing the compounding effect implicit in a rollover from a 90-day to a 180-day investment. Because the investor recovers the original investment plus interest after the first 90 days, there is somewhat more principal to reinvest over the subsequent 180-day period. Thus, one can afford to invest over the subsequent 180-day period at a rate slightly lower than 3% and still realize a total return of 3% over the entire 270-day term.

EXHIBIT 6.4 Calculating Implied Forward Rates

	90-Day Rate	270-Day Rate	IFR
Steep yield curve	2.75%	3.00%	3.10%
Inverted yield curve	3.25%	3.00%	2.85%
Flat yield curve	3.00%	3.00%	2.98%

Futures as Mirror of Yield Curve

The point to our discussion about IFRs is that Eurodollar futures should price at levels that reflect these IFRs. In other words, Eurodollar futures prices directly reflect, and are a mirror of, the yield curve. This is intuitive if one considers that a Eurodollar futures contract represents a 3-month investment entered into N days in the future. And, if Eurodollar futures did not reflect IFRs, an arbitrage opportunity would present itself.

Example Consider the following interest rate structure in the Eurodollar (euro) futures and cash markets. Which is the better investment for the next six months: (1) invest for six months at the current spot rate of 2.75%; (2) invest for three months at the current spot rate of 2.55% and buy March Eurodollar futures, or (3) invest for nine months at the current spot rate of 2.96% and sell June euro futures? It is December, and let's assume that these investments have terms of 90 days (0.25 years), 180 days (0.50 years), or 270 days (0.75 years).

Mar euro futures	97.00 (3.00%)
Jun euro futures	96.70 (3.30%)
Sep euro futures	96.50 (3.50%)
3-month investment	offer @ 2.55%
6-month investment	offer @ 2.75%
9-month investment	offer @ 2.96%

The second investment option implies that you invest at 2.55% for the first three months and lock in a rate of 3.00% by buying March Eurodollar futures for the subsequent three months. This implies a return of 2.78% over the entire six-month period.

$$1 + R(.5) = [1 + 0.0255\,(0.25)][1 + 0.03\,(0.25)]$$
$$R = \frac{([1 + 0.0255\,(0.25)][1 + 0.03\,(0.25)]) - 1}{0.5}$$
$$= 2.78456\%$$

The third alternative means that you invest for the next 270 days at 2.96% and sell June Eurodollar futures at 3.30%, effectively committing to sell the spot investment 180 days hence when it has 90 days until maturity. This implies a return of 2.77% over the next six months.

$$[1 + R\,(0.5)][1 + .033(0.25)] = [1 + 0.0296\,(0.75)]$$
$$R = \frac{([1 + 0.0296\,(0.75)]/[1 + .033\,(0.25)]) - 1}{0.5}$$
$$= 2.7672\%$$

Thus, the second alternative provides a slightly greater return at slightly more than 2.78% than does the third alternative yielding almost 2.77% versus the outright six-month investment at 2.76%.

Eurodollar futures prices are a reflection of IFRs because of the possibility that market participants may pursue arbitrage opportunities when prices become misaligned. In our preceding examples, one might have sold the six-month investment at 2.75% while buying the three-month investment and buying March Eurodollar futures for a return of 2.78%. In this example, there is a 3 basis point profit to be had without considering the transaction costs associated with an arbitrage. The net result of such transactions is that these related cash and futures markets achieve a state of equilibrium pricing where arbitrage opportunities do not exist.

Strips

A Eurodollar futures strip may be bought or sold by buying or selling a series of futures maturing in successively deferred months, often in combination with a cash investment in the near term. The initial cash investment is often referred to as the "front tail," or "stub," of the strip transaction. Referring to the second investment alternative evaluated earlier, we created a six-month strip of rolling investments by investing at the spot or cash rate for the first six months while buying a March Eurodollar futures. Similarly we could have created a nine-month strip by adding on a long June futures contract, or a one-year strip by adding on a September futures contract.

Buying a 1-Year Strip

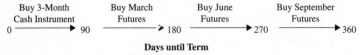

Days until Term

The value of this strip may be calculated as essentially the compounded rate of return on the components of the strip.

Example Returning to our previous example, which strategy is preferable, to (1) buy a nine-month investment yielding 2.96%, or (2) enter into the 3-month investment, buy March futures, and buy June futures? Our analysis suggests that the nine-month strip yields slightly more than 2.97% relative to 2.96% on the nine-month investment.

Mar euro futures	97.00 (3.00%)
Jun euro futures	96.70 (3.30%)
3-month investment	offer @ 2.55%
9-month investment	offer @ 2.96%

$$1 + R\,(0.75) = [1 + 0.0255\,(0.25)][1 + 0.03\,(0.25)][1 + 0.033\,(0.25)]$$

$$R = \frac{([1 + 0.0255\,(0.25)][1 + 0.03\,(0.25)][1 + 0.033\,(0.25)]) - 1}{0.75}$$

$$= 2.9717\%$$

In our example, there is no compelling advantage to buy the strip relative to a straight term advantage to the extent that the yields are virtually the same. However, if the rates were sufficiently divergent, one might buy the strip and sell (or borrow) the term investment to finance the strip or sell the strip and buy the term investment. This represents a form of arbitrage that ensures Eurodollar futures represent a consistent reflection of the curve.

Note that, to the extent that Eurodollar futures are listed out 10 years into the future, one may create 1-year, 2-year, 3-year, . . . , up to 10-year strips that may be compared to comparable term securities. In fact these values are often compared to term Treasury securities and to swap rates as discussed in more detail later.[3]

Packs and Bundles

Because strips have proven to be popular trading instruments and because of the complexities associated with their purchase or sale, the exchange has developed the concept of "packs" and "bundles" to facilitate strip trading. A pack or bundle may be thought of as the purchase or sale of a series of Eurodollar futures representing a particular segment of the yield curve.

Packs and bundles should be thought of a building blocks used to create or liquidate positions along various segments of interest along the yield curve. Packs and bundles may be bought or sold in a single transaction, eliminating the possibility that a multitude of orders in each individual contract goes unfilled.

Note that the popularity of these concepts is reflected in Eurodollar volume and open interest patterns. Unlike most futures contracts, where virtually all volume and open interest is concentrated in the nearby or lead month, Eurodollar futures have significant volume and open interest in the deferred months going out 10 years along the yield curve.

The exchange offers trading in 1-, 2-, 3-, 4-, 5-, 6-, 7-, 8-, 9-, and 10-year bundles. These products may be thought of as Eurodollar futures strips (absent the front tail or stub investment) extending out 1, 2, 3, . . . , 10 years into the future. For example, one may buy a one-year bundle by purchasing the first four quarterly expiration Eurodollar futures contracts. Or, one may sell a three-year bundle by selling the first 12 quarterly expiration Eurodollar futures contracts.

The price of a bundle is typically quoted by reference to the average change in the value of all Eurodollar futures contracts in the bundle since the prior day's settlement price. For example, if the first four quarterly Eurodollar contracts are up 2 basis points for the day and the second four quarterly Eurodollar contracts are up 3 basis points for the day, then the two-year bundle may be quoted as + or up 2.5 basis points.

After a trade is concluded at a negotiated price, prices are assigned to each of the various legs (i.e., Eurodollar futures contracts) associated with the bundle. These prices must be within the daily range for at least one of the component contracts of the bundle. This assignment is generally administered through an automated system operated by the exchange.

Packs are similar to bundles in that they represent an aggregation of a number of Eurodollar futures contracts traded simultaneously. But they are constructed to represent a series of four consecutive quarterly Eurodollar futures.

For example, one may buy a pack by buying the four front contracts—March, June, September, and December 2006 Eurodollar futures contracts, constituting the front pack. Or, one may sell a "Red" pack by selling the fifth through eighth cycle month contracts—March, June, September, and December 2007 Eurodollar futures contracts. Second-year contracts are also referred to the as "Red" contracts. Packs are quoted and prices are assigned to the individual legs in the same manner that one quotes and assigns prices to the legs of a bundle.

SPECULATING ON SHAPE OF YIELD CURVE

Because Eurodollar futures are a mirror of the yield curve, one may spread these contracts to take a position on the relative changes associated with long- and short-term yields (i.e., to speculate on the shape of the yield curve).

If the yield curve is expected to steepen, the recommended strategy is to "buy the curve" or "buy a Eurodollar calendar spread" by purchasing near-term and selling longer-term or deferred Eurodollar futures. If the opposite is expected to occur, that is, if the yield curve is expected to flatten or invert, then the recommended strategy is to "sell the curve" or "sell a Eurodollar calendar spread" by selling near-term and buying deferred Eurodollar futures.

Expectation		Action
Yield curve expected to steepen	→	"Buy the curve" (i.e., buy nearby and sell deferred futures)
Yield curve expected to flatten or invert	→	"Sell the curve" (i.e., sell nearby and buy deferred futures)

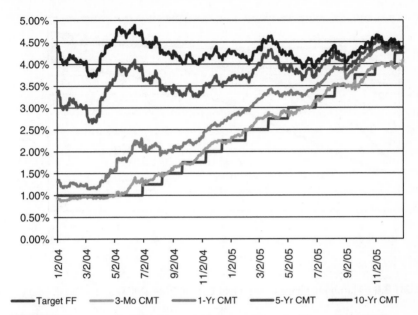

EXHIBIT 6.5 Target Fed Funds versus Constant Maturity Treasuries (CMT)

Let's examine how the shape of the yield curve has fluctuated over the previous year or so. Entering 2009, many analysts assumed that the Federal Reserve (the Fed) would continue to hold rates stable, noting that the target Fed Funds rate had been held at 1.00% since the Fed's quarter point easing of June 25, 2003.

In particular, analysts may have taken note of the Fed's stated concerns with respect to disinflation expressed at the October 28, 2003, Federal Open Market Committee (FOMC) meeting. Thus, the short-end of the yield curve, driven by Fed monetary policy, was holding firm, as seen in Exhibit 6.5.

Still, snippets of encouraging economic news had been filtering out albeit on an uneven basis. Although short-term rates are driven fundamentally by monetary policy, longer-term rates are driven by inflationary expectations. As such, longer-term rates had started to rally as depicted in our chart of Constant Maturity Treasury (CMT) yields relative to the target Fed Funds rate. See Exhibit 6.6.

Longer-term rates were rising while short-term rates remained anchored in early 2004. That is, the yield curve began to steepen. This development was reflected in the Treasury curve and was likewise mirrored in Eurodollar futures as shown in Exhibit 6.7. One may take advantage

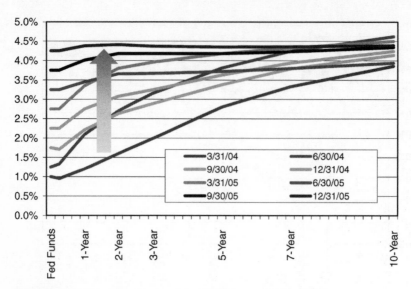

EXHIBIT 6.6 Flattening Shape of the Yield Curve (2004–2005)

of anticipation of a steepening yield curve environment by buying the curve or buying a Eurodollar futures calendar spread (i.e., simultaneously buying a nearby and selling a deferred Eurodollar futures contract at a price differntial).

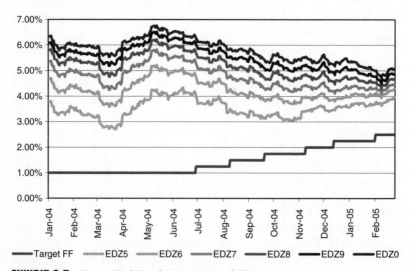

EXHIBIT 6.7 Target Fed Funds versus Eurodollar Futures

Example On February 10, 2004, one may have bought the curve by buying March 2005 and selling March 2010 Eurodollar futures. The spread was quoted on February 10, 2004, at 3.395%. By March 31, 2004, the spread may have been liquidated at 3.655% for a profit of 26 basis points, or $650 per spread.

	March 2005 EDs	March 2010 EDs	Spread
February 10, 2004	Buy @ 97.620 (2.380%)	Sell @ 94.225 (5.775%)	3.395%
March 31, 2004	Sell @ 98.135 (1.865%)	Buy @ 94.480 (5.520%)	3.655%
	+0.515 or +$1,287.50	−0.255 or −$637.50	0.260 or +$650.00

Interestingly, the yield curve steepened in our preceding example while forward rates represented in Eurodollar futures were generally declining. In this case, near-term rates declined a bit faster than longer-term rates. This may be attributed to the fact that monetary policy was still considered stagnant during this period. See Exhibit 6.8.

As such, sentiment shifted and the marketplace began to anticipate a reversal in FOMC monetary policy from a neutral to a tightening stance. Accordingly, the yield curve started to shift with short-term rates

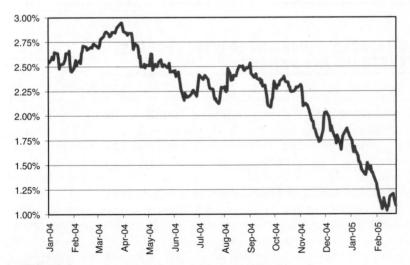

EXHIBIT 6.8 Dec 2010 versus Dec 2005 Eurodollar Spread

increasing, although longer-term rates held reasonably steady (i.e., a flattening of the yield curve).

But even stronger economic news was soon to emerge. Notably, March 2004 Non-Farm Payroll (NFP) figures were released on April 2, reporting the creation of some 308,000 new jobs. This figure was well above expectations that some 123,000 new jobs would be created.

Investor sentiment was subsequently proven correct when on June 30, 2004, the Fed tightened by 25 basis points, raising the target Fed Funds rate from 1.00% to 1.25% and raising the discount rate from 2.00% to 2.25%.

Example   On December 6, 2004, one may have sold the curve by selling December 2005 and buying December 2010 Eurodollar futures. The spread is quoted on December 6, 2004, at 1.985%. By February 28, 2005, the spread may have been liquidated at 1.18% for a profit of 80.5 basis points, or $2,012.50 per spread.

	December 2005 EDs	December 2010 EDs	Spread
December 6, 2004	Sell @ 96.565 (3.435%)	Buy @ 94.580 (5.420%)	1.985%
February 18, 2005	Buy @ 96.125 (3.875%)	Sell @ 94.945 (5.055%)	1.180%
	+0.440 or +$1,100.00	+0.365 or +$912.50	0.805 or +$2,012.50

TERM TREASURY/EURODOLLAR (TED) SPREADS WITH FUTURES AND OPTIONS

Treasury/Eurodollar (TED) spreads have been studied and traded since 1981 concurrent with the introduction of Eurodollar futures. Note that these spreads had originally been constructed with use of CME Group 91-day Treasury bill futures versus CME Group 90-day Eurodollar futures contracts. As such, the spread was a very direct measure of marketplace perception of the credit risk implied by a private investment (in Eurodollars) versus the so-called risk-free rate implied by a Treasury bill.

The popularity of the TED spread was enhanced by various credit events affecting the marketplace over the years. Notable events we might cite include the Continental Illinois Bank crisis of 1984, the savings and loan failures and subsequent bailout of the late 1980s, the Asian currency crisis followed by the Russian debt default in 1997–1998, the U.S. Treasury's comments questioning their level of financial support for the housing agencies (i.e., Freddie, Fannie) in 2000, the bursting of the "dotcom" bubble in 2001, and the subprime mortgage crisis beginning in 2007. All these events and others have created "pops" in the yield spread between private and public debt instruments.

Although CME Group's T-bill futures contract has fallen into disuse as the popularity of Eurodollar futures has transcended all other domestic STIR contracts, the TED lives on as a popular device for trading credit risks. The TED is sometimes referred to as a "swap spread" or a spread between interest rate swap (IRS) rates and a risk-free government rate. Noting the close relationship between IRSs and Eurodollar futures as a pricing mechanism and hedging tool, one may readily substitute Eurodollar futures as a proxy for a swap.

Thus, TED spreads are often constructed with the use of Eurodollar futures versus cash Treasury notes. Or, one may facilitate the trade with use of 2-year, 5-year, 10-year Treasury note futures versus Eurodollar futures. This section explores the use of Eurodollar and T-note futures as components of a quick and easy term TED spread. Then we extend the discussion to the use of options on Eurodollar and T-note futures for the same purposes.

Comparing Yields

Not all yields are created equal. The yield quoted on a money market instrument such as LIBOR is calculated using somewhat different assumptions than the yield quoted on a coupon-bearing instrument such as a T-note. Fixed income traders need be careful to assure that they are comparing "apples with apples."

Yields associated with Eurodollar or LIBOR quotes are known as money market yields (MMYs). Note that Eurodollars are so-called add-on instruments where one invests the stated face value and receives the original investment plus interest at term. Thus, one's interest may be calculated as a simple function of the face value (FV), rate (R), and days to maturity (d).

$$\text{Interest} = FV\,[R \times (d/360)]$$

Example If one were to purchase a $1 million face-value Eurodollar time deposit with MMY = 3.00% and 270 days until maturity, one would receive the original $1 million face-value (FV) investment plus interest (i) of $22,500 at the conclusion of 270 days.

$$\text{Interest} = \$1,000,000 \, [0.03 \times (270/360)]$$
$$= \$22,500$$

MMYs suffer from the mistaken assumption that there are but 360 days in a year (a "money-market" year!). As such, MMYs are not completely comparable to the bond equivalent yield (BEY) quoted on T-notes that imply periodic coupon payments. The following adjustment may be made to render the two quotes comparable:

$$\text{BEY} = \text{MMY} \times (365/360)$$

Example Assume you have a 90-day money market instrument yielding 3.00%. Let's convert that figure to a bond-equivalent yield. Note that the BEY of 3.0417% slightly exceeds the MMY.

$$3.0417\% = 3.00\% \times (365/360)$$

Complicating the calculation is the fact that notes and bonds offer semi-annual coupon payments. Thus, money market instruments that require the investor to wait until maturity for any return do not permit interim compounding. This means that the formula just provided is only valid for instruments with less than six months (183 days) to term. If there are 183 or more days until term, use the following formula where P = price or original investment and i = interest.

$$\text{BEY} = \frac{(-d/365) + \sqrt{([d/365]^2 - [(2d/365) - 1][1 - ((FV + i)/FV)])}}{[(d/365) - 0.5]}$$

Example Let's return to our example of a 270-day Eurodollar investment quoted at a MMY = 3.00%. Note from our preceding example that the interest accrued on a $1 million investment would be $22,500. The BEY may be calculated as 3.027% and slightly higher than the MMY = 3.00%.

$$\text{BEY} = \frac{(-270/365) + \sqrt{([270/365]^2 - [(2 \times 270/365) - 1][1 - ((\$1,000,000 + \$22,500)/\$1,000,000)])}}{[(d/365) - 0.5]}$$

$$= 3.027\%$$

Swap Spreads

Let's examine the recent performance of credit spreads between Treasuries and longer-term Eurodollar futures, the term TED spread. We could examine the compounded value of a strip of Eurodollar futures, converted to a bond equivalent basis to the yield on Treasuries. But for ease of exposition, we will take a few liberties. In particular, we will use 1-, 2-, 5- and 10-year interest rate swap (IRS) rates as proxies for strips or bundles of Eurodollar futures. This is reasonable to the extent that swaps are frequently priced on the basis of, and hedged with, strips or bundles of Eurodollar futures. Secondly, we will ignore the finer points of yield calculations for these purposes and simply compare those swap rates to Treasury yields.

Over approximately the past year prior to this writing, short-term yields have been on the rise. Swap rates can be expected to exceed, but nonetheless largely parallel, the yield on comparable maturity Treasuries. Exhibit 6.9 illustrates these points nicely.

Although short-term yields have generally been rising, longer-term yields have actually been rather stable and the yield curve has been flattening as discussed in the prior section regarding yield curve plays. Beyond that, credit spreads, as represented in the 1-year, 2-year, 5-year, and 10-year swap over comparable maturity Treasury spreads and depicted in the nearby graphic, have generally converged into the 35 to 40 basis point range. Notice that the 1-year swap spread has rallied to some extent, whereas the 10-year swap spread, after spiking in the spring of 2004, has actually been moderating.

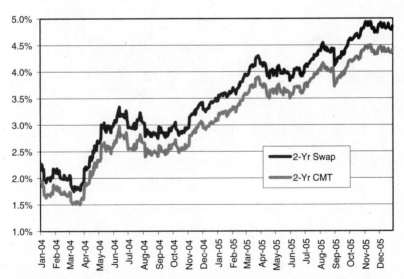

EXHIBIT 6.9 2-Year Swap versus Constant Maturity Treasury (CMT) Rates

Let's focus on the two-year spread. Notice that it was widening in the spring of 2004 from the 25 to 30 basis point (bip) range up to 40 to 45 bips. Subsequently in the summer of 2004, the spread reversed from 40 to 45 bips falling back into the vicinity of 25 to 30 bips.

Fundamental conditions leading to the widening action in the spring include the release of a surprisingly vibrant Non-Farm Payroll figure in April and growing speculation that the Fed might begin to tighten. As such, participants in the interest rate swap markets may have become more interested in buying swaps (as fixed-rate payers and floating rate receivers). See Exhibit 6.10.

Of course the Fed did in fact begin to tighten during the summertime. But as it did so, the marketplace became concerned about rising federal budget deficits and growing corporate debt issuance. Note that while short-term rates were pushed up by the Fed, longer-term rates that reflect inflationary expectations were stable or even moderating. Thus, the credit spread began to moderate as interest rate swap players may have become more interested in selling swaps (paying floating rates and receiving fixed rates), possibly anticipating that the Fed might be stopped short in its tracks.

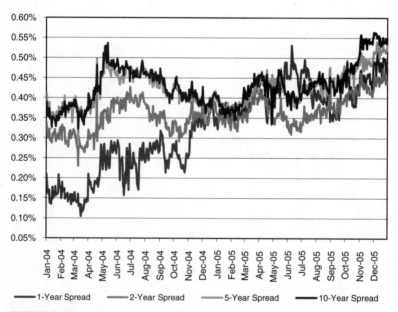

EXHIBIT 6.10 Spread: Swaps less Treasuries

Quick and Dirty Treasury/Eurodollar Spread

How best to take advantage of those conditions? Presumably, one might attempt to trade a strip of Eurodollar futures (i.e., a series of futures in successively deferred delivery months as a proxy for the value of an interest rate swap) versus a spot or cash Treasury note. However, the construction of a Eurodollar strip, possibly in the form of Eurodollar bundle, may be a bit cumbersome. Rather, we examine a streamlined method using a Eurodollar pack.

A Eurodollar futures pack represents an aggregation of four quarterly expiration Eurodollar futures in consecutive months traded simultaneously. For example, one may buy a pack by buying the March, June, September, and December 2006 Eurodollar futures contracts, constituting a pack. Or, one may sell a pack by selling the March, June, September, and December 2007 Eurodollar futures contract, constituting yet another pack.

Packs are often referred to by color designations. The "white pack" refers to the first four quarterly expiration Eurodollar futures; the "red pack" is the subsequent four futures; the "green pack" is the next four futures, the "blue pack" is the fourth year strip, and a "gold pack" represents four quarterly Eurodollar futures going out five years on the curve.

Just as it may be cumbersome to use a strip of Eurodollar futures in the context of a TED spread, it may likewise be cumbersome to use cash Treasury securities. In particular, Treasury note futures are available and may conveniently be spread against a Eurodollar pack. Note that since the merger of the CME and Chicago Board of Trade in 2007 under the auspices of the CME Group, both futures contracts are traded on the CME Globex platform and cleared through the CME Group Clearing House, which allows one to avail special spread margins that reflect the risk of the combination of the two partially offsetting legs of the spread.

In other words, let's use Eurodollar packs as a proxy for interest rate swap rates and two-year T-note futures as a proxy for cash or spot Treasury securities. One might buy the credit spread (buy T-note futures/sell Eurodollar futures) in anticipation of a widening TED spread. Or, one may sell the TED spread (sell T-note futures/buy Eurodollar futures) in anticipation of a narrowing credit spread. This is the essence of our "quick and dirty TED spread."

Long the TED Spread	→	Buy T-Note Futures & Sell Eurodollar Pack
Short the TED Spread	→	Sell T-Note Futures & Buy Eurodollar Pack

Weighting the Spread

To assure that the "quick and dirty" TED spread will really reflect the relative credit risks implied by the private versus public debt sectors, it will become necessary to weight the spread.

Thus, we must endeavor to match the risk exposure associated with the two instruments given an assumption that the yields on the paired futures contract positions move in a parallel manner (i.e., balance the risk associated with T-note futures with an appropriately offsetting number of Eurodollar packs to balance any change (Δ) in the value of the T-note futures with an opposite change in the value of the Eurodollar pack, given an equivalent shift in yields.

$$\Delta \text{ Value of T-Note Futures} \approx \Delta \text{ Value of Eurodollar Pack}$$

But we can't manage what we can't measure. Basis point value (BPV) measures the monetary change in the value of an instrument in response to a one basis point (0.01%) change in yield as follows. BPVs may be used as a proxy for the more abstract concept of change such that $BPV \approx \Delta$.

The BPV for a money market instrument such as those represented by Eurodollar futures may be calculated as follows where FV = face value of instrument and d = days to maturity.

$$BPV_{ED} = FV \times (d/360) \times 0.01\%$$

Example Find the basis point value (BPV) of a $1 million face-value 90-day exposure as represented by one Eurodollar futures contract.

By plugging these values into our equation as shown, we may calculate the basis point value associated with one $1 million face-value 90-day Eurodollar futures contract (BPV_{ED}) as $25.00 ($BPV_{ED}$ = $25.00).

$$
\begin{aligned}
BPV_{ED} &= FV \times (d/360) \times 0.01\% \\
&= \$1,000,000 \times (90/360) \times 0.01\% \\
&= \$25.00
\end{aligned}
$$

The BPV associated with a money market instrument such as a LIBOR investment may be found as a simple linear function of the face value (FV) and the term in days (d) of the instrument. Thus, the basis point value of a pack of four Eurodollar futures (BPV_{pack}) is simply $100 ($BPV_{pack}$ = $4 \times \$25$).

Likewise, we must find the BPV associated with a T-note futures contract. However, the calculations are a bit more complex. Note that 2-year T-note futures permit the delivery of $200,000 face value of U.S. Treasury notes with an original maturity no greater than 5 years, 3 months, and a remaining term until maturity between 1 year, 9 months, and 2 years, regardless of coupon. At any given time, there will be a number of T-notes that will be eligible for delivery or deliverable.[4]

The conversion factor (CF) invoicing system is (theoretically) designed to render equally economic the delivery of any eligible T-note. In practice, however, a single security stands out as most economic or cheapest to deliver (CTD) in light of the difference between cash values and the invoice price a buyer would pay to seller upon delivery calculated as a function of the futures price multiplied by the conversion factor: Invoice Price = Futures Settlement × CF plus any accrued interest.

The point is that it is necessary to identify the CTD security and its basis point value (BPV_{ctd}). The effective basis point value of a T-note futures contract (BPV_{t-note}) is equal to the basis point value of the CTD security divided by the conversion factor: $BPV_{t-note} = BPV_{ctd} \div CF_{ctd}$.

Once the CTD security is identified, we must identify its basis point value (BPV_{ctd}) and divide by its conversion factor (CF_{ctd}) to find the futures basis point value (BPV_{t-note})[5]

$$BPV_{t-note} = BPV_{ctd} \div CF_{ctd}$$

Example On April 16, 2004, the cheapest to deliver two-year T-note was the 2.25% of April 2006. It had a BPV of \$34.66 per \$200,000 face value and a conversion factor for delivery into the June 2004 two-year futures contract of 0.9358.[6] Thus, the effective BPV of the futures contract may be calculated as \$37.04.

$$\begin{aligned} BPV_{t-note} &= BPV_{ctd} \div CF_{ctd} \\ &= \$34.66 \div 0.9358 \\ &= \$37.04 \end{aligned}$$

Armed with this information, we may identify the appropriate hedge ratio (HR) that would balance a TED spread constructed using Eurodollar packs versus two-year T-note futures. The HR that indicates the appropriate number of T-note futures to trade versus Eurodollar packs may be calculated as follows:

$$HR = BPV_{pack} \div BPV_{t-note}$$

Example How many September two-year T-note futures must be traded to balance a single Eurodollar pack? In our previous discussion, we had calculated a $BPV_{pack} = \$100.00$ and a $BPV_{t-note} = \$37.04$. Plugging this information into our formula, we calculate a ratio of 2.7, or roughly 27 two-year T-note futures for every 10 packs.

$$HR = BPV_{pack} \div BPV_{t\text{-}note}$$
$$= \$100.00 \div \$37.04$$
$$= 2.699 \text{ or } \approx 27 \text{ 2-year T-note futures vs. 10 packs}$$

Term Treasury/Eurodollars with Futures

Now that we know how to weight the spread, let's look at some examples of how the spread may have been applied in 2004. Note once again that the two-year swap spread was rallying in the spring only to decline in the summer months.

Example　TED spreads were rallying in the spring of 2004. On April 16, 2004, one may have gone long or bought the two-year term TED spread by buying 27 September two-year T-note futures at 106 and 01/32nds and selling 10 red packs composed of the June 2005, September 2005, December 2005, and March 2006.[7] The four legs of the pack were priced at 97.23, 96.85, 96.51, and 96.225, respectively, for an average price of 96.705 (3.295%). Note that the two-year swap spread was at 30.1 basis points.

By July 15, 2004, the two-year swap spread was seen at 39.7 basis points, an advance of 9.6 basis points. September two-year T-notes were down 15/32nds to 105 and 18/32nds for a loss of \$25,312.50 on the 27-lot long position. The four legs of the Eurodollar pack were priced at 96.83, 96.49, 96.18, and 95.955, respectively, for an average price of 96.36375 (3.63625%). The 10 short packs could have been covered at a profit of \$38,675.00 while the 27 long T-note futures generated a loss of \$25,312.50. Adding it all up, this spread generated a profit of \$13,362.50.

	Sept 2004 2-Year T-Note Futures	Red Eurodollar Pack	Swap Spread
April 16, 2004	Buy 27 @ 106 and 01/32nds	Sell 10 @ 96.7050 (3.2950%)	0.301%
July 15, 2004	Sell 27 @ 105 and 18/32nds	Buy 10 @ 96.36375 (3.63625%)	0.397%
	−15/32nds or −\$25,312.50	+0.38675 or +\$38,675.00	+\$13,362.50

The spread between two-year T-note futures and the Eurodollar packs operated as a reasonable proxy for the two-year swap spread. The spread between the implicit yield on the pack and two-year note futures moved from 42 bips (=3.295% − 2.875%) up to 52.6 bips (=3.63625% −

3.11%) for an advance of 10.6 bips, approximately equal to the 9.6 bip movement in the two-year swap spread.

Note that this example had us put on 10 packs or 40 Eurodollar futures at $25 per basis point. Thus, the spread had an implicit BPV = $1,000. The spread, by whatever reference, moved approximately 10 bips and resulted in a profit of approximately $10,000 at $1,000/bip (actually $13,362.50).

Example   TED spreads were starting to slip by the summer months of 2004. On July 15, 2004, one may have gone short or sold the two-year term TED spread by selling 25 December two-year T-note futures at 105 and 04.5/32nds and selling 10 red packs composed of the September 2005, December 2005, March 2006, and June 2006 contracts.[8] The four legs of the pack were priced at 96.49, 96.18, 95.955, and 95.765, respectively, for an average price of 96.0975 (3.9025%). Note that the two-year swap spread was at 39.7 basis points.

	Dec 2004 2-Year T-Note Futures	Red Eurodollar Pack	Spread
July 15, 2004	Sell 25 @ 105 and 045/32nds	Buy 10 @ 96.0975 (3.9025%)	0.397%
September 30, 2004	Buy 25 @ 105 and 197/32nds	Sell 10 @ 96.66 (3.34%)	0.312%
	−152/32nds or −$23,828.12	+0.5625 or +$56,250.00	+$32,421.87

By September 30, 2004, the two-year swap spread was seen at 31.2 basis points, a decline of 8.5 basis points. September two-year T-notes were down 15.2/32nds to 105 and 19.7/32nds for a loss of $23,828.12 on the 25-lot short position. The four legs of the Eurodollar pack were priced at 96.99, 96.75, 96.54, and 96.36, respectively, for an average price of 96.66 (3.34%). The 10 long packs could have been liquidated at a profit of $56,250. Adding it all up, this spread generated a profit of $32,421.87.

Note that in this case, our quick and dirty term TED was not a particularly accurate tracker of the two-year swap spread. The spread between the implicit yield on the pack and two-year note futures moved from 58 bips (= 3.9025% − 3.322%) down to 26 bips (= 3.34% − 3.082%) for a decline of 32 bips, much larger than the 8.5-big decline in the two-year swap spread. It might be argued that futures traders had perhaps overestimated the Fed's aggression in pursuing a tightening policy by July, only to moderate perceptions by September.

INTEREST RATE SWAP MARKET

An interest rate swap represents a contractual agreement whereby two counterparties agree to exchange, or swap, periodic payments for a specific period of time based on a notional amount of principal. This principal value may be considered "notional" insofar as the counterparties never actually exchange the principal amount. Rather the counterparties periodically exchange monies calculated on the basis of that notional, principal value.

Dating to the early 1980s, interest rate swaps are now commonly used by banks, pension funds, insurance companies, and corporations as a means to alter the structure of their balance sheet and thereby manage financial risks. The Bank for International Settlements (BIS) estimated the total outstanding notional value of interest rate swaps at $309.7 trillion USD as of December 2008, as illustrated in Exhibit 6.11. The seminal swap transaction occurred in 1981 when IBM and the World Bank agreed to swap fixed for floating rate debt payments.

Although that transaction was completed directly between the two principal counterparties, most swaps are transacted through swap dealers, typically large banks or other financial institutions that show bids and offers to buy or sell swaps. This practice mitigates credit risk on the part of the counterparties who may be unfamiliar with the other's credit stature. See Exhibit 6.12.

EXHIBIT 6.11   Growth of Global Interest Rate Derivatives Marketplace (Billions USD)

	Dec-03	Dec-04	Dec-05	Dec-06	Dec-07	Dec-08
Interest rate derivatives TOTAL	141,991	190,502	211,970	291,581	393,138	385,896
Forward rate agreements (FRAs)	10,769	12,789	14,269	18,668	26,599	35,002
Interest rate swaps (IRS)	111,209	150,631	169,106	229,693	309,588	309,760
Options	20,012	27,082	28,596	43,221	56,951	41,134

Source: Bank for International Settlements (BIS).
NOTE: Approximately a third of these totals are originated in USD.

EXHIBIT 6.12 Turnover in Interest Rate Derivatives Marketplace (Billions USD)

	1998	2001	2004	2007
Interest rate swaps (IRS)	$155	$331	$621	$1,210
Options	$36	$29	$171	$215
Forward rate agreements (FRAs)	$74	$129	$233	$258
Other	$0	$0	$0	$1
OTC derivatives total	$265	$489	$1,025	$1,684
Exchange-traded interest rate derivatives	$1,371	$2,170	$4,521	NA

Source: Bank for International Settlements (BIS).

Structure of Swap Transaction

The most typical form of interest rate swap contemplates the exchange of a series of payments determined by applying a *fixed* rate of interest to the notional principal value versus a series of payments determined by using a *floating* rate of interest (i.e., an exchange of fixed payments for floating payments). Exhibit 6.13 depicts a typical fixed-for-floating rate swap transacted through a dealer.

Note that a dealer often assumes the role of middleman in the transaction, not only by finding the two counterparties and arranging the deal but also by passing through the periodic payments through from one counterparty to the other. This practice mitigates credit risk on the part of the counterparties, who may be unfamiliar with the other's credit stature. These dealers typically do not act as "brokers" per se insofar as they do not accept a commission for their services. Rather, they hope to profit by taking the bid/offer spread.

One may also swap a series of cash flows, both of which may float based on different reference rates. For example, one might swap a series of payments determined by reference to LIBOR rates with a series of payments determined by reference to commercial paper rates, or T-bill rates or other short-term reference rates. This type of interest rate swap is referred to as a basis or money market swap. More exotic swaps may be based on a commodity or an equity index as opposed to a strict interest rate swap.

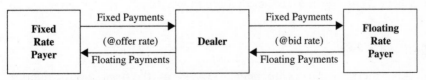

EXHIBIT 6.13 Interest Rate Swap Dealer Transaction

Terms of a Generic Swap Agreement

We turn our attention to those "generic," or "vanilla," fixed-for-floating rate swap agreements that are the subject of the exchange's swap futures contract. This type of swap contemplates the exchange of payments based on a fixed rate for a variable rate that may be reassessed periodically. The terms of such a transaction specify the notional principal amount, which is the basis for the transaction, along with a schedule of reset dates at which point the floating or variable rate is to be reassessed and the payment dates.

Generally, that fixed rate is determined by reference to the prevailing rate on Treasury securities of a term equal to that of the swap. The floating rate is typically determined by reference to three- or six-month LIBOR rates. The term, or "tenor," of a swap has been known to vary between 1 and 30 years. The fixed-rate payer is referred to as the buyer and is "long the swap." The floating-rate payer is the seller and is "short the swap."

The process of concluding a swap transaction may stretch over several days. The terms of the deal are typically negotiated on the "trade date" for settlement two business days hence, the "settlement date." "Par" swaps may be concluded without any initial payments between the two counterparties; "non-par" swaps entail a payment from one counterparty to the other on the settlement date. One begins to accrue interest on the "effective date" of the swap, generally the same date as the settlement date, although sometimes the effective date is pushed forward, a "forward swap."

Swap transactions contemplate the reset of the floating rate at periodic "reset dates" with payments swapped on a series of "payment dates" or "settlement dates." In the case of a swap tied to three-month LIBOR rates, these reset dates are typically established at three-month intervals; a swap tied to six-month LIBOR rates would typically be reset every six months. These reset intervals are of course subject to negotiation.

The associated payment dates may occur at three-month, six-month, or one-year intervals, although it is typical to establish payment dates at six-month intervals to mimic the coupon payment structure associated with Treasury securities. Although not always the case, it is commonplace to swap the fixed and floating-rate payments. As such, notice in Exhibit 6.14 that only the net payment or difference between the fixed- and floating-rate payment is passed between the counterparties.

Quoting a Swap

Because there are two components to the swap, the fixed and the floating rates, there are likewise two elements associated with the swap quote.

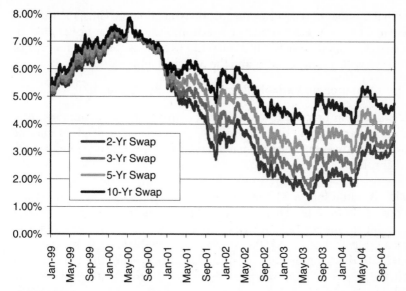

EXHIBIT 6.14 U.S. Swap Rates

The floating rate is generally pegged to a common STIR such as three-month LIBOR rates. Sometimes the floating rate is quoted on a "flat" basis, and sometimes the floating rate is adjusted upward or downward by some fixed margin, for example, three-month LIBOR plus 50 basis points (+0.50%).

The fixed rate may be quoted at a specific value (e.g., 6.50%). Or the fixed rate may be quoted on the basis of a specific reference rate. For example, one might quote a 10-year swap at 50 basis points (0.50%) above the prevailing rate associated with on-the-run or the most recently auctioned 10-year U.S. T-note. In other words, to transact the swap such that the fixed-rate payment is established at 50 basis points above the current rate on a 10-year T-note.

Once one determines the value of the fixed and floating rates, one may calculate the periodic payments between the counterparties. Let us apply a 30/360 day-count assumption (i.e., each month has 30 days and a year is composed of 360 days). Thus, the fixed-rate payment may be calculated as a function of the principal amount (P) and the fixed interest rate (R_{fixed}):

$$\text{Fixed Payment} = P \times R_{fixed} (180/360)$$

It is typical to calculate the payment tied to the floating or variable rate using the actual/360-day count convention (i.e., suggesting that we refer to that actual number of days since the prior payment date). Thus, the variable rate payment may be calculated as a function of the floating or variable interest rate ($R_{variable}$), presumably a reference to LIBOR rates, the number of days (d) since the prior payment and the principal amount (P):

$$\text{Floating or Variable Payment} = P \times R_{variable} \, (d/360)$$

It is common practice to require the payment of the net amount from one counterparty to the other counterparty upon payment. This may be complicated, however, when the fixed- and floating-rate payment dates are not synchronous.

Example   Assume that a $10 million swap is quoted at 3% versus a flat six-month LIBOR rate. There are 182 days to the first payment date at which point six-month LIBOR rates were quoted at 2.75%. The fixed payment may be calculated at $150,000 while the variable rate payment is only $139,028. In this example, our payment dates are synchronous, and the net of $10,972 is passed from the fixed-rate payer to the floating or variable rate payer.

$$
\begin{aligned}
\text{Fixed Payment } (R_{fixed}) &= \$10,000,000 \times 0.03 \times (180/360) &= \$150,000 \\
\text{Floating Payment } (R_{floating}) &= \$10,000,000 \times 0.0275 \times (182/360) &= \underline{\$139,028} \\
\text{Net Payment} & &= \$10,972
\end{aligned}
$$

Pricing Interest Rate Swaps

We turn our attention to the pricing of those generic or "plain vanilla" fixed-to-floating interest rate swaps, which are the subject of the exchange's interest rate swap futures contract. Conceptually, this exercise relies on the assumption that the present value of the future streams of fixed-rate payments (PV_{fixed}) and the present value of the future streams of variable-rate payments ($PV_{floating}$) should equate ($PV_{fixed} = PV_{floating}$). Or, at least in the case of a par swap that will be the primary topic of our discussion, where no monies change hands on the initial consummation of the transaction. In the case of a non-par swap, that non-par payment (NPP) passed from one counterparty to the next upon the initial conclusion of the swap transaction is used to balance the equation ($NPP = PV_{floating} - PV_{fixed}$).[9]

It is relatively easy to identify the present value of a stream of fixed payments, armed with the knowledge of the fixed rate, payment dates, and discount factors. Presumably, these discount factors may be identified by reference to the yield curve for returns associated with zero coupon securities of maturities that match the fixed-rate payment dates.

It is, however, a bit more difficult to assess the present value of those future streams of variable-rate payments. We cannot know what those variable payments will be. Still, the marketplace offers much information regarding interest rates that may be used to impute these future income streams and, in turn, to assess the value of a swap transaction.

In particular, one may study the yield curve to glean valuable information regarding the market's implicit assessment of future interest rates, or "implied forward rates" (IFRs). An IFR may be imputed if one can identify the term rate associated with the inception and conclusion of a loan. For example, if one has information regarding the term six-month rate and the one-year rate, one may impute the IFR for a six-month rate six months hence. This calculation is based on the assumption that an investor will be indifferent between a one-year term investment and a six-month investment rolled over into another subsequent six-month investment, aggregating to a one-year term.

These IFRs may be used as a proxy to calculate the variable-rate payments on future payment dates. Actually, IFRs of a sort are available by direct reference to the exchange's Eurodollar futures market that lists contracts extending out 10 years into the future. The rate implied in the Eurodollar futures quote effectively represents an IFR itself. As such, swap traders frequently reference Eurodollar pricing as a proxy for those future variable rates and in turn use swap rates as a benchmark for other fixed-income securities.

Thus, it is possible to assess the present value of the futures streams of both fixed- and variable-rate payments and, as discussed earlier, to identify the value of the swap as the difference in the two sums. In a par swap, that difference is zero: No monies change changes when the swap is initially concluded.

However, the value of a swap represented in the difference between these net present values is expected to fluctuate over time as a function of market conditions. For example, if yields are generally rising, this will result in advancing IFRs. Thus, the present value of the variable rate payments will advance, noting that the fixed payments are fixed, of course. This advantages the fixed-rate payer.

We can expect that the performance of an interest rate swap will reflect the performance of a coupon-bearing security with a maturity equal to the term of the swap less the term of the rate to which the variable payments are tied. For example, a 10-year swap tied to six-month LIBOR may perform akin to a 10-year term security, depending on how close one is to the next variable-rate reset date.

If one seeks to terminate a swap agreement prematurely, presumably with one's dealer, this implies either a profit or loss and a concluding receipt or payment of monies represented by the updated difference in the present values. As such, non-par swap transactions are often used prematurely to terminate a previous swap transaction, whether the original transaction was concluded at par or otherwise.

In any event, the initial pricing of a par swap reduces to this question: What fixed rate will cause the two streams of future income to balance? Essentially, that is the rate represented when one references the International Swap and Derivatives Association (ISDA) benchmark rates associated with par swaps of any particular term.

Credit Risk Considerations

Credit risk is implied in a swap insofar as the two counterparties are obligated periodically to swap monies, often for a considerable term into the future. But because there is no exchange of the principal or nominal amount up front, and because those payments are typically netted so that only the difference between the fixed- and variable-rate payment is actually exchanged, credit risks are reduced relative to a typical debt obligation. In other words, what is at risk in the event of a default on a swap agreement is the difference between the original cost of the swap and the current cost of a swap with a term equal to the remaining term of the original, i.e., the replacement cost.

The practice of netting is a significant convenience in this process. As the swap market developed and matured from the early 1980s, swap dealers found that they were frequently conducting business with the same counterparties. This led to the accumulation of large books of outstanding swaps.

Rather than administer each one of these swap transactions separately, these dealers' back offices wrote contracts that permitted them to consolidate all outstanding swaps, netting all payments between the dealer and a particular counterparty. A default in any one swap agreement would give the aggrieved counterparty the option to cancel all outstanding swaps. Eventually ISDA developed and made available standardized master agreements and netting agreements that are in near universal use in the OTC trading community.

Of course, swap dealers, many of which are banks and are therefore accustomed to assessing credit risks, can identify a poor credit counterparty, so they may attempt to manage credit risk through the imposition of collateral requirements. These collateral requirements may be administered in a manner not dissimilar from the way in which futures margins are administered, although mark-to-market adjustments would likely be required less frequently than daily.

Utility of Interest Rate Swaps

Interest rate swaps have been actively used by a wide variety of financial institutions including pension funds, mutual funds, insurance companies, banks, corporations (both domestic and abroad), and government entities. Swaps have been used to manage risk exposures, to reduce the cost of funding or increase the return on an investment, and for speculative purposes.

Interest rate swaps are used because they convey important financial benefits. Broadly speaking, these transactions convey value because they allow market participants to (1) exploit situations where they have a comparative advantage, (2) exploit information advantages or asymmetries; and (3) avoid prepayment "penalties" implicit in the structure of many debt instruments.

The theory of comparative advantage suggests that various fixed-income market participants may enjoy the ability to borrow or lend at advantageous terms in particular markets. A swap provides the means to convey those benefits from one counterparty to the other, in return perhaps for a similar favor.

Consider, for example, the possibility that credit spreads, or the difference in loan rates paid by less creditworthy borrowers versus more creditworthy borrowers, may be steeper with regard to fixed-rate as opposed to floating-rate loans, and they may rise as a function of the loan's term. Thus, a company with a relatively low credit rating may seek to borrow in the credit markets at a floating rate where the company has a comparative advantage but hedge the risk of rising rates by entering a swap transaction as the fixed-rate payer.

Some critics have sought to punch holes in the theory of comparative advantage. In particular, such critics suggest that arbitrage activity in the capital markets may serve to do away with such comparative advantages, detracting thereby from the usefulness of swap transactions. Although there is some validity in this criticism, it is not clear that capital markets are completely efficient in this sense or that the theory of comparative advantage does not at least partially explain the utility of swaps.

A second explanation for the utility of swap transactions may be identified as informational advantages. An example of such informational advantages might be found in a situation where a firm had information not generally available suggesting that its credit rating may deteriorate. As such, a firm may seek to fund its activities with floating-rate debt but hedge the risk of rising funding costs by entering a swap transaction as the fixed-rate payer. Or, a firm may enter into the same transaction simply because it anticipates rising short-term rates in the future.

A third explanation for the popularity of swaps might be found by examining the structure of most fixed-rate debt obligations. Often, fixed-rate debt is issued with a callable provision. A corporation may, for example, issue a note that is callable at par at the discretion of the corporation. This provision protects the borrower against the possibility that rates will fall and the borrower will be saddled with high-rate debt for an extended period of time. But such protection comes at a cost. In particular, the borrower will offer somewhat elevated rates to attract interest in such an obligation than would otherwise be the case.

By contrast, there is no such prepayment penalty or premium associated with a swap transaction. A swap may, however, be terminated prior to maturity by payment of the current value of the swap, reflecting the present value of the differential payment stream reflected in the original versus the current swap rate.

GROWING UP TOGETHER

The introduction of Eurodollar futures was (more or less) synchronized with the introduction of the interest rate swap (IRS) market.[10] Since the early 1980s, Eurodollar futures, the IRS market, and a generation of financial managers have grown up together—to the point where we simply cannot divorce Eurodollar futures (or more specifically Eurodollar strips and "prepackaged" strips in the form of packs and bundles) from the IRS market. See Exhibit 6.15.

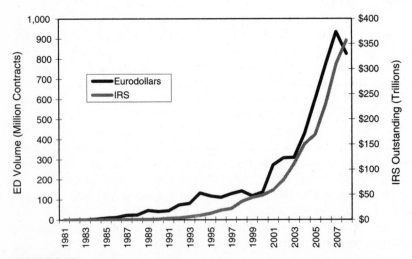

EXHIBIT 6.15 ED Futures and IRS Growth

And Eurodollar futures have thrived with the growth and development of the IRS marketplace. The tables provided earlier depict the growth in notional value outstanding (open interest) and turnover (volume) in OTC and exchange-traded interest rate derivatives. Although the notional value outstanding in Eurodollar futures is dwarfed by the OTC markets, futures nonetheless take the lead in terms of volume.

Asset and Liability versus Swap Applications

Actually, initial institutional use of Eurodollar futures was limited largely to asset and liability (A&L) management and general speculative applications. These A&L applications involved hedging asset/liability mismatches within an institution's book. In the early 1980s, most banks and savings institutions applied the "risk bucket" approach where assets and liabilities were categorized and compared by maturity. Risk was incumbent wherever a mismatch between assets and liabilities within any particular bucket was identified. Eurodollar futures became handy tools to balance these mismatches and allay risks.

In subsequent years, with the advent of cheap computing power and generalized appreciation for more sophisticated financial modeling techniques including duration, vector autoregression (VAR), and so on, the risk bucket method of analysis was largely supplanted. Nonetheless, Eurodollar futures remain an important tool for A&L managers.

Interest Rate Swap Applications

Swap traders routinely reference Eurodollar pricing as a proxy for future variable rates and in turn use swap rates as a benchmark for other fixed-income securities.

> *The interest-rate swap curve—a series of rates across the maturity spectrum, which are pegged to the Chicago Mercantile Exchange's Eurodollar futures—has established itself as an emerging alternative to Treasurys as a benchmark for measuring the relative value of other debt classes. . . . The swap curve is becoming "more influential, and we're certainly interested in swap movement as it relates to the corporates, asset-backed and mortgage-backed securities that we own," said Tom Marthaler, a portfolio manager with Chicago Trust Co.[11]*

Consider that OTC derivatives are marketed actively by derivatives dealers to insurance companies, hedge funds, and corporations. These

EXHIBIT 6.16   10-Year Credit Spread

dealers in turn manage their books with the use of futures. In other words, OTC derivatives dealers effectively package or repackage risks for sale to their customers that are managed with the use of Eurodollar futures.

To summarize, the lion's share of institutional customer use of Eurodollar futures is swap related, some is A&L, and some is spec and sundry applications. Although we cannot confidently provide proportions, we might broadly speculate that 50% of institutional customer usage of Eurodollars is swap related, another 25% is A&L related, and the remaining 25% is general speculation and sundry applications.

Deteriorating Credit Quality

Credit quality in the institutional marketplace, certainly among OTC derivatives dealers, has generally deteriorated over the past decade or two. It is no longer possible to find AAA-rated institutions; even AAs are few and far between. Accordingly, credit had become paramount in the minds of many traders. And, of course, swap traders had been scrambling to lock themselves in as floating-rate payers. This is reflected in the recent spike in the spread between swap and Treasury rates as depicted in the nearby graphic of the 10-year swap versus Treasury spread.

Many have turned to the burgeoning credit default swap (CDS) market as a way to manage credit risks. However, a non-negligible proportion of exercised CDSs culminate in a court battle. This underscores the utility of multilateral clearing services such as those offered by CME Group. Note that a multilateral clearing facility secured by collateral has the effect of homogenizing stellar and poor credits alike. See Exhibit 6.16.

PRICING RELATIONSHIP

The value of an IRS may readily be determined by recognizing that the instrument's structure may be broken down into a series of cash flows. As discussed earlier, the fair value of an IRS may be determined as the fixed rate that assures that the present value of all cash flows between the fixed-rate payer and the floating-rate payer are equally balanced. Interestingly, the forward rates implied in Eurodollar futures prices may be used as a significant reference in these calculations.

Let us consider the structure of a so-called International Monetary Market (IMM)-dated IRS. An IMM swap is constructed such that the periodic rate fixing dates fall on the maturation dates for Eurodollar futures contracts and the floating rate is pegged to current three-month LIBOR rates. Further, let us apply an "actual/360" day count convention for both legs of the swap transaction.

There are other swap structures that we may discuss, but this is a particularly convenient structure to price and hedge and will serve as the basis for our illustrations. Let the principal or notional value of the transaction be denoted as "P," the present value of $1 received i days ("$d_i$") in the future is denoted as "PV_i," the variable or floating three-month LIBOR rates expected to be prevailing d_i days in the future are denoted at "R_i."

We are of course interested in pricing the swap as the fixed rate R_{fixed} that assures that the net present value of all fixed-rate payments equates to the net present value of all floating-rate payments, i.e., the non-par payment of the swap equals zero (NPP = $0.00). The generalized solution to our problem may be found as follows.

$$\sum_{I=1}^{n} PV_i \, (R_{fixed}/4)P = \sum_{I=1}^{n} PV_i \, R_i \, (d_i/360)P$$

Solving for R_{fixed} . . .

$$R_{fixed} = 4 \sum_{I=1}^{n} PV_i \, R_i(d_i/360) / \sum_{I=1}^{n} PV_i$$

Conveniently, the specific numbers we require to solve for R_{fixed} will largely be supplied by reference to the Eurodollar futures market. As discussed earlier, Eurodollar futures prices represent the implied forward rate (i.e., the market's expectation regarding rates that may prevail in the future). Thus, we may reference those rates as an indication for the three-month LIBOR rates at which the variable payments may be established, or R_i. The appropriate present value discount factor (PV_i) may likewise be found in the Eurodollar futures market structure. Specifically, the reciprocal of the compounded value of a Eurodollar futures strip is comparable to the value of a zero coupon bond and may be used as the discounting factor PV_i, or the present value of $1 received i days in the future.

Example Let's find the value of a two-year IMM-dated swap with a $10 million notional or principal amount. Assume that the swap settles on December 13, 2004, and Eurodollar futures are priced as shown in Exhibit 6.17.

Applying our formula as just shown, we may calculate the appropriate fixed rate on our two-year swap as 3.6686%. This implies a quarterly fixed payment of $91,715.00 [= $10,000,000 (0.036686 ÷ 4)].

$$
\begin{aligned}
R_{fixed} = {} & 4\,[(0.9925)(0.030)(91/360) + (0.9843)(0.033)(91/360) \\
& + (0.9750)(0.035)(98/360) + (0.9662)(0.036)(91/360) \\
& + (0.9579)(0.037)(84/360) + (0.9481)(0.038)(98/360) \\
& + (0.9388)(0.039)(91/360) + (0.9295)(0.040)(91/360)] \\
& \div [0.9925 + 0.9843 + 0.9750 + 0.9662 + 0.9579 \\
& + 0.9481 + 0.9388 + 0.9295] \\
= {} & 3.6692\%
\end{aligned}
$$

We can confirm that the fixed and floating payments are balanced such that the present value of the fixed-rate payments equals the present value of the floating-rate payments ($PV_{fixed} = PV_{floating} = \$705,490.93$). This is another way of saying that the non-par payment equals zero (NPP = $0). See Exhibit 6.18.

EXHIBIT 6.17 Calculating Discount Factors

Instrument	Expiration Date	Day Span	Futures Price	Yield (R)	Compound Value	Discount Factor (PV)
EDZ4	12/13/04	91	97.0000	3.0000	1.0076	0.9925
EDH5	3/14/05	91	96.7000	3.3000	1.0160	0.9843
EDM5	6/13/05	98	96.5000	3.5000	1.0257	0.9750
EDU5	9/19/05	91	96.4000	3.6000	1.0350	0.9662
EDZ5	12/19/05	84	96.3000	3.7000	1.0439	0.9579
EDH6	3/13/06	98	96.2000	3.8000	1.0547	0.9481
EDM6	6/19/06	91	96.1000	3.9000	1.0651	0.9388
EDU6	9/18/06	91	96.0000	4.0000	1.0759	0.9295

EXHIBIT 6.18 Balancing Present Values

Payment Date	Fixed Payments	Discount Factor (PV)	PV of Fixed Payments	Floating Payments	Discount Factor (PV)	PV of Floating Payments
3/14/05	$91,715.00	0.9925	$91,024.73	$75,833.33	0.9925	$75,262.59
6/13/05	$91,715.00	0.9843	$90,271.72	$83,416.67	0.9843	$82,103.97
9/12/05	$91,715.00	0.9750	$89,419.75	$95,277.78	0.9750	$92,893.36
12/19/05	$91,715.00	0.9662	$88,613.36	$91,000.00	0.9662	$87,922.54
3/20/06	$91,715.00	0.9579	$87,854.88	$86,333.33	0.9579	$82,699.72
6/12/06	$91,715.00	0.9481	$86,955.38	$103,444.44	0.9481	$98,076.11
9/18/06	$91,715.00	0.9388	$86,106.51	$98,583.33	0.9388	$92,554.83
12/18/06	$91,715.00	0.9295	$85,244.59	$101,111.11	0.9295	$93,977.81
			$705,490.93			$705,490.93

HEDGING TECHNIQUES

As demonstrated earlier, there is a close pricing relationship between Eurodollar futures and interest rate swaps. Thus, it is intuitive that Eurodollar futures provide an ideal hedging vehicle for swaps.

Matching Changing Values

The essence of hedging is to match the risk exposure associated with an instrument such as an IRS or some other asset or liability with an equal and opposite risk exposure in a derivative marketplace such as futures (i.e., to balance any change (Δ) in the value of the IRS with an opposite change in the value of the futures position).

$$\Delta \text{ Value of Hedged Instrument} \approx \Delta \text{ Value of Futures Position}$$

But we can't manage what we can't measure. And a common way of measuring the change in the value of fixed-income items including short-term assets, liabilities, and swaps is by reference to the basis point value (BPV) associated with the instrument. BPV measures the monetary change in the value of an instrument in response to a one basis point (0.01%) change in yield. The BPV associated with a money market instrument such as a LIBOR investment may be found by reference to the face value (FV) and the term in days (d) of the exposure as follows:

$$BPV = FV \times (d/360) \times 0.01\%$$

Example　Find the BPV of a $1 million face-value 90-day exposure as represented by one Eurodollar futures contract. By plugging these values into our equation as shown, we may calculate the BPV associated with one futures contract ($BPV_{futures}$). We find that $BPV_{futures} = \$25.00$.

$$
\begin{aligned}
BPV_{futures} &= \$1,000,000 \times (90/360) \times 0.01\% \\
&= \$25.00
\end{aligned}
$$

Let us substitute the concept of BPV for the somewhat more abstract concept of change in value ($BPV \approx \Delta$ Value). By comparing the BPV of a short-term exposure that is the subject of our hedge with the $25 BPV associated with one Eurodollar futures contract, we may identify the appropriate number of futures that may be used to offset that exposure. This is known as the hedge ratio (HR).

$$HR = \Delta \text{ Value of Hedged Instrument} \div \Delta \text{ Value of One Futures Contract}$$
$$= BPV_{hedged} \div BPV_{futures}$$
$$= [FV \times (d/360) \times 0.01\%] \div \$25$$

Example Find the appropriate number of Eurodollar futures contracts needed to match the risks associated with a $25 million, 180-day LIBOR investment. Note that the BPV of the investment equals $1,250 [= $25,000,000 × (180/360) × 0.01%]. This implies that one should sell 50 Eurodollar futures contracts to match the BPVs of each position and thereby hedge the risk of loss associated with rising rates and falling values.

$$HR = [\$25,000,000 \times (180/360) \times 0.01\%] \div \$25$$
$$= 50 \text{ contracts}$$

Exhibit 6.19 provides a summary of the BPVs associated with securities ranging in terms of maturity and face value. We have highlighted the BPV associated with our $1 million face-value 90-day futures contract. This table underscores the fact that the risk associated with a short-term security will change over time, specifically by declining as we move forward in time and the remaining days until contract maturity wind down. This, of course, has an impact on the HR, which likewise diminishes over time for any particular short-term instrument.

EXHIBIT 6.19 Basis Point Values of Money Market Instruments

	Face Value						
Days	$500,000	$1 MM	$5 MM	$10 MM	$20 MM	$50 MM	$100 MM
1	$0.14	$0.28	$1.39	$2.78	$5.56	$13.89	$27.78
7	$0.97	$1.94	$9.72	$19.44	$38.89	$97.22	$194.44
15	$2.08	$4.17	$20.83	$41.67	$83.33	$208.33	$416.67
30	$4.17	$8.33	$41.67	$83.33	$166.67	$416.67	$833.33
60	$8.33	$16.67	$83.33	$166.67	$333.33	$833.33	$1,666.67
90	$12.50	$25.00	$125.00	$250.00	$500.00	$1,250.00	$2,500.00
120	$16.67	$33.33	$166.67	$333.33	$666.67	$1,666.67	$3,333.33
150	$20.83	$41.67	$208.33	$416.67	$833.33	$2,083.33	$4,166.67
180	$25.00	$50.00	$250.00	$500.00	$1,000.00	$2,500.00	$5,000.00
270	$37.50	$75.00	$375.00	$750.00	$1,500.00	$3,750.00	$7,500.00
360	$50.00	$100.00	$500.00	$1,000.00	$2,000.00	$5,000.00	$10,000.00

Hedging the Cash Flows of a Swap

The risks associated with an IRS position and the hedging strategy appropriate to offset those risks are summarized here. The fixed-rate payer ("long the swap") is exposed to the risk of falling rates and rising prices. A long Eurodollar futures position may generally address those risks. The floating-rate payer ("short the swap") is exposed to the risk of rising rates and falling prices. A short Eurodollar futures position may generally be applied to address these risks.

Of course, we need to delve deeper into the mathematics of the swap to identify how to apply the appropriate hedging strategy. Fortunately, the identical underlying logic that was applied in the prior section may likewise be applied to the concept of hedging an IRS instrument by dissecting the swap into its various component cash flows. To identify the effective BPV associated with an IRS, or more specifically, the BPV associated with each individual cash flow of the swap, we might apply the same mathematics as shown in our earlier example where we priced a swap. Notice Exhibit 6.20.

Again, the non-par payment (NPP) associated with a swap, essentially the price or value of the swap, may be found by comparing the present value of all the fixed cash flows (PV_{fixed}) to the present value of all the variable cash flows ($PV_{floating}$) or $NPP = PV_{floating} - PV_{fixed}$. Of course, this value will change as a function of fluctuations in the variable interest rate. By assuming that rates rise by 1 basis point at all points along the yield curve, we may calculate the NPP or price of the swap.

Example Find the BPV associated with a the two-year IMM-dated swap with a $10 million notional or principal amount as discussed in the prior section. To do this, we might compare the original value of the swap where NPP = $0 to the value of the swap calculated assuming that yields advance by a uniform 1 basis point (0.01%).

Note in Exhibit 6.21 that the present value of the fixed payments declines slightly ($PV_{fixed} = \$705,411.42$) whereas the present value of the floating payments advances slightly ($PV_{floating} = \$707,120.16$). The

EXHIBIT 6.20 Hedging Interest Rate Swap Positions

Position	Risk	Hedge
Fixed rate payer ("long the swap")	Rates fall and prices rise	Buy Eurodollar futures
Floating rate payer ("short the swap")	Rates rise and prices fall	Sell Eurodollar futures

EXHIBIT 6.21 Present Values of Fixed and Floating Payments

Payment Date	Fixed Payments	Discount Factor (PV)	PV of Fixed Payments	Floating Payments	Discount Factor (PV)	PV of Floating Payments
3/14/05	$91,715.00	0.9924	$91,022.45	$75,833.33[a]	0.9924	$75,260.70
6/13/05	$91,715.00	0.9842	$90,267.19	$83,669.44	0.9842	$82,348.64
9/12/05	$91,715.00	0.9749	$89,412.85	$95,550.00	0.9749	$93,151.58
12/19/05	$91,715.00	0.9661	$88,604.31	$91,252.78	0.9661	$88,157.76
3/20/06	$91,715.00	0.9578	$87,843.88	$86,566.67	0.9578	$82,912.84
6/12/06	$91,715.00	0.9480	$86,942.14	$103,716.67	0.9480	$98,319.23
9/18/06	$91,715.00	0.9387	$86,091.25	$98,836.11	0.9387	$92,775.70
12/18/06	$91,715.00	0.9293	$85,227.35	$101,363.89	0.9293	$94,193.70
			$705,411.42			$707,120.16

[a]Note that the first payment in March 2005 is fixed as of the date on which the transaction is originally concluded. Thus, there is no change in the floating payment and no real risk associated with the first set of cash flows.

difference in these values or the non-par payment has declined such that $NPP = PV_{floating} - PV_{fixed} = \$707,120.16 - \$705,411.42 = \$1,708.75$.

The result shown in our example suggests that the seller of the swap (the floating-rate payer) might hedge against the risk of rising interest rates by selling 68 Eurodollar futures contracts ($\approx BPV_{hedged} \div BPV_{futures} = \$1,708.75/\$25$). However, this analysis begs the question, sell futures in which contract month? This leads us to the possibility that we can do better yet by selling futures matched to each dated cash flow along the yield curve.

Example   Find the BPV of each of the eight cash flows associated with the two-year IMM-dated swap with a $10 million notional or principal, as in Exhibit 6.22. To do so, we might match up the present values of the fixed and floating payments on each date. For example, per the original pricing, the present value of a June 2005 fixed-rate payment exceeds the present value of the fixed-rate payment by $8,167.75. But if rates were to increase by 1 basis point, this decreases to $7,918.55, resulting in a profit to the fixed-rate payer (who is "long the swap") and a loss to the floating-rate payer ("short the swap") of $249.20. The floating-rate payer might have hedged that very specific risk by selling 10 or 11 of the June 2005 futures contracts.

Or the floating-rate payer might completely hedge his or her exposure to the risk or rising rates by selling 10 of the June 2005 futures, selling 11 of the September 2005 futures, selling 10 of the December 2005 futures, selling 9 of the March 2006 futures, selling 10 of the June 2006 futures, selling 9 of the September 2006 futures and selling 9 of the December 2006 futures. This hedge position includes a total of 68 short Eurodollar futures contracts.

Note that as each of the successive quarterly payment dates goes by, the Eurodollar futures contracts expiring on that date are settled in cash and are stricken from the books. Thus, this "strip" of futures is self liquidating and winds itself down as the risks associated with swap reset dates go by. Note that one might conveniently place and manage this hedge with the use of packs or bundles on the CME.

The risks associated with a rise in rates to the swap seller may be attributed to one major and one relatively minor factor. The major effect on the floating-rate payer is the simple fact that as rates rise, the amount payable to the fixed-rate payer increases.

Rising rates also exert an effect, albeit a minor effect, on the discount factors applied to a swap's cash flows. As rates rise, future value factors rise, but discount factors decline, and more so in the deferred payment periods than in the early payment periods, reducing the present value of all cash flows. This represents a detriment to the floating-rate payer in the early payment periods where the fixed-rate payments exceed the floating-rate

EXHIBIT 6.22 Calculating Hedge Ratios

Payment Date	Original Scenario			Rates + 1 Basis Point				
	(1) PV of Fixed Payments	(2) PV of Floating Payments	(3) Float-Fixed (2)-(1)	(4) PV of Fixed Payments	(5) PV of Floating Payments	(6) Float-Fixed (5)-(4)	(7) Diff in Cash Flows (6)-(3)	(8) Hedge Ratio (7)÷$25
3/14/05	$91,024.73	$75,262.59	($15,762.14)	$91,022.45	$75,260.70	($15,761.75)	$0.40	0.0
6/13/05	$90,271.72	$82,103.97	($8,167.75)	$90,267.19	$82,348.64	($7,918.55)	$249.20	10.0
9/12/05	$89,419.75	$92,893.36	$3,473.61	$89,412.85	$93,151.58	$3,738.73	$265.12	10.6
12/19/05	$88,613.36	$87,922.54	($690.82)	$88,604.31	$88,157.76	($446.55)	$244.27	9.8
3/20/06	$87,854.88	$82,699.72	($5,155.17)	$87,843.88	$82,912.84	($4,931.04)	$224.13	9.0
6/12/06	$86,955.38	$98,076.11	$11,120.73	$86,942.14	$98,319.23	$11,377.09	$256.36	10.3
9/18/06	$86,106.51	$92,554.83	$6,448.32	$86,091.25	$92,775.70	$6,684.46	$236.13	9.4
12/18/06	$85,244.59	$93,977.81	$8,733.22	$85,227.35	$94,193.70	$8,966.35	$233.13	9.3
	$705,490.93	$705,490.93	$0.00	$705,411.42	$707,120.16	$1,708.75	$1,708.75	68.3

payments. But it represents an advantage to the floating-rate payer in the deferred payment periods where the floating-rate payments tend to exceed the fixed-rate payments.

Convexity

Unfortunately, our hedger's tasks are not necessarily complete once the hedge is placed. Whereas the BPV associated with Eurodollar futures contracts remain static such that $BPV_f = \$25.00$, the BPV associated with the swap that is the subject of our hedge (BPV_{hedged}) is dynamic. This is illustrated in the table where we have calculated the NPP or price of the swap given a range of movement in interest rates. Note that the span or change in the value of the swap is in fact *not* constant.

This table illustrates the concept of *convexity*, a property embedded in the pricing structure of many interest rate instruments including interest rate swaps. And, as we may see from our illustration, it implies that the swap becomes more sensitive to changing rates as rates fall and less sensitive to changing rates as rates rise. This further implies that *more* futures contracts are needed to maintain a balanced hedge in a falling rate environment, whereas *fewer* futures contracts are needed in a rising rate environment. That is, HRs increase as rates fall and decrease when rates rise.

This phenomenon may tend to benefit the floating-rate payer who is short the swap and hedged with a short futures position. Specifically, this implies that she may become "overhedged" when rates rise. She is losing value in the swap at a decelerating pace but more than offsetting it with her short futures hedge. She becomes "underhedged" when rates fall—the swap is gaining value at an accelerating pace—the futures hedge position is losing value at a constant pace relative to the general change in rates.

By contrast, this phenomenon may work to the detriment of the fixed- rate payer who is long the swap and hedged with a long futures position. As rates rise, the swap is gaining value at a decelerating pace while the value of the long futures position is declining at a constant pace relative to the general change in interest rates: He is becoming "overhedged." As rates decline, the swap is losing value at an accelerating rate while the value of the short futures position is advancing at a constant pace relative to the general change in interest rates: He is becoming "underhedged."

Convexity is a relatively subtle effect but potentially quite significant when the size of one's positions becomes large. Thus, hedgers frequently attempt to manage the size of the futures hedge position on a dynamic basis in response to realized and anticipated market trends.

	NPP		Δ
−25 BPs	($42,858.34)		
		}	$8,593.19
−20 BPs	($34,265.15)		
		}	$8,582.41
−15 BPs	($25,682.73)		
		}	$8,571.65
−10 BPs	($17,111.08)		
		}	$8,560.91
−5 BPs	($8,550.17)		
		}	$8,550.17
Unchanged	$0.00		
		}	$8,539.45
+5 BPs	$8,539.45		
		}	$8,528.75
+10 BPs	$17,068.20		
		}	$8,518.05
+15 BPs	$25,586.25		
		}	$8,507.37
+20 BPs	$34,093.62		
		}	$8,496.71
+25 BPs	$42,590.33		

CONCLUSION

Eurodollar futures are extraordinarily versatile financial tools serving myriad applications. They may be used for the simple purpose of gaining exposure to possible trends in the level of STIRs. They may be utilized for purposes of taking a position on the possible shape of the yield curve. They may even be used as one leg of a spread intended to capitalize on changing credit conditions.

Eurodollar futures are likewise very useful in a variety of hedging applications. Perhaps the single most important patrons of Eurodollar futures include interest rate swap dealers. In particular, Eurodollar futures provide an excellent vehicle per which to price and hedge interest rate swaps, so much so that these two markets have grown over the years on a strikingly parallel path.

Because of this extreme versatility, we often characterize Eurodollar futures as fundamental building blocks in the STIR market.

TECHNICAL APPENDIX: COMPLICATIONS AND SHORTCUTS FOR PRICING AND HEDGING SWAPS

For expositional clarity, some practical aspects of pricing and hedging interest rate swaps are suppressed in the preceding text. Although covering all relevant details is impossible, we nonetheless intend to highlight some important complications that arise in practice and outline some shortcuts for addressing those issues.

Pricing by Anticipated Cash Flow versus Back-to-Back Notes

We illustrated the pricing of an interest rate swap, that is, determining the fixed coupon rate of the swap, by considering the anticipated *net* cash flow of the swap and setting the net present value of the cash flow to zero using the Eurodollar curve for discounting purposes. Although this is a perfectly legitimate way of pricing swaps, the method suffers from poor flexibility. This deficiency becomes very evident as the complexity of the structure of the swap grows (e.g., different basis, different day count convention, different payment frequency, etc.).

An elegant alternative for the pricing exists by recognizing the nature of swaps as back-to-back notes. That is, the "receive-fix" party in the swap is simultaneously long a fixed coupon note and short a floating coupon note with the same notional amount. Thus, at the inception of the swap, the net present value of the two notes must be equal because no cash changes hands. Further, the floating coupon note with the coupon set at the current market interest rate, (e.g., three-month LIBOR), must possess a net present value equaling the face value. Thus, the fixed coupon rate is nothing more than the current market coupon rate for a bullet note issue with maturity coinciding with the tenure of the swap. As such, we have reduced the problem to a very manageable one, even when more complexities are piled onto the swap structure.

A further benefit for using the back-to-back notes approach will be very evident when we discuss hedging interest rate swaps using Eurodollar futures. With a back-to-back notes structure, the hedges for the fixed and floating coupon notes are determined separately. Netting the hedges will give us the correct hedging strategy for the swap. We will demonstrate with an illustration in a later section.

Interpolating Eurodollar Curve

For simplicity, examples of swaps in this section are deliberately chosen to have a start date[12] coinciding with a particular Eurodollar futures contract. This situation occurs once every three months. For the rest of the days, one would inevitably need to account for the discrepancy. In this appendix, we illustrate a method based on log-linear interpolation of the discount factors. There are various advantages in interpolation based on discount factors:

1. Discount factors have a physical interpretation: It is, in fact, the price of a zero coupon note with a face value of one dollar. For example, assuming three-month LIBOR equal to 2.50%, and a count of 90 days for the three-month period, the corresponding discount factor is simply $1/[1 + 2.5\% \times (90/360)] = 0.993789$. Indeed, a three-month zero-coupon note with face value of $1 is worth exactly $0.993789. Discount factors and zero coupon prices are equivalent concepts.

2. Discount factors (zero coupon prices) are well behaved. As a function of time, a discount factor will always be between one and zero and decrease with time/maturity, starting with a value of one at the current value date.[13] That is, the discount factor for a payment three months from now will always be greater than that for a payment three months and two days from now.

Given discount factors associated with any two days, the (forward) rate between the two days can be easily determined. This has been illustrated in the article already.

Given the prices of all the traded instruments (e.g., Eurodollar futures of various expirations, cash LIBOR deposits, etc.), only so many points on the discount factor curve can be determined unambiguously. For the intervening points on the curve, some estimation or interpolation is required. Given the well-behaved nature of the curve (i.e., always between zero and one and is decreasing), there are many possible choices of interpolation techniques, among them linear and log-linear interpolation.

We choose log-linear interpolation for the following reasons: (1) it preserves the convex nature[14] of the discount factor curve, and (2) it provides a tractable hedging calculation with a tidy day-count-based hedging formula for non-IMM-dated swaps. Having mentioned these considerations, however, you are free to choose any curve interpolation method. With the advances in the capabilities of the computers, a closed-form hedging formula is not a necessity.

More precisely, suppose we know the discount factors (zero-coupon prices) associated with the dates March 16, 2005, and June 15, 2005. We denote these discount factors as $ZCP_{3/16/05}$ and $ZCP_{6/15/05}$, respectively. These two dates are 91 (calendar) days apart. Also, denote the natural logarithmic function by *ln*. Suppose we want to estimate the discount factor (zero-coupon price) associated with April 12, 2005, denoted by $ZCP_{4/12/05}$, via log-linear interpolation. Given that there are 27 and 64 days between April 12, 2005, and March 16, 2005, and between April 12, 2005, and

June 15, 2005, respectively, we have the following:

$$ln\,ZCP_{4/12/05} = (6/15/05 - 4/12/05)/91 \times ln\,ZCP_{3/16/05}$$
$$+ (4/12/05 - 3/16/05)/91 \times ln\,ZCP_{6/15/05}$$

OR

$$ln\,ZCP_{4/12/05} = (64/91) \times ln\,ZCP_{3/16/05} + (27/91) \times ln\,ZCP_{6/15/05}$$

With the interpolation scheme in place, we can trace out the discount factor/zero-coupon curve fairly easily provided that we have all the values associated with all the Eurodollar futures. We demonstrate this technique with the following example:

Example On January 10, 2005, the first upcoming quarterly Eurodollar futures contract is the March 2005 contract. This contract expires on March 14, 2005, and settles to the three-month LIBOR rate determined on that day, with a value date of March 16, 2005. The next quarterly Eurodollar contract expires on June 13, 2005, settles to the three-month LIBOR with a value date of June 15, 2005.

For simplicity, we assume that the three-month LIBOR rate with a value date of March 16, 2005, covers the period between March 16, 2005, and June 15, 2005. Therefore, if we have the discount factor associated with March 16, 2005, and the March 2005 Eurodollar futures price, we will be able immediately to determine the discount factor for June 15, 2005.

The period from the current value date (January 12, 2005, in this example) leading to the value date of the leading Eurodollar futures contract is known as the *stub*. The discount factor for the stub can be derived using the spot LIBOR deposit rates. Notice Exhibit 6.23.

EXHIBIT 6.23 Calculating ZCP Values

	Start Date	End Date	Day Count	Rate	ZCP	*ln* ZCP
LIBOR: 1W	1/12/05	1/19/05	7	2.32875	0.99955	(0.00045)
LIBOR: 1M	1/12/05	2/14/05	33	2.44	0.99777	(0.00223)
LIBOR: 2M	1/12/05	3/14/05	61	2.53	0.99573	(0.00428)
LIBOR: 3M	1/12/05	4/12/05	90	2.62	0.99349	(0.00653)
Stub	1/12/05	3/16/05	63	2.5388	0.99558	(0.00443)

The first row in the preceding table shows the spot 1-Week LIBOR deposit rate to be 2.32875%. Thus, the discount factor associated with January 19, 2005, or the end date of the 1-week deposit, is determined by $1/[1 + 2.32875\% \times (7/360)] \approx 0.99955$. Similarly, other cash deposit rates provide the discount factors associated with their respective end dates in rows 2 to 4.

The last row in the table shows the stub period. The natural logarithm of $ZCP_{3/16/05}$ is first determined by linear interpolation between March 14, 2005, and April 12, 2005. $ZCP_{3/16/05}$ is then determined by applying the exponential function to the interpolated natural log of $ZCP_{3/16/05}$. Finally, the equivalent interest rate of 2.5388% is determined by varifying that $1/[1 + 2.5388\% \times (63/360)] = 0.99558$. (i.e., $ZCP_{3/16/05}$).

With the discount factor associated with the stub period determined, we turn to the rest of the Eurodollar curve. Again, we illustrate by a continuation of the example.

Example The following table shows the first eight quarterly Eurodollar futures contracts (EDH5 – EDZ6) and the respective periods for which the interest rates underlying the futures contracts cover. The start, end dates, and the day counts are in columns 2 to 4. Column 6 shows the prices of the futures contract. Based on the futures prices, the implied future interest rates (i.e., 100 – futures price) are shown in column 5. Column 7 shows the zero-coupon prices (discount factors) associated with the respective "end dates." Although we do not need the *ln* ZCP here, we show it in Exhibit 6.24 for the sake of completeness.

To illustrate how the ZCPs are determined, we look at the row corresponding to EDH5. The start date for the period is March 16, 2005. The ZCP associated with the period January 12, 2005, to March 16, 2005, has already been determined on the row immediately above it (i.e., the stub.) As such, the ZCP associated with the June 15, 2005, end date is simply:

$$ZCP_{6/15/05} = ZCP_{3/16/05} \times 1/(1 + 2.96\% \times (91/360))$$
$$= 0.995577 \times 1/(1 + 2.96\% \times (91/360)$$
$$= 0.988183$$

The rest of the ZCPs are determined using this bootstrapping procedure. With these ZCPs serving as anchors to the curve, we can estimate the ZCP for any day via the previously described log-linear interpolation method or any other interpolation method.

Determining Fixed Coupon Rate

Suppose we would like to determine the current fixed coupon rate for a two-year interest rate swap with a quarterly reset/interest payment schedule.

EXHIBIT 6.24 Calculating ZCP Values

	Start Date	End Date	Day Count	Implied Rate	Futures Price	ZCP	*ln* ZCP
STUB	1/12/05	3/16/05	63	2.538774		0.995577	(0.00443)
EDH5	3/16/05	6/15/05	91	2.960	97.040	0.988183	(0.01189)
EDM5	6/15/05	9/21/05	98	3.280	96.720	0.979438	(0.02078)
EDU5	9/21/05	12/21/05	91	3.535	96.465	0.970763	(0.02967)
EDZ5	12/21/05	3/15/06	84	3.735	96.265	0.962376	(0.03835)
EDH6	3/15/06	6/21/06	98	3.855	96.145	0.952382	(0.04879)
EDM6	6/21/06	9/20/06	91	3.945	96.055	0.942978	(0.05871)
EDU6	9/20/06	12/20/06	91	4.025	95.975	0.933481	(0.06883)
EDZ6	12/20/06	3/21/07	91	4.110	95.890	0.923882	(0.07917)

EXHIBIT 6.25 Calculating ZCP Values

Coupon Dates	Day Count	ZCP	*ln* ZCP
4/12/05	90	0.99349	(0.00653)
7/12/05	91	0.98577	(0.01434)
10/12/05	92	0.97743	(0.02283)
1/12/06	92	0.96856	(0.03195)
4/12/06	90	0.95951	(0.04133)
7/12/06	91	0.95020	(0.05108)
10/12/06	92	0.94067	(0.06116)
1/12/07	92	0.93105	(0.07145)

Example Consider the trade date of January 10, 2005, and value date of January 12, 2005. We have already sketched out the discount factor/zero-coupon curve. Based on log-linear interpolation, we have arrived at the following ZCP values for the cash flow dates associated with the two-year swap as shown in Exhibit 6.25.

Column 1 shows the dates on which interest payments are exchanged. Column 2 shows the actual day counts for the corresponding coupon periods. Columns 3 and 4 show the ZCP and *ln* ZCP values based on the log-linear interpolation.

As we have explained earlier, determining the fixed coupon rate for the swap is fairly straightforward. It is nothing more than the coupon value that would have the bullet two-year note trading at par:

$$1 = \sum_{\text{all coupon periods}} C \times \frac{DC_i}{360} \times ZCP_i + 1 \times ZCP_{1/12/2007},$$

Where C denotes the fixed coupon rate, DC_i denotes the day count associated with each interest payment period, and ZCP_i denotes the zero coupon price for each interest payment date. Only C is unknown in this equation. With the data in the preceding table, it is straightforward to determine that C equals 3.53%.

Hedging Swaps Using Eurodollar Futures

As we mentioned earlier, viewing an interest rate swap as back-to-back notes affords a particularly easy hedge calculation. The hedges for the fixed coupon note and the floating coupon notes can be calculated separately and netted for the entire interest rate swap.

The logic of the hedge calculation is pretty straightforward, equating the basis point value of the fixed (or floating) rate note vis-à-vis the particular futures rate to the corresponding futures basis point value. Suppose the notional value of our two-year swap is $100 million. Because the swap is priced at the market, the fixed coupon note carries a net present value equal to the notional value of $100 million. By nudging the EDH5 price up by 1 basis point, the net present value of the note should increase by a certain amount.

This calculation is accomplished by recalculating the ZCP curve based on the new set of Eurodollar prices. This change in the net present value is the basis point value of the fixed coupon note vis-à-vis the EDH5 futures contract. Because each Eurodollar contract carries a basis point value of $25, dividing the basis point value of the note by $25 yields the correct hedge. Repeating this calculation with the other futures expiration (and stub rate) will yield the full set of futures hedges for the fixed coupon note.

The foregoing does not rely on the specifics of the curve interpolation schemes and thus is applicable to any interpolation scheme at one's disposal. If we choose to use the log-linear interpolation scheme as described in the previous sections, we can derive a simple hedging formula. Specifically, the Eurodollar prices affect the net present value of the note through the ZCPs. Thus, we can calculate the total effect of a particular Eurodollar price change by summing the changes in corresponding to each ZCP (interest payment date.) By applying the logic of calculus, we have the relationships shown in Exhibit 6.26.

The first table shows basis point value of each cash flow for the fixed coupon note vis-à-vis each Eurodollar futures contract (and the stub rate).[15] Column 1 shows the date of the cash flow. Column 2 shows the amount of the cash flow, including both the coupon as well as the face value on the last cash flow date. Column 3 shows the ZCP corresponding to each date. The rest of the columns show the basis point value vis-à-vis each Eurodollar contract for each cash flow. They are calculated by multiplying the corresponding cash flow to the changes in the ZCP per basis point as determined by the formulas in the preceding table.

Summing up the basis point value across all the cash flow vis-à-vis each futures expiration provides a total basis point value. Dividing the basis point value by the basis point value per Eurodollar contract ($25) provides the correct number of contracts for delta-hedging the fixed coupon note.

The same exercise is applied to the floating-rate note. Observe that at the next reset, the floating-rate note will carry the then-market rate. Thus, the market value of the note will be at par at the next reset. Thus, the total "cash flow" of the note at the next reset is the sum of the coupon payment (the current three-month LIBOR, which has been determined already) plus face value.

EXHIBIT 6.26 Calculating Changes in ZCP

If the period for which the ED futures contract covers falls	Changes in the ZCP per basis point change in the futures price
Before the date corresponding to the ZCP, e.g., EDH5 (covering 3/16/05–6/15/05) vs. $ZCP_{7/12/05}$	$-ZCP \times \dfrac{DC_i/36000}{1 + R_i \times DC_i/36000} \times 0.01$
Contains the date corresponding to the ZCP, e.g. EDM5 (covering 6/15/05–9/21/05) vs. $ZCP_{7/12/05}$	$-ZCP \times \dfrac{DC_i/36000}{1 + R_i \times DC_i/36000} \times 0.01 \times Frac$
Beyond date corresponding to the ZCP, *e.g.* EDU5 (covering 9/21/05–12/21/05) vs. $ZCP_{7/12/05}$	0

DC_i = Number of days in the period covered by the interest rate underlying the futures contract, for example, $DC = 91$ for EDH5 (3/16/05 – 6/15/05).

R_i = Future interest rate implied by the Eurodollar contract (i.e., 100 – futures price).

Frac = Fraction of the period covered by the futures relevant to the date corresponding to the ZCP. For example, in the case of EDM5 versus $ZCP_{7/12/05}$, Frac is the ratio of the day count of the period 6/15/05 to 7/12/05 versus the day count of the period 6/15/05 to 9/21/05 (i.e., 27/98 = 0.27551).

The second table illustrates the corresponding hedge calculations for the floating rate note. Netting the fixed coupon note against the floating-rate note provides the net futures hedge for the interest rate swap.

Before moving on to the next topic, you can observe that although we have a self-contained formula for the calculation of basis point value, it is not necessarily easy to implement. Given the possibility of the "perturbation" method and the enormous computing power at the user's disposal, one may elect to abandon these formulas in favor of the more computationally intensive method.

Executing the Hedge

Inspecting the hedging strategy prescribed by the hedge calculation, one can readily conclude that the tailored hedge may be very hard to execute in practice. It involves different number of contracts for each contract month. Simultaneous order execution on eight quarterly contracts is very hard to manage, with the markets in different contract months possessing different liquidity. Various strategies are available for simplifying the execution of the hedging strategy. See Exhibits 6.27 and 6.28. Depending on your confidence of the correlation among various contract months, you may prefer to use a particular method.

EXHIBIT 6.27 Eurodollar Futures Hedges for Fixed Coupon Note

Coupon Dates	Cash Flow ($ million)	ZCP	STUB	EDH5	EDM5	EDU5	EDZ5	EDH6	EDM6	EDU6	EDZ6
4/12/2005	0.8826	0.99349	$15	$7							
7/12/2005	0.8924	0.98577	$15	$22	$7						
10/12/2005	0.9022	0.97743	$15	$22	$24	$5					
1/12/2006	0.9022	0.96856	$15	$22	$24	$22	$5				
4/12/2006	0.8826	0.95951	$15	$21	$23	$21	$20	$7			
7/12/2006	0.8924	0.95020	$15	$21	$23	$21	$20	$23	$5		
10/12/2006	0.9022	0.94067	$15	$21	$23	$21	$20	$23	$21	$5	
1/12/2007	100.9022	0.93105	$1,637	$2,357	$2,535	$2,354	$2,173	$2,531	$2,351	$2,351	$594
Total Basis Point Value			$1,742	$2,494	$2,657	$2,444	$2,237	$2,583	$2,377	$2,356	$594
Hedge (no. of contracts) = Total Basis Point Value/$25			69.69	99.74	106.29	97.78	89.49	103.32	95.10	94.24	23.76
Rounded to nearest contracts			70	100	106	98	89	103	95	94	24

EXHIBIT 6.28 Netting Fixed vs. Floating Rate Coupon Notes to Derive Net Hedge for Swap

Coupon Dates	Cash Flow	ZCP	STUB	EDH5	EDM5	EDU5	EDZ5	EDH6	EDM6	EDU6	EDZ6
4/12/2005	100.6550	0.99349	$1,742	$744							
Floating Rate Note Hedge = Total Basis Point Value/$25			69.69	29.78	—	—	—	—	—	—	—
Fixed Coupon Note Hedges			69.69	99.74	106.29	97.78	89.49	103.32	95.10	94.24	23.76
Net Interest Rate Swap Hedges			0.00	69.96	106.29	97.78	89.49	103.32	95.10	94.24	23.76
Rounded to nearest contract			0	70	106	98	89	103	95	94	24

- *Stack All Contracts in Same Expiration:* Stacking the contracts in a single month provides the easiest order execution, at the expense of the likely degradation of hedging performance due to the less than perfect correlation among different expirations. Generally speaking, more temporally separated expirations exhibit lower degree of correlations. When stacking the hedges, one usually chooses a contract month with good market liquidity that also occupies the middle ground temporally to maximize the correlation among contracts.
- *Bundles:* In this example, one can choose to use a two-year bundle, essentially an equally weighted strip of Eurodollar contracts as opposed to an unequally weighted strip prescribed by the hedge calculation. Bundles, especially up on five years, are easy to execute. Although the liquidity in bundles could be lower than a single contract month, it is usually compensated by having better hedging performance by more closely matching the ideal weighted strip by stacking.
- *Combination colored packs:* If one is willing to further sacrifice ease of execution for better tracking performance, a combination of white pack (one-year bundle) and various deferred packs can be used. In the example, a combination of a one-year bundle and a red pack hedge better approximates the unequally weighted strip. See Exhibit 6.29.

Hedging Performance

Once again, we illustrate how well the hedges work by a continuation of the ongoing example. Suppose two weeks have passed and interest rates

EXHIBIT 6.29 Stacking a Hedge

Contract Month	Weighted Strip	Stacking	White + Red Pack	2-year Bundle
EDH5	70		91	85
EDM5	106		91	85
EDU5	98		91	85
EDZ5	89	679	91	85
EDH6	103		79	85
EDM6	95		79	85
EDU6	94		79	85
EDZ6	24		79	85
Total no. of contracts	679	679	680	680

EXHIBIT 6.30 Calculating Discount Factors

| Coupon Dates | Cash Flow ($mm) | | | ZCP |
	Receive Fix	Pay Float	
4/12/05	0.883	(100.655)	0.99426
7/12/05	0.892		0.98610
10/12/05	0.902		0.97739
1/12/06	0.902		0.96815
4/12/06	0.883		0.95875
7/12/06	0.892		0.94910
10/12/06	0.902		0.93922
1/12/07	100.902		0.92925
NPV ($mm)	99.82	(100.077)	
Swap P/L ($)	(260,308)		
ED P/L ($)	254,625		
Net ($)	(5,683)		

P/L of the hedge swap position after 15-bip increase in interest rates.

have risen in general. To simulate the effects, we adopt a hypothetical increase of 15 basis points in 1-week, 1-, 2-, and 3-month LIBOR, as well as 15-basis point declines in Eurodollar futures *prices* for all eight relevant expirations.

To assess the effectiveness of the futures hedge, one needs to recalibrate the discount factors based on the new interest rates and futures prices. Column 4 of Exhibit 6.30 shows the discount factors (zero coupon prices) for the relevant value date of January 26, 2005.

The unrealized gain/loss of the swap that has been seasoned by two weeks can once again be determined by considering the net present value of hypothetical fixed- and floating-rate notes. Suppose we have engaged in the swap to "receive fixed," the hedge would have been to short the relevant strip of Eurodollar futures. The interest rate increase will hit the fixed coupon side harder than the floating coupon side; therefore the swap as a whole would have an unrealized loss.

Given our assumption of a uniform 15 basis point decline in Eurodollar futures prices, there is little to choose among the four hedging strategies aside from a one contract difference in hedge ratios due to rounding. We would have gained $25 \times 15 = \$375$ per contract from the futures position, contributing a total futures gain equal to $\$375 \times 679 = \$254,625$ (or $\$375 \times 680 = \$255,000$). Netting the futures gains from the unrealized loss from the swap, the net hedged loss is $5,683, a very small fraction of the unrealized loss in the swap position.

EXHIBIT 6.31 Calculating Discount Factors

	Cash Flow ($mm)		
Coupon Dates	Receive Fix	Pay Float	ZCP
4/12/05	0.883	(100.655)	0.99489
7/12/05	0.892		0.98747
10/12/05	0.902		0.97949
1/12/06	0.902		0.97097
4/12/06	0.883		0.96225
7/12/06	0.892		0.95328
10/12/06	0.902		0.94407
1/12/07	100.902		0.93477
NPV ($mm)	100.390	(100.140)	
Swap P/L ($)	250,207		
ED P/L ($)	(254,625)		
Net ($)	(4,418)		

P/L of the hedge swap position after 15-bip decrease in interest rates.

Repeating the exercise per a uniform 15 basis point decline in interest rates (a 15 basis point increase in all futures prices), the results may be illustrated below. The results are similar: The swap position shows an unrealized gain of $250,207 and, after the offsetting loss of $254,625 in the futures position, the net P/L is a loss of $4,418, a very small fraction of the swap P/L in magnitude.

This hedging strategy works to the extent that the bulk of the interest rate risk associated with the swap position has been eliminated. As discussed in Exhibit 6.31, there are rounding errors in the hedge ratios as well as mismatches of "convexity" between the swap and the Eurodollar futures contract, the latter of which does not exhibit any convexity. Thus, even the most accurately constructed Eurodollar futures hedges could not completely eliminate portfolio risks.

In the foregoing discussion, much has been simplified in the interest of expositional clarity. In particular, the issue of convexity adjustments has been suppressed. Due to the effect of convexity mismatches, it is well known that the interest rates implied by Eurodollar futures are higher than the equivalent forward contracts. As such, swap prices implied by futures prices would be biased in absence of an adjustment for the convexity mismatches. The magnitude of the bias, not surprisingly, increases significantly with the tenure of the swap. It is advisable to address this issue for any practical implementation of a pricing or hedging strategy.

NOTES

1. The IMM, or International Monetary Market, was established as a division of the CME many years ago. The distinction is seldom made today because CME operates as a unified entity, but references to IMM persist today.
2. Please note that although these observations are generally true, they may not be absolutely true. Consider that as early as 2005, the Fed had been pushing STIRs higher while longer-term rates remained relatively stable. As such, the yield curve was in the process of tightening while many analysts still expected the Fed to continue tightening.
3. Note that for purposes of this exposition, we have simplified our analysis a bit. For example, we have not discussed the fact that compounding of interest implies that one will have more principal to invest upon each rollover date.
4. Note that T-note futures are quoted in 32nds or fractions of a 32nd. One thirty-second of the $200,000 face-value unit deliverable against a two-year T-note futures contract equals $62.50. Quotation devices may show a quote of 106% of par plus 16 thirty-seconds as 106-16. If you add 1/64th, the quote may appear as 106-16+ or as 106-165. Add a 1/128th, and the quote may appear as 106-162. Add 3/128ths and the quote may appear as 106-167. In the two latter cases, the trailing "5" is typically truncated.
5. Commercially available quotation devices such as the Bloomberg system may be referenced as a convenient way of identifying the CTD security at any given time, as well as its BPV.
6. Note that the two-year T-note futures contract is based on a $200,000 face-value delivery unit.
7. In this example, we are using September two-year T-notes. However, we are applying the hedge ratio calculated based on a June 2004 two-year T-note delivery. We have taken this liberty in keeping with the spirit of our "quick and dirty" approach and in light of the fact that the 2.25% T-note of April 2006 was in fact not eligible for delivery against the September 2004 futures contract as it would have slipped out of the 1.75 to 2-year maturity delivery window. In fact, a different security ultimately was cheapest to deliver against the September contract but that was unknown in April. Note that the BPV of the T-note futures contract can and will change in response to shifts in the CTD, possibly necessitating an adjustment of the hedge ratio.
8. The hedge ratio has changed to the extent that the CTD has shifted. In July 2004, the 2.75% note of June 2006 was CTD. It had a BPV = $38.10 per $200,000 face value and a CF = 0.9467 for delivery into September 2005 futures (noting that it was not ultimately deliverable against December 2005 futures). Thus, the $BPV_{t\text{-note}} = \$40.24$ suggests a HR = 2.48 or 25 two-year T-note futures for every pack (= $100 ÷ $40.24).
9. If these present values were not made to balance, the swap would advantage a particular counterparty over another, presumably creating an arbitrage opportunity. And, in an efficient market, we presume that such arbitrage opportunities are quickly and decisively exploited with the result that such opportunity disappears.

10. Noting that the seminal swap transaction occurred in 1981 when IBM and the World Bank agreed to swap fixed for floating-rate debt payments.
11. "Interest-Rate Swap Curve Is Emerging as Alternative to Treasury's Benchmark," *Wall Street Journal*, February 22, 2000.
12. More precisely, the value date of the swap coincides with the value date of a three-month LIBOR Eurodollar deposit corresponding to a Eurodollar futures contract.
13. LIBOR/Swap market observes a T + 2 arrangement. Thus, the discount factor associated with the current value date is 1.
14. Because the discount factor curve originates with a value one is decreasing but never falls to zero, the curve is necessarily convex if the curve is continuous. That is, the value of the curve at any point is lower than corresponding point on the chord linking points to either side of the point. Choosing log-linear interpolation preserves this feature.
15. Generally speaking, assuming the stub rate movement correlates well with the leading Eurodollar contract, one may choose to stack the hedges for the stub on the leading quarterly Eurodollar contract.

CHAPTER 7

Understanding U.S. Treasury Futures

John W. Labuszewski
Frederick Sturm

This chapter provides an overview of the fundamentals of trading U.S. Treasury bond and note futures.[1] We assume only a cursory knowledge of coupon-bearing Treasury securities, providing a grounding in cash Treasury markets, some detail regarding the features of the U.S. Treasury futures contracts, and a discussion of risk-management applications with U.S. Treasury futures.

COUPON-BEARING TREASURY SECURITIES

U.S. Treasury bonds and notes represent a loan to the U.S. government. Bondholders are creditors rather than equity holders or shareholders. The U.S. government agrees to repay the face, or principal or par amount, of the security at maturity, plus coupon interest at semiannual intervals.[2] Treasury securities are often considered "riskless" investments given that the "full faith and credit" of the U.S. government backs these securities.

The security buyer can either hold the bond or note until maturity, at which time the face value becomes due, or the bond or note may be sold in the secondary markets prior to maturity. In the latter case, the investor recovers the market value of the bond or note, which may be more or less than its face value, depending on prevailing yields. In the meantime, the investor receives semiannual coupon payments every six months.

For example, assume that you purchase $1 million face value of the 4 1/2% note maturing in May 2017. This security pays half its stated coupon, or 2.25% of par on each six-month anniversary of its issue. Thus, you receive $22,500 semiannually. Upon maturity in May 2017, the $1 million face value is repaid and the note expires.

Price/Yield Relationship

A key factor governing the performance of bonds in the market is the relationship of price and yield movement. In general, as yields increase, bond prices decline; as yields decline, bond prices rise. In a rising rate environment, bondholders witness market value erosion; in a declining rate environment, the market value of their bonds increases.

>   IF Yields Rise ↑ THEN Prices Fall ↓
>   IF Yields Fall ↓ THEN Prices Rise ↑

This inverse relationship may be understood when one looks at the marketplace as a true auction. Assume an investor purchases a 10-year note with a 6% coupon when yields are at 6%. Thus, the investor pays 100% of the face, or par, value of the security. Subsequently, rates rise to 7%. The investor decides to sell the original bond with the 6% yield, but no one will pay par because notes are now quoted at 7%. Now he must sell the bond at a discount to par in order to move the bond. That is, rising rates are accompanied by declining prices.

Falling rates produce the reverse situation. If rates fall to 5%, our investment yields more than market rates. Now the seller can offer it at a premium to par. Thus, declining rates are accompanied by rising prices. Should one hold the note until maturity, one would receive the par, or face, value. In the meantime, of course, one receives semiannual coupon payments.

Quotation Practices

Unlike money market instruments (including bills and Eurodollars) that are quoted on a yield basis in the cash market, coupon-bearing securities are frequently quoted in percent of par to the nearest 1/32nd of 1% of par. For example, one may quote a bond or note at 106-20 (see Exhibit 7.1). This equates to a value of 106% of par plus 20/32nds percent of par. The decimal equivalent of this value is 106.625. Thus, a $1 million face-value security might be priced at $1,066,250. If the price increases by 1/32nd of 1% from 106-20 to 106-21, this equates to a price increase of $312.50 (per million-dollar face value).

But often these securities, particularly those of shorter maturities, are quoted in finer increments than 1/32nd. For example, one may quote the

EXHIBIT 7.1 Quotation Practices

Cash Market Quote	Means	Decimal Equivalent	Futures Market Quote
106-20	106-20/32nds	106.625% of par	106-20
106-202	106-20/32nds + 1/128th	106.6328125% of par	106-202
106-20+	106-20/32nds + 1/64th	106.640625% of par	106-205
106-206	106-20/32nds + 3/128ths	106.6484375% of par	106-207

security to the nearest 1/64th. If the value of our bond or note in the preceding example were to rally from 106-20/32nds by $1/64^{th}$ of one percent, it may be quoted at 106-20+. The trailing "+" may be read as $+1/64^{th}$ of one percent.

Or you may quote to the nearest $1/128^{th}$ of one percent. If, for example, our bond were to rally from 106-20/32nds by 1/128th, it might be quoted on a cash screen as 106-202. The trailing "2" may be read as +2/8ths of 1/32nd, or +1/128th. If the security rallies from 106-20/32nds by 3/128ths, it may be quoted as 106-206. The trailing "6" may be read as +6/8ths of 1/32nd, or +3/128ths.

Futures quotation practices are similar but not entirely identical. A quote of 106-202 is the same no matter whether you are looking at a cash or a futures quote. It means 106% of par plus 20/32nds plus 1/128th. But in the case of the cash markets, that trailing "2" means 2/8ths of 1/32nd = 1/128th. In the case of the futures markets, that trailing "2" represents the truncated value of 0.25 × 1/32nd or 1/128th. A quote of 106-20+ in the cash markets is equivalent to 106-205 in the futures market. That trailing "5" represents 0.5 × 1/32nd or 1/64th. A quote of 106-206 in the cash markets is equivalent to 106-207 in the futures market. In the case of futures markets, the trailing "7" represents the truncated value of 0.75 × 1/32nd = 3/128ths.

The normal commercial "round-lot" in the cash markets is $1 million face value. Anything less might be considered an "odd-lot." However, you can purchase Treasuries in units as small as $1,000 face value. Of course, a dealer's inclination to quote competitive prices may dissipate as size diminishes. Ultra Treasury bond, Thirty-year Treasury bond, Ten-year Treasury note, and five-year Treasury note futures, however, are traded in units of $100,000 face value. Three-year and two-year Treasury note futures are traded in units of $200,000 face value.

Accrued Interest and Settlement Practices

In addition to paying the (negotiated) price of the coupon-bearing security, the buyer also typically compensates the seller for any interest accrued between the last semiannual coupon payment date and the settlement date of the security.

For example, assume it is Wednesday, August 25, 2007. You purchase $1 million face value of the 4.5 percent security of May 2017 (a 10-year note) for a price of 96-27 ($968,437.50) to yield 4.90%, for settlement on Thursday, August 26, 2007. In addition to the price of the security, you must further compensate the seller for interest of $8,804.35 accrued during the 72 days between May 15, 2007, (the issue date) and the settlement date of August 26. This interest is calculated relative to the 184 days between the issue date of May 15 and the next coupon payment date of November 15, or $8,804.35 [=(72/184) × ($45,000/2)]. The total purchase price is $977,241.85, as seen in Exhibit 7.2.

Typically, securities are transferred through the Fed wire system from the bank account of the seller to that of the buyer versus cash payment. That transaction is concluded on the settlement date, which is generally one business day after the transaction date.

Unlike the futures market where trades are settled on the same day they are transacted, it is customary to settle a cash transaction on the business day subsequent to the actual transaction. Thus, if you purchase the security on a Thursday, you typically settle it on Friday. If purchased on a Friday, settlement generally occurs on the following Monday. Sometimes, however, a "skip date" settlement is specified. For example, one may purchase a security on Monday for a skip date settlement on Wednesday, or a "skip-skip date" settlement on Thursday, or a "skip-skip-skip date" settlement on the Friday, and so on. Theoretically, there is no effective limitation on the number of days over which one may defer settlement. Thus, these cash securities may effectively be traded as a forward.

Treasury Auction Cycle

Treasury securities are auctioned on a regular basis by the U.S. Treasury, which accepts bids on a yield basis from security dealers. A certain amount of each auction is set aside, to be placed on a noncompetitive basis at the

EXHIBIT 7.2 Total Purchase Price

Price of note	$968,437.50
Accrued interest	$8,804.35
Total	$977,241.85

average yield filled. Prior to the actual issuance of specific Treasuries, they may be bought or sold on a "WI," or "When Issued," basis. Prior to the actual auction, WIs, bids, and offers are quoted as a yield. As a security is auctioned and the results announced, the Treasury affixes a particular coupon to bonds and notes that is near prevailing yields. At that time, coupon-bearing bonds and notes may be quoted on a price rather than a yield basis, although bills continue to be quoted and traded on a yield basis. Trades previously concluded on a yield basis are settled against a price on the actual issue date of the security, calculated per standard price-yield formulas.

Security dealers purchase these securities and subsequently market them to their customers including pension funds, insurance companies, banks, corporations, and retail investors. The most recently issued securities of a particular maturity are referred to as "on-the-run" securities. On-the-runs are typically the most liquid and actively traded of Treasury securities, and therefore they are often referenced as pricing benchmarks. Previously issued securities are known as "seasoned" or "off-the-run" securities and tend to be less liquid.

The Treasury currently issues 4-week, 13-week, 26-week, and 52-week T-bills; 2-year, 3-year, 5-year, 7-year, and 10-year T-notes; and 30-year T-bonds on a regular schedule. In the past, the Treasury had also issued securities with a 4-year and 20-year maturity. Further, the Treasury may issue very short-term cash management bills along with 5-year, 10-year, and 30-year Treasury Inflation-Protected Securities, or TIPS, as seen in Exhibit 7.3. The

EXHIBIT 7.3 U.S. Treasury Auction Schedule

	Maturity	Auctioned
Cash management bills	Usually 1–7 days	As needed
Treasury bills	4-, 13-, and 26-Week	Weekly
	52-Week	4 Weeks
Treasury notes	2-, 3-, 5-, and 7-Year	Monthly
	10-Year	February, May, August, and November with reopenings other eight months
Treasury bonds	30-Year	February, May, August, and November with reopenings other eight months
Treasury Inflation-Protected Securities (TIPS)	5-Year	April and October
	10-Year and 30-Year	January, April, July, and October

Treasury adjusts both the maturity structure and scheduling of Treasury security auctions to reflect their current financing requirements

The "Run"

If you were to ask a cash dealer for a quotation of "the run," he or she would quote yields associated with the on-the-run securities from the current on-the-run 4-week bill to the 30-year bond. The most recently issued 30-year bond is sometimes referred to as the "long bond" because it is the longest maturity Treasury available.

The most recently issued security of any tenor may be referred to as the "new" security. Thus, the second most recently issued security of a particular original tenor may be referred to as the "old" security, the third most recently issued security is the "old-old" security, the fourth most recently issued security is the "old-old-old" security. See Exhibit 7.4.

As of July 25, 2007, the most recently issued 10-year note may be identified as the 4 1/2% note maturing on May 15, 2017; the old note is the 4 5/8% note of February 15, 2017; the old-old note is the 4 5/8% of November 15, 2016; the old-old-old note is the 4 7/8% of August 15, 2016. Beyond that, one is expected to identify the security of interest by coupon and maturity. See Exhibit 7.5. For example, the "5 1/8s of '16" refers to the note with a coupon of 5 1/8% maturing on May 15, 2016. As of this writing there were not any "WI" or "when issued" 10-year notes. Note, however, that WIs typically trade on a yield basis in anticipation of the establishment of the coupon subsequent to the original auction.

One important provision is whether or not the security is subject to call. A "callable" security is one where the issuer has the option of redeeming the bond at a stated price, usually 100% of par, prior to maturity. If a bond is callable, it may be identified by its coupon, call, and maturity date. That is,

EXHIBIT 7.4   Quoting 'the Run' (as of July 25, 2007)

	Coupon	Maturity	Bid	Ask	Chg	Ask Yield
1-week bill	Na	8/02/07	4.93%	4.92%	+0.01	5.01%
3-month bill	Na	10/25/07	4.84%	4.83%	−0.03	4.97%
6-month bill	Na	1/24/08	4.85%	4.84%	−0.01	5.04%
2-year note	4 7/8%	6/30/09	100-07+	100-08	—	4.74%
3-year note	4 1/2%	5/15/10	99-12+	99-13	+00+	4.73%
5-year note	4 7/8%	6/30/12	100-13	100-13+	+01+	4.78%
10-year note	4 1/2%	5/15/17	96-27	96-28	+01	4.90%
30-year bond	4 3/4%	2/15/37	95-22+	99-23+	+00+	5.03%

EXHIBIT 7.5 Most Recently Issued 10-Year T-Notes (as of July 25, 2007)

	Coupon	Maturity	Price	Yield
WI				
On-the-run note	4 1/2%	5/15/17	96-26	4.913%
Old note	4 5/8%	2/15/17	97-24	4.923%
Old-old note	4 5/8%	11/15/16	97-26+	4.918%
Old-old-old note	4 7/8%	8/15/16	99-20	4.926%
	4 1/2%	2/15/16	97-06	4.906%
	5 1/8%	5/15/16	101-13+	4.923%
	4 1/2%	11/15/15	97-09	4.902%
	4 1/4%	8/15/15	95-24	4.894%
	4 1/8%	5/15/15	95-02+	4.890%
	4%	2/15/15	94-15	4.884%
	4 1/4%	11/15/14	96-09	4.860%
	4 1/4%	8/15/14	99-14	4.836%
	4 3/4%	5/15/14	99-16	4.836%

the 11 3/4% of November 2009-14 is callable beginning in November 2009 and matures in 2014. Prior to the February 1986 auction, the U.S. Treasury typically issued 30-year bonds with a 25-year call feature. That practice was discontinued at that time, however, as the Treasury instituted its "Separate Trading of Registered Interest and Principal on Securities," or STRIPS, program with respect to all newly issued 10-year notes and 30-year bonds.[3]

Quoting "the Roll" and the Importance of Liquidity

Clearly, traders who frequently buy and sell are interested in maintaining positions in the most liquid securities possible. As such, they tend to prefer on-the-run as opposed to off-the-run securities.

It is intuitive that on-the-runs offer superior liquidity when one considers the "life cycle" of Treasury securities. Treasuries are auctioned, largely to broker-dealers, who subsequently attempt to place the securities with their customers. Often these securities are purchased by investors who may hold the security until maturity. At some point, securities are "put away" in an investment portfolio until their maturity. Or they may become the subjects of a strip transaction per the STRIPS program.

In any event, as these securities find a home, supplies may become scarce. As a result, bid/offer spreads may widen and the security becomes somewhat illiquid. Liquidity is a valuable feature to many fixed income market participants. Thus, you may notice that the price of on-the-runs tends to be bid up, resulting in reduced yields, relative to other similar maturity securities. This relative increase in price tends to be most noticeable with respect to the 30-year bond, and is referred to as the liquidity premium.

Traders frequently quote a "roll" transaction where one sells the old security in favor of the new security. The "old note" in our preceding table was quoted at a yield of 4.923%; the "new note" was seen at 4.913%. Clearly, someone is willing to give up a basis point (0.01%) in yield for the privilege of holding the new note versus the old note. In other words, liquidity has some observable value. Dealers may quote a bid/offer spread in this transaction, offering the opportunity to sell the old note/buy the new note or buy the old note/sell the new note, in a single transaction.

Repo Financing

Leverage is a familiar concept to futures traders. Just as one may margin a futures position and thereby effectively leverage one's capital, the Treasury markets likewise permit traders to use "repo" financing agreements to leverage Treasury holdings. A repurchase agreement, repo or simply RP, represents a facile method by which one may borrow funds, typically on a very short-term basis, collateralized by Treasury securities. In a repo agreement, the lender wire-transfers same-day funds to the borrower; the borrower wire-transfers the Treasury security to the lender with the provision that the transactions are reversed at term with the lender wiring back the original principal plus interest.

The borrower is said to have executed a repurchase agreement; the lender is said to have executed a reverse repurchase agreement. Many banks and security dealers offer this service once the customer applies and passes a requisite credit check. The key to the transaction, however, is the safety provided the lender by virtue of the receipt of the (highly marketable) Treasury security. These repo transactions are typically done overnight but may be negotiated for a term of one week, two weeks, or one month. Overnight repo rates are typically quite low, in the vicinity of Fed Funds.

Any Treasury security may be considered "good" or "general" collateral. Sometimes when particular Treasuries are in short supply, dealers announce that the security is "on special" and offer below-market financing rates in an effort to attract borrowers.

TREASURY FUTURES DELIVERY PRACTICES

Although one might refer to Treasury bond futures as "30-year bond futures," that reference is a bit misleading. Treasury bond futures permit the delivery in satisfaction of a maturing contract of *any* U.S. Treasury security provided that it does not mature and is not callable for a period of at least 15 years from the date of delivery. It is likewise tempting to refer to U.S. Treasury bond futures as "6% bond contracts." This, too, may be somewhat misleading. T-bond futures are based *nominally* on a 6% coupon security. But in point of fact, the contract permits the delivery of *any* coupon security, again provided that it meets the maturity specification mentioned earlier. In other words, shorts are not necessarily required to deliver 6% coupon bonds and, of course, there may come a time when in fact there may be no eligible for delivery bonds carrying a 6% coupon!

Because of the rather broadly defined delivery specifications, a significant number of securities, ranging widely in terms of coupon and maturity, may be eligible for delivery. This applies with equal effect to 2-, 3-, 5-, and 10-year Treasury note and Ultra Treasury bond futures as well.

Conversion Factor Invoicing System

Securities with varying characteristics, such as coupon and maturity, of course are more or less valued by the investment community. High-coupon securities, for example, naturally command a greater price than comparable low-coupon securities.

These differences must be reflected in the futures contract. In particular, when a short makes delivery of securities in satisfaction of a maturing futures contract, the long will pay a specified invoice price to the short. As discussed earlier, the futures contract permits the delivery of a wide range of securities at the discretion of the short. That invoice value must be adjusted to reflect the specific pricing characteristics of the security that is tendered. Accordingly, Treasury futures use a "conversion factor" invoicing system to reflect the value of the security that is tendered by reference to the 6% futures contract standard (see Exhibit 7.6). In particular, the "Principal Invoice Amount" paid from long to short upon delivery may be identified as the Futures Settlement Price multiplied by the Conversion Factor (CF) multiplied by $1,000 (to reflect the $100,000 face value futures contract size).

$$\text{Principal Invoice Price} = \text{Futures Settlement} \times \text{Conversion Factor} \times \$1,000$$

Any interest accrued since the last semiannual interest payment date is added to the principal invoice amount to equal the "total invoice amount."

$$\text{Total Invoice Amount} = \text{Principal Invoice Amount} + \text{Accrued Interest}$$

EXHIBIT 7.6A Treasury Contracts Summary

	2-Year Note Futures	3-Year Note Futures	5-Year Note Futures	10-Year Note Futures
Contract size	$200,000 face-value U.S. Treasury notes		$100,000 face-value U.S. Treasury notes	
Delivery grade	T-notes with original maturity of not more than 5 years and 3 months and remaining maturity of not less than 1 year and 9 months from first day of delivery month but not more than 2 years from last day of delivery month	T-notes with original maturity of not more than 5 years and 3 months and a remaining maturity of not more than 3 years but not less than 2 years, 9 months from last day of delivery month	T-notes with original maturity of not more than 5 years and 3 months and remaining maturity of not less than 4 years and 2 months as of first day of delivery month.	T-notes maturing at least 6 and 1/2 years but not more than 10 years, from first day of delivery month.
Invoice price	Invoice price = settlement price × conversion factor (CF) plus accrued interest, CF = price to yield 6%			
Delivery method	Via Federal Reserve book-entry wire transfer			
Contract months	March quarterly cycle: March, June, September, December			
Trading hours	Open Auction: 7:20 AM to 2:00 PM, Monday to Friday; Electronic: 6:00 PM to 4:00 PM, Sunday to Friday (Central Times)			
Last trading and delivery day	Business day preceding last seven business days of month; last delivery day is last business day of delivery month			
Price quote	In percent of par to one-quarter of 1/32nd of 1% of par ($15.625 rounded up to nearest cent)		Quoted in percent of par to one-half of 1/32nd of 1% of par ($15.625 rounded up to nearest cent)	

EXHIBIT 7.6B Treasury Contracts Summary

	30-Year Bond Futures	Long-Term "Ultra" U.S. Treasury Bond Futures
Contract size	$100,000 face-value U.S. Treasury bonds	
Delivery grade	T-bonds not callable for 15 years from first day of delivery month; if callable, a minimum maturity of 15 years from first day of delivery month	T-bonds with a remaining term to maturity of at least 25 years.
Invoice price	Invoice price = settlement price × conversion factor (CF) plus accrued interest, CF = price to yield 6%	
Delivery method	Via Federal Reserve book-entry wire transfer	
Contract months	March quarterly cycle: March, June, September, December	
Trading hours	Open Auction: 7:20 AM to 2:00 PM, Monday to Friday; Electronic: 6:00 PM to 4:00 PM, Sunday to Friday (Central Times)	
Last trading and delivery day	Business day preceding last seven business days of month; last delivery day is last business day of delivery month	
Price quote	Quoted in percent of par to 1/32nd of 1% of par ($31.25)	

A conversion factor may be thought of as the price of the delivered security as if it were yielding 6%. Clearly, high-coupon securities tend to have high CFs and low-coupon securities tend to have low CFs. In particular, bonds with coupons less than the 6% contract standard have CFs that are less than 1.0; bonds with coupons greater than 6% have CFs greater than 1.0.

The conversion factor for delivery of the 4 3/4% Treasury note of 2014 versus September 2007 10-year Treasury note futures is 0.9335. This suggests that a 4 3/4% security is approximately valued at 93% as much as a 6% security. Assuming a futures price of 106-19, the principal invoice amount may be calculated as follows:

$$\text{Principal Invoice Amount} = 106\text{-}19 \ (106.59375) \times \$1,000 \times 0.9335$$
$$= \$99,505.27$$

The conversion factor for delivery of the 5 1/8% Treasury note of 2016 versus September 2007 10-year Treasury note futures is 0.9424. This suggests that a 5 1/8% security is approximately valued at 94% as much as a 6% security. Assuming a futures price of 106-19, the principal invoice amount may be calculated as follows:

$$\text{Principal Invoice Amount} = 106\text{-}19 \ (106.59375) \times \$1,000 \times 0.9424$$
$$= \$100,453.95$$

To arrive at the total invoice amount, one must further add any accrued interest from the last semiannual interest payment date through the Treasury futures delivery date to the principal invoice amount.

Cheapest-to-Deliver

The intent of the conversion factor invoicing system is to render equally economic the delivery of any eligible-for-delivery Treasury notes or bonds. Theoretically, the short that has the option of delivering any eligible security should be indifferent as to the selection. However, the CF system is imperfect in practice because we find that a particular security will tend to emerge as "cheapest-to-deliver" (CTD) after studying the relationship between cash security prices and principal invoice amounts.

On July 25, 2007, one might have been able to purchase the 4 3/4% -14 at 99-16 ($99,500.00 per $100,000 face value unit); at the time, the 5 1/8%-16 was valued at perhaps 101-13+ ($101,421.87 per $100,000 face value unit). Compare these cash values to the principal invoice amounts in Exhibit 7.7.

EXHIBIT 7.7 Return on Delivery

	4 3/4%-14	5 1/8%-16
Futures	106-19	106-19
× CF	0.9335	0.9424
× $1,000	$1,000	$1,000
= Invoice	$99,505.27	$100,453.95
− Cash	$99,500.00	$101,421.87
= Return	$5.27	($967.92)

Our analysis suggests that a slight gain of $5.27 may be associated with the delivery of the 4 3/4%-14 and a loss of $967.92 might be associated with the delivery of the 5 1/8%-16. One might conclude that the 4 3/4%-14 note is cheaper or more economic to deliver than the 5 1/8%-16. If one were to run this analysis for *all* eligible-for-delivery securities, one might identify *the* cheapest-to-deliver (CTD) security as the security with the lowest "gross" basis. It is important to identify the CTD security to the extent that Treasury futures tend to price or track or correlate most closely with the CTD. This has interesting implications from the standpoint of a "basis trader" or a hedger, as displayed in Exhibit 7.8.

EXHIBIT 7.8 10-Year T-Note Futures Basis Relationships (as of July 25, 2007)

Coupon	Maturity	Price	Yield	Sep-07 CF	Gross Basis	Dec-07 CF	Gross Basis
4 1/2%	5/15/17	96-26	4.913%	0.8926	53.3	0.8946	51.9
4 5/8%	2/15/17	97-24	4.923%	0.9034	46.5	0.9054	45.1
4 5/8%	11/15/16	97-26+	4.918%	0.9054	42.2	0.9074	40.8
4 7/8%	8/15/16	99-20	4.926%	0.9242	35.6	0.9259	35.3
5 1/8%	5/15/16	101-13+	4.923%	0.9424	31.0	0.9436	32.5
4 1/2%	2/15/16	97-06	4.906%	0.9034	28.5	0.9058	25.8
4 1/2%	11/15/15	97-09	4.902%	0.9058	23.3	0.9080	21.3
4 1/4%	8/15/15	95-24	4.894%	0.8927	19.0	0.8955	14.8
4 1/8%	5/15/15	95-02+	4.890%	0.8881	13.2	0.8910	8.6
4%	2/15/15	94-15	4.884%	0.8837	8.7	0.8870	2.8
4 1/4%	11/15/14	96-09	4.860%	0.9012	7.0	0.9040	2.9
4 1/4%	8/15/14	96-14	4.836%	0.9040	2.5	0.9069	−2.0
4 3/4%	5/15/14	99-16	4.836%	0.9335	−0.2		

September 2007 10-year T-note futures were valued at 106-19; December 2007 10-year T-note futures were valued at 106-13.

The Basis

Typically we expect to find a single security, or perhaps a handful of similar securities, emerge as CTD. This identification has important implications for basis traders who arbitrage cash and futures markets. Basis traders seek out arbitrage opportunities or situations where they might be able to capitalize on relatively small pricing discrepancies between cash securities and Treasury futures by buying "cheap" and selling "rich" items.

Arbitrageurs track these relationships by studying the "basis." The gross basis describes one relationship between cash and futures prices and may be defined as the cash price less the "adjusted futures price" where the adjusted futures price is equal to the futures price multiplied by the conversion factor. The net basis is defined as the gross basis minus "carry," where carry reflects the net income less payments associated with holding a Treasury note or bond through the Treasury futures delivery date. Both the gross basis and net basis may be expressed in 32nds. For example, 1 1/4 points might be shown as 40/32nds.

$$\text{Gross Basis} = \text{Cash Price} - \text{Adjusted Futures Price}$$
$$\text{Adjusted Futures Price} = \text{Futures Price} \times \text{Conversion Factor}$$
$$\text{Net Basis} = \text{Gross Basis} - \text{``Carry''}$$

The adjusted futures price is essentially equivalent to the principal invoice amount except that the adjusted futures price is typically expressed in percent of par, whereas the principal invoice amount may be expressed in dollars per $100,000 face-value unit. Earlier we studied principal invoice amounts less cash values, noting that the gross basis is analogous because it compares the cash price less the adjusted futures price.

As of July 25, 2007, a comparison of cash and adjusted futures prices ($\approx$ principal invoice amount) provides us with a quote for the gross basis associated with the 4 3/4%-14 and the 5 1/8%-16, as seen in Exhibit 7.9.

EXHIBIT 7.9 Calculating the Gross Basis

	4 3/4%-14	5 1/8%-16
Cash Price	99-16	101-13+
−Futures Price	106-19	106-19
×CF	0.9335	0.9424
(Adjusted Futures Price)	≈99-162	≈101-15+
=Gross Basis	≈−0.2/32nds	≈31/32nds
Return on Delivery	$5.26	($967.92)

The gross basis of $\approx -0.2/32$nds associated with the 4 3/4%-14 corresponds to a slight gain on delivery of $5.26 while the gross basis of $\approx 31/32$nds associated with the 5 1/8%-16 corresponds to a loss on delivery of $967.92. As a general rule, the security with the lowest gross basis, that is, the largest gain or smallest loss on delivery, may be considered CTD. Clearly, the 4 3/4%-14 is cheaper-to-deliver than the 5 1/8%-16. By examining the preceding table depicting the gross basis for all eligible-for-delivery securities, one may confirm that in fact the 4 3/4%-14 was *the* CTD, although there are quite a few securities, not coincidentally with similar coupons and maturities, which are near CTD. In fact, the entire battery of eligible for delivery securities features similar coupons and maturities.

Why Is One Issue Cheapest-to-Deliver?

If the conversion factor invoicing system were to perform flawlessly, all eligible-for-delivery securities would have a similar net basis and be equally economic to deliver. As suggested earlier, however, a single security or several similar securities tend to emerge as CTD. The CF invoicing system is imperfect because it is implicitly based on the assumption that all eligible for delivery securities have the same yield and that yield is 6%. There are any number of "cash market biases" that impact the yield of a Treasury security. Further mathematical biases in the CF calculation will tilt the field toward securities of particular coupons and maturities when yields are greater than or less than the 6% contract standard.

Cash market biases may be used as a catch-all phrase for anything that impacts the relative yields of bonds. Perhaps *supply-demand considerations* is an equally appropriate term. A key concept is that shorts will elect to deliver securities that are somehow inferior to others that they would prefer to retain in their portfolios. Some specific reasons why securities, even those with similar coupons and maturities, may carry somewhat different yields include the shape of the yield curve, reinvestment risks, liquidity preferences, tax considerations, and so on.

For example, in an upwardly sloping or "normal" yield curve environment, longer-term securities may carry somewhat higher yields (lower prices) than comparable shorter-term securities, and, the lower the price (relatively speaking), the greater the likelihood that a short will wish to dump the security through the delivery process. This factor may not exert a tremendous impact on deliveries unless the yield curve shows some reasonable slope to it either upwardly sloped or negatively sloped (inverted). In fact, we observe that the yield curve has historically been rather flat the past 15 years and, therefore, this factor has had little impact on the delivery of bonds into the 30-year T-bond contract. In our preceding example, however, we see there is an approximate 8 basis point difference between the yield on the most recently issued 10-year note and the shortest maturity security that is still eligible for delivery. Thus, the shallow slope of the Treasury yield curve in the 7-year to 10-year region is in fact providing some bias toward the delivery of short maturity securities versus the 10-year T-note contract.

Low or generally falling yields may prove problematic to the security investor to the extent that a significant component of one's return is attributable to reinvestment income. Coupon payments, once received, will be reinvested, presumably at prevailing short-term rates. When reinvestment risks become noticeable, investors may prefer lower-coupon securities, generating less coupon income and reduced reinvestment risk, over high-coupon securities. Thus, those high-coupon securities may become CTD.

As discussed earlier, recently issued, or "on-the-run," securities generally offer enhanced liquidity relative to "off-the-run" securities. Consequently, on-the-run bond prices may be bid up, their yields pushed down, and may, therefore, be unlikely candidates to become CTD. Likewise, tax considerations have the potential to tilt deliveries toward high-coupon as opposed to low-coupon securities.

Perhaps more important than these cash market factors, there are observable biases associated with the mathematics of the conversion factor system, or *conversion factor biases*. For example, it is clear that long duration, that is, low-coupon, long-maturity securities, will become CTD when yields are greater than the 6% contract standard. When yields fall below the 6% contract standard, these factors will bias toward the delivery of short-duration i.e., high-coupon, short-maturity securities.

> IF yields > 6% → Bias to long duration (i.e., low-coupon, long-maturity) securities
>
> IF yields < 6% → Bias to short duration (i.e., high-coupon, short-maturity) securities

Duration is explained more thoroughly later, but you can think of duration as a measure of risk. When yields are rising and prices are declining, investors gravitate toward less risky or short-duration securities. They want to dump riskier long-duration securities, creating a delivery bias in favor of long-duration bonds. However, when yields are declining and prices rising, investors prefer those riskier long-duration securities. They wish to dump less aggressive short-duration securities, creating a delivery bias in favor of short-duration securities.

As already indicated, the 4 3/4%-14 was CTD as of July 2007. This security had a relatively low duration compared to the field of eligible for delivery securities against the 10-year Treasury note contract by virtue of the fact that it was the shortest maturity security that was eligible for delivery. Further contributing to its relatively short duration is the fact that its coupon at 4 3/4% was greater than all but two other eligible for delivery securities. Note that yields were in the range of approximately 4.8% to 4.9% and well below the 6% futures contract standard. As a result, conversion factor biases were exerting a bias toward the delivery of short-duration securities, specifically the shortest duration yet still eligible for delivery security in the form of the 4 3/4%-14.

Note that in the period from March to June 2007, futures prices were generally declining while yields were rising up toward the 6% futures contract standard. As a result, these conversion factor biases were diminishing, and we witnessed some very slight crossovers such that the basis for a somewhat longer duration security in the form of the 4 1/4%-14 became CTD at least temporarily. In fact, the basis for securities of an even longer duration including the 4 1/2%-17 and the 5 1/8%-16 were declining during this period as well as a function of diminishing conversion factor biases. See Exhibit 7.10.

Subsequently during the period from June and into August 2007, prices began to rally back and yields fell farther below the 6% futures contract standard. Note that during that period, the shortest duration security in the form of the 4 3/4%-14 reestablished itself as CTD. Note further that the basis for other eligible for delivery securities such as the 4 1/2%-17 and the 5 1/8%-16 started to advance as conversion factor biases began to exert a larger influence. See Exhibit 7.11.

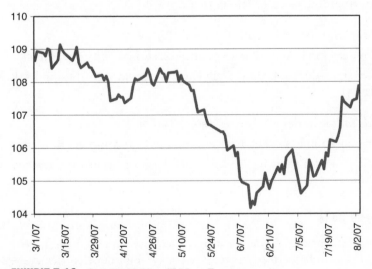

EXHIBIT 7.10 Sep-07 10-Year T-Note Futures

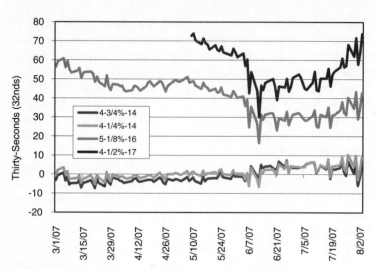

EXHIBIT 7.11 10-Year T-Note Basis Relationships

Thus, it is clear that the performance of the basis is strongly driven by directional price movement in the Treasury markets. This suggests that buying the basis (buying a cash Treasury and selling futures with the possibility of subsequently making delivery) or selling basis (selling a cash Treasury and buying futures with the possibility of subsequently repossessing the security by standing long in the delivery process) may be motivated by expectations regarding rising or falling yields.

IF yields rising above 6% (prices falling) THEN

Sell long-duration basis (sell long-duration securities and buy futures)

OR, buy short-duration basis (buy short-duration securities and sell futures)

IF yields falling under 6% (prices rising) THEN

Buy long-duration basis (buy long-duration securities and sell futures)

OR, sell short-duration basis (sell short-duration securities and buy futures)

Implied Repo Rate

We often suggest that the eligible for delivery security with the lowest gross basis is CTD. But to be perfectly correct, we may point out that the structure of coupon receipts and reinvestment of such coupon income (or carry) plays some (generally small) part in establishing a particular security as CTD as well. Hence, traders often calculate the "implied repo rate" (IRR) associated with eligible for delivery securities to account for such factors.

The IRR is calculated as the annualized rate of return associated with the purchase of a security, sale of futures, and delivery of the same in satisfaction of the maturing futures contract. This calculation indeed takes into account all the cash flows associated with the security. The assumption that the basis for any particular security may completely converge to zero is implicit in the IRR calculation.

As a general rule, the security with the lowest net basis likewise exhibits the highest implied repo rate. This is indeed the case with respect to the 4 3/4%-14 with an IRR at 4.66% for delivery into the September 2007 futures contract. Buying the basis, or buying the cash T-note and selling T-note futures with the option of making delivery in satisfaction of the maturing futures contract, may be considered as comparable to other investment alternatives of a similar term. For example, we might compare the 4.66% IRR on the CTD as comparable to the prevailing 13-week T-bill yield of 4.83%. Thus, the IRR is slightly below prevailing rates of a similar term. The disparity between the IRR of other non-CTD deliver securities is even greater. See Exhibit 7.12.

Consider the discrepancy with respect to the CTD to represent a risk premium of sorts. If one buys the CTD security and sells futures with the intention of making delivery, the worst case scenario has the basis converging fully

EXHIBIT 7.12 10-Year T-Note Futures Basis Relationships (as of July 25, 2007)

Coupon	Maturity	Price	Yield	Sep-07 CF	Gross Basis	IRR
4 1/2%	5/15/17	96-26	4.913%	0.8926	53.3	−5.27%
4 5/8%	2/15/17	97-24	4.923%	0.9034	46.5	−3.69%
4 5/8%	11/15/16	97-26+	4.918%	0.9054	42.2	−2.93%
4 7/8%	8/15/16	99-20	4.926%	0.9242	35.6	−1.45%
5 1/8%	5/15/16	101-13+	4.923%	0.9424	31.0	−0.42%
4 1/2%	2/15/16	97-06	4.906%	0.9034	28.5	−0.60%
4 1/2%	11/15/15	97-09	4.902%	0.9058	23.3	0.31%
4 1/4%	8/15/15	95-24	4.894%	0.8927	19.0	0.87%
4 1/8%	5/15/15	95-02+	4.890%	0.8881	13.2	1.79%
4%	2/15/15	94-15	4.884%	0.8837	8.7	2.53%
4 1/4%	11/15/14	96-09	4.860%	0.9012	7.0	3.01%
4 1/4%	8/15/14	96-14	4.836%	0.9040	2.5	3.87%
4 3/4%	5/15/14	99-16	4.836%	0.9335	−0.2	4.66%

September 2007 10-year T-note futures were valued at 106-19; December 2007 10-year T-note futures were valued at 106-13.

to zero and the hedger essentially locking in a return equal to the IRR, in this case 4.66%. But if market conditions should change such that another security becomes CTD, this implies that the basis may advance or at least fail to completely converge to zero. As a result, the trader may realize a rate of return that is in fact greater than the currently calculated IRR.

Optionality in the Basis

In other words, there is a certain degree of optionality associated with the purchase or sale of the basis. Buying the basis is analogous to buying an option, which, of course, implies limited risk. Buying the basis implies limited risk to the extent that under the worst of circumstances you make delivery of the security that is effectively equivalent to the possibility that the basis fully converges to zero. But crossovers may occur such that the basis converges at a slower rate than otherwise anticipated or actually advances. As a result, this short-term investment may generate a return that is (at least theoretically) unbounded on the upside. Limited risk accompanied by unbounded upside potential is reminiscent of the risk/reward profile of a long option position, thus the analogy between a long basis position and a long option.

The best outcome one may hope for by selling the basis, or selling securities and buying futures with the possibility of effectively replacing the sold security by standing long in the delivery process, is that the basis fully converges to zero. This implies limited profit potential. But in the event of significant changes in market conditions, the basis may advance sharply, exposing the seller of the basis to (theoretically) unbounded risks. Limited profit potential accompanied by unbounded risk is reminiscent of the risk/ reward profile of a short option position, thus the analogy between a short basis position and a short option.

As discussed earlier, the basis even for the CTD security tends to be in excess of cost of carry considerations. This is manifest in the fact that the IRR even for the CTD is typically a bit below prevailing short-term rates. This premium in the basis essentially reflects the uncertainties associated with which a security may become CTD in the future. Thus, the basis performs much akin to an option. Like any other option, the basis will be affected by considerations including term, volatility, and strike price. The relevant term in this case is the term remaining until the presumed delivery date versus the futures contract. Market volatility affects the probability that a crossover may occur. Rather than speak of a strike or exercise price, it is more appropriate to assess the market's proximity to a "crossover point" or a price/yield at which one might expect an alternative security to become CTD.

Consider the purchase or sale of the CTD basis. The degree to which this basis performs like a call or a put option is contingent on the relationship between market prices and the 6% futures contract standard.

If yields are below the 6% futures contract standard, the CTD basis may be expected to advance if interest rates rise (prices decline) toward 6% or decline if interest rates fall (prices increase). Thus, buying the CTD basis when rates are below 6% is akin to the purchase of a put option. Conversely, the sale of the CTD basis when rates are less than 6% is akin to the sale of a put option where the value of transaction is capped if prices should advance while losses may be unbounded if prices should decline.

If yields are above the 6% futures contract standard, the CTD basis may be expected to advance if interest rates decline (prices rise) toward 6% or decline if interest rates increase (prices fall). Thus, buying the CTD basis when rates are above 6% is akin to the purchase of a call option. Conversely, the sale of the CTD basis when rates are above 6% is akin to the sale of a call option where the value of transaction is capped if prices should decline while losses may be unbounded if prices should advance.

Finally, if rates are close to the 6% futures contract standard, the basis for what is currently CTD may be dictated by considerations apart from conversion factor biases. Thus, there may be significant crossovers regardless of whether rates rise or fall. Buying the CTD basis under these considerations may be considered akin to the purchase of an option straddle (i.e., the simultaneous purchase of call and put options). Under these circumstances the basis buyer may be indifferent between advancing or declining prices but has an interest in seeing prices move significantly in either direction. Selling the CTD basis when rates are near the 6% contract standard is akin to selling a straddle (i.e., the simultaneous sale of both call and put options). The basis is sold under these circumstances because the trader anticipates an essentially neutral market. Of course, the basis premium over carry should accrue to the short basis trader under circumstances of continued price stability. But the short basis trader is exposed to the risk of dramatic price movements in either direction. See Exhibit 7.13.

EXHIBIT 7.13   The Basis as an Option

	Buy CTD Basis	Sell CTD Basis
Yields <6%	Buy put option	Sell put option
Yields = 6%	Buy straddle	Sell straddle
Yields >6%	Buy call option	Sell call option

MEASURING RISK OF COUPON-BEARING SECURITIES

"You can't manage what you can't measure" is an old saying with universal application. In the fixed-income markets, it is paramount to assess the volatility of one's holdings in order reasonably to manage them. The particular characteristics of a coupon-bearing security clearly impact its volatility. Two readily identifiable ways to define coupon-bearing securities is in terms of their maturity and coupon. Defining volatility as the price reaction of the security in response to changes in yield:

The Longer the Maturity ↑ the Greater the Volatility ↑

The Higher the Coupon ↑ the Lower the Volatility ↓

All else held equal, the longer the maturity of a bond, the greater its price reaction to a change in yield. This may be understood when one considers that the implications of yield movements are felt over longer periods, the longer the maturity. However, high coupon securities will be less impacted, on a percentage basis, by changing yields than low-coupon securities. This may be understood when one considers that high-coupon securities return a greater portion of one's original investment sooner than low-coupon securities. Your risks are reduced to the extent that you hold the cash! There are several ways to measure the risks associated with coupon-bearing (and money market) instruments including basis point value (BPV) and duration.

Basis Point Value

Basis point value represents the absolute price change of a security given a one basis point (0.01%) change in yield. These figures may be referenced using any number of commercially available quotation services or software packages. Basis point value is normally quoted in dollars based on a $1 million (round-lot) unit of cash securities. Exhibit 7.14 depicts the BPVs of various on-the-run Treasuries as of July 25, 2007.

This suggests that if the yield on the 30-year bond were to rise by a single basis point (0.01%), the price should decline by some $1,481.80 per $1 million face-value unit.

Duration

If BPV measures the absolute change in the value of a security given a yield fluctuation, duration may be thought of as a measure of relative or

EXHIBIT 7.14   Measuring Volatility (As of July 25, 2007)

	Coupon	Maturity	Bid	Ask	BPV	Modified Duration
1-week bill	Na	8/23/07	4.93%	4.92%	$8.06	0.08
3-month bill	Na	10/25/07	4.84%	4.83%	$25.56	0.26
6-month bill	Na	01/24/08	4.85%	4.84%	$50.83	0.51
2-year note	4 7/8%	Jun-09	100-07+	100-08	$182.70	1.86
5-year note	4 7/8%	Jun-12	100-13	100-13+	$435.70	4.32
10-year note	4 1/2%	May-17	96-27	96-28	$756.60	7.74
30-year bond	4 3/4%	Feb-37	95-22+	95-23+	$1,481.80	15.15

percentage change. The modified duration of a fixed income security (typically quoted in years) measures the expected percentage change in the value of a security given an absolute (e.g., 100 basis points) change in yield.

Actually, there are two measures of duration - Macauley's duration and modified duration. Macauley duration measures the expected percentage price change in the price of a fixed income security given a percentage change in yields. Modified duration is often used in fixed income hedging applications as it measures the anticipated percentage price change in a fixed income security given an absolute change in yield.

Duration is calculated as the average weighted maturity of all the cash flows associated with the bond (i.e., repayment of "corpus" or face value at maturity plus coupon payments, all discounted to their present value).

The 30-year bond has a modified duration of 15.15 years. This implies that if its yield advances by 10 basis points (0.10%), we estimate a 1.515% decline in the value of the bond. This is, however, only an estimate as the sensitivity of a Treasury price to fluctuating yields will change as a function of yield levels. This is a phenomenon known as "convexity."

In years past, it was commonplace to evaluate the volatility of coupon-bearing securities simply by reference to maturity. But this is quite misleading. For example, if one simply examines the maturities of the current 2-year note and 10-year note, one might conclude that the 10-year is five times as volatile as the 2-year. But by comparing modified durations, we reach a far different conclusion. The 10-year note (duration of 7.74 years) is only about 4.2 times as volatile as the 2-year note (duration of 1.86 years). The availability of cheap computing power and duration functions included in most spreadsheet software has made duration analysis as easy as it is illuminating.

RISK MANAGEMENT WITH TREASURY FUTURES

Treasury futures are intended to provide risk-averse fixed-income investors with the opportunity to hedge or manage the risks inherent in their investment activities. Effective use of these contracts, however, requires a certain grounding in hedge techniques. Most pointedly, one may attempt to assess the relative volatility of the cash item to be hedged relative to the futures contract price. This relationship is often identified as the futures *hedge ratio* (HR). Hedge ratios reflect the expected relative movement of cash and futures and provide risk managers with an indication as to how many futures to use to offset a cash exposure.

Conversion Factor Weighted Hedge

The most superficial way to approach identification of the appropriate hedge ratio is simply to match the face value of the item to be hedged with the face value of the futures contract. For example, if one owned $10 million face value of a particular security, the natural inclination is to sell or short 100 $100,000 face-value futures contracts for a total of $10 million face value. However, this approach ignores the fact that securities of varying coupons and maturities have different price volatility characteristics.

Conveniently, Treasury futures contract specifications provide a facile means by which to assess the relative risks associated with cash and futures. As discussed earlier, the conversion factor (CF) represents the price of a particular bond as if it were to yield 6%. In other words, the CF reflects the *relative value* and, by implication, the *relative volatility* between cash and futures prices.

For example, it is July 25, 2007, and you go long $10 million face value of the 5 1/8%- 16 bond at 101-13+ to yield 4.925% for settlement on July 26. This security has a conversion factor for delivery against September 2007 10-year Treasury futures contract of 0.9424. This implies that this security is roughly 94% as valuable and 94% as volatile as a 6% coupon security. Thus, one might sell 94 10-year note bond futures against that position as a hedge.

Assume that yields uniformly rise 20 basis points (0.20%) and this hedge is held until August 28. In other words, the 4.923% yield on the 5 1/8% -16 rises to 5.125% and its price falls to 100-00. If one liquidates the portfolio at that time, there is a net profit of $16,864.13 on the series of transactions, or 1.80% on an annualized basis over the 33 days between July 25 and August 28.

EXHIBIT 7.15   Comparing Hedge Results

	Return in $s	Percentage Return
CF weighted hedge	$16,864.13	1.80%
Unhedged	−$96,229.62	−10.25%

7/25/07	Hold $10,000,000 5 1/8%-16 @ 101-13 + (4.925%)	$10,142,187.50
	Accrued interest on 7/26/07	$101,664.40
	Sell 94 Sep-07 futures @ 106-19	—
	Initial Portfolio Value or Investment	$10,243,851.90
8/28/07	Hold $10,000,000 5 1/8%-16 @ 100-00(5.125%)	$10,000,000.00
	Accrued interest on 8/28/07	$147,622.28
	Coupon income	$0
	Buy 94 futures @ 105-12+	$113,093.75
	Final Portfolio Value	$10,260,716.03
	Profit/Loss	$16,864.13

$$\text{Return} = (\text{Profit/Loss} \div \text{Initial Investment}) \times (360 \div \text{Holding Period})$$
$$= (\$16,864.13 \div \$10,243,851.90) \times (360 \div 33)$$
$$= 1.80\%$$

This is certainly superior to the unhedged loss of $96,229.62, which equates to −10.25% annualized. But bearing in mind that short-term rates were closer to 5%, you could have and probably should have done a bit better, as seen in Exhibit 7.15.

Basis Point Value Weighted Hedge

A conversion factor weighted hedge is likely to be quite effective under one particular circumstance, specifically, if you are hedging the CTD security. Treasury futures tend to price or track or correlate most closely with the CTD security. But other securities with varying coupons and maturities may react to changing market conditions differently. To understand the most effective techniques with which to apply a hedge, let us consider the fundamental objective associated with a hedge. A hedge is ideally intended to balance any loss (profit) in the cash markets with an equal and opposite profit (loss) in futures. Our goal, therefore, is to find a HR that allows one to balance the change in the value of the cash instrument to be hedged (Δ_H) with any change in the value of the futures contract (Δ_F).

$$\Delta_H = HR \times \Delta_F$$

Or, solving for the hedge ratio (HR) . . .

$$HR = \Delta_H \div \Delta_F$$

Unfortunately, this equation is abstract and cannot be directly applied. Let us, therefore, backtrack a bit and discuss the relationship between Treasury futures and cash prices. We know that the principal invoice amount paid from long to short upon delivery will be equal to the price of the Treasury futures contract multiplied by its conversion factor. Rational shorts, of course, elect to tender the CTD security. Thus, we might designate the futures price and the conversion factor of the CTD as P_f and CF_{ctd}, respectively.

$$\text{Principal Invoice Amount} = P_F \times CF_{CTD}$$

Because the basis of the CTD is generally closest to zero, relative to all other eligible securities, we might assume that the futures price level and, by implication, any changes in the futures price level (Δ_F) will be a reflection of any changes in the value of the CTD (Δ_{CTD}) adjusted by its conversion factor (CF_{CTD}) . . .

$$\Delta_F \approx \Delta_{CTD} \div CF_{CTD}$$

Substituting this quantity into our equation specified earlier, we arrive at the following:

$$HR = \Delta_H \div (\Delta_{CTD} \div CF_{CTD})$$

Or rearranging the equation:

$$HR = CF_{CTD} \times (\Delta_H \div \Delta_{CTD})$$

Unfortunately, the concept of "change" is abstract. Let us operationalize that concept by substituting the basis point value of the hedged security (BPV_H) and the basis point value of the CTD (BPV_{CTD}) for that abstract concept. Recall from our earlier discussion that a basis point value represents the expected change in the value of a security, expressed in dollars per $1 million face value, given a one basis point (0.01%) change in yield. Thus, we identify the "basis point value hedge ratio":

$$BPV\ HR = CF_{CTD} \times (BPV_H \div BPV_{CTD})$$

Note that our analysis implicitly assumes that any changes in the yield of the hedged security and that of the cheapest-to-deliver security will be identical. That is, we will experience parallel shifts in the yield curve. This analysis further presumes you are able to identify the CTD security and that it will remain CTD. The latter assumption, of course, is questionable in a dynamic market.

Let us find the basis point value HR associated with the 5 1/8%-16 security discussed in our previous example. It carried a BPV of some $713.50 per million. Recall that, as of July 25, 2007, the CTD security was identified as the 4 3/4%-14. This security had a BPV of $572.30 per million and a conversion factor of 0.9335 versus September 2007 10-year Treasury futures. The HR may be identified as 116 contracts per $10 million face value of the 5 1/8%-16.

$$\text{BPV HR} = 0.9335 \times (\$713.50 \div \$572.30)$$
$$= 1.1638$$

Note that the HR of 116 contracts is significantly greater than the 94 contracts suggested by reference to the conversion factor. This is due to the fact that the CTD 4 3/4%-14 security carries a relatively short duration of 5.70 years compared to the duration associated with the hedged security of 6.90 years. It is no coincidence that the ratio of durations is roughly equal to the ratio between the BPV and CF hedge ratios or $(6.90 \div 5.70) \approx (116 \div 94)$. In other words, the futures contract is pricing or tracking or correlating most closely with a shorter duration security. Consequently, futures prices will react rather mildly to fluctuating yields. Therefore one requires more futures to enact an effective hedge.

What would our hedge ratio be if the CTD security was the 4 1/2%-16 with a duration of 6.86 years? Note that this security has a BPV of $680.10 and a conversion factor for delivery versus September 2007 10-year T-note futures of 0.9034. Our analysis suggests that one might hedge with 95 contracts per $10 million face value of the 5 1/8%-16.

$$\text{BPV HR} = 0.9034 \times (\$713.50 \div \$680.10)$$
$$= 0.9478$$

Note that this hedge ratio of 94 contracts is significantly less than the 116 contracts suggested by the BPV hedge ratio and actually quite similar to the 94 contracts suggested by the CF hedge ratio. This can be explained by the fact that the 4 1/2%-16 has pricing characteristics that are quite similar to 5 1/8%-16 security, which is the subject of the hedge. In particular, the 4 1/2%-16 had a modified duration of 6.86 years relative to the 6.90

year modified duration of the 5 1/8%-16. Because of the similar risk characteristics of the CTD and hedged security, the CF will do a reasonable job of identifying an appropriate HR.

This further suggests that if there is a crossover in the CTD from a short duration security to a longer duration security, the number of futures needed to hedge against the risk of declining prices is decreased. This may be a favorable circumstance for the hedger who is long cash Treasuries and short futures in a ratio prescribed by the BPV technique. Consider that as prices decline and longer duration securities become CTD, one is essentially overhedged in a declining market. If, however, prices advance and even shorter duration securities become CTD, the appropriate HR will tend to increase. Thus, the long hedger becomes underhedged in a rising market.

Another way of saying this is that there is a certain degree of "convexity" inherent in these relationships that favors the long hedger or long basis trader (long cash and short futures). Conversely, this convexity tends to work to the disadvantage of the short hedger or short basis trader (short cash and long futures). Once again, we may liken the basis to an option to the extent that the premium structure of options is also affected by convexity. Further, because the long basis trader effectively owns the option, he or she pays an implicit premium in the difference between prevailing short-term yields and the return on the basis trade as simulated in the absence of any CTD crossovers. The short basis trader is effectively short an option and receives this implicit premium.

Returning to our preceding example, let's simulate assuming that you sell 116 futures by reference to the basis point value HR. Once again, assuming that yields rise 20 basis points (0.20%) and this hedge is held until November 30, we simulate a net profit of $148,663, or 4.77%, on the hedged portfolio.

7/25/07	Hold $10,000,000 5 1/8%-16 @ 101-13 + (4.925%)	$10,142,187.50
	Accrued interest on 7/26/07	$101,664.40
	Sell 116 Sep-07 futures @ 106-19	-
	Initial Portfolio Value or Investment	$10,243,851.90
8/28/07	Hold $10,000,000 5 1/8%-16 @ 100-00(5.125%)	$10,000,000.00
	Accrued interest on 8/29/07	$147,622.28
	Coupon income	$0
	Buy 116 futures @ 105-12+	$139,562.50
	Final Portfolio Value	$10,287,184.78
	Profit/Loss	$43,332.88

$$\begin{aligned} \text{Return} &= (\text{Profit/Loss} \div \text{Initial Investment}) \times (360 \div \text{Holding Period}) \\ &= (\$43{,}332.88 \div \$10{,}243{,}851.90) \times (360 \div 33) \\ &= 4.61\% \end{aligned}$$

EXHIBIT 7.16 Comparing Hedge Results

	Return in $s	Percentage Return
BPV weighted hedge	$43,332.88	4.61%
CF weighted hedge	$16,864.13	1.80%
Unhedged	−$96,229.62	−10.25%

Note that this return of 4.61% is closer to the vicinity of prevailing 3-month T-bill yields as depicted above. Still, this return is slightly less than overnight repo rates, which were trading close to 5.10%, a benchmark against which a hedged return might most appropriately be compared. See Exhibits 7.16 and 7.17.

Once again, this is offered with the caveat that the BPV of a debt security is dynamic and subject to change given fluctuating yields. As a general rule, BPV declines as a function of maturity; and, as yields increase (decrease), BPVs decline (advance). This implies that the hedge ratio is likewise dynamic. Over a limited period of time, however, these long-term HRs are reasonably stable, provided there is no crossover in the CTD.

Although it is common to calculate and apply these BPV weighted hedge ratios, some prefer to base their calculations on modified durations. Modified duration and BPV are closely related figures. Modified duration

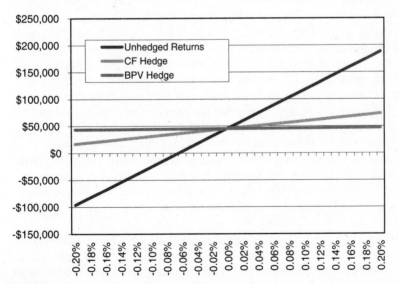

EXHIBIT 7.17 Hedged and Unhedged PL

measures the expected percentage change in the value of a security in response to an absolute change in the security's yield, whereas BPV measures the expected monetary change in value given a one basis point change in yield. Thus, it is fair to state that Modified Duration $\approx$ BPV $\div$ Price; or, BPV $\approx$ Modified Duration $\times$ Price $\times$ 0.0001. Given this relationship, it is easy to substitute Modified Duration $\times$ Price $\times$ 0.0001 for BPV in our equation. Either method will suffice and generate similar results, although we tend to prefer the simplicity of the BPV weighted hedge.

$$\text{Modified Duration HR} = CF_{CTD} \times (Price_H \times \text{Modified Duration}_H)$$
$$\div (Price_{CTD} \times \text{Modified Duration}_{CTD})$$

For sake of brevity the value of one basis point, 0.0001 has been factored out of both numerator and denominator in the Modified Duration HR expression

Locking In a Short-Term Rate of Return

It is significant that the 4.61% rate of return associated with the BPV weighted hedge is similar to prevailing T-bill rates but somewhat lower than repo rates at 5.10%. Consider the implications of a hedge, specifically that by selling futures against a long-term bond, one commits (at least temporarily) to the delivery of the security in the short term. In other words, one effectively turns a long-term investment into a short-term investment. Accordingly, one cannot expect to earn a long-term rate of return but rather should anticipate earning a short-term rate of return.

Given a normal, upwardly sloping yield curve, long-term rates exceed short-term rates. Thus, the 4.61% return earned through the hedge falls a bit short of the prevailing yield on the hedged security in our example of 4.923%. Of course, we are aware that the shape of the yield curve defines the "carry relationship." In a normal upwardly sloping yield curve environment where long-term rates exceed short-term rates, there is a positive result to buying and carrying a bond on a leveraged basis. In other words, coupon income received (represented by long-term rates) is greater than financing costs (represented by short-term rates). As such, "positive carry" prevails and bond futures can be expected to trade at successively lower and lower levels in deferred months.

In the event of an inverted or negatively sloped yield curve where short-term rates exceed long-term rates, "negative carry" is said to prevail. In other words, coupon income (represented by long-term rates) is less than the financing costs (represented by short-term rates) associated with buying and carrying a bond. As a result, bond futures can be expected to trade at successively higher and higher levels in deferred months.

When positive carry prevails, the bond basis will be positive. That is, cash prices will exceed adjusted futures prices (futures price × conversion factor). When negative carry prevails, the bond basis may become negative (i.e., cash prices will be less than adjusted futures prices). Typically, the yield curve is upwardly sloped and the basis is quoted as a positive number.

Carry can be calculated in terms of the payout on the bond less finance costs between the current date and the anticipated date of delivery. Note that when the yield curve is positive and positive carry prevails, then shorts, which have the option of making delivery on any business day of the delivery month, can be expected to defer delivery until late in the month. When the yield curve is inverted and negative carry prevails, then shorts can be expected to deliver early in the delivery period to minimize negative carry.

Theoretically, the gross basis for the CTD security should by approximately equal to its cost of carry. Yet it is typical in practice that the gross basis for even the CTD security will exceed its cost of carry. And this is the *best* that one might do considering that the adjusted gross basis for all other eligible-for-delivery securities is higher. Why, therefore, would anyone ever wish to make delivery?

Let us suggest that this premium of gross basis over cost of carry represents the uncertainty as to what will be CTD by the time the delivery month rolls around. As market conditions change, for example as yields rise or fall, other securities may "cross over" to become CTD. The premium of the gross basis over cost of carry essentially represents the "reverse probability" that a particular security may become CTD. The greater the premium, the less likely that a security will become CTD. This is sometimes referred to as a "switching option."

This uncertainty works to the advantage of a hedger who is long cash and short futures (i.e., long the basis). Consider that when rates are greater than the 6% contract standard, there will be a bias toward the delivery of long-duration securities; when rates fall below the 6% standard, there will be a bias toward the delivery of short-duration securities.

If one puts on a hedge using the proper BPV weighted ratio, then one is well positioned to take advantage of a crossover or switch. If, for example, rates rise above 6% and there is a crossover toward long-duration securities, the effective BPV of the futures contract, represented by the $BPV_{CTD} \div CF_{CTD}$, as discussed earlier, should rise. In other words, the futures contract will become increasingly sensitive to further yield advances (price declines). Thus, the futures contract will decline at a faster rate in a falling market. The basis widens, and the hedger who is long the basis (long cash/short futures) benefits.

If, for example, rates decline below 6% and there is a crossover toward the delivery of short-duration securities, the effective BPV of the futures contract should decline. The futures contract becomes desensitized to further rate declines (price advances). Futures advance at a slower rate in a rising market. Once again, the basis widens, and the hedger who is long the basis benefits.

In other words, buying the basis using the proper hedge ratio is analogous to buying an option. If yields exceed 6% and the contract is tracking long-duration securities, there is a probability that yields will fall (price rise), a crossover is realized, and the basis widens. That is, the basis performs like a call option. If yields are less than 6% and the contract is tracking short-duration securities, there is a probability that yields will rise (prices fall), a crossover is realized, and the basis likewise widens. That is, the basis performs like a put option.

The premium of gross basis over cost of carry, at least for the CTD security whose basis might be expected to converge to zero, may be thought of as akin to an option premium. Of course, other eligible-for-delivery securities will likely not experience complete convergence or they would become CTD! Thus, the implied option premium is *not* directly represented by the premium of the gross basis over cost of carry for non-CTD securities.

In our example, the implied option premium is represented in the approximate 50 basis point shortfall between the return on the hedged transaction near 4.61% versus prevailing repo rates near 5.10%. If there is no crossover, the implied premium may be lost through the process of basis convergence in the absence of a little "pop" in the basis. Thus, someone who is long the basis may realize a return that is somewhat less than prevailing repo or Fed Funds rates. Our example was simulated under the assumption that what was CTD would remain CTD (i.e., no crossovers).

MACRO HEDGING WITH TREASURY FUTURES

Thus far, our discussion has centered on comparisons between a single security and a Treasury futures contract, a "micro" hedge, if you will. But it is far more commonplace for an investor to become concerned about the value of a portfolio of securities rather than focus on a single item within a presumably diversified set of holdings. How might one address the risks associated with a portfolio of securities (i.e., how to execute a "macro" hedge)?

Let's begin with a hypothetical set of holdings as illustrated in Exhibit 7.18. We have arbitrarily assumed that an investor holds a variety

EXHIBIT 7.18 A Hypothetical Treasury Portfolio on 7/25/07

Holdings	Yield	Value	Acc Int	BPV	Dur
$30 mil of 4-7/8%-09 @ 100-08	4.74%	$30,075,000	$103,329	$5,481	1.86
$20 mil of 4-7/8%-12 @ 100-13+	4.78%	$20,084,375	$68,886	$8,714	4.32
$18 mil of 4-1/2%-17 @ 96-28	4.90%	$17,437,500	$158,478	$13,619	7.74
$14 mil of 4-3/4%-37 @ 99-23+	5.03%	$13,962,813	$295,760	$20,745	15.15
TOTAL		$81,559,688	$626,452	$48,559	5.97

of Treasuries distributed among 2-, 5-, 10-, and 30-year Treasuries. Of course we may assess the risks associated with any portfolio constituent by reference to their respective BPVs and modified durations. Further, we may sum the BPVs or take the weighted average of the modified durations to find the portfolio BPV and portfolio duration. In this example, our aggregate BPV suggests a loss on the order of $48,559 in response to a general 1 basis point advance in yields. The portfolio modified duration of 5.97 years suggests a 5.97% decline in the value of the portfolio given a uniform 1% advance in yields.

The techniques associated with a macro hedge are actually quite similar to those that might be applied to the hedge of a single security. In particular, the BPV hedge ratio calculation remains quite relevant. However, one might apply the ratio to the aggregate BPV instead of the BPV associated with any individual security within the portfolio. But which Treasury futures contract is most appropriate, noting that our portfolio includes constituents of a 2-, 5-, 10-, and 30-year original maturity?

To begin, let's calculate the appropriate BPV weighted hedge ratios for our hypothetical Treasury portfolio versus 2-, 5-, 10-, and 30-year Treasury futures. The results are shown in Exhibit 7.19 and, consistent with intuition, suggest that one needs fewer contracts as a function of the lengthening maturity of the futures contract. Note that the 2-year Treasury contract in fact calls for the delivery of $200,000 face value of securities and, therefore, one requires fewer futures contracts than one might otherwise presume.

Bullets and Barbells

As a first pass, one might hedge a Treasury portfolio with the use of Treasury futures that correspond most closely in terms of duration to the average

EXHIBIT 7.19 Calculating Hedge Ratios

	CTD	CF_{CTD}	×	[BPV_{port}	÷	BPV_{CTD}]	= HR
2-Yr	4 7/8%-09	0.9815	×	[$48,559	÷	$36.58]	= 1,303 contracts
5-Yr	4 1/2%-11	0.9453	×	[$48,559	÷	$38.65]	= 1,188 contracts
10-Yr	4 3/4%-14	0.9335	×	[$48,559	÷	$57.23]	= 792 contracts
30-Yr	7 5/8%-22	1.1593	×	[$48,559	÷	$123.07]	= 457 contracts

weighted portfolio modified duration. For example, if one held a portfolio with an average weighted modified duration of 4 years, it would be natural to look to 5-year Treasury note futures as a suitable risk layoff vehicle. Of if the portfolio modified duration were 8 years, that would correspond most closely to the modified durations associated with 10-year Treasury notes and point one in the direction of 10-year Treasury note futures.

This analysis would tend to work well when the portfolio is constructed predominantly of securities that were close in terms of their modified durations to the average portfolio modified duration. Certainly if the entire portfolio were populated with a variety of recently issued five-year T-notes, it would behoove the hedger to use five-year Treasury note futures as a hedge, minimizing basis risk and the need for any subsequent hedge management. A portfolio constructed in such a manner might be labeled a "bullet" portfolio to the extent that it contains reasonably homogeneous securities in terms of maturity and presumably coupon. Under these circumstances, one might simply "stack" the entire hedge in a single Treasury futures contract that most closely conforms to the modified duration of the portfolio constituents.

Of course, one may attempt to introduce a certain speculative element into the hedge by using longer- or shorter-term futures contracts as the focus of the hedge. If the yield curve were expected to steepen, a hedge using longer-term futures (e.g., 10- or 30-year Treasury futures rather than 5-year futures) would allow one to capitalize on movement in the curve beyond simply immunizing the portfolio from risk. If the yield curve is expected to flatten or invert, a hedge using shorter-term futures (e.g., two-year or three-year Treasury futures rather than five-year futures), could likewise provide yield enhancement.

But a portfolio need not necessarily be constructed per the "bullet" approach. Consider a portfolio with a modified duration of four years that is constructed using a combination of 2- and 10-year notes and no 5-year notes whatsoever. A portfolio constructed in such a manner may be labeled a "barbell" portfolio to the extent that it is "weighted" with two extreme duration securities with no intermediate duration securities at all. If one were to simply stack the hedge into 5-year Treasury note futures, the investor becomes exposed to the risk that the shape of the yield curve becomes distorted such that 5-year yields sag below yields in the 2- and 10-year sectors of the curve.

The holder of a barbell portfolio might instead attempt to use a combination of various tenored Treasury futures that is weighted with an eye to the proportion of the portfolio devoted to each sector of the yield curve. As such, the hedger may insulate from the risks that the shape of the yield curve will shift. In our example, we might use a combination of 2-, 5-, 10-, and 30-year Treasury futures, applying the BPV weighted HR technique to each of the four securities within the portfolio. If, however, the investor wished to introduce a speculative element into the hedge, the use of longer- or shorter-maturity Treasuries driven by an expectation of a steepening or flattening yield curve, respectively, may be in order.

Targeting Portfolio Duration

Thus far, we have assumed that the hedger wishes to immunize risks altogether with the use of futures by effectively reducing the security or portfolio duration to zero. This may be unlikely in practice where investment managers are frequently committed to a particular investment strategy for the long haul and may not be completely at liberty to alter the portfolio duration so dramatically.

Rather, it may be more commonplace to use futures to shade the portfolio duration downward in anticipation of rising rates or perhaps upward in anticipation of declining rates. After all, risk management does not necessarily mean that the investor will always pursue a risk abatement strategy. Taking on some additional risk in pursuit of yield, within some institutionally mandated parameters, is a frequently accepted practice.

Finding the requisite number of futures contracts that will effectively extend or contract the portfolio modified duration from the current modified duration ($D_{current}$) by some desired degree to the target modified duration (D_{target}) may readily be identified through a simple modification of the BPV hedge ratio calculation.

$$HR = \left[\left(D_{target} - D_{current} \right) \div D_{current} \right] \times CF_{CTD} \times \left(BPV_{portfolio} \div BPV_{CTD} \right)$$

Building from our prior example, assume you wish to extent the modified duration of the portfolio from 5.97 years to a target modified duration of 7 years in anticipation of falling rates and rising prices. Our analysis suggests the purchase of 137 10-year Treasury note futures for these purposes.

$$\text{Ratio} = [(7.00 - 5.97) \div 5.97] \times 0.9335 \times [\$48,559 \div \$57.23]$$
$$= 137 \text{ contracts}$$

Assume you wish to reduce risk by contracting the modified duration of the portfolio to a target level of four years. This suggests the sale of 261 10-year Treasury note futures.

$$\text{Ratio} = [(4.00 - 5.97) \div 5.97] \times 0.9335 \times [\$48,559 \div \$57.23]$$
$$= -261 \text{ contracts}$$

HEDGING CORPORATES WITH TREASURY FUTURES

Corporate debt markets are by some measures the fastest growing segment of the capital markets with tens of thousands of issues outstanding. Clearly corporate bonds or notes share many structural characteristics in common with Treasury securities. For example, both types of instruments call for periodic coupon payments with a final payment of the corpus, or principal, at maturity. It should be noted, however, that corporate debt instruments are often issued with many features that may distinguish them from a Treasury, such as call features, convertibility into other debt or equity structures, or other forms of optionality. Most significantly, however, they do differ from Treasuries in terms of credit risk. That is, the risk characteristics of a AA-rated or perhaps a BBB-rated corporate bond are certainly divergent from the presumed "riskless" character of government debt. Of course, once we venture past "investment grade" debt rated BBB or better by the rating agencies, we may encounter speculative grade or "high-yield" corporate bonds that entail even greater credit risks.

Ideally, one may look to a liquid corporate bond derivative contract as a means of managing the risks attendant to these instruments. As of this writing, however, the futures industry has generally failed in its attempts to introduce a risk-management vehicle of this nature successfully. Not for lack of trying and, of course, we believe that further attempts will be launched in the future. Nonetheless, these circumstances often cause corporate investors to look to the Treasury futures market as a vehicle for shifting these risks.

In its most elemental form, and limiting our analysis to generally highly rated corporates entailing lower credit risks without any significant optionality, hedging a corporate note or bond with the use of Treasury futures is largely analogous to hedging a Treasury with Treasury futures. In particular, one might begin by examining a BPV or duration weighted HR as a start.

Consider the General Electric (GE) corporate bond with a coupon of 5% maturing in February of 2013. As of July 25, 2007, this security had a

EXHIBIT 7.20 Calculating Hedge Ratios

	CTD	CF_{CTD}	×	$[BPV_{port}$	÷	$BPV_{CTD}]$	= HR
2-Yr	4 7/8%-09	0.9815	×	[$461.30	÷	$36.58]	= 12.4 contracts
5-Yr	4 1/2%-11	0.9453	×	[$461.30	÷	$38.65]	= 11.3 contracts
10-Yr	4 3/4%-14	0.9335	×	[$461.30	÷	$57.23]	= 7.5 contracts
30-Yr	7 5/8%-22	1.1593	×	[$461.30	÷	$123.07]	= 4.3 contracts

*Note that 2-year and 3-year T-note futures call for delivery of $200,000 face value securities. All other contracts are based on a $100,000 face-value unit.

modified duration of 4.631 years with a BPV equal to $461.30 per million. Because its maturity and duration are similar to that associated with a 5-year Treasury, one might hedge this security with 5-year Treasury futures. Or, one may consider the use of longer-term Treasury futures (such as 10 years or 30 years) to speculate on a possible steepening of the yield curve. Likewise, one may introduce a speculative element into the hedging equation with the use of shorter-term futures (such as 2-year Treasury futures) to speculate on a flattening or inverting yield curve. Applying the BPV hedge ratio as discussed earlier, we may find hedge ratios for a $1 million face-value unit of the 5%-13 GE corporate note using 2-, 5-, 10-, or 30-year Treasury futures as shown in Exhibit 7.20.

Use of the BPV weighted HR implies an expectation that yields on the hedged security and CTD will move in parallel. But, as discussed earlier, the credit quality of a corporate bond may be quite different than that associated with a "riskless" Treasury investment. Of course, yields on low-rated bonds exceed the yields on otherwise comparable high-rated bonds. Accordingly, we may presume that the volatility in low-rated bond yields might exceed the volatility in higher-rated bond yields. See Exhibit 7.21.

Accordingly, the industry has often reverted to a regression analysis technique empirically to assess the relationship between yields on the hedged security versus yields on the Treasury securities from which Treasury futures are derived. The most significant product of that analysis may be the "yield beta" (β), which may define, with some factor for error, the relationship between movements in corporate yields versus movements in Treasury yields.

$$Y = a + \beta(x) + e$$

where Y = Yield movements in corporates
       x = Yield movements in Treasuries

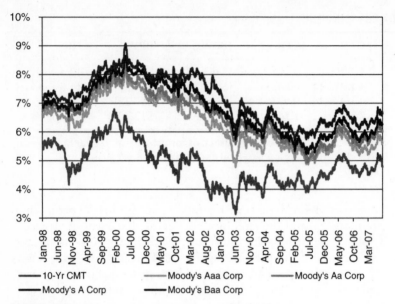

EXHIBIT 7.21 Treasury versus Corporate Bond Yields

Once discovered, the yield beta may be applied as an adjustment to the BPV weighted HR. Although this technique is often applied in the context of a hedge of corporate or other types of non-Treasury securities versus Treasury futures, some have also found the technique useful when attempting to hedge cash Treasuries with Treasury futures.

$$\text{Adjusted HR} = \beta \times \text{BPV HR}$$

Relationships between corporates and Treasuries are, of course, subject to change. Because of the vagaries associated with any specific corporate issue, traders sometimes use reasonably broad characterizations of risk referenced by credit ratings. It may be more useful to use a regression of the yields on a corporate bond index distinguished by rating (i.e., AA, A, BBB, etc.) rather than performing a regression using any particular corporate bond. To the extent that corporate bonds tend to be issued and "put away" in investment portfolios for extended periods of time, the period during which they are marketable and actively traded tends to be rather brief subsequent to their original issuance. As such, one may not be able to accumulate a sufficient data history to conduct a reasonable regression analysis for a particular corporate issue.

In any case, a reasonable rule of thumb might be to use a yield beta in the vicinity of perhaps 1.02 for Aaa-rated issues, ranging up to β 1.10 for Baa-rated issues. Of course, these relationships may be unstable,

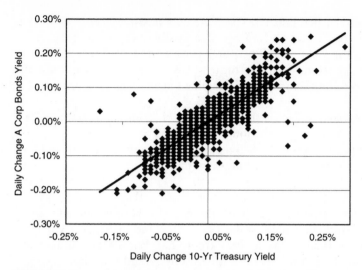

EXHIBIT 7.22 Yield Changes in Treasuries versus A Corporate Bonds

particularly during times of credit distress (e.g., subprime mortgage credit crisis of 2007/2009 or the Asian financial crisis of 1998). A scatter diagram like the one shown in Exhibit 7.22 may provide one with a feel for the stability of the relationship and the error one introduces into the hedge equation by using these techniques.

TRADING THE YIELD CURVE WITH TREASURY FUTURES

Treasury futures are strategically tied to key points along the Treasury yield curve, specifically to the 2-, 3-, 5-, 10-, and 30-year sectors. When a Treasury trader requests a quote on "the run," he or she routinely expects to examine quotations for the most recently issued Treasury security of these tenors. Of course, the associated Treasury futures contracts call for the delivery of a wide variety of issues, and it is a rather infrequent occurrence when the on- the-run issue becomes CTD. So although Treasury futures do not quite represent the most frequently quoted reference points along the Treasury yield curve, tied as they are to the CTD security, they are nonetheless very reasonable proxies for those key reference points. As a result, and in light of the extreme liquidity provided by Treasury futures, these contracts are frequently used in the form of intermarket spreads (e.g., 2-year versus 10-year or 5-year versus 10-year), as a means to speculate on the shape of the yield curve over a particular span of the curve.

As discussed earlier, one may speculate on a possible steepening or flattening of the curve. To take advantage of a possible steepening of the curve, one may "buy the yield curve" by purchasing short-term Treasury futures and selling longer-term Treasury futures. Conversely, one may "sell the yield curve" by selling short-term and buying longer-term Treasury futures.

| Yield curve expected to steepen | → | "Buy the curve," i.e., buy short-term and sell long-term futures |
| Yield curve expected to flatten or invert | → | "Sell the curve," i.e., sell short-term and buy long-term futures |

Of course, it is also possible to speculate on the changing shape of the curve over a particular span with the use of other instruments, notably Eurodollar futures traded in the form of an intramarket or calendar spreads. This is facilitated to the extent that Eurodollar futures are listed out a full 10 years into the future. Why would one choose to use Treasury futures as the vehicle for this speculation as opposed to Eurodollar futures?

Fundamentally, longer-term securities are driven by prevailing inflationary expectations, whereas shorter-term securities are more closely tied to, and driven by, Federal Open Market Committee (FOMC) monetary policy. Although this may be a bit of an oversimplification, it is reasonable to use intramarket Eurodollar spreads when one believes that the shape of the curve will change due to shifting Fed monetary policies. However, if one believes that other factors apart from Fed policies are likely to be the driving force behind a shift in the shape of the yield curve, it becomes reasonable to look to intermarket Treasury spreads as the means to express one's expectations.

PREMISE		THUS
Short end of yield curve largely anchored by FOMC monetary policy	→	Use intramarket (calendar) spreads on Eurodollar futures to trade shape of yield curve when movement driven by Fed monetary policy
Long end of yield curve driven by inflationary expectations and other supply/demand factors	→	Use intermarket spreads between Chicago Board of Trade (CBOT) Treasury futures to trade curve shape if movement driven by other factors

A Steepening Yield Curve

In May and June of 2007, Fed monetary policy had been in a holding pattern for some time. The target Fed Funds rate was essentially frozen in place at 5.25%. However, there were growing tensions between monetary policies and the longer end of the yield curve. In fact, Treasury rates at all strategic points along the Treasury yield curve were much lower than the target Fed Funds rate. See Exhibit 7.23.

By the first quarter of 2007, GDP growth had slowed to +0.7%, or +1.9% for the previous four quarters. This was down considerably from the figure of +3.7% reported in the first quarter of 2006 and covering the previous four quarters. Concerns accumulated regarding the general and dramatic downturn in the housing sector, mounting trade deficits, and over-built inventories. But U.S. consumer demand remained reasonably strong in May and June of 2007. GDP growth had not actually turned negative. In fact, the consensus among economists was calling for expanded growth in the 3 to 4% range by the second quarter 2007.

Asian investment in Treasuries on a very large scale certainly had contributed to the prior inversion in the yield curve. But some Asian central banks were becoming concerned regarding their concentrated holdings in U.S. Treasuries and weakening U.S. dollar. In particular, we note a landmark deal such that China invested some $3 billion in Blackstone, a large and diversified investment management concern. Many believed this to be a

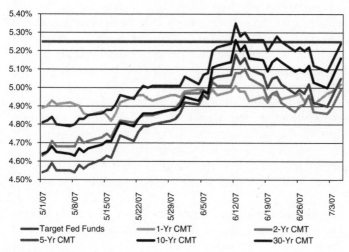

EXHIBIT 7.23 CMTs versus Target Fed Funds

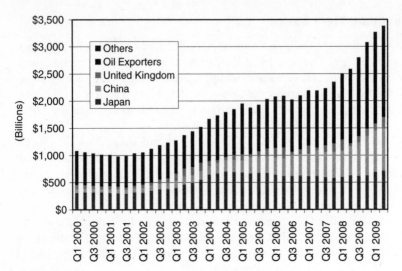

EXHIBIT 7.24 Overseas Holdings of U.S. Treasuries

harbinger of further diversification away from U.S. Treasuries on the part of Asian investors holding significant U.S. dollar–denominated reserves. See Exhibit 7.24.

Reasonably resilient domestic economic conditions coupled with mounting international reluctance contributed to a general decline in Treasury prices and resulting advance in Treasury yields during this period. On the short end of the curve, the FOMC was holding the target Fed Funds rate steady at 5.25%. Of course, there had been concern expressed that the Fed Funds target rate was (artificially) held at too high a level relative to market-determined long-term term rates.

As a result of these tensions, the yield curve shifted from a generally negative to a positive slope during May–June 2007. Typically we expect that any inversion of the yield curve will right itself into a generally upward slope as a result of Fed easing, noting that an inverted curve is often a harbinger of recession. But the yield curve inversion that had existed in 2006 and 2007 had not actually culminated in a recession. See Exhibit 7.25.

Just as these factors were reflected in the cash or spot Treasury markets, they were likewise reflected in Treasury futures markets. During much of May through mid-June 2007, the yields on 2-, 5-, and 10-year Treasuries increased and both Treasury cash and futures prices declined accordingly. See Exhibit 7.26.

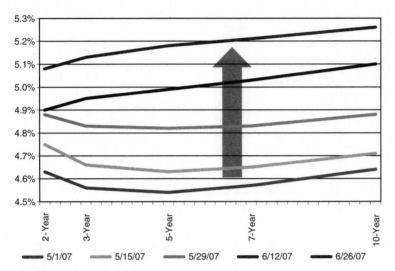

EXHIBIT 7.25 Steepening Shape of Yield Curve

The generalized steepening of the yield curve was observable by studying the spread, quoted in yields between key points along the Treasury yield curve. But that steepening was most consistent and readily observed in the span between two- and five-year Treasury futures. See Exhibit 7.27.

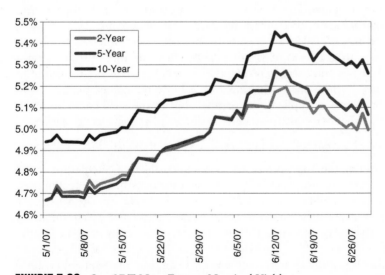

EXHIBIT 7.26 Sep-07 T-Note Futures Nominal Yields

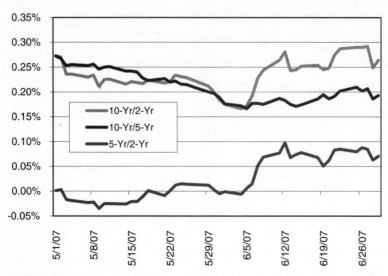

EXHIBIT 7.27 Treasury Note Futures Spreads

Finding the Right Spread Ratio

It is extremely convenient to quote Treasury spreads along any particular span of the yield curve on a yield basis. Yields are readily comparable one to the next. But of course Treasury futures are not traded or quoted on a yield basis; rather they are quoted on a percent of par basis. Because 2-, 3-, 5-, 10-, and 30-year as well as Ultra Treasury futures offer very different risk exposures on an outright basis, it is not possible to trade these products on a one-for-one basis and achieve results that parallel movements measured in yield spreads. Rather, one must weight or balance the contemplated spread so no profit or loss is implied by a parallel shift in the yield curve, in much the same way that one constructs a HR as discussed at some length earlier.

Δ Value of 2-Year T-Note Futures $\approx \Delta$ Value of 5-Year T-Note Futures.

Determining the appropriate ratios is analogous to a calculation of the BPV hedge ratio as discussed before in the context of hedging techniques. Thus, this exercise entails an identification of the CTD security versus the particular Treasury securities referenced in the spread and a determination of the effective BPV associated with the futures contract by reference to the BPV of the cheapest (BPV_{CTD}) divided by its conversion factor (CF_{CTD}).

On May 15, 2007, the 4%-09 was CTD against the September 2007 two-year Treasury futures. This security had a BPV of $34.48 per $200,000 face value with a CF equal to 0.9672. Thus, the basis point value of the two-year futures contract ($BPV_{2\text{-Yr Futures}}$) may be calculated as \$35.65.

$$
\begin{aligned}
BPV_{2\text{-Yr Futures}} &= BPV_{CTD} \div CF_{CTD} \\
&= \$34.48 \div 0.9672 \\
&= \$35.65
\end{aligned}
$$

The 4 1/2%-11 was CTD against September 2007 5-year Treasury futures. It had a BPV = \$40.13 per \$100,000 face value with a CF of 0.9453. Thus, the $BPV_{5\text{-Yr Futures}} = \$42.45$.

$$
\begin{aligned}
BPV_{5\text{-Yr Futures}} &= BPV_{CTD} \div CF_{CTD} \\
&= \$40.13 \div 0.9453 \\
&= \$42.45
\end{aligned}
$$

The 4 3/4%-14 was CTD against the September 2007 10-year Treasury futures with a BPV = \$61.18 per \$100,000 face value and a CF = 0.9335. Thus, the $BPV_{10\text{-Yr Futures}} = \$65.53$.

$$
\begin{aligned}
BPV_{10\text{-Yr Futures}} &= BPV_{CTD} \div CF_{CTD} \\
&= \$61.18 \div 0.9335 \\
&= \$65.53
\end{aligned}
$$

How many two-year T-note futures are needed to balance one five-year T-note futures contract? We may apply the following equation noting that the $BPV_{2\text{-Yr}} = \$35.65$ while the $BPV_{5\text{-Yr}} = \$42.45$.

$$
\begin{aligned}
\text{Spread Ratio} &= BPV_{5\text{-Yr}} \div BPV_{2\text{-Yr}} \\
&= \$42.45 \div \$35.65 \\
&= 1.19 \\
&\quad \text{6:5 two-year versus five-year T-note futures}
\end{aligned}
$$

Similarly, the 10-year versus 2-year spread ratio equals 1.84, or roughly 9:5 2-year versus 10-year T-note futures. The 10-year/5-year spread ratio equals 1.54, or roughly 15:10 five-year versus ten-year T-note futures.

Trading the Curve with Treasury Futures

Applying the ratios as calculated in our examples, we may track the dollar value of the three yield curve spreads that may be constructed using 2-, 5-, and 10-year T-note futures. See Exhibit 7.28.

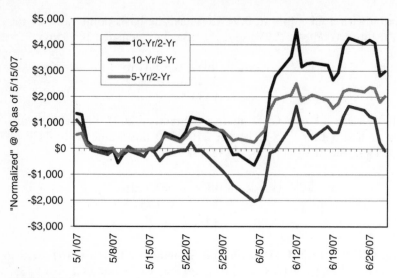

EXHIBIT 7.28   Dollar Value of Spread

Focusing on the span of the yield curve between the 2- and 5-year sectors, we may construct an example of a yield curve play. On May 15, 2007, one may have "bought the curve" buying 6 two-year and selling 5 five-year T-note futures. Holding the spread until June 26, 2007, the yield spread rallied from −0.021% to 0.088% (+10.9 bips) for a profit of $2,375.

	Sep-07 CBOT 2-Yr T-Note Futures	Sep-07 CBOT 5-Yr T-Note Futures	Spread
5/15/07	Buy 6 @ 102-092/ 32nds (4.786%)	Sell 5 @ 105-14/ 32nds (4.765%)	−0.021%
6/26/07	Sell 6 @ 101-266/ 32nds (5.024%)	Buy 5 @ 103-28/ 32nds (5.112%)	0.088%
	−14+/32nds or −$5,437.50	+50/32nds or +$7,812.50	+10.9 bips or +$2,375.00

CONCLUSION

Treasury futures serve an essential role in helping asset managers address the risks associated with volatile interest rates. This function is more essential than ever before in light of growing borrowing demands on the part of the U.S. Treasury.

Treasury futures may be used as part of a "basis trade" versus cash Treasury securities. Because of the unique construction of the contract, there are many interesting wrinkles associated with basis trading. More than a simple arbitrage, these transactions are affected by directional price movement and may be likened to options in some respects. Buying the basis entails the purchase of cash securities coupled with the sale of futures. This is essentially the same position that an asset manager intent on addressing the risks of possibly rising rates and falling prices might face. The same factors that impact the basis likewise impact the performance of hedging strategies.

Beyond hedging Treasuries or portfolios of Treasuries, these contracts likewise may be used to address the risks associated with corporate bonds under some conditions and with some adjustments. Finally, like Eurodollar futures, these products may be used to take advantage of anticipated changes in the shape of the yield curve.

NOTES

1. These contracts were originally introduced on the Chicago Board of Trade (CBOT). CBOT was merged with Chicago Mercantile Exchange (CME) in July 2007 and is now operated as a unit of the CME Group (CMEG).
2. Inflation-Indexed Treasury Securities were introduced in 1997. These securities are offered with maturities of 30 years, 10 years, and 5 years. They are sold with a stated coupon but promise the return of the original principal adjusted to reflect inflation as measured by the Consumer Price Index over the period until maturity. Thus, their coupons are typically established at levels that reflect the premium of long- or intermediate-term interest rates relative to inflation. Clearly, these have some investment appeal to those concerned about the long-term prospects for inflation.
3. The STRIPS program was created to facilitate the trade of zero-coupon Treasury securities. Prior to 1986, a variety of broker dealers including Merrill Lynch and Salomon Bros. issued zero-coupon securities collateralized by Treasuries under acronyms such as TIGeRs and CATS. For example, if you buy a 10-year Treasury, you can create zero-coupon securities of a variety of maturities by marketing the component cash flows. By selling a zero collateralized by a coupon payment due in five years, one creates a 5-year zero; or, one may create a 10-year zero by selling a zero collateralized by the principal payment. They engaged in this practice because the market valued the components of the security more dearly than the coupon payments and principal payment bundled together. Today, one might notice that the yield on a Treasury STRIP is usually less than a comparable

maturity coupon-bearing Treasury. Beginning with 10s and 30s issued in February 1986, the Treasury began assigning separate CUSIP numbers to the principal value and to tranches of coupon payments associated with these securities. A CUSIP number is a code unique to each security and is necessary to wire-transfer and, therefore, market a security. Thus, the Treasury STRIPS market was created. These securities are most popular when rates are high and, therefore, the price of the zero may be quite low.

CHAPTER 8

Commodities: Backbone of the Futures Industry

John W. Labuszewski
Paul E. Peterson

The futures market was originally developed and matured in the context of the basic commodity markets including grains, livestock, energy, and precious metals products. Although futures now extend into financial markets, we still frequently refer to our markets as "commodity futures markets" out of force of long habit. We could rightly characterize commodities as the backbone of the futures industry on which all else was based.

Arguably, financial futures had achieved status as perhaps the largest portion of the futures industry by the early 1980s. However, the recent global commodity boom occasioned by the rapid economic development of third world economies has placed new strains on commodity markets, driving prices to record highs in 2008. As such, institutional, corporate, and governmental sectors of our economy have focused intense interest in these markets in recent years.

Our intent is to review the characteristics of commodities in general with a specific focus on the principal commodity products offered on CME Group facilities including CBOT grains, CME livestock, NYMEX energy products, and COMEX metals. We discuss the pricing patterns of these products and some common trading strategies. We conclude by describing some recent developments as the CME Group extends its services into the realm of over-the-counter (OTC) derivatives, specifically by coupling OTC transaction execution with the financial sureties of a multilateral, centralized clearing system under the auspices of the CME ClearPort system.

WHAT ARE COMMODITIES?

From the outset, let us pause to consider a very simple question: What is a commodity? Commodities are products that are substantially identical regardless of the producer or originator. They are typically thought of as minimally processed products that serve as raw materials or inputs for the production of more refined products. Commodities are not branded but can, and typically do, conform to commonly accepted industrywide grades or standards.

Commodities are said to be homogeneous. As a result of this homogeneity or uniformity, one unit of a particular commodity is perfectly substitutable with another unit of the same commodity. In other words, and in the industry vernacular, the product is *fungible*.

Ideal of Perfect Competition

The market structure for commodities is typically highly diffuse with myriad producers and consumers. As such, the price and available quantities of commodities are driven by market factors rather than by the dictates of an individual or a concentrated group of producers and/or consumers.

These industries approach the economic ideal of "perfect competition" where prices are driven entirely by the interaction of the forces of supply and demand, or, more simply, market fundamentals. Industries that approach that ideal of perfect competition are characterized by a large number of both buyers and sellers where no particular player is significant enough to unduly influence prices. These markets typically feature very low-cost barriers to entry, and the concept of profit maximization tends to drive decisions.

Unfortunately, the so-called invisible hand of perfect competition may imply negligible economic profits in the long term. All producers of a fungible commodity may receive the same market price for their product. As a result, decisions that individual producers make about such commodities are dictated very strongly by the costs associated with production.

It follows that the most common way in which any individual market participant may increase profits is by reducing costs. Becoming a large or larger producer and enjoying the benefits of economies of scale represents an obvious way to reduce production costs. Consolidation among producers may achieve such economies but may further result in higher fixed costs. Still, in the final analysis, the lowest cost producer in the long term is the winner.

Are Commodities an "Asset Class"?

A commonly asked question is whether commodities constitute an "asset class" in the same sense as equities or fixed-income investments. Some suggest that the answer to this question might be irrelevant and that the better question is "can I expect a systematically positive and attractive return by holding commodities even if they are held on a purely passive or 'buy-and-hold' basis?" Let's review some of the commonly cited reasons to hold a commodity portfolio or at least to devote a portion of one's investment portfolio to commodities.

The three most commonly cited reasons include (1) commodities may represent a reasonable hedge against inflationary pressures; (2) commodities efficiently diversify one's portfolio to the extent that they exhibit negative or reasonably low correlation with traditional investments such as stocks and bonds; and (3) commodities provide attractive returns in their own right, particularly if one is willing to leverage one's investment and possibly to deploy an actively managed as opposed to a passive buy-and-hold approach to the investment.

Commodity Indexes

But before we can reasonably address these questions, we must discuss what specific products constitute the commodity marketplace. Further, are there any commonly referenced benchmark measures of commodity performance? We use two common references for commodity market performance as found in the S&P/GSCI Index and the Dow Jones-UBS (DJ-UBS) Commodity Index (formerly DJ-AIG Commodity Index).

The S&P/GSCI is a popular index that tracks the value of the most actively traded physical commodities, including energy, industrial metals, precious metals, agricultural, and livestock products. It is periodically reweighted by reference to the average production value of commodities within the past five years. Accordingly, the weightings of the S&P/GSCI Index provide a convenient measure for the significance of energy products relative to other popularly traded physical commodities. Most, although not all, of these markets are operated by CME Group through its CME, CBOT, NYMEX, and COMEX operations. See Exhibits 8.1. and 8.2.

Note that energy products accounted for approximately 70% of world production values of the physical commodities represented in the S&P/GSCI Commodity Index. Energy products are perhaps the most significant commodities of any category as measured by their worldwide production value. In fact, the significance of energy products has been exacerbated in recent years by advances in energy prices driven largely by relatively newfound demand in emerging economies including China and India.

An alternate commodity index that has similarly achieved widespread recognition as a benchmark measure of performance is found in the Dow Jones-UBS Commodity Index (DJ-UBS Index). Like the S&P/GSCI Index,

EXHIBIT 8.1 S&P/GSCI Weightings (as of 5/18/09)

Crude oil	38.49%	Gold	2.91%
Brent crude oil	13.47%	Silver	0.32%
RBOB gasoline	4.87%	Precious metals	**3.23%**
Heating oil	4.25%	Wheat	3.70%
Gasoil	4.64%	Red wheat	0.78%
Natural gas	3.91%	Corn	3.40%
Energy	**69.63%**	Soybeans	2.68%
Aluminum	2.26%	Cotton	1.10%
Copper	3.06%	Sugar	2.20%
Lead	0.46%	Coffee	0.75%
Nickel	0.77%	Cocoa	0.35%
Zinc	0.60%	Agriculture	**14.96%**
Industrial metals	**7.16%**	Live cattle	2.89%
		Feeder cattle	0.60%
		Lean hogs	1.54%
		Livestock	**5.02%**

the DJ-UBS references the values of a broad diversity of products covering the major commodity sectors, including energy, agriculture, precious and industrial metals, and livestock. See Exhibits 8.3. and 8.4.

But unlike the S&P/GSCI Index, which references 24 futures markets, the DJ-UBS focuses on just 19 futures markets, all of which are represented in the S&P/GSCI. Also unlike the S&P/GSCI Index, the DJ-UBS Index is weighted by reference to both the liquidity of the various futures contracts as well as production values. In fact, the DJ-UBS Index relies more heavily on liquidity than production values on a 2:1 bias.

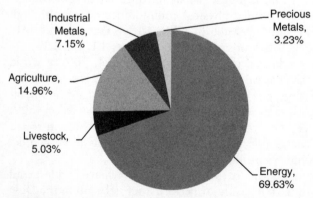

EXHIBIT 8.2 S&P/GSCI Weightings

EXHIBIT 8.3   2009 DJ-UBS Weightings

Crude oil	13.75%	Gold	7.86%
RBOB gasoline	3.71%	Silver	2.89%
Heating oil	3.65%	**Precious metals**	**10.75%**
Natural gas	11.89%	Wheat	4.80%
Energy	**33.00%**	Corn	5.72%
Aluminum	7.00%	Soybeans	7.60%
Copper	7.31%	Soybean oil	2.88%
Nickel	2.88%	Cotton	2.27%
Zinc	3.14%	Sugar	2.99%
Industrial metals	**20.33%**	Coffee	2.97%
		Agriculture	**29.23%**
		Live cattle	4.29%
		Lean hogs	2.40%
		Livestock	**6.68%**

   Of course, many other important and widely referenced commodity indexes are available. Noteworthy indexes include but are not necessarily limited to the Rogers International Commodity Index (RICI), Reuters/Jefferies CRB Index, Deutsche Bank Liquid Commodity Index (DBLCI), and the Merrill Lynch Commodity Index eXtra (MLCX).

   All of these indexes are constructed using their own take on most relevant constituents and weighting procedures, but all purport to represent the same essential quality, that is, the performance of the commodity markets in general. Although all of these indexes are valuable in their own unique

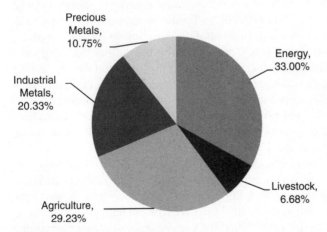

EXHIBIT 8.4   2009 DJ-UBS Weightings

ways, we limit ourselves to references to the S&P/GSCI and DJ-UBS Indexes for convenience.

It is noteworthy that it is eminently possible to take positions in the S&P/GSCI and DJ-UBS Indexes. Of course, one might re-create the indexes by taking positions in all index constituents. Or one might simply take a position in S&P/GSCI or DJ-UBS futures contracts. These are contracts that are cash-settled versus the value of the respective indexes. Another alternative is to enter into an OTC swap transaction based on either of these two indexes, although this avenue may be limited to so-called eligible contract participants (ECPs), who may generally be thought of as institutional and professional traders as opposed to a typical retail trader.

Hedge against Inflation?

Investors have frequently viewed physical commodities as a fundamental store of value against the potential ravages of inflationary pressures. Precious metals including gold and silver have traditionally been accumulated for this very reason, although other commodities with strategic value including energy and foodstuffs have likewise been viewed in this way as well.

Although the futures markets today are largely dominated by the financial futures markets, which started to spring up in the early 1970s, the decade of the 1970s was nonetheless dominated by the trade of physical commodity futures. It was during this era after the Vietnam War and Great Society social programs that the U.S. government started to spend far more than was being taken in by tax receipts.

During the 1970s, Federal Reserve policy was to maintain stable interest rates, and therefore the deficit was funded by growth in money supply more so than issuance of federal debt. A fundamental economic equation has a nation's gross domestic product (GDP) equating to money supplies, which in turn equate to the price, multiplied by the production of goods and services. If money supply increases without a proportionate advance in productivity, the result is rising prices, or inflation. By 1979, the Consumer Price Index (CPI) experienced its only recorded double-digit advance.

Against this backdrop, physical commodity futures, notably including gold, silver, and grains, were being purchased by largely retail investors as a hedge against inflation. But is this a "good hedge?"

The empirical evidence suggests there is indeed a positive correlation between commodity prices as measured by the major commodity indexes and inflation as measured by the CPI. However, that correlation is not terribly strong or particularly consistent. However, the evidence suggests there is a much stronger correlation between the performance of these commodity indexes and "unexpected inflation" or the differences between the market's

EXHIBIT 8.5 Commodity Correlation with Inflation

	Correlation with CPI (1995–2005)	Correlation with Unexpected Inflation (1995–2005)
S&P/GSCI	0.13	0.28
DJ-UBS	0.14	0.30
S&P 500	−0.10	0.01
Barclays Capital Aggregate Bond Index	−0.06	−0.01
Barclays Capital US Corporate High-Yield Bond Index	−0.08	−0.01
S&P/GSCI Ag Sub-Index	−0.04	0.06
S&P/GSCI Energy Sub-Index	0.12	0.26
S&P/GSCI Industrial Metals Sub-Index	0.00	0.13
S&P/GSCI Livestock Sub-Index	0.08	−0.07
S&P/GSCI Precious Metals Sub-Index	0.10	0.22

Source: "The Benefits of Commodity Investment: 2006 Update," Center for International Securities and Derivatives Markets, August 2006.

aggregate consensus on the likely value of the next CPI release versus the actual figure. See Exhibit 8.5.

Thus, one might conclude that physical commodities may broadly follow inflationary trends. Certainly there is better correlation between commodities and CPI than between other traditional asset classes, including stocks (as measured by the Standard & Poor's 500, or S&P 500) or bonds (measured by the Barclays Capital Aggregate Bond Index, formerly the Lehman Government/Corporate Bond Index, or the Barclays Capital U.S. Corporate High-Yield Bond Index, formerly the Lehman High-Yield Bond Index), against which relatively weak negative correlations are observed. But commodities are far from perfect or even particularly efficient hedging vehicles for inflation.

Diversification Benefit

A far more enticing benefit of commodity investment, even on a passive buy-and-hold basis, is the fact that commodities historically have displayed a low or even negative correlation with traditional investments including stocks and bonds. This is evidenced by our table in Exhibit 8.6 depicting correlations between the S&P/GSCI and DJ-UBS versus the S&P 500, the Barclays Capital Aggregate Bond Index, and 30-Day Treasury bills.

EXHIBIT 8.6   Correlation from Jan-91 through Jun-07

	S&P/ GSCI	DJ-AIG	S&P 500	Lehman Bond Index	30-Day T-Bill
S&P/GSCI	1.00				
DJ-UBS	0.88	1.00			
S&P 500	−0.02	0.08	1.00		
Barclays Capital Aggregate Bond Index	0.04	0.01	0.08	1.00	
30-Day T-Bill	−0.04	−0.04	0.10	0.16	1.00

Source: Morningstar.

The capital asset pricing model (CAPM) suggests that diversification of one's portfolio among low or uncorrelated assets provides significant benefits. This is underscored by a recent study that simply examined the performance of various benchmarks representing major asset classes during months when equities, as measured by the S&P 500, experienced their sharpest monthly losses of the year.

The data clearly suggest that commodities as measured by the S&P/GSCI and DJ-UBS Indexes tend to post favorable returns during the months when the S&P 500 performs worst. Clearly, this could be of major benefit to any investment portfolio largely invested in traditional asset classes such as stocks and bonds. See Exhibit 8.7.

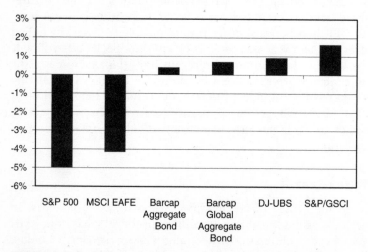

EXHIBIT 8.7   Average Return during Largest Monthly Decline in S&P 500 (1991–2006)
Source: "The Benefits of Commodity Investment: 2006 Update," Center for International Securities and Derivatives Markets, August 2006.

EXHIBIT 8.8   Investment Portfolio Performance (1995–2005)

Portfolio	Annualized Returns	Annualized Std Dev	Sharpe Ratio	Maximum Drawdown
50% stocks, 50% bonds	9.68%	7.77%	0.74	−16.07%
40% stocks, 40% bonds, 20% S&P/GSCI	10.26%	7.51%	0.85	−13.91%
40% stocks, 40% bonds, 20% DJ-UBS	9.78%	7.03%	0.84	−11.85%

Source: "The Benefits of Commodity Investment: 2006 Update," Center for International Securities and Derivatives Markets, August 2006.

The same study attempted to identify the explicit benefits associated with holding commodities on a passive buy-and-hold basis in portfolios constructed largely using stocks and bonds (as measured by the S&P 500 and Barclays Capital Aggregate Bond Index) in combination with an investment in either the S&P/GSCI or DJ-UBS Indexes. See Exhibits 8.8 and 8.9.

The study clearly demonstrated that diversification into commodities provided tangible benefits in terms of enhanced annualized returns, diminished variability of returns as measured by the standard deviation of monthly portfolio returns, an enhanced Sharpe ratio (measuring return as a function of risk), and a muted maximum monthly drawdown.

But the study further demonstrated that the performance of commodities is very "period dependent." In other words, commodities might perform quite well in some periods but perhaps not so well in other periods. Certainly commodities, driven by demand from emerging markets such as China and India, performed extremely well during the period from 2001 to 2005. However, commodities performed with somewhat less flair during the longer period from 1995 to 2005.

EXHIBIT 8.9   Investment Portfolio Performance (2001–2005)

Portfolio	Annualized Returns	Annualized Std Dev	Sharpe Ratio	Maximum Drawdown
50% stocks, 50% bonds	3.67%	7.06%	0.22	−14.63%
40% stocks, 40% bonds, 20% S&P/GSCI	5.33%	7.05%	0.45	−12.90%
40% stocks, 40% bonds, 20% DJ-UBS	5.09%	6.60%	0.45	−11.72%

Source: "The Benefits of Commodity Investment: 2006 Update, Center for International Securities and Derivatives Markets, August 2006.

Attractive Returns?

It is all well and good to suggest that a passive investment in commodities might represent at least a weak hedge against inflation. Or that a traditionally invested portfolio may benefit from the diversification afforded by at least a modest investment in commodities. But the results of the study just referenced beg the larger and perhaps most important question: are commodities, even when held on a passive buy-and-hold basis, a good investment in and of themselves?

Actually, it may be difficult to track the value of most commodities over extremely extended periods of time. Fortunately, gold is an exception to that rule because it is possible to gather data going back to the fourteenth century. In particular, we may examine the performance of gold in real or inflation-adjusted terms.

We find that although prices have experienced some rather extreme episodes, including the great bullion famine of the fifteenth century and the 1979 episode in which the Hunt Brothers allegedly caused a major run-up and subsequent sharp crash in the price of precious metals. Certainly there were periods during which the price of gold trended upward or downward for extended periods of time. But at the end of the day, or rather the end of some seven centuries, the value of gold has appreciated only about 20% beyond inflationary considerations. See Exhibit 8.10.

Gold, of course, is a single commodity. How would a diversified investment in commodities as represented by a commodity index have performed

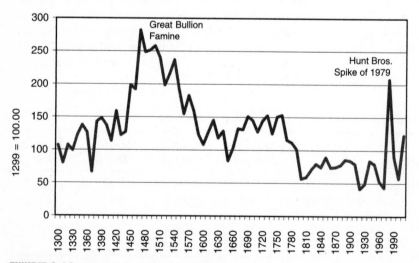

EXHIBIT 8.10   Real Value of Gold (1300–2006)

historically? If one had invested $100 in the commodities that constitute the S&P/GSCI Index in the prescribed proportions as indicated by the index weights at the conclusion of 1969, that $100 would have grown to $472.26 by the conclusion of 2008. That represents growth of 3.43% on an annual compounded basis. However, that same $100 invested at a rate that equaled the CPI would have grown to $580.95, for an annual compounded growth of 4.11%.

However, these results are really very period dependent. Had one invested that $100 at the conclusion of 1969 and liquidated the position at the conclusion of 2007, it would have grown to $882.57. That represents growth of 5.56% on an annual compounded basis and nicely exceeds the $559.68, or 3.99% growth, in CPI.

In other words, timing is very important. Calendar year 2008 was generally a very bad period in which to be invested in commodities, noting that energy and grain products had been driven to extreme highs by approximately midyear only to decline sharply as the subprime mortgage crisis broke and severely dampened global demand for many products including commodities. See Exhibit 8.11.

This point may be underscored by examining the rates of return associated with the major asset classes of stocks and bonds versus commodities in recent years. Commodities, as measured by the S&P/GSCI and DJ-UBS Indexes, generally posted very attractive returns in the period from 1995 to

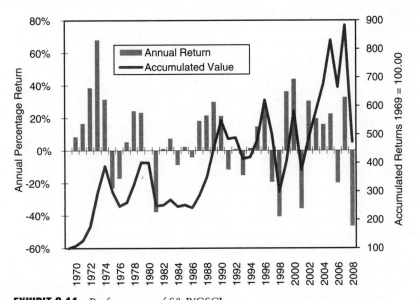

EXHIBIT 8.11   Performance of S&P/GSCI

EXHIBIT 8.12   Risk and Return in Various Asset Classes

	1995–2005			2001–2005		
	Annual Return	Annual Std Dev	Max Drawdown	Annual Return	Annual Std Dev	Max Drawdown
S&P/ GSCI	10.50%	20.65%	−48.25%	9.83%	22.23%	−34.06%
DJ-UBS	9.25%	13.38%	−36.20%	10.03%	13.67%	−20.05%
S&P 500	11.40%	15.10%	−44.73%	0.54%	14.94%	−38.87%
Barcap Agg Bond	7.29%	4.42%	−4.57%	6.10%	4.86%	−4.57%

Source: "The Strategic and Tactical Value of Commodity Investing," Campbell Harvey, Duke University, December 2007.

2005 and in the subperiod 2001 to 2005. Likewise, equities as measured by the S&P 500 performed quite well in the period from 1995 to 2005. However, we note that the S&P 500 performed poorly during the period from 2001 to 2005. See Exhibit 8.12.

Thus, it is possible to earn returns, even on a passive buy-and-hold basis, in commodities that are equity-like in magnitude. It is even possible, depending heavily on the period selected, to realize returns in the commodity markets that exceed returns realized in equities.

Similarly, the risks associated with commodities, as measured by either the annual standard deviation or the maximum realized drawdown, may be similarly equity-like. This is intuitive in the sense that returns in an investment are generally proportionate to the attendant risks. The foregoing analysis focuses on market risk as a readily measurable variable. But risk comes in many varieties.

For example, one may examine the sovereign risk associated with a particular investment. This refers to the risk that one purchases fixed- income or equity securities in a foreign country whose government or regulatory authorities intervene in some unforeseen way to erode or even abrogate the value of the investment. For example, a foreign government might suspend or defer coupon or principal payments associated with its debt securities. Or it may amend its foreign exchange regulations to impede the repatriation of invested capital. Stocks and bonds may clearly be affected by sovereign risks but to the extent that commodities might be considered transnational in a certain sense, perhaps they might be relatively immune.

Bankruptcy risk refers to the risk that the corporation that issues a particular equity or fixed-income security fails and is unable to meet its

EXHIBIT 8.13   Types of Risk Exposure

	Sovereign Risk?	Bankruptcy Risk?	Inflation Risk?
Stocks	Yes	Yes	?
Bonds	Yes	Yes	No
Commodities	No	No	?

obligations. Clearly, stocks and bonds carry this risk. Of course, the definition of a commodity implies that they are produced by a wide variety of sources and, therefore, might be insulated from the bankruptcy of any particular producer, at least in an aggregate sense. See Exhibit 8.13.

Finally, we may discuss inflation risk. Fixed-income securities, at least in theory, will be valued to provide a premium over inflation. It is not quite so clear whether stocks or commodities are not affected by these risks.

Thus, we return full circle to our original question: Does a passive buy-and-hold investment in commodities produce an attractive return? Our conclusion is "sometimes." Again, commodity investment is very much a period-dependent proposition. Certainly there are some periods during which passive commodity investments have performed very well but other periods when such an investment has performed quite poorly. Sometimes commodities may trend reliably for extended periods of time, sometimes even decades and often in pronounced boom-and-bust cycles.

This may largely be attributed to inelasticity associated with the supply and demand for commodities. For example, it may require considerable time for oil companies to develop new fields and increase production in response to increased demand. Certainly, the demand from emerging economies for basic commodities such as energy and grains had been driving the markets sharply higher until the 2008 market break occasioned by the subprime mortgage crisis and a resulting sharp downturn in economic conditions.

Perhaps the real moral of the story is that commodities are driven by the fundamental forces of supply and demand. Thus, rational traders, certainly those who are trading on a reasonably long-term basis, are advised closely to study the interaction of these market forces as a precursor to commodity investment. Further, it may be possible to achieve attractive positive returns by actively or selectively managing a portfolio of individual commodity futures contracts, held either long or short.

Commodity Investing Industry

Investors have taken notice that commodities can be, at least under some circumstances, an attractive investment alternative. Some have invested using a passive buy-and-hold strategy, but many others have sought professional trading services applied in an actively managed methodology.

The "managed futures" approach has been in operation for more than 60 years. The first managed futures account is attributed to the noted technician Dick Donchian, dating back to perhaps 1948. Much of the early interest came from retail investors who would open up separately managed accounts with particular professional commodity traders, commonly referred to as commodity trading advisors (CTAs).

In more recent years, however, institutional investors such as corporate and public pension funds, endowments, trusts, and even banks have driven the expansion of the managed futures industry, recognizing that managed futures represent an important component of a well-diversified portfolio.

Although one may still access CTAs by opening separately managed accounts, it has become more commonplace to participate in a fund or limited partnership designed to facilitate speculative futures investments and managed by a single CTA or multiple CTAs under the direction of a commodity pool operator (CPO).

Managed futures funds, commodity funds, or *commodity pools* (these various terms are generally synonymous) aggregate the monies of multiple investors for the purpose of speculating in futures and options markets. These funds or pools are organized and managed by CPOs. CTAs may be employed by the CPO to direct the day-to-day trading of the fund or a portion of it. This leaves the CPO free to concentrate on other significant activities, including fundraising, accounting, evaluation, and ongoing monitoring of CTA performance, relying on the professionalism and experience of CTAs devoted to trading activities.

A CTA may be thought of as performing the same function as a stock manager or mutual fund manager. Investors effectively employ, or assign power of attorney over their funds to, the CTA to manage their investments on a discretionary basis. CTAs typically use the global futures markets as their primary investment or trading vehicles in the pursuit of profitable opportunities.

Managed futures investments may also be referred to as commodity funds, futures funds, or commodity pools. The terms *CTA, CPO*, and *commodity pool* are U.S. regulatory designations originating with the Commodity Exchange Act (CEA) but may generally be applied to describe these specialized endeavors. Other regulatory jurisdictions may apply somewhat different nomenclature to describe these activities.

Consistent with the growth of the futures industry in general, investment in managed futures has grown impressively since the early 1980s. *Managed Accounts Reports* (MAR) is a publication that covers the industry and estimates that investment in managed futures grew from less than $310

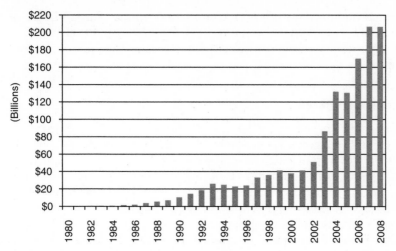

EXHIBIT 8.14 Funds under Management by CTAs

million in 1980 to an estimated $206.4 billion as of the fourth quarter 2008. See Exhibit 8.14.

Note that these CTAs may trade in physical commodities such as grains, livestock, energy, and metals products. But they may also trade in a variety of financial futures contracts as well. Some specialize in certain markets, whereas others apply their methodologies generally over a wide spectrum of commodity and financial futures.

The trading activity of CTAs is generally quite active rather than passive. Although some CTAs use fundamental market analysis to guide their investment decisions, CTA trading activities are more frequently guided by so-called technical trading systems. These systems are based on historical price patterns and may include moving average, price channel, and momentum systems. Generally speaking, these systems may be thought of as trend following in nature, noting that the ability to detect reversals in market momentum, that is, to apply contrarian systems successfully, is rather rare and extraordinary.

The next several sections of this chapter provide an overview of the major commodity sectors, including grains, livestock, energy, and precious metals products as well as the fundamental that drive these markets.

GRAIN MARKETS

The history of the futures industry in the United States is inextricably intertwined with the development of the grain markets. CME Group grain futures and options represent legacy products from the Chicago Board of Trade (CBOT), which has roots dating back formally to 1848. Therefore, it may be appropriate to begin any discussion of specific commodities by considering grains.

Categorizing Grains

Grains might be categorized on the basis of whether they are "feed grains" or "food grains." Feed grains are products fed primarily to animals and generally characterized as high in starch or energy content. These grains include corn, sorghum (milo), oats, and barley. They are also known as "coarse grains." Food grains are primarily consumed by humans but might be fed to animals if they become sufficiently cheap. These commodities include wheat and rice.

Some products within the grain family might further be categorized as oilseeds, which are processed, or crushed, primarily to produce vegetable oils. This includes soybean oil, sunflower oil, canola oil, and safflower oil. Sometimes products such as palm oil and palm kernel oil are likewise included in this category.

Although corn and cotton might be processed to produce corn oil and cottonseed oil, respectively, we do not typically include them as oilseeds because these products are not primarily produced for their oil content. The key word here is "primarily." In any event, each of these oils has its own unique properties and resulting uses that distinguish it from other oils.

The residual material left over from the crushing process is a high-protein meal such as soybean meal, sunflower meal, canola meal, and so on. These products are primarily fed to animals. Or they may be combined with other grains to produce a hybrid product. For example, corn is combined with soybean meal to produce a balanced protein with an amino acid profile to be fed to hogs or chickens.

Active futures contracts are available on a variety of grains, although we focus on the most actively traded CME Group products, including corn, wheat, soybeans, soybean oil, and soybean meal. The futures contract terms and conditions for these five most active grain futures are included in the appendix to this chapter.

Supply and Demand Balance Sheet

The price of these grains is fundamentally driven by the interaction of supply and demand. Supply and demand may be measured by reference to tables produced by the U.S. Department of Agriculture (USDA) World Ag Outlook Board. These tables may alternatively be referred to as balance sheets, supply/demand, or supply and use tables. They depict world and

EXHIBIT 8.15 U.S. Corn Supply and Use

			2008/09 Projections	
	2006/07	2007/09 Est.	February	March
	MILLION ACRES			
Area planted	79.3	93.5	96.0	96.0
Harvested	70.6	96.5	79.6	79.6
	BUSHELS			
Yield per harvested acre	149.1	150.7	153.9	153.9
	MILLION BUSHELS			
Beginning stocks	1,967	1,304	1,624	1,624
Production	10,531	13,039	12,101	12,101
Imports	12	20	15	15
Supply, total	12,510	14,362	13,740	13,740
Feed and residual	5,591	5,939	5,300	5,300
Food, seed, and industrial	3,490	4,363	4,900	5,000
Ethanol for fuel	2,119	3,026	3,600	3,700
Domestic, total	9,081	10,302	10,200	10,300
Exports	2,125	2,436	1,750	1,700
Use, total	11,207	12,737	11,950	12,000
Ending stocks, total	1,304	1,624	1,790	1,740
CCC inventory	0	0	0	0
Free stocks	1,304	1,624	1,790	1,740
Outstanding loans	116	106	200	200
Avg. farm price ($/bu)	3.04	4.20	3.65–4.15	3.90–4.30

Source: U.S. Department of Agriculture.

U.S. estimates for all major U.S. crops and are updated monthly including an accompanying narrative. See Exhibit 8.15.

Such information generally carries the greatest impact during the growing season or so-called weather months. It is during the growing season that market participants focus carefully on supply issues including acreage, weather conditions, possible yields, and so on.

During nonweather months, of course, the focus shifts to demand issues, including domestic consumption, export demand, and possibly growing conditions in other parts of the world, notably including South America that has grown to become a major rival to U.S. grain production. Traders frequently pay very close attention to statistics including ending stocks and ending stocks as a percentage of total use. Of course, each of the major grain crops including corn, wheat, and soybeans are affected by their own unique characteristics as summarized next.

Corn

Corn is primarily produced in the central states including Illinois, Iowa, and adjacent regions. It is planted in the spring and harvested in the fall. A successful crop and a high yield is contingent on factors including a timely planting in the spring, periodic rainfall during the season, moderate temperatures and adequate moisture when the corn is pollinating in July and August, and, finally, the absence of any deleterious early frost.

Corn yields and acreage devoted to its planting has grown over recent years. In particular, growing demand for renewable fuels such as ethanol has diverted much product from feedstock use.

CBOT corn futures call for the delivery of 5,000 bushels of #2 yellow corn with grades #1 and #3 also acceptable for delivery at a premium or discount to #2 yellow, respectively. They are traded for delivery during the months of March, May, July, September, and December. Corn futures are quoted in cents per bushel in minimum increments of ¼ cent per bushel ($12.50 per contract). For example, one might see at quote of 425.500, or $4.2550 per bushel. This implies that single futures contract is nominally valued at $21,275.00 (= 5,000 bushels × $4.255). (See the appendix for detailed futures and option contract specifications.)

Wheat

The two major categories of wheat are the winter and spring varieties, with several different classes of wheat within those two categories. Wheat is a very resilient crop and capable of tolerating severe weather much better than other grains. It tends to be planted in areas that may be too dry or harsh to support corn or soybean production. Of course, each category and class of wheat thrives best under its own unique conditions, has its own particular uses and, therefore, its own specific supply and demand drivers.

Winter wheat is planted in the fall and goes dormant during the winter. In fact, winter wheat requires a blanket of snow cover to serve as insulation and prevent freezing during the winter months. Growth resumes in the spring, and it is harvested in early summer. Winter wheat production is concentrated in a belt centered in Kansas. Soft red winter wheat is used for the production of baked goods such as cookies and crackers that do not need to rise. This is the type of wheat that is deliverable against the CBOT wheat futures contract. See Exhibit 8.16.

Hard red winter wheat is used for baked goods that do need to rise such as bread. This is the type of wheat that is deliverable against the Kansas City Board of Trade (KCBT) wheat futures contract. Spring wheat is planted in the spring and harvested in the fall. Production of spring wheat is concentrated

EXHIBIT 8.16   U.S. Wheat Supply and Use

	2006/07	2007/09 Est.	2008/09 Projections	
			February	March
	MILLION ACRES			
Area planted	57.3	60.5	63.1	63.1
Harvested	46.9	51.0	55.7	55.7
	BUSHELS			
Yield per harvested acre	38.6	40.2	44.9	44.9
	MILLION BUSHELS			
Beginning stocks	571	456	306	306
Production	1,909	2,051	2,500	2,500
Imports	122	113	110	120
Supply, total	2,501	2,620	2,915	2,925
Feed and residual	939	947	950	925
Food, seed, and industrial	92	99	90	79
Ethanol for fuel	117	15	230	230
Domestic, total	1,137	1,050	1,260	1,233
Exports	909	1,264	1,000	990
Use, total	2,045	2,314	2,260	2,213
Ending stocks, total	456	306	655	712
CCC inventory	41	0	0	0
Free stocks	415	306	655	712
Outstanding loans	14	1	10	10
Avg. farm price ($/bu)	4.26	6.49	6.70–6.90	6.70–6.90

Source: U.S. Department of Agriculture.

in a region centered in North Dakota and Minnesota. Hard red spring wheat is the type of wheat that is deliverable against the Minneapolis Grain Exchange (MGE) wheat futures contract. Durum wheat is used generally for pasta; white wheat is used in cereals and other specialty food products.

CBOT futures call for the delivery of 5,000 bushels of wheat of the #2 soft red winter variety. Alternative grades are also acceptable for delivery at specified premiums or discounts. They are traded for delivery during the months of March, May, July, September, and December. KCBT and MGE wheat futures also call for the delivery of 5,000 bushels of hard red winter and hard red spring wheat, respectively. See Exhibit 8.17.

CBOT wheat futures are quoted in cents per bushel in minimum increments of ¼ cent per bushel ($12.50 per contract). For example, one might see a quote of 562.750, or $5.6275 per bushel. This implies that a single futures contract is nominally valued at $28,137.50 (= 5,000 bushels × $5.6275). (See the appendix for detailed futures and option contract specifications.)

EXHIBIT 8.17   2009 U.S. Wheat by Class, Supply, and Use

Year beginning June 1	Hard Winter	Hard Spring	Soft Red	White	Durum	Total
2007/08 (estimated)			**MILLION BUSHELS**			
Beginning stocks	165	117	109	44	21	456
Production	956	450	352	221	72	2,051
Supply, total	1,121	615	475	275	134	2,620
Domestic use	446	242	211	68	94	1,050
Exports	539	305	209	170	42	1,264
Use, total	984	547	420	239	126	2,314
Ending stocks, total	139	69	55	37	8	306
2008/09 (Projected)						
Beginning stocks	138	69	55	37	8	306
Production	1,035	512	614	254	95	2,500
Supply, total	1,174	630	694	298	130	2,925
Domestic use	458	242	346	106	90	1,233
Exports	438	205	190	130	17	990
Use, total	896	449	536	236	99	2,213
Ending stocks, total						
March	279	192	159	62	33	712
February	249	160	153	74	21	655

Source: U.S. Department of Agriculture.

Soybeans

Soybeans are planted in the spring and harvested in the fall. They are easy to grow, enjoy a long blooming period, and are capable of withstanding some rather severe weather conditions. Soybeans thrive in the same regions as corn and are typically grown in a rotation to protect against disease and insect infestation. In fact, beans compete for acreage with corn with potential profitability generally serving as the determining factor. Beans may further be double-cropped with winter wheat and thereby use the land more completely.

Soybeans are processed, or "crushed," to produce two major by-products in the form of soybean oil and soybean meal. The average "crush ratio" or yield of by-product per single bushel (60 pounds) of soybeans equals 11 pounds of soybean oil, 47 pounds of soybean meal (48% protein content), with 2 pounds of residual material including hulls. Soybean futures are often traded versus opposite positions in soybean meal and soybean oil futures to gain exposure to the crush margin. This is essentially a speculation on how crushers will adjust production in response to dynamic market conditions. See Exhibit 8.18.

Although the United States remains the single largest soybean-producing nation on earth, Argentina and Brazil have become very significant sources as well. A fair proportion of this production is consumed in the producing country, but soybeans are a global product and nations including China, the European Union, Japan, and Mexico are large importers of the product. Thus, it is important to be cognizant of the global as well as domestic fundamentals. In particular, the development of Southern Hemisphere sources of supply has significantly altered the previously very seasonal nature of supply in the global market. See Exhibit 8.19.

CBOT soybean futures call for the delivery of 5,000 bushels of #2 yellow soybeans with premiums and discounts established for the delivery of alternate grades. They are traded for delivery in the months of January, March, May, July, August, September, and November. Soybean futures are quoted in cents per bushel in minimum increments of ¼ cent per bushel ($12.50 per contract). For example, one might see a quote of 1046.000 or $10.46 per bushel. This implies that a single futures contract is nominally valued at $52,300.00 (= 5,000 bushels × $10.46). See Exhibit 8.20 for grain pricing trends.

Soybean oil futures calls for the delivery of 60,000 pounds of oil during the months of January, March, May, July, August, September, October, and December. They are quoted in cents per pound in minimum increments of 1/100 cent ($0.0001) per pound ($6.00 per contract). Thus, a quote of 37.130 equals $0.3713 cents per pound and implies a futures contract value of $22,278 (= 60,000 pounds × $0.3713).

Soybean meal futures call for the delivery of 100 short tons of meal during the months of January, March, May, July, August, September, October, and December. Soybean meal futures are quoted in dollars and cents per short ton in minimum increments of 10 cents per short ton ($10.00 per contract). A quote of 405.20 may be interpreted as $405.20 per ton and implies a futures contract value of $40,520.00. (See the appendix for detailed futures and option contract specifications for soybeans, soybean oil, and soybean meal.) See Exhibit 8.21 for meal and oil pricing trends.

LIVESTOCK MARKETS

Livestock futures were originally developed on the CME in the 1960s. In fact, the CME is often referred to as the "exchange that pork bellies built" in reference to the first successful livestock-related futures contract

EXHIBIT 8.18   U.S. Soybeans Supply and Use

			2008/09 Projections	
	2006/07	2007/09 Est.	February	March
SOYBEANS	MILLION ACRES			
Area planted	75.5	64.7	75.7	75.7
Harvested	74.6	64.1	74.6	74.6
	BUSHELS			
Yield per harvested acre	42.9	41.7	39.6	39.6
	MILLION BUSHELS			
Beginning stocks	449	574	205	205
Production	3,197	2,677	2,959	2,959
Imports	9	10	9	9
Supply, total	3,655	3,261	3,173	3,173
Crushings	1,908	1,901	1,650	1,640
Exports	1,116	1,161	1,150	1,195
Seed	90	93	90	90
Residual	77	0	73	73
Use, total	3,091	3,056	2,963	2,999
Ending stocks	574	205	210	195
Avg. farm price ($/bu)	6.43	10.10	9.75–9.75	9.85–9.85
SOYBEAN OIL	MILLION POUNDS			
Beginning stocks	3,010	3,095	2,493	2,493
Production	20,499	20,569	18,810	19,645
Imports	37	65	50	50
Supply, total	23,536	23,719	21,343	21,178
Domestic	19,575	19,327	17,600	16,900
For methyl ester	2,762	2,991	2,900	2200
Exports	1,977	2,909	1,500	1,500
Use, total	20,451	21,235	19,100	19,400
Ending stocks	3,095	2,493	2,243	2,778
Average price (c/lb)	31.02	52.03	31.00–34.00	29.50–31.50
SOYBEAN MEAL	THOUSAND SHORT TONS			
Beginning stocks	314	346	294	294
Production	43,054	42,242	39,991	39,941
Imports	156	141	165	165
Supply, total	43,524	42,729	39,450	39,300
Domestic	34,374	33,155	30,750	30,600
Exports	9,904	9,290	9,400	9,400
Use, total	43,179	42,435	39,150	39,000
Ending stocks	346	294	300	300
Average price ($/s.t.)	205.44	335.94	265.00–305.00	265.00–305.00

Source: U.S. Department of Agriculture.

EXHIBIT 8.19 World Soybeans Supply and Use (Million Metric Tons)

Region	Supply			Use			
	Beginning Stocks	Production	Imports	Crush	Total	Exports	Ending Stocks
				2006/07			
World	53.09	237.54	69.16	195.90	225.60	71.50	62.69
United States	12.23	97.00	0.25	49.20	53.47	30.39	15.62
Total foreign	40.96	150.54	69.92	146.70	172.13	41.12	47.07
Major exporters	33.27	114.00	2.05	66.24	70.90	37.54	40.99
Argentina	16.47	49.90	1.99	33.59	35.09	9.56	22.61
Brazil	16.64	59.00	0.05	31.11	34.02	23.49	19.19
Major importers	5.92	19.53	55.41	59.33	74.99	0.52	4.35
China	4.57	15.97	28.73	35.97	46.12	0.45	2.70
EU-27	0.73	1.23	15.29	14.67	16.09	0.05	1.12
Japan	0.26	0.23	4.09	2.93	4.31	0.00	0.27
Mexico	0.04	0.08	3.94	3.90	3.93	0.00	0.04
				2007/09 (Estimated)			
World	62.69	220.88	79.95	201.66	229.75	79.48	53.19
United States	15.62	72.96	0.27	49.02	51.57	31.60	5.58
Total foreign	47.07	149.02	79.58	152.64	179.19	47.99	47.61
Major exporters	40.98	114.00	3.11	69.06	72.71	44.27	41.11
Argentina	22.61	46.20	2.95	34.61	36.16	13.93	21.77
Brazil	19.19	61.00	0.15	31.94	34.79	25.36	19.19
Major importers	4.35	16.02	64.12	62.99	79.46	0.53	5.51
China	2.70	14.00	37.92	39.52	49.92	0.45	4.25
EU-27	1.12	0.73	15.15	14.97	16.14	0.04	0.92
Japan	0.27	0.23	4.01	2.99	4.22	0.00	0.29
Mexico	0.04	0.09	3.65	3.70	3.74	0.00	0.03

(Continued)

EXHIBIT 8.19 (Continued)

Region	Supply				Use			Ending Stocks
	Beginning Stocks	Production	Imports	Crush	Total	Exports		
			2008/09 (Projected)					
World Feb	53.21	224.15	73.99	196.22	226.62	74.95		49.97
Mar	53.19	223.27	74.03	195.34	225.74	74.91		49.95
U.S. Feb	5.58	90.54	0.25	44.91	49.35	31.30		5.71
Mar	5.58	90.54	0.25	44.63	49.08	32.25		5.03
Total foreign Feb	47.63	143.61	73.74	151.31	177.27	43.55		44.16
Mar	47.61	142.74	73.79	150.70	176.65	42.56		44.92
Major exporters Feb	41.11	104.90	1.97	66.47	71.20	40.00		36.67
Mar	41.11	104.00	1.97	66.47	71.20	39.00		69.97
Argentina Feb	21.77	43.90	1.90	33.72	35.30	12.70		19.47
Mar	21.77	43.00	1.90	33.72	35.30	11.70		19.67
Brazil Feb	19.18	57.00	0.05	31.20	34.21	24.90		17.12
Mar	19.18	57.00	0.05	31.20	34.21	24.90		17.12
Major importers Feb	5.51	19.92	60.54	62.33	79.09	0.52		6.36
Mar	5.51	19.92	60.54	61.93	77.59	0.52		6.86
China Feb	4.25	16.90	36.00	41.10	51.50	0.45		5.09
Mar	4.25	16.90	36.00	40.60	51.00	0.45		5.59
EU-27 Feb	0.92	0.75	13.55	13.05	14.28	0.03		0.91
Mar	0.92	0.75	13.55	13.05	14.28	0.03		0.91
Japan Feb	0.29	0.23	4.00	2.94	4.26	0.00		0.26
Mar	0.29	0.23	4.00	2.94	4.26	0.00		0.26
Mexico Feb	0.03	0.16	3.40	3.52	3.55	0.00		0.04
Mar	0.03	0.16	3.40	3.52	3.55	0.00		0.04

Source: U.S. Department of Agriculture.

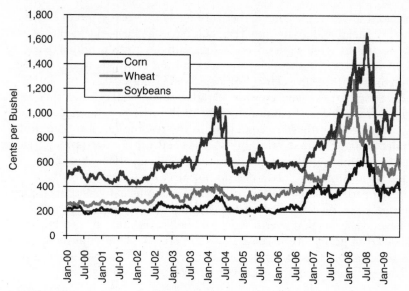

EXHIBIT 8.20   Grain Prices (Jan-00 to Jun-09)

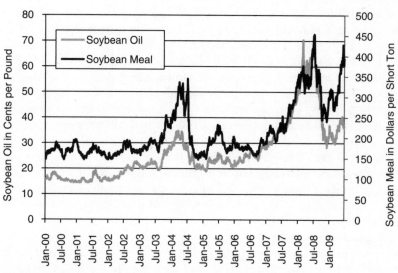

EXHIBIT 8.21   Soybean Oil and Meal (Jan-00 to Jun-09)

introduced in 1961. Of course, there are many different types of livestock including sheep and goats; poultry, including chickens, ducks, geese and turkeys; and fish and seafood, including salmon, catfish, tilapia, shrimp, and many others. But the major livestock futures contracts traded at CME Group today include live cattle, lean hogs, and feeder cattle.

Livestock futures were considered rather revolutionary when they were originally introduced. Traditionally, one of the criteria believed to characterize commodities that are conducive to the trading of futures contracts included near unlimited "storability," or shelf life. Under proper conditions, for example, grains can be stored for very long although certainly not infinite periods of time. Livestock do not meet our storability criteria and are in fact perishable. Further, it may not be economical to continue feeding an animal once it has reached market weight.

Beyond the fact that livestock are perishable, they may further be distinguished from grains in the sense that they produce continuously and not on a seasonal basis. As a result, one must resort to different tools for the fundamental analysis of livestock relative to the analysis of grains.

Live Cattle

Cattle are valued for their beef, a popular meat product throughout the world. But before we review the production process, a primer regarding cattle terminology may be appropriate. The different categories of cattle include calves, heifers, cows, bulls, and steers. *Calf* is a reference to an immature animal of up to a year old of either sex. A *heifer* is a female that has yet to produce a calf; a *cow* is a female that has previously produced a calf or "has calved." A *bull* is a sexually intact male. *Steers* are neutered males. The procedure is undertaken to improve the temperament and meat quality of the animal. The term *head* refers to any individual animal of any age or sex.

Breeding herds, or cows and bulls held for reproductive purposes, tend to number 40 head on average, although half of beef cows are produced in herds of 100 head or more. Some 16 to 18% of cows held in breeding herds are culled from the herd and slaughtered each year for a variety of reasons, including failure to breed, old age, weather, and feed supplies or market conditions. The number of replacement heifers coming into the breeding herd varies depending on profitability and stage in the production cycle.

The production cycle is broken down into the cow-calf stage; the stocker, or growing, stage; and the feedlot, or finishing, stage. This cycle culminates with the slaughter of the animal for meat production purposes.

The cow-calf stage begins as heifers of perhaps one to two years of age initially are bred to bulls. Breeding generally takes place during the summer months with a resultant nine-month gestation period. Typically, a breeding herd may have perhaps 1 mature bull or male for every 20 to 25 females. Most calves are born in the spring and weigh in at perhaps 60 to 100 pounds. Spring-born calves are generally weaned from their mothers in the fall at the age of six to eight months and are 300 to 500 pounds at that time. The stocker, or growing, stage commences as calves that will not be retained for breeding purposes are placed into a stocker or grazing program. These animals may be fed grass, winter wheat, or other high-fiber, low-energy roughages. The purpose is to grow and develop skeletal and muscle structures. Typically these animals may gain 1 to 1.5 pounds in weight daily. This stage generally lasts 6 to 10 months until the cattle weigh in at perhaps 600 to 800 pounds. These "yearlings" are then known as "feeder cattle."

Finally, during the feedlot or finishing stage, feeder cattle are placed in a feedlot. Some 40% of these cattle are kept in feedlots of 32,000 head or more. They are fed corn and other high-energy feed grains with the goal of completing the growing phase and depositing fat (or "marbling") to improve the quality of the meat product. Feeder cattle may gain some 3 to 4 pounds in weight daily. This stage may require four to six months, and the cattle weigh 1,200 to 1,500 pounds when they are ready for market. These final market weights are contingent on genetics, weather, and market conditions.

Once the product is up to weight, they are sent to meatpacking plants, which are typically located close to the feedlots, and slaughtered to produce a carcass consisting of the animal minus head, hooves, hide, and internal organs. Carcasses are split down the backbone into right and left halves, or "sides," then "ribbed," or cut at the 12th rib, and graded (e.g., prime, choice, select, etc.). Little is wasted because the "drop," including the hides and offal materials (organs, glands, fat, bones, blood, etc.), can serve many purposes and represents a significant source of revenue for packers. See Exhibit 8.22.

Sides are subsequently cut, or "broken," into primal cuts, including chuck, loin, rib, round, and so on. Primals may be cut into subprimals that are vacuum packed in plastic, weighed, and sorted into various weight categories for each cut (e.g., 12 to 14 pounds, 14 to 16 pounds, etc.). Then they are packaged into boxes containing 40 to 60 pounds of the same cut, weight, and grade. These boxes are marketed to grocery stores and restaurants, which slice the subprimal cuts into steaks, roasts, and other serving-size pieces.

Because the production of livestock varies so fundamentally from the production of grains, somewhat different tools are required to examine the relationships between the forces of supply and demand. Key to an

EXHIBIT 8.22 Cattle and Calves, Number by Class and Calf Crop, United States, January 1, 2008–2009

Class	2008 (1,000 head)	2009 (1,000 head)	2009 as % of 2008
Cattle and calves	95,035	94,491	98%
Cows and heifers that have calved	41,692	41,005	98%
Beef cows	32,435	31,671	98%
Milk cows	9,257	9,333	101%
Heifers 500 pounds and over	19,854	19,586	99%
For beef cow replacement	5,647	5,526	98%
Expected to calve	3,414	3,357	98%
For milk cow replacement	4,415	4,410	100%
Expected to calve	2,923	2,909	100%
Other heifers	9,793	9,650	99%
Steers 500 pounds and over	17,163	16,774	98%
Bulls 500 pounds and over	2,207	2,184	99%
Calves under 500 pounds	15,118	14,943	99%
Cattle on feed	14,827	13,851	93%
Calf crop	36,759	36,113	98%

Source: U.S. Department of Agriculture.

understanding of these relationships is the ability to track the production cycle, or "cattle pipeline." The USDA publishes the cattle inventory report biannually.

Beyond the cattle inventory report, the USDA monitors the number of cattle on feed on a monthly and quarterly basis. This report covers perhaps 85% of all U.S. cattle feeding and slaughter activity. *Placements* refers to the number of cattle moving into feedlots and placed "on feed." *Marketings* refers to the number of cattle moved out of feedlots to slaughter. See Exhibit 8.23.

The production cycle may further be tracked by reference to the number of cattle being slaughtered. The USDA Livestock Slaughter report provides definitive information in this regard. One may cross-reference the number of head slaughtered against marketings as reported by the USDA Cattle on Feed report as a check See Exhibit 8.24.

Average weight figures are a useful check to see if marketings are on schedule or not. Finally, note that the number of head multiplied by the average weight equals beef production. Possible future pricing clues are provided by comparing these figures regarding total beef supply versus red meat and total meat supplies. See Exhibit 8.25

EXHIBIT 8.23 Cattle on Feed: Number on Feed, Placements, Marketings, and Other Disappearance, 1,000+ Capacity Feedlots, United States, March 1, 2008–2009

Item	2008 (1,000 head)	2009 (1,000 head)	2009 as % of 2008
On feed Feb 1	11,966	11,288	94%
Placed on feed during Feb	1,723	1,678	97%
Fed cattle marketed during Feb	1,776	1,682	95%
Other disappearance during Feb	60	56	93%
On feed Mar 1	11,853	11,228	95%

Source: U.S. Department of Agriculture.

Another factor in determining supply is found in any "leaks" into or out of the production pipeline. Specifically, exports account for about 5% of total U.S. beef supply; imports provide about 10% of domestic supplies. Production or supply represents one side of the pricing equation. The other side is demand. Drivers of beef demand include disposable incomes, the price of substitute meats such as pork and chicken, and consumer tastes and preferences. See Exhibit 8.26.

Of course, the price of cattle is derived from the price of beef. Thus, changes in wholesale beef prices, or sales by packers to retailers, may result in parallel fluctuations in cattle prices. The USDA offers reports regarding the value of boxed beef cuts to provide another insight into the fundamentals of cattle pricing.

CME Live Cattle futures call for the delivery of 40,000 pounds of cattle with specific characteristics during the delivery months of February, April, June, August, October, and December. The contract is quoted in cents per pound in minimum increments of $0.00025 per pound ($10.00 per contract). Thus, one might see a quote of "84.600," which means $0.84600 per pound. This implies that the value of one futures contract would equate to $33,840 (= 40,000 pounds × $0.84600). (See the appendix for detailed futures and option contract specifications.) See Exhibit 8.27 for livestock price trends.

Lean Hogs

Pork, derived from hogs, represents another very popular meat selection. Like cattle, the industry uses its own terminology that we review here. *Pig*

EXHIBIT 8.24 Livestock Slaughter, Number, and Average Weights, United States

Species	Unit	Feb 2008	Jan 2009	Feb 2009	Feb 09 % of		Jan-Feb		
					Feb 08	Jan 08	2008	2009	09% of 08
				Cattle No.					
Fed Insp.	Thous	2,597.9	2,668.1	2,478.8	95%	93%	5,445.4	5,146.9	95%
Other	Thous	44.8	50.3	48.5	108%	96	96.7	98.8	102%
Comm'l	Thous	2,642.7	2,718.4	2,527.3	96%	93	5,542.1	5,245.7	95%
				Live Wt/Hd					
Fed Insp.	Lbs	1,287	1,309	1,314	102%	100%	1,291	1,311	102%
Other	Lbs	1,147	1,141	1,131	99%	99%	1,145	1,136	99%
Comm'l	Lbs	1,285	1,306	1,310	102%	100%	1,288	1,308	102%

Source: U.S. Department of Agriculture.

EXHIBIT 8.25 Commercial Red Meat Production, United States

Type	Feb 2008	Jan 2009	Feb 2009	Feb 09 % of		Jan-Feb		
				Feb 2008	Jan 2008	2008	2009	09 % of 08
	Million Pounds			Percent		Million Pounds		Percent
Beef	2,038.6	2,118.4	1,985.2	97%	94%	4,271.4	4,103.6	96%
Veal	11.0	12.0	11.0	100%	92%	22.3	23.0	103%
Pork	1,902.7	2,026.0	1,816.1	95%	90%	4,061.7	3,842.1	95%
Lamb and mutton	15.0	13.3	12.8	85%	96%	29.7	26.0	88%
Total red meat	3,967.4	4,169.6	3,825.1	96%	92%	8,385.1	7,994.8	95%

Source: U.S. Department of Agriculture.

EXHIBIT 8.26 U.S. Meats Supply and Use

Item	Supply				Use		Disappearance	
	Beginning Stocks	Production	Imports	Total Supply	Exports	Ending Stocks	Total	Per Capita
				Million Pounds				
BEEF								
2007	630	26,523	3,052	30,205	1,434	630	28,141	65.3
2008 Est. Feb	630	26,666	2,497	29,793	1,880	627	27,286	62.7
Mar	630	26,663	2,537	29,830	1,888	642	27,300	62.8
2009 Proj. Feb	627	26,212	2,680	29,519	1,880	595	27,044	61.6
Mar	642	26,477	2,680	29,799	1,880	605	27,314	62.2
PORK								
2007	514	21,962	968	23,444	3,141	536	19,767	50.8
2008 Est. Feb	536	23,367	803	24,706	4,719	635	19,352	49.3
Mar	536	23,367	831	24,734	4,668	641	19,425	49.5
2009 Proj. Feb	635	22,999	810	24,444	4,000	640	19,804	50.0
Mar	641	23,030	840	24,511	4,000	640	19,871	50.2

Source: U.S. Department of Agriculture.

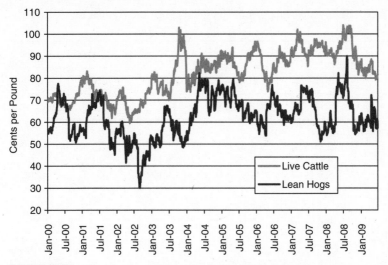

EXHIBIT 8.27   Live Cattle and Lean Hogs (Jan-00 to Jun-09)

is a reference to a young animal of either sex; *hog* is a reference to an older animal. A *sow* is a female that has already borne a litter of pigs or has *farrowed*; a *gilt* is a female that has not yet borne pigs. A *boar* is a sexually intact male; a *barrow* is a male that has been neutered for temperament and/ or for meat quality, sometimes referred to as *boar odor*.

Hogs are produced throughout the United States but with major concentrations in lower Minnesota and upper Iowa and in eastern regions of North Carolina. Much like the production of cattle, there are several stages to the production cycle of hogs. This includes the farrowing stage, the growing/finishing stage, and finally slaughter.

Females including sows and gilts may be bred year round, although conception rates tend to be highest during the spring and fall seasons. Conception may be natural or artificial. This is followed by a 144-day (3 months, 3 weeks, and 3 days) gestation period. The typical litter size is 9 to 10 pigs, and a female may bear two or more litters during the course of a single year. Sows are typically culled from the breeding herd and brought to slaughter after bearing four to six litters. The resulting pigs are weaned a few weeks subsequent to birth. See Exhibit 8.28.

During the growing/finishing stage, pigs are fed high-energy, high-protein feed typically consisting of corn and soybean meal supplemented by vitamins and minerals. Unlike cattle, hogs are not easily capable of digesting roughage because their digestive tracts are similar to that of humans. The protein content of feed is gradually reduced as the animals get larger from

EXHIBIT 8.28 Farrowings, Number of Sows, Pig Crop, and Pigs per Litter, United States, 2007–2009

				2009 as % of	
	2007	2008	2009	2007	2008
Item		1,000 Head		Percent	
Sows Farrowing					
Dec-Feb	2,905	3,071	2,978	103%	97%
Mar-May	3,030	3,052	2,962	98%	97%
Dec-May	5,935	6,123	5,940	100%	97%
Jun-Aug	3,133	3,075	2,952	94%	96%
Sep-Nov	3,180	2,990			
Jun-Nov	6,312	6,065			
Pig Crop					
Dec-Feb	26,395	28,387	28,230	107%	99%
Mar-May	27,870	28,630			
Dec-May	54,266	57,017			
Jun-Aug	29,095	29,240			
Sep-Nov	29,513	28,410			
Jun-Nov	58,608	57,650			
Pigs per Litter					
		Number		Percent	
Dec-Feb	9.09	9.24	9.48	104%	103%
Mar-May	9.20	9.38			
Dec-May	9.14	9.31			
Jun-Aug	9.29	9.51			
Sep-Nov	9.28	9.50			
Jun-Nov	9.28	9.51			

Source: U.S. Department of Agriculture.

20% or more at the point of initial weaning to approximately 13% protein just before slaughter. The goal is to grow and develop the animal's skeletal and muscle structure without putting on significant fat. Average daily weight gains run from perhaps 1.5 to 1.8 pounds during this stage. Hogs are ready for slaughter at the age of five to six months and after achieving a weight of 260 to 280 pounds.

Finally, hogs are slaughtered by packers to produce a carcass that generally weighs 190 to 200 pounds. Meatpacking plans are often located strategically near hog production areas. Carcasses are split down the backbone into right and left halves, or "sides." They are then cut, or "broken," into primal cuts including the shoulder, picnic, loin, ham, and so on. Subprimals are

EXHIBIT 8.29 Hogs and Pigs, Inventory Number by Class, Weight Group, and Quarter, United States, 2008–2009

Item	2008 (1,000 head)	2009 (1,000 head)	2009 as % of 2008
March 1 Inventory			
All hogs and pigs	67,218	65,389	97%
Kept for breeding	6,200	6,011	97%
Market	61,018	59,378	97%
Market Hogs and Pigs by Weight Groups			
Under 60 pounds	22,137	21,458	97%
60–119 pounds	14,490	14,126	97%
120–179 pounds	13,193	12,862	97%
180 pounds and over	11,199	10,932	98%

Source: U.S. Department of Agriculture.

vacuum-packed in plastic, weighed, and sorted into various weight categories for each cut (e.g., 12 to 14 pounds, 14 to 16 pounds, etc.). These subprimals are packaged in boxes of 40 to 60 pounds of the same cut, weight, and grade and marketed to groceries and restaurants that slice the meat into serving sizes. Like cattle, significant revenue may be realized from the "drop," or "offal," materials including organs, glands, fat, bones, blood, and so on.

Like cattle, the hog pipeline is monitored and reported by the USDA. The farrowing report provides information regarding the number of pigs produced over time. The inventory reports provides information regarding the number of hogs and pigs in inventory broken out by those retained for breeding purposes and those intended for market by weight class as an indication of how far along in the production process the inventory may be. See Exhibit 8.29.

Unlike beef, which tends to be marketed quickly after slaughter, significant quantities of pork are stored in frozen form for future use. These quantities held in cold storage tend to act as a shock absorber of sorts to smooth out any supply situations that may occur. The USDA Cold Storage report provides detailed data in this regard. See Exhibit 8.30.

Like cattle, several factors impact the demand for pork including disposable incomes, the price of substitute meat sources such as beef and chicken, exchange rates that impact the export demand for the product, and consumer tastes and preferences that may be the most important of these factors.

CME Lean Hog futures are settled in cash at the value of the CME Lean Hog Index. The index is constructed using data sampled over a

EXHIBIT 8.30 Stocks in Cold Storage, by Commodity, United States, February 2009

Commodity	Stocks in All Warehouses			Percent of		Public Warehouse Stocks
	Feb 28, 2008	Jan 31, 2009	Feb 28, 2009	Feb 2008	Jan 2009	Feb 28, 2009
	1,000 Pounds			Percent		1,000 Lbs
Frozen Beef						
Boneless	359,145	391,691	369,094	103%	94%	
Beef cuts	77,404	70,956	65,072	84%	92%	
Total	436,549	462,647	434,166	99%	94%	422,882
Frozen Pork						
Picnics, bone-in	18,102	8,992	12,071	67%	134%	
Hams, total	92,884	87,537	97,304	105%	111%	
Bone-in	49,768	44,022	47,141	95%	107%	
Boneless	43,116	43,515	50,163	116%	115%	
Bellies	79,282	69,166	77,748	98%	112%	
Loins, total	47,351	51,357	45,752	97%	89%	
Bone-in	18,270	20,608	20,144	110%	98%	
Boneless	29,081	30,749	25,608	88%	83%	
Ribs	83,769	87,854	92,727	111%	106%	
Butts	25,332	20,940	25,289	100%	121%	
Trimmings	70,604	66,610	66,102	94%	99%	
Other	105,570	111,024	111,533	106%	100%	
Variety meats	32,480	25,074	27,645	85%	110%	
Unclassified	56,456	78,382	80,437	142%	103%	
Total	611,830	606,936	636,608	104%	105%	555,587
Other						
Veal	6,107	7,177	7,559	124%	105%	
Lamb and mutton	18,157	19,469	17,742	98%	91%	
Total	24,264	26,646	25,301	104%	95%	24,747
Total	1,072,643	1,096,229	1,096,075	102%	100%	1,003,216

Source: U.S. Department of Agriculture.

two-day period ending on the last trading day of the futures contract. The sample represents the value of hog (barrow and gilt) carcasses as reported in the USDA's National Daily Direct Hog Prior Day Reported-Slaughtered Swine Report.

The futures contract is based on the value of 40,000 pounds of hogs and is traded for cash settlement during the months of February, April, May, June, July, August, October, and December. The contract is quoted in cents per pound in minimum increments of $0.00025 per pound ($10.00 per contract). Thus, one might see a quote of "73.4500," which means $0.7345 per pound. Thus, one futures contract might be valued at $29,380 (= 40,000 pounds × $0.7345). (See the appendix for detailed futures and option contract specifications.)

ENERGY PRODUCTS

Today's modern world is powered by energy from a wide variety of sources, and the well-established industrial economies as well as emerging economies are placing vast demands on these resources. As such, energy markets represent perhaps the most strategic of all commodity markets. Accordingly, these markets have emerged as the most actively traded of all physical commodity markets. This notably includes energy staples such as crude oil, natural gas, gasoline, and heating oil. But it also includes many other fossil fuels, biofuels, and related products such as electricity.

Spot or cash markets for these products have been active, of course, since the time that these products originally emerged as sources of fuel. But despite the fact that agricultural commodity futures had been actively traded in the United States at least since the 1840s, it was not until 1978 that the first successful energy futures contract was introduced in the form of heating oil futures on the New York Mercantile Exchange (NYMEX).

Since that time, many other energy-related futures and OTC derivatives markets have been introduced as well. In 2008, the NYMEX was merged into the CME Group, unifying energy trading with the trading venue for CME legacy commodities such as livestock futures along with CBOT legacy products, notably including grain futures.

Along the way, trading activity has grown substantially while the ways in which trade is conducted have changed as well. Most energy futures trading is now conducted on the CME Globex electronic trading venue as opposed to the traditional face-to-face open outcry method of trade.

Energy Sources and Uses

Petroleum or oil, natural gas, and coal are the primary energy sources in use in the United States and globally. Renewable energy sources including solar, biomass, geothermal, hydroelectric, and wind power comprise a relatively

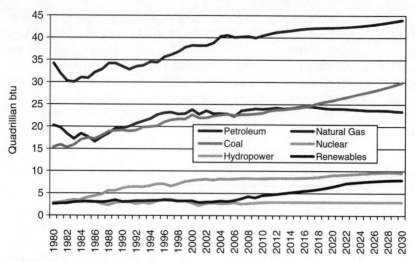

EXHIBIT 8.31   Past and Projected U.S. Energy Consumption
Source: U.S. Department of Energy.

small proportion of energy production. Growth in nuclear energy applications has generally been arrested by concerns regarding the attendant hazards. Energy is applied to various applications generally categorized as transportation; industrial, residential, and commercial applications; and the generation of electrical power.

These fossil fuels are expected to remain the primary contributors to the energy mix for decades to come despite growing concerns regarding possible global climate change and the attendant environmental implications.

This mix is reflected in the products that serve as the basis for the most popular energy futures contracts available today. Crude oil futures stand out as the most popular of these derivatives contracts followed by natural gas and the petroleum by-products of gasoline and heating oil futures.

Derivatives based on electrical power or biofuels such as ethanol have enjoyed relatively limited popularity to date. Although derivatives based on coal have been made available from time to time, they have not proven to be quite as viable due to the myriad standards for the product, the difficulties associated with evaluating the product, and a high transport cost-to-value ratio. See Exhibit 8.31.

Petroleum and Its By-Products

Petroleum formed in the earth's crust as prehistoric organisms died and settled to the ocean floor. Over time, those organic deposits were buried under sand and silt. Pressure, heat, and time combined to convert this material to oil and natural gas over the course of millions of years.

Pennsylvania is often identified as the birthplace of the petroleum industry. Oil oozed to the surface of the earth in "seeps," and it was discovered that this material could easily be collected and refined into kerosene, replacing whale oil in lamps. Edwin Drake sunk the first successful commercial oil well near Titusville, Pennsylvania, in 1859. This well was only 69 feet deep and produced a scant 25 barrels per day, minuscule by today's standards. But soon the first commercial crude oil refinery was built in Pittsburgh and a new industry has born.

Today, most domestic oil is produced in the states of Texas, Alaska, California, Louisiana, and Oklahoma from both on- and offshore facilities. The United States consumed 20.7 million barrels of petroleum per day in 2007 but U.S. production sources cannot meet this demand. Thus, the United States was dependent on foreign sources for some 58.2% of its consumption on a net basis in 2007. These imports are brought in from Canada (the largest single source, accounting for 18.2% of oil imported into the United States in 2007) followed by Mexico (11.4%), Saudi Arabia (11.0%), Venezuela (10.1%), Nigeria (8.4%), Algeria (5.0%), and others.

Crude oil is generally categorized by reference to its density (heavy or light) and its sulfur content (sweet or low sulfur content versus sour or high sulfur content). Lighter and sweeter varieties of crude oil generally command a higher market value because it is easier for oil refiners to extract high-value products from these oils.

The density of oil may be measured by its American Petroleum Institute (API) gravity, which is a comparison to the density of water. The API of water is 10, and the scale is inverse with higher values associated with lighter materials and lower values associated with heavier materials. Crude oil API measures in the vicinity of 40 to 45 tend to be the most highly valued.

Sulfur content is related to the quality of oil to the extent that sulfur may interfere with certain refining processes and is corrosive. Thus, low sulfur oils (sweet oil) command a higher market price than high sulfur oils (sour oil).

West Texas Intermediate (WTI) crude oil is a high-quality product produced, as its name implies, in the southwestern states. It is characterized by a relatively high API gravity of 39.6 and a low sulfur content of 0.24%. WTI yields a high proportion of gasoline and is referred to as light, sweet crude oil. Brent represents a blend of crude oil produced from a variety of different offshore oil fields in the North Sea. It has an API gravity of 38.3 degrees and a sulfur content of 0.37%. Brent is suitable for the production of gasoline and a variety of middle distillates.

NYMEX's most popular crude oil futures contract calls for the delivery of WTI despite the fact that WTI today accounts for a small proportion of crude oil produced in the United States. Brent was first traded in the form of futures on the International Petroleum Exchange in London, which was acquired by the Intercontinental Exchange (ICE) in 2005. NYMEX lists a Brent-based futures contract as well.

Historically, WTI has priced at a premium of perhaps $1 to $2 per barrel over Brent due to its preferred characteristics, and it is the world's foremost benchmark against which oil prices are pegged. However, local conditions of supply and demand can sometimes reverse these circumstances as observed in 2007 when supply shortages pushed Brent to a $1 to $3 per barrel premium over WTI.

The 2008 *International Crude Oil Market Handbook* recognized some 191 varieties of crude oil produced in all corners of the globe. Some of the popular varieties include Nigeria's Bonny Light, Dubai, and Saudi Light. Generally speaking, the prices of all these grades track each other reasonably closely. See Exhibit 8.32.

Once produced from domestic or imported from foreign sources, oil moves within the United States and Canada via a system of pipelines to an oil refinery for processing. Cushing, Oklahoma, is the most significant hub for oil pipelines traversing the lower 48 United States.

Crude oil is actually a mixture of many different hydrocarbon-based molecules, or "chains." But oil sourced from varying locations may have very different chemical compositions. Light oils have shorter molecular chains and lower specific gravities; heavy oils have longer chains and are of higher specific gravity. The refining process must be adjusted to account for these differences in molecular composition. The refining process breaks down the various compounds in a barrel of crude oil and reconstitutes the material into new products. The process may be broken down into the separation, conversion, and treatment stages.

Crude oil refining begins with a process known as *fractional distillation*, designed to separate the oil into various by-products, as illustrated in Exhibit 8.33. The raw oil passes through pipes in which it is heated by exposure to pressurized steam at temperatures of 600°C and enters the distillation chamber or tower.

The materials rise through the tower, are cooled, and condense on trays located at various heights within the tower. Because the various hydrocarbon molecules have different boiling points, the heavier hydrocarbons with greater density may be extracted from the lower levels of the tower, whereas the lighter hydrocarbons with less density rise to the upper levels of the tower.

EXHIBIT 8.32 Origin and Grades of Crude Oil

Abu Dhabi	Chad	Iraq	Norway	United States
Murban	Doba	Basrah Light	Asgard	Alaska North Slope
Umm Shaif	China	Kirkuk	Balder	Heavy Louisiana Sweet
Upper Zakum	Daqing	Kazakhstan	Draugen	Light Louisiana Sweet
Zakum	Liuhua	CPC Blend	Ekofisk	Mars Blend
Algeria	Nanhai Light	Karachaganak Condensate	Grane	Southern Green Canyon
Algerian Condensate	Panyu	Kashagan	Gullfaks	West Texas Intermediate
Saharan Blend	Peng Lai	Kumkol	Heidrun	West Texas Sour
Zarzaitine	Shengli	Kuwait	Norne	Venezuela
Angola	Colombia	Kuwait	Oseberg	BCF-17
Cabinda	Cano Limon	Libya	Sleipner Condensate	Boscan
Dalia	Cusiana	Abu Attifel	Statfjord	Cerro Negro
Gimboa	Congo	Al-Jurf	Troll	Hamaca
Girassol	Djeno	Amna	Oman	Mesa-30
Greater Plutonio	N'Kossa	Bouri	Oman	Petrozuata
Hungo	Cote d'Ivoire	Brega	Qatar	Tia Juana Light
Kissanje Blend	Baobab	El-Sharara	Al-Shaheen	Zuata Sweet
Kuito	Denmark	Es Sider	Condensates	Vietnam
Mondo	DUC Blend	Mellitah	Dukhan	Bach Ho
Nemba	Dubai	Sarir	Qatar Marine	Rang Dong
Palanca	Dubai	Sirtica	Russia	Yemen
Xikomba	Ecuador	Zueitina	Siberian Light	Marib
Argentina	Napo	Malaysia	Sokol	Masila
Medanito	Oriente	Bintulu Condensate	Urals	
Australia	Egypt	Kikeh	Vankor	
Bayu-Undan	Belayim Blend	Labuan	Vityaz	
Cossack	Suez Blend	Miri	Saudi Arabia	
Enfield	Equatorial Guinea	Tapis	Arab Extra Light	

(*Continued*)

EXHIBIT 8.32 (*Continued*)

Abu Dhabi	Chad	Iraq	Norway	United States
Gippsland	Alba	Mexico	Arab Heavy	
Mutineer-Exeter	Ceiba	Isthmus	Arab Light	
North West Shelf Condensate	New Zafiro Blend	Maya	Arab Medium	
Stybarrow	Gabon	Olmeca	Arab Super Light	
Vincent	Mandji	Neutral Zone	Sudan	
Azerbaijan	Rabi Light	Eocene	Dar Blend	
Azeri (BTC)	Indonesia	Khafji	Nile Blend	
Azeri Light	Belanak	Wafra	Syria	
Brazil	Cepu	New Zealand	Souedieh	
Albacora Leste	Cinta	Tui	Syrian Light	
Marlim	Duri	Nigeria	Turkmenistan	
Roncador	Handil Mix	Agbami	Turkmen Blend	
Brunei	Minas	Akpo	United Kingdom	
Champion	Senipah Condensate	Amenam Blend	Alba	
Seria Light	West Seno	Antan Blend	Beryl	
Cameroon	Widuri	Bonga	Brent	
Kole	Iran	Bonny Light	Captain	
Canada	Azadegan	Brass River	Clair	
Athabasca Oil Sands	Doroud	EA	Flotta	
Bow River	Foroozan	Erha	Foinaven	
Cold Lake	Iran Heavy	Escravos	Forties	
Hibernia	Iran Light	Forcados	Schiehallion	
Syncrude Sweet Premium	Lavan Blend	Okono	Triton	
Terra Nova	Nowruz-Soroush	Oso Condensate		
Western Canadian Select	Sirri	Pennington		
White Rose		Qua Iboe		
		Yoho		

Source: International Crude Oil Market Handbook (2008).

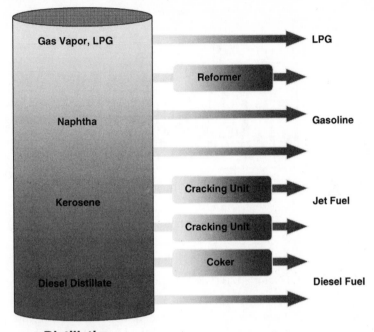

Distillation

EXHIBIT 8.33 Crude Oil Refining Process (Simplified)

Reconstitution of the resulting separated molecules is accomplished during the conversion stage of refining. This stage adds value to the finished product and is accomplished through several processes including cracking, coking, and alkylation.

Cracking, the most common conversion process, is accomplished by the application of heat and pressure to break complex hydrocarbons into smaller chains. A cracking device consists of a network of furnaces and heat exchangers. This process is typically applied to medium gas oil to create liquid petroleum gas (LPG) and gasoline and to heavy gas oil to create motor gasoline, jet fuel, and diesel fuel.

Coking is another form of cracking that breaks down heavy residuals into industrial fuels. Alkylation or reforming is the reverse of cracking in the sense that it creates heavier molecules from previously cracked lighter chains. Residual materials cracked into naphtha are sometimes exposed to this process to produce high-octane gasoline components.

During the final treatment stage, previously distilled materials are blended to produce a final product such as gasoline with the desired characteristics (e.g., octane, necessary additives for marketing in particular areas, etc.).

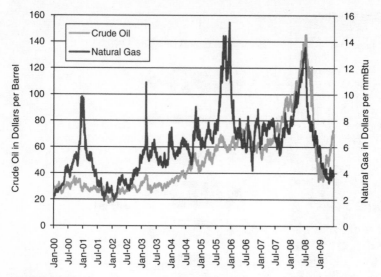

EXHIBIT 8.34 Crude Oil and Natural Gas (Jan-00 to Jun-09)

Refined products are then moved via pipeline systems to distribution terminals (or "racks") located strategically around the United States. These products are further moved by rail, barge, or truck to the point of use.

There are myriad analytical tools to gain insight into possible fluctuations in the value of crude oil and its various by-products. The sheer quantity of data available on the U.S. Department of Energy web site is daunting. But like other commodity products such as grains and livestock, supply and demand is the fundamental driving factor. See Exhibit 8.35.

Demand for energy products tends to be rather inelastic. However, high prices result in gradually reduced consumption over time. It is also important to consider that as new technologies (e.g., energy savings technologies) come online that affect demand, they are unlikely ever to be reversed. Energy markets do tend to be quite sensitive to possible supply shocks. Thus, analysts often pay close attention to information including political events, weather conditions, and operational considerations that may result in a disruption of supply.

The benchmark NYMEX Crude Oil futures call for the delivery of 1,000 barrels of West Texas Intermediate crude oil at Cushing, Oklahoma. They are traded for delivery in every month of the year extending out several years into the future with June and December contracts listed with even further deferred maturities. The contract is quoted in dollars and cents per barrel in minimum increments of $0.01 per barrel (or $10.00 per tick). Thus, a quote of $69.55 implies that a single futures contract may be valued

EXHIBIT 8.35 U.S. Crude Oil Supply and Disposition (000 Barrels)

	Aug-08	Sep-08	Oct-08	Nov-08	Dec-08	Jan-09
Supply						
Field production (commercial)	151,744	118,805	143,993	148,152	158,822	162,627
Alaskan	16,878	20,432	22,193	21,846	21,765	21,039
Lower 48 states	134,866	98,373	121,800	126,306	137,057	141,588
Imports	318,791	252,205	313,454	297,700	291,995	305,416
Commercial	318,791	252,205	313,454	297700	291,995	305,416
Strategic Petroleum reserve (SPR)						
Imports into SPR by others						
Adjustments (commercial)	1,050	9,957	3,151	1838	−985	1,184
Disposition						
Stock change	6,984	−2,988	8,201	8,635	3,485	30,625
Commercial	6,987	1,789	8,805	8,638	3,490	28,662
Strategic Petroleum Reserve (SPR)	−3	−4,777	−604	−3	−5	1,963
Refinery net inputs	463,367	382,782	451,076	438,139	444,933	437,480
Exports	1,234	1,173	1,321	916	1,413	1,122
Products supplied	0	0	0	0	0	0
Ending Stocks						
Ending stocks	1,008,724	1,005,736	1,013,937	1,002,572	1,026,057	1,056,682
Commercial	301,512	303,301	312,106	320,744	324,234	352,896
Cushing, OK	18,167	14,502	17,607	23322	32,886	32,394
Strategic Petroleum Reserve (SPR)	707,212	702,435	701,831	701,828	701,823	703,786

Source: U.S. Department of Energy.

at \$69,550 (= 1,000 barrels × \$69.55 per barrel). (See the appendix for detailed futures and option contract specifications.)

There are also active futures contracts in a variety of crude oil by-products. Although many energy futures contracts are available, the most actively traded of these products are based on RBOB Gasoline and #2 heating oil. See Exhibit 8.36. We should note that only about 5% of crude oil is used to produce heating oil, which in turn is used for both residential and commercial purposes. Heating oil is really only in prominent use in the northeastern United States and has been largely replaced by natural gas most everywhere else in the country. But the futures contract continues to

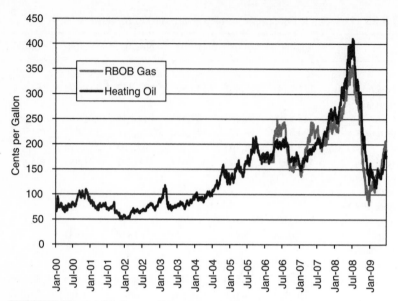

EXHIBIT 8.36 RBOB Gas and Heating Oil (Jan-00 to Jun-09)

flourish as a result of momentum and the fact that it may serve as a general proxy for diesel fuel values.

The gasoline contract calls for the delivery of 42,000 gallons (or 1,000 barrels at 42 gallons per barrel) of reformulated regular gasoline blendstock for oxygen blending (RBOB) with 10% denatured fuel ethanol at New York Harbor. They are traded for delivery in consecutive contract months extending out three years into the future. The contract is quoted in cents per gallon in minimum increments of $0.0001 per gallon (or $4.20 per tick). Thus, a quote of 193.22 implies that a single futures contract may be valued at $81,152.40 (= 42,000 gallons × 193.22 cents/gallon).

The heating oil contract calls for the delivery of 42,000 gallons (or 1,000 barrels at 42 gallons per barrel) of #2 heating oil at New York Harbor. Contracts are offered for delivery in consecutive contract months extending out three years into the future. The contract is quoted in cents per gallon in minimum increments of 0.01 cents per gallon ($4.20 per tick). Thus, a quote of 179.40 implies that a single futures contract may be valued at $75,348.00 (= 42,000 gallons × 179.40 cents/gallon).

Natural Gas

Natural gas is formed under nearly the same conditions as crude oil and often discovered in conjunction with oil deposits. Natural gas is methane with a chemical designation of CH_4. Natural gas flows up from wells under pressure. The product is transported via pipeline to processing plants where impurities are removed. The so-called dry, or processed, gas is then ported into transmission or distribution pipelines for immediate use. Or it may be moved into underground storage facilities for later use.

Natural gas is extracted from wells in the United States, Canada, and Mexico and transported via pipeline for use in the United States. But some natural gas is imported into the United States in the form of a supercooled liquid or liquefied natural gas (LNG). LNG is formed by cooling the product to $-260°F$ when it contracts to approximately 1/600th the original volume. It may be transported by specially equipped ocean freighters, warmed on arrival, and reconstituted in its gaseous state.

Natural gas is used primarily for purposes of heating and power generation. More than half of the homes in the United States are heated with gas. It is also applied to a variety of industrial processes as a feedstock for the production of more refined chemical products. Unlike petroleum, the U.S. is nearly self-sufficient in terms of natural gas production. Imports comprise approximately 15% of total domestic use and are brought in largely from Canada.

Volumes of gas are measured in billion cubic feet (bcf) and the energy content is measured in British thermal units (Btu). One cubic foot of natural gas generates 1,028 Btus or approximately 1,000 Btus. Thus, 1 billion cubic feet by volume is the rough equivalent of 1 trillion Btus; 1 trillion cubic feet is the rough equivalent of 1 quadrillion Btus, or a "quad."

Pipelines are the primary way in which natural gas is transported. The most significant nexus for transporting natural gas is found at Henry Hub, Louisiana, which serves as an interconnection point for multiple pipelines. Because of its significance, Henry Hub serves as the benchmark pricing point for natural gas. Pipelines may be accessed for purposes of transmission or the movement of large commercial quantities over long distances. Pipelines are also used for purposes of distribution or the movement of smaller retail quantities over shorter distances.

Production of natural gas tends to be quite stable to the extent that gas wells cannot readily be turned on and off in response to fluctuating demands. Thus, surplus gas is "injected" into underground storage facilities and withdrawn as needed. Storage facilities have physical limitations on how much gas may be stored (total storage capacity), how much may be injected daily (injection capacity), and how much may be withdrawn daily (deliverability). See Exhibit 8.37.

These volumes are measured by reference to the "total gas," or amounts in storage. The term *base gas* refers to permanent inventories in storage or volumes needed to maintain adequate pressure in the system; *working gas* refers to volumes available to the marketplace or total gas less

EXHIBIT 8.37 Underground Natural Gas Storage by All Operators (Million Cubic Feet)

	Aug-08	Sep-08	Oct-08	Nov-08	Dec-08	Jan-09
Natural gas in storage	7,094,399	7,393,547	7,634,108	7,577,567	7,068,944	6,376,863
Base gas	4,227,740	4,230,559	4,234,974	4,231,339	4,228,511	4,235,866
Working gas	2,866,659	3,162,989	3,399,134	3,346,228	2,840,433	2,140,997
Net withdrawals	−350,108	−300,367	−242,413	57,283	504,854	698,266
Injections	441,603	398,313	333,887	193,595	109,911	79,346
Withdrawals	91,495	97,946	91,474	250,878	614,765	777,612
Change in Working Gas from Same Period Previous Year						
Volume	−150,611	−152,730	−167,724	−95,805	−38,826	85,538
Percent	−5.0	−4.6	−4.7	−2.8	−1.4	4.2

Source: U.S. Department of Energy.

base gas. Other popular measures that are closely tracked by the market include the ratios of (1) total gas in storage to total capacity, (2) working gas versus working gas capacity, and (3) current working gas relative to historic levels of working gas. See Exhibit 8.38 for an example of weekly working gas in underground storage.

Demand for natural gas tends to be reasonably stable on a year-to-year basis. However, there tends to be much fluctuation in demand on a month-by-month basis. See Exhibit 8.39. Demand for heating purposes on both a commercial and residential basis is subject to the vagaries of the weather with heaviest demand during the coldest winter months. Use of natural gas for power generation purposes tends to peak during the summer when weather conditions lead to high demand for air conditioning.

The NYMEX Natural Gas futures contract calls for the delivery of 10,000 million British thermal units (mmBtu) of natural gas at Henry Hub, Louisiana. Contracts are offered for delivery in consecutive contract months

EXHIBIT 8.38 Weekly Working Gas in Underground Storage (Billion Cubic Feet)

	3/6/09	3/13/09	3/20/09	3/27/09	4/3/09	4/10/09
Total lower 48 states	1,681	1,651	1,654	1,654	1,674	1,695
East region	703	677	664	641	647	651
West region	288	276	281	282	283	288
Producing region	690	698	709	731	744	756

Source: U.S. Department of Energy.

EXHIBIT 8.39 U.S. Natural Gas Monthly Supply and Disposition Balance (Billion Cubic Feet)

	Aug-08	Sep-08	Oct-08	Nov-08	Dec-08	Jan-09
Gross withdrawals	2,187	1,966	2,202	2,212	2,276	2,254
Marketed production	1,859	1,601	1,801	1,802	1,862	1,854
Extraction loss	77	62	74	72	66	74
Dry production	1,781	1,540	1,727	1,730	1,796	1,781
Supplemental gaseous fuels	5	5	5	5	6	6
Net imports	257	255	252	226	254	252
Net storage withdrawals	−350	−300	−242	57	505	698
Balancing item	1	−36	−104	−160	−172	−35
Consumption	1,694	1,464	1,636	1,859	2,389	2,702

Source: U.S. Department of Energy.

extending out eight years into the future. The contract is quoted in dollars per mmBtu in minimum increments of $0.001 (0.1 cent) per mmBtu ($10.00 per tick). Thus, a quote of 4.065 implies that a single futures contract may be valued at $40,650.00 (= 10,000 mmBtu × $4.065 per mmBtu). In addition to the Henry Hub delivery contract, there are many other natural gas contracts that price gas at various strategic locations and are priced at a spread or "basis" the benchmark Henry Hub contract.

PRECIOUS METALS

Precious metals are unique commodities because they are valued not only for commercial or industrial applications like other commodities, but also as an investment or store of value. Thus, rather than being produced simply for purposes of consumption, these products are produced for purposes of accumulation. Gold, silver, and other metals are actively traded at the COMEX, a division of NYMEX, all of which was merged into CME Group in 2008.

Gold and silver are the best known precious metals, but the group also includes platinum and palladium. These metals are characterized by high values and are priced by the troy ounce (14.6 troy ounces = 1 pound). Industrial metals are valued at reduced levels compared to precious metals and are typically quoted in dollars per ton. This group includes ferrous metals such as iron and steel and nonferrous metals including copper, aluminum, zinc, lead, nickel, and others. Although there are viable markets for many of these commodities, our discussion largely focuses on gold and silver as the most actively traded of metals.

Sometimes these commodities are categorized as base metals or noble metals. A *base metal* is inexpensive and chemically defined as metals that are subject to corrosion or oxidization. This includes metals such as iron, lead, zinc, and copper. *Noble metals* are defined chemically as metals that do not corrode or oxidize (i.e., they remain shiny over time). This grouping includes gold, silver, platinum, palladium, rhodium, ruthenium, osmium, and iridium.

Metals of any sort are primarily produced through mining. In addition to mining as a primary source, recycling has long been an important secondary source of metal. Recycled material may be categorized as "new scrap" or by-products of manufacturing processes (e.g., cutoffs, scraps, shavings, etc.). Metal may also be recovered from old scrap or postconsumer use sources.

There are several types of mining operations, including the surface mine, also known as an open pit or strip mine, and subsurface mines consisting of underground shafts, tunnels, and so on. Ore, or rock that contains trace amounts of a valued metal, is extracted from these mines. Ore may be found in lodes or concentrations of metal in veins, beds, or seams. It may further be found in placer deposits or sands and gravels that contain particles of the valued metal.

Once extracted, the ores are typically crushed into fine powders and the valued metals are removed from the powder using a variety of methods usually involving the application of chemicals, heat, or electricity. The valued metal is refined to the desired purity, melted, and cast into ingots. These processes typically have some negative environmental impact and often leave behind unwanted tailings.

Mining can be a very capital-intensive process, and the market for any particular metal tends to be dominated by a relatively concentrated number of large vertically integrated firms. Annual mine production tends to be relatively stable because it can be costly and difficult to adjust production in response to fluctuating demands. Thus, surplus production is stored until needed.

Although supplies tend to be relatively stable, demand may be quite variable. Production tends to be geographically concentrated in certain regions, but demand is widely dispersed and global in nature. Analyzing market trends by reference to supply and demand statistics should be relatively straightforward. Unfortunately, reliable and timely data are difficult to obtain. With the exception of gold, warehouse stocks are reported on a spotty basis. The London Metals Exchange (LME) reports on LME stocks and is closely followed, but this covers only a fraction of the market. The

EXHIBIT 8.40 Aluminum (Data in thousand metric tons of metal unless otherwise noted)

	2004	2005	2006	2007	2008
Production:					
Primary	2,516	2,481	2,284	2,554	2,640
Secondary (from old scrap)	1,160	1,080	1,260	1,600	1,400
Imports for consumption	4,720	5,330	5,180	4,490	4,300
Exports	1,820	2,370	2,820	2,840	3,800
Consumption, apparent	6,060	5,990	5,980	5,110	3,700
Price, ingot, average U.S. market (spot) cents per pound	84.0	91.0	121.4	125.2	132.3
Stocks					
Aluminum industry, year-end	1,470	1,430	1,410	1,400	1,300
LME, U.S. warehouses, year-end	116	209	228	463	860
Employment, number	57,500	58,400	57,300	56,600	55,000
Net import reliance as a percentage of apparent consumption	39	41	31	19	

Source: U.S. Geological Survey.

U.S. Geological Survey is another source of (noncomprehensive) data. See Exhibit 8.40 for an example of aluminum.

Thus, analysts may be compelled to use what spotty data is available as a general barometer and supplement it with economic data that is more readily available. For example, one may study the correlations between gold versus inflation, copper versus GDP, or platinum and palladium versus automobile sales.

Gold

Gold has many important properties that make it valuable. It is the most malleable and ductile of all metals. A single ounce may be flattened into a sheet covering 300 square feet. It is an excellent conductor of electricity, resists corrosion, and is readily combined with other metals. Major sources of production in 2008 included China (13%), South Africa (11%), United States (10%), Australia (10%), Peru (8%), Russia (7%), Canada (4%), Indonesia (4%), and other countries (33%).

It has all the defining characteristics that make it an important store of value. Specifically, it is rare, durable, divisible, fungible, and identifiable. Thus, it has been used for many centuries in coinage. More recently, it has been used to backstop the issuance of paper currency. In 1844, Great Britain adopted the gold standard with the passage of the Charter Bank Act that tied the value of notes issued by the Bank of England to gold. This implied that the national treasury could print paper money in proportion to the quantity of gold held on deposit. This represents a means to control inflation and prevents manipulation of currency values.

These gold reserves are typically held in the form of bullion or metal in bulk form. Gold bars or ingots typically are cast in weights of anywhere from 400 troy ounces (approximately 27 pounds) down to 1 kilogram. However, it is most common to find ingots in bars weighing in the vicinity of 100 ounces or 1 kilo. Coins or "rounds" may be minted in weights from 1 troy ounce to 1/10th of a troy ounce. Other shapes and sizes may be found in weights as low as 1 gram. But regardless of the shape or size, these castings generally identify the manufacturer or refiner, the weight, and the purity (e.g., 0.995, 0.999, etc.).

Industrial or commercial use of gold is dominated by jewelry applications (80%), followed by electronics (8%) and dental and other miscellaneous applications (12%). Pure gold (24 karat) may be very soft and easily deformed or damaged. Thus, jewelers typically alloy gold with copper to produce yellow gold, or with nickel, platinum, and palladium to produce white gold. Most jewelry is 22 karat or less.

COMEX gold futures call for the delivery of 100 troy ounces ($\pm$5%) of gold of a minimum 0.995 fineness and cast in one 100-ounce bar or three 1-kilogram bars. Contracts are offered in every month of the year and are quoted in dollars and cents per troy ounce in minimum increments of $0.01 per ounce (or $10.00 per tick). Thus, a quote of 941.20 implies that a single futures contract may be valued at $94,120.00 (= 100 troy ounces × $941.20 per troy ounce).

Silver

Like gold, silver is also extremely malleable and ductile, although not quite so as gold (see Exhibit 8.41 for a pricing comparison of the two). Silver has the highest level of electrical conductivity and reflectivity of all metals, although it is somewhat susceptible to tarnish and corrosion. Most silver is mined in conjunction with gold, copper, lead, or zinc. Major sources of production in 2008 included Peru (17%), Mexico (14%), China (12%), Chile (10%), Australia (9%), Poland (9%), United States (5%), Canada (4%), and other countries (23%).

Silver is generally cast in an industrial size ingot of 1,000 troy ounces (approximately 68 pounds) of 0.999 fineness. Sterling silver used for jewelry and silverware is typically of 0.925 fineness and consists of an alloy of

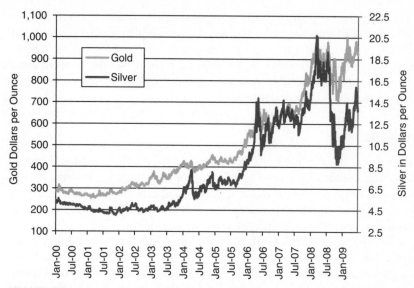

EXHIBIT 8.41 Precious Metals (Jan-00 to Jun-09)

92.5% silver and 7.5% copper. Beyond use in jewelry, silver is also used in applications including industrial and medical, photographic, and silverware, coins, and medals.

COMEX Silver futures call for the delivery of 5,000 troy ounces (±6%) of silver of a minimum 0.999 fineness and cast in 1,000 or 1,100 troy ounce bars. Contracts are offered in every month of the year and are quoted in dollars and cents per troy ounce in minimum increments of $0.005 per ounce (or $25.00 per tick). Thus, a quote of 14.200 implies that a single futures contract may be valued at $71,000.00 (= 5,000 troy ounces × $14.200 per troy ounce).

THE FORWARD CURVE

Casual observers who inspect a table depicting futures prices in various contract or delivery months are sometimes confused. Specifically, they might ask. "Why does any particular commodity have many prices instead of a single price?" Of course, the future or forward value for any particular product may vary considerably at various points in time extending out into the future. This set of relationships between prices for different future or forward deliveries is known as the *forward curve* for the commodity.

A great deal of information is implicit in the forward curve for any commodity. The forward curve is driven by a multiplicity of forces, possibly including market expectations as well as cost of carry relationships. The degree to which one or the other set of considerations drives the forward curve is generally a function of the facility with which one may construct an arbitrage between cash or spot commodities and futures.

Cost of Carry

The term *cost of carry* refers to the costs associated with buying and storing a particular commodity over a specific future time period. This may also be referred to as the *theory of storage*, which suggests the difference between spot and futures commodity prices has three distinct components including finance charges, storage fees, and a convenience yield.

Financing costs are important if one intends to borrow funds to purchase a commodity on a leveraged basis. Finance costs are generally reflected in short-term interest rates such as LIBOR rates or some premium over a floating LIBOR rate. Beyond the cost of financing, the storage of a commodity often implies a fee. For example, if one orders grain into a public grain elevator, the elevator operator charges a fee. Or if one deposits gold or silver bullion in a bank vault, there will also be a monthly fee. We reserve our explanation of the convenience yield for now.

Thus, a proponent of the theory of storage would suggest that the fair value or cost of carry futures price is a function of spot commodity values, finance charges, storage fees, and convenience yields as follows.

Cost of Carry Futures Price = Spot Price + Finance Charges + Storage Fees
+ Convenience Yield

The basis, or the relationship, between spot and futures prices is calculated as the futures price less the spot price. The basis calculated thus normally results in a positive quotation to the extent that finance costs and storage fees should always be positive, driving futures prices to a premium to spot prices. (However, this is not universally true to the extent that we have not fully considered the possible impact of the convenience yield.)

Basis = Futures Price − Spot Price

Another way of presenting this is to suggest that the basis is a function of finance charges, storage fees, and the convenience yield.

Basis = Finance Charges + Storage Fees + Convenience Yield

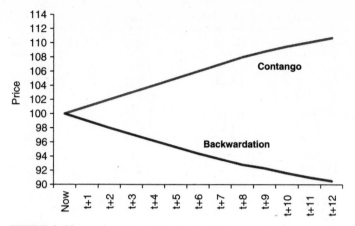

EXHIBIT 8.42 Contango and Backwardation

In practice, we may observe that some commodity futures systematically trade at higher and higher levels in successively deferred months in the future. This is known as a *contango*, or a normal carrying charge market. But other futures contracts may trade at lower and lower levels in successively deferred months extending into the future. This is known as a *backwardation*. See Exhibit 8.42.

Expectations Expressed in Pricing Curve

Let's examine the situation that prevailed in agricultural markets in June 2009. At the time, we might have found corn futures trading at higher and higher levels in successively deferred months reaching into the future (i.e., a contango). Interestingly, we witnessed soybean futures pricing at lower and lower levels in successively deferred months into the future (i.e., a backwardation). See Exhibits 8.43 and 8.44.

This appears rather strange, at least superficially, to the extent that corn and soybeans are affected by many of the same factors such as weather, noting that they are grown in the same geographic regions and indeed in the same fields on a rotating basis.

A number of fundamental factors contributed to the situation in mid-2009. Soybeans were in relatively short supply largely because of strong demand for soybean oil. In fact, soybean meal was trading at a backwardation as the future demand for meal was expected to diminish because hog and poultry producers were expected to cull herds and flocks. Tellingly, soybean oil was trading at a healthy contango.

EXHIBIT 8.43   CBOT Corn Futures in Contango (June 29, 2009)

Month	Settlement	Change	Volume	Open Interest
Jul-09	377	−7 1/4	94,936	43,628
Sep-09	384 1/2	−7 1/4	57,232	297,419
Dec-09	397 1/4	−7	94,298	403,216
Mar-10	409 1/2	−6 1/2	6,050	62,357
May-10	418	−6 1/2	1,407	16,353
Jul-10	425	−6 1/4	3,345	38,125
Sep-10	420	−3 1/2	2,074	4,942
Dec-10	413 3/4	−2	3,778	64,199
Mar-11	423 1/4	−2 1/2		526
May-11	428 1/4	−2 1/2		2
Jul-11	433 1/4	−2 1/2	15	629
Sep-11	430	−2 1/4		
Dec-11	426 3/4	−2	16	4,800
Jul-12	441 3/4	−2		5
Dec-12	428 3/4	−2	5	33
TOTAL			263,156	936,234

EXHIBIT 8.44   CBOT Soybean Futures in Backwardation (June 29, 2009)

Month	Settlement	Change	Volume	Open Interest
Jul-09	1215	+14	46,952	16,888
Aug-09	1122	−6	29,638	70,320
Sep-09	1036	−10	5,903	19,963
Nov-09	983 1/2	−7 1/2	52,993	246,891
Jan-10	986 1/2	−5 1/2	1,781	25,527
Mar-10	979 1/2	−7	1,052	17,600
May-10	964 1/2	−3 1/2	964	10,264
Jul-10	964	−3	970	15,490
Aug-10	951	−4		5
Sep-10	930	−7		2
Nov-10	915 1/2	−4 1/2	371	17,071
Jan-11	920	−4		26
Mar-11	922	−4		22
May-11	923	−4 1/2		
Jul-11	923	−6		7
Aug-11	923	−6		
Sep-11	915	−14		
Nov-11	910	−7		434
TOTAL			140,624	440,520

A second powerful fundamental factor that explains the fact why corn can be trading at a contango while soybeans were in a backwardation is that grain farmers were expected to rotate their crops from corn to soybeans. This expectation was based in part by concerns that the Renewable Fuels Mandate that had subsidized the production of corn-based ethanol might be in political jeopardy.

Thus, one might conclude that marketplace expectations can play a central role in establishing either a contango or a backwardation in a particular market. But this conclusion seems to fly in the face of our theory of storage and a cost of carry pricing model.

Arbitrage Activity

Arbitrage activity is key to holding commodity prices to a "pure" cost of carry pricing model. In a pure "carrying charge market," futures should consistently trade at a contango, or at higher and higher levels in successively deferred months into the future. The forward curve for some commodities including gold or silver is affected almost exclusively by cost of carry considerations including finance and storage costs. This may be explained by the facility with which one may purchase and carry gold or silver as part of an arbitrage.

Such arbitrage actually was extremely popular in the 1970s as retail investors scrambled to buy gold and silver futures as a possible hedge against inflation that was rampant at the time. The demand was so great that gold and silver futures were often pushed to premiums above levels dictated by cost of carry considerations. Professional traders would step in to buy physical bullion and sell (overpriced) futures. It was quite easy to hold the bullion until the futures contract matured and make delivery of the physical metal against the maturing futures contract. This was known as the cash-and-carry trade.

To illustrate this arbitrage, consider conditions prevailing on September 12, 2007, in the gold spot and futures markets. See Exhibit 8.45. The value of spot gold was quoted at \$711.60 per troy ounce. There were 106 days (d) until maturity of the December COMEX gold futures contract on December 27, 2007, while short-term interest rates (r) were at 5.70%. Applying our cost of carry formula, we could calculate that the "fair value" of gold should be \$723.54.

$$\text{Futures} = \text{Spot Gold} \times (1 + [r \times d/360])$$
$$= \$711.60 \times (1 + 0.0577 \times 106/360])$$
$$= \$723.54$$

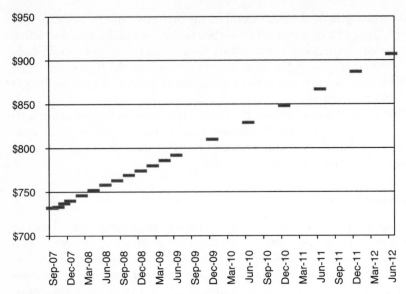

EXHIBIT 8.45   Gold Futures (as of 9/12/07)

Thus, we might expect the basis or the difference between futures and spot values to be tracking near $11.94 (= Futures − Spot = $723.54 − $711.60). If the basis were much lower than this level (implying that spot gold was "cheap" relative to futures that are trading "rich"), one might expect arbitrageurs to buy spot gold and sell futures. By tendering bullion against the maturing futures contract, one may complete the transaction and dispose of the bullion.

If the basis were much higher than this level (spot gold is "rich" relative to futures that are "cheap"), one might expect arbitrageurs to sell bullion, presumably out of inventory, and buy futures. By standing long for delivery against the futures contract, one essentially replaces the previously sold bullion.

Because of the facility with which one may execute this arbitrage in the context of gold or silver, these markets typically trade quite precisely in sync with the shape of the short-term interest rate yield curve. In fact, some traders have been known to trade gold or silver spreads as a proxy for trading short-term interest rates.

Not only are these relationships reflected in the basis or the spread between futures and spot commodity values, they are also implicit in calendar spreads or the difference between values prevailing in one futures delivery month versus another futures delivery month.

EXHIBIT 8.46 Calendar Spread with COMEX Gold Futures

	Oct-07 Gold Futures	Dec-07 Gold Futures	Spread	3-Month LIBOR
6/29/07	Sell @ $657.00	Buy @ $663.20	$6.20	5.36%
9/12/07	Buy @ $714.00	Sell @ $720.70	$6.70	5.70%
	−$57.00	+57.50	+$0.50	+34 bips

Thus, if one expected short-term interest rates to advance in June 2007 (as shown in Exhibit 8.46), one might have sold a calendar spread in COMEX gold futures by selling a nearby October 2007 contract at $657.00 and buying a deferred December 2007 contract at $663.20. The spread of $6.20 (= $663.20 less $657.00) advanced over the next several months to $6.70 in response to increasing short-term interest rates.

Arbitrage Breakdown

But the ease with which one may conduct an arbitrage may affect the structure of the commodity pricing curve. In particular, where arbitrage activity is difficult or even impossible to conduct, so-called convenience yields may dictate the structure of the commodity pricing curve.

The convenience yield may exert either a positive or a negative influence on the pricing structure of commodities extending into the future. In essence, convenience yields reflect the option of either holding inventories of commodities for future use or consuming said commodities currently. In a very real way, the convenience yield may be thought of as another way of suggesting that expectations are reflected in the pricing curve where arbitrage becomes difficult.

Convenience yields may strongly be affected by where we might be in terms of the business cycle. In particular, there tends to be an inverse relationship between inventory levels and convenience yields. Thus, when we find ourselves in a weak segment of the business cycle, demand for any particular commodity may decline and inventories may increase. Convenience yields are low and the economic system becomes inclined to consume inventories currently rather than hold them for fear of future price declines. When the business cycle is strong, demand for commodities may increase and draw down inventories. Convenience yields are high and producers may become inclined to hoard inventories of storable commodities in anticipation of future price advances.

Convenience yields are further correlated very positively with volatility or risk. As a general rule, short-term commodity futures contracts exhibit greater volatility and convenience yields than do long-term contracts. This is known as the *Samuelson effect* in tribute to Paul Samuelson, who first articulated the theory in the 1960s.

The Samuelson effect reflects the observation that commodities tend to be more heavily affected by short-term economic factors than long-term factors. In the short term, as the theory goes, the ability of commodity producers to ramp up or curtail production may be rather limited. Thus, price action becomes the engine through which commodities are allocated among competing end uses. But in the long term, production levels will be adjusted to reflect perceived market demand, introducing a naturally stabilizing long-term effect. By contrast, financial instruments such as stocks and bonds tend to be more heavily affected by longer-term expectations regarding economic growth and stability.

A related theory, often attributed to Anderson and Danthine, addresses seasonality in commodity prices, suggesting the volatility is heavily related to the flow of pertinent information.

The grain markets provide a nice example of a seasonal commodity to the extent that they are produced seasonally. Specifically, and at least in the Northern Hemisphere with a nod to the growing importance of South American grain production, crops are harvested in the fall. Price volatility tends to peak during the summer months during which time the crops are growing in the fields and subject to the vagaries of weather. Thus, grain traders often refer to those volatile "weather months."

Grains may be held in elevators literally for years before the product experiences deterioration and loss in nutritional value. But beyond the seasonality implicit in grain production, these markets are also affected by the crop year phenomenon. Although demand may continue throughout the calendar year, supplies of grain can only be augmented at harvest time. Thus, we sometimes witness sudden fractures in the grain pricing curve across the crop year or in the fall harvest period. As such, it may become risky to hold grains in storage across crop years as part of an arbitrage transaction.

Livestock production and meat consumption tends to be relatively consistent during winter and summer months and, therefore, may not exhibit any marked seasonal patterns. Still, it may become problematic to hold animals for extended periods of time to the extent that, once they are up to market weight, there is usually little economic sense in continuing to hold the product.

Like grains, gasoline and heating oil are also heavily affected by seasonal considerations. But whereas grain production is seasonal, it is the consumption or demand pattern of energy products that is affected by seasonal weather considerations. Demand for gasoline tends to peak during the

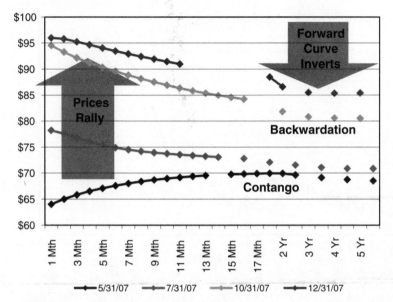

EXHIBIT 8.47 WTI Crude Oil Forward Curves

summer "driving months"; demand for heating oil peaks during the cold winter months. Thus, volatility and prices may be seasonally high in the summer for gasoline and high in the winter for heating oil.

Beyond these factors, energy products may be difficult to hold on the part of arbitrageurs. Although grains may be held in public grain elevators, storage facilities for crude oil at Cushing, Oklahoma, are owned and operated by a handful of large companies. Thus, the average trader would not be advised to attempt to participate in a delivery. As such, the cost of carry model breaks down and the forward curve is affected more heavily by convenience yields or market expectations.

This may be illustrated by examining the forward curves for crude oil during the year 2007. See Exhibit 8.47. In late May 2007, spot oil was trading just below $65 per barrel and the forward curve exhibited a contango. One might interpret that contango as an indication that traders held the belief that prices might advance in the future.

By December 2007, spot prices had indeed advanced up to just above $95 per barrel. By that point, the forward curve showed a strong inversion or backwardation, as if to suggest that traders believed that prices would decline in the future. Of course, spot crude oil values eventually approached $150 per barrel before declining sharply in late 2008 as a result of a general economic pullback and declining global demand. See Exhibit 8.48.

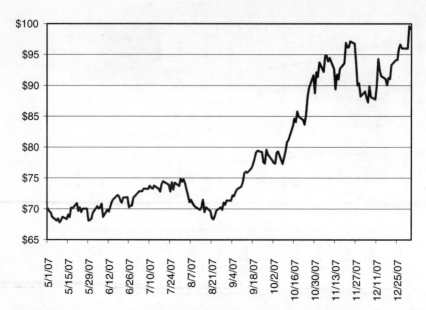

EXHIBIT 8.48   Feb-08 WTI Crude Oil Futures

Thus, some believe that the shape of the forward curve, particularly in markets that are not easily "arbed," provides a general indication of market sentiment. Although the accuracy of such sentiments should be questioned, it is nonetheless an appealing concept.

Roll Returns

A passive long investment in commodities offers two sources of return including spot commodity price performance and so-called roll returns. Understanding roll relationships can be the key to generating superior returns even in a passive long commodity investment.

Futures are not perpetual like a stock but rather expire periodically. This implies that one must roll one's holdings by liquidating nearby futures as contract maturity approaches and reestablishing positions in deferred futures contracts. Accordingly, the shape of the forward curve can exert a major impact on the profitability of a passive long investment.

Consider the costs of rolling a crude oil futures position from one month to the next under conditions of contango versus backwardation (Exhibit 8.49). Rolling a long position from July 2007 to September 2007 futures during a contango implies the purchase of a deferred futures contract trading at a $1.82 per barrel premium over the nearby contract. But rolling the long position forward from February 2008 to April 2008 futures

EXHIBIT 8.49 2009 Crude Oil Contango and Backwardation

Contango on 5/31/07	Backwardation on 12/31/07
Sell Jul-07 crude oil @ $64.01	Sell Feb-08 crude oil @ 95.98
Buy Sep-07 crude oil @ $65.83	Buy Apr-08 crude oil @ 95.24
−$1.82/bbl	+$0.74/bbl

during a backwardation implies the purchase of a deferred contract trading at $0.74 per barrel discount to the nearby contract.

Thus, one may conclude that holding passive long positions during a backwardation is less costly than in a contango. So we might recommend the maintenance of long positions in nearby months when in backwardation and deferred months when in contango. Of course, and as we discussed earlier, a contango is often accompanied by tight inventories and prospects for rising prices, whereas a backwardation may occur when inventories are more plentiful.

A study by Campbell in 2007 found that, during the period from October 1997 through February 2007, it was optimal to hold crude oil futures contracts extending out approximately six months into the future as opposed to any more nearby or deferred contracts.

This conclusion was extended into a study of passive positions in the S&P/GSCI Index as well. See Exhibit 8.50. The standard S&P/GSCI Index

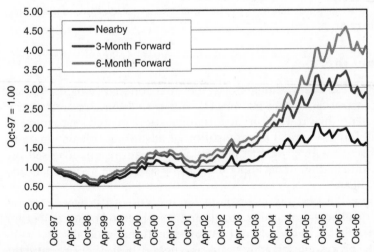

EXHIBIT 8.50 S&P/GSCI Performance (Oct-97 to Feb-07)
Source: "The Strategic and Tactical Value of Commodity Investing," Campbell Harvey, Duke University, December 2007.

implicitly represents positions in nearby futures. However, it is possible to construct the index assuming that one holds positions in deferred contract months in the 28 constituent futures contracts. For example, one may construct the index by populating it with futures contracts extending out approximately three months, six months, or one year into the future.

Noting that energy products comprise a large proportion of the index by weight, it is not surprising that superior returns would have been generated by holding passive positions in the S&P/GSCI Index using futures contracts extending out some six months into the future. The difference in returns is not trivial. If one had invested passively in nearby contracts, one would have realized an annualized return of 7.40% from 1997 to 2007. By investing in the three-month or six-month forward series, those returns would have been enhanced to 13.54% or 16.73%, respectively.

INTERMARKET COMMODITY SPREADING

Calendar or intramarket spreads across different contract delivery months are driven by the shape of the forward pricing curve as already discussed. But in addition to these types of trades, the market focuses keenly on any number of intermarket spreads that are driven by fundamental factors such as the interplay of supply and demand along the production cycle from raw to refined product or the substitutability of one commodity with another related commodity. This section highlights a few of these relationships including the soybean crush spread, various energy crack spreads, and the gold-to-silver ratio.

Crush Spread

The crush spread can be thought of as a transaction that (roughly) reflects the soybean crusher's profit margin. Of course, soybeans are used to produce two major by-products in the form of soybean oil and soybean meal. One might buy the spread in anticipation of advancing crushing margins by purchasing the by-products and selling soybeans or one may sell the spread in anticipation of declining margins by selling the by-products and buying soybeans.

This spread is typically accomplished in the ratio of 10 soybean futures contracts to 11 soybean meal contracts and 9 soybean oil contacts, but for simplicity some use a ratio of 1:1:1. A soybean crusher generally prefers to think of the processing spread in terms of cents per bushel. But because the three contracts are quoted in somewhat different terms, some conversions are necessary to arrive at that convenient quote.

Soybean oil is quoted in cents per pound; soybean meal is quoted in dollars per short ton. Finally, soybeans are quoted in cents per bushel. The crushing process generally produces about 11 pounds of oil per bushel and 44 pounds of soybean meal. Thus, one may convert a soybean oil quote in cents per pound to cents per bushel by multiplying the price by 11. It is a bit more complicated with soybean meal quoted in dollars per short ton. There are 2,000 pounds in a short ton, 44 pounds per bushel, and 100 cents per dollar. Thus, one must multiply by 2.2 ($= 100/[2,000 \times 44]$).

As such, the crush spread may be calculated and quoted in cents per bushel by using the following formula. Assume that nearby soybean futures are quoted at 1,191.00 cents per bushel, nearby soybean meal is at \$393.8 per short ton, and nearby soybean oil is quoted at 36.70 cents per pound. Thus, the crush spread is quoted at 79.06 cents per bushel.

$$\begin{aligned}
\text{Crush Spread} &= (2.2 \times \text{Soybean Meal}) + (11 \times \text{Soybean Oil}) \\
&\quad - (\text{Soybeans}) \\
&= (2.2 \times 393.8) + (11 \times 36.70) - (1,191.00) \\
&= 79.06 \text{ cents per bushel}
\end{aligned}$$

The value of the soybean crush is widely followed as an important indicator of possible future market developments. Like any other businesspeople, soybean crushers would prefer to maintain a healthy and stable profit margin and are likely to adjust production in response to inordinate movements in the spread. Thus, they are likely to increase production and resulting supplies in the end products when the spread becomes rich and decrease production when the spread becomes thin. Thus, the action of soybean crushers naturally tends to moderate extreme price movements at least in the long term. See Exhibit 8.51.

Crack Spreads

The petroleum crack spread is analogous to the soybean crush spread. As described earlier, crude oil is refined, or "cracked," into various products including gasoline and heating oil among many others. Thus, the spread between the crude oil futures contract as the raw input and a combination of gasoline and heating oil futures contracts as representative of the finished product roughly reflects oil refiners' profit margins.

To construct the three-leg spread between crude oil on one side versus gasoline and heating oil on the other side, one must identify the relative quantity of by-product generated by a barrel of crude. Although this ratio is very rough, the market applies the assumption that three barrels of crude may generate two barrels of gasoline and one barrel of heating oil.

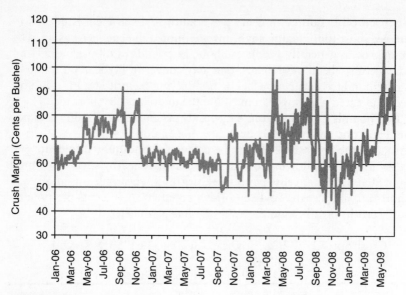

EXHIBIT 8.51 Nearby Soybean Crush

Thus, if one anticipated that refining margins would increase, one might (1) buy two RBOB gasoline futures, (2) buy one #2 heating oil futures contracts, and, (3) sell three crude oil futures contracts. Or if one anticipated that refining margins would decrease, (1) sell two RBOB gasoline futures, (2) sell one #2 heating oil futures, and (3) buy three crude oil futures.

Crude oil futures are based on the delivery of 1,000 barrels of product and are quoted in dollars per barrel. RBOB gasoline and #2 heating oil futures call for the delivery of 42,000 gallons (or 1,000 barrels at 42 gallons per barrel) of product and are quoted in dollars per gallon. A simple algebraic conversion is required to quote the crack spread in dollars per barrel.

Assume that nearby gasoline futures are trading at $1.8633 per gallon, nearby heating oil futures are at $1.7689 per gallon, and nearby crude oil was at $69.53 per barrel. The crack spread may be quoted as follows.

$$
\begin{aligned}
\text{Crack Spread} &= (2 \times 42 \times \text{Gas}) + (1 \times 42 \times \text{Heating Oil}) - (3 \times \text{Crude Oil}) \\
&= (2 \times 42 \times \$1.8633) + (1 \times 42 \times \$1.7689) - (3 \times \$69.53) \\
&= \$22.221 \text{ per barrel}
\end{aligned}
$$

As an alternative to the 3:2:1 crude, gasoline, and heating oil spread, one may simply trade one crude oil futures contract versus one gasoline futures contract or one crude oil futures versus one heating oil futures. The market likewise prefers to quote these spreads on a uniform basis in dollars per barrel.

$$\begin{aligned}
\text{Crude Oil/Gasoline Spread} &= (42 \times \text{Gas}) - \text{Crude Oil} \\
&= (42 \times \$1.8633) - \$69.53 \\
&= \$8.7286 \text{ per barrel}
\end{aligned}$$

$$\begin{aligned}
\text{Crude Oil/Heating Oil Spread} &= (42 - \text{Heating Oil}) - \text{Crude Oil} \\
&= (42 \times \$1.7689) - \$69.53 \\
&= \$4.7638 \text{ per barrel}
\end{aligned}$$

All three of these crack spreads are quite seasonal. As a general rule, the demand for gasoline increases sharply during the summer driving season, pushing the value of gasoline relatively higher. Thus, we clearly see pronounced pops in the gas/heating oil/crude spread and in the crude/gas spread during the summers of 2006, 2007, and 2008. See Exhibit 8.52.

Of course the demand for heating oil is greatest during the winter months. But we do not see terribly obvious seasonal patterns in the heating oil/crude spread, probably because heating oil has largely been replaced by natural gas as a major source of heat and is only in heavy use in the Northeast.

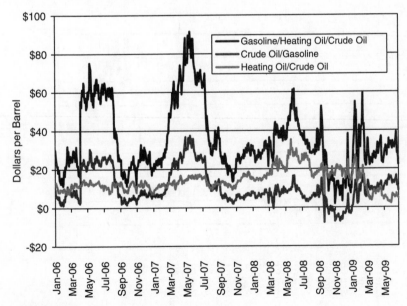

EXHIBIT 8.52   Nearby Energy Crack Spreads

Gold-to-Silver Ratio

Gold and silver have both been used as a standard for monetary exchange over the millennia. Thus, although they may not be substitutable for industrial purposes, they might broadly be considered substitutable in at least one sense. The gold-to-silver ratio is simply calculated as the number of ounces of silver required to purchase a single ounce of gold. Thus, if gold were trading at \$983.30 per troy ounce with silver at \$13.875 per troy ounce, the gold-to-silver ratio could be calculated at 70.8.

$$\begin{aligned}
\text{Gold Silver Ratio} &= \text{Gold} \div \text{Silver} \\
&= \$983.30/\text{troy oz} \div \$13.875/\text{troy oz} \\
&= 70.8
\end{aligned}$$

Today, the ratio floats as a function of the fundamental forces of supply and demand in gold relative to silver (see Exhibit 8.53). Historically, however, the gold-to-silver ratio has sometimes been pegged by government fiat. For example, during the time of the Roman Empire, the ratio was set at 12. In the late nineteenth century, bimetalism, or the economic policy that calls for money to be backed by fixed quantities of either gold or silver, became a rallying cry of the U.S. Populist Party. However, advocates of a monometalism policy prevailed by 1896 with the election of President McKinley

EXHIBIT 8.53   Gold-to-Silver Ratio

when the ratio stood at 15. Since then, the ratio has generally increased, peaking near 100 in 1991.

The ratio is useful as a general indication of relative value. Thus, if the ratio becomes "high," this may suggest that one consider the sale of gold versus the purchase of silver. Or if the ratio becomes "low" by historical standards, consider buying gold and selling silver. These trades would generally be weighted or balanced such that one may buy and sell equal dollar values of both metals. This strategy may best be pursued during stressful economic or political periods when fears of deflation or currency devaluation are most pronounced.

CLEARPORT OVER-THE-COUNTER CLEARING FACILITY

In addition to offering a very wide variety of commodity contracts for trading through conventional facilities such as the CME Globex electronic trading platform or via open outcry in a trading pit, CME Group also offers clearance of a wide variety of OTC derivatives through the CME ClearPort facility.

Although this concept may be applied to any number of commodity and financial markets, the service has been most widely accepted to date within the context of the NYMEX energy markets. In fact, the ClearPort facility was originated in the early 2000s at NYMEX but was relabeled CME ClearPort subsequent to the CME Group acquisition of NYMEX Holdings, Inc. in August 2008.

What Is CME ClearPort?

CME ClearPort should not be thought of as a trading platform or as a clearing service. Rather it is best understood as an Internet or web-based gateway through which transactions executed bilaterally may be submitted (or "novated") to the CME Clearing House for centralized processing and clearing.

CME ClearPort has historically been applied and is most widely known in the context of energy markets. The CME ClearPort system currently provides traders an unparalleled flexibility to conduct their own transactions in a slate of hundreds of energy, metals, and other contracts off-exchange, negotiate their own prices, and submit the transactions through the CME ClearPort gateway to the CME Group Clearing House.

As a general rule, these transactions are executed off-exchange in a bilateral transaction directly between buyer and seller. This is akin to the execution of any other OTC derivatives contract. Subsequently, the transaction is submitted or novated to the CME Clearing House for purposes of processing and clearance. This is accomplished through a procedure known alternatively as an exchange of futures for physicals (EFP) or an exchange for swap (EFS) or a substitution (SUB) transaction.

The net result is that the original OTC derivative is extinguished in favor of a corresponding futures position with economically equivalent terms and conditions. Once the transaction is accepted and processed in the exchange's multilateral clearing system, it is subject to initial and periodic variation margin requirements like any other futures contract. Like any other futures contract and unlike an OTC derivatives contract, it may be offset with an opposite transaction with any other counterparty and not just with the original counterparty.

By submitting one's OTC transactions to the CME ClearPort process, one enjoys the financial sureties afforded by the CME Clearing House. Thus, one may effectively address counterparty credit risks, which naturally become heightened in the wake of the so-called subprime mortgage crisis.

Markets Covered

CME ClearPort currently facilitates the processing of a very wide variety of contracts linked to natural gas; crude oil; petroleum by-products; ethanol, freight rates; "green" products; electricity; coal; metals; currencies; "softs" including coffee, cocoa, and sugar; commodity indexes including the S&P/GSCI index; uranium; petrochemicals; and grains.

These contracts may be based on the outright values for these products or may use alternative structures. For example, a "basis swap" is a very common structure that essentially represents a spread between the value of a commodity at two different locations. For example, one might trade a basis swap between the value of natural gas at the benchmark Henry Hub location versus the Houston ship channel. Index swaps, swing swaps, and options may also be available.

Moving forward, it will not be a service offered exclusively for energy or even just physical commodity traders. Rather, this service may be applied in a wide variety of asset classes including interest rates, foreign exchange, equities, and others.

The needs and demands of each of these markets may be somewhat unique. CME ClearPort is sufficiently flexible to address the varied requirements of traders in many different asset classes. In some markets this may mean that a bilaterally executed transaction is used to create a position that is subsequently carried and treated as a futures contract for regulatory and bookkeeping purposes. In other cases, it may mean that a bilaterally executed transaction may continue to carried as an OTC derivative for regulatory purposes but still enjoy the financial sureties and processing efficiencies implied by centralized counterparty clearing.

In some instances, CME ClearPort may be used to conduit transactions into the Clearing House that can be transacted exclusively on a bilateral basis or on a "cleared-only" basis. In the case of more mature and highly standardized markets, CME ClearPort may be used to augment an actively traded contract such that bilaterally negotiated and on-exchange contacts may ultimately reside in the same clearing system.

But the unifying feature of CME ClearPort will be the coupling of an OTC-style, bilateral execution with futures-style, multilateral clearing services. CME ClearPort is the conduit or mechanism through which the value-added services of dealers may be coupled with the financial safeguards and capital efficiencies of a central counterparty clearing model.

Benefits of Centralized Counterparty Clearing

The CME ClearPort facility effectively extends the benefits of the exchange or centralized or multilateral clearing model to participants in the OTC derivatives markets. Those benefits may be cataloged as follows.

- *Automated bookkeeping processes:* Automated, rather than manual, processes ensure timely and accurate confirmation of transactions.
- *Mark-to-market:* CME Group clearing features a twice daily mark-to-market (MTM) regime with performance bond requirements adjusted as required based on volatility and market events. This effectively means that unrealized losses cannot accrue or go unnoticed, assuring confidence for market participants.
- *Capital efficiencies through cross-margining:* CME Group offers an extraordinarily wide array of products covering the interest rate, equity, currency, energy, agricultural, metals, and alternative investment asset classes. Significant capital efficiencies in the form of reduced performance bond or margin requirements are implied by bringing correlating OTC and on-exchange products under one roof.
- *Financial sureties:* The CME Group Clearing House acts as buyer to every seller and seller to every buyer. Thus, we provide for the separation of trading counterparties from credit counterparties. Further, the CME Group Clearing House provides for the most effective customer protection system in the world, segregating customer funds and positions from those of the bank or broker. Finally, and perhaps most importantly, central counterparty clearing guarantees the performance of every transaction, both on-exchange or OTC, backed by the exchange's extensive financial safeguard system.

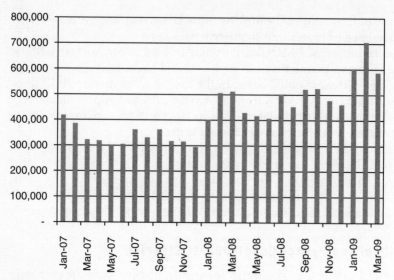

EXHIBIT 8.54 ClearPort Average Daily Volume (ADV)

These benefits are underscored by the general advance in ClearPort volumes in 2008 and into 2009 in the wake of the subprime mortgage crisis and heightened concerns regarding counterparty credit risks. See Exhibit 8.54.

CONCLUSION

The futures industry grew up on the back of the physical commodity markets. Over the last century, the domestic futures markets expanded from its original base in the grain trade to include livestock, metals, energy products, and many other items.

Commodities have increasingly become recognized as an asset class in addition to traditional asset classes such as stocks and bonds. Accordingly, many institutional and individual investors have allocated portions of their investment holdings to these markets, often in the form of passive long allocation to commodity index instruments and sometimes in the form of actively managed investments within the managed futures segment of the industry. Commodities tend to be uncorrelated with traditional assets such as stocks and bonds and therefore provide investors with diversification.

Savvy traders may study the fundamental factors that affect various commodity markets by staying abreast of supply and demand considerations. This knowledge may be applied to outright trades based on anticipated directional price movement or to a variety of intra- and intermarket spreading activities. In particular, the forward curve in futures markets extending out into successively deferred contract months is telling with respect to anticipated price movements and intermarket or calendar spreads.

Beyond offering the widest array of commodity futures in the world, CME Group also offers clearance of OTC executed commodity derivatives through its CME ClearPort facility.

APPENDIX: MAJOR COMMODITY MARKET SPECIFICATIONS

The following exhibits are summaries of futures and options contract specifications for the major commodities discussed in this chapter. Since these specifications are subject to change, readers are advised to consult the relevant Rulebook for the most current specifications and other rules governing these contracts.

EXHIBIT 8.55   CBOT Corn Futures and Options

	Futures	Options
Trading Unit	5,000 bushels (~127 metric tons)	One corn futures contract of 5,000 bushels
Price Quote	In cents per bushel in minimum increments of 1/4 cent per bushel ($12.50 per contract)	In cents per bushel in minimum increments of 1/8th of one cent per bushel ($6.25)
Trading Months	March (H), May (K), July (N), September (U), and December (Z)	March (H), May (K), July (N), September (U), and December (Z). Also, a monthly (or serial) option is listed when front month is not standard month. Serials exercise into nearby futures contract (e.g., October option exercises into December futures).

(Continued)

EXHIBIT 8.55   (*Continued*)

	Futures	Options
Trading Hours	On CME Globex from 6:00 PM to 6:00 AM the following day and 9:30 AM to 1:15 PM (Central Time) on Sundays through Fridays. Via open outcry on trading floor from 9:30 AM to 1:15 PM Mondays through Fridays	
Strike Price Intervals	NA	Five cents per bushel or ten cents per bushel as specified by Exchange Rule
Last Trading Day	Business day prior to 15th calendar day of contract month	For standard options: last Friday preceding first notice day of corresponding corn futures contract month by at least two business days. For serial options: last Friday preceding by at least two business days last business day of month preceding option month.
Delivery	Requires physical delivery of #2 Yellow at contract price, #1 Yellow at 1.5 cent/bushel premium, #3 Yellow at 1.5 cent/bushel discount. Delivery may occur on any day at discretion of short from first business day of month to second business day following last trading day of delivery month	Option longs may exercise on any business day prior to expiration by giving notice to clearinghouse by 6:00 PM (Central Time). In-the-money options on last trading day are automatically exercised. Unexercised options expire at 7:00 PM on last day of trading.
Daily Price Limit	$0.30 per bushel expandable to $0.45 and to $0.70 when market closes at limit bid or limit offer. No price limits on current month contract on or after second business day preceding first day of delivery month.	

EXHIBIT 8.56 CBOT Wheat Futures and Options

	Futures	Options
Trading Unit	5,000 bushels (~136 metric tons)	One wheat futures contract of 5,000 bushels
Price Quote	In cents per bushel in minimum increments of 1/4 cent per bushel ($12.50 per contract)	In cents per bushel in minimum increments of 1/8th of one cent per bushel ($6.25)
Trading Months	March (H), May (K), July (N), September (U), and December (Z)	March (H), May (K), July (N), September (U), and December (Z). Monthly (serial) option is listed when front month is not standard month. Serials exercise into nearby futures contract (e.g., October option exercises into December futures).
Trading Hours	On CME Globex from 6:00 PM to 6:00 AM the following day and 9:30 AM to 1:15 PM (Central Time) on Sundays through Fridays. Via open outcry on trading floor from 9:30 AM to 1:15 PM Mondays through Fridays	
Strike Price Intervals	NA	Five (5) cents per bushel or ten (10) cents per bushel as specified by Exchange Rule
Last Trading Day	Business day prior to 15th calendar day of contract month	For standard options: last Friday preceding first notice day of corresponding corn futures contract month by at least two business days. For serial options: last Friday preceding by at least two business days last business day of month preceding option month.
Delivery	Physical delivery of #2 Soft Red Winter at contract price, #1 Soft Red Winter at 3 cent/bushel premium, other deliverable grades specified by Rule. Delivery may occur on any day at discretion of short from first business day of month to second business day following last trading day of delivery month	Option longs may exercise on any business day prior to expiration by giving notice to clearinghouse by 6:00 PM (Central Time). In-the-money options on last trading day are automatically exercised. Unexercised options expire at 7:00 PM on last day of trading.
Daily Price Limit	$0.60 per bushel expandable to $0.90 and to $1.35 when market closes at limit bid or limit offer. No price limits on current month contract on or after second business day preceding first day of delivery month.	

EXHIBIT 8.57   CBOT Soybeans Futures & Options

	Futures	Options
Trading Unit	5,000 bushels (~136 metric tons)	One soybean futures contract of 5,000 bushels
Price Quote	In cents per bushel in minimum increments of 1/4 cent per bushel ($12.50 per contract)	In cents per bushel in minimum increments of 1/8th of one cent per bushel ($6.25)
Trading Months	January (F), March (H), May (K), July (N), August (Q), September (U), and November (X)	January (F), March (H), May (K), July (N), August (Q), September (U), and November (X). Monthly (or serial) option is listed when front month is not standard month. Serials exercise into nearby futures contract (e.g., October option exercises into November futures).
Trading Hours	On CME Globex from 6:00 PM to 6:00 AM the following day and 9:30 AM to 1:15 PM (Central Time) on Sundays through Fridays. Via open outcry on trading floor from 9:30 AM to 1:15 PM Mondays through Fridays	
Strike Price Intervals	NA	Ten cents per bushel or 20 cents per bushel as specified by Exchange Rule
Last Trading Day	Business day prior to 15th calendar day of contract month	For standard options: last Friday preceding first notice day of corresponding soybean futures contract month by at least two business days. For serial options: last Friday preceding by at least two business days last business day of month preceding option month.
Delivery	Requires physical delivery of #2 Yellow at contract price, #1 Yellow at a 6 cent/bushel premium, #3 Yellow at a 6 cent/bushel discount. Delivery may occur on any day at	Option longs may exercise on any business day prior to expiration by giving notice to clearinghouse by 6:00 PM (Central Time). In-the-money options on last trading day

EXHIBIT 8.57 (*Continued*)

	Futures	Options
	discretion of short from first business day of month to second business day following last trading day of delivery month.	automatically exercised. Unexercised options expire at 7:00 PM on last day of trading.
Daily Price Limit	$0.70 per bushel expandable to $1.05 and to $1.60 when market closes at limit bid or limit offer. No price limits on current month contract on or after second business day preceding first day of delivery month.	

EXHIBIT 8.58 CBOT Soybean Oil Futures and Options

	Futures	Options
Trading Unit	60,000 pounds (~27 metric tons)	One soybean oil futures contract of 60,000 pounds
Price Quote	In cents per pound in minimum increments of 1/100 cent ($0.0001) per pound ($6.00 per contract)	In cents per pound in minimum increments of 5/1,000 cents per pound ($3 per contract)
Trading Months	January (F), March (H), May (K), July (N), August (Q), September (U), October (V), and December (Z)	January (F), March (H), May (K), July (N), August (Q), September (U), October (V), and December (Z). Monthly (serial) option is listed when front month is not standard month. Serials exercise into nearby futures contract (e.g., November option exercises into December futures).
Trading Hours	On CME Globex from 6:00 PM to 6:00 AM the following day and 9:30 AM to 1:15 PM (Central Time) on Sundays through Fridays. Via open outcry on trading floor from 9:30 AM to 1:15 PM Mondays through Fridays.	
Strike Price Intervals	NA	Generally 1/2 cent per pound; see Exchange Rules for details

(*Continued*)

EXHIBIT 8.58 (*Continued*)

	Futures	Options
Last Trading Day	Business day prior to 15th calendar day of contract month	For standard options: last Friday preceding first notice day of corresponding soybean futures contract month by at least two business days. For serial options: last Friday preceding by at least two business days last business day of month preceding option month.
Delivery	Physical delivery of crude soybean oil meeting Exchange-approved grades and standards per Exchange Rules. Delivery may occur on any day at discretion of short from first business day of month to business day following last trading day of delivery month.	Option longs may exercise on any business day prior to expiration by giving notice to clearinghouse by 6:00 PM (Central Time). In-the-money options on last trading day automatically exercised. Unexercised options expire at 7:00 PM on last day of trading.
Daily Price Limit	2.5 cents per pound expandable to 3.5 and to 5.5 when market closes at limit bid or limit offer. No price limits on current month contract on or after second business day preceding first day of delivery month.	

EXHIBIT 8.59 CBOT Soybean Meal Futures and Options

	Futures	Options
Trading Unit	100 short tons (~91 metric tons)	One soybean meal futures contract (of a specified month) of 100 short tons
Price Quote	In dollars and cents per short ton in minimum increments of 10 cents per short ton ($10.00 per contract)	In dollars and cents per short ton in minimum increments of 5 cents per short ton ($5 per contract)
Trading Months	January (F), March (H), May (K), July (N), August (Q),	January (F), March (H), May (K), July (N), August (Q),

EXHIBIT 8.59 *(Continued)*

	Futures	Options
	September (U), October (V), and December (Z)	September (U), October (V), and December (Z). Monthly (serial) option is listed when front month is not standard month. Serials exercise into nearby futures contract (e.g., November option exercises into December futures).
Trading Hours	On CME Globex from 6:00 PM to 6:00 AM the following day and 9:30 AM to 1:15 PM (Central Time) on Sundays through Fridays. Via open outcry on trading floor from 9:30 AM to 1:15 PM Mondays through Fridays.	
Strike Price Intervals	NA	$5 per short ton when strike price <$200 per short ton; $10 per short ton when strike price is ≥$200 per short ton.
Last Trading Day	Business day prior to 15th calendar day of contract month	For standard options: last Friday preceding first notice day of corresponding soybean futures contract month by at least two business days. For serial options: last Friday preceding by at least two business days last business day of month preceding option month.
Delivery	Physical delivery of 48% protein soybean meal meeting various requirements specified by Exchange Rule. Delivery may occur on any day at discretion of short from first business day of month to business day following last trading day of delivery month.	Option longs may exercise on any business day prior to expiration by giving notice to clearinghouse by 6:00 PM (Central Time). In-the-money options on last trading day automatically exercised. Unexercised options expire at 7:00 PM on last day of trading.
Daily Price Limit	$20 per short ton expandable to $30 and to $45 when market closes at limit bid or limit offer. No price limits on current month contract on or after second business day preceding first day of delivery month.	

EXHIBIT 8.60 CME Live Cattle Futures and Options

	Futures	Options
Trading Unit	40,000 pounds (~18 metric tons)	One live cattle futures contract (of a specified month) of 40,000 pounds
Price Quote	In cents per pound in minimum increments of $0.00025 per pound ($10.00 per contract)	In cents per pound in minimum increments of $0.00025 per pound ($10 per contract) or $0.000125 per pound ($5 per contract)
Trading Months	February, April, June, August, October, and December	February, April, June, August, October, and December. Also monthly or serial option listed for January, March, May, July, September, and November. Serials exercise into nearby futures contract. E.g., November option exercises into December futures.
Trading Hours	On CME Globex from 9:05 AM on Monday to 1:55 PM on Friday with trading halt from 4:00 PM to 5:00 PM daily. Via open outcry on trading floor from 9:05 AM to 1:00 PM Mondays through Fridays.	On CME Globex from 9:05 AM on Monday to 1:55 PM on Friday with trading halt from 4:00 PM to 5:00 PM daily. Via open outcry on trading floor from 9:05 AM to 1:02 PM Mondays through Fridays.
Strike Price Intervals	NA	$0.02 for all months and $0.01 for front 2 months only
Last Trading Day	At 12:00 PM (Central Time) on last business day of contract month	At 1:00 PM (Central Time) on first Friday of contract month
Delivery	Physical delivery of 55% Choice, 45% Select, Yield Grade 3 live steers. Delivery may occur on any business day of contract month and the first seven business days	Option longs may exercise on any business day prior to expiration by giving notice to clearinghouse by 7:00 PM (Central Time). In-the-money options on

EXHIBIT 8.60 (*Continued*)

	Futures	Options
Daily Price Limit	of succeeding calendar month per Exchange Rules. $0.03 per pound above or below previous day's settlement price	last trading day are automatically exercised. None

EXHIBIT 8.61 CME Lean Hogs Futures and Options

	Futures	Options
Trading Unit	40,000 pounds (~18 metric tons)	One lean hog futures contract (of a specified month) of 40,000 pounds
Price Quote	In cents per pound in minimum increments of $0.00025 per pound ($10.00 per contract)	In cents per pound in minimum increments of $0.00025 per pound ($10 per contract); or, $0.000125 per pound ($5 per contract)
Trading Months	February, April, May, June, July, August, October, and December	
Trading Hours	On CME Globex from 9:05 AM on Monday to 1:55 PM on Friday with trading halt from 4:00 PM to 5:00 PM daily. Via open outcry on trading floor from 9:05 AM to 1:00 PM Mondays through Fridays.	On CME Globex from 9:05 AM on Monday to 1:55 PM on Friday with trading halt from 4:00 PM to 5:00 PM daily. Via open outcry on trading floor from 9:05 AM to 1:02 PM Mondays through Fridays.
Strike Price Intervals	NA	$0.02 for all months and $0.01 for front two months only
Last Trading Day	At 12:00 PM (Central Time) on 10th business day of contract month	
Delivery	Cash settlement based on CME Lean hog Index for two-day period ending on last trading day. Sample represents value of hog (barrow and gilt) carcasses	Option longs may exercise on any business day prior to expiration by giving notice to clearinghouse by 7:00 PM (Central Time). In-the-money options on

(Continued)

EXHIBIT 8.61   (*Continued*)

	Futures	Options
	as reported in USDA National Daily Direct Hog Prior Day Reported-Slaughtered Swine Report.	last trading day are automatically exercised.
Daily Price Limit	$0.03 per pound above or below previous day's settlement price	None

EXHIBIT 8.62   NYMEX Crude Oil Futures and Options

	Futures	Options
Trading Unit	1,000 US barrels (42,000 gallons)	Exercisable into one futures contract
Price Quote	In dollars and cents in minimum ticks of $0.01 (1 cent) per barrel ($10.00/contract)	
Trading Months	Each month in current year and next five (5) calendar years; June and December listed in years 6 to 9	
Trading Hours	Open Outcry from 9:00 AM to 2:30 PM; traded on CME Globex from 6:00 PM to 5:15 PM Sundays through Fridays with 45-minute halt between 5:15 PM and 6:00 PM daily (Eastern Time)	
Last Trading Day	On third business day prior to 25th calendar day of month preceding delivery month	Option trading ends three business days before termination of futures trading
Strike Price Intervals	NA	20 strike prices in $0.50 per barrel intervals above and below at-the-money strike price plus next 10 strikes in $2.50 increment above highest and below lowest strike for at least 61 strikes
Delivery	Physical delivery via FOB seller's facility at Cushing, OK, at any pipeline or storage facility with pipeline access to TEPPCO, Cushing storage, or Equilon Pipeline	Exercisable into one futures contract

EXHIBIT 8.62 (*Continued*)

	Futures	Options
	Co. by in-tank transfer, in-line transfer, book-out, or interfacility transfer (pump over)	
Delivery Period	All deliveries ratable over course of delivery month, must be initiated on or after first calendar day and completed by last calendar day of delivery month	Exercise may occur on any day prior to expiration. Clearing member required to notify clearinghouse no later than 4:30 PM or 45 minutes after daily futures settlement price is posted
Delivery Grades	Specific domestic crudes with 0.42% sulfur by weight or less, not less than 37° nor more than 42° API gravity. Deliverable grades include West Texas Intermediate, Low Sweet Mix, New Mexican Sweet, North Texas Sweet, Oklahoma Sweet, South Texas Sweet. Specific foreign crudes also acceptable per Exchange Rules.	Exercisable into one futures contract

EXHIBIT 8.63 NYMEX Natural Gas (Henry Hub) Futures and Options

	Futures	Options
Trading Unit	10,000 million British thermal units (mmBTUs)	Exercisable into one futures contract
Price Quote	In minimum ticks of $0.001 (0.1 cent) per mmBtu ($10.00/contract)	
Trading Months	Listed on CME Globex: every month in current year plus next 8 years. Via open outcry: every month in the current year plus the next 12 years	Consecutive months for balance of current year plus five additional years

(*Continued*)

EXHIBIT 8.63   (*Continued*)

	Futures	Options
Trading Hours	Open Outcry from 9:00 AM to 2:30 PM; traded on CME Globex from 6:00 PM to 5:15 PM Sundays through Fridays with 45-minute halt between 5:15 PM and 6:00 PM daily (Eastern Time)	
Last Trading Day	On third business day prior to first calendar day of delivery month	Trading ends on business day immediately preceding expiration of underlying futures
Strike Price Intervals	NA	Generally in $0.05 per mmBtu intervals per Exchange Rules
Delivery	The Sabine Pipeline Co. Henry Hub in Louisiana, seller is responsible for movement of gas through the Hub; the buyer, from the Hub; the Hub fee paid by seller	Exercise may occur on any day prior to expiration. Clearing member required to notify clearinghouse no later than 4:30 PM or 45 minutes after daily futures settlement price is posted
Delivery Period	Must be initiated on or after first calendar day and completed by last calendar day of delivery month	Exercisable into one futures contract

EXHIBIT 8.64   NYMEX RBOB Gasoline Futures and Options

	Futures	Options
Trading Unit	42,000 gallons (1,000 barrels)	Exercisable into one futures contract
Price Quote	In minimum ticks of $0.0001 (0.01 cent) per barrel ($4.20/ contract)	
Trading Months	First 36 consecutive months	
Trading Hours	Open Outcry from 9:00 AM to 2:30 PM; traded on CME Globex from 6:00 PM to 5:15 PM Sundays through Fridays with 45-minute halt between 5:15 PM and 6:00 PM daily (Eastern Time)	

EXHIBIT 8.64 (*Continued*)

	Futures	Options
Strike Price Intervals	NA	Generally in $0.01 per gallon intervals per Exchange Rules
Last Trading Day	On last business day of month preceding delivery month	Trading ends three business days before last trading day of underlying futures
Delivery	FOB seller's facility in New York harbor ex-shore with all duties, entitlements, taxes, fees, and other charges paid. Seller's shore facility must be capable of barge delivery; delivery may also be completed by pipeline, tanker, book transfer, or inter- or intrafacility transfer.	Exercisable into one futures contract
Delivery Period	Deliveries may be initiated the day after the fifth business day and complete by the last business day of the delivery month	Exercise may occur on any day prior to expiration. Clearing member required to notify clearinghouse no later than 4:30 PM or 45 minutes after daily futures settlement price is posted
Delivery Grades	Conform to industry standards for reformulated regular gasoline blendstock for oxygen blending (RBOB) with 10% denatured fuel ethanol (92% purity) as listed by Colonial Pipeline Co. specs for fungible F grade for sales in New York and New Jersey	Exercisable into one futures contract

EXHIBIT 8.65 NYMEX No. 2 Heating Oil Futures and Options

	Futures	Options
Trading Unit	42,000 gallons (1,000 barrels)	Exercisable into one futures contract
Price Quote	In minimum ticks of $0.0001 (0.01 cent) per barrel ($4.20/contract)	
Trading Months	Every consecutive month out 36 months	
Trading Hours	Open Outcry from 9:00 AM to 2:30 PM; traded on CME Globex from 6:00 PM to 5:15 PM Sundays through Fridays with 45-minute halt between 5:15 PM and 6:00 PM daily (Eastern Time)	
Strike Price	NA	Generally in $0.01 per gallon intervals per Exchange Rules
Last Trading Day	On last business day of month preceding delivery month	Trading ends three business days before last trading day of underlying futures
Delivery	FOB seller's facility in New York harbor ex-shore with all duties, entitlements, taxes, fees, and other charges paid. Seller's shore facility must be capable of barge delivery; buyer may request truck delivery if available and pays surcharge; delivery may also be completed by pipeline, tanker, book transfer, or inter- or intrafacility transfer	Exercisable into one futures contract
Delivery Period	Deliveries may be initiated the day after the fifth business day and complete by the last business day of the delivery month	Exercise may occur on any day prior to expiration. Clearing member required to notify clearinghouse no later than 4:30 PM or 45 minutes after daily futures settlement price is posted
Delivery Grades	Conform to industry standards for fungible #2 heating oil	Exercisable into one futures contract

EXHIBIT 8.66 COMEX Gold Futures and Options

	Futures	Options
Trading Unit	100 troy ounces of gold	Exercisable into one futures contract
Price Quote	In dollars and cents in minimum ticks of $0.10 (10 cents) per troy ounce ($10.00/contract)	
Trading Months	Traded for delivery in the first three calendar months; any February, April, August, and October during the next 23 months; and June and December within the next 60 months.	Nearest six contract months of February, April, June, August, October, and December; January, March, May, July, September, and November listed two months before expiration; June and December contracts may be listed 60 months out
Trading Hours	Open Outcry from 8:20 AM to 1:30 PM; traded on CME Globex from 6:00 PM to 5:15 PM Sundays through Fridays with 45-minute halt between 5:15 PM and 6:00 PM daily (Eastern Time)	
Last Trading Day	On third to last business day of maturing contract month	Option trading ends four business days before termination of futures trading
Strike Price Intervals	NA	$10 apart for strikes ≤$500; $20 apart for strikes >$500 and up to $1,000; $50 apart for strikes>$1,000; see Exchange Rules for more details.
Delivery	Delivered gold must bear serial number and identifying stamp of exchange-approved refiner with delivery from exchange-licensed depository	Exercisable into one futures contract
Delivery Period	Delivery from first to last business day of contract month	Exercise may occur on any day prior to expiration. Clearing member required to notify clearinghouse until one hour after market close or 4:30 PM (Eastern time) on expiration day.
Delivery Grades	100 troy ounces (±5%) of refined gold not assaying less than 0.995 fineness, cast as one bar or in three 1-kg bars	Exercisable into one futures contract

EXHIBIT 8.67 COMEX Silver Futures and Options

	Futures	Options
Trading Unit	5,000 troy ounces of gold	Exercisable into one futures contract
Price Quote	In dollars and cents in minimum ticks of $0.005 (1/2 cent) per troy ounce ($25.00/contract)	
Trading Months	Traded for delivery in the first three calendar months; any January, March, May, and September during the next 23 months; and June and December within the next 60 months.	Nearest five contract months of March, May, July, September, and December; January, February, April, June, August, October, and November listed 2 months before expiration; June and December contracts may be listed 60 months out
Trading Hours	Open outcry from 8:25 AM to 1:25 PM; traded on CME Globex from 6:00 PM to 5:15 PM Sundays through Fridays with 45-minute halt between 5:15 PM and 6:00 PM daily (Eastern Time)	
Last Trading Day	On third to last business day of maturing contract month	Option trading ends four business days before termination of futures trading
Strike Price Intervals	NA	10 cents and 25 cents apart for strikes ≤$8.00; 25 cents for strikes >$8 and up to $15; 50 cents for strikes >$15 during first six nearby months; see Exchange Rules for more details.
Delivery	Delivered silver must bear serial number and identifying stamp of exchange-approved refiner with delivery from exchange-licensed depository	Exercisable into one futures contract
Delivery Period	Delivery from first to last business day of contract month	Exercise may occur on any day prior to expiration. Clearing member required to notify clearinghouse until one hour after market close

EXHIBIT 8.67 (*Continued*)

	Futures	Options
Delivery Grades	5,000 troy ounces (±6%) of refined silver not assaying less than 0.999 fineness, in 1,000 or 1,100 troy ounce bars	or 4:30 PM (Eastern time) on expiration day. Exercisable into one futures contract

CHAPTER 9

Alternative Investment Market Fundamentals

John W. Labuszewski
Paul E. Peterson
Charles Piszczor

Successful futures contracts tend to be based on benchmarks, that is, products or indexes that represent the standard measure of performance in whatever asset class they purport to represent. Contract designers employed by derivatives exchanges study the potential to develop derivatives based on these various asset classes and attempt to identify or create benchmark measures of performance. Of course, the most commonly referenced asset classes include equities and fixed-income securities. And for good reason: stocks and bonds account for vast investment amounts of monies. But stocks and bonds are not the only asset classes worth considering.

In recent years, many investors, certainly investors active in developed economies, have experienced a certain level of frustration with traditional passive investment strategies deployed in traditional asset classes such as stocks and bonds. In many cases, returns available in these markets have simply not been sufficient to meet the obligations of particular types of investors such as pension funds. Accordingly, investors have increasingly looked to "alternative investments" as a potential source of attractive returns.

The "typical" or "average" pension fund in the United States will look to diversify their assets over particular asset classes to achieve an attractive mix of investments. A typical mix might include an approximate 60% allocation to stocks, 30% to fixed-income securities, and 10% to "alternative" assets. These alternative assets may include a diverse range of investments

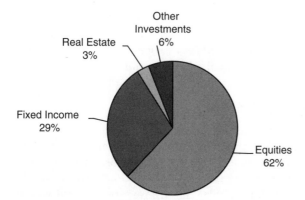

EXHIBIT 9.1   Typical Market Exposure of S&P 500 Defined Benefit Pension Plans ($1.3 billion in assets, 12/04)
Source: Crédit Suisse Asset Management, "Alpha Management Revolution or Evolution, A Portable Alpha Primer," November 2005.

including real estate, commodities, fine art, antique automobiles, or any number of exotic items or derivative instruments. See Exhibit 9.1.

The futures industry has taken notice and, over the years, has been building up its capabilities in this regard, recognizing that alternative investments are indeed a legitimate and increasingly important form of asset or asset class. This has resulted in some rather imaginative new products on CME Group including futures on weather conditions, losses from hurricane damages, and real estate and economic indicators. We highlight some of the more noteworthy of these new developments by reviewing some of the staples of CME Group's alternative investment offerings including those covering weather, real estate, and economic indicators.

WEATHER

It has been estimated that weather exerts a significant impact on approximately a third of U.S. economic activity.[1] Noting that the U.S. gross domestic product (GDP) totaled some $13.9 trillion in 2007, this suggests that weather conditions exerted an influence over some $4.6 trillion in GDP in 2007. The impact that weather has on businesses such as energy and agriculture is particularly acute.

This realization actually motivated the energy industry to commence development of over-the-counter (OTC) weather-based derivatives by the late 1990s. In 1998, CME began development of what has grown to become a well-rounded family of weather derivatives including tempera-ture, hurricane, frost- and snowfall-based futures and option contracts. These contracts are currently listed based on weather conditions in diverse locations within the United States, Canada, Europe, and Asia.

Historical Market Developments

The development of the weather derivatives markets represents an interest-ing case study of sorts regarding the linked and complementary nature of OTC and exchange-traded derivatives. This market was originally inspired by a transaction that was consummated in July 1996 between Aquila Energy and Consolidated Edison Co. Per this transaction, ConEd would buy electricity from Aquila. The unique feature was a clause that provided for a discount if weather was cooler than anticipated. In particular, the transaction referenced weather conditions measured at Central Park in New York City. This prompted Enron Capital & Trade Resources to trans-act the first documentable derivatives trade in mid-1997 tied to fluctuations in weather conditions. It was not long after that CME Group became inter-ested in weather derivatives and launched the first weather futures and op-tion markets in 1999.

In the early going, the two most popular instruments to emerge in-cluded option contracts based on heating degree days (HDD) and cooling degree days (CDD). HDD and CDD represent energy industry standard measures of the extent to which average temperatures during a particular day deviate from a benchmark of 65°F. The concept of a heating degree day (HDD) index was developed by engineers who observed that commercial buildings were frequently heated to maintain an indoor temperature of 70°F whenever daily mean (average) outdoor temperatures fell below 65°F. Each degree of mean temperature below 65°F is counted as "one heating degree day." Conversely, air conditioning may be employed when tempera-ture rise much above the 65°F standard. Thus, each degree of mean temperature above 65°F is counted as "one cooling degree day." These con-cepts are expressed mathematically as follows:

HDD = Max(0, 65°F − daily average temperature)

CDD = Max(0, daily average temperature − 65°F)

For example, if the average of a day's maximum and minimum temper-ature on a midnight-to-midnight basis is 35°F, that day's HDD is 30 and the CDD is zero (0).

CME began gathering market intelligence on weather-related deriva-tives with an eye toward the development of weather-based futures contracts in late 1997. Because OTC derivatives may be highly customized subject to the bilateral agreement of the two counterparties, a variety of trade practices had evolved among the major energy firms and broker/dealers that represented the core players in the OTC markets. Thus, prospective market participants were interviewed regarding ways to construct standardized weather futures contracts. Issues included how contracts might be settled, which index providers might provide reliable references, and the timing associated with contract settlements. Because weather is a localized phenomenon, further study centered about the most likely regions or cities on which to base futures contracts.

Four significant energy firms, including Aquila Energy, Enron Capital & Trade Resources, Koch Supply & Trading, and Southern Co. Energy Marketing, represented the most active OTC weather derivative traders. Input was further solicited from a broad group of prospective commercial contract participants including utilities, fuel suppliers, propane distributors, hydroelectric generators, Florida orange growers, Colorado ski resort operators, and municipalities concerned about the expense of snow removal.

Contract specifications were drafted based on this market intelligence and subsequently validated with the major players. Of critical importance was the selection of a data provider who would maintain the indexes and whose participation was supported by OTC derivative traders. Earth Satellite Corporation (EarthSat), of Rockville, Maryland, was selected as the data provider based on its experience and reputation as an internationally recognized service firm specializing in the development and the application of remote sensing and geographic information technologies. EarthSat's responsibilities include updating weather files via the web on a daily basis and maintaining historical records of data pertaining to CME Group weather products.

Heating and Cooling Degree Day Futures

CME received approval from the Commodity Futures Trading Commission (CFTC) to list HDD and CDD futures in August 1999. The very first weather futures contracts listed in September 1999 were based on HDDs to the extent that this coincided with the beginning of the heating season. CDD-based contracts were subsequently introduced in January 2000. These contracts were amended and listings expanded over the years; current terms and conditions are described in Exhibit 9.2.

The original HDD and CDD futures are based on the cumulative value of HDDs or CDDs throughout a specific subject month. To illustrate, an average daily temperature of 45°F is associated with an HDD of 20 (= 65°F − 45°F). If the average daily temperature was in excess of 65°F, the HDD for that day would be zero. A monthly contract is cash settled at the

EXHIBIT 9.2 Monthly and Seasonal HDD/CDD Contract Specifications

	Futures	Options
Contract Size	$20 × HDD/CDD Index	One futures contract
Minimum Tick Size	1.00 Degree Day Index Point = $20	
Monthly Contract × s	Monthly HDD contracts are available for the contract months of October, November, December, January, February, March, and April. Monthly CDD contracts are available for the contract months of April, May, June, July, August, September, and October.	
Seasonal Strip Contracts	Seasonal "strip" contracts created by linking from 2 to 7 consecutive months. For example, an HDD seasonal strip may be created based on cumulative HDDs in months of October, November, December, and January. A CDD seasonal strip may be created based on cumulative CDDs in months of June, July, and August.	
Listed Cities	HDD and CDD contracts are available for the following U.S. cities: Atlanta, Baltimore, Boston, Chicago, Cincinnati, Colorado Springs, Dallas, Des Moines, Detroit, Houston, Jacksonville, Kansas City, Las Vegas, Little Rock, Los Angeles, Minneapolis-St. Paul, New York, Philadelphia, Portland, Raleigh, Sacramento, Salt Lake City, Tucson, and Washington, DC.	
Last Trading Day	Last exchange business day of a calendar month	
Final Settlement Day	The second exchange business day immediately following the last day of calendar month	
Final Settlement Price	Settled in cash at monthly HDD/CDD Index as calculated by EarthSat	Exercisable into one futures contract
Option Exercise	NA	European style
Strike Prices	NA	Strike prices listed "on demand"
Trading Hours	Traded on CME Globex electronic trading platform nearly 24 hours a day	Offered on the floor of the exchange

cumulative value of HDDs recorded on each day of the month. For example, assume the month had 31 days and the average daily temperature for all of those days was 45°F. Accordingly, the cumulative monthly HDD would equal 620 (= 31 days × 20). The futures contract value would be identified by multiplying that figure by $20. In this example, the cash value of the contract would be $12,400 (= $20 × 620).

A seasonal strip contract is based on the cumulative HDD or CDD values during two to seven months within the season. The traditional heating season runs from November through March; the traditional cooling season runs from May through September. October and April are transition, or "shoulder," months for which both HDD and CDD values are calculated, and therefore October and/or April may be included in a seasonal strip.

For example, an HDD seasonal strip may be created based on cumulative HDDs in the months of October, November, December, and January. Or a CDD seasonal strip may be created based on cumulative CDDs in the months of June, July, and August. These contracts are identified by the first month and the number of months within the season as constructed. Seasonal strip contracts provide the same type of risk exposure as monthly HDD and CDD contracts but offer the convenience of being able to trade a bundled package of months when one seeks coverage over several months during the heating or cooling season.

A further refinement of this concept was introduced with the development of weekly weather contracts based on average temperatures between Monday through Friday of a particular week.

The concept of temperature-linked futures has likewise been expanded to include international coverage in Europe (Amsterdam, Barcelona, Berlin, Essen, London, Madrid, Oslo, Paris, Rome, and Stockholm), Asia (Tokyo and Osaka), and Canada (Calgary, Edmonton, Montreal, Toronto, Vancouver, and Winnipeg). These contracts are based on cumulative monthly temperatures during the cooling season and HDD readings during the heating season. These contracts are denominated in British pounds, euros, Japanese yen, and Canadian dollars in the case of the European-, Asian-, and Canadian-based contracts, respectively. They use contact multipliers of GBP 20, EUR 20, JPY 2,500 and CAD 20.

These contracts further depart from the U.S. standards in the sense that temperature readings are recorded on the Celsius rather than Fahrenheit scale. Rather than reference a base of 65°F, these indexes reference a base of 18°C. As a matter of nomenclature, the European cooling contracts are based on a so-called Cumulative Average Temperature (CAT) index rather than a CDD to the extent that the term CDD is not in use in the context of European OTC weather markets.

Risk-Management Applications

HDD and CDD futures and options are employed by a wide variety of enterprises, largely operating in the context of the energy industry, to manage their temperature-related risks.

Energy companies, for example, have been known to sell HDD or CDD contracts to manage the risk of diminished revenues under mild weather conditions, noting that the quantity of energy sold is heavily contingent on consumer demand driven by temperatures. Large-scale energy consumers including automobile manufacturers and large residential building operators may buy HDD or CDD contracts to hedge against the risk of rising utility costs under extreme weather conditions.

Retailers whose sales are sensitive to weather conditions might control inventory costs more effectively through the use of HDD or CDD contracts. Beer consumption reaches a seasonal peak in the summer, and cool weather can put a dent in beer sales. According to "The 2000 Preliminary Report for SABMiller," "history shows that on a summer day with the temperature over 25 degrees Celsius, sales can be more than 50% greater than on a day where the temperature is under 20 degrees."[2]

Amusement parks rely on favorable weather, noting that people stay home if conditions are too hot or cold. It is a simple matter for parks to correlate temperatures to attendance and construct a "collar" to hedge revenues should temperatures fall outside a preferred range.

Let's focus on the use of temperature contracts on the part of utility companies. Utilities may use HDD or CDD futures and options to guard against so-called volumetric risks. These volumetric risks are based on the quantity of energy that might be expected to be marketed throughout the course of a heating or cooling season. These transactions rely on the intuitive and well-documented relationship between power consumption and temperature extremes.

Thus, if the daily average temperatures during the course of a winter season were abnormally high, utility firms might face depressed demand for heating. Utilities have traditionally increased consumer prices to offset lower retail consumption volume. However, intensifying competition caused by ongoing deregulation has made it increasingly difficult for utilities to raise prices arbitrarily.[3] Therefore, it becomes necessary for utility firms to address volumetric risks using other means such as HDD or CDD futures and options.

A simple numerical example is presented here to illustrate the hedging application of HDD futures. Let us assume that ABC Utility Co. sells electricity in the Chicago area at $0.08/kilowatt hour (kWh). Under normal winter weather conditions, ABC may forecast sales of 1 billion kWh with a projected revenue of $80 million. However, ABC is concerned about the possibility of El Niño weather effects and would like to use HDD futures to hedge against the possibility of warmer than expected winter conditions.

To construct a hedging strategy, it will become necessary to quantify the relationship between economic outcomes (such as sales revenues) and weather conditions (as implied in weather futures prices). In particular, one wants to find an appropriate hedge ratio (HR) that might balance the anticipated change in revenues (denoted as ΔRevenues) with the changing value of the subject derivatives contracts (ΔValue of Futures). A statistical regression between revenues and weather conditions is frequently useful in assessing these quantitative relationships.

Assume that, based on historical regressions, ABC finds that its sales are positively correlated with the CME Group Chicago HDD Index with a sensitivity ratio of 0.80. That is, a 1% change in HDD may drive a 0.8% change in ABC's anticipated $80 million in revenues. Assuming futures are trading at 1,250.00, an effective hedge ratio may be calculated as follows:

$$
\begin{aligned}
\text{Hedge Ratio(HR)} &= \Delta\text{Revenues} \div \Delta\text{Value of Futures} \\
&= (\$80,000,000 \times 0.8\%) \div (1,250 \times \$20 \times 1\%) \\
&= 2,560 \text{ futures contracts}
\end{aligned}
$$

This suggests that ABC might sell 2,560 futures to hedge the risks of higher than expected temperatures and lower than expected revenues. Assume that temperatures are mild and that the HDD Index settles at 1,150. This decline of 100 HDDs (8% of original value of 1,250) implies that sales may decline from 1 billion to 936 million kWh for sales of $74,880,000 ($0.08/kWh × 936,000,000 kWh). This implies a revenue shortfall of $5.12 million. But this shortfall is offset by a corresponding $5.12 million profit in futures, as illustrated in Exhibit 9.3.

Note that this analysis is based on an assumption that the relationship between sales and temperatures is linear when, in fact, it is more likely that a nonlinear relationship exists such that energy demands will increase (decrease) exponentially as a function of rising (falling) HDDs. In other words, the HR becomes rather dynamic and may therefore require active adjustment in response to changing conditions.

EXHIBIT 9.3 Hedging with Weather Futures

	Revenues	Futures
Now	Expected revenues of $80 million or 1 billion kWh @ $0.08/kWh	Sell 2,560 futures @ 1,250
Later	Realized revenues of $74,880,000 Revenue shortfall of $5,120,000	Futures settled @ 1,150 Profit of 100 HDDs or $5,120,000 (= 2,560 × 100 × $20)

Proper use of temperature-related contracts not only enables utility firms to stabilize revenue streams but may also be used to provide at least a partial hedge to the cost side of the equation. Note that most utility firms operate under inherent capacity limitations. In particular, electricity represents a nonstorable commodity. If temperatures suddenly rise or decline dramatically, utility firms may need to deploy less efficient generators to meet the sudden jump in demand or may be compelled to purchase electricity from the power grid in the face of soaring demands and rising prices. This implies that energy prices may increase and transmission costs may grow simultaneously. In this case, utility firms may find both weather derivatives and energy contracts useful to stabilize economic outcomes (i.e., to hedge both volumetric- and cost-based risks).

Hurricane Products

Hurricanes represent perhaps the most prevalent and certainly the most devastating type of risk faced by property insurance companies. This was clearly in evidence in the wake of Hurricanes Andrew and Katrina. Hurricane Katrina in 2005 was the costliest hurricane on record with insured damages estimated (by one source) at $96 billion in the wake of this storm. Hurricane Andrew hit Florida before sweeping through the Gulf of Mexico and striking Louisiana in 1992 and was the second most costly storm with an estimated $26 billion in insured damages. Some scientists believe that the global warming phenomenon will be responsible for increased hurricane risk in the Atlantic in the years to come.

The difficulty of managing these risks, of course, is responsible for a good deal of the growth witnessed in the reinsurance business. Hurricane-related risk has also inspired the development of OTC products including catastrophe bonds and other related products. Actually, the Chicago Board of Trade (CBOT) had pioneered the development of hurricane-related derivatives in the 1990s with the introduction of futures tied to accumulated insurance losses. But this market was probably a little ahead of its time. The product was also, paradoxically, a little behind its time in the sense that it was pegged to stated insurance losses that could not be fully accounted for until well after the hurricane. Thus, the product lost some of the "economic immediacy" that characterizes the futures markets.

Prompted by the difficulty of managing hurricane-related risks, CME Group introduced futures and options based on the Carvill Hurricane Index, since renamed the CME Hurricane Index (CHI) beginning in 2007. These contracts are designed to address the risk of storm damage as precisely as possible and are available in a number of structural configurations.

Measuring Hurricane Intensity

The Saffir-Simpson scale (Exhibit 9.4) was devised in 1971 to measure the potential for damage associated with hurricanes. Storms are rated on a scale from 1 through 5 and provide a crude indication of the potential for wind- and flood-related damage as a result of a hurricane landfall. Wind speed is the predominant factor in the rating, noting that flooding is contingent on various physical characteristics at the point of landfall including water depth and shape of the shoreline.

Unfortunately, the extremely analog character of a 1 to 5 scale renders the Saffir-Simpson scale just a bit clumsy. As a result, meteorologists have taken to describe storms with finer gradations (e.g., a "weak" category 3 storm or a "strong" category 2). Although the Saffir-Simpson scale considers wind speed as the primary cause of property damage, it does not take into account other significant characteristics of a hurricane such as the size or area over which a hurricane extends or the amount of precipitation that accompanies the storm. Working at the University of Colorado, Professor Lakshmi Kantha published a paper in 2006 suggesting some alternatives to the Saffir-Simpson Index that incorporate these other factors that impact the amount of damage inflicted by a storm.

Researchers at the ReAdvisory Group of Carvill America subsequently extended the tenets of Kantha's work to develop the CHI. The CHI takes explicit account of the radius of hurricane force winds as well as wind speed as follows: where V = maximum sustained wind speed velocity, V_0 = a velocity reference value calibrated to 74 mph, R = the radius of hurricane force winds, and R_0 = a radius reference value calibrated to 60 miles.

$$\text{CHI} = (V \div V_0)^3 + \left[1.5 \times (R \div R_0) \times (V \div V_0)^2 \right]$$

EXHIBIT 9.4 Saffir-Simpson Index

	Max Sustained 1-Minute Wind Speed	Storm Surge	Pressure (millibars)	Damage Description
Category 5	>156 mph	>18 feet	<920	Catastrophic
Category 4	131–155	13–18	920–945	Extreme
Category 3	111–130	9–12	945–965	Extensive
Category 2	96–110	6–8	965–980	Moderate
Category 1	74–95	4–5	>980	Minimal
Tropical storm	39–73			
Tropical depression	<39			

EXHIBIT 9.5 Rating Hurricanes on CHI Scale

	Estimated Damages	Saffir-Simpson Scale at Landfall	Wind Speed Velocity	Radius	CHI
Katrina (2005)	$96.0 bil	4	145 mph	120 mi	19.0
Charley (2004)	15.0	4	145	30	10.4
Wilma (2005)	14.4	3	125	90	11.2
Ivan (2004)	14.2	3	130	105	13.5
Rita (2005)	9.4	3	120	85	9.9
Frances (2004)	8.9	2	105	75	6.6
Jeanne (2004)	6.9	3	115	70	8.0

To illustrate, consider Hurricane Katrina, which achieved a sustained wind speed velocity of 145 mph over a 120-mile radius. The CHI for Katrina is calculated as 19.0 as follows:

$$\text{Katrina CHI} = (145 \div 74)^3 + \left[1.5 \times (120 \div 60) \times (145 \div 74)^2\right]$$
$$= 19.0$$

Sometimes two storms of the same rated intensity along the Saffir-Simpson scale imply very different destructive force. Both Hurricanes Katrina and Charley were rated category 4 storms with identical maximum sustained wind speed velocities of 145 mph. But Katrina encompassed a radius of 120 miles, whereas Charley was relatively small at only 30 miles. As illustrated in Exhibit 9.5, Katrina generated an estimated $96 billion in insured damages; Charley resulted in only $15.0 billion in damage.

Although the Saffir-Simpson scale did not distinguish Katrina and Charley, Katrina was rated at 19.0, whereas Charley was at 10.4 per the CHI. In fact, the correlations between insured damages and the CHI are much stronger than the correlations between insured damages and the Saffir-Simpson categorizations. Many other factors that are not referenced in the CHI can certainly influence the value of hurricane-related damage, notably whether or not a hurricane makes landfall at a heavily developed urban as opposed to a sparsely developed rural area. Still, the CHI represents a superior measure of the destructive potential associated with a hurricane than does the classic standard of measurement.

CME Hurricane Index Futures and Options

Accordingly, CME Group built its family of hurricane-related products on the CHI. One version is based on named storms, noting that the United States Weather Service started naming hurricanes in 1953. These contracts are generally cash settled based on a value of $1,000 \times$ the applicable CHI. For example, a hurricane contract based on a particular named storm achieving a CHI equal to 8.5 may be settled at a final cash value of $8,500. See Exhibit 9.6.

In addition to a series of contracts based on named storms as they are observed, a series of CHI-based contracts are structured a bit differently to address somewhat different risk-management purposes including contracts based on named storms.

For example, seasonal contracts are based on activity in broad regions along the East and Gulf coasts. Their payouts are determined based on the aggregate or accumulated CHI for all named storms that reach landfall in that particular area over the course of a season. Seasonal maximum contracts are based on the highest CHI reading associated with all storms that reach landfall in a particular area. Other variations on these themes have been offered from time to time as well.

Other Esoteric Weather Products

In addition to temperature- and hurricane-related contracts, CME Group also offers futures and options based on somewhat more esoteric aspects of the weather including frost and snowfall.

Frost days are referenced in the Netherlands by unions that represent construction workers. Union contracts are such that construction workers are routinely excused in the event of frost. This creates risks on the part of construction companies that may lose valuable time due to unscheduled frost-related work stoppages. These frost contracts are tied to temperatures observed during a month or a season but confined to working hours and days excluding holidays and weekends.

It is estimated that snow removal costs U.S. municipalities up to $1 million for every inch of snowfall, the bulk of which cost is tied to labor. Snowfall is readily measured, and CME Group offers monthly and seasonal contracts based on snow recorded in New York's Central Park and LaGuardia Airport, Boston's Logan International Airport, Chicago's O'Hare International Airport, Detroit's Metro Airport, and the Minneapolis/St. Paul International Airport.

RESIDENTIAL HOUSING FUTURES

The significance of a residential housing or home real estate futures contract stems from the sheer size of real estate as an asset class. Federal Reserve Flow of Funds data suggest that the value of residential real estate held by households and nonprofit organizations totaled $22.6 trillion[4] by the conclusion of

EXHIBIT 9.6   Hurricane Contract Specifications

	Futures	Options
Contract Size	$1,000 × CME Hurricane Index (CHI)	One futures contract
Minimum Tick Size	0.10 Index Point = $100	
Named Storm Contracts	Contracts are issued for trading on named hurricanes that occur from June 1 through November 30. Final settlement of these contracts is based on the CHI associated with the particular named storm as it achieves landfall.	
Seasonal Contracts	Seasonal contracts available for the following regions: Gulf Coast (Brownsville TX to AL/FL Border), Florida (AL/FL Border to Fernandina Beach FL), Southern Atlantic Coast (Fernandina Beach FL to NC/VA Border), Northern Atlantic Coast (NC/VA Border to Eastport ME), Eastern US (Brownsville TX to Eastport ME). Cash settlement of these contracts is based on the aggregate CHI for all hurricanes that achieve landfall in the particular area between June 1 and November 30.	
Seasonal Maximum Contracts	Seasonal contracts available for the following regions: Gulf Coast (Brownsville TX to AL/FL Border), Florida (AL/FL Border to Fernandina Beach FL), Southern Atlantic Coast (Fernandina Beach FL to NC/VA Border), Northern Atlantic Coast (NC/VA Border to Eastport ME), Eastern US (Brownsville TX to Eastport ME). Cash settlement of these contracts is based on the maximum CHI for any hurricanes that achieve landfall in the particular area between June 1 and November 30th.	
Contract Expiration	In case of contracts based on named storms, trading terminates at 9:00 AM (CT) on first business day that is at least two calendar days following last forecast/advisory issued by National Hurricane Center for named storm. In case of seasonal contracts, trading terminates at 9:00 AM (CT) on first business day that is at least two calendar days following November 30.	
Option Exercise	NA	American style
Strike Prices	NA	Strike prices listed "on demand"
Trading Hours	Traded on CME Globex electronic trading platform nearly 24 hours a day	

2006, essentially on par with the $18.1 trillion held in domestic equities[5] and $27.4 trillion in fixed-income assets.[6] As such, residential real estate represents perhaps a third of the total value of these highly significant and visible asset classes. See Exhibit 9.7. Unlike the markets for stocks and bonds, however, there was no liquid market or facile means of hedging the attendant real estate risk.

Thus, Case, Shiller, and Weiss articulated the concept of real estate futures in 1992: "[f]utures and options markets should be established that are cash settled based on indices of real estate prices, and there should be separate markets for each of the major geographic regions . . . at present no real estate futures contract exists in the world; nor are there good substitutes for such markets."[7]

Futures and options based on the S&P/Case-Shiller Home Price Indices ("S&P/CS Indices" or "the Indices") at CME Group (CME Housing futures and options) launched in early 2006, represent the fulfillment of that vision and an historic financial event, forging the creation of a novel derivatives asset class. CME Housing futures and options are designed to provide a facile way for institutional and individual investors to gain exposure to real estate risk and effectively diversify their portfolios. Commercial and private asset holders are afforded an efficient hedging mechanism. In the process, this novel market may have the effect of reducing transaction costs for trading real estate.

We discuss the economic circumstances that lend impetus to this initiative; a discussion of the S&P/Case-Shiller Home Price Indices, as published by Fiserv CSW Inc. (CSW), which serve as the subject of CME Housing

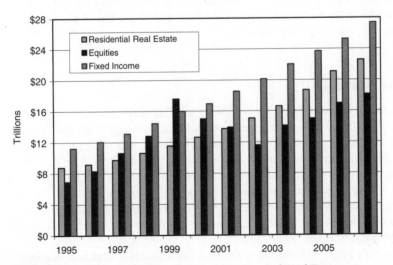

EXHIBIT 9.7 Value of U.S. Fixed Income, Equity, and Real Estate

futures and options, and we review the use and characteristics of CME Housing futures and options.

The Housing Boom and Bust

Certainly a driving force behind the development of CME Housing futures and options has been the "housing boom" of the early 2000s followed by a subsequent "housing bust." By July 2006, the median value for a home across the United States was valued at $230,900, representing an advance of close to 52% over the past five-year period, according to data from the National Association of Realtors (NAR). The charge had been led by housing prices on the West and East coasts with the more stolid Midwest booking the most modest advances.

At the time, there was much talk in the media and among the public to the effect that the U.S. housing market was in the midst of a housing "bubble." This bubble was fueled by high income growth and (arguably) over-aggressively low mortgage rates. Much concern had been expressed that the bubble might burst, resulting in homeowner distress and financial uncertainties. Sharp and unanticipated declines in housing values are not unprecedented, noting that Los Angeles home prices fell 41% in real terms from 1989 to 1997, and on the opposite coast, Boston home values declined 29% between 1987 and 1994.

Subsequent dramatic declines in housing activity and values were in fact realized, a housing "bust," if you will. By February 2008, the NAR estimated the median value of a U.S. home at $193,900, approximately 16% off the highs from mid-2006. Just as the East and West coasts experienced the most dramatic advances in values, these markets likewise exhibited the most severe declines.

Housing Affordability

The housing boom of the early twenty-first century reflected growing affordability driven by low long-term rates and income growth. Thirty-year fixed-rate mortgages had fallen to a nationwide average of 5.39% by July 2003, the lowest rates seen at any time reaching back to the 1960s. However, the continual advance in housing prices offset that decline in mortgage rates to a degree, with the median single-family home value in the United States breaking the $200,000 barrier by December 2004. According to statistics from the NAR, the median single-family home value peaked at $230,900 by July 2006.

Although home values had risen, and risen sharply, that had not been enough to offset the effect of falling mortgage rates and rising family

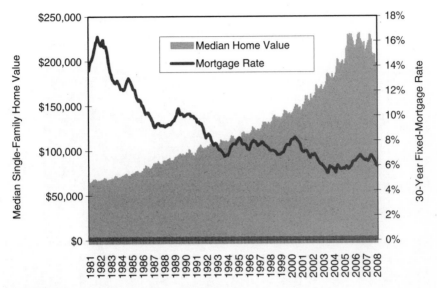

EXHIBIT 9.8 Home Prices versus Mortgage Rates

incomes. Principal and interest payments (P&I) on a median single-family home were reported by NAR at just $795 per month, or $9,540 annually, by February 2003, representing just 18.2% of median family income of $52,303. That figure has been generally declining over the course of the past 25 years from a high of 39.1% in November 1981 (when mortgage rates soared to 16.38%) to a low of 17.8% in February 1999 (and prior to the boom of the early 2000s). See Exhibit 9.8.

But the proportion of household income consumed by housing costs began to rise as a function of rising home values coupled with rising mortgage interest rates. By July 2006, 30-year fixed-rate mortgages had advanced to 6.82% and median home valued peaked at $230,900. Median monthly P&I increased to $1,207 a month, or $14,484 annually, to consume 25.1% of median household income of $57,685. See Exhibit 9.9.

As a result, the NAR's Housing Affordability Index, which was as high as 137.1 in February 2003, plummeted to 99.6 by July 2006. Note that the higher the index, the more affordable housing is deemed to be. In particular, any figure in excess of 100 suggests that the median household can afford to purchase a median single-family home. See Exhibit 9.10.

Homeownership rates were particularly high during the course of the housing boom. The U.S. Census Bureau reported homeownership as high as 69.2% by the second quarter of 2004, and up dramatically from a low of 63.8% in 1986. This figure was bolstered by the fact that as many as

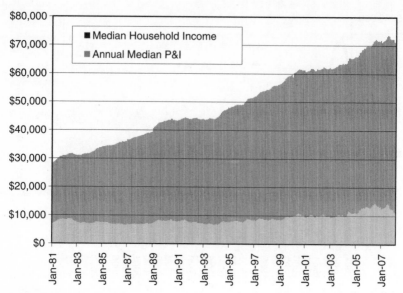

EXHIBIT 9.9   Median Annual P&I versus Household Income

5 million former renters had become empowered to purchase their own homes as a result of the affordability just discussed. Longer term home-owners had been moving up to higher priced housing.

Real estate speculation had likewise become a factor. Fannie Mae reported that investors had accounted for up to 12.2% of purchases in the

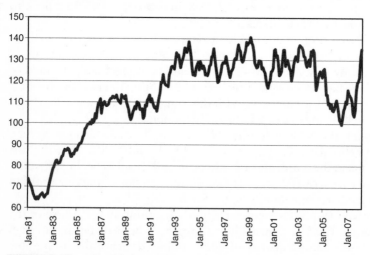

EXHIBIT 9.10   Affordability Index

conventional mortgage market by 2005 compared to an average of 6.9% in 2002. These proportions were much higher in other venues, including Miami, where investors were behind upward to 70% of home purchases by the height of the boom. By the fourth quarter 2007, however, U.S. home-ownership rates had slipped to 67.8% as the housing bubble burst.

Still, housing affordability as measured by the NAR Housing Afford-ability Index is rebounding sharply in the midst of the housing bust. By February 2008, the median home price had declined to $193,900 with 30-year fixed-mortgage rates down to 5.94%. Median P&I payments declined to just $924 a month, or 18.5% of median household income at $59,967 a year. Thus, the Affordability Index had rebounded to 135.2 and in the vicinity of the high-water mark of 137.1 recorded in February 2003.

Housing Stock

Housing volume figures, whether measured by building permits, housing starts, or housing completions, had been strong and had, in fact risen to all-time highs by late 2005 or early 2006. House prices had concurrently surged to historic highs with Arizona, Nevada, Hawaii, and California lead-ing the way. Florida, the District of Columbia, Maryland, and Virginia like-wise witnessed strong appreciation. Colorado, Ohio, Oklahoma, Indiana, and Texas showed the least appreciation. This reflects a restricted supply of buildable land on U.S. coasts. In particular, and spurred on by the tech boom, coastal California housing took off as early as 1995 along with de-mand in other favorable climes.

But all of these measures of housing market robustness came crashing down in early 2006. The same largely coastal markets that had experienced the greatest strength during the boom subsequently exhibited the greatest weakness during the bust. By early 2008, there were no indications in housing stock figures that suggested the downward trend might be approaching a conclusion. See Exhibit 9.11.

Home Finance Trends

The rising prices early in the decade of the 2000s meant that financing the purchase of a home was becoming increasingly difficult. Thus, buyers sought out ways to hold down monthly payments with the use of inter-est-only or adjustable-rate mortgages. These loans became quite attractive to the extent that short-term interest rates were very low, anchored by Fed monetary policy holding the target Fed Funds rate at just 1% in 2003 and 2004. The situation was exacerbated in some cases as lenders offered low initial "teaser" rates to mortgage borrowers. As such, adjustable-rate

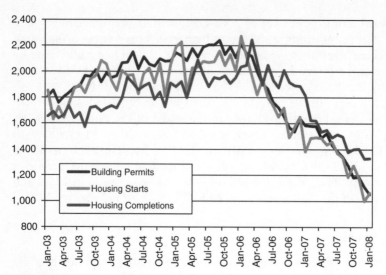

EXHIBIT 9.11   Monthly Housing Activity

mortgages were priced very low relative to 15- or 30-year fixed-rate mortgages that were tied to longer term rates. In other words, the shape of the yield curve was upwardly sloped, encouraging mortgage lending tied to those very low short-term, as opposed to longer-term, interest rates.

Lenders who were faced with increased competition because of excess capacity were accommodating with respect to their loan standards. Many buyers opted for the most lenient loan terms to acquire a larger home, in the hopes of profiting more from further appreciation. Others leveraged themselves to acquire multiple homes. These aggressive lending practices shifted price risk, particularly in inflated markets, onto buyers and mortgage insurance companies.

But by 2004 through 2006, the yield curve began to flatten. Although long-term rates and fixed-rate mortgages remained relatively stable, we saw short-term rates and adjustable-rate mortgage rates increase sharply to levels comparable to long-term rates. This curve flattening put sharp pressure on overextended homeowners and their mortgage companies. This, in turn, led to a spate of foreclosure activity all over the country but particularly in those coastal areas that had witnessed the greatest amount of price appreciation or in markets where real estate speculation was most prevalent. Subprime borrowers subject to premium mortgage rates suffered even further as their resources were strained, forcing many into foreclosure situations and kicking off the so-called subprime mortgage crisis by mid-2007.

Fed Action

Alan Greenspan, addressing a joint congressional committee on June 9, 2005, stated, "exceptionally low interest rates on ten-year Treasury notes, and hence on home mortgages, have been a major factor in the recent surge of homebuilding and home turnover, and especially in the steep climb in home prices. Although a 'bubble' in home prices for the nation as a whole does not appear likely, there do appear to be, at a minimum, signs of froth in some local markets."

Similarly, Fed Governor Don Kohn had discussed imbalances in the U.S. economy with a specific focus on the housing market: "people should now be aware of risks in the real estate market . . . there is a role that monetary policy plays in reacting to these imbalances and this inevitable unwinding. . . . By increasing the return to saving and dampening upward momentum in house prices, rising rates should induce an increase in the personal savings rate and thereby lessen one of the significant imbalances we have noted." It appeared that Kohn is advocating the use of monetary policy to induce a housing downturn and presumably thereby encouraging less spending and more personal savings.

In retrospect, of course, the Fed's focus on the housing sector was not unjustified. Indeed, it was estimated that the housing boom had generated over 800,000 new jobs in the homebuilding, real estate marketing, and durable consumer goods sectors in the early 2000s. Still, the Fed's tightening actions beginning in 2004 had done little to affect long-term fixed-rate mortgages. While target Fed Funds was increased from 1 to 5 1.4% by 2005, the long end of the yield curve remained stable or even declined slightly in terms of yield. Of course, it was the short end of the yield curve that was affected by Fed action. As such, Fed action did not necessarily keep new long-term borrowers out of the housing market but rather caused current homeowners on adjustable-rate mortgages to see their costs spiral higher. See Exhibit 9.12.

By July 2007, the subprime mortgage crisis kicked off with a spate of reported large losses by some significant hedge funds. By September 2007, the Federal Reserve started to ratchet down short-term rates; significantly some of the easings were in 50 basis point increments as opposed to the previous standard 25 basis point adjustment. Fed Chairman Bernanke acknowledged in testimony to Congress that "global financial losses have far exceeded even the most pessimistic estimates of the credit losses on these loans . . . creating significant market stress." Bernanke further suggested that the Fed would take measures to prevent abusive or bad lending practices: "the Federal Reserve takes responsible lending and consumer protection very seriously. Along with other federal and state agencies, we are

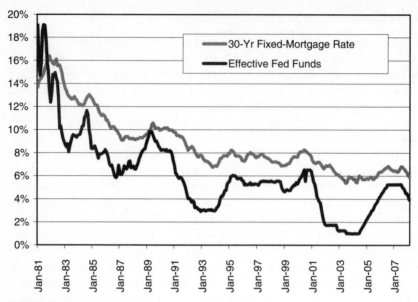

EXHIBIT 9.12 Mortgage Rates versus Fed Funds

responding to the subprime problems on a number of fronts. . . . We are committed to preventing problems from recurring while still preserving responsible subprime lending."

By the spring of 2008, the crisis was still in full swing highlighted by a bailout of Bear Stearns and legislation on the table that might provide homeowners with some relief. As of this writing draft legislation to this effect was being developed in the Senate. In the meantime, many speculate that the United States is already in the throes of a recession, possibly to be confirmed by forthcoming economic reports.

S&P/Case-Shiller Home Price Indices

The S&P/Case-Shiller Home Price Indices as published by Fiserv CSW Inc. (CSW) are widely recognized as the most reliable and authoritative measures of residential housing price movements for a variety of purposes, including loan portfolio due diligence, customer retention, loss reserve reviews, market surveillance, mortgage default, and loss and prepayment analyses. The S&P/Case-Shiller Home Price Indices represent market- specific time series designed to track residential home values accurately.

The development of the indices was pioneered in the 1980s by CSW's research principals, Karl E. Case and Robert J. Shiller. In particular, Case and Shiller developed the repeat sales pricing technique, a methodology that is recognized as the most reliable means to measure housing price movement and a technique that has been applied by other home price index publishers, notably the Office of Federal Housing Enterprise Oversight (OFHEO).

Case and Shiller were initially motivated by the sheer size and value of home equity in the United States and the impact it exerts on consumer behavior patterns. As suggested earlier, the value of residential real estate held by households and nonprofit organizations totaled $22.6 trillion at the end of 2006, rivaling the value of the domestic equity and fixed-income markets. Although the significance of the marketplace cannot be disputed, there simply were no truly accurate measures of home value movements available at the time.

Accordingly, Case, Shiller Weiss, Inc. was founded in 1991 to provide a practical outlet for this work. The firm was subsequently acquired by Fiserv, Inc. in 2002 and now operates as Fiserv CSW, Inc. (CSW). In 2006, Standard & Poor's (S&P) stepped in to rebrand and eventually assume responsibility for marketing the tradable indexes as the S&P/Case-Shiller Home Price Indices.

CSW is built on a firm foundation of leading edge data collection, filtering, analysis, and modeling of home values. In the process of researching home values, the firm has accumulated an extensive nationwide database of residential real estate information. This data comprises the REdex Library of home pricing indices and related metrics and CASA, an automated property valuation service.

The indices are fundamentally based on observed changes in home values. In particular, CSW collects data regarding transactions on all residential properties during the time period in question. Next, CSW conducts a search of its accumulated database to find information regarding any previous sales for the same home. If this search is successful, this data point is examined in order to eliminate from consideration data points that might distort the calculations. Specifically, these transactions would include non-arm's-length transactions (e.g., the surnames of the seller and buyer match); foreclosure sales by mortgage lenders; transactions where the property type designation is changed (e.g., properties originally recorded as single-family homes are subsequently recorded as condominiums); and suspected data errors where the order of magnitude in values change dramatically.

The sale pair is thereupon aggregated along with all other sales pairs found in a particular region to create the index. CSW uses both published and unpublished index calculation techniques created by Case, Shiller, and CSW's research staff to arrive at the index value.[8]

The indices are established with a base value of 100.00 in the quarter ending March 2000 (the "base year"). The indices are generated for geographic areas located across the entire United States and categorized on the basis of property type and price level. These geographic areas include U.S. Census Divisions, states, Metropolitan Statistical Areas (MSAs), counties, and ZIP codes. The figures are produced quarterly and released near the conclusion of the second month of each calendar quarter representing activity in the previous calendar quarter.

Distinct indices are published for both single-family homes and condominiums. Further distinctions may be made, as permitted by specific market conditions, on the basis of three price tiers: high-, moderate- and low-priced homes. Tiering is established at levels that represent approximately a third of the housing stock within the geographic region being measured. The indices may be accessed via CSW's index-based Portfolio Valuation Services. See Exhibit 9.13.

Quality data is the cornerstone of any index, and CSW approaches the tasks of accumulating and screening raw data rigorously. Long-term

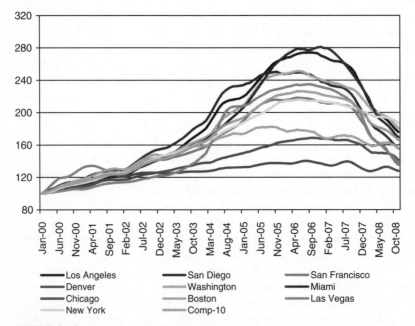

EXHIBIT 9.13 S&P Case-Shiller Home Price Indexes

contracts are maintained with multiple redundant sources to ensure access to data in all geographic regions. In the process, CSW has vastly expanded its library of data without compromising quality. CSW further filters the raw data per proprietary methodologies to ensure accuracy, given the some-times uneven quality of data from various public databases. CSW meticu-lously scans its database for possible errors and cross-checks data from its multiple data suppliers. CSW standardizes residential home addresses per U.S. Postal Service specifications.

The S&P/Case-Shiller Home Price Indices are not the only housing price indices available. In addition, NAR publishes the NAR housing indi-ces. Similarly, housing indices are published by the OFHEO.

The NAR indices are quoted in terms of median home values and there-fore might not actually measure the potential investment return of homeown-ers. Median values may be deceptive and may readily be skewed if, for example, homes are remodeled or new luxury or low-cost housing is con-structed in the area. Further, high-end homes tend to sell most heavily in the summer months when high-income homeowners are more willing to move their children from one school to the next. Thus, there is a certain degree of seasonality in the NAR series. As a result of these considerations, there may be dramatic changes in the value of these indices that have little to do with the actual price fluctuations of homes. The indices use a repeat sales method-ology that is more robust and speaks directly to homeowners' wealth.

The OFHEO indices use a repeat sales methodology applying the work of Case and Shiller. But they are based on a geometric, not an arithmetic average, which introduces certain biases to the data. Further, sampling is confined to Fannie and Freddie conforming mortgages and is therefore biased toward lower end rather than higher end housing. Note that only perhaps a sixth of all California home sales conform. The indices draw upon much larger sample sizes. Further, OFHEO references appraisal data to supplement actual transactions. Because the S&P/Case-Shiller indices are not confined to conforming mortgages, they incorporate a wider sample and do not resort to use of appraisal data. Note that appraisal data are often biased on the high side. OFHEO indices typically undergo multiple adjust-ments and restatements because they are released two months after the con-clusion of the quarter.

A Unique Asset Class

Modern investment theory underscores the benefits of diversification. Resi-dential real estate represents a rather unique asset class, the returns on which are distinguished from other major asset classes including stocks and bonds.

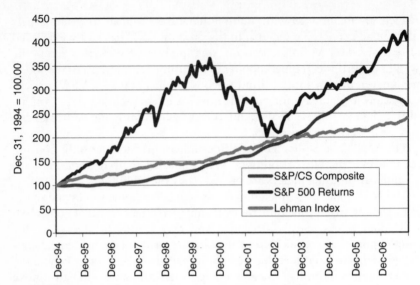

EXHIBIT 9.14 Housing versus Other Assets (Jan-95 to Nov - 07)

Exhibit 9.14 depicts the performance of the S&P/Case-Shiller 10-City Composite Index versus stock performance represented by the S&P 500 versus the bond market represented by the Lehman Aggregate Bond Index. (Note that these values were normalized at a value of 100.00 as of December 31, 1994, for purposes of this comparison.)

During the approximate 12-year period from January 1995 through November 2007, the returns on these three assets were reasonably similar, as shown in Exhibit 9.15. But the three different asset classes achieved those returns in very different ways. In particular, housing experienced the least volatility of returns as measured by the standard deviation of monthly percentage returns.

It is also interesting to note that housing displayed a negative correlation with the other three asset classes over the past 10 years as depicted in

EXHIBIT 9.15 Performance of Asset Classes (Jan-95 thru Nov-07)

	Average Monthly Return	Volatility (Standard Deviation of Monthly Returns)
Housing	0.64%	0.73%
Bonds	0.57%	1.05%
Stocks	0.99%	4.11%

EXHIBIT 9.16 Correlation of Various Asset Classes (Jan-95 through Nov-07)

	Housing	Bonds	Stocks
Housing	—		
Bonds	−0.106	—	
Stocks	−0.150	−0.039	—

Exhibit 9.16. Accordingly, housing as an asset would imply some important benefits in terms of diversification.

Housing Futures and Options

CME Group began offering futures and option contracts based on the S&P/ Case-Shiller Home Price Indices as published by Fiserv CSW, Inc. (CME Housing futures and options) in early 2006. But the real estate asset class is different from other asset classes such as stock or bonds in that real estate is frequently held for use over protracted intervals of time. Homeowners who expect to live in the same home for the rest of their lives or businesses whose real estate holdings are very stable through time may think they do not need to hedge. In fact, however, there are substantial variations in the disposition of real estate assets through time that ought to generate hedging demand.

Real estate futures hold appeal to some homebuyers to hedge their risks. Builders who have a supply of homes to sell may want to hedge the inventory. Builders who have a supply on the market may also immediately want to offer some kind of value warranty to homebuyers, who may be suddenly wary about buying in a market that appears possibly to be peaking, as an inducement to buy.

Other users include holders of mortgage portfolios. Mortgage insurers currently hold a significant exposure to home prices because a sustained decline combined with high loan-to-value (LTV) ratios could result in dangerous levels of mortgage defaults. Government-sponsored entities (GSEs), agencies, and other issuers of mortgages also would benefit from these markets to address the risk inherent in their portfolios.

Without a futures market, a period of rising rates combined with general home price declines can be catastrophic for the issuers. As evidenced by the subprime mortgage crisis, events that impacts the agencies can create a crisis that cuts through the entire U.S. economy. Finally, investors at large will find CME Housing futures and options useful to provide exposure to a very important asset class without incurring the difficulties of actually executing real estate transactions.

Economic Benefits

On a macroeconomic level, futures based on home prices may add stability to the economy by allowing institutions to hedge their exposure to home prices and diversify the potential impact of sustained declines in home prices. As articulated by Case, Schiller, and Weiss,

> *Nowhere in the world today are there markets that would allow investors to invest in a widely diversified portfolio of real estate without incurring enormous transaction costs. Since they cannot invest in a widely diversified portfolio of real estate, they cannot invest in a truly diversified portfolio at all. Thus, the presumed diversification that is supposed to be practiced by all investors according to modern financial theory just isn't happening.*
>
> *Nor are there markets that would allow individuals and institutions with large exposure to specific real estate risk to hedge these risks. Individuals for various reasons usually prefer to own their own homes, rather than rent them from institutions, and firms usually prefer to own real estate that they use in connection with their operations. But they cannot easily hedge the risk of these holdings.*
>
> *In order to hedge their portfolio, these owners of real estate should sell real estate futures or buy put options that are closely correlated with the real estate that they live in or operate. At the same time, everyone should invest in a broad portfolio of real estate futures and options, which they can do by holding a portfolio of the opposite sides of the futures and options contracts that those who own real estate concentrated in a certain area undertake.*
>
> *Thus, the long sides of any given futures or options contract should be taken by a wide spectrum of investors, presumably primarily institutional, who invest in many futures contracts and options as a means of diversifying their portfolios; the short side should be taken by owners of region-specific real estate: individual homeowners, managers of rental properties, developers, corporation, and farmers.*[9]

Further, it is possible and perhaps even likely that the availability of real estate futures may facilitate the introduction of a variety of risk-management products that may be made available to individuals, such as home equity insurance or mortgages with guaranteed down payments. Institutions that offer such retail products will want to hedge their interests in futures markets. In fact, we might speculate that these institutions are unlikely to appear until liquid futures markets are in place. We would expect that over a period of years after the introduction of real estate futures a substantial risk-management industry will develop that will be intensive users of real estate futures. In the process, the costs associated with real estate transactions might be reduced on an institutional and on a retail level alike.

> *The establishment of real estate futures and options contracts might be described as having the effect of spectacularly lowering transactions costs for trading real estate. The modern theory of the transaction costs (see for example Demsetz [1968], Akerlof [1970], Gammill and Perold [1989], and Gorton and Pennachi [1991]) stresses the importance of traders with superior or inside information: dealers must announce bid-asked spreads wide enough that they are not routinely "picked off" by more informed traders. Baskets of corporate stocks and other financial assets are inherently subject to lower bid-asked spreads than are individual assets because there is less informed trading about the aggregates. The same would be true about the baskets of real estate on which the index is used to settle real estate futures and options contracts is based. Those who invest in real estate would be spared the concern that they are buying lemons, they can thereby forego the enormous costs and risks associated with buying individual properties.[10]*

Tradable Indices

CME lists futures and options based on "tradable" S&P/Case-Shiller Home Price Indices as opposed to the more comprehensive set of "standard" Case-Shiller Indices as described above. The tradable S&P/Case-Shiller Home Price Indices, which are the subject of CME futures and options, are released monthly on the last Tuesday of the month. They reflect housing sale data from the quarter ending approximately seven weeks before or an approximate two-month "look-back" basis. For example, the indices released on the last Tuesday of February 2008 include data from October-November-December 2007; the indices released on the last Tuesday of January 2008 include data from September-October-November 2007. In other words, the indices represent "rolling three-month" snapshots of housing data. By contrast, the standard S&P/Case-Shiller Indices are only released quarterly representing the prior entire calendar quarter and are released near the end of the next calendar quarter on a three-month look-back basis.

Futures and options are available on tradable indices (see Exhibit 9.17) that represent matched sale prices for single-family residential

EXHIBIT 9.17   CME Housing Futures & Options

	Futures	Options on Futures
Contract Size	Each contract shall be valued at $250 times the S&P/ Case-Shiller Home Price Index (e.g., the value of the Los Angeles Index was reported at 264.78 in the fourth calendar quarter 2005, which equates to a contract value of $66,195 (= $250 × 264.78)	One futures contract
Minimum Price Fluctuation	0.10 index points ($25.00)	0.05 index points ($12.50)
Trading Hours	Offered exclusively on CME Globex on Sundays to Thursdays 5:00 PM to 2:00 PM the next day	Traded via open outcry in CME Eurodollar options pit Monday to Friday, 7:20 AM to 2:00 PM (Central Time)
Contract Months	February Quarterly Cycle of February, May, August, and November	
Final Settlement Date	Trading in expiring contract ceases at 12:00 noon (Central Time) on last Tuesday of contract month	
Cash Settlement	Cash settlement based on reported value of S&P/ Case-Shiller Home Price Indices of home prices as published by Fiserv CSW Inc. (CSW) for the cities of Boston, Chicago, Denver, Las Vegas, Los Angeles, Miami, New York, San Diego, San Francisco, Washington, DC, and an index that represents a composite of the 10 cities	Exercised into the associated futures contract
Strike Prices	NA	At one-point intervals above and below prevailing market price

dwellings in 10 metropolitan statistical areas (MSAs). The 10 MSAs include Boston, Chicago, Denver, Las Vegas, Los Angeles, Miami, New York, San Diego, San Francisco, and Washington, D.C. In addition, the exchange also lists futures and options based on a composite index of the 10 MSAs. However, there are additional indexes published including indexes that represent housing values in Atlanta, Charlotte, Cleveland, Dallas, Detroit, Minneapolis, Phoenix, Portland, Seattle, and Tampa. Finally, a composite of the 20 MSA-based indices as well as a national index is also available.

Note that the S&P/Case-Shiller New York Home Price Index is not based on an MSA but rather represents a customized index that measures single-family home values in select New York, New Jersey, and Connecticut markets with significant populations that commonly commute to New York City for employment purposes. The S&P/Case-Shiller Composite Home Price Index is a weighted average of the 10 MSA indices. Although the indices are intended to be representative of all single-family residential homes within the subject MSA, data for particular properties or component areas may be unavailable. Performance of individual properties or counties is not necessarily consistent with the MSA as a whole. County components are subject to change as a result of revisions by the U.S. Census Bureau or data insufficiencies.

ECONOMIC INDICATORS

CME Group began offering futures and options based on Nonfarm Payrolls (NFP) in April 2008. Nonfarm Payrolls represents the most anxiously anticipated and closely watched of all domestic economic indicators. Unexpected movements in NFPs can exert tremendous influence on fixed-income, equity, and currency markets.

Employment Reports

Nonfarm Payrolls are released by the Bureau of Labor Statistics (BLS) usually at 7:30 AM Central Time on the first Friday of each month, along with a battery of other employment information. Actually, two distinct reports are generated from separate surveys: the "Establishment Survey" of approximately 375,000 businesses used to generate NFPs and a "Household Survey" of approximately 60,000 households used for the unemployment rate. We focus on the Establishment Survey depicting the seasonally adjusted change in total NFPs.

Significance of NFPs

The Establishment Survey is one of the first major economic releases of the month that depicts economic activity in the prior month. Note that the Federal Reserve's implicit mission is to balance the risks of inflation with the goal of achieving maximum possible stable growth and employment. Thus, the Fed takes heed of the various labor market reports including the monthly change in NFPs, the unemployment rate, average workweek, overtime, and average hourly earnings. In turn, the market focuses on NFPs for clues regarding possible Fed intentions. The value of interest rate, equity, and currency markets might all be impacted accordingly.

Futures and Options

Despite the significance of the NFPs, there is no facile means by which to gain direct exposure to this figure for either speculative or risk-management purposes. CME Group's NFP futures and options address this issue. Futures are cash settled based on a value of $25 times the reported change in size of civilian labor force quoted in thousand jobs.

Although these numbers are sometimes revised in subsequent months, NFP futures and options are settled based on the preliminary or "headline" number regardless of any subsequent revisions. Because we quote the change in the number of jobs, this can result in quotation of negative prices or strike prices. These contracts expire in each calendar month and are based on the employment report for the prior calendar month. They are offered exclusively on the CME Globex electronic trading platform. See Exhibit 9.18.

EXHIBIT 9.18   Nonfarm Payroll (NFP) Futures and Options

	Futures	Options
Contract Size	$25 × change in NFPs as published by BLS	One futures contract
Quote	Quoted in thousands (e.g., May 2007 contract would have settled at +157, representing change in Nonfarm Payrolls [in 000s] from April to May 2007. Each minimum price fluctuation of 1 point (1,000 jobs) = $25.00	Quoted in 500 jobs or minimum fluctuation of 0.5 (= $12.50)
Contract Months	Contracts available for all NFP releases, listed on the Monday after the previous month's release	

Trading Hours	Offered exclusively on CME Globex electronic trading platform on Sundays through Thursdays from 5:00 PM to 4:00 PM Central Time	
Last Trading Day	Trading in an expiring contract concludes at 7:25 AM Central Time on the first Friday of the contract month or such other day on which NFP figures are scheduled to be released by the BLS	
Final Settlement	Settled in cash based on change in seasonally adjusted total NFPs reported by U.S. Dept. of Labor, Bureau of Labor Statistics Table B-1, Employees on nonfarm payrolls by industry sector and selected industry detail, seasonally adjusted change in total nonfarm payrolls for month prior to named contract month	American-style options may be exercised into one futures contract
Strike Prices	NA	Established at 10-point (or 10,000 jobs) intervals from −500,000 to +500,000 jobs
Price Limit	Price limit of ±200 points (200,000 jobs = $5,000) applied to final settlement price from previous business day's settlement price	Movement in value of a call (put) is effectively capped (floored) by virtue of price limit applied to futures contract

CONCLUSION

The term *alternative investments* has been applied to many diverse types of assets and instruments. CME Group is committed to exploring the possibilities and offering derivatives on exotic instruments that are useful in the execution of practical risk-management strategies. Thus, the exchange has been innovative in developing products including weather, real estate, and even derivatives based on economic indicators. Sometimes, because of the unique nature of these products, they have long gestation periods. Fortunately, electronic trading technologies tend effectively to extend the shelf life of new products, allowing them to take root over an more extended period of time. Inevitably, some of the products will flourish while others fall by the wayside. Still, we expect more of these products to be introduced over time to complement derivatives in traditional asset classes listed on the exchange.

NOTES

1. Per Dean John Dutton, Penn State University (2002).
2. 2000 Preliminary Report for SAB Miller.
3. The Comprehensive Electricity Competition Act, allows consumers to choose their electric company, thereby bringing consumer choice and retail competition to the largest regulated markets. This act was designed to replace the Public Utility Holding Company Act of 1935.
4. See Federal Reserve Statistical Release Z.1, Table B.100, Balance Sheet of Households and Nonprofit Organizations. This figure represents the market value of "[a]ll types of owner-occupied housing including farm houses and mobile homes, as well as second homes that are not rented, vacant homes for sale, and vacant land."
5. See New York Stock Exchange (NYSE) Fact Book, "Global comparison of market capitalization of domestic listed companies."
6. Estimates of the Securities Industry and Financial Markets Association (SIFMA).
7. Karl E. Case, Robert J. Shiller, and Allan N. Weiss, "Index-Based Futures and Options Markets in Real Estate," Cowles Foundation Discussion Paper 1006, 1992.
8. Sales pairs within a particular geographic area are statistically combined, creating a "price path" of all single-family homes in that area using an M-Index-Robust Interval- and Value-Weighted Arithmetic Repeat Sales Chain-After Base model to create a single home price index. The home need not be sold within one quarter to measure changing values in the current quarter. Rather, sales pairs spanning some time are referenced to estimate an index point for that period. But the value of individual homes may fluctuate for many reasons. For example, a home may be remodeled or abandoned and deteriorate with obvious implications with respect to value. These situations speak more to a change in the physical characteristics of the property than the change in market value. CSW addresses these concerns by weighting sales pairs using proprietary software that weights changing home values based on their statistical distribution in that geographic region. Specifically, CSW employs an "M-Index-Robust Weighting" methodology where M is a reference to M-Estimate class. As a first cut, if a large change in the sales pair is observed relative to the statistical distribution of all area sales pairs, the suspect pair may be discounted or removed altogether from the sampling. Data related to homes that sell very frequently are excluded to the extent that historical and statistical data suggest that such sales are usually not at arm's length. Sales pairs are further weighted based on the period between the two sales dates ("interval weighting"). When sales intervals are very long, it becomes more likely that a house may have experienced physical alteration, and therefore longer interval pairs are discounted. Finally, each sales pair is assigned a weight equal to the first sale price ("value weighting"). For more discussion regarding the repeat sales methodology, refer to Robert J. Shiller, "Arithmetic Repeat Sales Price Estimators," *Journal of Housing Economics* 1 (1991): 110–126.
9. Case, Shiller, and Weiss, "Index-Based Futures and Options Markets in Real Estate."
10. Ibid.

CHAPTER 10

Fundamental Market Indicators

John W. Labuszewski
Richard Co

Many factors impact the price performance and level of participation in any marketplace. But the most fundamental of factors may be found in the fundamentals! In other words, we may look to basic supply and demand indications in our markets as generally guiding price performance and market participation.

The flagship products offered by CME Group include Eurodollar, Treasury debt, and E-mini S&P 500 futures, representing primary benchmarks for interest rates and domestic equity values. The kinds of fundamental market indicators that drive these benchmark products may be found in a variety of economic indicators that describe the ebbs and flows of our economy.

Of course, many economic indicators are released by a variety of U.S. government agencies and various private sources. Some are more and some are less closely followed than others. But some of the most significant and widely followed of economic indicators include Nonfarm Payrolls (NFPs), Retail Sales, the Institute for Supply Management (ISM) Index, the Consumer Price Index (CPI), Durable Goods Orders, the Philadelphia Fed Index, and gross domestic product (GDP).

This chapter will help you understand the impact of the most significant economic indicators on CME Group flagship products in the form of volatility and trading volume.

WHY THESE INDICATORS?

There are many indicators on which this study could have focused. The degree to which the marketplace focuses on one or another indicator is subject to change over time and as a function of monetary and fiscal policy.

Significance Is Era Specific

In today's marketplace, most analysts agree that the BLS monthly Employment Report featuring NFP and unemployment rate statistics stands out as the single most significant economic release. NFP is anxiously anticipated because it is followed closely by the Federal Reserve System's (Fed) Federal Open Market Committee (FOMC), which attempts to balance inflationary pressures against economic growth. Further, it is released on the first Friday of each calendar month and therefore represents one of the first major fundamental releases that speaks to economic activity in the prior month.

But in the 1980s when Paul Volcker served as Fed chairman, the most anxiously anticipated economic indicator was the release of money supply figures, notably in the form of M1. Volcker, of course, will be remembered for directing the Fed and the nation through an extremely difficult period when inflation had soared to double-digit levels. Money supply targeting, as measured by M1, became the prime tool in the Fed's fight to control inflation. Although the Fed continues to establish target ranges for M2 and M3 growth, these numbers mean little, and the Fed is more likely to adjust its targets when it misses rather than adjust monetary policy in any significant way.

Grading the Indicators

Although the popularity of various economic indicators may be dynamic, we nonetheless consulted a popular economic calendar service in the form of Briefing.com to get an indication regarding the value of the various releases. Briefing.com offers ratings on a scale from A to F of the significance of each release. Note that NFPs were accorded the highest grade of an "A," whereas Money Supply has fallen tremendously in significance down to the lowest possible grade of an "F."

For purposes of this study, we did nothing more scientific than simply select seven of the most highly graded indicators, including NFPs, ISM Index, Retail Sales, CPI, Durable Orders, GDP, and the Philadelphia Fed Index. See Exhibit 10.1.

EXHIBIT 10.1 Grading Economic Indicators

Economic Indicator	Briefing.com Rating
Nonfarm Payrolls (NFP)	A
Institute for Supply Mgt (ISM) Index	A−
Retail sales	A−
Consumer Price Index (CPI)	B+
Chicago Purchasing Managers Index (PMI)	B
Durable goods orders	B
Gross domestic product (GDP)	B
Philadelphia Fed Index	B
Consumer confidence	B−
Housing starts and building permits	B−
Industrial production	B−
Non-Manufacturing ISM Index	B−
Producer Price Index (PPI)	B−
University of Michigan Consumer Survey	B−
Initial jobless claims	C+
New home sales	C+
Personal income and spending	C+
Trade balance	C+
Existing home sales	C
Auto and truck sales	C−
Business inventories	C−
Leading indicators	C−
Factory orders	D+
Productivity and unit labor costs	D+
Construction spending	D
Export/Import price	D
Treasury budget	D
Consumer credit	D−
Wholesale trade	D−
Money supply (M2)	F

Source: Briefing.com.

Forecast Error

Certainly the financial marketplace studies all of the subject indicators closely to determine likely implications for the state of the economy and impact on interest rate and equity markets. As a general rule, a robust number that portends a strong economy may cause interest rates to advance (fixed-income instrument prices to decline) and equity values to advance. Conversely, one would expect that an economic release that portends of a weaker economy may cause interest rates to decline (prices to advance) and equity values to decline.

EXHIBIT 10.2 Average Forecast Error (January 2001–August 2006)

	Average Absolute Forecast Error	Unit
Nonfarm Payrolls (NFP)	73.63	Change in thousands
Retail Sales	0.73%	Monthly % change
Inst Supply Mgt (ISM) Index	1.69	Index points
Consumer Price Index (CPI)	0.10%	Monthly % change
Durable Goods Orders	2.10%	Monthly % change
Philadelphia Fed	2.14	Index points
Gross Domestic Product (GDP)	0.39%	Quarterly % change

But the marketplace generally anticipates the level of significant economic indicators and acts accordingly in advance of the actual release. Generally, a consensus or forecast figure is reported that indicates the consensus expectation regarding the level of an impending fundamental release. Thus, it is the divergence between that forecasted figure and the actual release, the "forecast error" or the "surprise," that is most important in causing the marketplace to react by bidding market prices upward or offering them downward, as illustrated in Exhibit 10.2.

Some economic indicators may be more difficult to forecast with accuracy than others. For example, the average (absolute) forecast error observed between consensus expectations as reported by Briefing.com and the actual release of NFPs over the period January 2001 through August 2006 was 73.63 thousand jobs. By contrast, the average (absolute) forecast error for the Consumer Price Index (CPI) was only 0.10%. Although these indicators are reported in very different units of measurement, it is probably safe to conclude that CPI releases are a bit more predictable than NFP releases.

We focus on the effect that these forecast errors have on daily trading volume and volatility in E-mini S&P 500 (ES) and in Eurodollar (ED) futures. We use two simple measures of volatility for these purposes: the net change from close to close and the daily high-low range.

TRADING VOLUMES

Just as the significance of various economic indicators is era-specific, as discussed earlier, trading volumes likewise should not be assessed out of context. In other words, to differentiate "good" versus "poor" volume for any single day, we must compare that daily volume to "typical" volume in

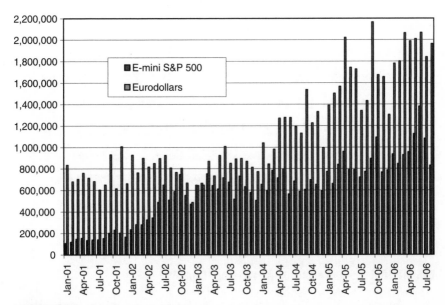

EXHIBIT 10.3 Average Daily Volumes

the surrounding time period. Thus, we reference daily volume in relationship to average daily volume during the entire calendar month during which an economic indicator is released.

Note that volume in E-mini S&P 500 and Eurodollar futures have been increasing rather dramatically during the period January 2001 through August 2006. Average daily volume (ADV) in E-mini S&P 500 futures has advanced from below 200,000 to nearly 1,000,000 contracts per day. Similarly, Eurodollar futures volume has advanced from nearly 800,000 to 2,000,000 contracts per day during the same five and a half years. See Exhibit 10.3.

As a first pass, we may identify the ADV on the release dates for our seven indicators versus average daily volume. Over the entire period from January 2001 through August 2006, ADV in E-mini S&P 500 futures was 601,346. Leading the pack is ADV on release dates for CPI at 673,539, followed by Retail Sales, Philadelphia Fed, and NFPs. Interestingly, ADVs on release dates for GDP, Durable Orders, and the ISM Index are actually less than the overall ADV. See Exhibit 10.4.

Our summary results are somewhat more decisive with respect to ADV in Eurodollar futures. ADVs over the entire January 2001 through August 2006 period were 1,139,767. ADV on the release dates for all seven of our indicators exceeded the overall average, often by a wide margin. NFP release dates lead the pack with 1,743,380, followed by CPI, Retail

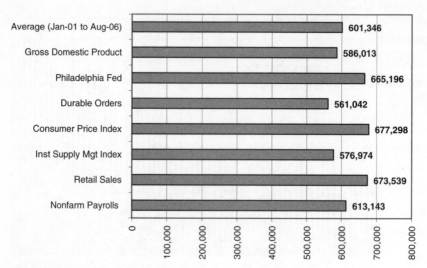

EXHIBIT 10.4   E-mini S&P 500 (ES) Average Daily Volume

Sales, Philadelphia Fed Index, ISM Index, GDP, and Durable Orders. See Exhibit 10.5.

This suggests that interest rate traders seem to take the release of economic indicators a bit more seriously in general than equity traders do. As such, we might expect that economic indicator releases may generate a

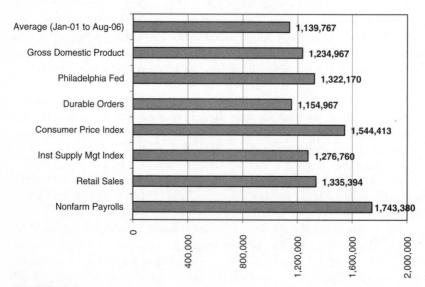

EXHIBIT 10.5   Eurodollar (ED) Average Daily Volume

greater impact on the pricing and volatility of interest rate instruments than equity markets.[1]

VOLATILITY: DAILY NET CHANGE

One very simple measure of volatility may be found in the daily net change or price change from close to close. On average, the absolute value of the daily net change in E-mini S&P 500 futures from January 2001 through August 2006 was 10.05 index points.

The economic indicator that exerted the greatest impact on net change was NFPs with an average net change of 10.74 index points, followed by the ISM Index. Unexpectedly, all of our other economic indicators seemed to have little impact on daily net changes in the equity market, averaging less than the overall total over the period January 2001 through August 2006. See Exhibit 10.6.

Although E-mini S&P 500 futures appear rather insensitive to economic releases, Eurodollars performed much closer to our expectations. NFPs seem to exert the greatest impact on market volatility with an average absolute net change of 9.8 basis points compared to the overall average of 4.9 basis points. NFP was far beyond any other indicator in this regard, although all of our indicators inspired movement at least slightly in excess of the overall average. See Exhibit 10.7.

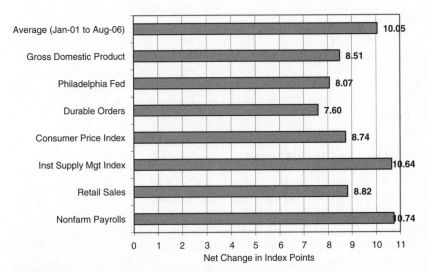

EXHIBIT 10.6 E-mini S&P 500 (ES) Absolute Daily Net Changes

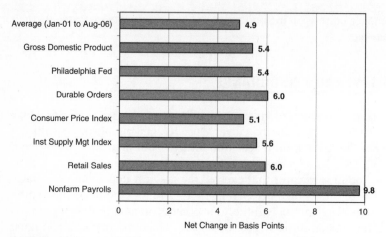

EXHIBIT 10.7 Eurodollar (ED) Absolute Daily Net Changes

VOLATILITY: DAILY HIGH-LOW RANGE

Another simple measure of volatility is found in the daily high-low range. The average daily high-low range in E-mini S&P 500 futures during the period January 2001 through August 2006 was 20.56 index points. However, not a single one of our economic indicators could generate such a wide high-low range. Nonfarm payrolls came close at 20.12 index points, but ranges on the release of all our other indicators fell short, sometimes rather far short. See Exhibit 10.8.

The impact of economic indicator releases on the daily high-low range in Eurodollar futures was a bit more predictable with NFPs leading the way at 15.5 basis points relative to the overall average of 9.5 basis points. Still, only Durable Goods Orders and CPI could exceed the overall average figure with ISM, Retail Sales, GDP, and the Philadelphia Fed Index falling short. See Exhibit 10.9.

Correlation and Significance

Finally, we apply a single variable ordinary least-squares or regression analysis to test correlations and significance of economic indicator forecast error on volume and volatility in E-mini S&P 500 and Eurodollar futures. We can gain an intuitive understanding of the relationship between forecast error and volume volatility by inspecting simple scatter diagrams. In particular, we focus on scatter diagrams depicting forecast errors for NFPs versus daily net changes in ES and ED futures. See Exhibit 10.10 and 10.11.

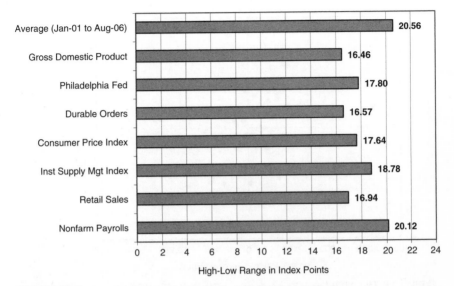

EXHIBIT 10.8 E-mini S&P 500 (ES) Average Daily High-Low Ranges

We might expect that forecast errors greater than zero, indicative of stronger than expected economic conditions, would portend stronger equity values and higher interest rates (lower fixed-income instrument prices). Forecast errors less than zero, indicative of weaker than expected economic

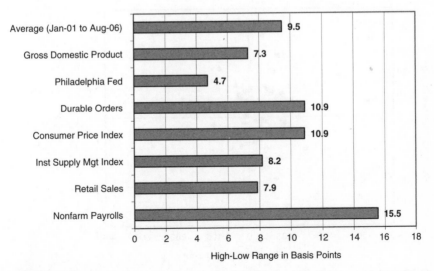

EXHIBIT 10.9 Eurodollar (ED) Average Daily High-Low Range

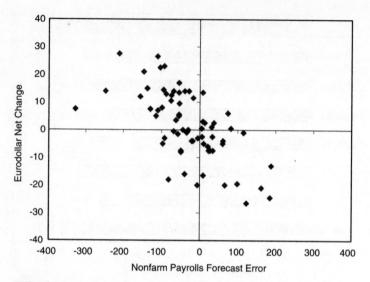

EXHIBIT 10.10   NFP Error Forecast versus ED Daily Net Change

conditions, may portend weaker equity values and lower interest rates (higher fixed-income prices).

This relationship appears evident in our scatter diagram for Eurodollar futures where positive forecast errors typically result in falling prices (rising

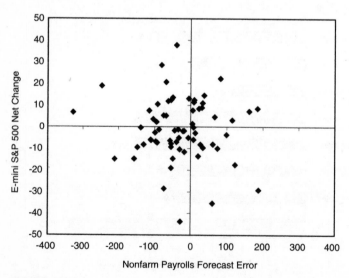

EXHIBIT 10.11   NFP Forecast Error versus ES Net Change

rates), whereas negative forecast errors are more typically associated with rising prices (falling rates). However, the scatter diagram in the context of E-mini S&P 500 futures exhibits a pronounced shotgun effect with no particular causal relationship in evidence.

We further test the significance of any relationships by running a simple regression analysis, focusing on R^2 and the t-Stat associated with the coefficient for the single independent variable. The only relationship in the context of E-mini S&P 500 futures that rises to the level of statistical significance is that between (absolute) NFP forecast error and volume. See Exhibit 10.12.

The indicator that clearly exerts the most impact on Eurodollar futures is NFPs. Note that there is a markedly significant relationship between absolute NFP forecast error and volume, NFP forecast error and net change, and absolute NFP forecast error and range. There are further significant relationships between forecast errors for ISM, Philadelphia Fed Index, and GDP versus both net change and range.

EXHIBIT 10.12 Regression Results vs. Economic Indicator Forecast Error R^2 and (t-Stat)

	E-mini S&P 500 (ES)			Eurodollars (ED)		
	Volume	Net Change	Range	Volume	Net Change	Range
Nonfarm Payrolls (NFP)	0.074 (2.295)*	0.006 (−0.652)	0.000 (0.023)	0.149 (3.401)*	0.419 (−6.902)*	0.109 (2.836)*
Retail Sales	0.002 (−0.403)	0.001 (−0.308)	0.000 (−0.161)	0.011 (−0.872)	0.030 (−1.441)	0.000 (0.113)
Inst Supply Mgt (ISM) Index	0.003 (−0.410)	0.003 (0.481)	0.000 (0.069)	0.003 (0.458)	0.253 (−4.726)*	0.070 (2.223)*
Consumer Price Index (CPI)	0.011 (0.866)	0.033 (−1.509)	0.010 (−0.834)	0.019 (1.126)	0.002 (−0.389)	0.001 (0.204)
Durable Orders	0.001 (−0.230)	0.003 (0.463)	0.002 (0.359)	0.009 (−0.792)	0.004 (−0.492)	0.026 (1.326)
Philadelphia Fed	0.000 (−0.125)	0.014 (−0.982)	0.000 (−0.155)	0.000 (0.136)	0.280 (−5.062)*	0.080 (2.394)*
Gross Domestic Product (GDP)	0.006 (0.619)	0.004 (0.496)	0.030 (−1.436)	0.020 (1.163)	0.135 (−3.208)*	0.046 (1.781)

*Statistically significant result.

CONCLUSIONS

Nonfarm Payrolls are clearly and predictably the most significant economic indicator that impacts the performance of CME Group flagship products in the form of E-mini S&P 500 and Eurodollar futures. Actually, the relationships between economic releases and ES futures are rather tenuous.[2] These relationships are far stronger in the context of Eurodollar futures.

Although NFPs may be the most significant of these indicators, Durable Goods Orders appear to be the least significant of these indicators as a general rule. Finally, one may observe that although CPI releases tend to be accompanied by high volumes, the indicator's impact on price movement is perhaps a bit muted, possibly attributed to the rather predicable nature of CPI and generally low forecast errors.

APPENDIX: ECONOMIC INDICATOR DESCRIPTIONS

This appendix provides a description of the seven economic indicators that are the subject of this study.

Nonfarm Payrolls

Nonfarm Payrolls (NFPs) are released by the Bureau of Labor Statistics (BLS) at 7:30 AM (Central Time [CT]) on the first Friday (but generally on the second Friday if the first Friday is the first business day of the month) of each month along with a battery of other employment information. Actually, two distinct reports are generated from separate surveys: a survey of approximately 375,000 businesses (the establishment survey) that is used to generate NFPs and a survey of approximately 60,000 households (the household survey) used to generate the unemployment rate. The unemployment report is one of the first major economic releases of the month that depicts economic activity in the prior month. The Federal Reserve typically focuses keenly on the employment report, including NFPs, the unemployment rate, average workweek, overtime, and average hourly earnings.

Retail Sales

The retail sales report is published by the Census Bureau of the Commerce Department. It is released at 7:30 AM (CT) on or about the 13th of the month and represents data for the prior calendar month. It is a measure of the total receipts of retail stores. The figure is closely monitored as a useful indication of consumer spending. Analysts frequently study the report on an "ex-autos" basis, noting potentially dramatic advances and declines in auto sales driven by discounting tactics on the part of the automakers. Food and energy components of the index are likewise often discounted as volatile but not necessarily always sustainable drivers. Note that services are not included in retail sales and that the figures may be volatile and subject to wide revisions.

ISM Index

The Institute for Supply Management releases its ISM Index at 9:00 AM (CT) on the first business day of the month, representing the prior calendar month. The ISM Index is generated from a nationwide poll of purchasing managers. The index is weighted to incorporate new orders (30%), production (25%), employment (20%), deliveries (15%), and inventories (10%). An index in excess of 50% suggests economic expansion relative to the prior month; an index less than 50% is indicative of economic contraction relative to the prior month. The ISM Index is perhaps the most significant privately generated economic report.

Consumer Price Index

CPI is compiled by the Bureau of Labor Statistics (BLS) of the U.S. Department of Labor and released at 7:30 AM (CT) on or about the 13th of the month. CPI measures prices of a fixed market basket of goods and services purchased by consumers and is widely used to determine cost of living adjustments (COLAs) in the context of public and private labor agreements. Analysts often study CPI excluding volatile food and energy prices, which are often seasonal or cyclical, leaving one with a reading of "core" inflation. Fed policy is tied to a core inflation rate rather than the aggregate inflation rate. These figures may tend to exaggerate the true impact of inflation in the sense that astute consumers tend to find substitutes for overly inflated goods and services, patterns that are not recognized per the CPI statistics.

Durable Goods Orders

Durable goods orders are released by the Census Bureau of the Commerce Department at 7:30 AM (CT) on or about the 26th of each month representing data from the prior month. This figure represents orders, shipments, and unfilled orders of durable goods. A durable good is considered one that may last for three years or better. These figures are frequently distorted by large defense or aircraft orders; hence many market participants pay closer attention to the non-defense capital goods component of Durable Goods. Still, durable orders are considered an important indicator of manufacturing activity.

Philadelphia Fed Index

The index is released by the Philadelphia Federal Reserve Bank at 11:00 AM (CT) on the third Thursday of the month. It is one of several manufacturing surveys generated by the regional branches of the Federal Reserve. However, the Philly Fed Index is considered a leading indicator in the sense that it is first Fed index to be released and represents activity for the month in which it is reported. An index level greater than zero indicates growth, whereas an index level less than zero is indicative of contraction.

Gross Domestic Product

Gross domestic product (GDP) is compiled by the Bureau of Economic Analysis (BEA), an arm of the U.S. Commerce Department, and is the broadest measure of economic activity. The figures represent activity in a previous calendar quarter. Actually, the figures are reported in stages. There is an "advance" announcement in the first month of each calendar quarter representing activity in the prior calendar quarter; revised by a "preliminary" release during the middle month of the quarter; capped by a "final" revision during the last month of each calendar quarter. Revisions can be significant and may impact figures reflecting activity several years in the past.

GDP is often quoted as an annualized percent change basis. The most significant components of GDP include consumption, investment, net exports, government purchases, and inventories. Consumption is the single most important of these components. The BEA further publishes GDP deflators or measurements of the change in prices of GDP components and is considered a key indicator of inflationary pressures. The GDP deflator might be considered a bit more useful than CPI in the sense that it is not tied to a fixed basket of goods and services but rather represents the actual mix of goods and services produced.

NOTES

1. Most of the subject economic indicators are published at 8:30 AM Eastern Time (7:30 AM Central Time) during regular trading hours of Eurodollar futures but prior to the commencement of regular trading hours in E-mini S&P 500 futures. A possible conjecture is that the impact of these economic indicators manifests

itself in Eurodollar futures through continuous trading, whereas E-mini S&P 500 futures react at the opening of regular trading hours, thus absorbing the market impact. As such, volume in stock index futures may be less dramatically affected.

2. Although it is difficult to argue that these economic indicators do not provide market moving information, perhaps their directional impact on E-mini S&P 500 futures is less certain than in Eurodollar futures where a direct monetary policy linkage is evident.

CHAPTER 11

Technical Analysis Primer

John W. Labuszewski

Technical analysis covers an extremely broad spectrum of concepts and techniques. Many technical methods are quite complex, relying on reams of statistical information. Other technical methods may be simple and are based on visual interpretation of a price chart.

It is clear that technical analysis is commonplace in financial markets, prominently including futures markets. In fact, it is not an exaggeration to suggest that technical forecasting methods may be more widely followed and form the basis for more trading activity in the context of futures markets than any fundamental indicators.

This is evident when you consider there are thousands of commodity trading advisors (CTAs) and macro hedge funds offering their funds management services largely on the strength of their technical market forecasting expertise. Many of these traders are using the most modern computerized trading technologies to program mechanical or automated trading systems, sometimes under the banner of algorithmic trading methods. In any event, the market frequently is driven by these technical factors. Accordingly, we suggest that astute traders cannot afford not to pay attention to these interesting and potentially quite rewarding technical forecasting methods.

WHY TECHNICAL ANALYSIS?

Technical forecasting techniques have been in use, in one form or another, at least as long as organized markets have been in existence. But technical methods are not the only means by which one may attempt to gain an insight into potential future market movements. This section answers the question "Why should I be interested in technical analysis?" by discussing the distinction between a technical and fundamental approach to market forecasting as well some of the origins of technical trading methods.

Fundamental and Technical Analysis

Technical and fundamental analysts have often been at odds regarding the validity and relevance of the two approaches to market forecasting. Let's discuss the role that each method may play in a trading situation and why technical analysis plays so prominent a role in many futures trading applications.

Fundamental analysts are most concerned with the question "why?" Why does the market move the way it does? What fundamental economic conditions may cause the market to fluctuate upward or downward? Thus, fundamental analysts busy themselves studying cause-and-effect relationships.

Technical analysts believe the market price already incorporates all known fundamental information. As new economic data are released, they are incorporated into the market price level efficiently and almost instantaneously. Therefore, it becomes difficult to trade profitably on the strength or weakness of known fundamental information. Thus, you should focus on a study of the price level and patterns in price movements directly!

The market trades from day to day on the strength or weakness of unknown fundamental factors. More specifically, on the strength or weakness of what traders believe these factors will portend as they become known. More than anything else, therefore, the market trades on the basis of market psychology or the bullish or bearish attitudes of market participants in the aggregate.

Many academics question the validity of technical trading methods. In fact, these same academics frequently embrace the so-called random walk theory, which suggests market prices respond as fundamental market information is made known quickly, efficiently, and without serial autocorrelation. The absence of serial autocorrelation in a price series, or more specifically in a series of price movements, is said to occur because today's fundamental economic release may bear little correlation to tomorrow's fundamental economic release. Random walk theorists believe, therefore, that market prices fluctuate unpredictably and randomly over time.

But this is not inconsistent with the technical viewpoint that the market may fluctuate considerably between the points in time at which fundamental information is made known. During those intervals, market perceptions become more important than the most recently issued bit of fundamental market news.

Random walk theorists may assert that market movements are random and unpredictable. But a simple inspection of any chart book will probably satisfy most observers that the market is apt to move in trends. Not only does the market move in trends, but pricing patterns tend to repeat themselves and are witnessed over and over again. There are very few if any traders, for example, who have never seen a so-called head and shoulders formation. And very few who are unfamiliar with the traditional interpretation and pricing implications of the pattern.

If the market trends and behaves in accordance with repeating patterns, then traders will take action accordingly. If many traders rely on similar technical systems (and there is evidence to suggest that most trend-following systems trigger buy or sell recommendations in rough unison), then technical analysis becomes a kind of "self-fulfilling prophecy." If you believe the market will advance or decline and buy or sell accordingly, then the market may very well tend to rise or fall. This may be particularly true if there are a large number of like-minded traders.

Many of the so-called principles of technical analysis are quite unusual and might even seem to lack a commonsensical basis. But if enough traders believe that a given technique will work, it may very well work. If technical analysis is useful at all, therefore, it is because traders believe it will provide useful information. Their subsequent actions enforce those predictions. This implies that one should only be concerned about methods that fall in the mainstream of technical thought. Other, more arcane methods cannot work because too few traders will use those methods and, therefore, enforce their predictions.

Technical Analysis and the Futures Markets

Most of the technical work that has been done throughout the years has centered on the stock markets. In particular, famous analysts such as Dow and Elliott concentrated exclusively on equity markets. Nonetheless, a case may be made that technical analysis is more relevant in the context of the futures markets than in any other segment of the marketplace.

This is due largely to the fact that futures trade on low margin or performance bond requirements relative to the value of the underlying instrument. It is not uncommon for the margin on a futures contract to be anywhere between 1% and 5% of the total value of the delivery instrument. Compare that to the minimum 50% margin requirement associated with stocks. As such, futures traders enjoy extreme leverage compared to equity traders. But these comparisons do not tell the entire story.

When you buy stock, that 50% minimum margin requirement represents a down payment on the purchase price of the stock. The balance is typically borrowed at interest from the broker. This is appropriate because when you purchase stock, you acquire an equity interest in the issuing firm.

But when you buy (or sell) futures, the difference between the value of the commodity and the margin or the "unpaid balance" is not lent at interest. This is because the margin associated with futures transactions serves an entirely different purpose than a stock margin. A futures margin simply represents a "good faith deposit" or "performance bond." It is intended to secure the integrity of the contract by covering the risk associated with a single day's price movement. The margin need only cover a single day's maximum possible risk because margins are administered daily. That is, there are no paper profits or losses because traders are "marked-to-market" daily. Profits or losses are distributed or paid daily and in cash.

But the initial margin is deposited in the form of collateral, and this collateral is often accepted in the form of securities, generally T-bills, on which the futures trader continues to earn the interest. Thus, there is no explicit opportunity cost associated with the initial purchase or sale of futures. So futures traders enjoy 100% leverage. Because of this extreme leverage, futures traders generally cannot afford the luxury of a "buy-and-hold" strategy. Equity traders may buy a stock and hold it in the face of adverse market movements because they know they have already paid the full purchase price. But futures traders may not be able to fund variation cash payments associated with a losing futures position.

Futures trading, therefore, is much more of a short-term proposition. Because futures positions are not likely to be held for an extended period of time, timing is paramount! A futures trader who is right in the long term but wrong in the short term loses money. Futures traders who are wrong in the long term but right in the short term usually make money. The trick, so to speak, is to be right in the short term.

This means that technical analysis may be much more important than fundamental analysis in the futures markets. Fundamental analysis may provide useful insights in the long term. But often short-term market trends run contrary to long- term trends. Technical analysis is a tool that is much more useful in the short term.

Dow Theory

If any single individual may be credited with the introduction of modern technical thought, it is probably Charles Dow. He was an owner and editor of the *Wall Street Journal* in its early formative years. Dow's so-called theory appeared in a series of editorials carried by the paper in the late 1800s until Dow's death in 1904. Some people may question the relevance of Dow's ideas in an age of advanced telecommunications, computerized trading methods, and extremely fast-paced markets. Yet much of his work endures today and has heavily influenced vastly disparate schools of financial thought.

Among Dow's achievements was the introduction of a series of stock market indexes, one of which became known as the Dow Jones Industrial Average (DJIA). The first of Dow's stock averages, published initially on July 3, 1884, was an 11-stock rail average. In 1885, that average was expanded to include 12 rail stocks and 2 industrials. By 1896, the composition of the average was altered so it contained exclusively industrial stocks. Finally, by October 7, 1896, Dow created two averages: a 12-stock industrial and a 20-stock rail index.

Dow relied heavily on these indexes for technical forecasting purposes. In particular, Dow believed it was more worthwhile to study the movement of the indexes rather than movement in any individual stock. Dow believed the price of any individual stock may be affected heavily by unique factors that may not impact other firms. To identify broad market trends, therefore, it was important to focus on the averages. Further, Dow believed bullish movement in either the rail or industrial average should be confirmed by similar action in the other index.

Although Dow is not generally credited with the idea, it is clear he recognized that the risks associated with any individual stock were a function of general economic conditions as well as conditions that might uniquely impact a given stock. That is, Dow recognized early on what has become an axiom in modern financial thought: The total risk associated with any given stock is composed of systematic and unsystematic market risks. *Systematic risks* refer to those general economic factors that impact all stocks to one degree or another. *Unsystematic risks* may uniquely affect a given firm with little or no impact on other firms.

These ideas represent a cornerstone of the capital asset pricing model (CAPM). The CAPM was hammered out largely in the 1950s and early 1960s by a variety of academics who might have had little sympathy for many of Dow's theories. Nonetheless, they owe a large debt of gratitude to Dow. In particular, it is interesting to note that systematic market risks are today measured by stock market averages or indexes such as the DJIA or the Standard & Poor's 500 (S&P 500).

Not only did Dow's thought feed into the CAPM; his work also deeply affected other financial theorists of a quite different ilk. Ralph Nelson Elliott, a leading technician of the 1930s whose theories, known cumulatively as the Elliott wave theory, are in common use today, was an ardent student of Dow theory.

Dow believed that market movements may be categorized as minor, secondary, or primary trends. A minor or "near-term" trend may broadly be considered as movement that lasts anywhere from two to three days to two to three weeks. A secondary or "intermediate-term" trend may last from two to three weeks to two to three months. A primary, major, or "long-term" trend may last upward from two to three months.

Note: In today's world of futures trading, characterized by high-velocity electronic trading techniques, our horizons may be shortened a bit relative to Dow's world of 100 years ago. Thus, we might trade futures on an intra-day basis; "swing" trades may be characterized as those lasting from a day or two or three upward to two to three weeks. Beyond that, long-term futures trades may be held for two to three weeks and beyond.

Elliott believed that he refined these ideas considerably. In particular, Elliott was far more specific in identifying various trends. In addition to the primary, secondary, and minor trend, Elliott refers to trends of smaller du-ration: the minute, minuette, and subminuette. Further, Elliott has identi-fied trends of larger degree in the cycle, supercycle and grand supercycle, which may last upward of 200 years!

Dow also suggested that a primary trend breaks down into three stages: (1) the accumulation stage, (2) the technical trend-following stage, and (3) the distribution stage. Let's consider a primary bull trend. The accumu-lation stage represents the initial stage of a primary market movement. This is where the "smart money" begins to take a position by buying the bull trend. The technical trend-following stage occurs later when a variety of technical trading systems confirm the existence of a trending market and trigger buys. The distribution stage is the final upward surge where the "smart money" begins to take its profits.

Elliott wave theory is based primarily on the idea that the market moves in distinguishable patterns. In particular, the market may rally in a bull market in a five-step pattern and subsequently correct itself in a three-step pattern. As illustrated in Exhibit 11.1, these "5s" and "3s" represent the core of the Elliott wave theory.

The five-step upward movement is denoted with the numbers 1, 2, 3, 4, and 5. The subsequent corrective phase is denoted with the letters a, b, and c. Hence, these 5s and 3s may be referred to as the "numbered" and the subsequent corrective "lettered" phases. The numbered phase breaks down into three "impulse waves," specifically waves 1, 3, and 5 in the general direction of the market trend. The intervening waves 2 and 4 represent "corrective waves." The point is that these three impulse waves 1, 3, and 5 are highly reminiscent of Dow's accumulation, technical trend-following, and distribution phases.

It is difficult to imagine two schools of financial thought more diver-gent than the capital asset pricing model and Elliott's wave principle. Yet both of these concepts owe much to the original work of Charles Dow, the "great-great-grandfather of technical analysis."

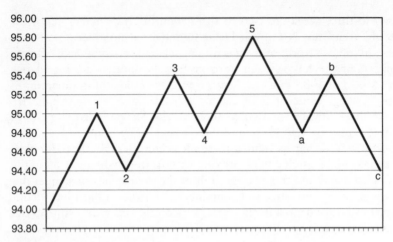

EXHIBIT 11.1   Elliott's 5's and 3's

INTERPRETING CHARTS

Technical analysts have often been distinguished into two camps: chartists and statisticians. A *statistician* relies on a numerical approach to technical market forecasting. A *chartist* relies on trends and patterns observed in a graphic representation of market behavior.

Bar charts are one of the most commonly referenced types of charts. A bar chart provides a vast wealth of information about market price movements, volume, and open interest. It is characterized by a series of vertical bars that depict the lowest price traded on a given day and the highest price traded on a given day against a horizontal axis depicting sequential dates. Off to the right of the bar, a short tick, or slash, is used to indicate the closing or settlement price of the day. Sometimes a similar slash is used off to the left of the bar to indicate the opening price of the day. Bar charts also might incorporate information regarding volume (in the form of bars at the bottom of the chart) and open interest (a line running through the bars at the bottom of the chart). In addition to providing information about price, volume, and open interest, bar charts provide information about market volatility and timing. Volatility may be observed in the height of the vertical bars. Timing may be observed in terms of the horizontal length over which a trend or pricing pattern persists.

A close cousin to the classic bar chart is the Japanese candlestick chart. The candlestick chart likewise depicts the open, high, low, and close. However, the candlestick chart may be a bit easier to read at a glance to the

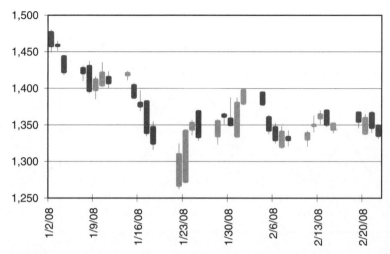

EXHIBIT 11.2   Candlestick Chart: March 2008 S & P 500 Futures

extent that the body of the daily entry is thickened between the opening and closing prices. Although conventions may be a bit different in different parts of the world, it is commonplace in the United States to fill in the body of the graph in green if the close is higher than the open or in red if the close should fall lower than the open. Candlestick charts, like that of Exhibit 11.2, date back several centuries in Japan, and a complete body of interpretative constructions have been developed around the candlestick chart. To a large extent, classic Japanese interpretations are paralleled in classic Western interpretations. For our purposes, we adopt a hybrid approach by generally using Japanese candlesticks charts while applying classic chart interpretations of Western origin.

The Trend

The first and foremost issue in the minds of many technical traders centers on the existence or nonexistence of a trend. A *trend* may be bullish, bearish, or sideways (neutral). A bullish trend is indicated by a series of successively higher and higher peaks coupled with a series of successively higher and higher troughs, (i.e., higher highs and higher lows). A bearish trend is indicated by a series of successively lower and lower troughs coupled with a series of successively lower and lower peaks (i.e., lower lows and lower highs). The trend is found by studying peaks and troughs in market movements. A bullish trend is characterized by a series of higher peaks and higher troughs; a bearish trend is confirmed by a series of lower troughs and lower peaks.

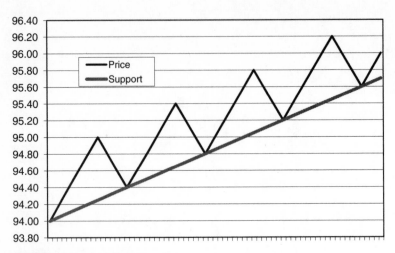

EXHIBIT 11.3 A Bullish Trend

Trends may be enforced by the existence of support or resistance in a bullish or bearish market, respectively. *Support* may be thought of as buying pressure as the market falls into a trough, or a "reaction low." *Resistance* may be thought of as selling pressure as the market rallies into a peak, or a "reaction high." Areas where support or resistance may be encountered may be estimated by drawing a *trendline* on the chart. A bullish trendline (support) may be found by connecting a straight line under a series of higher and higher troughs. See Exhibit 11.3. A bearish trendline (resistance) may be found by connecting a straight line over a series of lower and lower peaks. See Exhibit 11.4.

When connecting just two troughs or two peaks, you have established a tentative trendline. Subsequently, you will look for a third return to the trendline to confirm the tentative trendline. The strength of a potential support or resistance area on the chart may be estimated on the basis of a number of factors: volume, duration, recency, and round numbers.

Trends may, for example, be confirmed by advancing volume driving prices up to a peak in a bullish market or advancing volume driving prices down to a trough in a bearish market. Volume should fall off on a reaction low in a bull market and on a reaction high in a bear market. The more volume traded as the market approaches the support or resistance levels, the stronger those support or resistance levels are considered.

Another way of assessing the strength of a support or resistance level is to watch the amount of time spent trading near such an area. The longer time spent trading at or near these areas, the more significant that area may be considered. This is intuitive because if the market spends a great deal of

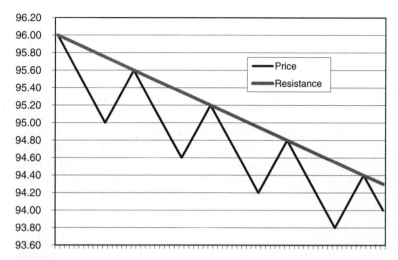

EXHIBIT 11.4 A Bearish Trend

time "testing" a support or resistance and it still holds, this suggests great strength. The more recently you have been trading near a support or resistance area, the stronger that area is likely to be. This is intuitive in the sense that if support or resistance at any particular area has held firm in the recent past, it is likely to remain firm in the near future.

Finally, traders often associate a great deal of significance to round numbers. For example, a Treasury note futures quote of 100% of par (100-00) is more likely to have some psychological significance than a quote like 99-23. In fact, the famous commodity and stock analyst W. D. Gann spent a great deal of time looking at the value of round numbers. Gann would break a range into halves, thirds, quarters, and eighths, assessing less and less significance to each successively finer and finer division. Consider, for example, a situation in which Eurodollar futures are trading between 95.00 and 96.00. Gann might break that range into halves, identifying 95.50 as a potentially significant support or resistance level. Other potentially significant areas might be 95.33 and 95.67 (thirds), 95.25 and 95.75 (quarters), or 95.12, 95.37, 95.63 and 95.88 (eighths).

How can you tell whether these levels will represent support or resistance? If the market is above the level, then it may provide support, but if the market is below the level, it may provide resistance. This is a variation of the idea that once broken, support becomes resistance; once broken, resistance becomes support. As a rule, it is probably best to avoid placing limit orders precisely at a support or resistance level that is deemed significant. If a significant support or resistance level is hit, the market may react strongly with a sharp advance or decline. This may mean that your broker will be unable to fill a limit order at the specified price.

It is usually best to place a limit buy order just above a support level and a limit sell order just below a resistance level in order to assure a fill. But why should these perceived support or resistance areas be expected actually to hold? Some observers say there are three kinds of market participants: longs, shorts, and the uncommitted. All three groups are psychologically committed to enforcing support in a bull market. Longs are looking for the next dip to a support level to add to an existing profitable long position. Shorts are looking for the next dip as a good opportunity to cut their losses. Finally, the uncommitted are looking for the next dip to establish a new position and participate in the bullish trend. See Exhibits 11.5 and 11.6 for trends with channels.

Support and resistance are said to be characteristic of a bull and a bear market, respectively. Many traders, however, identify lines that run parallel to bull and bear trendlines. By connecting a series of higher and higher peaks in a bull market, you have identified a bullish channel. A series of lower and lower troughs may be connected in a bear market and identified as a bearish channel.

A channel is found by studying peaks and troughs in market movements. A bullish channel is identified by connecting a series of higher and higher peaks in a bull market; a bearish channel is identified by connecting a series of lower and lower troughs in a bear market. Although channels are

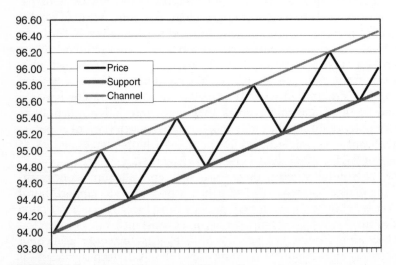

EXHIBIT 11.5   A Bullish Trend with Channels

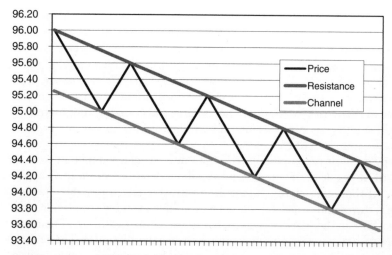

EXHIBIT 11.6 A Bearish Trend with Channels

frequently identified in bull and bear markets, they are generally weaker and more "ragged" than the support or resistance levels that they parallel.

These channels should run parallel to the support or resistance levels and may provide a useful indication of where to take profits. For example, a long in a bull market may buy on the troughs and take profits on the peaks; a short in a bear market may sell on the peaks and take profits on the troughs. But the market may not always reach the channel level. Often, the first sign of a reversal is the failure of the market to achieve a channel level.

What happens if a trendline should be broken? A broken support or resistance level is a necessary condition to signal a reversal of the market trend. But it is not a sufficient condition. Trendlines are often penetrated and yet the market continues to trend in a bullish or bearish direction. As a result, many analysts apply *filters* to help them determine whether any given penetration constitutes a legitimate break of the trendline. For example, a penetration of a trendline on an intraday basis is generally not regarded as significant. Many analysts look for a penetration of a trendline on the market close or settlement. Some analysts are not convinced unless the market trades through a support or resistance level for two or three consecutive days. Others are not convinced unless that break accounts for perhaps 2 to 3% of the previous market trend, measured from the lowest trough to the highest peak achieved during the duration of the trend.

Assume, however, that a trendline is broken, satisfying the added rigor of a filter application. This still does not necessarily suggest that the trend itself is broken. It may simply mean the trendline as drawn is "unsustainable."

A trendline can be unsustainably steep or even unsustainably shallow. A "sustainable" rate of advance or decline is thought to be measured as a 45-degree angle. Forty-five degrees may be meaningless, however, to the extent that the size of one's window on a computer screen could make a great deal of difference with respect to the angle. Call this the "classic wisdom" with respect to this point. But if a sufficient number of traders might subscribe to this classic wisdom, it may become self-fulfilling and, therefore, this might suggest the use of commonly available charting systems or tools to assure a common reference.

In any event, it is commonplace to "fan-up" trendlines drawn initially at too shallow an angle or to "fan-down" trendlines drawn at too steep an angle. One rule of thumb, however, is that once you have penetrated three fanned trendlines, then trend reversal is imminent. Call this the three-strikes rule.

How far can the market be expected to travel on a valid trend penetration? Many analysts rely on "percentage retracement" guides. The first issue is to ask, "How far can a market trend be retraced?" Obviously a movement can only be retraced up to 100% of the original movement. But once a retracement or reversal begins, analysts often look for a one-third, one-half, or two-thirds retracement. Assume that Eurodollar futures have experienced a rally from 95.00 to 96.00, measured from the lowest trough to the highest peak. But now the market shows signs of reversing or retracing that 100 basis point movement. Look for support at the one-third retracement level (95.67), the one-half retracement level (95.50), and the two-thirds retracement level (95.33).

Other analysts disagree with respect to the one-third, or 33%, level and the two-thirds, or 67%, level. Some claim that it is more appropriate to identify the 38% (support at 95.62) and 62% (support at 95.38) retracement levels. These alternative 38% and 62% levels are derived from the so-called Fibonacci number series. The Fibonacci number series goes 1, 2, 3, 5, 8, 13, 21, 34, 55, 89, 144 . . . . Note that each number is derived by adding together the prior two numbers. This number series has some interesting and unique properties. For example, if you divide any number in the series by the prior number, the result will be remarkably consistent at about 1.618. (This only works well after the first few numbers in the series.) See Exhibit 11.7.

By dividing any number in the series by the next number, the result will be remarkably consistent at about 0.618. The reciprocal of 0.618 (1/0.618) is 1.618. The reciprocal of 1.618 (1/1.618) is 0.618. We will say more about the remarkable properties of the Fibonacci number series later. The point is that traders often attribute significance to these numbers. The 62% retracement level is derived from the number 0.618. The 38% retracement level is simply 100% less the 62% figure.

EXHIBIT 11.7   Properties of Fibonacci Numbers

2/1 = 2.000	1/2 = 0.500
3/2 = 1.500	2/3 = 0.667
5/3 = 1.667	3/5 = 0.600
13/8 = 1.625	8/13 = 0.615
21/13 = 1.615	13/21 = 0.619
34/21 = 1.619	21/34 = 0.618
55/34 = 1.618	34/55 = 0.618
89/55 = 1.618	55/89 = 0.618
144/89 = 1.618	89/144 = 0.618

Reversal Patterns

A reversal pattern is a formation, identified on a bar chart, whose initial stages may suggest that a reversal of a market trend is imminent. A top may occur at the completion of a sustained bull movement, signaling an imminent bear market. A bottom occurs at the completion of a sustained bear movement, signaling the beginning of a bull movement. A reversal represents a formation on a chart that indicates the end of a sustained movement and the beginning of a new movement. A top indicates the conclusion of a bull movement and the inception of a bear movement. A bottom indicates the conclusion of a bear movement and the inception of a bull movement.

It is important to be able to distinguish a reversal from a consolidation pattern. A *consolidation pattern* is simply an area on the chart where the market takes a pause before it can continue to trend in the previously established direction. A *reversal pattern* indicates that the market is now ready to trade in a direction opposite the previously established direction.

The first early warning sign associated with a market reversal is a penetration of a trendline. This suggests, of course, that the market had previously been trending either up or down. Of course, a simple penetration may or may not signal a reversal. It may simply indicate that the trend is moving at an unsustainable angle and that your trendlines require adjustment.

This section explores five commonly referenced reversal patterns. Those five patterns include the (1) head and shoulders, (2) triple top or bottom, (3) double top or bottom, (4) rounded bottom, and (5) spike or "V" top.

The head and shoulders (H&S) formation is the most widely recognized of the five reversal patterns just named. The H&S pattern is typified by three peaks, or a "left and right shoulder" coupled with a higher peak known as the "head" in between. Perhaps the best way to describe the H&S formation is to examine the chart closely, identifying early warning signs that may portend the coming reversal. In the early stages of the H&S, there are generally no warning signs at all that a reversal might be on the horizon. Volume may in fact surge upward on the bullish movement up to the left shoulder associated with a topping H&S.

Subsequently, one may see the market decline to the nape of the "neck-line," or the trough between the left shoulder and head, on reduced volume. Still, there is no indication of a reversal because the market has simply returned to a support trendline as might normally be expected. The next surge upward to the head still provides no clear indication of a possible reversal. Sometimes, however, volume on this upward surge falls short of the volume on the prior upward surge to the left shoulder. The market then declines through the support level, down to the nape of the neckline or the trough between the head and the right shoulder. See Exhibit 11.8.

Once the two troughs between the head and the right and left shoulders are formed, one may draw in a neckline. It is important to identify the slope of this neckline. The neckline associated with a true H&S formation tends to slope in the general direction in which the market was trending before entering the pattern. If the neckline slopes downward in a topping H&S, then one may suspect that the formation may actually turn out to be a consolidation, rather than a reversal, pattern. On the next upward surge to the right shoulder, expect to see light volume. Once broken, the roles of support and resistance are reversed. Thus, what was once support in a bullish market now becomes resistance. The market bounces down off the resistance level and races through the neckline. The penetration of the neckline completes the H&S pattern.

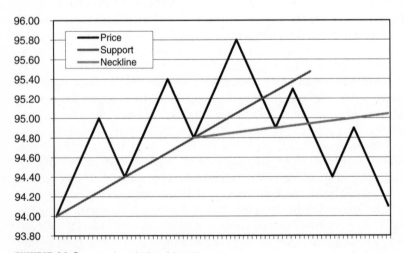

EXHIBIT 11.8   Head and Shoulders Top

It is important to measure the strength of the downward surge through the neckline. This strength or weakness may be assessed by looking at the volume traded on the break and the degree to which the neckline is penetrated. If that downward surge is strong (heavy volume and a so-called clean break of the neckline), then it is less likely to be a false break. When volume on the neckline break is weak, then it may be likely that the market will rally to test the neckline before resuming a downward trend (if the movement in fact results in a reversal).

Once the neckline is broken, you should begin looking for support at the one-third, one-half, and two-thirds retracement levels (or, at the 38%, 50%, or 62% levels if you prefer). But there is an even more direct way of identifying the vertical movement subsequent to a break in the neckline. The minimum expected movement on the break of a neckline may be estimated by measuring the vertical distance from the peak of the head downward to the neckline.

This suggests that the size of the pattern is an important indication of the expected subsequent market movement. The size of the pattern may be measured in two dimensions including vertical height and horizontal width. The vertical measure of the pattern is an indication of volatility. The horizontal width of the pattern is an indication of duration or time spent while trading in the pattern.

As a general rule, market tops, or the reversal of a bullish trend, tend to be more volatile but take less time to form. That is, tops tend to be characterized by large vertical height but relatively narrow width. Market bottoms, or the reversal of a bearish trend, tend to be less volatile but take a longer time to form. That is, bottoms tend to be characterized by relatively low vertical height but relatively wider width. This suggests that bottoms may be a bit easier to trade than tops because you will generally have more early warning signals when there is less volatility.

The triple top or bottom strongly resembles a head and shoulders top or bottom with the exception that all three peaks (in a top) or troughs (in a bottom) are of relatively equivalent height. This, of course, represents an infrequently observed pattern to the extent that it would be rare to see three peaks all of very similar height.

The volume pattern associated with this formation is strikingly similar to that of a head and shoulders. In other words, you may see a strong volume surge up to the first peak (down to the first trough) in a topping (bottom) pattern. A bit less volume may be observed on the next surge with very low volume on the final surge. Finally, volume should increase on a break of the neckline, which may be drawn by connecting the troughs (on a top) or the peaks (on a bottom). The minimum price movement on the break is thought to be equal to the maximum vertical height of the pattern. (This

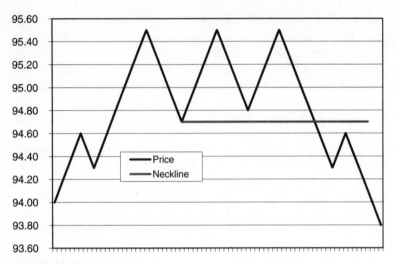

EXHIBIT 11.9   Triple Top

is consistent with the idea that the larger the pattern, the greater the subsequent price movement.) See Exhibit 11.9.

The double top or bottom is a very common kind of reversal. It is similar to the triple reversal except, as suggested by its name, it is characterized by only two roughly equal peaks (in a top) or troughs (in a bottom). In general, you expect volume to be a bit lighter on the second peak or trough relative to the first peak or trough. Subsequently, the market may break through the support or resistance (in a bull and bear market, respectively). Then, the market may break below (above) the trough (peak) formed between the two peaks (troughs). These breaks should be on increased volume to confirm the reversal. See Exhibit 11.10 for a double top.

A rounded bottom is a pattern characterized by low volatility and relatively long duration. These features are more characteristic of a bottom pattern than a topping pattern, however. As such, this rounded reversal formation is generally thought of as typical of the reversal of a bear rather than a bull trend. Volume and volatility fall off while the market is in this pattern. While the market is trading in a rounding bottom, it is essentially being "lulled to sleep" over an extended period of time. Little or no fundamental information may be released during this period.

Subsequently, the market break is accompanied by a burst of volume and a flurry of activity. This volume is said to be "stored up" during the lull. Often this break is the result of new fundamental information that becomes known in the marketplace. It is difficult to trade a rounding

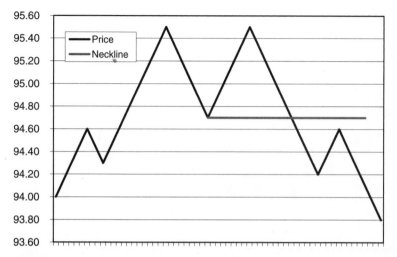

EXHIBIT 11.10   Double Top

bottom because there is generally little indication with respect to when the market will break. Nor is there any indication with respect to the magnitude of that break.

A rounding pattern is much more common in the "traditional" futures markets (grains, livestock, metals) relative to the financial markets. This may be attributed to the fact that fundamental news that impacts the agricultural markets, for example, is not released with the same frequency as is news that impacts the financials. See Exhibit 11.11 for a rounding bottom.

Almost every day a news release regarding some fundamental measure of economic activity, inflation, or government fiscal or monetary policy hits the financial markets. But soybean crop reports, for example, are not made known with the same kind of frequency even in the growing season. In the winter months, many agricultural markets can become quite inactive. Thus, the possibility of a rounding pattern with low volume and volatility over an extended period of time becomes quite possible. If the rounded bottom is more typical of a "traditional" futures market than a financial futures market, a "V" formation is more typical of a financial rather than a traditional market. In this and in other respects, the V, or spike pattern, is the antithesis of the rounding bottom.

A V, or spike, pattern more commonly occurs at a top than a bottom. It is characterized by high volatility over an extremely short period of time. Because the reversal occurs so sharply, it is often referred to as a "V" or, to be more precise, an inverted "V" formation. In fact, the pattern may begin and end within the course of a single day. This single day is sometimes

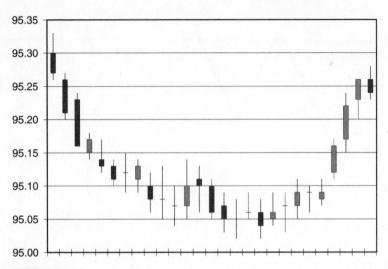

EXHIBIT 11.11 Rounding Bottom

referred to as the "key reversal day." A great deal of volume and volatility is realized on a key reversal day. A key reversal often results in a limit movement. Generally, the market reaches a new high on the key day followed by a sudden decline, often as a result of new fundamental news. The market may close at or near the low of the day that extends below the low for the previous day or two. See Exhibit 11.12 for a spike or V top.

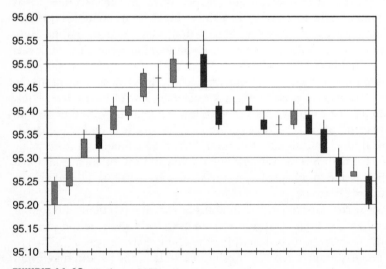

EXHIBIT 11.12 Spike or V Top

Like the rounded bottom, there is little or no warning before the reversal takes place so it is difficult to trade profitably. But sometimes, there are early warning signs. Market gaps are reasonably commonplace before and after key reversal days. A market gap is an area on the chart where no trading takes place. If you see the market gap upward on light volume, this may portend a subsequent reversal. Sometimes, the market gaps down on heavy volume subsequent to a key reversal. In that case, the formation may be referred to as an "island reversal." We say more about gaps later in this text.

Another sign of a possible reversal may be extremely high open interest. Growth in open interest in a volatile market may be unsustainable. In the long term, volume tends to rise and open interest falls in a volatile market environment. The reason is intuitive: Opportunities are frequently available in a volatile market, and you need not hold positions overnight to take advantage of it. When the market is trending upward on high volatility with growing open interest, any "crack" in those long positions may result in a panic sell situation. That is, if a significant number of the longs start to "take profits" by selling, others may follow, accelerating the decline.

Consolidation Patterns

A consolidation pattern represents an interruption of a trend. The market trades sideways for a while before it can continue in its bullish or bearish pattern. A consolidation pattern occurs when the market trades in a neutral holding pattern for a limited period of time before resuming the direction in which it was trending before entering the pattern. There are a number of common consolidation patterns including (1) pennants and flags; (2) symmetrical, ascending, descending, or expanding triangles; (3) wedge or diagonal triangle; and (4) sideways channel.

The pennant or flag is a very common consolidation pattern, as illustrated in Exhibit 11.13. Essentially, it is an indication of a market that has moved too far too fast. Market participants may be tempted to take some profits, to rethink their strategies, to regroup before continuing to trade aggressively.

A pennant differs from a flag in that the flag is more rectangular and the pennant more closely resembles a triangular pattern. Both patterns tend to slant or point away from the general market direction. If the market is generally bullish, for example, a flag or pennant will trend in a bearish direction. If the market is generally bearish, the flag or pennant will trend in a bullish direction.

But this trend against the market direction tends to be short lived. Flags and pennants are generally completed within two to three weeks or less

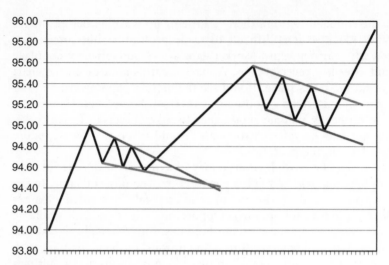

EXHIBIT 11.13   Pennant and Flag

from the time that the pullback begins. Subsequently, these patterns are thought to be very reliable in the sense that they almost invariably result in a continuation of the prior market trend. One old market saying is "Flags and pennants fly at half-mast." This suggests that flags and pennants may be observed about midway in a major market movement. But this way of thinking may be incompatible with Elliott wave theory.

Elliott wave theory suggests that the market may ratchet up in a five wave pattern including three "impulse" waves (waves 1, 3, and 5) with two intervening "corrective" waves (waves 2 and 4). If waves 2 and 4 take the form of a flag or a pennant, then it is clear that these patterns cannot "fly at half-mast." But what if the second wave "b" of the following three-step corrective phase (a, b, and c) takes the form of a flag or pennant? Under those circumstances, the flag or pennant may in fact "fly at half-mast."

Triangles are very similar in shape to pennants. Yet they differ in a number of key respects. Foremost among these differences is that a triangle is generally thought of as a longer-term consolidation pattern, a pattern that may take several different, yet similar, forms. A triangle is characterized by converging support and resistance levels that meet at a point referred to as the "apex." But this triangle may take the shape of a symmetrical triangle, ascending triangle, or descending triangle.

A *symmetrical* triangle is characterized by an upward sloping support trendline coupled with a downward sloping resistance trendline, as seen in Exhibit 11.14. An *ascending triangle*, as illustrated in Exhibit 11.15, is

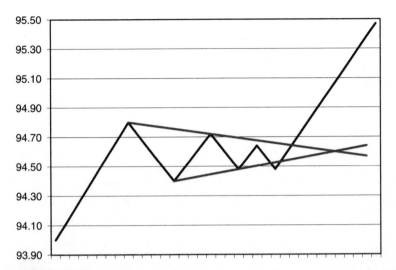

EXHIBIT 11.14 Symmetrical Triangle

characterized by a flat resistance trendline and an upwardly sloping support level. Finally, a *descending triangle* is characterized by a flat support trendline and a downwardly sloping resistance level, as illustrated in Exhibit 11.16. Despite the somewhat different inclinations associated with these three kinds of triangles, they all share some common characteristics.

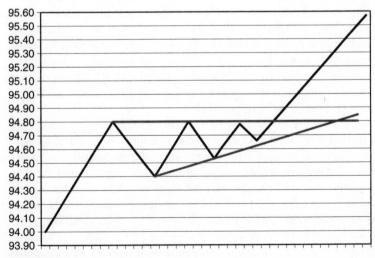

EXHIBIT 11.15 Ascending Triangle

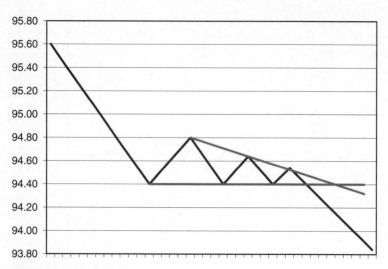

EXHIBIT 11.16 Descending Triangle

Volume and volatility, for example, are expected to decline as you trade into any of these three triangular formations. Subsequently, the triangle is concluded with a sharp, sudden breakout as the market begins, once again, to trend.

But the direction in which this breakout may occur is unknown. Triangles are generally thought of as consolidation patterns. As such, it is believed that triangles are most likely to result in a continuation of the trend that had been established before the formation of the triangle. Sometimes triangles result in a reversal rather than a continuation of the trend. Many analysts would attach perhaps a two-thirds probability to the possibility of a continuation with a one-third probability to the possibility of a subsequent reversal. Many analysts would attach probability a bit greater than two-thirds to an upward or downward break on the conclusion of an ascending or descending triangle, respectively.

Triangles are generally thought of as rather longer-term patterns. By this we mean that a triangle may continue for perhaps upward of two to three weeks. What market conditions may portend a breakout? Technical analysts often measure a triangle horizontally from the beginning of the formation out to the apex (where the support and resistance trendlines converge). The breakout is believed to be likely to occur somewhere between the halfway point and three-quarters of the way to the apex. Elliott wave theory provides an even more complete description of the nature of a triangle. According to Elliott, a triangle is composed of five waves so let us refer to these waves as A, B, C, D, and E. Thus, one might start anticipating a breakout as the market trends into the one-half to three-quarters to the apex area and as the market completes a fifth wave within the triangle.

Because the market is essentially neutral while trading in a triangle, traders may prefer to apply neutral option trading strategies (short straddles, short strangles). Unfortunately, it is only when three legs (A, B, and C) and four points are formed that one may identify a triangle. One cannot identify a triangle without four points to form converging support and resistance levels. By the time four points are formed and the triangle identified, the triangle may be close to achieving a breakout. Thus, it may be risky to sell straddles and strangles at this point. But when a breakout is imminent, many traders prefer to buy straddles and strangles in anticipation of a big market break.

Similar to the reversal patterns just discussed, the triangle provides an indication with respect to the size of the movement upon a breakout. By measuring the vertical height of the triangle at its widest point (at the inception of leg A), you can estimate the minimum expected movement on the break. Sometimes, however, the market does not break out at all. If the market drifts past the three-quarters of the way point or the apex itself, many analysts believe that the market will continue to drift indeterminately.

Sometimes, the triangle takes on a fourth, most unusual form as an expanding triangle. An expanding triangle looks like a symmetrical triangle with the exception that it is backward. That is, support and resistance trendlines expand rather than converge to an apex. The expanding triangle, like in Exhibit 11.17, is unlike most of the reversal and consolidation

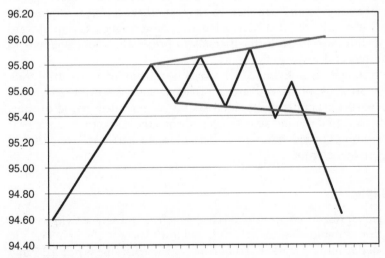

EXHIBIT 11.17   Expanding Triangle

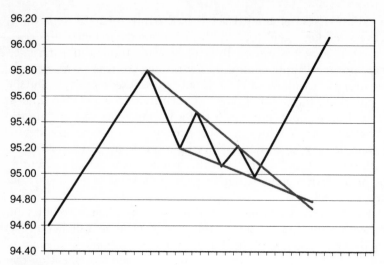

EXHIBIT 11.18   Wedge

patterns considered thus far in the sense that it is accompanied by generally increasing, rather than decreasing, volume and volatility. This formation is extremely difficult to trade because it is characteristic of a market that is desperately searching without success for direction. There is no really reliable way of identifying the prospects for an upward or a downward break.

The wedge, like in Exhibit 11.18, strongly resembles a triangle in terms of its shape with one notable exception. The wedge generally slants against the general market trend quite sharply. In most other aspects, it is quite like a triangle. It may be thought of as a longer-term formation taking upward of two to three weeks to form. It tends to break out about one-half to three-quarters of the way to the apex.

The rectangle, as in Exhibit 11.19, may be thought of as a neutral trading range. Strong support and strong resistance are evident, which means that the market generally drifts sideways for an extended period of time. Generally increased trading activity occurs when the market is trading near either the support or resistance levels. These levels are used to establish new positions and take profits.

Price Gaps

A price gap represents an area on the chart where no trading activity occurs. Assume, for example, that today's high and low was at 95.36 and 95.28 in the Eurodollar futures market. Tomorrow, the market opens at 95.25 and continues to trend downward. The area between 95.25 and 95.28

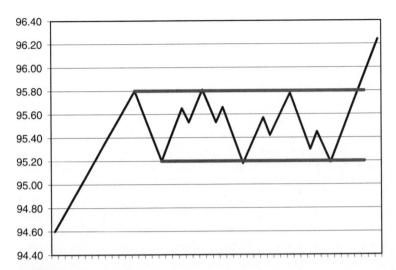

EXHIBIT 11.19 Rectangle

represents a price gap. A *gap* represents an area on a chart characterized by an absence of any trading activity. A gap may have a great deal of significance or it may be essentially meaningless. As such, one may identify two basic kinds of gaps: pattern and nonpattern gaps.

A *nonpattern gap* is sometimes referred to as a "common gap." This kind of gap may appear often in an illiquid or thinly traded market or when the market is drifting along in a rectangular pattern with no clear market direction. It is characterized by little interest and low volume. From a predictive standpoint, the best advice is simply to discount a nonpattern gap. It usually provides little indication about the strength or weakness of a market trend. In fact, it may appear frequently in a basically trendless market. As such, a common gap is often *filled*. That is, the market will subsequently trade within that area in which the gap was observed.

Pattern gaps are altogether different. A *pattern gap* is generally suggestive of subsequent market movements. Pattern gaps usually occur in very active, liquid markets, often when these active markets are experiencing a great deal of volatility. There are three types of pattern gaps: the breakaway, the runaway, and the exhaustion gap.

The *breakaway gap* signals the completion of a prior trend and the commencement of a new market trend. It is likely to occur early in the initial stages of a market movement in the so-called accumulation phase of a market trend. The breakaway gap may occur suddenly with little or no warning, often on the release of explosive fundamental market news. The breakaway gap is not filled. (If it is subsequently filled, then it could not have been a breakaway gap in the first place!) The breakaway gap is characterized by a sudden surge of volume and high volatility. The stronger the volume on the break (particularly on a movement to the upside), the stronger the subsequent market movement.

This gap may be difficult to trade because the market may move dramatically on the initial surge. Unless traders are extremely astute, in fact, they may have no opportunity to establish a position prior to the gapping movement. Because this initial surge may be extremely strong, the market often needs to consolidate before continuing onward. This may discourage traders from taking a position in anticipation of subsequent movement in the direction of the gapping surge. See Exhibit 11.20.

The *runaway gap* generally occurs later in the sequence of events that witness a market movement unfolding. It is generally thought to mark the midway point of a major market movement. Like the breakaway gap, it is characterized by heavy volume. In fact volume may be even heavier on a runaway gap than a breakaway gap. This is intuitive when you consider the phase of the trend in which a runaway gap may occur.

A runaway gap observed about midway into a major market movement may be realized in the so-called technical trend following phase of the market. The technical trend following phase generally enjoys broader participation and therefore may be much stronger than the initial accumulation phase. This suggests that the runaway gap may be very strong.

The *exhaustion gap* is generally characterized by weak volume and portends a subsequent market reversal or at least a consolidation. An

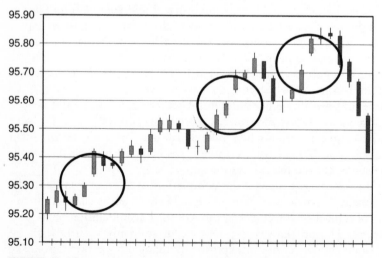

EXHIBIT 11.20   Breakaway, Runaway, and Exhaustion Gaps

exhaustion gap represents the last gasping movement in a major trend. But be careful insofar as an exhaustion gap does not necessarily mean you should reverse your position. It may suggest, however, that you adopt a less aggressive posture and be poised to liquidate that position when clearer reversal signals appear.

Actually, gaps may have become rather difficult to identify in today's market environment that is characterized by near 24-hour per day trading in many markets. Where there is near continuous trading of particular markets, of course, there tends to be little opportunity for gaps to form overnight. Thus, the only gaps that might be observed would tend to be as a result of the release of economic news that exerts a major impact on market prices. In other words, gaps may be more relevant in today's marketplace than they were in years past when trading may have been confined to the daylight business hours in the region where the trading venue was located.

ELLIOTT WAVE THEORY

Ralph Nelson Elliott completed his major works in the 1930s. Nonetheless, Elliott's wave theory represents one of the most influential schools of thought affecting the marketplace today. Elliott's influence has been felt quite keenly since the late 1970s when Robert Prechter, perhaps the best known and leading advocate of Elliott's theory, reintroduced the subject with his book *Elliott Wave Principle: Key to Market Behavior*. In the most fundamental sense, Elliott wave theory is based on three elements: patterns, ratios, and time. Far and away the most significant of these three elements is pattern.

Fives and Threes

The fundamental premise (as indicated earlier) is that the market moves in the direction of the overall trend in a series of five waves followed by three waves that fluctuate against the general trend. Waves 1, 3, and 5 fluctuate with the trend and are referred to as "impulse waves." Waves 2 and 4 represent pullbacks from the trend and are referred to as "corrective waves." The subsequent three-wave correction denoted with a, b, and c represents a correction of the prior five-wave trend. Because the fives are denoted with numbers and the threes denoted with letters, these phases are referred to as the numbered and lettered phases.

But Elliott indicates there are trends within the trend. For example, impulse wave 1 followed by a subsequent corrective wave 2 breaks down into fives and threes of one lesser degree. These waves break down into even smaller patterns of fives and threes of yet one lesser degree.

EXHIBIT 11.21 Labeling Waves

	5s with Trend	3s vs. Trend
Supercycle	(I) (II) (III) (IV) (V)	(A) (B) (C)
Cycle	I II III IV V	A B C
Primary	① ② ③ ④ ⑤	(a) (b) (c)
Intermediate	(1) (2) (3) (4) (5)	(a) (b) (c)
Minor	1 2 3 4 5	a b c
Minute	i ii iii iv v	- - -

As discussed earlier, Elliott categorized trends on the basis of general duration. In addition to the primary, secondary, and minor trends that Dow identified, Elliott referred to trends of smaller degree including the minute, minuette, and subminuette and trends of a longer degree including the cycle, supercycle, and grand supercycle. Prechter developed a notation system that is commonly used to reference these trends, summarized in the accompanying table. The grand supercycle is of such extremely long duration that it is considered to be of "no practical significance" by Prechter and is not labeled. Similarly, Prechter leaves the labeling of the minuette and subminuette to the imagination of his readers.

To some, Elliott's ideas may appear to be unfounded. But the basis of Elliott's thoughts is the Fibonacci number series. Note that 5 and 3 are both Fibonacci numbers in Exhibit 11.21. If you add them together, the resulting figure 8 is also a Fibonacci number. When you break a series of fives and threes down into fives and threes of one lesser degree, the resulting figure 34 is also a Fibonacci number.

Pursuant to this theme, Elliott also believed that major reversal days in the market may be predicted by counting the number of days forward from the last previous major reversal. Pay particular attention to Fibonacci numbers. The next day on which a significant reversal day may occur should fall on a Fibonacci number. See Exhibit 11.22.

Variations on an Impulse Wave

Fives and threes represent the normally expected pattern. But Elliott's theories are flexible to the extent that they propose a basic theme and some possible variations on the theme. Let us consider the alternative ways in which impulse waves (waves 1, 3, and 5) may form, in particular extensions, wedges, and failures.

As a general rule, impulse waves tend to be of approximately equal size. (Size can be measured by the vertical height or price movement of a pattern

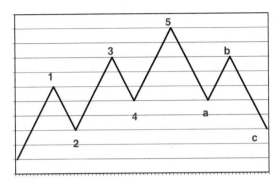

EXHIBIT 11.22   Elliott's 5's and 3's

and in terms of its horizontal width or duration.) This is the "rule of wave equality." But sometimes, even often, one of the impulse waves is larger in terms of its height and width than the other two approximately equal impulse waves. This represents *wave extensions*, which tend to break down into a series of five smaller waves. Extensions are thought to be most likely to occur during the third impulse wave. This is intuitive to the extent that this wave may represent the "technical trend following" phase of the market, that is, the wave that surges forth on the weight of a great deal of technical market participation.

Because wave 3 is generally the strongest and most likely to extend, Elliott suggests that although wave 3 is often the longest, it is never the shortest of the three impulse waves. Because wave 3 is so strong, the downward movement on the subsequent corrective wave 4 should generally not cover the same territory as wave 1 did. That is, waves 1 and 4 should not typically overlap. See Exhibit 11.23.

In fact, Elliott's "depth of corrective waves" hypothesis suggests that corrections, particularly fourth wave corrections, tend to stop within the span of movement of the previous fourth wave movement of one lesser degree. In other words, a fourth wave correction of primary degree should cease before it hits the trough established by the fourth wave movement of intermediate degree within the third impulse wave.

The wave least likely to extend is the first impulse wave. This is due to the fact that the first impulse wave generally represents the weakest impulse movement. The subsequent corrective wave number 2 may, in fact, give back almost all of the movement on impulse wave number 1. Wave 5 is the second most likely or second least likely (depending on your perspective) wave to extend. Elliott developed some interesting guidelines that may be useful for forecasting how market movements may unfold subsequent to a fifth wave extension. In particular, a fifth wave extension is said to be retraced twice.

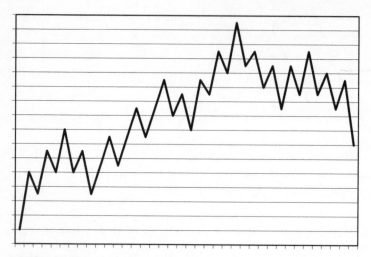

EXHIBIT 11.23 Trends with the Trend

Assume you have reached a market top at the completion of the fifth wave of the fifth wave. The market is now expected to begin a three-wave corrective phase. The first corrective wave is expected to fall or retrace to the beginning of the extension. The second corrective wave b is thereupon expected to advance to the previously established market top or beyond before falling off as wave c is established. As such, the top of the fifth-wave extension cannot represent the completion of the upswing as the market is likely to break down and then rally to the same level or possibly to a new high. As discussed later, this lettered phase takes the form of an irregular correction. See Exhibit 11.24.

As indicated earlier, impulse waves are normally expected to be approximately equal in magnitude (the magnitude of a movement may be measured in terms of volatility or vertical height and time or horizontal width). An extended wave is of greater magnitude than the two nonextending waves. In particular, it may be expected to be about 1.618 times greater in vertical height than the nonextending waves. (The number 1.618 comes from the Fibonacci number series.)

A "wedge" or "diagonal triangle" may be mistaken for an extension because this triangle is generally played out in a series of five waves. But unlike a fifth-wave extension, this wedge may rise on reduced volume and volatility. In other words, the market is becoming exhausted. It has traveled a bit too sharply and must display a bit of a consolidative movement. Similar to a triangular correction (discussed later, this wedge breaks down into a 3-3-3-3-3 pattern or a series of five waves that break down into three smaller waves each.

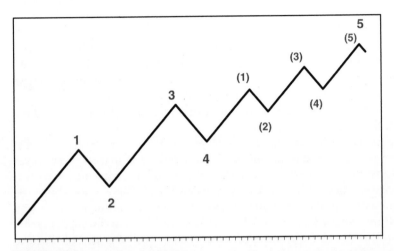

EXHIBIT 11.24 Extended Fifth Wave

A *failure* represents an instance where the fifth impulse wave fails to clear the top of the third impulse wave. Many analysts may mistake this formation as a lettered corrective phase. But the fourth corrective wave and the subsequent fifth wave failure may be distinguished from the beginning of an a-b-c corrective phase. The distinction lies in the fact that this fifth impulse wave may break down into a series of five waves of smaller degree. It is, therefore, distinguished from wave b of an a-b-c correction in that wave B should break down into three, rather than five, smaller waves. See Exhibit 11.25.

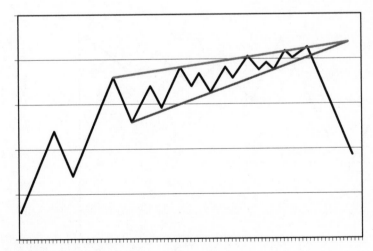

EXHIBIT 11.25 Diagonal Triangle or Wedge

Corrective Waves

Just as impulse waves often take on alternative forms apart from the norm, the subsequent a-b-c lettered phase often takes on alternative forms as well. Let's illustrate the so-called normal correction and its variations. These variations may be referred to as "flats," "triangles," "double threes" and "triple threes." These issues are complicated further by the fact that there are several variations on the variations.

The normal a-b-c correction is sometimes referred to by its technical term, the *zigzag*. The normal zigzag is characterized in that its three waves break down into smaller waves with five, three, and five movements, respectively. Notice that wave b of the normal zigzag does not rally above the peak established at the beginning of wave a (or the top of the previous fifth wave). Elliott suggests that, as a general rule, the vertical distance traveled by wave b tends to be about 61.8% of the vertical distance of wave a. Waves a and c tend to be of about equal magnitude. See Exhibit 11.26.

This means that the zigzag carries the market into an area well below the top established at the beginning of wave a. But other kinds of corrections such as the flats cannot be expected to carry the market into quite so low areas. Whereas the zigzag is characterized as a 5-3-5 formation, the flat is characterized as a 3-3-5 formation (i.e., three waves that break down into smaller movements of three, three, and five waves, respectively). See Exhibit 11.27.

This breakdown suggests strength in the previous market trend. Strength is indicated in the fact that the first wave breaks down into only

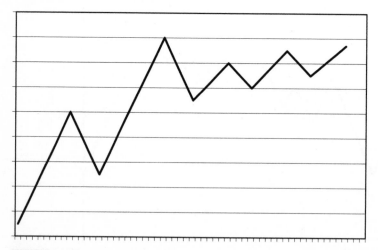

EXHIBIT 11.26   Fifth Wave Failure

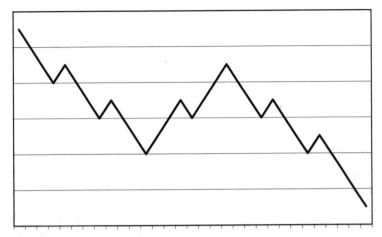

EXHIBIT 11.27 Zigzag Correction

three, rather than five, waves. The market's downward force during wave a is insufficient to create five waves.

In a normal flat, the subsequent upward wave b may fully retrace the movement of wave a (i.e., the market may match its previous high established at the beginning of wave a or the conclusion of wave 5). Wave c thereupon drives the market to a point that is below the low established at the conclusion of wave a. But in addition to the normal flat, there are three other types of flats: the "irregular flat no. 1," "irregular flat no. 2," and the so-called running correction. See Exhibit 11.28.

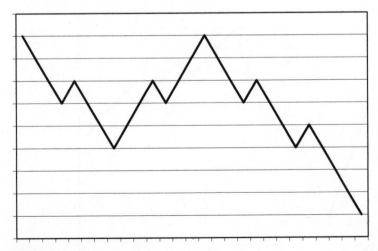

EXHIBIT 11.28 Normal Flat Correction

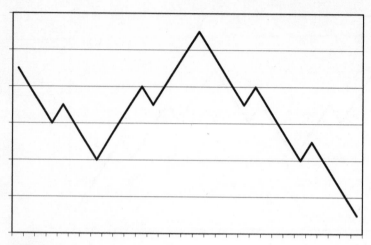

EXHIBIT 11.29   Irregular Flat No. 1

Pursuant to the irregular flat number 1, as in Exhibit 11.29, the market rallies not only to meet, but to exceed, the highs established at the beginning of wave a or the conclusion of wave 5. The subsequent third wave c falls below the low established at the conclusion of wave a. The irregular flat number 1 indicates great strength insofar as wave b rallies over the previously established highs. But it also indicates volatility as the market trades in successively wider ranges with each wave.

Irregular flat number 2 likewise in Exhibit 11.30 shows strength but perhaps not such great strength as in irregular flat number 1. This is

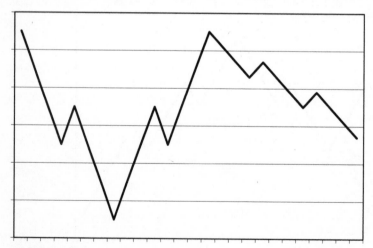

EXHIBIT 11.30   Irregular Flat No. 2

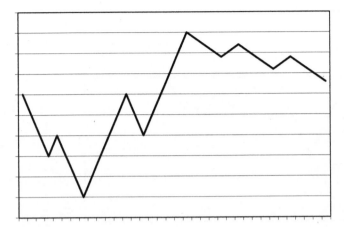

EXHIBIT 11.31 Running Correction

observed insofar as wave b meets but does not typically exceed the top established at the beginning of wave a. The subsequent fifth wave c pushes the market down but not so far as to break the lows established at the bottom of wave a. In other words, the irregular flat number 2 shows strength, but volatility is falling rather than rising.

Finally, a *running correction*, as in Exhibit 11.31, is indicative of very great strength in the market. This is indicated in the fact that a running correction positively carries the market into new higher ground. In fact, wave c often concludes at a price level in excess of the top established at the beginning of wave a or conclusion of wave 5.

In addition to zigzags and flats, corrective phases may take on the form of a triangle. Like the flat, a triangle can take on a number of forms (discussed in the context of traditional bar charting theory earlier). These forms include the ascending, descending, symmetrical, and expanding triangles. See Exhibits 11.32 to 11.35.

Elliott's interpretations of these triangles are quite similar to traditional interpretations discussed earlier (i.e., triangles are continuation or corrective patterns). Ascending, descending, and symmetrical triangles generally tend to be accompanied by falling volatility and volume, whereas expanding triangles are accompanied by rising volatility and volume.

The break at the conclusion of an ascending, descending, or symmetrical triangle is expected to be roughly equivalent to the width of the triangle at its widest point. Unlike traditional bar charting theory, Elliott's triangles are much more closely defined in terms of their pattern. All of these triangles are expected to break down into five waves (let's refer to these five as waves a, b, c, d, and e).

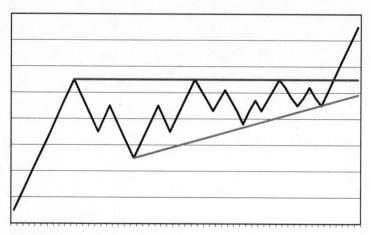

EXHIBIT 11.32   Ascending Triangle

These five waves in turn break down into three smaller waves. In the ascending, descending, and symmetrical triangles, the vertical height of each successive wave is expected to represent approximately 61.8% of the prior wave.

Finally, Elliott indicates that a three-stage corrective phase may take on a more complex or compound form such as a "double 3" or a "triple 3." These formations may be thought of as two or three zigzags or flats strung together. They are strung together by a three-step upswing referred to as "x." These formations indicate that the market needs an extended period of

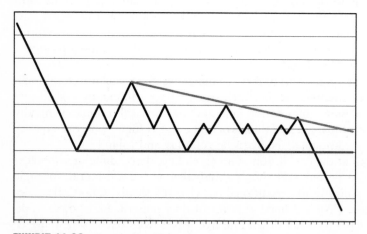

EXHIBIT 11.33   Descending Triangle

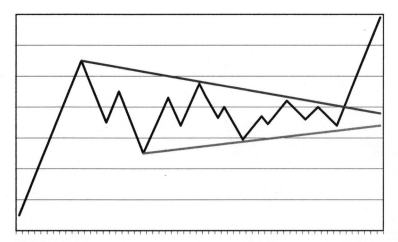

EXHIBIT 11.34 Symmetrical Triangle

time to correct itself. Insofar as this formation is mostly horizontal, a double or triple three is a market that is searching for direction.

Look for these patterns to be composed of different types of corrective movements. For example, a double three may be composed of a zigzag and some type of flat. Or a triple three may be composed of a zigzag and two different kinds of flats. Elliott believed that patterns do not repeat themselves successively. If the last correction (in wave 2 of a five-step rally, for example) was a flat, expect the next correction (wave 4) to represent

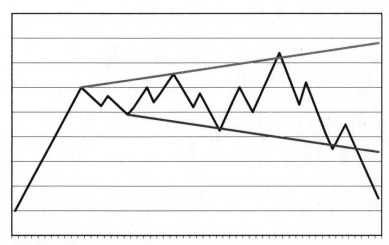

EXHIBIT 11.35 Expanding Triangle

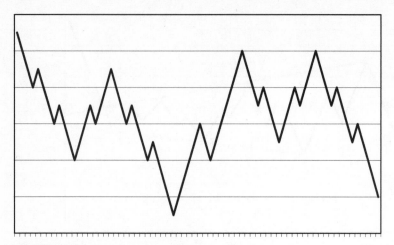

EXHIBIT 11.36   Double Threes: Zigzag and Flat

something other than a flat such as a zigzag or triangle. This "rule of alternation" applies with equal respect to the "threes" that make up a double or triple three in the lettered phase of a market movement as well as to the corrective waves in the numbered phase of the market.

As suggested earlier, Elliott believed that the strength of a trend may be assessed not so much by watching the trend itself but by studying corrective patterns within the trend. The various corrective patterns discussed here all give rise to an interpretation with respect to the strength of the trend within the market.

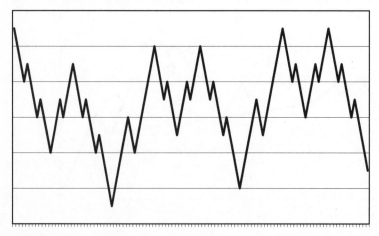

EXHIBIT 11.37   Triple Threes: Zigzag, Flat, and Zigzag

For example, a zigzag is indicative of normal strength in the market. The normal and the irregular flats indicate more strength in the market. The running correction is indicative of very great strength. Ascending, descending, and symmetrical triangles indicate more strength than does the zigzag, culminating in a swift but relatively short-lived breakout. Double and triple threes show strength but of a tentative nature.

INTRADAY TRADING TECHNIQUES

Many analysts find that the charting techniques we have discussed can be extremely useful for the purposes of interday trading. On an intraday basis (within the same day), these techniques may be somewhat less useful. Some analysts, for example, do not make use of intraday charts. If we believe that technical analysis works because it represents a "self-fulfilling prophecy," then it would be unwise to rely on charting techniques that are not commonly referenced. As a result, analysts often rely on other methods for purposes of intraday trading. Some of these classic methods discussed here include point and figure charting and "pivot point" analysis.

Point and Figure Charting

Point and figure charting is a frequently referenced charting technique that may be used to plot price fluctuations on an inter- or intraday basis. For our purposes, however, we restrict our consideration to intraday data. Point and figure charts are characterized by a series of "Xs" and "Os" arranged in columns. "Xs" represent price advances and "Os" represent price declines.

Point and figure charts are considered to be useful because, if properly constructed, they "filter out" spurious price fluctuations. Because of the filtering mechanism intrinsic to the chart, it does not provide full information with respect to all (or at least small) fluctuations. Nor does it provide any information with respect to the time at which particular fluctuations took place.

Let's consider how one might construct a point and figure chart and how to interpret the chart. One begins a point and figure chart with a piece of graph paper showing a series of columns and rows. The next and most critical step is to identify one's box size and reversal criterion.

The *box size* refers to the number of ticks represented by each row. You may identify a box size from a single tick upward. Assume that you were to plot T-note futures prices. One might designate a 2-tick box size (e.g., each box represents 2/32nds or $62.50). The reversal criterion refers to the number of boxes by which the market must reverse before a reversal is recognized and the chart changes from "Xs" to "Os" or vice versa. That is, the reversal criterion provides the filtering mechanism by which one discounts relatively small breaks in the trend. It is most common to designate a three-box reversal criterion. If the box size is designated as two ticks, this suggests that the market must reverse itself by a full six ticks before such a reversal is recognized.

How does one construct a point and figure chart? Begin by placing a dot in the box corresponding to the first price observed. Assume that the market opens at 94-00 and begins to rally. As the market rallies in two-tick increments, fill in successively higher boxes. But only if the market rallies by a full two-tick box! Thus, if prices rise to 104-07, the highest box that is filled corresponds to 104-06. Only if the market rallies to 104-08 is the next highest box filled. Does a subsequent decline to 104-01 constitute a reversal? No! Only if prices fall a full six ticks or three boxes off the highest box filled in at 104-06 is a reversal recognized.

Now assume the market falls all the way to 103-24. When the market hits 104-00, you move one column to the right and begin filling in "Os" down to 103-24. A subsequent rally back to 103-30 covers a full three boxes, and therefore you move one column to the right and fill in a series of "Xs" up to 103-30. Another reversal takes the market in our example down to 103-22, indicated by a column of "Os." But the subsequent rally to 103-25 does not cover three full boxes. The market settles back to 103-22, but the rally to 104-05 constitutes a reversal. As soon as the market hit 103-28 on the way up, you move one column to the right and begin filling in "Xs."

Constructing a Point and Figure Chart

104-00 → 104-07 → 104-01 → 104-06 → 103-24 →
103-30 → 103-22 → 103-25 → 103-22 → 104-05 →

104-08				
104-06	X			
104-04	X	O		X
104-02	X	O		X
104-00		O		X
103-30		O	X	X
103-28		O	X	O	X
103-26		O	X	O	X
103-24		O		O	X
103-22				O
103-20				

The simplest way of using a point and figure chart is to buy whenever you begin a new column of "Xs." Cover your longs and take a short position on a new column of "Os." As such, it is tremendously important to identify a workable box size and reversal criterion. This kind of trading system may work if the market exhibits clear trending tendencies. If, however, the market is quite choppy and reverses frequently, the system will result in a series of losses, albeit relatively modest losses on any given trade.

Although the point and figure chart is sometimes used as indicated above, traders sometimes look for patterns in the charts just as you would look for patterns in a bar chart. Because this method filters out spurious information automatically, patterns sometimes stand out much more clearly in a point and figure chart than in a bar chart.

Let's consider some of the more commonly recognized patterns. You will note that many of these point and figure patterns are reminiscent of the bar chart patterns discussed earlier. The patterns shown in the accompanying diagrams are restricted to buy signals. Sell signals may be generated by similar formations that are simply reversed (i.e., invert these diagrams by rotating along a horizontal axis).

Break of Triple Top   Ascending Triple Top

```
                                        X
                                        X
                    X                   X
                    X                   X
                    X           X       X
        X     X     X     X     X  O    X
  O  X  O  X  O  X  O  X  O  X  O  X
  O  X  O  X  O  X  O  X  O  X  O
  O     O     O     O     O  X
                             O
```

Symmetrical Triangle   Spread Triple Top

```
X                     X                     X
X  O                  X                     X
X  O  X               X                     X
X  O  X  O            X                     X
X  O  X  O  X  O  X  X     X                 X
X  O  X  O  X  O  X  X  O  X  O  X           X
X  O  X  O  X  O        X  O  X  O  X  O  X
X  O  X  O  X              O        O  X  O  X
O  X  O  X  O                       O        O
O  X  O  X
O  X  O
O  X
```

Once the market breaks, how far can it be expected to move? One may get an indication for the expected movement by counting the number of columns over which the pattern formed. Look for the vertical market movement to equal the horizontal movement while the pattern formed.

Ascending Triangle Bull Resistance

```
                                                                    X
                                    X                               X
                                    X                               X
                                    X                               X
X       X       X       X       X                                   X
X   O   X   O   X   O   X   O   X                               X    X
X   O   X   O   X   O   X   O   X                       X       X O  X
X   O   X   O   X   O   X   O                       X       X O X O  X
X   O   X   O   X   O   X           O   X       X O X O X O  X
X   O   X   O   X   O               O X O X O X O   O
X   O   X   O   X                   O X O X O
X   O   X   O                       O       O
X   O   X
X   O
X
```

Bear Resistance Catapult

```
X                                   X                               X
X   O   X                           X                               X
X   O   X   O                       X                       X       X
    O   X   O   X                   X                       X O     X
    O           O   X   O   X       X                       X O     X
                O   X   O   X   O   X   X                    X O     X
                O   X   O   X   O   X O X X         X        X O     X
                O       O           O X O X X O X O X O      X O
                                    O X O X X O X O X
                                    O X O X     O       O
                                    O X O
                                    O
```

Pivot Point Analysis

Pivot point analysis represents another technique that is frequently used on an intraday basis. This method allows one to identify potential levels of support or resistance. It relies on high, low, and closing price information from the preceding day. The central pivot may be calculated as the average of the high (H), low (L), and closing (C) price levels.

$$Pivot = (H + L + C) \div 3$$

Depending on whether the market is above or below this pivot, it may act as either a support or resistance level. Other potential areas of support or resistance may be found with similar measures. In particular, one may calculate the "1st support" and the "1st resistance" levels or the "2nd support" and "2nd resistance" levels. Look for support or resistance on the following day at these levels on the next trading day.

1st Support $= (2 \times Pivot) - H$

1st Resistance $= (2 \times Pivot) - L$

2nd Support $= Pivot - (H - L)$

2nd Resistance $= Pivot + (H - L)$

Example: On February 15, 2008, EuroFX futures for delivery in March 2008 settled at 1.4657 U.S. dollars per euro. The low for the day was posted at 1.4654, the high at 1.4695. The pivot points may be calculated as follows:

> 2nd Resistance $= 1.4710$
> 1st Resistance $= 1.4684$
> Pivot Point $= 1.4669$
> 1st Support $= 1.4643$
> 2nd Support $= 1.4628$

TREND-FOLLOWING SYSTEMS

Many (if not most) technical trading methods represent "trend-following" systems to one extent or another. In other words, they do not attempt to predict the advent of a new trend. Rather, they are intended to identify the existence of a trend and recommend action on the expectation of a continuation of the same. "Moving averages" represent some of the most common trend-following devices. Used in combination with oscillators, they provide some very interesting and potentially useful technical tools.

Moving Averages

A *moving average* (MA) represents an average market price over a recent time period. Moving averages are constructed to identify "the trend" by filtering or "smoothing out" unusual or temporary price aberrations. Two issues that must be addressed include how to calculate a MA and, once constructed, how to interpret the statistic.

On the first pass, one might assume there is a single straightforward method of calculating a moving average. In actuality, however, there are a number of very different means by which one may construct an MA. To calculate an MA, you must decide exactly what statistic you wish to average. For example, you may elect to take an average of a series of market opening prices, highs, lows, or closes. Some analysts prefer to take an average based on the midpoint of the high/low range or on the pivot, or the average, of the high, low, and closing prices. Most analysts, however, use the close or settlement prices.

There are also several different ways of calculating a moving average. These means include (1) a simple or arithmetic average, (2) a geometric average, (3) a weighted or linear-weighted average, and (4) an exponentially weighted average. Let's consider each method in turn along with its respective advantages and disadvantages.

An arithmetic average simply refers to the kind of average with which we are all very familiar: Take the summation of a series of prices (P) divided by the number of observations (n).

$$MA = \sum_{i=1}^{n} (P_i) \div n$$

Example   Consider the following data series and construct a simple average of the data:

i	Day	Price
1	Wednesday	96.10
2	Tuesday	96.00
3	Monday	95.90

$$MA = (96.10 + 96.00 + 95.90) \div 3$$
$$= 96.00$$

A geometric moving average means that you take the nth root of the multiplicative sum of the numbers:

$$MA = \left[\prod_{i=1}^{n} P_i \right]^{\frac{1}{n}}$$

Example   Find the geometric average of the number series just illustrated.

$$MA = (96.10 \times 96.00 \times 95.90)^{1/3}$$
$$= 95.99$$

As is apparent, a geometric average tends to be downwardly biased (i.e., it consistently tends to understate the arithmetic average). A weighted average is intended to accord greater emphasis to more recent, as opposed to less recent, observations. The rationale is simply that recent observations provide information that may be more relevant to forthcoming price movements than "stale" or old observations.

$$MA = \sum_{i=1}^{n} (W_i \times P_i) \div \sum_{i=1}^{n} W_i$$

The weights (W) in a scheme such as that illustrated above may be determined arbitrarily by the user.

Example   Let's arbitrarily establish weights of 10, 5, and 2 for the most recent and successively less recent observations.

i	Day	Price	Weight
1	Wednesday	96.10	10
2	Tuesday	96.00	5
3	Monday	95.90	2

Find the weighted moving average:

$$MA = [(10 \times 96.10) + (5 \times 96.00) + (2 \times 95.90)] \div (10 + 5 + 2)$$
$$= 96.05$$

A criticism of this method is that our weights are being established in a strictly arbitrary manner. Some analysts prefer to identify weights on a "linear" basis. This means that you weight the most recent price with a number corresponding to the number of observations (n). The next most recent observation is given a weight of n − 1; the second most recent observation is given a weight of n − 2, and so on.

Example   Find the linear moving average for the price series shown above. This means that you will weight these prices with 3, 2, and 1 as depicted below.

i	Day	Price	Weight
1	Wednesday	96.10	3
2	Tuesday	96.00	2
3	Monday	95.90	1

Find the linear-weighted moving average:

$$MA = [(3 \times 96.10) + (2 \times 96.00) + (1 \times 95.90)] \div (3 + 2 + 1)$$
$$= 96.03$$

Another weighting scheme is known as an exponentially weighted moving average. This method provides weights that are graduated on an exponential basis as shown next.

$$MA = \sum_{i=1}^{n} \left[(1-a)^i \times P_i \right] \div \sum_{i=1}^{n} (1-a)^i$$

Where $0 < a < 1$.

Example Find the exponentially weighted moving average for the price series just shown. Set "a" equal to 0.5. This means that you will weight these prices with 1, 0.5, and 0.25, respectively.

i	Day	Price	$(1-0.5)^i$
1	Wednesday	96.10	0.5
2	Tuesday	96.00	0.25
3	Monday	95.90	0.125

Find the exponentially weighted moving average:

$$MA = [(0.5 \times 96.10) + (0.25 \times 96.00) + (0.125 \times 95.90)] \div (0.5 + 0.25 + 0.125)$$
$$= 96.04$$

Once calculated, what do you do with a moving average? Let's explore three different systems that may be used to trigger buy or sell orders in the futures markets. These systems include a double crossover, a triple crossover, and a double crossover system with bands.

See Exhibit 11.38. A double crossover system is quite straightforward. Simply calculate two moving averages including a "fast" moving average

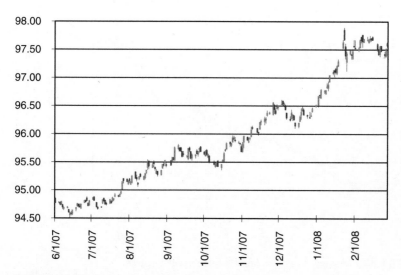

EXHIBIT 11.38 September 2008 Eurodollar Futures

MA(f) incorporating a relatively small number of observations and a "slow" moving average MA(s) incorporating a relatively large number of observations. A fast MA will be more reactive to recent market movements relative to a slow moving average that may tend to smooth out unusual or discrepant price movements. (The ultimate in "fast" moving averages is a one-day "mover.") How many observations should be used to construct a moving average? Enough observations such that the average is "representative" but not so many as to incorporate old stale data!

But a better answer is to calculate moving averages in such a way as to maximize your return given the trading system you wish to employ. You will only know this answer through the process of simulation over a historical time period. And, unfortunately, there is no guarantee that a particular system that produced good results over some past period will continue to produce profitable results. See Exhibit 11.39.

This system may trigger a buy or sell upon a "crossover." That is, when the fast MA crosses up over the slow MA, this may trigger the placement of a buy order (covering any existing short positions at the same time). Should the fast MA cross down below the slow MA, then put in a sell order, covering any existing long positions.

If MA(f) > MA(s) → Cover any shorts and buy.

If MA(f) < MA(s) → Cover any longs and sell.

EXHIBIT 11.39 Moving Averages: Sep-08 Eurodollar Futures

This represents a trend following system. If the market is trending, you may expect large profits. But if the market is generally directionless or choppy, you may expect to make a relatively large number of trades, many of which may result in small losses. That is, you will suffer from whipsaws.

Losses tend to be cut short to the extent that a sudden reversal may result in a crossover. But when the market is trending, the fast moving average may remain on the upside or the downside of the slow MA for a lengthy period of time. Thus, you tend to let your profits run. This is consistent with the old saying in the futures markets: "Let your profits run and cut your losses short."

The triple moving average is intended to provide the benefits of the double moving average system while minimizing losses as a result of whipsaw markets. It does so by attempting to identify buy and sell as well as neutral situations (where the best advice is to stay out of the futures market altogether). See Exhibit 11.40.

As its name implies, this system uses three different moving averages, including a fast average MA(f), an intermediate average MA(i), and a slow average MA(s). When the fast mover breaks above both the intermediate and slow mover, then buy futures. When the fast mover breaks below both the intermediate and the slow mover, then sell futures. When the fast moving average is between the slow and intermediate averages, stay on the sidelines.

If MA(f) > MA(i), MA(s) → Buy futures

If MA(f) < MA(i), MA(s) → Sell futures

If MA(f) between MA(i) and MA(s) → Cover any longs or shorts

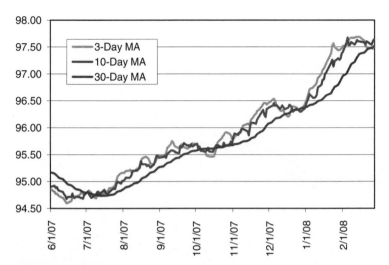

EXHIBIT 11.40   Moving Averages: Sep-08 Eurodollar Futures

Another way of attempting to minimize whipsaws and to take advantage of true trends is to use a variation of the double crossover system: a double crossover with "volatility bands." This means you will compare a fast moving average to a slow moving average plus or minus some "band." This band may be established at some fixed arbitrary amount. For example, take the slow moving average plus or minus 1 point.

Example   A moving average based on the last 30 days in the Eurodollar ("ED") futures market is at 95.34. Find an upper and lower band calculated as the 30-day MA plus or minus 15 ticks or 0.15. Obviously, the upper band equals 95.49 and the lower band equals 95.19.

Sometimes it is expressed as a percentage of the value of the slow moving average. For example, take the slow moving average plus or minus 2%.

Example   A moving average based on the last 30 days in the ED futures market is at 95.34. Find an upper and lower band calculated as the 30-day MA plus or minus 2% of the ED futures implied yield. These levels equal 95.43 on the upper side and 95.25 on the lower side. See Exhibit 11.41.

How can you use this system? The idea is to buy when the fast moving average crosses up over the upper band. Sell when the fast moving average crosses down below the lower band. Cover any longs or shorts and remain neutral if the fast moving average falls between the upper and lower bands.

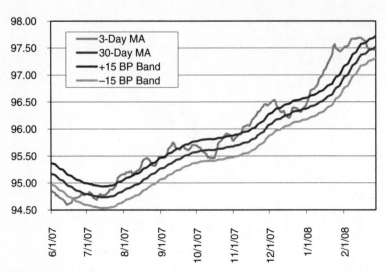

EXHIBIT 11.41 MAs with Bands: Sep-08 ED Futures

If MA(f) > MA(s) + band → Buy futures

If MA(f) < MA(s) − band → Sell futures

If MA(s) − band < MA(f) < MA(s) + band → Cover any longs or shorts.

Sometimes the system is used such that you cover any existing long position when the fast moving average crosses down below the slow moving average itself (rather than the slow moving average plus the band). And cover any existing short position when the fast moving average crosses up above the slow moving average (rather than the slow moving average less the band).

Which of these systems is best? Obviously, the answer to this question will vary from market to market. Moreover, different systems will produce different results over various time frames. The best answer is to simulate results using historical data and employ the system that seems to produce the most profitable and stable results over time.

Oscillators

Moving averages are quite useful in determining the direction of the trend. But sometimes, the trend moves "too far, too fast." If the market has rallied strongly, it may be overbought. If the market has been declining sharply, it may be oversold. In these cases, a consolidation, correction, or even a reversal becomes imminent. *Oscillators* represent statistics that may be used to identify these situations.

Oscillators may be used in conjunction with a way of thinking about the markets that is referred to as the school of "contrary opinion." This is the basic premise associated with contrary opinion: When everyone is bullish, then sell. The corollary when everyone is bearish is to buy. But this seems to contradict the idea that a trend, once in motion, tends to stay in motion. But let's consider two hypotheses that may explain the psychology of a trend in motion, in particular: market participants and the "strong hands" theory.

The three basic kinds of traders in the market are longs, shorts, and uncommitted. Assume the market is trending upward. To continue that trend, new participants must continue to enter the market on the long side. Likewise, new participants must continue to sell to sustain a bearish trend. In either case, these new long or short positions tend to drain the pool of uncommitted traders. When most or all of the uncommitted traders have committed themselves, there are no more traders to continue to push the market one way or the other. Finally, the bullish trend cannot be sustained and the market cracks. Or the bearish trend halts and the market rallies.

Further, let's consider which side of the market has the stronger position in a bullish or bearish trend. Assume that 90% of all market participants are bullish and that only 10% of the participants are bearish. This suggests that for every nine traders who are long, only a single trader is short (i.e., the shorts must have larger size positions than the longs).

Who has the stronger hand? If the shorts have been able to fade the market up so far, sustaining losses all the way up, they probably have the stronger hand. When the first of those longs decides to take his or her profit, the market cracks. Other longs, noticing that the market is falling, may start to take their profits as well. Soon, open interest starts to fall dramatically and the market falls quickly. Sometimes, the market may decline quickly in a panic sell situation.

How can you statistically assess whether the market is in an overbought or oversold condition? Let's review a variety of statistics such as momentum, double moving averages, and the relative strength index.

Momentum refers simply to the change in the price of the instrument in question (P) over some arbitrary time period. Momentum may represent a 1-day lag, a 2-day, 3-day, 5-, 10-, 30-day lag or any other period deemed appropriate.

$$\text{Momentum} = P_t - P_{t-i}, \text{ where } i = \text{days of the momentum lag}$$

Example Today's ED futures price is 94.88. Yesterday, the market was at 94.96. A one-day momentum may be calculated at positive eight ticks. Assume that the market was at 94.94 10 days ago. The 10-day momentum may be calculated at six ticks.

There is a tradeoff with respect to the lag. The longer the lag you select, the less the degree to which the statistic is unduly impacted by extraneous or spurious movements. The shorter the lag, the greater the degree to which the statistic is affected by fresh current data.

Does momentum exceed zero or fall short of zero? Is the market trending upward or downward? If momentum is above zero and rising, this suggests the market advance is accelerating. If momentum is above zero but flat, the market is rising at a stable rate. If momentum is above zero but falling, the market is rising at a declining rate. Likewise, acceleration or deceleration may be observed in a falling market. See Exhibit 11.42.

One of the unfortunate aspects about the use of the momentum statistic is that it tends to be choppy, particularly when using a short lag. Double moving averages tend to smooth out extraneous, choppy movements by comparing a fast moving average to a slow moving average.

$$\text{Double MA} = \text{MA(f)} - \text{MA(s)}$$

Example A three-day moving average of the ED futures price is quoted at 95.39. A 30-day moving average is quoted at 95.34. The 3/20 double moving average is quoted at positive 5 ticks. See Exhibit 11.43.

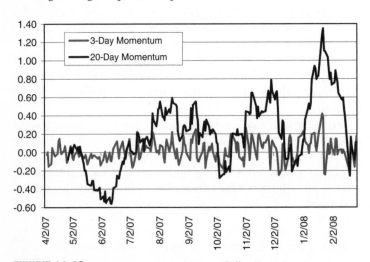

EXHIBIT 11.42 Momentum: Sep-08 Eurodollar Futures

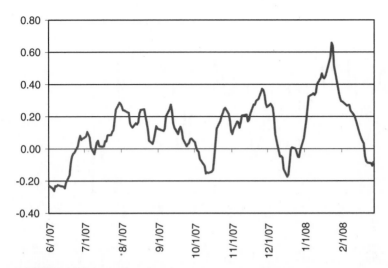

EXHIBIT 11.43   3-Day less 20-Day MA: Sep-08 ED Futures

The unfortunate aspect about the application of either a momentum or a double moving average statistic is that there is often difficulty in recognizing the danger zone, that is, how high must the statistic be in order to trigger an "overbought" signal? How low must the statistic be to trigger an "oversold" signal?

The relative strength index (RSI) was developed by a technician named Welles Wilder, and it is intended to provide a consistent overbought or oversold indicator. The statistic must range between 0 and 100. Wilder's original work suggested that when the statistic meets or exceeds 70, an overbought condition is indicated and the market may consolidate or reverse. Or if the statistic runs to 30 or below, an oversold condition is indicated. See Exhibit 11.44.

$$RSI = 100 - [100/(1 + Up/Down)]$$

Where: Up = Sum of price advances over past n days.
   Down = Sum of price declines over past n days.

Example   Find a nine-day RSI for Eurodollar futures given the data here. This RSI of 54.54 is relatively close to 50.00. As such, neither an overbought or oversold condition is indicated.

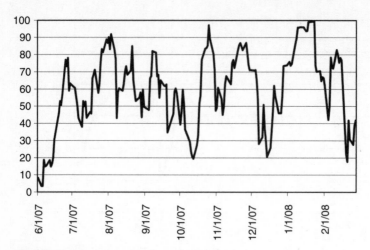

EXHIBIT 11.44   9-Day RSI Sep-08 ED Futures

Day	Price	Change
t	96.22	+0.02
t-1	96.20	+0.10
t-2	96.10	+0.04
t-3	96.06	+0.17
t-4	95.89	−0.28
t-5	96.17	−0.01
t-6	96.18	+0.15
t-7	96.03	−0.04
t-8	96.07	−0.07
t-9	96.14	

$$\text{Up} = 0.02 + 0.10 + 0.04 + 0.17 + 0.15 = 0.48$$
$$\text{Down} = 0.28 + 0.01 + 0.04 + 0.07 = 0.40$$
$$\text{RSI} = 100 - [100 \div (1 + (0.48/0.40))] = 54.545$$

Often when using an RSI with relatively few observations, it may be best to liberalize one's definitions of what constitute overbought and oversold conditions. Rather than 30 and 70, look for 25 and 75 or 20 and 80. Sometimes when the market is about to reverse, the RSI penetrates the danger levels significantly, backs off, and then penetrates the danger levels once again. This second penetration may or may not be as extreme as the first. It is often only after this second violation that the market reverses. This is intuitive in the sense that the market often trades in a reversal formation, or a sideways holding pattern, before reversing. The RSI may achieve an extreme level when initially entering the reversal pattern. Subsequently, the RSI may fall off those extreme levels and penetrate the danger levels again just prior to completing the reversal pattern.

CONCLUSION

Fundamental market conditions provide the basis for long-term movements in any marketplace. But fundamental information is quickly absorbed and incorporated in the price of efficient and liquid markets. Between the points in time when new fundamental information becomes known, markets trade on the basis of unknown fundamental information. Many observers ascribe certain patterns or tendencies in these movements.

The identification of these patterns or tendencies using a wide variety of techniques is the art of technical analysis. Although some dismiss technical analysis as a form of voodoo, it is nonetheless clear that a large proportion of the traders in any given marketplace rely on such techniques in their everyday trading activities. Thus, one cannot afford not to be aware of these techniques and the possible market impact they may exert.

CHAPTER 12

Fundamentals of Option Markets

John E. Nyhoff
John W. Labuszewski

In addition to operating the primary venue for the trade of futures, CME Group also offers options exercisable for futures for most of its major futures contracts, including options in interest rate, equity, currency, grain, livestock, energy, and metals contracts. Note that upon exercise, rather than delivering an actual commodity or financial asset, these contracts contemplate the establishment of a futures position. Options on futures contracts are accessible both through the CME Globex electronic trading platform and open outcry trading. Exchange-traded options are similar to exchange-traded futures with respect to their relatively high degree of standardization.

WHAT IS AN OPTION?

Options provide a very flexible structure that may be tailored to meet the risk management or speculative needs of the moment. Options may generally be categorized as two types, calls and puts, with two very different risk/reward scenarios.

Call options convey to the call option buyer the right, but not the obligation, to buy the underlying futures contract at a particular strike or exercise price on or before an expiration date. One may buy a call option, paying a negotiated price or premium in cash to the seller, writer, or grantor of the call. Alternatively, one may sell, write, or grant a call, thereby receiving that option premium as a cash credit to one's trading account.

Put options convey to the put option buyer the right, but not the obligation, to sell the underlying futures contract at a particular strike or exercise price on or before an expiration date. Again, one may buy or sell a put option, either paying the put premium in cash or receiving a negotiated premium or price as a cash credit to one's trading account.

As a matter or prudent risk management, it should be noted that the option premium received by writing either a call or put option becomes part of the option seller's margin requirement. In addition to the option premium, which is marked-to-market daily, the option seller must also post an additional risk margin to the trading account to reflect the potential change in value of the option premium during the next trading day. An option seller's total margin requirement varies as the option trades in- or out-of-the-money.

Options may be configured as European- or American-style options. A European-style option may only be exercised on its expiration date, whereas an American-style option may be exercised at any time up to and including the expiration date. CME Group offers options that are generally American style, but it also offers options that may be either American- or European-style. For example, both American- and European-style options on FX futures are listed for trading on the most popular currency futures.

Exhibit 12.1 uses options on FX futures for illustration purposes. Contract specifications for a selected listing of Options on FX futures contract are included in the table.

EXHIBIT 12.1 Specifications of Popular Options on FX Futures

	Options on EuroFX Futures	Options on Japanese Yen Futures	Options on British Pound Futures	Options on Swiss Franc Futures
Exercisable for	One 125,000 euro futures contract	One 12,500,000 yen futures contract	One 62,500 pound futures contract	One 125,000 franc futures contract
Minimum Price Fluctuation (Tick)	$0.0001 per euro ($12.50)	$0.000001 per yen ($12.50)	$0.0001 per pound ($6.25)	$0.0001 per franc ($12.50)
Price Limits	None			
Strike Interval	$0.005 per euro	$0.00005 per yen	$0.01 per pound	$0.005 per franc
Contract Months	Four months in the March cycle (March, June, September, and December) and two months not in the March cycle (serial months), plus four weekly expiration options			
CME Globex Trading Hours	Mondays to Thursdays from 5:00 PM to 4:00 PM the following day; Sundays and holidays from 5:00 PM to 4:00 PM the following day (Chicago times)			
Trading Ends	Quarterly & Serial Options: Second Friday before third Wednesday of contract month; Weekly Options: Close of trading is on the four nearest Fridays that are not also terminations for quarterly & serial options (2:00 PM Chicago time).			

Purchasing a call option is an essentially bullish transaction with limited downside risk. The maximum loss associated with a long call option position is the premium paid to enter the transaction. If the underlying futures market price should advance above the option's strike price, the call is considered *in-the-money*. One may exercise the call, thereby going long the underlying futures contract at the exercise price. This implies that an option's potential profit is diminished only by the premium paid up front to establish the option position. If the market should decline below the strike price, the option is considered *out-of-the-money* and may expire worthless, leaving the buyer with a loss limited to the option's premium.

The risks and potential rewards that accrue to the call seller or writer are opposite that of the call buyer. If the call option expires out-of-the-money, the option writer retains the premium and counts it as profit. If the market should rally above the call option's strike price, the call writer is faced with the prospect of being forced to sell the underlying futures contract at the strike price when the futures price is much higher, such losses cushioned to the extent of the premium received upon option sale.

Exhibit 12.2 illustrates the payoffs, or profit and loss profiles, for long and short call option positions, at expiration. Notice that the kinks, or sharp bends, in these call option payoff diagrams indicate the location of the call option's exercise price. The point at which the long call option and the short call option crosses is the call option's breakeven level, or zero profit point.

Buying a put option is essentially a bearish transaction with limited downside risk. The maximum loss associated with a long put option position is the premium paid to enter the transaction. If the market declines

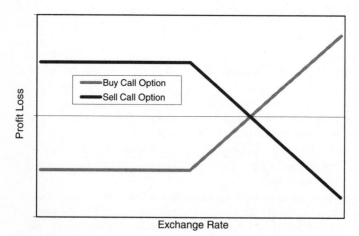

EXHIBIT 12.2 Profit/Loss for Call Option

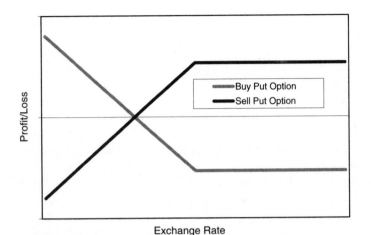

EXHIBIT 12.3   Profit/Loss for Put Option

below the put option's strike price, the put is said to be in-the-money and one may exercise the put thereby selling the underlying futures contract at the option's exercise price. If the market advances above the put option's strike price, the put option is out-of-the-money, implying a loss equal to the premium. See Exhibit 12.3.

The risks and potential rewards that accrue to the put writer are opposite that of the put buyer. If the put option expires out-of-the-money, the put writer retains the premium and counts it as profit. If the underlying futures price declines substantially, the put option may move into-the-money. In this case the put writer is faced with the prospect of being forced to buy the underlying futures contract at the strike price when the futures price is much lower. Losses incurred by the put writer will be cushioned to the extent of the premium received upon the put option's sale.

An option holder may dispose of a previously established option position either by exercising or abandoning (expiration sans exercise) the option. But it is important to remember that a trader may also liquidate or offset a previously established long/short option position through a subsequent option sale/purchase.

As such, option on futures traders may use a variety of mathematical pricing models to quantify appropriate premium values, not the least of which is a variation on the well-cited Black-Scholes, or Black option pricing model. Several factors, including the relationship between the underlying futures price and exercise price, term until expiration, market volatility, and interest rates, impact the option pricing model's value. Frequently, options are quoted in terms of volatility and converted into monetary terms with use of a specified option pricing model.

Because of the variety with which options are offered, including puts and calls with varying exercise prices and expiration dates, one may create an almost infinite variety of strategies that may be tailored to suit one's unique needs. Further, one may deploy a combination of options to achieve particular risk management requirements.

Option Pricing

Option pricing is at once one of the most complicated but perhaps the most significant topic that a prospective option trader can consider. The importance of being able to identify the fair value of an option is evident when you consider the meaning of the term *fair value* in the context of this subject.

A fair market value for an option is such that the buyer and seller expect to break even in a statistical sense, that is, over a large number of trials (without considering the effect of transaction costs, commissions, etc.). Thus, if a trader consistently buys overpriced or sells underpriced options, he or she can expect, over the long term, to incur a loss. By the same token, an astute trader who consistently buys underpriced and sells overpriced options may expect to realize a profit.

But how can a trader recognize over- or underpriced options? What variables impact this assessment? A number of option pricing models may be used to calculate these figures, notably including models introduced by Black-Scholes, Black, Merton, Cox-Ross-Rubinstein, and Whaley, among others. The purpose of this section, however, is not to describe these option pricing models but to introduce some of the fundamental variables that impact an option's premium and their effect.

Fundamentally, an option premium reflects two components: intrinsic value and time value.

$$\text{Premium} = \text{Intrinsic Value} + \text{Time Value}$$

The *intrinsic value* of an option is equal to its in-the-money amount. If the option is out-of-the-money or at-the-money, it has no intrinsic or in-the-money value. The intrinsic value is equivalent and may be explained by reference to the option's terminal value. The *terminal value* of an option is the price the option would command just as it is about to expire. Another way of viewing an option's intrinsic value is to consider it to be equal to the mark-to-market value of a futures contract position obtained as a consequence of the exercise of a long option position, assuming the option was either at- or in-the-money.

When an option is about to expire, an option holder has two alternatives available. On one hand, the holder may elect to exercise the option or,

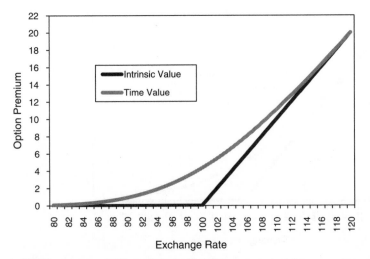

EXHIBIT 12.4   Intrinsic and Time Value of Call

on the other hand, may allow it to expire unexercised. Because the holder cannot continue to hold the option in the hopes that the premium will appreciate and the option may be sold for a profit, the option's value is limited to whatever cash flow it may generate upon exercise.

As such, the issue revolves entirely on whether the option is in-the-money or out-of-the-money as expiration draws near. If the option is out-of-the-money, then of course it will be unprofitable to exercise and the holder will allow it to expire unexercised or "abandon" the option. An abandoned option is worthless, and therefore the terminal value of an out-of-the-money option is zero. If the option is in-the-money, the holder will benefit upon exercise by the in-the-money amount, and therefore the terminal value of an in-the-money option equals the in-the-money value or amount. See Exhibits 12.4 and 12.5.

An American-style option should (theoretically) never trade below its intrinsic value. If it did, then arbitrageurs would immediately buy all the options they could for less than the in-the-money amount, simultaneously take an opposite risk position in the underlying futures contract, and exercise the option immediately. Arbitrageurs would realize a profit equal to the difference between the in-the-money amount and the premium paid for the option.

Time Value

An option contract often trades at a level in excess of its intrinsic value. This excess is referred to as the option's *time value* or sometimes as its *extrinsic*

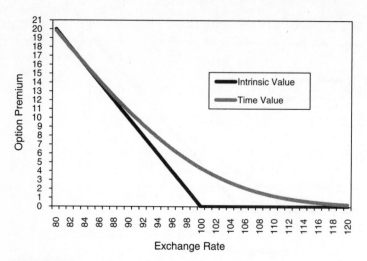

EXHIBIT 12.5 Intrinsic and Time Value of Put Option

value. When an option is about to expire, its premium is reflective solely of intrinsic value. But when there is some time until option expiration, there exists some probability that market conditions will change such that the option may become profitable (or more profitable) to exercise. Thus, time value reflects the probability of a favorable development in terms of prevailing market conditions that might permit a profitable exercise.

Generally, an option's time value will be greatest when the option is at-the-money. To understand this point, consider options that are deep in- or out-of-the-money. When an option is deep out-of-the-money, the probability that the option will ever trade in-the-money becomes remote. Thus, the option's time value becomes negligible or even zero.

When an option trends deep in-the-money, the leverage associated with the option declines. Leverage is the ability to control a large amount of resources with a relatively modest investment. Consider the extraordinary case where a call option has a strike price of zero. Under these circumstances, the option's intrinsic value equals the outright purchase price of the underlying instrument. There is no leverage associated with this option, and therefore the option trader might as well simply buy the underlying instrument outright. Thus, there is no time value associated with the option.

A number of different factors impact an option on future's time value in addition to the in- or out-of-the-money amount. These include (1) term until option expiration, (2) market volatility, and (3) short-term interest rates. Options exercisable for actual commodities or financial instruments are also affected by other cash flows or cost of carry considerations such as dividends (in the case of stock), coupon payments (bonds), and so on.

Term until Expiration

An option's extrinsic value is most often referred to as *time value* for the simple reason that the term until option expiration has a noticeable and dramatic effect on the option premium. All other things being equal, an option's premium always diminishes over time until option expiration. To understand this phenomenon, consider that options perform two basic functions: (1) they permit commercial interests to hedge or offset the risk of adverse price movement, and (2) they permit traders to speculate on anticipated price movements. See Exhibit 12.6.

The first function suggests that options represent a form of price insurance. The longer the term of any insurance policy, the more it costs. The longer the life of an option, the greater the probability that adverse events will occur; hence, the value of this insurance is greater. Likewise, when there is more time left until expiration, there is more time during which the option could potentially move in-the-money. Therefore, speculators will pay more for an option with a longer life.

Not only will the time value of an option decline over time, but an option's time value decay or erosion may accelerate as the option approaches

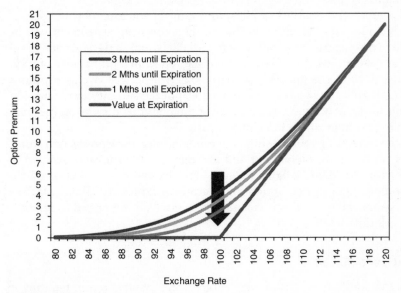

EXHIBIT 12.6 Time Value Decay

expiration. But be aware that accelerating time value decay is a phenomenon that is characteristic of at- or near-the-money options only. Deep in- or out-of-the-money options tend to exhibit a more linear pattern of time value decay.

Volatility

Option holders can profit when options trend into-the-money. For example, if currency values are expected to move upward by 10%, option traders would be inclined to buy call options. But if currency values were expected to move upward by 20% over the same time period, traders would become even more anxious to buy calls, bidding the premium up in the process.

It is not easy to predict the direction in which prices will move, but it may nonetheless be possible to measure volatility. Market volatility is often thought of as price movement in either direction, either up or down. In this sense, it is the magnitude, not the direction, of price movement that counts.

The standard deviation of daily percentage commodity price changes, or commodity price daily returns, represents a statistic that is often employed to measure price volatility or risk. For example, you may see an asset's volatility assessed or quoted at 10%, 15%, 20%, and so on. The use of this statistic implies that commodity or asset returns or percentage price movements may be modeled by a "normal probability distribution." The normal distribution is represented by the familiar bell-shaped curve.

To interpret a volatility of 20%, for example, you can say with approximately 68% certainty that the price of the underlying instrument will be within plus or minus 20% (or one standard deviation) of the current market price at the conclusion of a year. Or you can say with a probability of 95% that the price of the underlying instrument will be within plus or minus 40% (2 × 20%, or two standard deviations) of the current market price at the conclusion of one year. A good rule of thumb is that the greater the price volatility, the more an option will be worth.

One interesting relationship between volatility and options on futures prices is that at-the-money put and call options on futures are valued in proportion to their volatility level. For example, the value of an at-the-money put or call option on a futures contract at a 20% volatility level is approximately twice as large as the same option priced to reflect a 10% volatility level.

Short-Term Rates

Whenever someone invests in any venture, some positive return typically is expected. Accordingly, when an option exercisable for a futures contract is purchased, there is an investment equal to the premium. To the extent that the option is paid for up front and in cash, a return is expected on the investment. This implies that premiums must be discounted to reflect the lost opportunity represented by an investment in options. When the opportunity cost rises, as reflected in the rate at which funds may alternatively be invested on a short-term basis, the price of an option is discounted accordingly. When the opportunity cost decreases, the premium appreciates.

These remarks must be qualified by the following considerations. First, the effect described is applicable only to options on futures and not to options exercisable for actual instruments. In fact, rising short-term rates will tend to increase call premiums and decrease put premiums for options exercisable for actual instruments. Secondly, these remarks apply holding all other considerations equal. But of course we know that all else is never held equal. For example, if short-term rates are rising or falling, this suggests that bond futures prices will be affected. Of course, this consideration will also have an impact, often much greater in magnitude, than the impact of fluctuating short-term rates.

MATHEMATICAL OPTION PRICING MODELS

Options pricing theory is often thought of as a relatively recent development, but its seeds were sown more than 100 years ago. Louis Bachelier wrote his Ph.D. dissertation in 1900 on topics that included determining the value of stock options. During the 1960s James Boness and Paul Samuelson made progress on option pricing theory but were reliant on incorporating a risk premium into an option price evaluation process.

The widely cited Black-Scholes option pricing model was introduced in an academic paper published in the *Journal of Political Economy* in 1973 by Fisher Black and Myron Scholes. Concurrently, Robert Merton derived an option pricing model under alternative assumptions. In particular, Black and Scholes introduced risk-neutral assumptions that avoided any need to calculate the appropriate risk premium. Merton's paper was published in the *Bell Journal of Economics and Management Science*. What has become to be known as the Black-Scholes or Black-Scholes-Merton model demonstrates a method of pricing European-style options on non-dividend-paying equities.

Pricing Options on Futures

More importantly for options on futures contracts, in 1976 Fisher Black published a paper in the *Journal of Financial Economics* that demonstrated European-style options on commodities could be priced using an extension of the Black-Scholes-Merton option pricing model. The Black model has been widely used to price European-style options on futures contracts.

A discrete (and more easily appreciated by the novice student of options) option pricing model was published in 1979 by John Cox, Stephen Ross, and Mark Rubinstein. Their model follows a decision tree–like analytical framework and has come to be known as the Cox-Ross-Rubinstein (CRR) or "binomial" option pricing model. The CRR model is adaptable to price both European- and American-style options.

In 1987, Giovanni Barone-Adesi and Robert Whaley demonstrated an analytic approximation method for pricing the early exercise component of an American-style option on a futures contract. Because most exchange-traded options on futures contracts are American-style options, the Barone-Adesi/Whaley model has been widely adopted for pricing exchange-traded options on futures contracts.

The option pricing models just described represent seminal contributions to modern option pricing theory. There have been many additional refinements to the options pricing and risk-management literature that are far too numerous to be cited here.

As mentioned earlier, several factors influence an option on futures market value. These factors include the underlying futures price ("U"), the strike or exercise price ("E"), the term until option expiration ("t"), volatility of the underlying futures price ("σ"), and the risk-free short-term interest rate ("r"). An option pricing model adds great value to an option trader's toolbox in that it assists the market participant in observing how these five pricing factors interrelate to determine an option on futures contract theoretical or fair market value.

Black Model

The Black model equations used to price European-style put and call options on futures contracts are as follows:

$$C = e^{-rt}[UN(d_1) - EN(d_2)]$$

$$P = e^{-rt}[EN(-d_2) - UN(-d_1)]$$

$$d_1 = [\ln(U/E) + 0.5\,\sigma^2 t]/\sigma\sqrt{t}$$

$$d_2 = [\ln(U/E) - 0.5\,\sigma^2 t]/\sigma\sqrt{t} = d_1 - \sigma\sqrt{t}$$

Where: C = Call option premium
  P = Put option premium
  U = Underlying futures price
  E = Option exercise price
  N() = Cumulative normal probability (see standard normal cumulative distribution function table or use Excel NORMSDIST function)
  r = Short-term risk-free interest rate
  t = Time until option expiration (expiry) expressed in years, based on trading days
  σ = Annualized volatility of the underlying futures price returns
  e = Base of natural logarithm or 2.71828182845904523536

A variety of assumptions underlie the Black option pricing model. These assumptions include the following: (1) volatility is constant over the life of the option, (2) interest rates are constant and known over the life of the option, (3) markets are perfectly efficient with zero transactions costs and no taxes, (4) assets are perfectly divisible, and (5) futures prices are log-normally distributed and daily returns are normally distributed.

Needless to say, all of these assumptions are violated in the real world. Remember that the models cited here are models, not an actual depiction of the circumstances that underlie real-world trading. Nevertheless, both the Black and binominal option pricing models offer tremendous value when used to provide guidance for both trading and hedging strategies.

One of the key benefits of the Black option pricing model (or the Black-Scholes-Merton option pricing model) is that it is relatively easy to set up in an Excel spreadsheet using the NORMSDIST function to approximate the cumulative value of the standard normal distribution. Another benefit is that the only interest rate that must be known is the short-term risk-free interest rate, rather than a stock or option's risk-adjusted rate of return. Let's take a look at calculating the fair value of a slightly out-of-the-money yen call option.

Example Assume a September Japanese yen call option on futures contract is struck at 102 cents per 100 yen or ¥100 (E = 102). The futures market is at 100, that is, 100 cents per ¥100 (U = 100). There are three months or 0.25 years until option expiration (t = 0.25). Volatility is assumed to be 20% annually (σ = 20%). Domestic or U.S. short-term interest rates are equal to 0.80% (r = 0.80%). Find the price of this 102 call using the Black option pricing model:

$$C = e^{-rt}[UN(d_1) - EN(d_2)]$$
$$e^{-(.008)(.25)}[100(.4178) - 102(.38685)]$$
$$= 3.1001 \text{ or } 3.1001 \text{ cents per } 100 \text{ Yen or } ¥100$$

$$d_1 = [\ln(U/E) + 0.5\sigma^2 t]/\sigma\sqrt{t}$$
$$= \left[\ln(100/102) + 0.5(0.20)^2(0.25)\right]/(0.20)\sqrt{0.25}$$
$$= -0.14803$$

$$N(d_1) = N(-0.14803)$$
$$= 0.44116$$

$$d_2 = [d_1 - \sigma\sqrt{t}]$$
$$= [\ln(U/E) - 0.5\sigma^2 t]/\sigma\sqrt{t}$$
$$= -0.14803 - (0.20)\sqrt{0.25}$$
$$= -0.24803$$

$$N(d_2) = N(-0.24803)$$
$$= 0.40206$$

If a buyer of the 102 yen call option paid 3.1 cents (per 100 yen) for the right to go long yen futures (which call for the delivery of 12.5 million yen) at 102 cents, then the total out-of-pocket cost would be equal to $3,875 as shown below.

$$\text{Premium per Contract} = \text{Premium per } 100 \text{ yen} \times \text{Contract Size}$$
$$= 0.031 \text{ cents} \times 12,500,000$$
$$= \$3,875 \text{ per contract}$$

The 102 yen call option buyer's maximum loss is limited to the payment of the $3,875 premium (plus any trading commission). Meanwhile, the option buyer's maximum profit is effectively open ended should the yen rally substantially relative to the U.S. dollar. Conversely, the 102 yen call option seller's maximum profit is the $3,875 premium collected, whereas the call option seller's maximum loss is unlimited.

Another important statistic is found in the option delta. The 102 yen call option delta (for options on futures) may be derived by taking the first derivative of the Black option pricing equation with respect to the underlying futures price. More simply, the 102 yen call option delta may be calculated as follows:

$$Delta = e^{-rt} N(d_1)$$
$$= e^{-(0.008 \times 0.25)} 0.44116$$
$$= 0.440278$$
$$Where\ N(d_1) = N(-0.14803)$$
$$= 0.44116$$

$$d_1 = [\ln(100/102) + 0.5(0.20)^2(0.25)]/(0.20)\sqrt{0.25}$$
$$= -0.14803$$

Now that we have derived the theoretical value of a call option on yen futures and its related delta, you may be curious regarding the value of a put option at the same strike price. We can determine the value of the 102 yen put by taking notice of the "put-call parity" relationship.

Put-call parity allows us to identify the value of a put option at a given strike price if we know the price of the call option at the same strike price and the same expiration date. Conversely, put-call parity allows us to identify the value of a call option at a given strike price if we know the price of the put option at the same strike price and the same expiration date. Other than the call option premium, the only other information required is the level of the short-term risk-free interest rate.

$$C - P = e^{-rt}[U - E]$$
$$or\ P = C - e^{-rt}[U - E]$$
$$or\ C = P + e^{-rt}[U - E]$$

In our prior example we determined that the 102 yen call with three months until expiration had a fair value equal to 3.1001 cents per 100 yen (C = 3.1001). Hence, a yen put option on a futures contract with a 102 strike price with three months remaining until expiry may be valued as follows:

$$P = C - e^{-rt}[U - E]$$
$$= 3.1001 - 0.998 \times (100 - 102)$$
$$= 5.0961$$

Hence, the 102 put option's fair market value is equal to approximately 5.10 cents per 100 yen (P = 5.10). The 102 put option is more valuable than the 102 call option because the put option is two cents in-the-money (i.e., the immediate exercise value of the put is two cents). Correspondingly, the 102 yen call option is two cents out-of-the-money. If we had known the value of the 102 yen put, but not the 102 yen call, we could have used the put-call parity relationship to solve for the value of the 102 yen call. We could, of course, have determined the fair market value of the put directly by using the Black put option pricing formula as follows:

$$P = e^{-rt}[UN(-d_2) - EN(-d_1)]$$
$$= e^{-(.008)(.25)}[102(0.59794) - 100(0.55884)]$$
$$= 5.0961 \text{ or } 5.0961 \text{ cents per } 100 \text{ Yen or } ¥100$$

$$d_1 = [\ln(U/E) + 0.5\,\sigma^2 t]/\sigma\sqrt{t}$$
$$= [\ln(100/102) + 0.5(0.20)^2(0.25)]]/(0.20)\sqrt{0.25}$$
$$= -0.14803$$

$$N(d_1) = N(-0.14803)$$
$$= 0.44116$$

By symmetry
$$N(-d_1) = [1 - N(d_1)]$$
$$= [1 - 0.44116]$$
$$= 0.55884$$

$$d_2 = [d_1 - \sigma\sqrt{t}]$$
$$= [\ln(U/E) - 0.5\sigma^2 t]/\sigma\sqrt{t}$$
$$= -0.14803 - (0.20)\sqrt{0.25}$$
$$= -0.24803$$

$$N(d_2) = N(-0.24803)$$
$$= 0.40206$$

By symmetry
$$N(-d_2) = [1 - N(d_2)]$$
$$= [1 - N(0.40206)]$$
$$= 0.59794$$

The put delta may be found as follows:

$$\text{Delta} = e^{-rt}[N(d_1) - 1]$$
$$e^{-(0.008 \times 0.25)}[0.44116 - 1]$$
$$= -0.5577$$
Where $N(d_1) = N(-0.14803)$
$$= 0.44116$$

$$d_1 = [\ln(100/102) + 0.5(0.20)^2(0.25)]/(0.20)\sqrt{0.25}$$
$$= -0.14803$$

Binomial Model

An alternative method of evaluating the fair value for an option on a futures contract is to deploy the binomial option pricing model developed by Cox, Ross, and Rubenstein. Many students of options find the intuitive characteristics of the binomial model more accessible and understandable than either the Black or Black-Scholes model.

The basic attribute of the binomial model is how futures prices evolve over time. Assume we begin with or are given today's futures price. Then what may we anticipate tomorrow's futures price to be? The first assumption is that at any point the futures price can either go up (u) or down (d). The magnitude of the up or down movement will depend on how we determine market volatility, which is based on the annualized standard deviation of daily returns.

Let $u = e^{\sigma\sqrt{\Delta t}}$ represent the magnitude of an up-move in the futures price at any point in time, where σ = annualized volatility or standard deviation of returns, and Δt = the length of the time period over which the futures price will move. Further, let $d = (1/u)$ represent the magnitude of a down-move in the futures price at any point in time, and let F = starting futures price. Finally, let $p = (1 - d)/(u - d)$ = probability that the futures price moves higher at any interval in time. Conversely, the value $(1 - p)$ = probability that the futures price moves lower at any interval in time.

If we look at the evolution of a futures price over a one-year time horizon, where there are three intervals of price movement during that year ($\Delta t = 1/3$ year), then the three-period future price fluctuation path or three-period price lattice may appear as illustrated in Exhibit 12.7.

Let's look at how futures price might evolve over a one-year period of time. First we must define the model parameters. We assume that we are dealing with a European-style option that may only be exercised on its final expiration date.

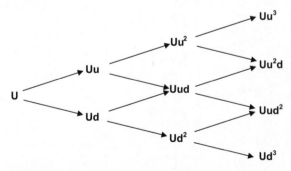

EXHIBIT 12.7 Upward or Downward Price Movement

Futures price ("U") = 100.00
Strike price ("E") = 100.00
Annualized volatility ("σ") = 15%
Time until expiration ("t") = 1 year
Time interval ("Δt ") = 1/3 of 1 year
Short-term interest rate ("r") = 3%

Per our scenario:

$$\text{Magnitude of any up-move ("u")} = e^{\sigma\sqrt{\Delta t}}$$
$$= e^{0.15\sqrt{\frac{1}{3}}}$$
$$= 1.09046$$

$$\text{Magnitude of any down-move ("d")} = (1/u)$$
$$= (1/1.0946)$$
$$= 0.91704$$

$$\text{Probability of an up-move ("p")} = (1-d)/(u-d)$$
$$= 0.4784$$

$$\text{Probability of a down-move } (1-p) = (1-0.4784)$$
$$= 0.5216$$

The lattice or tree in Exhibit 12.8 represents how futures prices may evolve at one-third yearly or four-month intervals over a one-year time horizon. Note that the underlying futures price either moves up or down by a constant multiplicative factor at each node of this lattice or tree.

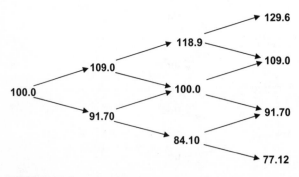

EXHIBIT 12.8 Possible Futures Prices

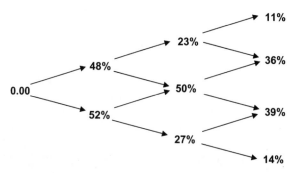

EXHIBIT 12.9 Probability of Reaching Any Node

Based on a 15% annualized volatility and a one-third year time interval, the underlying futures price moves higher by a multiplicative factor equal to 1.09046 at each stage of the tree or declines by a multiplicative factor equal to 0.91704 at each stage of the tree. The underlying futures price may achieve a level as high as 129.67 if the market moves higher at each of the three steps in this three-period tree. Alternatively, the underlying futures price may trade as low as 77.12 if the market trades lower at each of the three steps in this three-period tree.

Note that total upward price movement is greater than the total downward price movement in this tree. If we added additional steps to this binomial tree pricing pattern and determined the probability of achieving each terminal futures price, then the resulting price distribution would begin to look more and more like a log-normal price distribution, the typical assumption underlying a Black or Black-Scholes option pricing model.

The pattern of likelihood shown in the probability tree indicates that potential terminal futures prices closer to the current futures price have a much higher probability of occurrence than prices far removed from the current futures price. Again, this is representative of the outcomes associated with a log-normal price distribution.

Also, it is important to mention that a three-step lattice is used in Exhibit 12.9 for sake of brevity. A minimum of 50, and generally many more binomial steps is typically used to evaluate an option's fair value using the binomial model.

What we wish to determine is what would a call option or a put option be valued at based on the futures price, exercise price, volatility, short-term risk-free interest rate and time/time interval assumptions we have incorporated in this example.

First, let us define the terminal value or expiration day value of a call and put option. The terminal value of a call option ($C_{terminal}$) at expiration may be expressed as follows.

$$C_{terminal} = Max[(U - E); 0]$$

A call option is in-the-money when its underlying futures price is greater than its exercise price ($U > E$), and the call option terminal value is equal to its intrinsic value or ($U = E$) at expiration. When a call option is either at-the-money or out-of-the-money at expiration ($U \leq E$), then its terminal and intrinsic values are equal to zero (0).

The terminal value of a put option ($P_{terminal}$) at expiration may be expressed as follows:

$$P_{terminal} = Max[(E - U); 0]$$

A put option is in-the-money when its underlying futures price is less than its exercise price (i.e., $U < E$), and the put option terminal value is equal to its intrinsic value at expiration. When a put option is either at-the-money ($E = U$) or out-of-the-money ($U > E$) at expiration, then its terminal, and its intrinsic, value is equal to zero (0).

The method used to calculate the value of a call option, or a put option, using the binomial tree is to first determine the terminal value of the underlying futures price at the last stage of the tree, and then determine the terminal value of the option associated with the terminal futures price.

For example, if the terminal futures price in our example was 129.67, then the terminal value of a 100 strike price call option would be 29.67. If the terminal futures price was 109.05, then the terminal value of the 100 strike price call option would be 9.05. If the terminal value of the futures price is less than the call option strike price, then the call option is out-of-the-money at expiration and the terminal value of the call option is equal to zero. See Exhibit 12.10.

Next we need to move backward through the tree to determine the value of the call option at the nodes prior to expiration. As we move backward in the tree it is important to note that we must account for the time value of money. A payoff one period in the future does not have the same value today. Hence, we must take the present value of any expected future payoff to equate it to current-day value.

In the call tree we see that the value of a 100 strike price call with one period remaining to expiration (Cu^2), when the underlying futures price is equal to 118.91 (Uu^2), is equal to 18.73. How is this value derived? We need to recall the probability of an up-move or a down-move at any stage of the binomial tree as well as the present value of a dollar for a period of

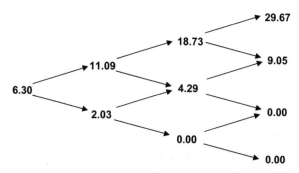

EXHIBIT 12.10 Pricing a European-style 100 Call Option

four months with an annual interest rate equal to 3%.

$$\text{Present value factor} = e^{-r \cdot \Delta t}$$
$$= e^{-3\% \cdot 0.333}$$
$$= 0.99005$$

Hence, the value of the call when the futures price is equal to 118.91 with one period to expiration may be calculated as 18.73.

$$Cu^2 = 0.99005 \times [(0.4784 \times 29.67) + (0.5216 \times 9.05)] = 18.73$$

Notice that when the futures price is equal to 84.10 or (Ud^2) with one period remaining to expiration that the call option has zero value. This is so because during the third and final period the futures price can't move to a level that will make for a positive valued call option at expiration.

For put options, if the terminal futures price in our example was 77.12, or (Ud^3) then the terminal value of a 100 strike price put option, or (Pd^3) would be 22.8. If the terminal futures price was 91.70, or (Uud^2) then the terminal value of the 100 strike price put option, or (Pud^2) would be 8.30. If the terminal value of the futures price is greater than the put option strike price, then the put option is out-of-the-money at expiration and the terminal value of the put option is equal to zero.

We continue to work iteratively backward through the tree, determining the value of the call at each node of the tree. We will ultimately determine that the 100 strike call in our example with one year remaining to expiration is valued at 6.30.

For put options, if the terminal futures price in our example was 77.12, then the terminal value of a 100 strike price put option would be 22.8. If the terminal futures price was 91.70, then the terminal value of the 100 strike

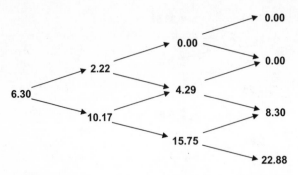

EXHIBIT 12.11 Pricing a European-style 100 Put Option

price put option would be 8.30. If the terminal value of the futures price is greater than the put option strike price, then the put option is out-of-the-money at expiration and the terminal value of the put option is equal to zero.

In the put tree in Exhibit 12.11, we see that the value of a 100 strike price put with one period remaining to expiration, when the underlying futures price is equal to 84.10, is equal to 15.75. How is this value derived? We need to recall the probability of an up-move or a down-move at any stage of the binomial tree as well as the present value of a dollar for a period of four months with an annual interest rate equal to 3%.

$$\text{Probability of an up-move (``p'')} = (1-d)/(u-d)$$
$$= 0.4784$$

$$\text{Probability of a down-move } (1-p) = (1-0.4784)$$
$$= 0.5216$$

$$\text{Present value factor} = e^{-r\cdot\Delta t}$$
$$= e^{-3\%\cdot0.333}$$
$$= 0.99005$$

Hence the value of the put when the futures price is equal to 84.10 with one period to expiration may be calculated as 15.75.

$$Pd^2 = 0.99005 \times [(0.4784 \times 8.30) + (0.5216 \times 22.88)] = 15.75$$

Notice that when the futures price is equal to 118.91 with one period remaining to expiration, the put option has zero value. This is so because during the third and final period the futures price can't move to a level that will make for a positive valued put option at expiration.

We continue to work iteratively backward through the tree, determining the value of the put at each node of the tree. We will ultimately determine that the 100 strike put in our example with one year remaining to expiration is valued at 6.30.

Note that the value of the at-the-money call is equal to the value of the at-the-money put in this example. This is an important attribute of options on futures; that is, at-the-money calls and at-the-money puts for the same expiration month have the same theoretical value.

Remember that we were pricing European-style options in our binomial example. What if we were pricing American-style options instead? If we were pricing an American-style option rather than a European-style option, we need to remember that the American-style option can be exercised at any time to realize the intrinsic value of the option, whereas a European-style option can only be exercised at expiration.

Notice the value of the 100 strike price put when the underlying futures price is trading at 84.10 is equal to 15.75. But the intrinsic value of the 100 put at this futures price is equal to 15.90. If this were an American-style option rather than a European-style option, then the minimum value for an option at any node on the binomial tree should not be less than the option's intrinsic value. If the intrinsic value of 15.90 is substituted into the tree for the former value of 15.75, then the earlier period valued for the put must be reevaluated to determine a new present-day put value.

The impact of the early exercise possibility is illustrated in Exhibit 12.12.

In this example, the American-style put has a slightly larger value (6.34 versus 6.30) relative to the European-style put. This serves to illustrate that American-style options are at least as valuable as European-style options and in general slightly more valuable.

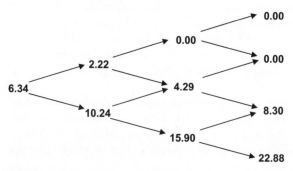

EXHIBIT 12.12 Pricing an American-style 100 Put Option

HISTORIC AND IMPLIED VOLATILITIES

One of the inputs into the Black option pricing model was the volatility of the underlying futures price. Volatility, in this context, refers to the anticipated dispersion or distribution of the underlying futures price, relative to the current futures price, during the remainder of an option's life. In this sense, volatility is a "nondirectional concept." *Volatility* refers to the magnitude of futures price movement rather than the prospect for either bullish or bearish price movement. Standard option pricing models implicitly apply several assumptions regarding the behavior of market-related prices as follows:

1. *Normal distribution:* The daily percentage price change (or daily returns) for futures contracts (on a continuously compounded basis) conform to a statistical "normal distribution" (i.e., take on the shape of the familiar bell-shaped curve). Two parameters including the current futures price (or "mean" of the distribution) and volatility ("standard deviation") are all that is required completely to describe a normal distribution.

2. *Log-normal distribution:* If the day-to-day returns in futures price (on a continuously compounded basis) may be described by reference to a normal distribution, then futures prices themselves are log-normally distributed. Two implications of a log-normal distribution are that the futures price may not decline below zero (remember we are talking about single market futures prices, not futures spreads), and futures prices are generally skewed toward higher price levels. In other words, futures or commodity prices typically trade at moderate levels but occasionally experience "spikes" to rather high extremes.

Volatility is generally expressed as a mathematical value or statistical parameter on an "annualized" basis. For example, options on yen futures volatility may be 20%. Or options on long-term Treasury futures volatility may be 10%. Volatility is a surrogate name for the standard deviation of the distribution of daily futures price returns. The standard deviation is equal to the square root of the variance of returns measured on an annual basis. This is useful because, as indicated earlier, a normally distributed random variable, such as futures price returns, is fully defined by reference to its mean and its standard deviation.

Volatility represents the annualized standard deviation of the natural log (ln) of price relatives. A price relative is equal to today's price divided by yesterday's price or P_t/P_{t-1}. Thus, one might think of volatility as representative of the variability in a series of logged price relatives or $\ln(P_t/P_{t-1})$.

Knowledge of a futures market's or option's volatility can be valuable in a hedging or trading context in that this awareness permits the approximation of the probability that an underlying futures price attains a value within a designated range.

For example, if we assume that yen futures returns are normally distributed and that the standard deviation of returns, or volatility, is equal to 16%, then there is an approximate 68% probability that the price will remain within a range bounded by the current futures price (the mean of the distribution) plus or minus 16% during the next year. There is also an approximate 95% probability that the futures price will remain within a range bounded by the current price plus or minus two times the volatility or 32% during the next year.

Dividing the 16% annual yen volatility by the square root of 252 (i.e., $16\%\frac{1}{\sqrt{252}}) = 1.0079\%$), converts the annual volatility into a daily volatility. Hence, we can say with approximately 68% confidence that the yen futures price may fall within a price interval bounded by the current yen futures price plus and minus 1% times the current yen futures price during the next trading day. With approximately 95% confidence, one may state that yen futures prices may fall within a price interval bounded by the current yen futures price plus and minus 2% times the current yen futures price during the next trading day.

Values for the standard normal probability distribution function can be found in virtually any probability and statistics book or by using the NORMSDIST function in Excel.

Historic Volatility

Futures price historical volatilities are often cited as a measure of futures market price movement. Note that a historical volatility calculation, as its name implies, represents futures price volatility observed over some period in the recent past. For example, futures prices may be observed over some period of time such as the last 10, 20, or 50 days. The volatility over the chosen historical time horizon can be calculated via the annualized standard deviation of the daily returns, or percentage price changes, based on the daily futures settlement prices observed during this historical period.

The first step when calculating futures price historical volatility is to convert futures market daily settlement prices into continuous daily rates of return. The following formula is typically referenced:

$$R_t = \ln(P_t/P_{t-1})$$

Where R_t = Daily rate of return or percentage price change in futures
            contract from day $t-1$ to day t
        P_t = Futures settlement or closing price on day t
        P_{t-1} = Futures settlement or closing price on day $t-1$

Example On September 2, 2008, the December 2008 yen futures settled at
92.12 cents per 100 yen. On the next trading day, September 3, 2008, the
December 2008 yen futures market advanced and settled at 92.48. Let P_{t-1} =
92.12 and let P_t = 92.48. The one-day or daily return from September 2 to
September 3 may be calculated as follows:

$$R_t = \ln(P_t/P_{t-1})$$
$$= \ln(92.48/92.12)$$
$$= 0.003900 \text{ or } 0.3900\%$$

After collecting a time series of daily returns as illustrated in Exhibit 12.13,
one may calculate a time period specific historic volatility (e.g., over the past

EXHIBIT 12.13 Calculating Daily Returns

Date	Price	Logged Return
9/2/08	92.12	
9/3/08	92.48	0.3900%
9/4/08	93.50	1.0969%
9/5/08	93.38	−0.1284%
9/8/08	92.62	−0.8172%
9/9/08	93.47	0.9135%
9/10/08	92.83	−0.6871%
9/11/08	93.73	0.9648%
9/12/08	92.74	−1.0618%
9/15/08	94.51	1.8906%
9/16/08	95.09	0.6118%
9/17/08	96.04	0.9941%
9/18/08	96.68	0.6642%
9/19/08	94.15	−2.6517%
9/22/08	95.59	1.5179%
9/23/08	95.67	0.0837%
9/24/08	95.24	−0.4505%
9/25/08	94.73	−0.5369%
9/26/08	95.03	0.3162%
9/29/08	96.61	1.6490%
9/30/08	94.98	−1.7016%

20 days) by taking the standard deviation (σ) of the data series and then annualizing by multiplying this standard deviation by the square root of 252 (the number of trading days in a typical calendar year). Note that 21 days of data are required to compute 20 days for daily returns. The standard deviation of the daily returns is easily calculated using the STDEV function in Excel.

$$\sigma = \sqrt{252} \times \sqrt{\left(\frac{1}{n}\right) \sum_i (R_i - \bar{R})^2}$$

Where R_t = Daily Return or $\ln(P_t/P_{t-1})$
$\quad\quad$ n = Number of days in sample

Example A 20-day historic volatility ($n = 20$) may calculated for December 2008 Japanese yen futures price per our previous example by applying the formula for standard deviations to the period from September 2 through September 30, 2008, as follows. The result is 18.05% using the formula and subsidiary calculations as illustrated in Exhibit 12.14.

$$
\begin{aligned}
\sigma &= \sqrt{252} \times \sqrt{\left(\frac{1}{n}\right) \sum_{i=1}^{n} (R_i - \bar{R})^2} \\
&= \sqrt{252} \times \sqrt{\left(\frac{1}{20}\right) \sum_{i=1}^{20} (R_i - 0.001529)^2} \\
&= \sqrt{252} \times \sqrt{\left(\frac{1}{20}\right) 0.002586} \\
&= 15.8745 \times 0.011371 \\
&= 18.05\%
\end{aligned}
$$

For readers familiar with Eurodollar futures or other short-term interest rate futures (STIRs) and their associated options, note that historic and implied volatilities are typically based on the yield implicit in the quoted Eurodollar futures price (or 100 less price) and not directly on the Eurodollar futures price. This departs from the typical practice of calculating historical and implied volatilities based on quoted futures prices. Short-term interest rate futures represent a special exception.

Mean Reversion

Although volatilities can vary quite considerably over time in the context of any given market, they often exhibit a tendency to hover toward a long-term mean or characteristic level. Option traders often find it useful to examine those average levels in the hopes of identifying mispriced options.

EXHIBIT 12.14 Calculating Historical Volatility

Date	Price	Logged Return	$\ln(R_t) - \bar{R}$
9/2/2008	92.12		
9/3/2008	92.48	0.3900%	0.0006%
9/4/2008	93.5	1.0969%	0.0089%
9/5/2008	93.38	−0.1284%	0.0008%
9/8/2008	92.62	−0.8172%	0.0094%
9/9/2008	93.47	0.9135%	0.0058%
9/10/2008	92.83	−0.6871%	0.0071%
9/11/2008	93.73	0.9648%	0.0066%
9/12/2008	92.74	−1.0618%	0.0148%
9/15/2008	94.51	1.8906%	0.0302%
9/16/2008	95.09	0.6118%	0.0021%
9/17/2008	96.04	0.9941%	0.0071%
9/18/2008	96.68	0.6642%	0.0026%
9/19/2008	94.15	−2.6517%	0.0787%
9/22/2008	95.59	1.5179%	0.0186%
9/23/2008	95.67	0.0837%	0.0000%
9/24/2008	95.24	−0.4505%	0.0036%
9/25/2008	94.73	−0.5369%	0.0048%
9/26/2008	95.03	0.3162%	0.0003%
9/29/2008	96.61	1.6490%	0.0224%
9/30/2008	94.98	−1.7016%	0.0344%
Average =		0.1529%	
Summation =			0.2586%

One quite simple and reasonably popular technique is to study the average (median) level of volatility observed in the marketplace over the past year or past three years. The tables that follow provide the median, maximum, and minimum levels of 30-day historic volatilities in a sampling of some of the most actively traded CME FX futures markets. These markets include the euro, Japanese yen, British pound, Swiss franc, Australian dollar, and Canadian dollar. Generally, we examine volatility in the lead or nearby month, which typically represents the most actively traded futures contract. See Exhibit 12.15.

One observation pattern gleaned from a comparison of the two historical volatility tables is that historical volatility is nonconstant and ever changing. The one-year period following the financial market turmoil of September 2008 (October 1, 2008, to September 30, 2009) demonstrated significantly higher historical volatility levels than the prior two-year period as illustrated in Exhibit 12.16. This is evidenced by the considerably higher

EXHIBIT 12.15 30-Day Historical Volatilities over 3-Year Window (10/1/06 to 9/30/09)

	Percentiles								
	Max	90%	75%	60%	Median	40%	25%	10%	Min
EuroFX	22.98%	18.30%	13.58%	10.13%	9.39%	8.00%	6.11%	5.07%	3.96%
Japanese Yen	26.39%	17.01%	14.95%	12.42%	11.38%	10.22%	8.62%	6.73%	3.32%
British Pound	26.77%	20.67%	13.93%	9.39%	8.73%	7.99%	6.82%	5.49%	3.75%
Swiss Franc	26.64%	17.59%	14.76%	12.52%	10.39%	8.70%	7.38%	6.42%	4.22%
Australian $	57.91%	32.69%	21.12%	14.97%	13.07%	11.64%	8.68%	7.04%	4.93%
Canadian $	30.40%	18.93%	14.87%	12.90%	11.33%	9.58%	7.19%	6.22%	4.85%

median historical volatilities during this period as well as the considerably higher minimum historical volatility during this period.

Also, take note of Exhibit 12.17 illustrating the 30-day yen futures historical volatility pattern from shortly before the financial crisis of September 2008 through the end of September 2009. The onset of the Fannie Mae and Freddie Mac technical defaults, the Lehman Brothers bankruptcy, and the AIG government bailout during early to mid-September 2008 gave rise to a significant repricing of risk. The rapid rise in Japanese yen 30-day historical volatility from 9% in early September 2008 to 26% in late October 2008 provides a strong indication of how rapidly market assessment of risk can change.

We might also compare these historical volatility levels to current implied volatilities in actively traded options to get a better feel for whether options are reasonably priced relative to historic averages. This statement begs for a discussion of option implied volatility (IV).

EXHIBIT 12.16 30-Day Historical Volatilities over 1-Year Window (10/1/08 to 9/30/09)

	Percentiles								
	Max	90%	75%	60%	Median	40%	25%	10%	Min
EuroFX	22.98%	21.16%	19.06%	17.10%	16.30%	14.49%	13.18%	10.24%	7.82%
Japanese Yen	26.39%	21.93%	16.82%	15.75%	15.45%	14.96%	13.85%	12.04%	8.03%
British Pound	26.77%	24.07%	21.97%	18.17%	16.45%	15.55%	13.62%	11.74%	8.89%
Swiss Franc	26.64%	24.51%	17.86%	16.76%	16.06%	15.09%	13.75%	11.80%	7.75%
Australian $	57.91%	49.32%	33.83%	30.68%	23.02%	22.13%	20.72%	14.27%	12.02%
Canadian $	30.40%	27.98%	20.34%	17.14%	16.01%	14.98%	14.03%	12.79%	11.28%

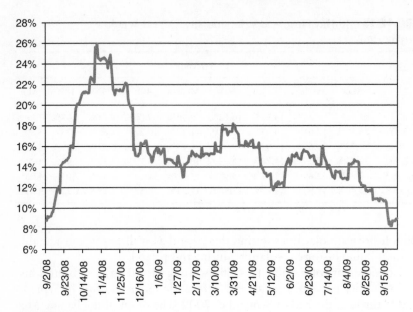

EXHIBIT 12.17   30-Day HV for Nearby JY Futures

Implied Volatility

Volatility is often viewed as the most significant input for an option pricing model. Surprisingly, it may also be viewed as one of the most important outputs from an option pricing model! We are referring to the practice of deriving an option's "implied" volatility (or "IV") for the purpose of measuring the level of risk embedded in the current level of an option's premium. This is the level of volatility that is implicit or embedded in the currently prevailing option premium.

As discussed earlier, five variables must be input into an option on futures pricing model including the underlying futures price ("U"), exercise price ("E"), time until expiration ("t"), volatility ("v"), and risk-free short-term interest rate ("r"). Plugging these values into a mathematical option pricing formula, one may calculate the fair value of the option premium.

$$\text{Premium} = f(U, E, t, v, r)$$

These five inputs into an option pricing model are readily observable in the market with the notable exception of volatility. However, it is not always necessary to calculate an option premium. Rather, one might observe that in liquid markets, the option premium may simply be observed by reference to the last trade price or perhaps by reference to the prevailing bid/offer spread.

An option's IV is calculated using those readily observable variables plus the market observable option premium level. Hence, IV represents the level of market risk implied by the market determined option premium:

$$\text{Implied Volatility} = f(\text{Premium}, U, E, t, r)$$

When one attempts to solve the Black pricing formula for volatility, unfortunately, one arrives at a polynomial expression that is not directly solvable. Numerical approximation techniques, such as the iterative Newton-Raphson method, can be employed to solve for the IV level that equates to the current level of an option's premium.

An option's IV may be described as a barometer of risk associated with anticipated movement in the underlying futures price. Just as it is worthwhile to study how the level of a market's historical volatility changes over time, it is also useful to compare how the IV level of an option behaves over time.

Note that whereas an option's IV represents anticipated risk or expected price change, historical volatility represents a measure of observed or past price change. Hence, it may be stated that whereas IV is a forward-looking assessment of underlying market price risk, historical volatility is a backward-looking assessment of where price risk has been. See Exhibit 12.18.

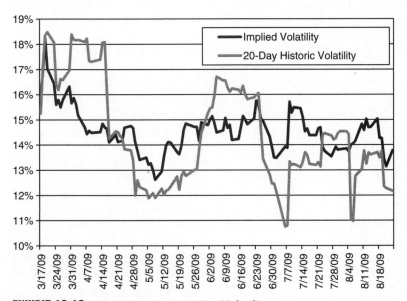

EXHIBIT 12.18 Measuring Japanese Yen Volatility

The chart in Exhibit 12.18 compares implied volatilities on near-the-money calls for September 2009 Japanese yen futures with 20-day historical volatilities for September 2009 Japanese yen futures. Note that implied volatilities were considerably more stable than the 20-day historical volatilities.

It may be useful to remember although the profit and loss associated with a futures contract depends solely on changes in the underlying futures price, an option's profit and loss depends on not only changes in the underlying futures price but on changes in the option's IV and time to expiration. Fluctuations in an option's IV may often be the most important factor influencing the change in an option's premium over a short period of time.

Many factors may influence an option's IV. The IV associated with options of a particular asset class such as interest rates, stock indices, or currencies may be bid up or move higher immediately prior to an anticipated government economic report or the earnings release associated with a bellwether equity as traders establish long option positions to express a market view, with limited risk.

Higher IV levels coincide with higher option premiums. If the information in the economic report or earnings release deviates substantially from market expectations, then significant futures price change may ensue, leading to even higher levels of IV. But should the information associated with the economic report or the earnings release not deviate substantially from expectations, then both IV and option premiums often decline as traders exit their long option positions.

If you established a long call position prior to the release of an important report, and the information content of the report was very bullish, the long call position will likely gain significant value in the short term due to both bullish underlying futures price impact as well as from a further increase in IV immediately after the report. In effect, the long call option benefited from both bullish futures price movement and a favorable increase in IV.

Alternatively, if a long call position was established prior to the release of an important report, and the information content of the report was only slightly bullish, a long call position may lose value in the short term due to a decline in IV immediately after the report. In effect, the long call option benefited from bullish futures price movement but was negatively impacted by a decline in IV.

A greater appreciation for how changes in an option's underlying price, time to expiration, and IV influence an option's premium can be attained by gaining an appreciation for the option Greeks in the next section.

Option Smile or Skew

Another interesting way to regard volatility is to study the implied volatilities associated with in-, at-, and out-of-the-money options. Option pricing theory assumes that IV is constant across all option strike prices, for a given option maturity. By charting this phenomenon, we may see that the constant IV assumption of the option pricing model is violated.

A plot or chart of actual IV across option strike prices is often referred to as the option "smile." The term *smile* refers to the characteristic shape of the IV curve where at-the-money options tend to sag in terms of their IVs relative to in- and out-of-the-money options with somewhat higher IVs. Exhibit 12.19 illustrates two variations on the volatility smile associated with December 2009 options on corn futures.

Other option market practitioners sometimes refer to the plot of option IV against option strike prices as the volatility "skew." As a general rule, the market tends to value cheap out-of-the-money options to the extent that they imply low risk in an absolute sense. Thus, option traders may bid up the value of cheap out-of-the-money calls and puts, particularly when they hold a bullish or bearish market perspective, respectively. By studying the smile, its changing level and dynamic shape, we might garner a few insights regarding aggregate market sentiment.

In trending currency or interest rate markets, a plot of option IV will often show a deviation from a typical smile pattern. The Japanese yen

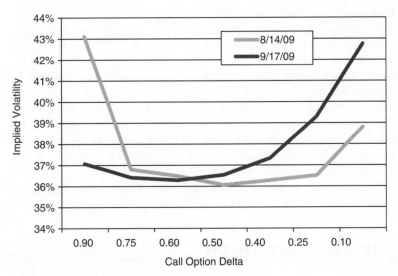

EXHIBIT 12.19   Dec-09 Corn IV "Smile"

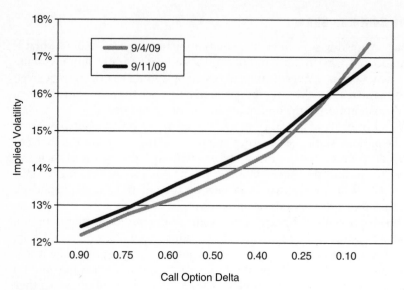

EXHIBIT 12.20   Dec-09 Japanese Yen IV "Skew"

option skew, shown in the chart in Exhibit 12.19, during September 2009 demonstrates that the market or traders were willing to pay higher volatility for out-of-the-money (or lower delta) Japanese yen calls to establish limited risk bullish option positions. See Exhibit 12.20.

Alternatively, in-the-money (or higher delta) yen calls were trading at lower IV levels, perhaps reflecting traders' willingness to sell out of the money puts as an alternative bullish strategy. This is often the case when any currency futures contract has experienced a sustained rally or the U.S. dollar has suffered sustained declines in value.

Options on stock index futures typically display a volatility skew pattern as depicted in Exhibit 12.21. The inclination of stock index portfolio hedgers to buy puts and/or to sell calls as a concerted part of their hedge programs offers one explanation for the higher IV volativity levels associated with in-the-money calls and out-of-the-money puts and conversely the lower IV levels associated with out-of-the-money calls and in-the-money puts.

MEASURING OPTION PERFORMANCE

Option traders often refer to a variety of "exotic" statistics, or "Greeks," that may be used to measure the prospective performance or risk of an

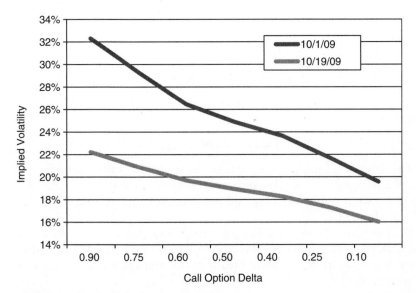

EXHIBIT 12.21   Dec-09 S&P 500 IV "Skew"

option in response to any one of the variables that affect its premium. In particular, the effects of movement in the underlying market price, the passage of time, and volatility are of great interest. These statistics may be calculated as a by-product of various mathematical option pricing models such as the Black model (1976).

Let us emphasize that movements with respect to the underlying market price are often the most obvious and influential factor affecting the option premium. Therefore, we begin our discussion of exotic option measures by examining delta and its close relative gamma. *Delta* is said to measure the influence of price movement on the option premium; *gamma* measures the influence of price movement on the option delta.

Subsequently, let us consider the influence of time and volatility on the option premium. Again, the Greek alphabet provides a ready source of inspiration for these measurements. The influence of time is measured by theta; the influence of volatility is measured by vega.

Delta

When the price of the underlying instrument rises, call premiums rise and put premiums fall. But how much will the call or put option premium change? Delta measures the change in an option's premium relative to a small change in the underlying futures price. An option's delta may be calculated as the first derivative of the option pricing model with respect to the underlying price. As shown earlier, the delta of a call option based on the Black model may be calculated as:

$$\text{Call Delta} = e^{-rt}\,N(d_1)$$

Likewise, the delta of a put option based on the Black model may be calculated as:

$$\text{Put Delta} = -e^{-rt}\,N(-d_1)$$

The delta of a long call option takes on a positive value, whereas the delta of a long put option takes on a negative value. The delta of short call option and short puts option take on negative and positive values, respectively. See Exhibit 12.22.

Delta is generally expressed as a number from zero to 1.0 (in absolute value). Deep in-the-money deltas will approach 1.0. Deep out-of-the-money deltas will approach zero. Finally at- or near-the-money deltas will run at about 0.50.

Deep In-the-Money	$\rightarrow$	Delta ≈ 1.00
At-the-Money	$\rightarrow$	Delta ≈ 0.5
Deep Out-of-the-Money	$\rightarrow$	Delta ≈ 0

It is easy to understand why a deep in- or out-of-the-money option may have a delta equal to 1.0 or zero, respectively. A deep in-the-money option's premium is reflective solely of intrinsic or in-the-money value. If the option moves slightly more or less in-the-money, its time value (which is zero) is unlikely to be affected. Its intrinsic value, however, reflects the relationship between the market price and the fixed strike price. Hence, a deep in-the-money call delta converges toward 1.0.

A deep out-of-the-money option has little or no value and is completely unaffected by slightly fluctuating market prices. Hence, a deep out-of-the-money option's delta is not significantly different from zero.

It is also important to note that delta is a dynamic concept. It will change as the market price moves upward or downward or as the option

EXHIBIT 12.22   Impact of Delta

Option Position	Call	Put
Long	+	−
Short	−	+

expiration date draws nearer. Hence, if an at-the-money call starts trending into-the-money, its delta will start to climb. Or, if the market starts falling, the call delta will likewise fall.

This changing value of an option's delta relative to movement in the underlying futures price is also illustrated by the three lines drawn tangent to the call option pricing curve in Exhibit 12.23. An out-of-the-money (OTM) call option delta is depicted by the slope of the flatter tangent line in this chart. Notice that the OTM option tangent line has a relatively small slope, which indicates that the OTM call option premium is relatively less responsive to futures price move than either the at-the-money (ATM) or in-the-money (ITM) call option.

The ATM call option delta is larger than that of the OTM call option, indicating that an ATM option premium changes more quickly than an OTM call option for equal changes in the underlying futures price. The more responsive nature of the ATM call option premium is depicted by the larger slope of the ATM call option tangent line relative to the slope of the OTM call option tangent line.

Finally the in-the-money (ITM) call option delta is larger than either the OTM or ATM call option deltas, indicating that the option premium associated with an ITM option is more responsive to underlying futures price change than either the OTM or ATM option. The higher delta associated

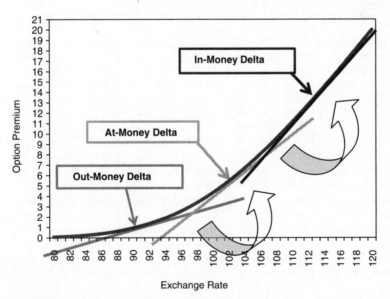

EXHIBIT 12.23 In-, At-, and Out-of-the-Money Deltas

with the ITM option may be discerned by the greater steepness of the tangent line See Exhibit 12.23.

In addition to movement in the underlying market price (as measured by an option's delta), other factors impact the option premium significantly, notably including time until expiration and marketplace volatility. A number of exotic Greek statistics including delta, gamma, vega, and theta are often referenced to measure the impact of these factors on the option premium. Underlying price movement stands out as perhaps the most obvious factor that impacts option premiums, and we have already discussed delta as the measure of such impact. Let's consider other statistics including gamma, vega, and theta.

Gamma

Gamma may be thought of as the "delta of the delta." Gamma measures the expected change in the delta given a change in the underlying market price. Gamma is said to measure a phenomenon known as *convexity*, which refers to the shape of the curve that depicts the total value of an option premium over a range in possible underlying market values. The curvature of that line is said to be convex, hence the term *convexity*. See Exhibit 12.24.

EXHIBIT 12.24 Options on EuroFX Futures (August 18, 2008)

Month	Put/ Call	Strike	Futures Price	Premium	Implied Volatility	Delta	Gamma	Theta	Vega
Sep-08	Call	1.4400	1.4675	0.0320	11.07%	0.7819	0.0810	20.61	9.57
Sep-08	Call	1.4450	1.4675	0.0281	10.95%	0.7407	0.0910	22.41	10.53
Sep-08	Call	1.4550	1.4675	0.0210	10.73%	0.6440	0.1060	25.29	12.12
Sep-08	Call	1.4600	1.4675	0.0178	10.60%	0.5901	0.1120	26.07	12.65
Sep-08	Call	1.4650	1.4675	0.0149	10.49%	0.5332	0.1160	26.40	12.94
Sep-08	Call	1.4700	1.4675	0.0123	10.40%	0.4747	0.1170	26.20	12.96
Sep-08	Call	1.4750	1.4675	0.0101	10.40%	0.4167	0.1150	25.68	12.71
Sep-08	Call	1.4800	1.4675	0.0081	10.30%	0.3592	0.1110	24.38	12.17
Sep-08	Call	1.4850	1.4675	0.0065	10.30%	0.3058	0.1040	22.87	11.42
Sep-08	Call	1.4900	1.4675	0.0051	10.28%	0.2560	0.0960	20.95	10.48
Sep-08	Put	1.4550	1.4675	0.0085	10.72%	0.3548	0.1065	25.31	12.12
Sep-08	Put	1.4600	1.4675	0.0103	10.59%	0.4088	0.1124	26.09	12.65
Sep-08	Put	1.4650	1.4675	0.0124	10.49%	0.4657	0.1161	26.41	12.94
Sep-08	Put	1.4700	1.4675	0.0148	10.40%	0.5242	0.1174	26.20	12.96
Sep-08	Put	1.4750	1.4675	0.0176	10.39%	0.5823	0.1152	25.63	12.71
Sep-08	Put	1.4800	1.4675	0.0206	10.31%	0.6395	0.1112	24.35	12.18
Sep-08	Put	1.4850	1.4675	0.0240	10.33%	0.6926	0.1042	22.89	11.43

(*Continued*)

EXHIBIT 12.24 (*Continued*)

Month	Put/ Call	Strike	Futures Price	Premium	Implied Volatility	Delta	Gamma	Theta	Vega
Dec-08	Call	1.4200	1.4605	0.0573	10.71%	0.6904	0.0407	9.55	27.78
Dec-08	Call	1.4300	1.4605	0.0506	10.63%	0.6483	0.0432	10.00	29.29
Dec-08	Call	1.4400	1.4605	0.0443	10.55%	0.6040	0.0453	10.32	30.47
Dec-08	Call	1.4500	1.4605	0.0384	10.45%	0.5579	0.0470	10.48	31.25
Dec-08	Call	1.4550	1.4605	0.0357	10.42%	0.5342	0.0474	10.54	31.49
Dec-08	**Call**	**1.4600**	**1.4605**	**0.0331**	**10.39%**	**0.5104**	**0.0478**	**10.54**	**31.61**
Dec-08	Call	1.4650	1.4605	0.0306	10.35%	0.4864	0.0480	10.51	31.62
Dec-08	Call	1.4700	1.4605	0.0283	10.34%	0.4625	0.0479	10.46	31.51
Dec-08	Call	1.4750	1.4605	0.0261	10.32%	0.4387	0.0476	10.37	31.29
Dec-08	Call	1.4800	1.4605	0.0240	10.30%	0.4150	0.0472	10.23	30.96
Dec-08	Call	1.4850	1.4605	0.0221	10.30%	0.3920	0.0465	10.09	30.52
Dec-08	Call	1.4900	1.4605	0.0203	10.30%	0.3693	0.0457	9.91	29.98
Dec-08	Call	1.4950	1.4605	0.0185	10.26%	0.3466	0.0449	9.66	29.33
Dec-08	Call	1.5000	1.4605	0.0169	10.25%	0.3248	0.0438	9.42	28.61
Dec-08	Put	1.4200	1.4605	0.0171	10.72%	0.3033	0.0407	9.74	27.78
Dec-08	Put	1.4250	1.4605	0.0186	10.66%	0.3237	0.0421	9.93	28.57
Dec-08	Put	1.4300	1.4605	0.0203	10.63%	0.3452	0.0432	10.13	29.29
Dec-08	Put	1.4350	1.4605	0.0220	10.57%	0.3668	0.0444	10.26	29.92
Dec-08	Put	1.4400	1.4605	0.0239	10.54%	0.3894	0.0454	10.39	30.46
Dec-08	Put	1.4450	1.4605	0.0259	10.50%	0.4123	0.0462	10.49	30.91
Dec-08	Put	1.4500	1.4605	0.0280	10.46%	0.4356	0.0469	10.54	31.25
Dec-08	Put	1.4550	1.4605	0.0302	10.41%	0.4592	0.0475	10.55	31.49
Dec-08	Put	1.4600	1.4605	0.0326	10.39%	0.4831	0.0478	10.55	31.61
Dec-08	Put	1.4650	1.4605	0.0351	10.36%	0.5070	0.0479	10.50	31.62
Dec-08	Put	1.4700	1.4605	0.0377	10.33%	0.5310	0.0479	10.41	31.51
Dec-08	Put	1.4750	1.4605	0.0405	10.32%	0.5548	0.0476	10.31	31.29
Dec-08	Put	1.4800	1.4605	0.0434	10.31%	0.5783	0.0472	10.16	30.96
Dec-08	Put	1.4850	1.4605	0.0464	10.29%	0.6016	0.0466	9.98	30.52
Dec-08	Put	1.4900	1.4605	0.0496	10.30%	0.6242	0.0457	9.79	29.98
Dec-08	Put	1.4950	1.4605	0.0528	10.27%	0.6467	0.0449	9.53	29.34
Dec-08	Put	1.5000	1.4605	0.0561	10.24%	0.6689	0.0439	9.23	28.60

Convexity is a concept that promises to benefit traders who purchase options to the detriment of those who sell or write options. Consider that as the market rallies, the premium of a call option advances at an ever-increasing rate as the delta itself advances. Thus, the holder of a call is making money at an increasing or accelerating rate. But if the market should fall, the call holder is losing money but at a decelerating rate.

On August 18, 2008, for example, the delta for a December 2008 1.4600 call (essentially at-the-money with December futures trading at

1.4605) was 0.5104. It had a gamma of 0.0478, suggesting that if the underlying futures price were to move upward (downward) by 1 cent, the value of delta would move upward (downward) by about 0.0478. This may be validated by noting that the call struck at 1.4500 has a delta of 0.5579 or 0.0475 higher than 0.5104. Or, that the call struck at 1.4700 has a delta of 0.4625 or 0.0479 lower than 0.5104. It is important to note that the gammas in our illustration are based on a 1 cent or $0.01 movement in the EUR/USD exchange rate.

Obviously, if the call buyer is making money at an accelerating rate and losing money at a decelerating rate, the call writer is experiencing the opposite results. Gamma tends to be highest when an option is at- or near-to-the-money. But gamma declines as an option trends in- or out-of-the-money. Notice that theta and vega are likewise greatest when the market is at or reasonably near to the money. These values decline when the option goes in- or out-of-the-money as discussed later. Thus, convexity as measured by gamma works to the maximum benefit of the holder of at-the-money options.

As shown in Exhibit 12.25, option buyers benefit from an option's positive convexity or gamma, whereas option sellers are negatively impacted by the effects associated with an option's gamma.

Theta

Theta measures time value decay or the expected decline in the option premium given a forward movement in time toward the ultimate expiration date of the option, holding all other variables (such as price, volatility, short-term rates) constant. Time value decay and the degree to which this decay or erosion might accelerate as the option approaches expiration may be identified by examining the change in the theta.

For, example, our December 2008 1.4600 call had a theta of 10.54. This suggests that over the course of seven days, holding all else equal, the value of this call option may fall 10.54 ticks or $0.0011 from its value of $0.0331. In other words, its value is expected to decline to $0.0320. Note that we are quoting a theta in ticks over the course of seven calendar days. It is also common to quote a theta over the course of a single day.

EXHIBIT 12.25 Impact of Gamma

Option Position	Call	Put
Long	+	+
Short	−	−

Theta is a dynamic concept and may change dramatically as option expiration draws nigh. At- or near-to-the-money options experience rapidly accelerating time value decay when expiration is close. Away-from-the-money options experience less time value decay as in-and out-of-the-money options have less time value than do comparable at- or near-the-money options. Thetas associated with moderately in- or out-of-the-money options may be relatively constant as expiration approaches signifying linear decay characteristics. Deep in- or out-of-the-money options will have very little or perhaps no time value. Thus, the theta associated with an option whose strike is very much away from the money may "bottom out" or reach zero well before expiration.

Time value decay works to the benefit of the short but to the detriment of the long. The same options that have high thetas also have high gammas. Convexity as measured by gamma works to the detriment of the short and to the benefit of the long. Near-the-money options will have high thetas and high gammas. As expiration approaches, both theta (measuring time value decay) and gamma (measuring convexity) increase.

As shown in Exhibit 12.26, both call and put option buyers will be negatively impacted from time decay. Hence, long options have negative thetas. However, option sellers benefit from the passage of time. Hence, short options have positive thetas.

An important point to remember is that you "can't have your cake and eat it too." In other words, it is difficult, if not impossible, to benefit from both time value decay and convexity simultaneously.

Vega

Vega measures the expected change in the premium given a change in marketplace volatility. Normally, an option's vega is expressed as the change in the option premium given a 1% movement in IV. For example, our December 2008 1.4600 call had a vega of 31.61. This suggests that its premium of $0.0331 might fluctuate by 31.61 ticks or $0.0032 if volatility were to move by 1% from the current IV of 10.39%.

EXHIBIT 12.26 Impact of Theta

Option Position	Call	Put
Long	−	−
Short	+	+

Vega tends to be greatest when the option is at- or reasonably near-to-the-money. In- and out-of-the-money options have generally lower vegas. However, this effect is not terribly great. Note that vega tends to fall, rather than rise, as a near-to-the-money option approaches expiration. This is unlike the movement of theta and gamma, which rise as expiration draws near.

Volatility and convexity are very similar properties. This can be understood when one considers that it is only when the market is moving, or when the market is volatile, that the effects of convexity are observed. Remember that when you buy an option, convexity works to your benefit no matter whether underlying price movements are favorable or not. If the market moves against you, you lose money but at a decelerating rate. If the market moves with you, you make money at an accelerating rate. Thus, the prospect of rising volatility is generally accompanied by beneficial effects from convexity (at least from the long's standpoint).

Earlier we suggested that it is generally impossible to enter an option strategy in which both time value decay and convexity work to your benefit simultaneously. Paradoxically, it may be possible to find option strategies where the prospect of rising volatility and time value decay work for you simultaneously (although convexity will work against you).

This is possible because vega falls as expiration approaches while theta and gamma rise. For example, one might buy a long-term option experiencing the ill effects of time value decay while selling a shorter-term option that benefits from time value decay. The benefits associated with the short-term option will outweigh the disadvantages associated with the longer-term option. And the strategy will generally benefit from the prospect of rising volatility because the long-term option will have a higher vega than the short-term option.

In summary, both call and put option buyers benefit from an increase in IV. Hence, long options have positive vegas. However, option sellers benefit when IV declines. Hence, short call or put option position possess negative vegas. See Exhibit 12.27.

EXHIBIT 12.27 Impact of Vega

Option Position	Call	Put
Long	+	+
Short	−	−

EXHIBIT 12.28   "Greek" Option Statistics

Delta	Measures the expected change in the option premium given a small change in the PRICE of the instrument underlying the option
Gamma	Measures the change in the DELTA given a small change in the PRICE of the instrument underlying the option (i.e., the "delta of the delta" measuring a phenomenon known as convexity)
Vega	Measures the expected change in the option premium given a small change in the IMPLIED VOLATILITY of the instrument underlying the option
Theta	Measures the expected change in the option premium given the forward movement of TIME

Putting It All Together

Options are strongly affected by the forces of price, time, and volatility/ convexity. (We often consider convexity and volatility to be one and the same property for reasons discussed earlier.) "Exotic" option statistics such as delta, gamma, theta, and vega are quite useful in measuring the effects of these variables.

As a general rule, when you buy an option or enter into a strategy using multiple options where you generally buy more than you sell, convexity and the prospect of rising volatility work to your benefit. Time value decay generally works against you in those situations. When you sell options or enter into strategies where you are generally selling more options than you buy, convexity and the prospect of rising volatility will work against you, although time value decay will work to your benefit. See Exhibit 12.28.

The key point is that these variables—price, time, and volatility—do not operate independently one from the other. Price may generally be considered the most important of these variables and will tend to dictate whether time value decay is more or less important than convexity and rising volatility. Changes in IV and the passage of time may also have considerable impact on the value of an options position. One can use this information to good effect when formulating a hedging strategy using options.

CONCLUSION

Options offer an alternative to futures to gain risk exposure or manage the risks associated with a wide variety of assets. Futures may be regarded as rather one-dimensional instruments to the extent that the payoff structure is a linear function of price movements in the underlying marketplace. But options are much more complex and might be considered three dimensional to the extent that they are affected by price movements, time value decay, and fluctuating market volatilities.

One may reference various mathematical option pricing models to calculate the fair value of an option. These models are also useful in modeling the sensitivity of options to the three dimensions of price, time, and volatility. In particular, so-called Greeks, including delta, gamma, vega, and theta, are useful risk assessment tools in this regard.

CHAPTER 13

Option Trading Strategies

John W. Labuszewski
John E. Nyhoff

Options can be incredibly flexible trading instruments that may be used to customize a strategy closely to conform to a straightforward or a complex market forecast. Part of that flexibility may be attributed to the fact that options are typically offered with many choices, put or call, with a variety of expirations and strike prices, American style versus European style. A derivatives trader may, of course, go long or short futures in anticipation of a strongly bullish or strongly bearish market scenario, respectively. But by combining options with those various characteristics, options permit traders to pursue much more subtle and complex trading strategies.

This chapter focuses on a wide variety of strategies applicable under a wide variety of circumstances. We discuss option spreads of various sorts including vertical, horizontal, and diagonal spreads as well as ratio and backspreads. We further discuss the use of various volatility strategies that are sensitive to factors including market volatility and the convexity inherent in an option.

Then we review how one may assess or measure the risks associated with an option trading strategy using the Greek-letter option statistics such as delta, gamma, vega, and theta. Finally, we consider the trade-offs that one implicitly accepts when pursuing a specific option trading strategy.

OPTION SPREADS

An option spread may be described as a strategy that requires you to buy and sell options of the same type, that is, to buy a call and sell a call or to buy a put and sell a put. Although the components of an option spread may be of the same type, these options may differ with respect to strike price, expiration date, or both.

Option spreads are really quite flexible trading strategies. They may be used to take advantage of strongly bull or strongly bear markets. But option spreads may also be used to capitalize on mildly trending markets or even neutral markets.

Let us consider the fundamentals and some of the finer points of trading specific types of option spreads. But before reviewing the specific strategies, we discuss the trade-offs that may be implicit in the pursuit of option spreads.

Option Trade-Offs

The pursuit of any specific option strategy is presumably driven by a market forecast. That forecast may incorporate various elements including price direction (of the underlying instrument for which the option may be exercised). But that forecast may also reference other variables that impact an option premium. Notable among these variables is time or term to expiration.

Thus, options are affected by (at least) two factors including price and time. Rational traders would naturally prefer to make all the variables that impact an option premium (and consequently, an option strategy) work to their benefit. But that may be difficult or impossible, and one must therefore consider the trade-offs implicit in an option strategy.

Consider that options with different characteristics experience differential rates of time value decay. See Exhibit 13.1. This is a function of the extent to which an option is in-the-money or out-of-the-money. It is further a function of the term or time remaining until option expiration.

Near-the-money options experience more decay and accelerated decay relative to in- or out-of-the-money options. Consider that at- or near-the-money options have more time value to decay from the start. Longer-term options typically have more time value than shorter-term options. But those long-term options may continue to hold on to their time value until option expiration begins to approach.

Near-the-money, near-term options exhibit a pattern of accelerating time value decay. But the time value associated with an away-from-the-money, near-term option may bottom out and therefore experience little or no time value decay. This is intuitive to the extent that time value fundamentally reflects the possibility that market trends may push an option

EXHIBIT 13.1 Differential Rates of Time Value Decay

	Near Term	Long Term
At- or Near-the-Money	Rapid acceleration	Slight acceleration
In- or Out-of-the-Money	Time value may bottom out	Linear decay

into-the-money or deeper into the money if it is already in-the-money. The extent to which this may occur is limited when options are well out-of-the-money, when there is a short period until expiration, or if volatility is very low.

Longer-term, near-the-money options experience slight time value decay but not on the same highly accelerated pace as their shorter-term counterparts. Finally, longer-term, away-from-the-money options may experience linear patterns of time value decay.

Of course, an option trader may consider the impact of decay when pursuing a spread that involves both the purchase and sale of options. Obviously, time value decay benefits the option writer but works adversely from the perspective of the long option holder. Time (or time value decay) may be on your side or may work against you on a net basis when putting on a spread depending on the characteristics of the particular options that comprise the spread.

Thus, option traders may be advised to carefully study the risk/reward profile associated with an option strategy. In particular, one may calculate the "Greeks" (or the delta, gamma, theta, vega, etc.) associated with each leg of the option strategy. Assign each Greek statistic a positive (+) or negative (−) value by reference to whether the attribute represents a positive or negative force on the strategy.

For example, when buying an option, time value decay represented by theta is a negative force over time. Assign the theta for that leg a negative value. When selling an option, time value decay represented by theta is a positive force. Assign that theta a positive value. Add up the thetas associated with each leg in the strategy to determine the net effect of that factor on the strategy as a whole.

Of course, most option spreads allow you to limit your risk to formulaically known parameters. Many of these strategies further entail strictly limited reward potential. Option traders may consider the ratio between potential reward and risk (maximum reward/maximum risk).

But you must be cognizant of the probability of achieving any particular profit or loss. In general, these probabilities will balance out any asymmetry between risk and reward. Thus, a strategy with a high reward-to-risk ratio generally means that you have a low probability of large profit and a relatively high probability of a relatively small loss. A strategy with a low reward-to-risk ratio generally means that you have a high probability of small profit and a relatively low probability of large loss.

When trying to take advantage of time value decay, you generally pursue strategies of the latter nature: strategies where you have a high probability of small profit, low probability of large loss. Fortunately, an astute option trader can often trade out of a situation where a large loss is imminent—to limit the loss. There is very little an option trader can do, however, to stop the forward march of time.

An option trader should think about when to hold and when to liquidate a position. By familiarizing oneself with the dynamics of an option strategy, you can tell when it is best advised to hold or fold an option strategy. The dynamics of an option strategy reflect the possible movements of the option strategy in response to the various dimensions including underlying market price and time that affect individual legs of a strategy as well as the strategy taken as a whole.

The "high-probability" strategy just discussed relies more on one's judgment regarding when to hold and when to liquidate than does the "low-probability" strategy. This is because the latter strategy usually requires more active management than the former strategy. The option trader who pursues the former strategy must be prepared to trade the position frequently.

Finally, it is well to note that option spreads entail (at least) two positions relative to a single outright option position with the implication that one's trading costs including slippage and commissions are typically greater than the costs incurred in an outright strategy involving a single instrument. Find strategies with sufficient payoff probabilities to assure that commissions are wisely spent.

Vertical Option Spreads

A *vertical option spread* entails the purchase and sale of two options of the same type (i.e., purchase and sale of two call options or purchase and sale of two put options) with the same expiration but different strike prices. You can, generally speaking, scan option quotes in the pages of financial reports or on electronic quotation devices vertically to identify options that comprise vertical spreads. (Note that option months are often displayed horizontally along the tops of columns with strikes shown vertically along rows.)

One may categorize vertical spreads along two dimensions: (1) whether they are essentially bullish or bearish (see Exhibit 13.2), and (2) whether they result in an initial net payment of premium, a debit spread, or in an initial net receipt of premium, a credit spread. See Exhibit 13.3.

EXHIBIT 13.2 Constructing Vertical Spreads

	Low Struck Option	High Struck Option
Bull Vertical Spread	Buy	Sell
Bear Vertical Spread	Sell	Buy

EXHIBIT 13.3 Constructing Vertical Spreads

	Debit Spread	Credit Spread
Bull Vertical Spread	Call	Put
Bear Vertical Spread	Put	Call

Bull Vertical Call Spread

As a general rule, you create a bullish vertical spread by buying the option with the low strike price and selling the option with the high strike. This rule of thumb is valid regardless of whether you are using call or put options to construct the spread. Bearish vertical spreads are created by selling the option with the low strike price and buying the option with the high strike. Again, this applies regardless of whether you are working with call or put options. See Exhibit 13.3.

Example December CME Eurodollar futures are trading at 95.695 on March 23, 2005. You may have constructed a vertical bull call spread by buying a 95.75 December call at 0.2000 ($500.00) and selling a 96.00 December call at 0.1075 ($268.75) for an initial net debit of $231.25. See Exhibit 13.4.

You may confirm that the position is essentially bullish by examining the net delta. Note that we have assigned a positive delta to the long call (a bullish position) and a negative delta to the short call (a bearish position). Our net delta of 0.16 suggests that if the market were to advance by one full point (1.00), the net premium might advance by 0.16 points. As indicated earlier, however, deltas are actually only valid over small price movements. Thus, we might interpret the net delta as suggesting that if the market were to advance by 0.10 index points (10 basis points), the net premium might advance by 0.016 index points (1.6 basis points).

Likewise, we may assign positive or negative signatures to gamma, theta, and vega to identify the net effect that the convexity, time value decay, and

EXHIBIT 13.4 Vertical Bull Call Spread

	Prem	Vol	Delta	Gamma	7-Day Theta	Vega
Buy 1 95.75 Dec-05 Call	−0.2000	15.70%	+0.43	+0.671	−0.0029	+0.0144
Sell 1 96.00 Dec-05 Call	+0.1075	16.20%	−0.27	−0.548	+0.0027	−0.0123
	−0.0925 ($231.25)		0.16	0.123	−0.0002	0.0021

(rising) volatility may exert on the net spread. We assign a positive gamma and positive vega to the long call to the extent that convexity and (rising) volatility benefit the long. We assign a negative gamma and negative vega to the short call to the extent that convexity and (rising) volatility detracts from short positions. Again, convexity and rising volatility tend to work together.

Finally, we assign a negative theta to the long call to the extent that time value decay will erode the value of long positions. A positive theta is assigned to the short call to the extent that time value decay will benefit a short position.

Note that we have a net positive gamma and vega and a net negative theta. That is, the effects of convexity and (rising) volatility will exert a positive influence on the value of the position. However, time value decay represents a negative factor.

The nearby graphic illustrates the profit or loss that would accrue if this position were held until June, September, or expiration in December. Assuming that the market trades below the lower of the two strikes (95.75) by expiration, both calls expire out-of-the-money and are worthless. Thus, the trader is left with the initial net debit of $231.25.

If, however, the market rallies above the upper of the two strikes (96.00), both options are in-the-money and exercised. Thus, you buy futures at 95.75 and sell at 96.00 for a net profit of 25 basis points ($625 = 25 bips × $25) less the initial net debit of $231.25 for a net gain of $393.75. If the market trades between the two strikes by expiration, the long 95.75 call is in-the-money and exercised for some gain, whereas the short 96.00 call falls out-of-the-money and expires worthless. See Exhibit 13.5.

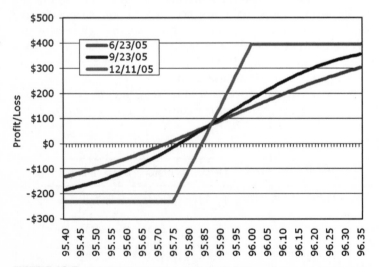

EXHIBIT 13.5 95.75/96.00 Vertical Bull Call Spread

EXHIBIT 13.6   Vertical Spread Parameters

	Bull Vertical Call Spread	Bear Vertical Call Spread
Results in	Initial net debit	Initial net credit
Maximum Loss	Initial net debit	Difference in strikes less net credit
Maximum Profit	Difference in strikes less net debit	Initial net credit
Breakeven (B/E) Point	Low strike plus maximum loss	Low strike plus maximum profit

The risk and reward parameters of this spread, assuming it is held until expiration, may be defined in Exhibit 13.6.

Bear Vertical Call Spread

Note that the spread depicted earlier resulted in the initial net payment of premium or an initial net debit. This is referred to as a *debit spread.* If one were to execute a trade that were exactly opposite to the bull call spread with initial net debit, the result would be a bear call spread with an initial net credit. The risks and rewards would be defined in opposite terms. See Exhibit 13.7.

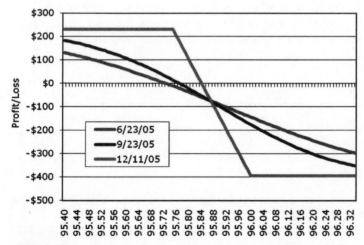

EXHIBIT 13.7   95.75/96.00 Vertical Bear Call Spread

Bear Vertical Put Spread

One may create bull and bear spreads with call options. Or, one may create similar risk exposures using put options. Like the call spreads, put spreads may result in an initial net debit or an initial net credit.

Example December CME Eurodollar futures are trading at 95.695 on March 23, 2005. You may have constructed a vertical bear put spread by buying a 95.75 December put at 0.2550 ($637.50) and selling a 95.25 December put at 0.0700 ($175.00) for an initial net debit of $462.50. See Exhibit 13.8.

This position is essentially bearish as confirmed by the negative net delta of −0.33. This suggests that if the market price were to decline by one full point (1.00), the net premium on the bear put spread would advance by 0.33 or 33 basis points. To the extent that deltas change (as measured by gamma), the net delta only holds much predictive value over a relatively small price movement. Thus, we might interpret the delta as suggesting that if prices were to decline by 10 basis points, the net premium on the bear put spread might advance by approximately 3.3 basis points.

This position has a net positive gamma and vega and a net negative theta. That is, convexity and the prospect of (rising) volatility will exert a profitable impact on the transaction. As generally expected when convexity and (rising) volatility represent positive impacts, time value decay will work against this trade (all else held constant).

If the market should advance above the upper of the two strike prices (95.75), at expiration, both puts expire out-of-the-money and worthless. This leaves the trader with a loss equal to the initial net debit of $462.50. If the market should decline below the lower of the two strike prices (95.25), at expiration, both options fall in-the-money and are exercised.

EXHIBIT 13.8 Vertical Bear Spread

	Prem	Vol	Delta	Gamma	7-Day Theta	Vega
Sell 1 95.25 Dec-05 ED Put Option	+0.0700	14.680%	+0.23	−0.559	+0.0019	−0.0115
Buy 1 95.75 Dec-05 ED Put Option	−0.2550	15.780%	−0.56	+0.671	−0.0029	+0.0144
	−0.1850 ($462.50)		−0.33	+0.112	−0.0010	+0.0029

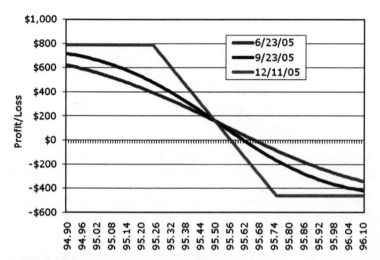

EXHIBIT 13.9 *95.25/95.75* Vertical Bear Put Spread

Thus, you sell futures at 95.75 and buy futures at 95.25 for a gross profit of 50 basis points ($1,250.00) less the initial net debit of $462.50 for a net profit of $787.50. If the market falls between the two strikes by expiration, the 95.75 long put is exercised while the 95.25 short put expires out-of-the-money and worthless. See Exhibit 13.9.

The risk/reward parameters of this spread assuming it is held until expiration may be defined in Exhibit 13.10.

Bull Vertical Put Spread

Like the bull call spread, the bear put spread results in the initial net payment of premium or an initial net debit: a "debit spread." If one were to execute a trade that were exactly opposite to the bear put spread with its initial net

EXHIBIT 13.10 Vertical Spread Parameters

	Bear Vertical Put Spread	Bull Vertical Put Spread
Results in	Initial net debit	Initial net credit
Maximum Loss	Initial net debit	Difference in strikes less net credit
Maximum Profit	Difference in strikes less net debit	Initial net credit
Breakeven (B/E) Point	High strike less maximum loss	High strike less maximum profit

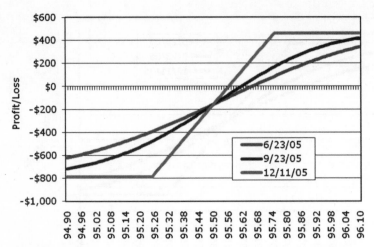

EXHIBIT 13.11   95.25/95.75 Vertical Bull Put Spread

debit, the result would be a bull put spread with an initial net credit. The risks and rewards would be defined in opposite terms. See Exhibit 13.11.

As is the case with call spreads, put spreads may result in an initial net debit or an initial net credit. As a rule, the bull call spread and bear put spreads are debit spreads; the bear call spread and the bull put spread result in initial net credits.

Selecting Vertical Spreads

Is it preferable to take advantage of a bullish market forecast using a bull (debit) call spread or a bull (credit) put spread? Consider the risks and rewards associated with 95.75/96.00 bull call and bull put spreads placed in March 2005. The bull call spread was described earlier in some detail. The 95.75/96.00 bull put spread could have been placed at an initial net credit of 0.1525 or $381.25.

Examining the potential magnitude of profit and loss with both these spreads we find, not unexpectedly, that they turn in very similar performance. The maximum loss with the bull call spread is calculated as $231.25, and the maximum loss associated with the bull put spread is $243.75. Similarly, the maximum possible profits are $393.75 and $381.25, respectively. The breakeven points are also nearly identical at 95.8425 and 95.8475, respectively.

Do the (slight) differences in the risk/reward parameters suggest that market inefficiencies are at play? Actually, the differences are at least partially explained by the fact that option spreads must be compensated to post a debit and effectively charged to take a credit from the marketplace.

The difference between the bull call spread's $393.75 maximum profit and the bull put spread's $381.25 maximum profit is related to the time value of money.

That $12.50 discrepancy ($393.75 − $381.25) essentially reflects the time value of money to the extent that the trader who puts on the bull put spread has $381.25 that may be reinvested at prevailing short-term interest rates, whereas the trader who puts on the bull call spread presumably must borrow that $231.25 debit at prevailing rates. To the extent that the discount does not truly reflect the time value of money may motivate one to pursue the bull call or bull put spread. See Exhibit 13.12.

Another consideration may be described simply as "control." If the market is trading between the two strike prices, the credit spread entails a short in-the-money option and a long out-of-the-money option. By contrast, the debit spread entails a long in-the-money and a short out-of-the- money option.

Because the short gives up control regarding the timing of a possible exercise, the credit spreader may find his or her strategy disrupted prematurely by exercise of the short option at a time when the long option is out-of-the-money. This may be particularly true when the short is trading near its intrinsic value (i.e., when term to expiration is short, volatility is low, or the option is relatively deep in-the-money). By contrast, the debit spread provides more control of the situation, which may have some value.

In addition to choosing between debit and credit spreads, option traders may also select among a variety of strike prices. Assume, for example, that you maintain a bullish outlook and wish to place a bull call spread. But which strike prices should you select?

EXHIBIT 13.12 Comparing Bull Vertical Spreads

	95.75/96.00 Bull Vertical Call Spread	95.75/96.00 Bull Vertical Put Spread
Results in	Initial net debit = 0.0925 or $231.25	Initial net credit = 0.1525 ticks or $381.25
Maximum Loss	Initial net debit = 0.0925 ticks or $231.25	Difference in strikes less net credit = $243.75 (= $625 − $381.25)
Maximum Profit	Difference in strikes less net debit = $393.75 (= $625 − $231.25)	Initial net credit = 0.1525 ticks or $381.25
Breakeven (B/E) Point	Low strike plus maximum loss = 95.8425 (= 95.75 + 9 1/4 ticks)	High strike less maximum profit = 95.8475 (= 96.00 − 15 1/4 ticks)

EXHIBIT 13.13 Choosing a Bull Vertical Spread (March 23, 2005)

Month	Strikes	Put/Call	Max Loss	B/E Point	Max Profit
Dec-05	95.50/95.75	Bull call spread	$318.75	95.6275	$306.25
Dec-05	95.50/96.00	Bull call spread	$550.00	95.7200	$700.00
Dec-05	95.50/96.25	Bull call spread	$805.00	95.8220	$1,070.00
Dec-05	95.75/96.00	Bull call spread	$231.25	95.8425	$393.75
Dec-05	95.75/96.25	Bull call spread	$486.25	95.9445	$763.75
Dec-05	96.00/96.25	Bull call spread	$268.75	96.1075	$356.25
Dec-05	95.00/95.25	Bull put spread	$531.25	95.2125	$93.75
Dec-05	95.00/95.50	Bull put spread	$993.75	95.3975	$256.25
Dec-05	95.00/95.75	Bull put spread	$1,318.75	95.5275	$556.25
Dec-05	95.00/96.00	Bull put spread	$1,562.50	95.6250	$937.50
Dec-05	95.25/95.50	Bull put spread	$462.50	95.4350	$162.50
Dec-05	95.25/95.75	Bull put spread	$787.50	95.5650	$462.50
Dec-05	95.25/96.00	Bull put spread	$1,031.25	95.6625	$843.75
Dec-05	95.50/95.75	Bull put spread	$325.00	95.6300	$300.00
Dec-05	95.50/96.00	Bull put spread	$568.75	95.7275	$681.25

Let's consider the placement of a 95.50/95.75 bull call spread versus a 95.75/96.00 bull call spread on March 23, 2005, when the underlying market was seen at 95.695. The lower struck spread entailed a bit more risk ($318.75) coupled with a bill less profit potential ($306.25) relative to the higher struck spread with less risk ($231.25) and more profit potential ($393.75).

But the market has a way of evening the odds. Note that with the market at 95.695, we are already over the breakeven point of the lower struck spread at 95.6275. In other words, if the market should remain perfectly static, the lower struck spread should result in a profit held until expiration with time value decay working to your benefit. However, the market needs to advance from 95.695 to 95.8425 to achieve the breakeven point of the upper struck spread. In this case, time value decay will work against the spread. See Exhibit 13.13.

In other words, you have a higher probability of achieving a reduced profit and a lower probability of achieving a somewhat greater profit with these two spreads. Clearly, one must be a bit more bullish to pursue the 95.75/96.00 bull call spread relative to the 95.50/95.75 bull call spread.

HORIZONTAL SPREADS

A horizontal spread entails the purchase of a put and the sale of a put or the purchase of a call and the sale of a call. The two options that comprise a horizontal spread share a common strike price but are distinguished

EXHIBIT 13.14   Constructing Horizontal Spreads

	Near-Term	Longer-Term
Horizontal Call Spread	Sell	Buy
Horizontal Put Spread	Sell	Buy

with respect to their expiration dates. You can scan option quotes in the pages of financial reports or on electronic quotation devices horizontally to identify options that comprise horizontal spreads. (Option months are usually quoted horizontally in columns with prices shown vertically along the rows.) Because the options that comprise the spread have different terms to expiration, these spreads may also be referred to as "time" or "calendar spreads."

We are interested primarily in a single type of horizontal spread: a *debit horizontal*. This spread is characterized by the sale of a shorter-term option (in the nearby month) and the purchase of a longer-term option (a deferred option). See Exhibit 13.14.

Horizontal Call Spread

A horizontal call spread typically results in an initial net debit to the extent that long-term options command greater premiums than do short-term options with the same strike. However, this rule may not work in the context of options on futures. This may be explained by the fact that the options on futures are exercisable for futures in two different months with implications that are explored later. The idea is simply to take advantage of the tendency for shorter-term options to exhibit more time value decay than longer-term options.

Example   On March 23, 2005, you might have sold a 96.00 call exercisable for September 2005 Eurodollar futures for 0.14 points or $350. By simultaneously buying a 95.75 December 2005 call for 0.20 or $500, you will have created a debit horizontal call spread at an initial net debit of $150 (= $500 − $350).

Actually, this does not quite conform to a textbook definition of a horizontal spread because the two strike prices are a bit different. Technically, it is a diagonal spread as described in Exhibit 13.14. But noting that September futures were at 95.98 and December futures at 95.695, the 96.00 September call and the 96.75 December call were the nearest-to-the-money options. Thus, the "Sep/Dec" spread may be quoted at 0.0285 (= 95.98 − 95.695). Assuming that the underlying futures spread is stable, it may be

EXHIBIT 13.15   Horizontal Call Spread

	Prem	Vol	Delta	Gamma	7-Day Theta	Vega
Sell 1 96.00 Sep-05 Call	+0.1400	13.51%	−0.46	−1.030	+0.0029	−0.0111
Buy 1 95.75 Dec-05 Call	−0.2000	15.70%	+0.43	+0.671	−0.0029	+0.0144
	−0.0600 ($150.00)		−0.03	−0.359	0.0000	+0.0033

more important to select options by reference to the relationship between the strike and market price than by the outright strike price alone. That is, select two options that are equivalently in-, out-of-, or near-to-the-money. Thus, we have slightly stretched our definition of a horizontal spread.

This spread is essentially price neutral as indicated by the net delta equal to −0.03. It also has a net theta that is near zero. But this may be a bit misleading. Consider that the net gamma is negative at −0.359. As a general rule, if the net gamma of a strategy is negative, the net theta will be positive and vice versa. That is, if convexity works against you, time value decay as measured by theta will (eventually) work to your benefit. In this case, time value decay will eventually work to your benefit.

What would happen if the strategy were held until expiration of the September options on September 19? The horizontal scale of our graphic depicts the value of September futures with the implicit assumption that the Sep/Dec spread remains stable. Likewise, for purposes of our simulated returns, we assume that the implied volatilities of the two options that comprise the spread remain stable. See Exhibit 13.16.

Profit is maximized in a horizontal spread when the market is reasonably stable and the near-term leg of the spread is trading at or near its strike price at expiration. Because the profit is contingent on the sale price of the long deferred call at expiration there is no convenient formula you can use to estimate the maximum profit. Rather, the profit must be approximated by simulation as just shown. In the foregoing example, the maximum profit was approximated at 15 basis points or $375.

Because profit is maximized in a stable environment when the nearby option expires at its strike price, it is advisable to use strikes that are near to where you believe the market may be trading at expiration of the nearby option. If you are mildly bearish, set strikes somewhat below the market. If you are mildly bullish, set the strikes a bit above the market. But don't set strikes too far from the money. This spread is intended to capitalize on the differential time value decay associated with short-term and long-term

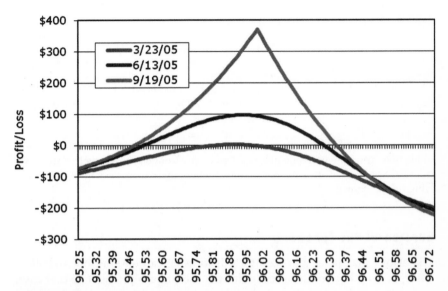

EXHIBIT 13.16   Sep/Dec Horizontal Call Spread

near-the-money options. It likely won't work if you use options that are too far from the money and do not experience the pattern of time decay normally associated with near-the-money options.

Just as the maximum profit cannot be calculated in a straightforward manner, the breakeven points can likewise only be approximated through the process of simulation. In this case, the breakevens are located around 95.49 and 96.33 (for the September contract holding the Sep/Dec spread constant).

If the market declines significantly by expiration of the September contract, the short Sep call will become worthless. Likewise, the long Dec call is driven deep out-of-the-money and may become worthless. Thus, the spread results in the loss of the initial net debit.

If the market advances significantly, losses accruing on the short near-term call equal the in-the-money amount. As the market advances, the long long-term call likewise moves deep in-the-money. At some point, a deep in-the-money option is worth nothing more than its intrinsic value. Thus, the loss on the short option is offset by profit on exercise of the long option, and the spreader is left with a loss equal to the initial net debit. However, this assumes that this is a true horizontal spread where both options are struck at equivalent levels. It also assumes that the spread between the two underlying legs is stable. We show these qualifications in more detail in Exhibit 13.17.

EXHIBIT 13.17   Horizontal Spread Parameters

	Horizontal Call Spread	Horizontal Put Spread
Results in	Initial net debit	
Maximum Loss	Approximated by initial net debit*	
Maximum Profit	Must be simulated but realized near the strike price of short option	
Breakeven (B/E) Points	Must be simulated	

*This only applies where one places a "true" horizontal spread where both strike prices are equivalent. It is further qualified where there is movement in the underlying futures spread.

Horizontal Put Spread

Just as one may place a horizontal spread using call options, one may likewise put on a horizontal spread with the use of put options. In either case, the results are quite similar.

Example   See Exhibit 13.18. On March 23, 2005, you could have sold a 96.00 put exercisable for September 2005 Eurodollar futures for 0.16 or $400. Simultaneously, buy a 95.75 December 2005 put for 0.255 or $637.50 to create a debit horizontal put spread at a debit of $237.50 (= $637.50 − $400). Again, this is technically a diagonal spread to the extent that the two strike prices are different. But it is consistent with the spirit of a horizontal spread to the extent that the two options were both reasonably close-to-the-money.

What happens if the strategy is held until expiration of the nearby September option? Our simulation assumes that the December long call is liquidated at prevailing market prices, that the Sep/Dec futures spread is

EXHIBIT 13.18   Horizontal Put Spread

	Prem	Vol	Delta	Gamma	7-Day Theta	Vega
Sell 1 96.00 Sep-05 Put	+0.1600	13.54%	+0.53	−1.030	+0.0029	−0.0111
Buy 1 95.75 Dec-05 Put	−0.2550	15.78%	−0.56	+0.671	−0.0029	+0.0144
	−0.0950 ($237.50)		−0.03	−0.359	+0.0000	+0.0033

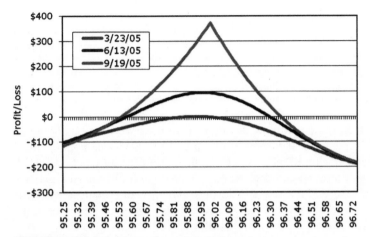

EXHIBIT 13.19   Sep/Dec Horizontal Put Spread

held constant, and that the options trade at constant volatilities into the future. See Exhibit 13.19.

Again, the maximum profit and breakeven points may be approximated through simulation. Your estimate depends on what you estimate the long-term put will be worth at expiration of the near-term put.

The maximum (upside) risk may be approximated as the initial net debit. If the market rallies sharply, both options fall deep out-of-the-money and become worthless. If the market declines sharply both options fall deep in-the-money. A loss equal to the in-the-money amount of the short put upon exercise is offset by the profit on exercise of the long put. This assumes that the long put will be worth only its in-the-money amount, which is typical for deep in-the-money options. Again, this is qualified by the assumption that you are placing a true horizontal spread with identical strikes and where the underlying futures spread is stable.

Underlying Futures Spread

We have indicated that the maximum risk associated with horizontal spreads may only be approximated by reference to the initial net debit. Why is this only an approximation?

Evaluating calendar spreads becomes complicated in the context of the task for options on futures relative to stock options. The reason is that the two legs of a horizontal spread using options on futures are exercisable for two different contracts. Of course, a 100-share lot of stock is the same regardless of whether the stock option expires in September or December. But a September futures contract is not the same as a December futures contract.

EXHIBIT 13.20 Effect of Futures Spread on Horizontal Spread

	Horizontal Call Spread	Horizontal Put Spread
Futures spread rallies	Negative effect	Positive effect
Futures spread declines	Positive effect	Negative effect

In our preceding example, September futures were at 95.98 while December futures were at 95.695 for a spread of 28.5 basis points. But if that futures spread should rally or decline, the option spread will be affected. If the Sep/Dec futures spread declines (i.e., September futures decline relative to December futures), the call spread may generate an enhanced profit. If the Sep/Dec spread advances (i.e., December falls relative to September), the value of the call spread declines. See Exhibit 13.20.

Note that our calendar call spread entails a nearby short call (a bearish position) and a deferred long call (a bullish position). Thus, if nearby futures should decline relative to deferred futures (if the futures spread should decline), this benefits the call spread. But if nearby futures rally relative to deferred futures (the futures spread rallies), this benefits the calendar call spread.

The same logic applies in reverse with respect to a put calendar spread. A put spread entails a nearby short put (bullish) and a deferred long put (bearish). Thus, the put spread benefits when the spread between nearby and deferred futures rallies and is adversely impacted when the underlying futures spread declines.

DIAGONAL SPREAD

A *diagonal spread* entails the purchase of a put and the sale of a put or the purchase of a call and the sale of a call. The two options that comprise a diagonal spread differ with respect to both strike price and expiration date. Because this spread involves options that differ with respect to both strike and expiration, it incorporates elements of both the vertical and horizontal spread.

Of course, our discussion centered about the use of options exercisable for futures contracts. To the extent that the two futures contracts may be trading at very different prices, we might modify our definitions here by focusing on the extent to which the two options that comprise a diagonal spread are in-, near-, or out-of-the-money.

A diagonal option spread is often constructed using the following strategy: (1) sell the nearby and buy the deferred option to capitalize on the accelerated time value decay associated with near-term options, (2) sell an at- or near-the-money option and buy a low struck option to enter a mildly

EXHIBIT 13.21 Constructing Diagonal Spreads

	Near-Term	Longer-Term
Diagonal Call Spread	Sell	Buy
Diagonal Put Spread	Sell	Buy

bullish position, and (3) sell an at- or near-the-money option and buy a high struck option to enter a mildly bearish position. See Exhibit 13.21.

Diagonal Call Spread

Vertical bull call spreads may be pursued given an expectation that the market may rise above particular breakeven point by expiration (i.e., a bullish position). The horizontal call spread might be pursued in anticipation that market prices will trade in a neutral range. The diagonal call spread is generally practiced in anticipation of a mildly bullish market scenario.

Example See Exhibit 13.22. On March 23, 2005, you could have sold a 96.00 call exercisable for September 2005 Eurodollar futures at 0.14 or $350. By concurrently buying a 95.50 December 2005 call for 0.3275 or $818.75, you have created a diagonal call spread. The spread entails an initial net debit of $468.75. September futures were at 95.98; December futures were at 95.695.

The maximum possible profit and the breakeven points must be identified through the process of simulation and the application of assumptions regarding volatility and the performance of the underlying futures spread. Specifically, one must simulate the possible sale price of the long low-struck deferred call in order to assess possible outcomes.

Like the horizontal spread, you can approximate the maximum potential loss by reference to the initial net debit. In our example, the maximum you can lose is approximately $468.75. This may be understood by

EXHIBIT 13.22 Diagonal Call Spread

	Prem	Vol	Delta	Gamma	7-Day Theta	Vega
Sell 1 96.00 Sep-05 Call	+0.1400	13.51%	−0.46	−1.030	+0.0029	−0.0111
Buy 1 95.50 Dec-05 Call	−0.3275	14.78%	+0.61	+0.703	−0.0026	+0.0140
	−0.1875 ($468.75)		+0.15	−0.327	+0.0003	+0.0029

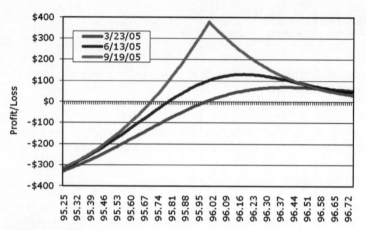

EXHIBIT 13.23 Sep/Dec Diagonal Call Spread

considering that if the market should fall sharply, both options fall out-of-the-money and become worthless. Thus, the spread trader is left with a loss equal to the initial net debit.

If the market should rally sharply, both options are driven into-the-money. The short 96.00 option will generate a loss equal to its in-the-money amount at expiration. Likewise, the in-the-money long 95.50 call will be worth its intrinsic value.

But the long call may have more intrinsic value than the short call to the extent that it is struck at a lower level. Of course, this is contingent on the possible performance of the underlying futures calendar spread. Thus, the returns associated with the spread in the event of a substantial rally may be expressed as the difference in strike prices less the initial debit. In the foregoing case that translates to a $781.25 ($1,250 − $468.75) profit.

Because "downside" returns (i.e., returns in the event of a market decline) are worse than "upside" returns (i.e., returns in the event of a market decline), this strategy is clearly somewhat bullish. See Exhibit 13.23.

Maximum profits, however, are still realized at the short strike price (96.00 in our example). This is attributed to the accelerated time value decay associated with near- or at-the-money options. As expiration approaches, holding September futures constant at 96.00, it is clear that the value of the spread appreciates at an accelerated pace. See Exhibit 13.24.

Diagonal Put Spread

The combination of a short nearby near-the-money call and a long deferred in-the-money call constitutes a diagonal call spread as already discussed. What if you used puts instead of calls?

EXHIBIT 13.24 Diagonal Spread Parameters

	Diagonal Call Spread	Diagonal Put Spread
Results in	Initial net debit	
Maximum Profit	Must be simulated but realized near the strike price of short option	
Maximum Downside Loss	Approximated by initial net debit*	Approximated by difference in strikes less initial net debit*
Maximum Upside Loss	Approximated by difference in strikes less initial net debit*	Approximated by initial net debit*
Breakeven (B/E) Points	Must be simulated	

*This assumes that the "underlying futures spread" is stable and does not fluctuate. If the underlying futures spread fluctuates, however, this will affect the returns on these spreads constructed using options on futures.

Example See Exhibit 13.25. On March 23, 2005, you could have sold a 96.00 put exercisable for September 2005 Eurodollar futures for 0.16 or $400 and purchased a 96.00 December 2005 put for 40.75 or $1,018.75. To the extent that this spread represents the combination of two options at the same strike price, many would recognize it as a horizontal spread. Note, however, that September futures were trading at 95.98 and December were trading at 95.695 at the time. Thus, the September 96.00 put is very near- the-money, whereas the December 96.00 put is in-the-money. As a result, we might (liberally) regard this as more of a diagonal than a horizontal spread.

EXHIBIT 13.25 Diagonal Put Spread

	Prem	Vol	Delta	Gamma	7-Day Theta	Vega
Sell 1 96.00 Sep-05 Put	+0.1600	13.54%	+0.53	−1.030	+0.0029	−0.0111
Buy 1 96.00 Dec-05 Put	−0.4075	16.30%	−0.72	+0.562	−0.0027	+0.0123
	−0.2475 ($618.75)		−0.19	−0.468	+0.0002	+0.0021

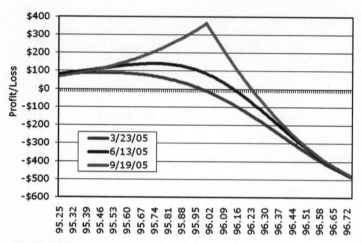

EXHIBIT 13.26   Sep/Dec Diagonal Put Spread

You can approximate the maximum "upside" loss by reference to the initial net debit. If the market rallies and both options run deep out-of-the-money, they might both become worthless leaving the spreader with a loss equal to the initial net debit of $618.75.

If the market should decline sharply, both options are driven deep in-the-money. The short 96.00 put generates a loss equal to its in-the-money amount by expiration. Likewise, the deep in-the-money long 96.00 put will be worth little more than its intrinsic or in-the-money value. See Exhibit 13.26.

If the underlying futures spread or the spread between September and December futures is at zero, the difference between the intrinsic values of the two puts will be indicated by the difference in option strike prices. Thus, the maximum "downside" loss may be approximated by the difference in strike prices less the initial net debit.

Of course, in our example, both options shared a strike price of 96.00 while the underlying futures spread was quoted at 28.5 ($= 95.98 - 95.695$). To the extent that the long December 96 put is already well in-the-money, and to the extent that the underlying futures spread remains stable in a market break, the downside loss might be approximated by the initial net debit less the value of that spread. In this case, that equals a profit of $93.75 calculated as the value of the futures spread of $712.50 ($= 28.5$ basis points $\times$ $25 per basis point) less the initial net debit of $618.75. Because the return on the "upside" (in the event of a market advance) is much worse than the return on the "downside" (in the event of a market decline), this strategy is somewhat bearish.

Profits tend to be maximized at the short strike price, or 96.00, in our example. This is attributed to the accelerated time value decay associated with near- or at-the-money options. As expiration approaches, holding September futures constant at 96.00, the value of the option spread will appreciate at an accelerated pace. The maximum profit simulated in our example is approximately $373.

Futures Spread Movement

Diagonal and horizontal spreads are very closely related and sometimes almost indistinguishable as we consider the nominal strike price versus in- or out-of-the-money values. Thus, just as the performance of the underlying futures spread may strongly impact the diagonal spread, it may likewise impact the value of the horizontal spread.

Our simulated returns are based on the assumption of a stable underlying futures spread. Of course, if that spread should fluctuate, the effect on a diagonal spread is similar to the effect on a horizontal spread.

Specifically, if the futures spread should decline ("Dec" rallies relative to "Sep"), this will exert a positive impact on horizontal and diagonal call spreads and a negative impact on horizontal and diagonal put spreads. If the spread should rally ("Dec" falls relative to "Sep"), this has a negative impact on both horizontal and diagonal call spreads and a positive impact on both horizontal and diagonal put spreads.

COMPARING VERTICALS, HORIZONTALS, AND DIAGONALS

It is interesting to compare and contrast the performance of vertical, horizontal, and diagonal spreads. In particular, let's compare the vertical bull call spread, the horizontal debit call spread, and the diagonal call spread illustrated in our preceding examples.

Even though it is only mildly bullish relative to a long futures position, the vertical call spread is generally considered the most bullish of the three option spreads. The horizontal spread is quite neutral, and the diagonal call spread is generally considered to fall somewhere in between. This is supported by examining the initial net deltas associated with our three spreads.

	Initial Net Delta
Vertical Call Spread	+0.16
Horizontal Call Spread	−0.03
Diagonal Call Spread	+0.15

The vertical spread in our example has a net delta of +0.16, which suggests that it represents the rough equivalent of buying 0.16 futures. The horizontal spread is quite neutral as evidenced by the delta of −0.03. Finally, the diagonal spread is somewhere in between with a net delta of +0.15.

As expiration draws near, deltas for in-the-money options will approach 1.0 while deltas for out-of-the-money options approach zero. Thus, as a general rule, the net deltas on the vertical and diagonal spreads tend to become more positive or bullish over time. Another way of expressing this is to suggest that these spreads become increasingly less stable and exhibit convexity as expiration approaches.

Our discussion has considered the merits of "high probability" strategies (i.e., strategies with a high probability of modest profit and low probability of a relatively larger loss). This generally implies that the strategy will allow you to take advantage of time value decay. Strategies that take advantage of time value decay are subject to the risks of convexity. This phenomenon is examined in greater detail next.

WEIGHTED SPREADS

Weighted spreads may be thought of as variations on the simple vertical spread. Vertical spreads entail the purchase of one call and sale of one call or the purchase of one put and sale of one put (i.e., a balanced 1-for-1 ratio). A *ratio spread* is a vertical spread except that you sell more options than you buy. A *backspread* is a vertical spread where you buy more options than you sell.

As a general rule, ratio spreads are thought of as tools that allow you to take advantage of time value decay. Backspreads are just the opposite and generally thought of as trading strategies dependent on a large market movement or volatility to succeed.

2-for-1 Ratio Call Spread

The "2-for-1" is the most common of ratio spreads. This strategy calls for the purchase of one option (put or call) and the sale of two options (puts or calls). Like the vertical spread, the long and short legs of the spread share a common expiration but differ with respect to strike prices.

Example See Exhibit 13.27. On March 25, 2005, a ratio call spread could have been placed by buying a December 95.75 call for 20 basis points or $500 and selling two December 96.00 calls for 10.75 basis points each,

EXHIBIT 13.27 2-for-1 Ratio Call Spread

	Prem	Vol	Delta	Gamma	7-Day Theta	Vega
Buy 1 95.75 Dec-05 Call	−0.2000	15.70%	+0.43	+0.671	−0.0029	+0.0144
Sell 2 96.00 Dec-05 Call	+0.1075	16.20%	−0.27	−0.548	+0.0027	−0.0123
	+0.0150 $37.50		−0.11	−0.425	+0.0025	−0.0102

which equates to $268.75 a piece or $537.50 for the two. Thus, the spread is placed at a total net credit of $37.50. December futures were trading at 95.695 at the time.

In our example, the 2-for-1 spread resulted in an initial net credit. Sometimes these spreads may result in a debit and sometimes in a credit. We typically think of strategies that result in the initial receipt of premium (net credit) as strategies to be pursued in an essentially neutral or reasonably calm market environment. Note that the net gamma is negative and the net theta is positive. Thus, the initial net credit is consistent with the implications associated with the net gamma and theta, although only by a small margin.

The initial net delta of −0.11 seems to suggest that this is a slightly bearish strategy, but this is a bit misleading. Actually, we would characterize this spread as slightly bullish to the extent that profits are maximized if the market rallies slightly to the 96.00 strike price by option expiration.

Let's summarize the risks and rewards associated with the strategy. Should the market fluctuate to the lower strike or below by expiration, both the 95.75 and 96.00 calls fall out-of-the-money. Thus, the trader is left with the original net debit or net credit. In this case, the initial placement of the spread resulted in the receipt of a modest credit of $37.50.

Profit is maximized at the upper of the two strike prices, or 96.00 in our example. If the market is at precisely 96.00, the single long call is 25 basis points in-the-money and worth $625. The two short higher struck calls are at-the-money and worthless. This implies a profit equal to the in-the-money amount of the long call, which may be expressed as the difference in strikes less any net debit or plus any net credit. In Exhibit 13.28, the maximum profit equals $662.50 (= $625 + $37.50).

If the futures rally above the upper of the two strike prices, the two short calls fall in-the-money. At some point, the losses that accrue from the exercise of the short options offset the profit from the single in-the-money long option. This is the breakeven point identified as the upper strike price

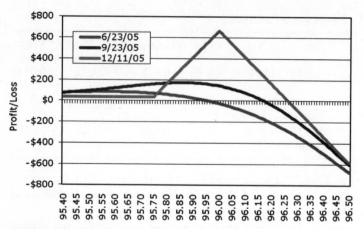

EXHIBIT 13.28 95.75/96.00 2-for-1 Ratio Call Spread

plus the maximum profit. In Exhibit 13.29, that equals 96.00 plus 26.5 basis points (= $662.50 at $25 per basis point), or 96.265.

We think of this spread as one that might be placed when the market is near or even under the lower of the two strikes. The idea is to find a situation where the market may be expected to gradually trade toward the short strike price by expiration. If the market price doesn't move upward, however, the spread's terminal value is limited to any initial net credit or debit. In our example, the placement of the spread resulted in an initial net credit so the prospect of a flat or declining market is not particularly distressing. The major risk is that the market will rally rapidly up to and through the upper breakeven, possibly leaving the upper trader with large losses.

2-for-1 Ratio Put Spread

Just as you can place a 2-for-1 ratio call spread in anticipation of a mildly bullish market, you can place a 2-for-1 ratio put spread in anticipation of a mildly bearish market.

EXHIBIT 13.29 2-for-1 Ratio Call Spread Parameters

	2-for-1 Ratio Call Spread
Downside Risk	Initial net debit or credit = $37.50
Maximum Profit	Difference in strikes plus or minus initial net credit or debit = $662.50 (= $625 + $37.50)
Upper Breakeven (B/E) Point	Upper strike price + maximum profit = 96.265 (= 96.00 + 0.265)

EXHIBIT 13.30 2-for-1 Ratio Put Spread

	Prem	Vol	Delta	Gamma	7-Day Theta	Vega
Sell 2 95.25 Dec-05 Put	+0.0700	14.68%	+0.23	−0.559	+0.0019	−0.0115
Buy 1 95.75 Dec-05 Put	−0.2550	15.78%	−0.56	+0.671	−0.0029	+0.0144
	−0.0115 ($287.50)		−0.10	−0.447	+0.0009	−0.0086

Example It is March 23, 2005, and a 2-for-1 ratio put spread is placed by buying a December 95.75 Eurodollar futures put for 25.5 basis points, or $637.50, and selling two 95.25 puts for 7 basis points apiece, or $350 in total. This results in an initial net debit of $287.50. December futures were trading at 95.695 at the time. See Exhibit 13.30.

If the market price is at or above the upper of the two strikes at expiration, both puts fall out-of-the-money and become worthless. Thus, the trader is left with either the original net debit or net credit. In our example, that implies a loss equal to the initial net debit of $287.50.

Profits are maximized at the lower of the two strike prices. Here, the single long put falls 50 basis points in-the-money and is worth $1,250. The two short lower struck puts are at-the-money and worthless. Thus, the profit equals the in-the-money amount of the long put plus any initial net credit or minus any initial net debit. In our example, that equals $962.50 (= $1,250 − $287.50). See Exhibit 13.31.

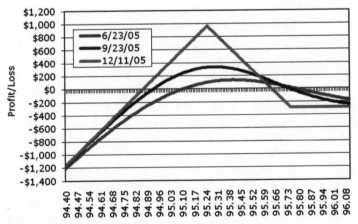

EXHIBIT 13.31 95.25/95.75 2-for-1 Ratio Put Spread

EXHIBIT 13.32 2-for-1 Ratio Put Spread Parameters

	2-for-1 Ratio Put Spread
Downside Risk	Initial net debit or credit = −$287.50
Maximum Profit	Difference in strikes plus or minus initial net credit or debit = $962.50 (= $1,250 − $287.50)
Lower Breakeven (B/E) Point	Lower strike price − maximum profit = 94.865 (= 95.25 − 0.385)

If the market price should trend below the lower of the two strike prices, two short puts fall in-the-money. At some point, losses that accrue from the exercise of the short options offset the profit from the single in-the-money long option. The loss associated with one of the two short puts offsets the profit from the single long put. Under the lower of the two strikes, it is as if you were long one futures contract in a falling market. The lower breakeven point is identified as the lower strike price less the maximum profit. In Exhibit 13.32, that equals 95.25 less 38.5 basis points ($962.5 at $25 per basis point) or 94.865.

Analogous to the ratio call spread, the ratio put spread is normally placed when the market is around or above the upper of the two strikes. Hopefully, the market will gradually trade toward the short strike price by expiration. The risk is that the market will decline rapidly down to or below the lower breakeven point.

3-for-1, 3-for-2 Ratios

Although the 2-for-1 ratio is the most common, other ratios are often employed as well. The 3-for-1 or 3-for-2 ratios are fairly common.

The risks and rewards associated with the 3-for-1 ratio call spread are similar to those associated with the 2-for-1. Like the 2-for-1 call spread, the "downside" risk below the lower of the two strike prices is identified as the initial net debit or credit. Similarly, the maximum profit equals the difference in strike prices plus or minus any initial net credit or initial net debit. But the upper breakeven point is calculated as the upper strike price plus half of the maximum possible profit.

The 3-for-2 ratio call spread likewise shares some parameters with the 2-for-1 ratio call spread. The "downside" risk in the event that the market falls below the two strike prices by expiration is defined as any initial net debit or initial net credit. Like the 2-for-1 spread, the upper breakeven point is defined as the upper strike price plus the maximum profit. But the

EXHIBIT 13.33 Other Ratio Spread Parameters

	3-for-1 Ratio Call Spread	3-for-2 Ratio Call Spread
Downside Risk	Initial net debit or credit	Initial net debit or credit
Maximum Profit	Difference in strikes plus or minus initial net credit or debit	Twice the difference in strikes plus or minus initial net credit or debit
Upper Breakeven (B/E) Point	Upper strike price + half of maximum profit	Upper strike price + maximum profit

maximum profit is equal to twice the difference in strike prices plus or minus any initial net credit or debit, respectively. See Exhibit 13.33.

Which of the three strategies (2-for-1, 3-for-1, 3-for-2) might be considered best? No single strategy dominates to the extent that risks and rewards generally tend to balance. The 3-for-2 spread is the most aggressive of the three strategies with the greatest maximum profit but also implies the greatest downside risk. The 2-for-1 strategy is the least aggressive in terms of its maximum potential profit but offers no explicit downside risk to the extent that it may have been put on at an initial net credit. See Exhibit 13.34.

Backspreads

A *backspread* is created by taking a vertical spread but by buying more options than are sold, or the opposite of a ratio spread. As you might expect, the risks and rewards associated with these strategies are precisely opposite those associated with similarly weighted ratio spreads.

In fact, you may simply rotate a ratio spread diagram along a horizontal axis to create a diagram illustrating a backspread. Similarly, you may rotate these graphics along a vertical axis and change the orientation from a put to a call or a call to a put. See Exhibits 13.35 and 13.36 for examples.

EXHIBIT 13.34 Comparing Ratio Spreads

	"Downside" Risk	Maximum Profit	Upper Breakeven
2-for-1	$37.50	$662.50	96.265
3-for-1	$306.25	$931.25	96.18625
3-for-2	($193.75)	$1,056.25	96.4225

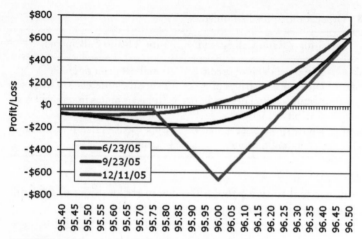

EXHIBIT 13.35   95.75/96.00 2-for-1 Call Backspread

VOLATILITY-DRIVEN STRATEGIES

One of the several factors that drive option prices is marketplace volatility. Of course, there are other factors, notably including the relationship of the market price to the option strike or exercise price and the term or time remaining until option expiration. All of these variables impact the option premium to one degree or another and therefore impact the outcome of one's option trading strategy.

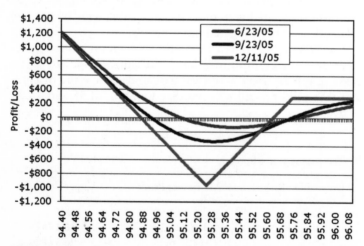

EXHIBIT 13.36   95.25/95.75 2-for-1 Put Backspread

Let's focus on a series of option strategies that are sometimes referred to as *volatility trades*. But although these trades may be called volatility trades, it is important to recognize the impact that price time and volatility wield on the particular strategy. Further, it is important to understand that these three variables are not independent but rather act in concert to offer the option trader a number of tradeoffs. Thus, one's strategy tends to be driven by a judgment regarding which of these factors is most likely to exert a heavy impact on the market.

The specific strategies we intend to highlight include straddles, strangles, guts, butterflies, and condors. All of these strategies are significantly affected by rising or falling volatilities. But as a practical matter, it may be difficult to isolate the impact of volatility on the strategy apart from the concerted impact of market price movement and the significance of time value decay. This is apparent when one considers that volatility is essentially defined by the degree of price movement over time.

As a general rule, short options are thought of as instruments that permit you to capitalize on stable prices, the onset of time value decay and falling volatility. Long options permit you to capitalize on heavily trending prices over short time periods and rising volatility.

Long Straddle

The terms *straddle* and *spread* are sometimes employed interchangeably in the context of futures, but this is not true when we speak of options. As discussed earlier, an option spread involves the purchase and sale of two calls or the purchase and sale of two puts (in other words, two options of the same type). A straddle is distinguished from an option spread in the sense that it uses both types of options (i.e., calls and puts). Specifically, a straddle entails the purchase of a call and a put or the sale of both a call and a put.

The calls and puts that constitute an option straddle share a common strike or exercise price and a common expiration date. A long straddle entails the purchase of a call and a put; a short straddle entails the sale of both a call and a put.

Example On March 23, 2005, you might have purchased a 95.75 December 2005 call exercisable for Eurodollar futures for 20 basis points, or $500, and purchased a 95.75 December 2005 put for 25.5 basis points, or $637.50. This long straddle entails an initial net debit of $1,137.50. See Exhibit 13.37.

The maximum loss associated with a long straddle may be identified as the initial net debit. If the market trades to the common strike price at expiration, both options are at-the-money and expire with zero in-the-money or

EXHIBIT 13.37 Long Straddle

	Prem	Vol	Delta	Gamma	7-Day Theta	Vega
Buy 1 95.75 Dec-05 Call	−0.2000	15.70%	+0.43	+0.671	−0.0029	+0.0144
Buy 1 95.75 Dec-05 Put	−0.2550	15.78%	−0.56	+0.671	−0.0029	+0.0144
	−0.4550 ($1,137.50)		−0.13	+1.342	−0.0058	+0.0288

intrinsic value. Thus, the options might be abandoned leaving the trader with a loss equal to the initial debit. In our example, this equals $1,137.50.

The maximum potential profit might be described as open-ended. It is limited only by the extent to which the market might trend away from the common strike price over the life of the trade. An upper and a lower break-even point may be identified as the common strikes price plus and minus the initial net debit, respectively. If the market rises to the strike price plus the initial net debit, the long call is in-the-money by an amount equal to the debit and the long put is out-of-the-money and worthless, resulting in breakeven. Similarly, if the market declines to the strike price less the debit, the long put is in-the-money by an amount equal to the debit while the long call is out-of-the-money, resulting in breakeven again.

In Exhibit 13.38, the breakeven points may be calculated as 96.205 and 95.295. These values are calculated as 95.75 + 45.5 basis points and 95.75 − 45.5 basis points (the initial net debit of $1,137.50 at $25 per basis point equals 45.5 basis points).

The long straddle may be characterized as a nondirectional trade in the sense that it can generate profits regardless of which direction the market moves. The initial net delta in our example was −0.13, which is certainly close to zero. But more telling is the initial net gamma and theta, which are

EXHIBIT 13.38 Long Straddle Parameters

	Long Straddle
Maximum Loss	Initial net debit = $1,137.50
Upper B/E	Strike price + Initial net debit = 96.205 (= 95.75 + 45.5 basis points)
Lower B/E	Strike price − Initial net debit = 95.295 (= 95.75 − 45.5 basis points)

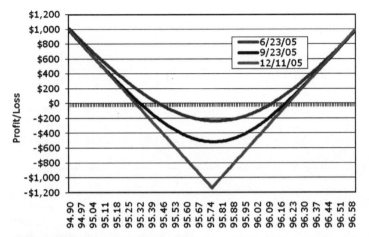

EXHIBIT 13.39   Long 95.75 Straddle

decidedly positive and negative, respectively. Thus, the trade will benefit from convexity in a volatile market environment but will experience time value decay resulting in loss in a neutral market. Finally, the net vega is also quite positive, suggesting that the long straddle will benefit from rising volatility. See Exhibit 13.39.

If you are slightly more bullish than bearish or bearish than bullish, you may wish to enter the straddle using options struck below the market (an in-the-money call and an out-of-the-money put) or struck above the market (an out-of-the-money call and an in-the-money put).

The bullish or bearish orientation of a long straddle is reflected in the net deltas and the relation of the upper and lower breakevens to the market. Thus, the 95.50 straddle that is struck low relative to the market price of 95.695 offers a lower breakeven point than the 95.75 or 96.00 straddle and a higher initial net delta. The 96.00 straddle is struck relatively high compared to the market price. It offers a relatively high lower breakeven point and a decidedly negative initial net delta. See Exhibit 13.40.

EXHIBIT 13.40   Comparing Straddles

	Long 95.50 Straddle	Long 95.75 Straddle	Long 96.00 Straddle
Maximum Loss	$1,156.25	$1,137.50	$1,287.50
Upper B/E	95.9625	96.205	96.515
Lower B/E	95.0375	95.295	95.485
Initial Net Delta	+ 0.23	−0.13	−0.45

EXHIBIT 13.41   Short Straddle

	Prem	Vol	Delta	Gamma	7-Day Theta	Vega
Sell 1 95.75 Dec-05 Call	+0.2000	15.70%	−0.43	−0.671	+0.0029	−0.0144
Sell 1 95.75 Dec-05 Put	+0.2550	15.78%	+0.56	−0.671	+0.0029	−0.0144
	+0.4550 $1,137.50		+0.13	−1.342	+0.0058	−0.0288

Short Straddle

Just as you can buy a put and a call to create a long straddle, you can sell both a put and a call to create a short straddle. A short straddle allows you to take advantage of the possibility that the market will trade in a range between the breakeven points or that volatility will decline.

Example   On March 23, 2005, you might have sold a 95.75 December 2005 call exercisable for Eurodollar futures for 20 basis points, or $500, and sold a 95.75 December 2005 put for 25.5 basis points, or $637.50. This short straddle entails an initial net credit of $1,137.50. See Exhibit 13.41.

The risk/reward parameters of the short straddle are exactly the opposite of those of the long straddle. Unlike the long straddle that requires the payment of premium or an initial net debit, the short straddle implies the receipt of premium for an initial net credit. See Exhibit 13.42.

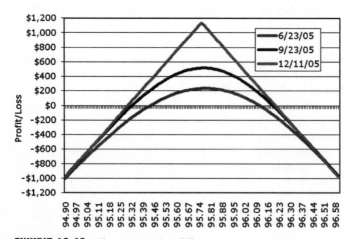

EXHIBIT 13.42   Short 95.75 Straddle

EXHIBIT 13.43 Short Straddle Parameters

	Short Straddle
Maximum Profit	Initial net credit = $1,137.50
Upper B/E	Strike price + initial net credit = 96.205 (= 95.75 + 45.5 basis points)
Lower B/E	Strike price − initial net credit = 95.295 (= 95.75 − 45.5 basis points)

This initial net credit represents the maximum possible profit presuming that the market trades to the common strike price at expiration. Under these circumstances, both options are at-the-money and worthless at expiration. Thus, you are left with the initial net credit, which, in our example, is equal to $1,137.50.

If the market rallies, the call runs into-the-money and will presumably be exercised at some point. Losses accruing from the exercise of the call will offset the initial receipt of the net credit, resulting in a breakeven situation. Thus, an upper breakeven point is found at the common strike plus the net credit. The lower breakeven point is found where the in-the-money value of the short put offsets the initial receipt of the net credit or at the common strike price less the net credit.

In Exhibit 13.43, those points are found at 96.205 and 95.295. They are calculated just as in the case of the long straddle as 95.75 + 45.5 basis points and 95.75 − 45.5 basis points (the initial net credit of $1,137.50 at $25 per basis point equates to 45.5 basis points).

Short straddles tend to be placed using strike prices that are at- or near-the-money just like long straddles. If, however, you were slightly bullish or bearish, you might consider the sale of straddles that are struck a bit above or a bit below the prevailing market price. But you likely would not use options struck very far from the money to the extent that the intent is to take advantage of time value decay. Options struck far-from-the-money tend not to exhibit much time value decay.

Long Strangle

Strangles are very similar to straddles in the sense that they entail the purchase of a call and put or the sale of both a call and a put option. Unlike a straddle, which entails the use of two options with the same strike price, a strangle entails the use of a high-struck call and a relatively low-struck put. Although the two options differ with respect to strike prices, they nonetheless share a common expiration date.

A *long strangle* entails the purchase of a high-struck call with the purchase of a relatively low-struck put. A *short strangle* entails the sale of a high-struck call with the sale of a relatively low-struck put. These trades are generally, although not necessarily, placed when the market is trading between the two strike prices. As such, this implies that a strangle involves two out-of-the-money options.

Example   You buy a long strangle on March 23, 2005, by buying a December 2005 96.00 call on Eurodollar futures at 10.75 basis points, or $268.75, and buying a December 2005 95.50 put on Eurodollar futures for 13.50 basis points, or $337.50. Thus, this strangle is placed for an initial net debit of $606.25. See Exhibit 13.44.

The long strangle performs much like a long straddle insofar as it permits you to take advantage of a market breaking sharply up or sharply down. But if the underlying futures price should remain between the two strikes prices, both options are out-of-the-money and worthless if held until expiration. Thus, the trader realizes a net loss equal to the initial net debit. In our example, that equates to a loss of $606.25.

If the market should rally over the upper of the two strike prices, the call runs into-the-money. At some point, the profit on exercise of the call offsets payment of the initial net debit. This is the upper breakeven point. If the market should break under the lower of the two strike prices, the put runs into-the-money and profits on exercise offset the initial net debit. This is the lower breakeven point. The upper and lower breakeven points may be defined as the call strike plus the net debit and the put strike less the net debit, respectively. In Exhibit 13.45, these breakeven points are calculated as 96.2425 (= 96.00 + 24.25 basis points) and 95.2575 (= 95.50 − 24.25 basis points).

The long strangle performs very much like the long straddle. It is a nondirectional volatility play that benefits from sharp movement either up or down but suffers from the phenomenon of time value decay. But

EXHIBIT 13.44   Long Strangle

	Prem	Vol	Delta	Gamma	7-Day Theta	Vega
Buy 1 96.00 Dec-05 Call	−0.1075	16.20%	+0.27	+0.548	−0.0027	+0.0123
Buy 1 95.50 Dec-05 Put	−0.1350	14.67%	−0.37	+0.695	−0.0025	+0.0144
	−0.2425 ($606.25)		−0.11	+1.243	−0.0052	+0.0267

EXHIBIT 13.45 Long Strangle Parameters

	Long Strangle
Maximum Loss	Initial net debit = $606.25
Upper B/E	Call strike price + initial net debit = 96.2425 (= 96.00 + 24.25 basis points)
Lower B/E	Put strike price − initial net debit = 95.2575 (= 95.50 − 24.25 basis points)

it might be considered a bit more conservative than the long straddle. See Exhibit 13.46.

To explain, assume that you buy a strangle when the market is midway between the two strikes or buy a straddle struck exactly at-the-money. At-the-money options are more responsive to time value decay and to shifting volatilities than are out-of-the-money options. Further, out-of-the-money options will cost less than an at-the-money option. This suggests that long strangles will generally entail a smaller initial net debit and less maximum risk than long straddles. Thus, the long strangle might be regarded as the more conservative of the two strategies.

You could also use strangles with wider or narrower strike price intervals if you wished to employ a more or less conservative strategy. As a general rule, the greater the strike price interval, the more conservative the strategy measured in terms of less initial cost and associated risk. You could further shade the strangle by using higher or lower strike

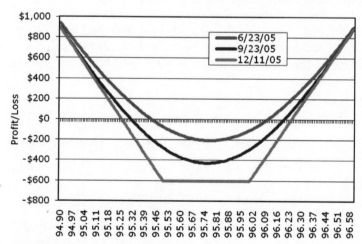

EXHIBIT 13.46 Long 95.50/96.00 Strangle

prices in anticipation of a bit more bearish or a bit more bullish market forecast, respectively.

Short Strangle

Just as you might buy a put and a call to create a long strangle, you can sell a put and a call to create a short strangle. Like a short straddle, the short strangle allows you to take advantage of a neutral market or declining volatility (i.e., to capitalize on time value decay).

Example   You sell a December 2005 call struck at 96.00 and sell a December 2005 put struck at 95.50 on March 23, 2005. The call is sold at 10.75 basis points, or $268.75, and the put is sold at 13.50 basis points, or $337.50. This generates an initial net credit of $606.25. See Exhibit 13.47.

Of course, the risk/reward parameters of the short strangle are the exact opposite of those of the long strangle. Like a short straddle, the short strangle allows you to receive premium equal to the initial net credit.

That initial net credit represents the maximum possible profit associated with the strategy. If the market should remain within the two strike prices, both options will become worthless when held until expiration. This leaves the trader with a profit equal to the initial net credit. In our example, that initial net credit was equal to $606.25.

If the market should rally, the put falls out-of-the-money and will expire worthless if held until its full term. But the call is going into-the-money and accumulating intrinsic value, which works to the detriment of the short. The upper breakeven is found at the upper strike price plus the initial net credit. If the market should decline below the lower of the two strike prices, the short call is out-of-the-money and may expire worthless. But the put is driven into-the-money and its intrinsic value will offset the receipt of the initial net credit at the lower breakeven point.

EXHIBIT 13.47   Short Strangle

	Prem	Vol	Delta	Gamma	7-Day Theta	Vega
Sell 1 96.00 Dec-05 Call	+0.1075	16.20%	−0.27	−0.548	+0.0027	−0.0123
Sell 1 95.50 Dec-05 Put	+0.1350	14.67%	+0.37	−0.695	+0.0025	−0.0144
	+0.2425 $606.25		+0.11	−1.243	+0.0052	−0.0267

EXHIBIT 13.48 Short Strangle Parameters

	Short Strangle
Maximum Profit	Initial net credit = $606.25
Upper B/E	Call strike price + Initial net credit = 96.2425 (= 96.00 + 24.25 basis points)
Lower B/E	Put strike price − Initial net credit = 95.2575 (= 95.50 − 24.25 basis points)

This lower breakeven is calculated as the lower strike price less the initial net credit.

In our example, the maximum loss was represented by the net credit of $606.25. The upper breakeven is found at 96.2425 or the upper of the two strike prices plus the initial net credit (= 96.00 + 24.25 basis points). The lower breakeven point is found at 95.2575 or the lower of the two strike prices less the initial net credit (= 95.50 − 24.25 basis points). See Exhibit 13.48.

Just as the long strangle is more conservative than the long straddle, the short strangle is likewise more conservative than the short straddle. The profitable range associated with a short strangle is a bit wider than that of a short straddle, but the maximum profit is reduced by virtue of the fact that the out-of-the-money options tend to cost less than at-the-money options, resulting in a relatively modest initial net credit.

Time value decay tends to be weaker for the out-of-the-money options that generally comprise a strangle than the near-to-the-money options associated with a straddle. This is counterbalanced by the reduced convexity generally associated with strangles. See Exhibit 13.49.

Long Guts

A *guts* trade is a close cousin to a straddle or a strangle. It too involves the purchase of a call and a put or the sale of a call and a put. We often think of straddles as the purchase or sale of at-the-money options and strangles as the purchase or sale of out-of-the-money options. Think of guts as the purchase and sale of in-the-money options (i.e., a high-struck put coupled with a relatively low-struck call). Like strangles, the two options that comprise a guts strategy share a common expiration date but differ with respect to strike price.

A *long guts* represents the purchase of a low-struck call coupled with the purchase of a high-struck put. A *short guts* is the opposite: the sale of a low-struck call along with the sale of a high-struck put. To the extent that

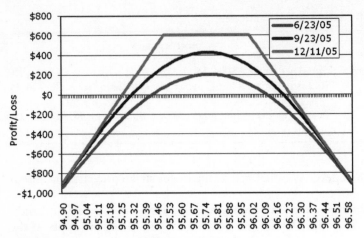

EXHIBIT 13.49   Short 95.50/96.00 Strangle

the market may be trading between the two strike prices, a guts trade involves two in-the-money options.

Example   You buy a 95.50 December 2005 call for 32.75, or $818.75, and buy a 96.00 December 2005 put for $1,018.75 on March 23, 2005. This implies an initial net debit of $1,837.50. See Exhibit 13.50.

The risk/reward profile of the long guts strongly resembles that of the long strangle. A fixed loss is realized between the two strikes, and profits may be realized if the market breaks in either direction. The magnitude of these profits and losses are similar.

If underlying market prices should remain within the two strikes by expiration, both options fall in-the-money and may be exercised. The total profit on exercise of the two options must equal the difference in strikes. Thus, the long guts generates a loss equal to the initial net debit less the

EXHIBIT 13.50   Long Guts

	Prem	Vol	Delta	Gamma	7-Day Theta	Vega
Buy 1 95.50 Dec-05 Call	−0.3275	14.78%	+0.60	+0.703	−0.0026	+0.0140
Buy 1 96.00 Dec-05 Put	−0.4075	16.30%	−0.71	+0.562	−0.0027	+0.0123
	−0.7350 ($1,837.50)		−0.11	+1.265	−0.0053	+0.0263

EXHIBIT 13.51   Long Guts Parameters

	Long Guts
Maximum Loss	Initial net debit − Difference in strikes = $587.50 (= $1,837.50 − $1,250)
Upper B/E	Call strike price + Initial net debit = 96.235 (= 95.50 + 73.5 basis points)
Lower B/E	Put strike price − Initial net debit = 95.265 (= 96.00 − 73.5 basis points)

difference in strikes as long as the market trades within the two strike prices by expiration.

To illustrate in the context of our example, assume that the underlying December Eurodollar futures market trades to 95.75 at option expiration. This is exactly midway between the 95.50 call and the 96.00 put strike price. Both options are in-the-money by 25 basis points, or $625 apiece. If both are exercised, that implies an aggregate profit of $1,250. Thus, the maximum potential loss equals $587.50 or the difference in strikes of $1,250 (50 basis points at $25 per basis point) adjusted by the initial net debit of $1,837.50.

Profits may result if market prices should advance or decline sharply in either direction. If the market should advance to the lower of the two strike prices plus the initial net debit, the low-struck call is exercised for an intrinsic value that exactly offsets that debit. This is the upper breakeven point. If the market should decline to the lower of the two strike prices less the initial net debit, then the long put might be exercised for an intrinsic value that offsets that debit. This is the lower breakeven point.

In our example, the upper and lower breakeven points may be calculated as 96.235 and 95.265, respectively. The upper breakeven point is calculated as the call strike of 95.50 plus 73.5 basis points (the initial net debit of $1,837.50 equates to 73.5 basis points at $25 per basis point). As shown in Exhibit 13.51, the lower breakeven point is calculated as the put strike of 96.00 less those 73.5 basis points.

Thus, a major difference between the long guts and long strangle is that the strangle results in a much reduced initial net debit. In other words, it requires less cash up front to finance a strangle even though both positions offer a very similar risk/reward posture. See Exhibit 13.52.

In other words, strangles offer enhanced leverage relative to guts. However, the market tends to compensate in the sense that the maximum loss associated with long guts trades tend to be slightly less than the maximum loss associated with a long strangle with the same strike prices. This implies

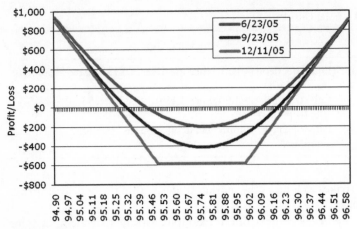

EXHIBIT 13.52　　Long 95.50/96.00 Guts

that breakeven points associated with a long guts strategy tend to be a bit narrower than that associated with a comparable long strangle.

Short Guts

Likewise, a short guts strategy is similar to a short strangle in terms of its risk/reward profile. The notable exception is that the short guts trade tends to generate a larger initial net credit. Presumably, traders will reinvest those funds at prevailing short-term rates, providing a bit more return.

Example　　You have traded a short guts on March 23, 2005, by selling a 95.50 December 2005 call and selling a 96.00 December 2005 put. The call might have been sold for 32.75 basis points, or $818.75, while the put might have been sold for 40.75 basis points, or $1,018.75. This implies an initial net credit in the amount of $1,837.50. See Exhibit 13.53.

EXHIBIT 13.53　　Short Guts

	Prem	Vol	Delta	Gamma	7-Day Theta	Vega
Sell 1 95.50 Dec-05 Call	+0.3275	14.78%	−0.60	−0.703	+0.0026	−0.0140
Sell 1 96.00 Dec-05 Put	+0.4075	16.30%	+0.71	−0.562	+0.0027	−0.0123
	+0.7350 $1,837.50		+0.11	−1.265	+0.0053	−0.0263

EXHIBIT 13.54 Short Guts Parameters

	Short Guts
Maximum Profit	Initial net credit − difference in strikes = $587.50 (= $1,837.50 − $1,250)
Upper B/E	Call strike price + initial net credit = 96.235 (= 95.50 + 73.5 basis points)
Lower B/E	Put strike price − Initial net credit = 95.265 (= 96.00 − 73.5 basis points)

The maximum possible profit associated with the short guts equals the initial net credit adjusted by the difference in strike prices. Consider that if the market should fall anywhere between the two strike prices, the intrinsic value of the two options must aggregate to the value of the difference in strike prices.

For example, if the market should be at 95.75, or exactly between the call struck at 95.50 and the put struck at 96.00, the intrinsic value of both options is equal to 25 basis points, or $1,250 in the aggregate. Because you are short both of these options in a short guts, you lose that amount cushioned by the initial receipt of the $1,837.50. This represents a net gain of $587.50, which is the maximum possible profit. See Exhibit 13.54.

The upper breakeven point is defined as the call strike price plus the initial net credit. If the market should rally about the call strike price, it falls in-the-money and may be exercised against the call writer. The upper breakeven point is found at the level where the intrinsic value of the call exactly offsets the initial net credit. The lower breakeven point is defined as the put strike price less the initial net credit. This is where the intrinsic value of the put exactly offsets the initial net credit.

In our example, the upper breakeven point is calculated as 96.235, or the call strike price of 95.50, plus the initial net credit of 73.5 basis points ($1,837.50 at $25 a basis point). The lower breakeven point is calculated as 95.265, or the put strike price of 96.00, less the initial net credit of 73.5 basis points. See Exhibit 13.55.

A short guts strategy entails a larger initial net credit relative to a short strangle with the same strike prices. But the short strangle trader is compensated with a bit higher maximum possible profit and a bit wider breakeven point.

Comparing Straddles, Strangles, and Guts

Let's compare the relative merits of entering the straddle, strangle, or guts trades as shown in our preceding examples. We restrict our consideration

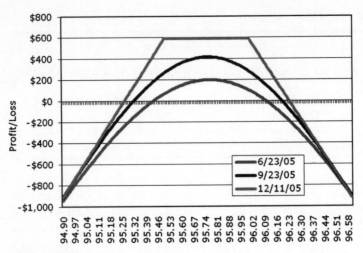

EXHIBIT 13.55 Short 95.50/96.00

to long strategies, although the principles are equally applicable to short strategies but in reverse.

Clearly, the straddle is the most aggressive of the three strategies. The long 95.75 straddle in our example entails much more risk than do the 95.50/96.00 strangle or the 95.50/96.00 guts. As might be expected, the straddle also offers narrower breakeven points. Thus, the increased maximum possible loss is offset by a greater probability that the market may trend sufficiently to generate a profitable disposition of the trade.

The differences between the results associated with the strangle and the guts strategies are much more subtle. The guts trade entails slightly reduced risk and somewhat narrower breakevens relative to the strangle. But it also requires a much greater initial net debit. There is an opportunity cost associated with the payment of a larger relative to a smaller initial net debit in the sense that cash deployed in an option trade might otherwise be earning short-term interest rates. See Exhibit 13.56.

EXHIBIT 13.56 Comparing Straddles, Strangles, and Guts

	Risk	Low Breakeven	High Breakeven
Long 95.75 Straddle	$1,137.50	95.2950	96.2050
Long 95.50/96.00 Strangle	$606.25	95.2575	96.2425
Long 95.50/96.00 Guts	$587.50	95.2650	96.2350

EXHIBIT 13.57   Greeks for Straddle, Strangle, and Guts

	Initial Net Debit	Net Delta	Net Gamma	Net Theta	Net Vega
Long 95.75 Straddle	$1,137.50	−0.13	+1.342	−0.0058	+0.0288
Long 95.50/96.00 Strangle	$606.25	−0.11	+1.243	−0.0052	+0.0267
Long 95.50/96.00 Guts	$1,837.50	−0.11	+1.265	−0.0053	+0.0263

We can also tell a great deal about these trades by examining the Greeks, or the net deltas, gammas, vegas, and thetas associated with the three trades. Most of these numbers are quite similar or in some cases identical from one strategy to the next. But there are some subtle differences worth noting. For example, the straddle is the most sensitive to fluctuating volatility levels as indicated by the net vega. In fact, the straddle is most sensitive to convexity as measured by gamma as well as time value decay measured by theta. This may be understood by considering that at-the-money options tend to be more sensitive to these factors relative to the out-of-the-money options that comprise the strangle or in-the-money options that comprise the guts strategy. See Exhibit 13.57.

All of these strategies are considered *volatility plays*. Thus, let's consider the results that may be realized in the event that implied volatilities were to advance by a uniform 1% in all three cases. We may do so through a simulation using option pricing models. In our example, the 95.75 long straddle is found to be marginally more responsive to a 1% advance in volatility relative to the strangle or guts. The straddle generated a simulated return of $72 relative to $66.75 and $65.75 on the long 95.50/96.00 strangle and the long 95.50/96.00 guts trade, respectively. Actually, this result was quite predictable simply by inspecting the net vegas of the three strategies. See Exhibit 13.58.

Although the straddle produces marginally superior absolute returns, the percentage profit associated with the strangle is by far the most attractive.

EXHIBIT 13.58   Comparing Leverage

	Vega	Profit	Investment	Return
Long 95.75 Straddle	+0.0288	~$72.00	$1,137.50	6.3%
Long 95.50/96.00 Strangle	+0.0267	~$66.75	$606.25	11.0%
Long 95.50/96.00 Guts	+0.0263	~$65.75	$1,837.50	3.6%

This underscores the superior leverage associated with out-of-the-money options as opposed to in-the-money options. In other words, those cheap out-of-the-money options provide greater elasticity on a dollar-for-dollar basis than do relatively more expensive at- or in-the-money options.

SPECIALTY OPTION STRATEGIES

Straddles and strangles are the most popular of so-called volatility plays. However, when you sell straddles and strangles in anticipation of declining volatility in an anticipated neutral market, you nonetheless open yourself up for open-ended risks in the sense that there is no limit on the maximum loss in the event of a major move either up or down. Thus, some traders prefer the use of butterflies or condors, which provide very similar risk/reward structures with the added benefit of limited risk should the market move sharply up or down.

Butterflies

Butterflies strongly resemble short straddles in the sense that returns are maximized at the strike price associated with the short options in the strategy. Unlike the short straddle, however, the butterfly represents a combination of four options rather than just two options. Further, all four of these options may be calls or puts. Or one may construct a butterfly with a combination of put and call options. These options share a common expiration date but differ in respect to strike prices.

The characteristic structure of a butterfly entails the purchase of two extreme struck options combined with the sale of two options with a strike price that falls between the two extremes. The strategy may be constructed by purchasing two extreme struck calls coupled with the sale of two calls at a common intermediate strike price or the purchase of two extreme struck puts coupled with the sale of two puts at an intermediate strike price.

Or one may combine a bull vertical call spread with a bear vertical put spread where the short components of the two vertical spread share a common strike price or the combination of a bull vertical put spread with a bear vertical call spread where the short options share a common strike price. Perhaps the easiest way of thinking about a long butterfly is that it represents the combination of a bull and a bear vertical spread, and it doesn't matter whether one uses call vertical spreads, put vertical spreads, or a combination of the two. In other words, there are many ways to piece together a butterfly.

Regardless of how the butterfly is constructed, the strategy is intended to capitalize on declining volatility or neutral markets. The strategy generally results in the payment of an initial net debit. Thus, we often refer to this as a "long" butterfly.

Example A long butterfly could have been created on March 23, 2005, by buying one 95.50 December 2005 call, selling two 95.75 calls, and buying one 96.00 call option. This strategy could have been placed at an initial net debit of $87.50. See Exhibit 13.59.

If the underlying futures market should fall at or below the lowest of the three strikes by expiration, all three call options fall out-of-the-money and expire worthless. Thus, the butterfly buyer is left with a loss equal to the initial net debit. In our example, this equates to a modest loss of $87.50.

If the market trades to the intermediate strike price by expiration, the lowest struck call falls in-the-money by an amount identified as the difference in strike prices. That long call may be exercised for its intrinsic value, which offsets the initial net debit. Thus, the maximum possible profit realized at the intermediate short strike price may be defined as the difference in strikes less any initial net debit. In our example, the maximum possible profit equals $625 (25 basis points at $25 per basis point) less the initial net debit of $87.50, or $537.50.

If the market should advance to the highest of the three strike prices by expiration, the lowest struck long call is in-the-money by an amount equal to the difference between the high and low strike prices. Thus, one may recover its in-the-money or intrinsic value through exercise. The two short intermediate struck options are likewise in-the-money by an amount equal to the difference between the highest strike and the intermediate strike. This

EXHIBIT 13.59 Long Butterfly

	Prem	Vol	Delta	Gamma	7-Day Theta	Vega
Buy 1 95.50 Dec-05 Call	−0.3275	14.78%	+0.60	+0.703	−0.0026	+0.0140
Sell 2 95.75 Dec-05 Calls	+0.2000	15.78%	−0.43	−0.671	+0.0029	−0.0144
Buy 1 96.00 Dec-05 Call	−0.1075	16.20%	+0.27	+0.548	−0.0027	+0.0123
	−0.0350 ($87.50)		+0.02	−0.091	+0.0005	−0.0025

EXHIBIT 13.60   Long Butterfly Parameters

	Long Butterfly
Maximum Profit	Difference in strikes − initial net debit = \$537.50 (= \$625 − \$87.50)
Upper B/E	Intermediate strike price + maximum profit = 95.965 (= 95.75 + 21.5 basis points)
Lower B/E	Intermediate strike price − maximum profit = 95.535 (= 95.75 − 21.5 basis points)
Maximum Loss	Initial net debit = \$87.50

results in a loss equal to the strike price span times two to the extent that they are two short calls. The net result is that the profit on exercise of the long low-struck call offsets the loss on exercise of the two short intermediate struck calls. This leaves one with a maximum loss equal to the initial net debit. In Exhibit 13.60, the initial net debit or maximum possible loss equates to \$87.50.

An upper and a lower breakeven point may be identified as the intermediate strike price plus and minus the maximum possible profit. In our example, the upper breakeven point is found at 95.965 (= 95.75 + 21.5 basis points or the maximum profit of \$587.50 at \$25 per basis point). The lower breakeven point is found at 95.535 (= 95.75 − 21.5 basis points).

The risk/return graphic of our long butterfly (shown in Exhibit 13.61) strongly resembles a short straddle with the exception that risk is limited if the market should rally above or break below the upper or lower of the three strike prices, respectively.

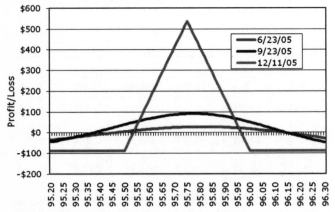

EXHIBIT 13.61   95.50/95.75/96.00 Butterfly

Condors

If a butterfly may the thought of as akin to a short straddle with limited risk, a *condor* is said to resemble a short strangle with limited risk. It too may be thought of as the combination of bullish and bearish vertical spreads except that the spreads do not share any common strikes. Thus, a condor may be composed of all calls, all puts, or a combination of both calls and puts. Like a long butterfly, the long condor is intended to capitalize on time value decay or a neutral market.

Example A long condor could have been created on March 23, 2005, by buying a 95.50 December 2005 call, selling a 95.75 call, selling a 96.00 call, and buying a 96.25 call. All of these options were exercisable for December 2005 Eurodollar futures. The strategy might have been placed at an initial net debit of $187.50. See Exhibit 13.62.

Provided that the underlying futures market price remains at or under the lower of the four strikes by expiration, all four options fall out-of-the-money and expire worthless. Thus, the condor buyer is left with a maximum loss equal to the initial net debit. In Exhibit 13.63, that represents a very modest risk of $187.50.

If the market trades to the lower intermediate strike price by expiration, the lowest struck call is in-the-money by an amount equal to the difference in strike prices and may be exercised for its intrinsic value. All other options in the condor are either at- or out-of-the-money and worthless. Thus, the maximum profit may be defined as the difference in strike prices less the initial net debit. In our example, that equals $437.50, or $625 less the initial net debit of $187.50.

EXHIBIT 13.62 Long Condor

	Prem	Vol	Delta	Gamma	7-Day Theta	Vega
Buy 1 95.50 Dec-05 Call	−0.3275	14.78%	+0.60	+0.703	−0.0026	+0.0140
Sell 1 95.75 Dec-05 Call	+0.2000	15.78%	−0.43	−0.671	+0.0029	−0.0144
Sell 1 96.00 Dec-05 Call	+0.1075	16.20%	−0.27	−0.548	+0.0027	−0.0123
Buy 1 96.25 Dec-05 Call	−0.0550	17.18%	+0.15	+0.371	−0.0022	+0.0037
	−0.0750 ($187.50)		+0.06	−0.145	+0.0008	−0.0037

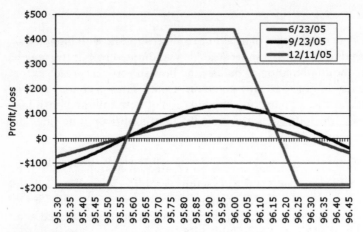

EXHIBIT 13.63   95.50/95.75/96.00/96.25 Condor

If the market should advance to the upper of the two intermediate strike prices by expiration, the lowest struck call is in-the-money by an amount equal to the difference between the high intermediate strike and the lowest strike and may be exercised for the same amount. The short call with the lower of the two intermediate strikes is also in-the-money but by an amount equal to the difference between the high intermediate and low intermediate strike prices. It may be exercised against the condor trader for a loss in that amount. On a net basis, the maximum profit is still defined as the difference between the low intermediate strike and lowest strike less the initial net debit. In our example, provided that the market remains between the two intermediate strike prices by expiration, the maximum possible profit equals $437.50, or $625 less the initial net debit of $187.50.

Finally, if the market should advance to or beyond the highest of all four strike prices, all four options may fall in-the-money and might be exercised. This results in a net wash and the trader is left with a maximum possible loss defined as the initial net debit. In Exhibit 13.64, this equals $187.50.

EXHIBIT 13.64   Long Condor Parameters

	Long Condor
Maximum Profit	Difference in strikes − initial net debit = $437.50 (= $625 − $187.50)
Upper B/E	Upper intermediate strike price + maximum profit = 96.175 (= 96.00 + 17.5 basis points)
Lower B/E	Lower intermediate strike price − maximum profit = 95.575 (= 95.75 − 17.5 basis points)
Maximum Loss	Initial net debit = $187.50

EXHIBIT 13.65   Comparing Butterfly and Condor

	Long Butterfly	Long Condor
Maximum Profit	$537.50	$437.50
Upper Breakeven (B/E) Point	95.965	96.175
Lower Breakeven (B/E) Point	95.535	95.575
Maximum Loss	$87.50	$187.50

Upper and lower breakeven points may be identified as the upper intermediate strike price plus the maximum profit and the lower intermediate strike price less the maximum profit. In our example, the upper breakeven equals 96.175 or the upper intermediate strike price of 96.00 plus 17.5 basis points (= maximum profit of $437.50 at $25 per basis point). The lower breakeven equals 95.575 or the lower intermediate strike price of 95.75 less 17.5 basis points (= maximum profit of $437.50 at $25 per basis point).

The condor is generally thought of as a bit more conservative than the butterfly. Butterflies generally offer a bit more maximum profit and a bit less maximum loss than do condors. But this is balanced by the fact that the breakeven points associated with condors are generally wider than those associated with butterflies. Thus, condors offer a greater probability of realizing a bit more modest return. These points are underscored by comparing the butterfly and condor strategies shown in Exhibit 13.65.

MATCHING STRATEGY AND FORECAST

We began by suggesting that options are remarkably flexible trading tools that provide you with the ability to tailor closely your trading strategy to a market forecast. When you trade futures, the implicit market forecast is really very straightforward. Buy futures if you anticipate a strongly bullish market or sell futures if you anticipate an essentially bearish market environment. But options provide the ability to take advantage of much more subtle forecasts that incorporate expectations regarding price, time, and volatility.

If you were strongly bullish, you might simply buy futures. Or you might consider the purchase of call options that provides unlimited participation in a bull market but with strictly limited risk in the event your forecast is in error. Sell futures if strongly bearish. Or you may consider the purchase of put options that likewise provides one with the ability to participate fully in a bear movement but again with strictly limited risk in the event your forecast is in error.

EXHIBIT 13.66 Matching Strategy to Forecast

Forecast	Option Strategy
Strongly bullish	Buy futures; buy calls
Neutral to mildly bullish	Sell puts, vertical bull spreads, ratio spreads
Neutral	Sell straddles or strangles
Neutral to mildly bearish	Sell calls, vertical bear spreads, ratio spreads
Strong bearish	Sell futures; buy puts
Bullish or bearish	Buy straddles or strangles
Specialty trades	Time and backspreads; butterflies and condors

More subtle forecasts include an expectation of a neutral to mildly bullish environment or a neutral to mildly bearish market scenario. In those cases, one might attempt to structure a trade that allows you to take advantage of time value decay with a bullish or bearish tilt. The sale of put options, vertical bull spreads, and ratio spreads are all reasonable alternative strategies in a neutral to mildly bullish environment. Likewise, the sale of calls, vertical bear spreads, or ratio spreads might be considered in a neutral to mildly bearish environment. See Exhibit 13.66.

But options are even more flexible insofar as they allow you to take advantage of a very neutral market by selling straddles or strangles. These strategies take advantage of time value decay at the risk of accepting negative convexity and the possibility of rising volatilities in a strongly rallying or breaking market. If your forecast was just the opposite and you anticipated that the market might rally or break strongly but were uncertain regarding the direction, consider the purchase of straddles or strangles. Some question how one might arrive at a "bullish or bearish" forecast. One possibility is that you expect the release of a significant piece of fundamental market information but are unsure about the direction in which that information may send market prices but are confident nonetheless in a strong reaction.

Finally, we may consider a variety of specialty trades including time spreads such as horizontal or diagonal option spreads, backspreads, butterflies, and condors.

The point is that options are extremely flexible and allow one to take advantage of possibly very elaborate market forecasts in ways that the blunter instruments represented by futures contracts simply cannot offer.

CONCLUSION

Options are very versatile trading tools that may be used to take advantage of many different market scenarios. When trading options, you must be cognizant of the fact that their values are impacted along three interwoven dimensions of price, time, and volatility. Of these three dimensions, price is probably most important to the extent that a price forecast generally dictates your beliefs with respect to time and volatility. That is, if one is strong bullish, this implies an expectation of rising volatility. If one is very neutral, this implies an expectation of declining volatility and suggests that you should attempt to take advantage of time value decay.

Many complex option strategies or combinations may be used to capitalize on these expectations, including vertical, horizontal, and diagonal spreads; ratio spreads; straddles, strangles, and guts; and a variety of specialty trades including butterflies and condors. In fact, the imagination is the only limitation when it comes to constructing option strategies.

CHAPTER 14

Hedging with Options

John W. Labuszewski
John E. Nyhoff

Options are extremely flexible trading and risk-management tools. We explore some practical considerations associated with the use of options for risk-management purposes. In particular, we compare how futures, puts, and calls may be used to hedge market exposure. In the process, we might ask what hedging strategy is best under what kind of market conditions. In other words, can we select an option strategy that may be well matched to prospective market conditions?

Although our examples focus on currency markets, the principles are readily generalizable to just about any market where futures and options are available whether it is an interest rate, equity, or commodity market.

BASELINE FUTURES HEDGE

To provide a comparison of various hedging strategies, let us quickly review the efficacy of a short futures hedge by revisiting a previous example when we discussed currency futures.

Recall that our hedger expected the receipt of €50,000,000, which at a spot USD/euro exchange rate of 1.4704 translated into a value of $73,520,000. Per this example, our hedger was concerned about protecting the value of those monies denominated in U.S. dollars. Thus, we recommended a strategy of selling 400 CME Group December 2008 EuroFX futures at the prevailing futures price of 1.4605 to cover that risk.

Assume that our hedger holds this position until December 5, 2008, at which point we might assume the basis becomes fully or near fully converged (i.e., spot and futures prices are equal). What would happen under these circumstances if the spot exchange rate were (hypothetically)

EXHIBIT 14.1 Hedging with Futures

	Spot USD/Euro	€50MM in USD	Dec '08 Futures	Basis
8/18/08	1.4704	$73,520,000	Sell 400 @ 1.4605	−0.0099
12/05/08	1.3200	$66,000,000	Buy 400 @ 1.3200	0.0000
		($7,520,000)	+$7,025,000	+0.0099
		Net Loss of $495,000		

to decline to 1.3200, remain essentially unchanged at 1.4700, or advance to 1.6200?

If the spot exchange rate declines to 1.3200, the value of the €50,000,000 falls to $66,000,000, which implies a loss of $7,520,000 (= $73,520,000 − $66,000,000). But having sold 400 futures at 1.4605, which converge to 1.3200, implies an offsetting profit of $7,025,000 for a net loss of $495,000. Exhibit 14.1 illustrates this example.

In fact, if we assume full basis convergence under all circumstances regardless of the final value of the spot market, we might simulate a net loss of $495,000 consistently whether the market declines to 1.3200, remains essentially unchanged at 1.4700, or advances to 1.6200. See Exhibit 14.2.

In other words, the sale of futures allows our hedger to lock in a specific return, subject to some basis risk, regardless of prevailing market trends. He is protected in an adverse market, although he forfeits the potential benefits of possibly favorable exchange rate movements. How does the use of options for hedging purposes stack up against this "baseline" futures hedge? See Exhibit 14.3.

BUYING PROTECTION WITH PUTS

The idea behind the purchase of puts is to compensate loss associated with the potentially declining value of a currency with the rising intrinsic value of the puts. As the market declines, puts go deeper and deeper in-the-money,

EXHIBIT 14.2 Comparing Unhedged and Hedged Returns

	Spot @ 1.3200	Spot @ 1.4700	Spot @ 1.6200
Unhedged	($7,520,000)	($20,000)	$7,480,000
Short Futures Hedge	($495,000)	($495,000)	($495,000)

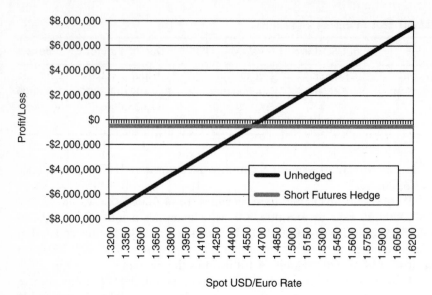

EXHIBIT 14.3 USD/Euro Hedged with Short Futures

permitting the put holder to exercise the options for a profit. Of course, if the market should rally instead, the puts go out of the money. However, having paid the option premium, the put holder's loss is limited thereto and, of course, the favorable underlying price movement should work to the benefit of the hedger.

Let's return to our example of the company that wishes to hedge the anticipated future receipt of €50,000,000 (or the equivalent of $73,520,000 at a spot exchange rate of 1.4704). Assume that the company purchases 400 at-the-money December 2008 puts with a strike price of 1.4600 (with futures at 1.4605) for 0.0326. This represents an initial net debit of $1,630,000 (= 400 × 125,000 × $0.0326). Note that we are using the same hedge ratio that was applied to the sale of futures in our short futures hedge described earlier.

Subsequently, assume that the spot exchange rate declines from 1.4704 to 1.3200, resulting in a loss of value of $7,520,000. Held until December 5, 2008, the put options are about to expire in-the-money and are valued at their intrinsic worth of 0.1400 (= futures price of 1.3200 relative to strike price of 1.4600). Thus, they might be exercised by selling futures at 1.4600 when they are actually valued at 1.3200, resulting in a net profit of $5,370,000 [= 400 × 125,000 × ($0.1400 − $0.0326)]. This partially but not completely offsets the loss of $7,520,000 in the unhedged cash value of the €50,000,000 receipt. See Exhibit 14.4.

EXHIBIT 14.4 Short Put Hedge

	Spot USD/ Euro	€50MM in USD	Dec '08 Puts
8/18/08	1.4704	$73,520,000	Buy 400 1.4600 Puts @ 0.0326
12/05/08	1.3200	$66,000,000	Exercise 400 1.4600 Puts @ 0.1400
		($7,520,000)	+$5,370,000
		Net Loss of $2,150,000	

Of course, if the spot market was to have remained essentially stable at 1.4700, then our hedger would have been left with slightly out-of-the-money and therefore worthless options by early December when expiration approached. Or, if the spot exchange rate had advanced, the hedger would likewise have essentially forfeited the initial $1,630,000 debit from the purchase of the 400 puts but would have benefited from the market advance.

As such, the long put hedge allows you to lock in a floor return while still retaining a great deal of the upside potential associated with a possibly favorable market swing, limited to the extent that you pay the premium associated with the purchase of the put options up front. See Exhibit 14.5.

Of course option premiums are impacted by a variety of factors, including the movement of price, time, and volatility. So although the purchase of put options in the context of a hedging application reduces price risks, it also entails the acceptance of other types of risk uniquely applicable to options. Still, price impact is the foremost of these factors.

The degree to which you immediately reduce price risk may be found by reference to the put delta. In our example, we used the purchase of at- or near-the-money put options with a delta of 0.4831 (or approximately 0.5). As such, we effectively reduce the immediate or near-term price risk by a factor of about one-half (using the appropriate futures hedge ratio). See Exhibit 14.6.

But delta is a dynamic concept. If the market falls and the option goes in-the-money, the delta will get closer to 1.0. If the market rises and the option goes out-of-the-money, the delta gets closer to zero. An

EXHIBIT 14.5 Comparing Returns

	Spot @ 1.3200	Spot @ 1.4700	Spot @ 1.6200
Unhedged	($7,520,000)	($20,000)	$7,480,000
Short Futures Hedge	($495,000)	($495,000)	($495,000)
Long Put Hedge	($2,150,000)	($1,650,000)	$5,850,000

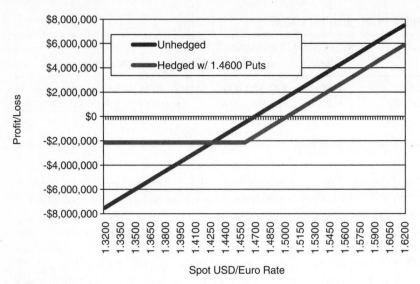

EXHIBIT 14.6   USD/Euro Hedged with Long Puts

in-the-money put with a delta of 0.60 suggests an effective 60% reduction in price risk, whereas the use of an out-of-the-money option with a delta of 0.40 suggests a 40% reduction in price risk.

The dynamic nature of delta represents convexity. Convexity benefits the holder of a put insofar as it promises more protection in a bear market when you need more protection and less protection in a bull market when you would prefer less protection. Unfortunately, you pay for convexity by accepting negative time value decay. As expiration approaches, a near-to-the-money option will exhibit more and more time value decay or "accelerating" time value decay or erosion. It is interesting that the same options that experience high and rising convexity (near-term, near-the-moneys) also experience high and rising thetas. Barring a mispricing, it is impossible to experience both a positive gamma and theta when trading options.

Thus, you must ask yourself if the market is basically volatile and therefore you should take advantage of convexity by buying options. Or is the market essentially stable, recommending a strategy of taking advantage of time value decay by selling options?

YIELD ENHANCEMENT WITH CALLS

If you believe the market is basically stable, you might pursue a *yield enhancement* or *income augmentation* strategy by selling call options

EXHIBIT 14.7 Covered Call Writing

	Spot USD/ Euro	€50MM in USD	Dec '08 Calls
8/18/08	1.4704	$73,520,000	Sell 400 1.4600 Calls @ 0.0331
12/05/08	1.3200	$66,000,000	Abandon 400 1.4600 Calls @ 0.0000
		($7,520,000)	+$1,655,000
		Net Loss of $5,865,000	

against a long cash or spot position. This is also known as *covered call writing* in the sense that your obligation to deliver the underlying currency or futures contract as a result of writing a call is covered by the fact that you already own the currency or futures contract.

Let's revisit our example of the company anticipating the receipt of €50,000,000 ($73,520,000 at a spot exchange rate of 1.4704). Assume that the company sells 400 at-the-money December 2008 calls with a strike price of 1.4600 (with futures at 1.4605) for 0.0331. This represents an initial net credit or receipt of cash of $1,655,000 (= 400 × 125,000 × $0.0331). Again, we employ the same hedge ratio that was applied to the short futures or long put hedges.

Assume that spot exchange rates fall from 1.4704 to 1.3200 for a loss of $7,520,000 (see Exhibit 14.7). Held until December 5, 2008, the 1.4600 calls options are out-of the-money, valued at zero, and therefore abandoned. Thus, our hedger retains the $1,655,000 to at least partially offset the loss of $7,520,000, or a net loss of $5,865,000.

Had the spot market remained stable at 1.4700, then our hedger would have had slightly in-the-money options that would be exercised against him such that he would have retained most of the initial net credit. Or if the spot exchange rate had advanced sharply to 1.6200, the benefits of the favorable exchange rate movement would essentially be offset by a loss in the value of the short calls, although the hedger would still benefit to the extent of the initial net credit of $1,655,00. See Exhibit 14.8.

EXHIBIT 14.8 Comparing Returns

	Spot @ 1.3200	Spot @ 1.4700	Spot @ 1.6200
Unhedged	($7,520,000)	($20,000)	$7,480,000
Short Futures Hedge	($495,000)	($495,000)	($495,000)
Long Put Hedge	($2,150,000)	($1,650,000)	$5,850,000
Short Call Hedge	($5,865,000)	$1,135,000	$1,135,000

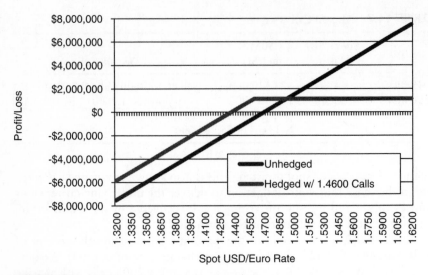

EXHIBIT 14.9 USD/Euro Hedged with Short Calls

The short call strategy (shown in Exhibit 14.9) implies that you lock in a ceiling return, limiting your ability to participate in any upside potential. The covered call writer is compensated, however, to the extent that he receives the option premium, which at least partially offsets downside losses. A long put hedge enables you to take advantage of convexity albeit while suffering the ill effects of time value decay. The short call hedge is just the opposite insofar as it allows you to capitalize on time value decay while suffering from the potentially ill effects of convexity.

Convexity and volatility are closely related concepts. It is only when the market is volatile, when it is moving either up or down, that the effects of convexity are actually observed. If the market is moving and volatility is rising, the short calls may rise in value, resulting in loss.

If the market should advance, the calls will go in-the-money, the delta approaching 1.0. The growing intrinsic value of the calls presumably offsets profit in the rising value of the cash security resulting in an offset. Fortunately, this return is positive by virtue of the initial receipt of the option premium. If the market should decline, the calls go out-of-the-money, eventually expiring worthless as the delta approaches zero. Still, the hedger is better off having hedged by virtue of the receipt of the premium upfront.

The short call hedge works best when the market remains basically stable. In this case, time value decay results in a gradual decline in the premium. Thus, you "capture" the premium, enhancing yield.

IN- AND OUT-OF-THE-MONEY OPTIONS

Thus far, we have focused on the use of at- or at least near-to-the-money options in the context of our hedging strategies. But let us consider the use of in- and out-of-the-money long puts or short calls as an alternative.

As a general rule, you tend to get what you pay for, as the saying goes. The purchase of the expensive in-the-money puts entails a much larger up-front investment, but you buy more protection in the event of a market downturn. For example, rather than buying the 1.4600 at-the-money puts for a premium of 0.0326, our hedger might have purchased in-the-money puts struck at 1.4900 for a premium of 0.0496. By contrast, the purchase of the cheaper out-of-the-money puts entails a much smaller upfront debit to your account. For example, our hedger might have purchased out-of-the-money puts with an exercise price of 1.4300 for a premium of 0.0203. But you get less protection in a downturn. For an example, see Exhibit 14.10.

The purchase of a put allows you to lock in a floor or minimum return. But that floor is only realized at prices at or below the strike price. The high-struck in-the-moneys provide protection at all levels from 1.4900 and down. The low-struck out-of-the-moneys provide protection only from levels of 1.4300 and below.

By contrast, the cheaper out-of-the-money puts allow you to retain greater ability to participate in possible upward price advances than do the

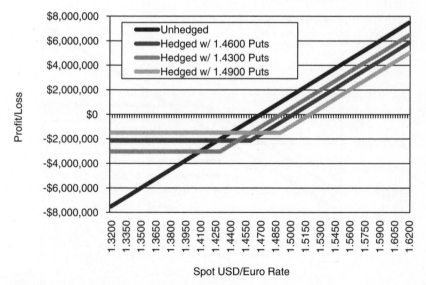

EXHIBIT 14.10   USD/Euro Hedged with Long Puts

expensive in-the-moneys. Remember that at all prices at or above the strike price, one's returns are restrained by the initial forfeiture of the option premium. The purchase of the expensive in-the-money puts place a greater burden on one's portfolio than do the cheap out-of-the-moneys.

The same general principles may be said to apply to the sale of expensive in-the-money calls versus the sale of cheap out-of-the-money calls. For example, rather than selling at-the-money 1.4600 calls for a premium of 0.0331, one might have sold in-the-money calls struck at 1.4300 for a premium of 0.0506 or out-of-the-money calls struck at 1.4900 for a premium of 0.0203.

One receives protection from downside risk by selling calls through the initial receipt of the option premium. Thus, the higher that premium, the greater the degree of protection. If the market should advance above the option strike price, however, the short calls go in-the-money and generate a loss that offsets the increase in the value of the cash securities.

Thus, the sale of in-the-money 1.4300 calls provides the greatest degree of protection in the event of a market decline. On the other extreme, the sale of out-of-the-money 1.4900 calls provides the thinnest margin of protection. But if the market should advance, the sale of the cheap out-of-the-money calls allows one to participate to a much greater degree in the rally. The sale of expensive in-the-money calls offers the least amount of upside participation. This is illustrated in Exhibit 14.11.

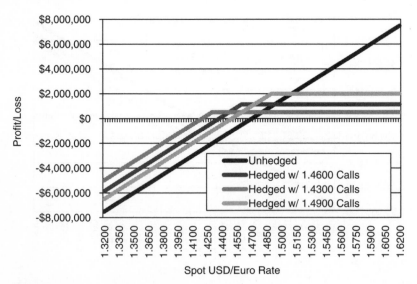

EXHIBIT 14.11 USD/Euro Hedged with Short Calls

Note, however, that the sale of calls options against a long spot position generally is considered a neutral strategy. One sells options to capitalize on time value decay in a stagnant market environment. Clearly, the sale of the at-the-moneys generates the most attractive return when yields remain stable. This makes sense because the at-the-moneys have the greatest amount of time value to begin and experience the greatest degree of time value decay as evidenced by their generally high thetas.

MATCHING STRATEGY WITH FORECAST

Note that by buying puts against a long cash portfolio, the risk/reward profile associated with the entire position strongly resembles that of an outright long call. As such, this strategy is sometimes referred to as a *synthetic long call*. Likewise, the combination of selling calls against a long securities portfolio will strongly resemble the outright sale of a put. Thus, we sometimes refer to this strategy as a synthetic short put.

Many textbooks draw a strong distinction between hedging or risk-management and speculative activity. We are not so sure that this distinction is warranted. Obviously, the same factors that might motivate a speculator to buy calls might motivate hedgers to buy puts against their cash portfolio. And the same factors that might motivate a speculator to sell puts might motivate hedgers to sell calls against their cash portfolio.

How might we define hedging versus speculative activity? Clearly a speculator is someone who might use futures and options in an attempt to make money. A hedger is someone who might use futures and options selectively in an attempt to make money and who already holds a cash position. Perhaps this distinction is a bit cynical. It is, however, thoroughly practical.

The conclusion you might reach from this discussion is that the necessity of making a price forecast is just as relevant from the hedger's viewpoint as it is from the speculator's viewpoint. Which one of our three basic hedge strategies— sell futures, buy puts, or sell calls—is best? Clearly, that depends on the market circumstances.

In a bearish environment, where the holder of a cash portfolio needs to hedge the most, the alternative of selling futures is clearly superior to that of buying puts or selling calls. In a neutral environment, the sale of calls is superior, followed by the sale of futures and the purchase of puts. The best alternative in a bull market is simply not to hedge. However, if one must attempt to limit risk, the best hedge alternative is to purchase puts, followed by the sale of calls and the sale of futures. See Exhibit 14.12.

EXHIBIT 14.12 Matching Hedging Strategy with Forecast

	Bearish	Neutral	Bullish
1	Sell futures	Sell calls	Buy puts
2	Buy puts	Sell futures	Sell calls
3	Sell calls	Buy puts	Sell futures

Note that no single strategy is systematically or inherently superior to any other. Each achieves a number 1, 2, and 3 ranking, underscoring the speculative element in hedging.

COLLAR STRATEGY

The concept of a long put hedge is very appealing to the extent that it provides limited downside risk while retaining at least a partial ability to participate in potential upside price movement. The problem with buying put options, of course, is the necessity to actually pay for the premium! Thus, some strategists have looked to strategies that might at least partially offset the cost associated with the purchase of put options.

You might, for example, combine the purchase of put options with the sale of call options. If you were to buy puts and sell calls at the same strike price, the resulting risks and returns would strongly resemble that of a short futures position. As a result, the combination of long puts and short calls at the same strike price is often referred to as a *synthetic short futures position*. Barring a market mispricing, however, there is no apparent advantage to assuming a synthetic as opposed to an actual futures position as part of a hedging strategy.

But if you were to sell near-to-the money calls and purchase lower struck and somewhat out-of-the-money puts, you could create an altogether different type of risk exposure. See Exhibit 14.13. This position might allow you to capture some premium in a neutral market as a result of the accelerated time value decay associated with the short calls while enjoying the floor return associated with the long put hedge in the event of a market decline. On the downside, this strategy limits your ability to participate in potential market advances. In other words, this strategy entails the elements of both a long put hedge and a short call hedge (i.e., one locks in both a floor and a ceiling return).

For example, assume you sell 400 of the 1.4600 at-the-money calls at 0.0331 for a credit of $1,655,000 and simultaneously buy 400 of the

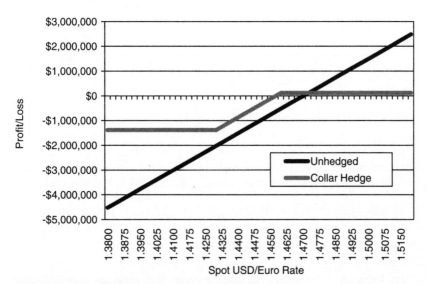

EXHIBIT 14.13 USD/Euro Hedged with Collar

1.4300 out-of-the-money puts at 0.0203 for a debit of $1,015,000. This results in a net credit or inflow of cash equivalent to $640,000.

A collar is most highly recommended when one has a generally neutral to negative market outlook. There are many variations on this theme, including the possibility of buying higher struck puts and selling lower struck calls or a "reverse collar." This strategy might enhance one's returns in a bear market but comes at the risk of reducing one's ability to participate in an upside market move.

DELTA-NEUTRAL HEDGE

Options are extremely versatile instruments, and there are many variations on the risk-management theme. In particular, it is always enticing to attempt to find a way to take advantage of the beneficial effects associated with options while minimizing the unfortunate effects that come as part of the package through a system of active management. Many of these systems rely on the concept of delta as a central measure of risk and are known as *delta-neutral* strategies.

For example, one may buy put options or sell call options against a long exposure with the intention of matching the net deltas. As an illustration, consider our hedger with the prospective receipt of €50,000,000 intent on hedging the risk of a falling euro versus the U.S. dollar. He may elect to sell 400 call options on EuroFX futures by reference to the futures hedge ratio. Or the hedge may be weighted by reference to delta. The appropriate delta-neutral hedge ratio is readily determined by taking the reciprocal of the delta.

$$\text{Delta Neutral Hedge Ratio} = \text{Futures Hedge Ratio} \div \text{Option Delta}$$

In our previous examples, we had considered the sale of 400 at-the-money 1.4600 call options with a delta of 0.5104. Employing a delta-weighted strategy, the hedger might elect to use 784 options instead.

$$\begin{aligned}\text{Delta Neutral Hedge Ratio} &= \text{Futures Hedge Ratio} \div \text{Option Delta}\\ &= 400 \div 0.5104\\ &= 784 \text{ call options}\end{aligned}$$

But because delta is a dynamic concept, this strategy implies some rather active management. For example, as the market rallies and the calls go into-the-money, the call delta will start to increase, resulting in accelerating losses if no action is taken. Thus, our hedger should reduce the size of the short call position as the market advances. For example, if the option delta advances from 0.5104 to 0.5500, this implies that the hedge ratio will decline to 727 positions ($= 400 \div 0.5500$). Thus, one might buy back or liquidate 57 call options as the market advances.

If the market declines, the calls will go out-of-the-money and the call delta will fall. This too will result in accelerating net losses to the extent that the options will provide increasingly less protection as the market breaks. Thus, our hedger might sell more options on the way down. For example, if the call delta declines to 0.4800, this implies that the hedge ratio will advance to 833 positions ($= 400 \div 0.4800$). Thus, one might sell an additional 49 calls as the market declines.

The application of a delta hedge strategy with the use of short calls implies an essentially neutral market forecast. This is intuitive to the extent that the sale of call options implies that one wishes to take advantage of time value decay in an essentially sideways trending market environment.

But sometimes the market does not cooperate. In particular, this strategy entails the risk of whipsaw markets (i.e., the possibility that one buys back positions on the way up and sells more on the way down). Thus, whipsaws may have one buying high and selling low as the market reverses from one direction to the other. The perils of a whipsaw market imply that one might couple this strategy with a diligent effort in creating market forecasting tools specifically to avoid the ill effects of whipsaws.

Instead of the use of call options as part of a delta neutral strategy, one might also consider the purchase of put options. For example, one might buy the at-the-money 1.4600 put options with a delta of 0.4831. Our formula suggests that one might use 828 options to neutralize one's risk exposure as measured by delta.

$$\text{Delta Neutral Hedge Ratio} = \text{Futures Hedge Ratio} \div \text{Option Delta}$$
$$= 400 \div 0.4831$$
$$= 828 \text{ put options}$$

As was the case with our delta neutral short call hedge, we know that the put delta will be sensitive to changing market conditions. If, for example, the market were to decline, the puts will go into-the-money and the delta will increase. This implies that one might liquidate some of the long puts to maintain a delta-neutral stance. Or if the market advances, this implies that the put options may go out-of-the-money and the delta will decrease. This may suggest that you purchase more puts to maintain a delta-neutral stance.

However, one might observe that as the market declines, the put options essentially provide more protection just when you need it most by virtue of the advancing delta. Or that the put options will provide less protection as the market advances by virtue of a declining delta at a point. This calls the question: Why adjust the hedge ratio when the options are "self-adjusting" in a beneficial way?

Of course, the risk of this strategy is that the market might simply remain stagnant and the hedger is subject to the ill effects of time value decay. As such, the use of long options is a hedging strategy most aptly recommended in a volatile market environment.

CONCLUSION

Options provide utility not only as a means of gaining speculative exposure to a market but they are also quite useful as a risk-management tool. The most important factor in the successful use of options as a speculative tool is to develop an outlook regarding market conditions and apply a strategy that matches those conditions. That outlook may reference possible price movements in combination with the impact of time value decay and fluctuating volatility. Likewise, prudent hedging strategies should match possible market conditions as well.

We have reviewed a variety of strategies beginning with a futures hedge as a baseline example. Instead of selling futures against a long risk exposure, other possible hedging strategies include the purchase of put options or the sale of calls. One may further adjust the strategy with the use of in-, at-, or out-of-the-money options with varying effects. Other more ambitious risk-management strategies are also possible with the use of options including collars and delta-neutral strategies.

About the Authors and Contributors

John W. Labuszewski is Managing Director of Research & Product Development at CME Group. Before coming to CME in 1998, Mr. Labuszewski was General Manager of Nikko International's U.S. Asset Management Division where he was responsible for the development and operation of managed futures and hedge funds. He has also worked for Virginia Trading Company, a subsidiary of Kleinwort Benson; Refco, Inc. and the Chicago Board of Trade. Mr. Labuszewski is the co-author of *Investing in Government Securities: Fundamental and Technical Analysis, Portfolio Management and Arbitrage*, John Wiley & Sons, 1994 (w/Frederick Barnett and Dennis Heskel); *Trading Options on Futures: Markets, Methods, Strategies & Tactics*, John Wiley & Sons, 1988 (w/John E. Nyhoff); *Trading Financial Futures: Markets, Methods, Strategies & Tactics*, John Wiley & Sons, 1988 (w/John E. Nyhoff); and, *Inside the Commodity Option Markets*, John Wiley & Sons, 1985 (w/Jeanne Sinquefield). He has written numerous articles for Journals including the *Financial Analysts Journal* and other trade and industry publications. He earned an MBA from the University of Illinois in 1978.

    John E. Nyhoff is Director, Financial Research and Product Development at CME Group. He is responsible for the Exchange's research & product development efforts in credit and fixed income derivative products. Prior to joining Chicago Mercantile Exchange in 2006, Mr. Nyhoff was Executive Vice President & Chief Economist with Tokyo-Mitsubishi Futures (USA), Inc. in Chicago. His responsibilities included alternative asset management, financial market research and trading strategy, as well as electronic trading systems. He began his derivatives industry career as a Senior Economist in the Chicago Board of Trade's Department of Economic Analysis. Mr. Nyhoff teaches financial futures and options at DePaul University's Kellstadt Graduate School of Business. He has co-authored (with John Labuszewski) two books on financial markets including *Trading Options on Futures: Markets, Methods, Strategies & Tactics*, John Wiley & Sons, 1988; and *Trading Financial Futures: Markets, Methods, Strategies & Tactics*, John Wiley & Sons, 1988. He holds a master's degree in applied financial economics from the University of Rochester.

Richard Co is Director, Financial Research and Product Development at the CME Group. Dr. Co is principally responsible for developing new financial products as well as managing the continual development of CME's current product lines, with specialization in index, FX and interest rate products. Dr. Co joined CME in 1999. He received master's and doctorate degrees in economics from the University of Chicago in 1995 and 2000, respectively. Dr. Co also holds the Chartered Financial Analyst charter.

Paul E. Peterson is Director, Commodity Research & Product Development of CME Group. He leads CME Group's new product development activities in livestock, meat, dairy, weather, and other commodities. Peterson joined CME in 1989 as an Economist. Before joining the company, he served as Vice President, Research for Brock Associates from 1988-89; Manager, Education and Marketing Services for the Chicago Board of Trade from 1986-88; and Manager, Market Analysis for the American Farm Bureau Federation from 1983-86. He earned a Ph.D. in agricultural economics from the University of Illinois, and has authored a number of articles in professional journals and business/trade publications.

Dale Michaels was appointed Managing Director, Credit & Risk Management of CME Group in August 2007. He is responsible for managing CME Clearing's exposure to counterparty risk, including monitoring market volatility, setting minimum performance bond requirements, enhancing CME's risk management systems and building new and enhanced margin algorithms. Previously, Mr. Michaels served as Director, Risk Management of CME since 2001. During his tenure, he has played a key role in CME's efforts to establish its historic clearing agreement with the Chicago Board of Trade including responsibility for margining issues, cross-margining agreement changes and development of new risk management tools. He also is responsible for the integration of NYMEX risk management and margins in conjunction with CME Group's acquisition of NYMEX. Mr. Michaels most recently led CME Clearing's development of financial safeguards and margin methodologies for clearing credit default swaps. Mr. Michaels joined CME in 1995 as an Investigator in the company's market regulation area. He joined the Clearing House's Risk Management area in 1996 as a Risk Management Analyst, and he has held numerous roles and leadership positions in Risk Management since that time. Before joining CME, Mr. Michaels worked as a Treasury bond futures and options trader and as a Staff Economist and Financial Analyst at CBOT. Mr. Michaels earned a bachelor's degree in finance and economics from Illinois State University and a MBA in finance from DePaul University. He also holds a Chartered Financial Analyst designation.

James Moran is Global Director of Market Regulation Strategic and Technology Initiatives for CME Group. Mr. Moran has worked in the derivatives industry for over 30 years, spending most of that time in the Regulatory area. Within CME Group's Market Regulation department, Mr. Moran has worked as a Surveillance Analyst, an Investigator, a manager of investigators, and he headed the Investigative and Disciplinary functions from 1997 to 2004. Mr. Moran currently specializes in electronic trading issues, and is in charge of Regulatory Systems development, regulatory data quality, OTC preparations, and merger integration.

Charles Piszczor is an Associate Director of Commodity Research and Product Development for CME Group. He is responsible for the development, design and maintenance of the weather futures and options contracts for the Exchange and works with weather traders, brokers and forecasting companies to develop new and innovative weather derivatives. He also participates on panels relating to weather derivatives. Mr. Piszczor has spent twelve years in the futures industry developing contracts. Prior to joining CME Group he spent ten years as an economist in the automotive field providing research to the industry. Mr. Piszczor holds an undergraduate degree in economics from Northwood University, Midland, Michigan and a Master Degree in economics from Roosevelt University, Chicago, Illinois. Mr. Piszczor is a member of the National Association of Business Economists and the Chicago Association of Business Economists.

Frederick Sturm is a Director in the Research & Product Development Department of CME Group. Between 1999 and July 2007, he served as Senior Economist with the Chicago Board of Trade. Prior to joining the CBOT, Mr. Sturm was First Vice President of Futures and Options Research with Fuji Futures (now Mizuho Securities USA) and an analyst with Carr Futures (now Newedge Group). Mr. Sturm earned the Bachelor of Arts degree in economics from Indiana University and the Master of Arts and Master of Philosophy degrees in economics from Columbia University.

Brett Vietmeier is Director, CME Equity Products with CME Group. In this capacity, he is responsible furthering the volume growth of the CME Group's futures and options on equity index futures traded on the Exchange. He is also responsible for managing the development, promotion, implementation and marketing of CME equity index product line to many audiences including pension plans, mutual funds, broker/dealers and proprietary trading firms. Mr. Vietmeier has over 18 years experience in the futures industry. Mr. Vietmeier earned a bachelor's degree in business from Illinois Wesleyan University in 1989 and received his MBA with a concentration in Finance from DePaul University in 1991.

Index